Digital and Cultural Influences on Media Narratives and Storytelling

Nur Emine Koç
Istanbul Aydın University, Turkey

Mine Demirtaş
İstanbul Beykent University, Turkey

Başak Gezmen
Istanbul Medipol University, Turkey

IGI Global
Scientific Publishing
Publishing Tomorrow's Research Today

Vice President of Editorial	Melissa Wagner
Director of Acquisitions	Mikaela Felty
Director of Book Development	Jocelynn Hessler
Production Manager	Mike Brehm
Cover Design	Jose Rosado

Published in the United States of America by
IGI Global Scientific Publishing
701 East Chocolate Avenue
Hershey, PA, 17033, USA
Tel: 717-533-8845
Fax: 717-533-7115
Website: https://www.igi-global.com E-mail: cust@igi-global.com

Library of Congress Cataloging-in-Publication Data

LCCN: 2025017396 (CIP Data Pending)
ISBN13: 9798337320236
Isbn13Softcover: 9798337320243
EISBN13: 9798337320250

British Cataloguing in Publication Data
A Cataloguing in Publication record for this book is available from the British Library.

Table of Contents

Preface xi

Chapter 1
The Influence of AI on Digital Storytelling and Media Narratives 1
Muhammad Usman Tariq, Abu Dhabi University, UAE & University College Cork, Ireland

Chapter 2
Audience Interactive Storytelling Anchors' Narrative Techniques in Opposition Television Channels in Turkey 27
Beril Sarılar, Istanbul Aydin University, Turkey

Chapter 3
Storytelling in Digital Games 57
Ayşe Nesrin Akören, Doğuş University, Turkey

Chapter 4
Shadows in the Stream: Turkish Horror, Gothic Storytelling, and Digital Narrative.. 87
Aman Deep Singh, Nirma University, India

Chapter 5
Analyzing Sahmaran as an Example of Transmedia Storytelling 115
Nur Emine Koç, İstanbul Aydın University, Turkey
Mine Demirtaş, Istanbul Beykent University, Turkey

Chapter 6
Exploring the Influence of Long-Form Narrative in Digital Journalism: The Model of "Scrolli.co" 141
Ahmet Serkan Okay, İstanbul Medipol University, Turkey

Chapter 7
An Exploration on Rousseau and Arendt's Accounts About Communication Listening, Voice, and Self 171
Tuğba Gülal, Istanbul Aydin University, Turkey

Chapter 8
An Essay on Digital Storytelling in the Art of Refik Anadol 197
Nazan Alioğlu, Istanbul Beykent University, Turkey

Chapter 9
Reading The Concept of Storytelling Within the Framework of Fashion Marketing Through Luxury Brands 229
Erdem Varol, Marmara Üniversitesi, Turkey
Merve Çelik-Varol, Istanbul Beykent University, Turkey

Chapter 10
The Role of Digital Storytelling in Transforming Consumption Motivations: "Not an Advertisement, Dubai Chocolate" 267
Başak Gezmen, Istanbul Medipol Universıty, Turkey
Asena Temelli Coşgun, Istanbul Medipol Universıty, Turkey

Chapter 11
Digital Self-Help Culture: How Social Media is Reshaping Psychological Discourse.. 299
Eser Levi, Istanbul Bilgi University, Turkey
Eda Aylin Genç, Manchester Metropolitan University, UK

Chapter 12
The Role of Storytelling in Creating a Country's Image on the Example of Eurovision Song Contest: How the "Rim Tim Tagi Dim" Rhythm Contributed to the Global Promotion of Croatia... 333
Tanja Grmuša, Zagreb School of Business, Croatia

Compilation of References 383

About The Contributors.. 433

Index.. 439

Detailed Table of Contents

Preface xi

Chapter 1
The Influence of AI on Digital Storytelling and Media Narratives 1
Muhammad Usman Tariq, Abu Dhabi University, UAE & University College Cork, Ireland

The outcome of artificial intelligence (AI) on digital and media stories will revolutionize the way stories are created, experienced, and consumed. This shift has gone beyond traditional linear storytelling formats, leading to dynamic, interactive content that allows viewers to shape and influence stories. AI also improves creating content by automating tasks such as scriptwriting, video production, character development, and more, making storytelling more efficient and creative. However, AI participation in the media also increases ethical considerations, particularly concerning bias, reliability, and the likelihood of misinformation. While AI is developing, it offers exciting opportunities for engaging and more diverse stories and challenges related to content accuracy and cultural representation. In this article, we will explore AI's effects and future directions through digital storytelling.

Chapter 2
Audience Interactive Storytelling Anchors' Narrative Techniques in Opposition Television Channels in Turkey 27
Beril Sarılar, Istanbul Aydin University, Turkey

This study analyzes the evolving news narratives and audience engagements of anchors delivering primary news bulletins on Turkey's most viewed opposition television stations (NOW TV, Sözcü TV, Halk TV) regarding the development of news presentations. The study employed a mixed-methods approach, analyzing the primary news bulletins from four distinct days aired on three different networks (NOW TV, Sözcü TV, Halk TV) during January and February 2025. The purposive sample strategy was employed to identify days unaffected by special agendas that could accurately depict the routine broadcast flow.

Chapter 3
Storytelling in Digital Games 57
Ayşe Nesrin Akören, Doğuş University, Turkey

In digital games, storytelling is an important element that enables the player to adapt more easily to the game world, ensures continuous follow-up, and enriches the gaming experience. These scenarios sometimes serve as entertainment and provide players with an emotional journey. Storytelling is the most crucial factor determining the structure of games. Therefore, it would be appropriate to distinctly separate and define the types of narratives in this section through examples. In digital games, storytelling develops in traditional follow-ups, which we can describe as linear narratives consisting of beginning, development, and conclusion sections. In this 'Linear' narrative style, players progress through a written script and witness pre-determined events of the story. Such scenarios are usually written for action, adventure, and role-playing (RPG) games. In conclusion, this book chapter will pay careful attention to addressing the deepening methods of interactions that digital games establish with individuals through the diversity of storytelling.

Chapter 4
Shadows in the Stream: Turkish Horror, Gothic Storytelling, and Digital Narrative.. 87
Aman Deep Singh, Nirma University, India

This paper explores the convergence of Turkish horror cinema with Gothic storytelling and the transformative impact of new media. It examines how digital platforms have reshaped the production, distribution, and reception of horror narratives in Turkey, focusing on adapting Gothic elements for contemporary audiences. Key themes, such as the supernatural and the uncanny, are analysed within a Turkish cultural context, alongside the influence of Islamic motifs like the concept of jinn. The role of streaming platforms in shaping viewing habits and promoting active audience engagement is also highlighted. Additionally, the portrayal of women in Turkish horror films is scrutinised, linking societal anxieties to gender representation. The chapter concludes by reflecting on the future of Turkish horror in the digital landscape, emphasising innovative narrative experiences and the genre's adaptation challenges. It integrates scholarly and cinematic sources to address significant themes related to this evolving genre.

Chapter 5
Analyzing Sahmaran as an Example of Transmedia Storytelling 115
Nur Emine Koç, İstanbul Aydın University, Turkey
Mine Demirtaş, Istanbul Beykent University, Turkey

Storytelling is a social and cultural activity. Transmedia storytelling, whose main elements include story, technology, and consumers, ensures that the previous plot is remembered by continuing the existing story and makes the audience experience the stories by identifying them with their period. An effective transmedia storytelling strategy interacts with popular culture. It produces a new perspective on the original meaning. The Sahmaran story, the subject of the study, is not only famous in Anatolia but also in many parts of the world. These legends have been known among the people from ancient times to the present day and are based on universal cultural foundations. The event patterns are continued with transmedia narration. As an example of transmedia storytelling, the Legend of Sahmaran and the Sahmaran series streamed on the Netflix platform in 2023, are analyzed by the content analysis method. It is revealed how the story fed from oral culture has changed on digital platforms and how it has moved away from its cultural story by incorporating Western elements.

Chapter 6
Exploring the Influence of Long-Form Narrative in Digital Journalism: The Model of "Scrolli.co" 141
Ahmet Serkan Okay, İstanbul Medipol University, Turkey

Digital journalism has progressed in a dynamic structure from Web 2.0 to the present, thanks to new communication and artificial intelligence technologies. In journalism, which has transformed into a dynamic structure, content has become enriched, and production is carried out with different narratives. Digital storytelling has also brought with it new narrative structures for news. Among these narrative structures, long-scroll news narratives have become a preferred type in digital news production. The aim of this study is to reveal the AI-supported structure of long-scroll narratives used in digital journalism in Turkey within the framework of story flow designs, as shaped by new communication technologies. The study also aims to demonstrate the impact of long-scroll narratives on digital news production under the umbrella of new communication and artificial intelligence technologies. Furthermore, the importance of this research lies in its potential to lead the way in examining long-scroll narrative structures in the field of digital journalism in Turkey.

Chapter 7
An Exploration on Rousseau and Arendt's Accounts About Communication Listening, Voice, and Self 171
Tuğba Gülal, Istanbul Aydin University, Turkey

In Rousseau's key works, including Émile or Treatise on Education (1918), and Reveries of a Solitary Walker (1992),the author examines the dimensions of communication, emphasizing engagement with oneself, others, and nature through silence.This paper utilizes Laverty's (2011) analysis of Rousseau's philosophy, which categorizes communication into three voices:articulate, melodic, and accentuated, representing different listening modalities,particularly in education.A central question emerges regarding the relationship between the self and the external world.I will compare Rousseau's model with Hannah Arendt's views on thinking and selfhood from The Human Condition, ultimately grouping their communication models into two categories: (i) the listening self (Rousseau) and (ii) the performative self (Arendt).Both authors contribute unique insights into communication and the role of silence.In conclusion, I propose the term "tacet sui," or "soundless self," to describe a form of storytelling relevant to both models,drawing on Moskalewicz's (2024) interpretation of Arendt's storytelling.

Chapter 8
An Essay on Digital Storytelling in the Art of Refik Anadol 197
Nazan Alioğlu, Istanbul Beykent University, Turkey

In this article, digital storytelling will be interpreted through the works of Refik Anadol, which are mainly "Machine Hallucination" (2019), Machine Memories (2021) and other works when necessary, in which he transforms machine learning into stories with algorithms, by relating it to technological determinism and Marshall McLuhan's motto "the medium is the message". As a philosophical essay on generative art, the article will analyze Refik Anadol's art in the context of concepts such as digital culture, digital storytelling, generative art, artificial intelligence and its aesthetics, technological sublime, technological determinism, using a qualitative method based on descriptive narration through the mentioned works.

Chapter 9
Reading The Concept of Storytelling Within the Framework of Fashion Marketing Through Luxury Brands 229
Erdem Varol, Marmara Üniversitesi, Turkey
Merve Çelik-Varol, Istanbul Beykent University, Turkey

This study is based on the analysis of how five luxury brands utilize the concept of storytelling in their fashion marketing strategies, employing the content analysis method. The concept of storytelling, a popular marketing strategy today, manifests as brand-specific narratives that convey the brands' histories, unique values, cultural heritage, and quality principles. In the current digital age, it is known that luxury brands frequently leverage storytelling in fashion marketing to establish a strong brand image. In this study, the stories in the campaigns of Louis Vuitton, Gucci, Rolex, Dior, and Prada are analyzed using the content analysis method within the fields of luxury branding, fashion marketing, and storytelling. The campaign analyses reveal that luxury brands not only offer expensive, high-quality, and rare goods and services but also present their consumers with stories that attribute a lifestyle, exclusivity, prestige, and emotional connection.

Chapter 10
The Role of Digital Storytelling in Transforming Consumption Motivations:
"Not an Advertisement, Dubai Chocolate" 267
Başak Gezmen, Istanbul Medipol Universıty, Turkey
Asena Temelli Coşgun, Istanbul Medipol Universıty, Turkey

In the digital world we live in today, the meanings produced by advertisements have changed and transformed with representations and discourses, and the functional stories about the product have been replaced by storytelling that emphasises emotional benefit and focuses on creating desire. Consumption motivations are reconstructed around these stories, meaning worlds and symbols. The current study aims to examine the role of storytelling in digital media in the transformation of consumption motivations. For this purpose, in-depth interviews will be conducted with 16 participants from the digital native generation, the most common users of digital media in Turkey. The findings to be obtained through in-depth interviews, one of the qualitative research methods frequently used in social sciences, will be analysed through descriptive analysis.

Chapter 11
Digital Self-Help Culture: How Social Media is Reshaping Psychological
Discourse.. 299
Eser Levi, Istanbul Bilgi University, Turkey
Eda Aylin Genç, Manchester Metropolitan University, UK

This chapter examines how social media has transformed psychological discourse from academic field to popular cultural phenomenon. Tracing the evolution from early self-help literature and TV psychotainment to digital platforms, it explores how psychological concepts migrated from clinical settings into everyday language through influencer culture and algorithmic amplification. Drawing on communication theories such as Framing, Parasocial Interaction, and Cultivation, the chapter analyzes how content creators package mental health content for viral reach. It examines the cultural impact of this shift, showing how terms like trauma or gaslighting enter mainstream use, while neoliberal values frame mental health as personal responsibility.

Though social media democratizes access to psychological knowledge, it also spreads misinformation, simplification, and pseudoscience. The rise of conspirituality where wellness merges with conspiracy exemplifies these risks, pointing to the need for regulatory frameworks while preserving benefits in digital mental health discourse.

Chapter 12
The Role of Storytelling in Creating a Country's Image on the Example of Eurovision Song Contest: How the "Rim Tim Tagi Dim" Rhythm Contributed to the Global Promotion of Croatia.......... 333
Tanja Grmuša, Zagreb School of Business, Croatia

The chapter explores the role of storytelling as a communication tool in the process of nation branding through music using the example of the Eurovision Song Contest. The motive for the above was Croatia's historic success at this popular music competition in 2024, where the performer Baby Lasagna won second place with his song "Rim Tim Tagi Dim". Recently, storytelling has been gaining more importance in the marketing context with the aim of better placing products and services, highlighting the strength of the brand and creating the soft power of states. In addition to focusing on the images and messages we want to send to others about ourselves, it is important to have an institutionalized approach to national branding, which Croatia as a country still needs in order to (re)maintain competitiveness. However, Croatia's image in the world is positively stable and is mainly associated with culture, natural beauty and lifestyle, which Baby Lasagna confirmed with his performance and contributed to the global promotion of Croatia in the world.

Compilation of References 383

About The Contributors 433

Index 439

Preface

Storytelling has accompanied humanity for centuries—first through oral traditions, later in written texts, and now in digital environments. The idea for this book emerged from a growing recognition that storytelling is not only persisting in the digital age, but evolving, adapting, and expanding into new fields. As researchers from diverse disciplines, we came together with the shared aim of understanding how storytelling shapes and is shaped by contemporary digital, cultural, and technological forces.

This volume brings together contributions from scholars across communication, media studies, journalism, marketing, philosophy, digital art, and game design. It reflects an interdisciplinary perspective on the diverse ways in which stories are constructed, circulated, and experienced in today's media ecosystems. From political journalism to children's literature, from AI-generated art to nation branding, the chapters in this book offer a multifaceted view of storytelling's enduring relevance and contemporary transformations.

We were particularly motivated to include both global and local perspectives—highlighting examples from Turkey, while also addressing international phenomena. This allowed us to explore how storytelling functions not only as a universal human practice but also as a culturally embedded and context-sensitive tool for expression and identity formation.

We would like to thank all the contributors for their intellectual generosity, collaborative spirit, and dedication throughout the process. Their work gives this volume its richness and diversity. We are also grateful to our readers—academics, students, and professionals—who continue to explore the evolving role of storytelling in media, culture, and society.

We hope this book contributes meaningfully to the conversation on digital and cultural storytelling, and that it inspires further research and critical reflection on the stories we tell—and the media through which we tell them.

INTRODUCTION

Digital and Cultural Influences on Media Narratives and Storytelling

Storytelling is one of humanity's oldest and most powerful tools of communication. Rooted in oral traditions, evolving through written forms, and today thriving in digital platforms, storytelling remains central to how we understand ourselves, relate to others, and make sense of the world. As societies change, so do the stories they tell—and the media through which they are told.

This book explores the transformation of storytelling in the context of digitalization, globalization, and cultural hybridization. It brings together interdisciplinary research from scholars across communication, journalism, media studies, marketing, philosophy, digital game design, and cultural studies. By combining theoretical insights with practical case studies, the chapters examine how digital storytelling shapes audience behavior, brand perception, national identity, self-image, and social discourse.

In Section 1, the volume explores the transformation of storytelling within contemporary media and journalism. The chapters examine the influence of artificial intelligence on narrative construction, the emergence of long-form digital journalism, and the rise of interactive and participatory storytelling practices. Further discussions include the adaptation of horror and gothic narrative traditions in Turkish digital media, the philosophical dimensions of communication through the perspectives of Rousseau and Arendt, and the articulation of transmedia storytelling exemplified by the reinterpretation of the Sahmaran myth in digital culture.

In Section 2, the focus shifts to the intersections of storytelling, marketing, and brand communication. This analysis examines the narrative strategies employed by luxury and fashion brands, the role of storytelling in shaping consumer motivation, and how digital media facilitate the construction of brand identity through localized cultural codes and emotional engagement.

In Section 3, the volume investigates storytelling as a tool of social discourse, digital self-representation, and soft power. Chapters address the rise of digital self-help culture, the reshaping of psychological discourse on social media, and the role of cultural events—such as the Eurovision Song Contest—in constructing and promoting national images within the global media sphere.

This compilation thus offers a comprehensive panorama of how storytelling operates in and across different domains—media, technology, culture, marketing, politics, and identity. It provides both theoretical frameworks and empirical observations that underscore the enduring relevance and transformative power of storytelling in a digitally mediated world.

By highlighting the Turkish context alongside international examples, the book offers not only a contribution to global academic discourse, but also a unique lens on the specific dynamics of digital storytelling in Turkey—a country marked by rapid digitalization, strong youth media culture, and deep historical narratives. It serves as a valuable reference for academics, students, and professionals in understanding how digital storytelling continues to evolve, connect, and influence the contemporary media ecosystem.

OVERVIEW OF CHAPTERS

Chapter 1 – The Influence of AI on Digital Storytelling and Media Narratives (Muhammad Usman Tariq)

Tariq investigates how artificial intelligence is transforming narrative structures, personalization, and content generation. He addresses both ethical implications and the creative opportunities AI introduces into media storytelling.

Chapter 2 – Audience Interactive Storytelling in Opposition Television Channels in Turkey (Beril Sarılar)

Focusing on political and oppositional media, this chapter examines how narrative techniques and audience interaction redefine television journalism in Turkey, with a critical look at affect, bias, and participation.

Chapter 3 – Storytelling in Digital Games (Ayşe Nesrin Akören)

Akören discusses how narrative construction within games contributes to emotional immersion, identity formation, and user engagement. The study highlights the narrative architecture of popular games and the role of interactivity.

Chapter 4 – Shadows in the Stream: Turkish Horror, Gothic Storytelling, and Digital Narrative (Aman Deep Singh)

This chapter explores gothic and horror elements in Turkish digital storytelling, emphasizing cultural codes, folklore influences, and the psychological dimensions of fear in the digital space.

Chapter 5 – Analyzing Şahmaran as an Example of Transmedia Storytelling (Nur Emine Koç & Mine Demirtaş)

Şahmaran is examined as a case of myth reinterpreted through contemporary platforms like Netflix. The chapter reveals how transmedia storytelling bridges cultural heritage and digital innovation.

Chapter 6 – Exploring the Influence of Long-Form Narrative in Digital Journalism: The Model of "Scrolli.co" (Ahmet Serkan Okay)

This chapter analyzes long-form digital journalism formats and how narrative flow, structure, and depth are reshaped by platforms like Scrolli.co, especially under the influence of AI and mobile-first reading habits.

Chapter 7 – An Exploration of Rousseau and Arendt's Accounts About Communication, Listening, Voice and Self (Tuğba Gülal)

This philosophical chapter compares Rousseau's and Arendt's reflections on communication and the formation of the self, situating storytelling within deeper ontological and ethical discussions.

Chapter 8 – An Essay on Digital Storytelling in the Art of Refik Anadol (Nazan Alioğlu)

Focusing on Refik Anadol's media art, this chapter investigates how storytelling is encoded in data sculptures, AI visuals, and architectural interfaces, revealing a new language of digital narrative art.

Chapter 9 – Reading the Concept of Storytelling within the Framework of Fashion Marketing Through Luxury Brands (Erdem Varol & Merve Çelik-Varol)

This chapter illustrates how storytelling is used to construct brand identity and emotional appeal in fashion marketing, exploring consumer imagination and symbolic meaning.

Chapter 10 – The Role of Digital Storytelling in Transforming Consumption Motivations (Başak Gezmen & Asena Temelli Coşgun)

This chapter traces the shift from rational advertisement to emotionally charged storytelling in digital marketing, explaining how desires and values are constructed through immersive narrative strategies.

Chapter 11 – Digital Self-Help Culture: How Social Media is Reshaping Psychological Discourse (Eser Levi & Eda Aylin Genç)

The authors explore how self-help narratives on platforms like Instagram and TikTok shape perceptions of mental health, agency, and wellness, using storytelling to reframe personal growth.

Chapter 12 – The Role of Storytelling in Creating a Country's Image: Eurovision and the Case of Croatia (Tanja Grmuša)

Grmuša shows how performances like "Rim Tim Tagi Dim" contribute to soft power and cultural storytelling, making Eurovision a stage for national identity construction and global narrative visibility.

Chapter 1
The Influence of AI on Digital Storytelling and Media Narratives

Muhammad Usman Tariq
https://orcid.org/0000-0002-7605-3040
Abu Dhabi University, UAE & University College Cork, Ireland

ABSTRACT

The outcome of artificial intelligence (AI) on digital and media stories will revolutionize the way stories are created, experienced, and consumed. This shift has gone beyond traditional linear storytelling formats, leading to dynamic, interactive content that allows viewers to shape and influence stories. AI also improves creating content by automating tasks such as scriptwriting, video production, character development, and more, making storytelling more efficient and creative. However, AI participation in the media also increases ethical considerations, particularly concerning bias, reliability, and the likelihood of misinformation. While AI is developing, it offers exciting opportunities for engaging and more diverse stories and challenges related to content accuracy and cultural representation. In this article, we will explore AI's effects and future directions through digital storytelling.

INTRODUCTION

Digital storytelling has changed significantly in the AI era, indicating a major departure from traditional narrative forms. This development is deeply intertwined with technological advances that media has shaped over the last decades. From the early days of static text to image-based storytelling to the dynamic and immersive experiences made possible by artificial intelligence, the trajectory of storytelling

DOI: 10.4018/979-8-3373-2023-6.ch001

is increasingly complex and interactive. In this modern landscape, the story is no longer linear or static. They are varied, responsive, and increasingly tailored to individual preferences and behaviors. Digital stories now serve as a means of communication and entertainment and a powerful means of creating commitment, conviction, education, and identity (Jiang et al., 2024). This transformation reflects a wider shift in media consumption, with users no longer being passive recipients but active participants in creating and distributing stories. Initially, media stories were primarily shaped by the limitations and possibilities of print, radio, and broadcast television. These platforms have determined one-to-many communication models where content makers control the structure and distribution of narratives. However, the advent of the Internet has shifted towards a more decentralized and democratized media environment. The story became more of a dialogue than mere communication (Kholifah and Hamzah, 2025). In this context, technological advancements served as tools and agents of narrative transformation that facilitated new forms of interactivity and multimodality, fundamentally changing the nature of storytelling. This personalization extends to the actual construction of the story. You can now create AI-powered tools, action lines, dialogs, and scripts based on specific parameters, user input, or real-time data. These skills question the traditional ideas of authors and creativity and the role of human agents in storytelling. Traditional narratives usually follow a linear progression with a clear beginning, center, and end. In contrast, storytelling available in AI can generate nonlinear, branched stories that develop in response to user choices or surrounding instructions. It is especially pronounced in interactive media such as video games, virtual reality (VR), and AI-controlled chatbots. These forms of storytelling blur the boundaries between fiction and reality immersively and experimentally (Kurian and Saad, 2024). Integrating natural language processing (NLP) and mechanical learning with these platforms enables real-time dialogue generation and reactive Quick storytelling that adapts to user input and creates a more engaging and personalized experience. This evolution refers to the shift from storytelling to dynamic systems as static art forms. On the aesthetic side, art, music, and videos with AI-generated creations are increasingly being used to improve the story's experience. This aesthetic controls and often combines human creativity with mechanically generated elements to create hybrid works that provide new sensory and emotional experiences. On the ethical side, using AI in storytelling raises important concerns about reliability, manipulation, and bias. When AI systems learn from existing data, they can incorrectly reproduce or reinforce social biases that lead to problematic representations and stories (Ngoi et al., 2024). These developments need to critically include the ethical impact of AI on storytelling, particularly in contexts such as journalism, education, and political communication. By automating content and translation, AI can make stories more accessible to various target groups, including those with disabilities or language impairments. For example, text-to-speech and speech-to-text technology allows visual or deaf users to process digital stories in new ways. Similarly, real-time translation tools can close language gaps and allow stories to reach global audiences. These advancements contribute to a more integrated storytelling environment, allowing you to express and hear several voices and perspectives. However, the inclusiveness granted by AI depends on the diversity of data and algorithms used. Without a conscious effort to meet representative equity in training data and system design, AI-controlled storytelling risks demand the demand to maintain existing inequality and marginalized underestimated groups (Pierosara, 2024).

In the educational context, we also saw the up-and-close use of AI in storytelling, particularly in developing personalized learning experiences. Through adaptive learning platforms, AI can include narrative elements that adapt educational content to students' individual needs and improve commitments and bonds. In this context, storytelling is not merely an educational tool but a mechanism that promotes empathy, critical thinking, and cultural understanding. Simulate tutors and chatbots using an AI-driven learning experience. However, interactive, story-based games allow more accessible and associated complex subjects. These applications highlight the potential for AI transformation in redesigning how stories are used to educate and enhance learners (Rachman et al., 2024). Nevertheless, they also raise questions about the role of educators, the quality of content that AI generates, and the impact on student data protection and autonomy. Brands increasingly rely on AI to analyze consumer data, predict trends, and create stories that match the value and effort of their audience. These stories spread across several platforms through personalized content, often creating consistent, emotionally resonating brand experiences. Here are some examples of how to use video generated by chatbots, virtual influencers, and AI to tell stories and create sensible interactions with consumers. AI's capabilities greatly enhance the change in emotional branding, with the story aimed at establishing deep psychological connections with the audience, understanding and responding to emotional information. This emotional intelligence is mechanically transmitted but allows for creating stories that feel more authentic and reliable, even if they are algorithmically generated. AI technology can analyze, archive, and revive traditional stories to ensure transgenerational and regional transmissions (Alqahtani et al., 2024). AI's digital story-counting platform allows communities to culture and share cultural stories in multimedia. It can promote intercultural dialogue and understanding.

Additionally, AI can support the revival of endangered species by supporting content creation and translation efforts. These applications highlight the possibilities of AI not only as an innovation tools but also as a medium of cultural continuity and expression (Jiang et al., 2024). However, it also causes reviews of cultural property and expression dynamics, mainly when used by external companies in the local government that AI systems want to represent. Writers, filmmakers, musicians, and artists experiment with AI and collaborate with stories that challenge traditional genres and formats. These collaborations often lead to hybrids that go beyond narrative structure and content limits. For example, A-generated poetry, scripts, and visual arts have been featured in festivals and exhibitions that spark discussions about creativity, originality, and writers. The use of AI in creative narratives is not without critics who argue that algorithmic processes lack the intuition, intuition, and emotional resonance of human creativity (Singh et al., 2024). However, supporters argue that AI can enhance human creativity through new perspectives, generating new ideas, and promoting experimentation. This dialectic emphasizes the developmental nature of AI-era, where storytelling becomes a venue for cooperation between human and mechanical intelligence. If AI technology is developed, we can expect a more sophisticated and emotionally intelligent system to understand context, sound, and subtext. This advancement allows for more personalized, emotionally resonating, ethically subtle, subtle, subtle stories. Integrating AI into new technologies such as Augmented Reality (AR), Virtual Reality (VR), and Metaverse further expands storytelling possibilities, creating an immersive narrative environment that includes several senses and traditional media boundaries. In these rooms, stories are consumed in real time and experienced, alive and put together. It challenges to rethink basic concepts such as author, creativity, and reliability while providing new tools and paradigms for representation, commitment, and communication (Thakkar et al., 2024).

Theoretical Foundations of Digital Storytelling

Stories in traditional and digital contexts represent fundamental human activities beyond cultural, temporal, and technical limitations. Storytelling conveys practices, experiences, ideas, values , and feelings through structured stories. In traditional contexts, storytelling was an oral, literary, and acting art form (Rachman et al., 2024). From mythology and folklore to generations, grand poetry, religious texts, and theatrical achievements, traditional storytelling has always served as a means of cultural preservation, identity formation, moral education, and entertainment. Its structure usually follows a linear trajectory, emphasizing causal effect sequences and character cards with well-defined settings and temporal frameworks. In particular, oral traditions were strongly based on memory, voice, gestures, and community participation, and storytellers often played a respected role in transferring collective knowledge and wisdom. In these contexts, the relationship between storytellers and audiences was direct and intimate; feedback was fed back in real time, and emotional responses formed a critical part of the storytelling experience. A digitally similar postponement introduced a new narrative, distribution, and reception mode. Digital storytelling includes multimedia elements such as text, images, audio, video, animation, and interactivity, enabling multi-sensory and multi-modal experiences. It also democratizes storytelling by reducing barriers to creation and distribution. Tools like blogging, social media platforms, video sharing services, interactive web applications, and more allow anyone to become a storyteller with internet access. This technological shift disperses narrative authority and diversifies the types of narratives that can be told (Tariq, 2025).

Additionally, digital storytelling includes nonlinear, fragmented hyperlink structures that often decouple from linearity and reflect the associative logic of digital networks. The digital age has led to new narrative genres such as video blogging, webcomics, transmedia storytelling, and interactive fiction. Each reflects the developed relationship between media technology and narrative forms (Thakkar et al., 2024). Denkers like Hannah Allend, Jean Jacques Rousseau, and Marshall MacLehan have given them rich insight into the impact of nature and storytelling. Hannah Arendt emphasized storytelling as the center of the human condition, especially when studying behavior and multiple. In the human state, Allend argues that storytelling is a political act, meaning human action, and preserves it in the public sector. Arendt has a story about how we make the world feel and each other. They are vehicles where we achieve identity and continuity during the contingencies of life. She viewed storytelling as a form that constructs meaning in an everyday world, allowing individuals to disclose themselves and their actions. This relational aspect of storytelling combines the ability to combine individuals with time and space to underpin its political and existential values. In works such as Confessions and Emile, Rousseau examined the role of storytelling in the design of personal and collective identity (Chubb et al., 2024). He was aware of the educational and moral possibilities of the story. However, he also warned of its ability to distort, manipulate, and alienate (Jiang, 2024). For Rousseau, storytelling crafts can conceal natural human impulses and contribute to social inequality and corruption. He was particularly critical of fictional stories encouraging passive consumption as a positive moral commitment. However, Torso recognized that a story based on authenticity and emotional truth can promote empathy, imagination, and a common sense of humanity. The emphasis on integrity and emotional expression laid the foundation for romantic and educational concepts after the story. His saying is that the medium is to sell the conviction that the message is told by the narrative, affecting human perceptions and is told about it.

In understanding media and other work, McLuhan argued that all new media alters users' cognitive and sensory commitments. Oral storytelling of the story emphasized hearing and city commitment print-promoted linear, logical thinking. Electronic media introduced immediacy and emotional responses. McLuhan predicted the emergence of digital media as a transformative power in storytelling (Bilici and Yilmaz, 2024). It allows for integrating oral and educated cultures into global electronic tribes. These philosophical perspectives jointly show that narrative telling is a dynamic, socially embedded practice deeply influenced by its technical and cultural context. At this point, artificial intelligence is a redefinition of the form and structure of the narrative that extends the concerns raised by Arendt, Rousseau, and McLuhan. AI systems range from natural language processors and generative models to recommended algorithms and chatbots so stories are created, experienced, and understood. One of the most notable changes is the automation of the story generation. Developing large-scale voice models, such as GPT and other generation AI tools, has allowed machines to generate consistent context-related stories with minimal human input. These stories of AI-generated stories can be used in the form of news articles, short stories, scripts, poetry, and even personalized sleep time stories (Sanabria Zepeda et al., 2024). The impact of this automation is profound as it challenges the traditional ideas of authors, originality, and creativity. In a world where machines can produce stories indistinguishable from people, questions about the role of storytellers, criteria for evaluating stories, and the cultural significance of narrative works (Tariq, 2025).

AI also changes narrative structure through interactivity and personalization. In contrast to traditional linear stories, AI-enabled storytelling can adapt in real-time to user input, preferences, and behavior. This dynamic storytelling is especially prevalent in the experiences of video games, interactive fiction, virtual reality, and educational platforms. These stories have not been decided. They branch, crush, and develop based on user decisions. It creates agency and immersion. AI algorithms analyze user data to predict and respond to emotional states, adapt content, and propose narrative paths. As a result, each user's experience in a story is unique, personalized, and context-related. This level of interactivity constitutes the relationship between storyteller and audience, blurring the boundaries between creation and consumption, author and reader, performance and participation. The digital room tells the story on several platforms that combine video, text, social media contributions, augmented reality, and live interaction. AI promotes this transmedia storytelling by organizing content, maintaining narrative consistency, and optimizing delivery across the channel (Gourlet et al., 2024). For example, AI can generate real-time virtual character interactions, synchronize content across platforms, and recommend narrative sequences catering to user interests. This modular form of storytelling reflects singularly written narrative changes to the collective, algorithmically conveyed narrative ecosystem. These ecosystems are fluid, develop further, and rely on users, data analysis, and machine learning processes. The philosophical influence of these developments is essential. Arendt's emphasis on storytelling as political and identity-preserving actions is complicated by the rise of algorithmic narratives that may not lack clear human authority or intentions. Who was generated or curated by AI? Who is responsible for their importance and impact? Lucy's concerns about stories' credibility and moral impact are reinforced in a world where deep dandruff, synthetic media, and emotional manipulation algorithms are increasing. The border between fiction and reality is increasingly blurred, raising concerns about deceptions, manipulation, and erosion of trust (Bansal et al., 2024).

In the meantime, McLuhan's insight is that medium-sized messages are more relevant than ever. AI is more than just a new tool for storytelling. It is a new medium with its logic, grammar, and aesthetics. It presents the sense, cognitive, and social aspects of the story's experience in how we first understand it. AI systems are trained on large data records reflecting social bias, so your stories can maintain stereotypes, exclusions, or misinformation. The opacity of algorithmic processes complicates accountability and transparency, particularly in journalism, education, and public communication (Woodruff et al., 2024). At the same time, AI has the potential to scale storytelling in a more powerful and integrated way. By activating real-time translation, language, language text, and adaptive interfaces from text, AI becomes more accessible to people with disabilities and language distinctions. Support marginalized voices by making content easy to create and distribute in various formats and languages. However, knowledge of this possibility requires intentional design of performance dynamics built into technical systems, integrated data records, and critical investigation.

In an educational environment, AI redefines storytelling as an educational strategy. Intelligent tutorial systems, story education games, and AI-driven simulations use stories to improve commitment, motivation, and understanding (Avello Martinez et al., 2024). To create personalized learning trips, these systems adapt stories to student profiles, learning styles, and performance data. The use of stories in this context is decorative and central to the cognitive and emotional learning process. Stories help learners understand complex information, refer to different perspectives, and maintain knowledge through emotional and context-related embedding. However, reliance on AI in education also raises questions about the learning experiences of surveillance, data protection, and marketing. Artists and writers use AI to generate ideas, create music, photos, and build stories. These collaborations often use machine logic to open up human intuition, open new aesthetic possibilities, and lead to hybrid works that challenge traditional artistic limits. The role of a storyteller is the role of a curator, editor, or co-creator who navigates between human vision and the algorithmic version. This author's new structure makes us rethink creativity as a distributed, interactive process. It changes how stories are designed, who tells them, how they are structured, and how they are experienced. Let's move further into the AI era. It is important to promote the critical literacy of digital stories based on AI performance and limitations, consciously and on the enduring human needs for a meaningful common narrative. Storytelling develops, but it develops a central function of understanding the world and combining it with others to introduce new opportunities. In this developing landscape, the challenge is not to resist technological change but to design it to preserve the narrative tradition's wealth, diversity, and humanity (Tariq, 2025).

AI and Narrative Construction in Media

The application of artificial intelligence in creating journalism, film, and digital content is one of the most transformative developments in the modern media landscape. Although technological advances accelerate, AI has transformed from behind-the-scenes tools to better players in designing production, distribution, and content consumption (Thakkar et al., 2024). In journalism, AI is used not only to automate tasks such as transcription interviews and data organization but also for more sophisticated features such as creating complete news articles, recognizing misinformation, personalizing news feeds, and creating editorial content. From the Associated Press to Reuters to the Washington Post, news organizations worldwide are including AI technology in their work processes to improve efficiency and accuracy and expand the story. Automated journalism, also known as robot journalism, uses algorithms (Avello Martínez et al., 2024). Tools run by AI can create large documents, social media contributions, or legal submissions to identify trends, identify anomalies, and record potential leads. These skills are invaluable in the media ecosystem, and the mere volume of information available can overwhelm even the most experienced journalists. Additionally, AI can support fact and inspection processes, scan content for inconsistencies, recognize Deeppfakes, and cross-reference with established databases. However, integrating AI into journalism raises complex ethical questions about the role of transparency, bias, accountability, and human judgment in editorial decision-making. As algorithms are increasingly shaping written, published, and recommended messages for readers, there is a growing need for oversight and public discourse about how these technologies affect journalistic standards and democratic processes. From scripting and casting to visual effects and public analysis, AI revolutionizes how films are designed, produced, and sold. AI control tools can support screenwriters by generating cracks, drawing arches, and co-writing scripts based on genre conventions and audiences. These tools are trained with huge data records in the tropics of scripts, dialogues, and films, allowing them to mimic the structure and stylistic nuances of the story. In some cases, AI-generated scripts are converted into short films, indicating potential and limitations on machine creativity. AI is also used to predict cash benefits, identify target demographics, and optimize marketing strategies. Through analysis of public data, social media trends, and previous viewing behavior, AI systems will allow studios to create advertising content, determine publishing data, and even influence casting decisions (Alqahtani et al., 2024).

Genetically controversial networks (geese) allow for creating surreal CGI signs, environments, and scenes. These technologies can cut off actors, create digital doubles, and simulate natural phenomena with unprecedented realism. AI-powered processing tools can analyze raw materials to identify the most impressive scenes, suggest cuts, and automatically assemble the pendant. In animated films, AI helps to use traits to rip the dialogue, reducing the time and work required in traditional animation workflows (Chubb et al., 2024). However, these advancements also require traditional roles and skills in the film industry, leading to discussions about changes in work by AI producers, authors, and performance credibility. Content makers now use AI to generate text, images, audio, and video, enabling them to create content on a scale and with minimal technical knowledge. Platforms like Tikk, Instagram, and YouTube increasingly contain content that AI has created or improved, at least in part. It ranges from AI-generated music tracks and deepfake videos to algorithmically curated visual aesthetics. Text-to-image generators such as OpenAI and other developer-developed users can create breathtaking visual content based on simple input requests, opening new ways of artistic representation and digital branding. AI helps you plan contributions, analyze engagement metrics, and optimize your content strategy to maximize the scope and interaction of your target group. This convergence of creativity and calculations only changes the aesthetics of digital content and the economy of rhythm and attention in the online world. These systems can generate human prose, mimic a particular writing style, and adapt the content to various platforms and audiences (Dai et al., 2024). Tools such as Wordsmiths and Heliographer were used in journalism. These bots can process raw data and generate grammatically modified stories in seconds. It is often associated with high accuracy. Entertainment and Marketing uses storytelling bots to create personalized content for your users. Advertising, interactive stories, or conversation scripts for virtual influencers. These bots return to user data and create emotional stories that improve commitment and brand loyalty.

Generation AI systems such as large-scale language models and diffusion-based image generators also catalyze a new era of creativity and media failure. These systems are refined and can produce poetry, novels, essays, songs, photos, and videos. Some platforms allow users to create a video scene based on textual descriptions with realistic signs, movements, and over-voice. In interactive storytelling, AI enables dynamic stories that develop according to user input, generating deep, immersive, personalized experiences. In virtual and expanded reality, AI contributes to worldviews, character behavior, and adaptive stories, making the digital environment faster and more reliable. Understanding AI's ability to understand context, emotions, and intentions is essential to improve and enable steadily more subtle and persuasive content (Kasemsarn et al., 2024). On the one hand, generative AI extends the limits of what is creatively possible, allowing us to democratize access to new forms of expression and powerful creative tools. It allows individuals and small teams to create high-quality content without extensive training or resources. It also allows for stronger personalization, creating stories of more relevant, engaging, and emotional responses for different target groups. On the other hand, rising generative AI maintains significant concerns about recognition reliability, trust, and manipulation. Suppose the content of AI-generated content is more persuasive. In that case, it becomes more difficult for viewers to distinguish between the people produced and the machine media (Bilici & Yilmaz,2024). This ambiguity can be used to distribute misinformation, deepfakes, or propaganda to undermine media literacy's epistemological foundation and public trust in digital content. These systems are trained with data that reflect social inequality, allowing them to accidentally replicate harmful tropical tropics, alienate certain voices, and normalize the tensions of exclusion. Commercial mandate that promotes AI development also takes precedence in commitment and virality from nuance and critical depth, spreading sensational or emotionally manipulative content. Audiences can be subtly influenced by algorithm curation. The information filters the information according to opaque criteria and generates an echo chamber or filter bubble (Ngoi et al., 2024). Active interpreters translate audience roles into data points in feedback loops optimized for attention and monetization. Who is the author when a machine creates poems, draws pictures, or writes scripts? How do you assess the artistic merits of such works, and on what criteria do you assess their cultural values? These questions sparked a centralized debate between artists, scientists, and engineers, revealing the deep tension between human-centered creative paradigms and arithmetic models of creativity. Some view AI as employees who can enhance human imagination, while others fear reducing human art's value and culture to many algorithmic versions (Ciğerci & Yıldırım, 2024). When AI is integrated through content creation, it is essential to equip people with instruments to understand, criticize, and ethically address the AI-generated media that AI has generated. It includes understanding how AI systems work, acknowledging limitations and biases, and verifying the content's reliability. It formulates the roles of creators and audiences, constitutes the aesthetics and economy of media production, and redefines narrative communication's ethical and epistemological contours (Thomas, 2024). The promise of AI lies in its ability to improve creativity, efficiency, and personalization. However, its dangers are based on the possibility of hiding the truth, increasing distortion, and avoiding cultural expression. Navigating this complex area requires a balanced approach to celebrating innovation while adjusting the sociotechnical dynamics of AI-controlled storytelling. We continue to study and shape the boundaries of this ambitious narrative, but the orders remain clear. It is to use the power of AI in ways that confirm people's dignity, promote diversity, and maintain the democratic and imaginative potential of the media.

AI's Role in Transmedia Storytelling

Netflix's adaptation of cultural folklore, particularly series such as Shahmaran, demonstrates how global streaming platforms use artificial intelligence and data control strategies to reject traditional narratives for international audiences. Rooted in Middle Eastern and Anatolia mythology, Sharmaran studies half-female legends related to wisdom, healing, and feminine power. Not only is the product of creative reinterpretation, but the series is also a case study of what stories should be adapted to how AI and Big Data build them for emotional and cultural responses and how they can be sold to a global audience. Like many content providers, Netflix uses demanding algorithms to analyze audience preferences, local interests, genre affinity, and observational behavior (Singh et al., 2024). These findings guide a platform for curating and generating content embedded in localized myths and packed with global appeal. Shahmaran's production reflects the strategic confluence of cultural idiosyncraticity and the universality elements of the narrative. It is based on identifying contacts for themes that use different demographic data. It notifies you of script development, character design, pace, and emotional modulation. It allows creators to adapt story counting techniques in real-time based on predictive analytics. For example, AI tools can evaluate early designs of scripts for speed and mood, compare them with successful templates, and provide feedback on character sheets and emotional effects. These systems are trained in a vast database by scripts, public responses, and film tropics, allowing us to characterize or suggest potential issues. In projects such as Shahmaran, this ability supports adapting folklore - often verbal, fragmented, consistent, persuasive visual narrative interpretations (Febriandy & Revolusi, 2024). The integration of AI ensures that these stories maintain their cultural essence while shaping them into a form that meets modern expectations of storytelling. This act of compensation for tradition and innovation is central to the role of AI development in narrative media. In the digital age, stories are no longer limited to a single medium. Instead, they develop through films, series, video games, social media, podcasts, virtual reality, and live experiences (Belda-Medina & Goddard, 2024). AI coordinates this transmedia ecosystem, ensuring narrative consistency, audience commitment, and content optimization.

By analyzing the interactions of target groups between platforms, AI helps creators determine which narrative elements resonate most, which characters create the strongest emotional connections, and which theme motives promote user commitment. These findings provide information on where the story universe is extended, how user interactions are structured, and how content can be adapted to different platforms. For shows like Shahmaran, this could mean developing interactive mobile phone games based on their mythology, creating a podcast that deals with the traditions behind the series, or creating a social media campaign inviting fans to contribute to the interpretation of the legend. This function is used in projects such as Netflix's Bandersnatch, where viewers choose a path to history and create results for several stories. While this technology is developing, delivering unique and personalized stories on scale will become increasingly possible (Kholifah & Hamzah, 2025). AI can adapt actions, interactions, and visual elements in real-time based on previous interactions and viewer psychographic profiles. It led to deep, urgent, and emotional resonance in knowledge, blurring the boundaries between passive consumption and positive co-creation. For global platforms that want to combine with different audiences, the ability to dynamically coordinate stories structurally and contextually is a powerful tool to promote cultural relevance and emotional depth. It may seem paradoxical, but with AI skills in linguistic translation, mood analysis, and cultural contextualization, narratives simultaneously overcome linguistic and cultural obstacles based on specific origins. Machine translation tools run by AI In addition to language accuracy, AI systems are currently trained to understand cultural references, idioms, and social information so that they can propose culturally appropriate adjustments (Pierosara, 2024). It is important to make content like Sharmaran accessible and wise to audiences worldwide without a stroll through cultural credibility. For example, AI analyzes various visual aesthetics, costume design, and time, suggesting changes that can improve the relativity of a particular market. In marketing and advertising, AI-driven tools can create localized trailers, posters, and social media content that address local flavors and trends. This hyperlocal approach to content promotion ensures that global publications are perceived as integrated, respectful, and coordinated rather than culturally slick or homogenized. By optimizing the delivery of culturally rich narratives for global audiences, AI can help increase local folklore and traditions to the international stage, helping to contribute to cultural exchange and mutual understanding.

Furthermore, AI contributes to narrative inclusiveness by identifying underrated voices and action lines. By analyzing gaps in existing content libraries and audience feedback, AI tools can highlight areas lacking diversity in terms of ethnicity, gender representation, socioeconomic perspective, or theme diversity. Content platforms can use this data to order stories that fill these gaps, ensuring a more integrated media situation (Jao et al., 2024). In reality, this could lead to lesser-known myths and legendary adaptations from marginalized communities, which increase the voices that mainstream media stories have historically excluded. Ethical frameworks and integrated values direct AI and have become a powerful cultural conservation, innovation, and democratization force. Improve storytelling by providing real-time feedback, allowing for rapid story idea prototyping, and optimizing production workflows. AI can create preliminary visualizations of scenes, simulate public responses, and even predict the potential success of various narrative arches. This predictive ability is especially valuable in industries that need to compensate for creative risks to financial realities (Nader et al., 2024). By reducing uncertainty and improving creative control, AI allows storytellers to study more experimental or culturally concrete stories without fear of commercial failure (Tariq, 2025).

However, integrating AI into the narrative process is not without its challenges. The causes of data protection, creative reliability, algorithm bias, and cultural appropriation remain at the top of the discussion about the role of AI in storytelling. There is a risk that stories may be too formulated or adjusted to suit algorithmic preferences, with unpredictability and emotional wealth characterized by large narratives (Bansal et al., 2024). Furthermore, using AI in a new package of cultural narratives for mass consumption raises ethical issues regarding property, representation, and marketing. Who will be told, and who will benefit from their stories? Platforms like Netflix continue to invest in culturally rooted content, so these questions must be answered through integrated production practices, fair reward models, and collaborative approaches to telling stories that include local creators, scientists, and communities. Stories are no longer static artifacts but dynamic systems characterized by data, algorithms, and global networks. They travel through the platform, morph in response to feedback from their audiences, and adapt to new technical services. In this liquid narrative landscape, AI works not only as a medium and as a message but also to experience, understand, understand, and appreciate how the story is told. The case of a similar project as Shahmaran shows that when it is thoughtfully used, AI enriches the gap between local traditions and global audiences, enriches the story, and promotes a more integrated and diverse narrative ecology (Habib & ElTarabishi, 2024). Rather than rethinking the role of storytellers as lonely geniuses, we invite ourselves as the knot of a huge, interrelated system of people and machine creativity. It asks us to use hybrids, test new narrative forms, and address cultural heritage with respect and vision. Understanding the meaning of telling stories and performing live shows digitally while AI develops.

Cultural Influences on AI-Generated Narratives

The integration of AI into storytelling revolutionized how stories are created and distributed and how cultural values and traditions are encoded and interpreted. At the heart of this transformation is the ability to process and analyze large quantities of text and visual data and audit data, which allows AI to recognize culturally important patterns, topics, and motifs. Suppose you are trained in culturally rich data records. In that case, you can learn from folk tales and myths to literature, music, and oral AI systems, recognize the nuances of specific traditions, and encode these discoveries into stories that generate these discoveries. This ability allows the digital preservation of intangible cultural heritage, including language, rituals, phrases, and beliefs. By embedding these elements into stories, AI acts as a channel of cultural communication, allowing the stories to be told and retold in a way that honors their origins and adapts to modern forms. The quality and expressivity of the training data are essential to the reliability and accuracy of the resulting story. The AI output reflects these flaws if the data is limited, distorted, or biased (Kurian & Saad, 2024). For example, AIs trained primarily in Western literature, allowing the media to try to present Indigenous perspectives and non-Western storytelling traditions genuinely. Culture's wealth lies in the complexity, contradictions, and diversity of depths that AI is challenging to grasp fully, especially when it is limited to data by simplified or stereotypical representations.

AI can reflect and strengthen cultural identity, but there is also the risk of flattening Vermorts in Vermont. The challenge is for AI systems to curate and expand the data records they are trained to include a more balanced, more integrated cultural narrative. Algorithms do not only reflect the data they are being trained. Enhance a particular pattern compared to other patterns based on optimized goals, such as maximizing engagement and click rates. These optimization goals misprise sensational, exotic, or well-known tropics at the expense of more subtle and authentic narratives (Hernandez-Martinez & Keane, 2024). As a result, marginalized communities can jointly present their stories of being misrepresented or deprived of context and agency. For example, colonial or patriarchal bias can be replicated and embedded in historical texts and media, maintaining obsolete stereotypes. Even the intentional use of AI can lead to cultural appropriation if the system does not recognize the origins of the narrative portrayed by the system or if you exclude the voices of these communities in storytelling. Combating these concerns requires technical solutions such as committee algorithms, culturally sensitive data, and structural changes in the development and delivery of AI tools (Zhao et al., 2024). These teams should include engineers, cultural scientists, artists, community leaders, and ethics professionals. It can lead the design and use of AI in a way that respects cultural integrity. Participatory design processes in which communities contribute to the development of AI counts help to tell care and accountable stories. In reality, this means collaborating with cultural institutions to invite local storytellers, cooperate with AI-generated myths, and digitize and comment on historical texts in ways that reflect local epistemology. In the foreground of the nature of narrative relationships and location, this approach emphasizes that culture is not a static resource but a living practice that must be used ethically and respectfully.

The role of cultural heritage in AI-driven narratives is significant in contexts where traditional knowledge is triggered. In many parts of the world, oral traditions are lost when younger generations hike in urban areas, take over globalized media, or lose language skills in regular language. AI can actively combat this erosion by detecting, maintaining, and reviving digital media traditions. For example, AI can teach children local legends, simulate old rituals in virtual reality, or create interactive stories that create music and poetry in endangered languages. These applications not only make cultural heritage accessible and more attractive but also encourage identity generation and learning pride. They help to pin people to their stories and navigate them with a root sense (de Lima et al., 2024). Who owns digital and coded stories in AI models? Who has the right to adapt, remix, or monetize them? These questions are severe when dealing with saint, ritual, or community-specific knowledge. Such digitization of knowledge and reproduction of algorithms can lead to mental or cultural damage if sensitivity is not addressed. The commercial interests that often drive AI development were conflicts with local governments, which encouraged the value of supporting traditional storytelling. Therefore, protecting cultural heritage in the digital age requires robust ethical framework conditions, legal protections, and city government mechanisms that maintain the rights and responsibilities of cultural managers. Despite these challenges, the potential of AI is to enrich cultural storytelling. It allows for multilingual stories on an unprecedented scale, reduces language barriers, and allows for the cycling of stories about different target groups. AI-generated subtitles, audio overs, and summaries make local narratives easier for a global audience to understand while maintaining a linguistic and emotional texture.

Furthermore, AI can promote intercultural dialogue by identifying theme similarities and general motifs in various traditions and helping audiences understand the universality of human experience. AI can promote a global sense of belonging rather than erasing it by illuminating the connection between West African people and Norse mythology, or between Ma Oli Haka and Japanese No performances. By creating nonlinear diagrams, adaptive arches, and interactive environments, AI invites audiences to participate in creating importance (Belda-Medina et al., 2024). This participatory spirit runs with many local people and non-Western traditions. There, stories about the story are interactive, municipal, and open. In these traditions, stories are not fixed texts but conversations that develop with everyone. AI has the potential to emulate and extend this fluidity, allowing stories to be adapted in real-time to entries of a variety of users, contexts, and cultural logic. Such dynamic narratives reflect the diversity of human representation and seek a dominant narrative format that will allow linearity closure and prioritize individual authors. It includes supporting local AI initiatives, establishing community-controlled data records, and developing open-source tools allowing cultural groups to create and manage their digital stories. It also implies that indicators of success in AI stories are related not only to views and sharing but also to cultural response, educational effectiveness, and community strengthening. Storytelling should be evaluated based on how well it is and how deeply connected, taught, healed, and inspired it. AI can increase these capabilities when guided by empathy, respect, and social justice values.

Finally, the role of AI in coding cultural values and traditions in storytelling is promising and burdened. It offers new opportunities to maintain, share, and reinterpret cultural heritage but also reveals the limitations and biases of technological infrastructure. The presentation of different stories in the content generated by AI depends on the inclusiveness of training data, the diversity of development teams, and the ethical framework conditions that influence the use of these tools. As AI is embedded in our cultural and creative ecosystem, we must remain vigilant against false presentations, spending, and homogenization risks. Instead, we must strive to make AI a medium for cultural blooming (Tosun et al., 2025). It reflects who we are and helps us become more careful, networked human storytellers. Through collaborative community-oriented practices, AI can contribute to a storytelling renaissance that honors the past, embraces the present, and imagines a more fair and integrated imagination.

AI in Gaming and Interactive Storytelling

Artificial intelligence revolutionizes video games' storylines by enabling profound, adaptive, and personalized experiences. Traditional players often follow linear or branched structures, which leads to limited statements in which players' choices are limited. It has enabled engaging storytelling, but the advent of AI has greatly expanded the possibilities for dynamic, player-driven stories that develop in real-time. AI can organically respond to player behavior and create immersion with agents who cannot fully achieve traditional scripting methods (Kendrick & Early, 2025). Natural Language (NLP) processing redefines the narrative limitations in interactive entertainment by producing procedural content (PCG) and machine learning algorithms. AI-driven NPCs have complex behaviors, emotional depth, and memories, which allow them to interact with players more realistically and wisely (Fan et al., 2024). In-game scenarios where players are repeatedly familiar with NPCs, AI can develop trustworthy relationships with players whose characters remind them of past interactions and adapt their dialogue and actions accordingly. This memory-based interaction creates continuity in the story's experience, bringing the world vividly and reactively. Games like The Elder Scrolls V: Skyrim and Red Dead Redemption 2 are beginning to implement rudimentary versions of such mechanics. However, AI progress can make this reactive storytelling more subtle and scalable. AI can generate environments, quests, and arches on the fly by analyzing player behavior and preferences. It increases repetition and is tailored to the gaming experience to make it feel personal and wise. For example, suppose players prefer stealth and diplomacy towards direct combat. In that case, AI can generate missions that require negotiation or lower classes, along with characters who deal with this strategic approach. AI can also interpret emerging stories that arise organically from the interaction between game systems and player decisions. It increases player narrative institutions and transforms them into active story-building participants, like pre-defined consumer behavior (Begus, 2024). The game with NLP allows players to participate in free dialogue with characters, leading to more natural and unwritten conversations. Projects such as AI dungeons and large model (LLMS) progress show whether players can write or speak their actions and intentions. AI creates dynamically relevant answers and behavior development. This type of interaction involves a traditional model of dialogue that restricts player input to several options, replacing it with an open story. In this story, the narrative path is just as different as the player's ideas. The ability of AI to understand and generate language in context improves immersion by allowing for richer character development and narrative depth. The main issue is the possibility that AI-generated content may reproduce or enhance harmful stereotypes, distortions, or misinformation.

Suppose an AI system is trained according to biased or incomplete data. In that case, the stories that create it reflect these biases, leading to problematic representations of breed, gender, culture, or morality. It is particularly affected in games of moral choice systems where AI can enhance discriminatory tropics or punish players for behaviors that deviate from normative moral frameworks. To remove this issue, you must carefully curate the training data, transparency in AI behavior, and include various voices in your design process (Beguš, 2024). AI-controlled storytelling relies heavily on data collection and analyzing player behavior, choices, and emotional responses. It allows for greater personalization but also raises data protection questions. Players need to let them know how their data is used, who can access it, and what protection measures are available to protect the information. Game developers are responsible for ensuring that data collection is transparent, mutually respectful, and respectful of players' autonomy. Additionally, there is a need to ethically limit how much emotional manipulation is permitted in the name of immersion. Suppose AI can predict and influence players' emotions. In that case, it can be used to create addictive gameplay loops or to use psychological weaknesses that cause serious ethical red flags. When the story's experience resonates with real and emotionality, players can develop deep attachments to fully generated characters and scenarios. While this can be a powerful tool for commitment and empathy, it also risks disruption between artificial and actual emotional experiences. Using AI to simulate relationships, sadness, or trauma, especially without clear boundaries or review mechanisms, can have psychological effects that are not yet fully understood. Game developers should consider ways to responsibly manage the emotional depth of AI-controlled stories and allow players to distinguish between them in their game and their real relationships. If players and AI create the story, does anyone belong to the resulting story? It is particularly relevant to user-generated content platforms and games, allowing players to share or monetize their experiences. Establishing a legal and ethical framework for AI-CO authors is important to protect both the creator and the user. Furthermore, even if AI is involved in the final product, writing the work of human writers, artists, and designers is important. AI should be seen as a tool to enhance human creativity, not as an alternative.

AI and the Transformation of Advertising Narratives

AI will change the landscape of ad counts by introducing a new era of deeper, personalized, data-driven storytelling for individual consumers. In digital marketing and branding, AI-controlled storytelling uses machine learning, natural language processing, and predictive analytics to create content that adapts to real-time consumer preferences, behaviors, and contexts. It shows a departure from traditional, one-size-fits-all ads toward dynamic, more intimate interactions for branded consumers. With AI, marketers can provide stories that are not only visually and emotionally persuasive but also highly relevant. Brands can now generate individual email campaigns, social media ads, and website experiences developed based on user behavior. For example, customers browsing eco-friendly products can use user-specific actions and product recommendations to show a story about a brand's sustainability travel. ChatGpt and Midjourney generate creative copies, visual assets, and even video scripts that match brand messaging but can quickly adapt to various segments. This massive personalization allows marketers to remain consistent and, at the same time, achieve detailed adaptation. It is not possible to use traditional methods alone. For example, Coca-Cola uses AI-generated visuals and user data to create hyper-oriented social media campaigns that speak directly to consumers' lives and efforts.

Nike combines AI with portable technology to tell stories about personal performance and motivation and translates user activity data into compelling stories about fitness and success. Similarly, Netflix uses AI to recommend content and create personalized trailers that match individual audience settings, effectively converting viewers into co-authors of entertainment experiences. These case studies show how AI refines the story's accuracy and extends the scope of a brand story with consumer voice and experience. AI promotes deeper emotional connections between brands and consumers by providing uniquely relevant stories. Personalized stories can induce trust, loyalty, and a sense of belonging. It is essential for long-term brand affinity.

Additionally, AI brand agile and responses – first stories can reflect changing trends, crises, or consumer moods. This ability to remain culturally and contextually aware increases brand reliability and relevance. However, using AI in storytelling also requires transparency and ethical responsibility. Consumers are increasingly aware of how data is used, and perceptions of manipulation and data protection breaches can undermine brand reliability. AI is essentially more than just a tool for optimizing advertising. It's the way brands tell stories and combine them with audiences. Transform static and static programs into dynamic, mutual interactions that develop with the audience and build brand identity through general and wise experiences.

AI in Cinema and New Media Narratives

Artificial intelligence will dramatically change a film's narrative, changing how films are created, distributed, and experienced. In traditional filmmaking, storytelling is guided by specific scripts and narrative arches, largely linear and fixed. However, with AI, filmmakers have tools that scriptwriters can improve. It can process film material more efficiently, analyze target group preferences, and generate visual and narrative elements. AI-powered software can support screenwriters by suggesting action changes, improving dialogue, and creating entire short films based on genre and emotional sound input. This technical intervention is not intended to replace human creativity but to improve filmmakers' Freans focus on vision and nuance. Instead, AI deals with patterns, predictions, and structural consistency. As a result, the film's narrative is tailored to adaptation, experimentation, and development of viewer expectations. In these formats, audiences receive institutions that influence direction and story outcomes, often in real-time.

AI algorithms help manage the narrative complexity behind such interactions and dynamically adapt actions based on audience choices. A similar project to Netflix's Black Mirror: Bandersnatch shows how AI can support seamless transitions between branching logic and interactive stories. This form of film has redesigned the meaning of turning passive viewers into active participants and dealing with the story. AI is an improvement in content and strategy for delivering content, ensuring that every method is consistent and emotionally satisfying, and user commitment to improving future interactions. Using Netflix, Amazon Prime, and Disney+, we use algorithms for machine learning to analyze observational habits, preferences, and behavioral data to recommend movies and series that may address individual users. These systems affect not only what viewers observe but also how filmmakers and studios design and develop new content. Genre, pace, topic, and cast decisions are characterized by predictive analytics, allowing them to promote formats and stories that suit consumer demand. This data-controlled approach to storytelling helps maximize platforms, commitments, and bonds but also raises concerns about the homogenization and marginalization of niche or experimental films. These innovations offer new creative opportunities and critical reflection on human authors' originality, diversity, and future role in film.

AI and Activism in Digital Storytelling

AI is increasingly important in activist narrative design and social movement dynamics. By analyzing a large amount of social media data, news content, and public sentiment, AI activists can help create targeted messages and identify strategic communication channels. These data-controlled findings allow campaigns to be more agile, recoiling, and persuasive, improving reach and response for advocacy stories. AI tools can also create compelling visual and textual content for protest media, videos, and slogans that match the real-time development of emotional and cultural references. Automated content creation allows for limited resource movements, increasing marginalized voices and creating high-quality material of interest that encourages collective action. However, using AI in digital advocacy groups raises considerable ethical concerns. There is a risk of misinformation, algorithm bias, and manipulation, especially when AI tools are trained according to imbalance or politically charged data. Furthermore, AI surveillance technology can be driven against activists who undermine the causes of AI. AI improves the strategic capabilities of campaigns for social justice but also requires strict ethical supervision and transparent use.

AI, Orientalism, and Self-Orientalism in Digital Narratives

AI's representation of Eastern and Western narratives often reflects the data and cultural biases embedded in its training sources. Since most AI models are developed using predominantly Western-centric data, their storytelling tends to align with Western values, aesthetics, and narrative structures. This skew can result in reductive or stereotypical portrayals of Eastern cultures, reinforcing orientalist tropes—such as mysticism, exoticism, or authoritarianism—that have long been criticized in global media. When AI is tasked with generating content about non-Western regions, it may unintentionally replicate these outdated narratives due to its exposure to biased historical texts, films, or media.

The perpetuation of orientalist imagery in AI-generated media is evident in outputs that romanticize or distort Eastern traditions while positioning Western perspectives as default or superior. For instance, AI-generated travel content or historical recreations may emphasize temples, martial arts, or spiritual rituals without proper cultural context, flattening diverse cultures into monolithic caricatures. Case studies such as AI-generated promotional videos for tourism in South Asia or East Asia reveal the recurrence of such themes. To counteract this, training AI systems on more culturally inclusive datasets and involving diverse creators in the development process is essential, ensuring global storytelling becomes more equitable, authentic, and respectful of cultural complexity.

Ethical and Philosophical Considerations in AI-Powered Storytelling

AI changes the boundaries of storytelling, truth, fiction, and credibility by creating stories that blur the boundaries between reality and imagination. Content that contains AI-generated content with deeper synthetic media and data-controlled stories can manipulate or manufacture truths that question traditional notions of reliability. For example, AI can create realistic news and documentaries that are displayed in truth and are entirely produced. It raises great concern about the reliability of information and the possibility of misinformation, as it can be difficult for the audience to recognize between the actual and correct content. In this context, truth becomes subjective, relying on systems and algorithms that curate and produce, undermining trust in media and storytelling.

Despite the growing influence of AI on narrative creation, human institutions remain essential. AI can create stories, but people are responsible for determining parameters, curating content, and making ethical decisions about the story. The role of human creativity in AI-controlled narrative management ensures that narratives reflect intention and responsibility, particularly in sensitive areas such as political discourse and cultural representation. Supervision is required to ensure the story maintains ethical integrity and respect for different perspectives when AI tools are developed. It certainly means that the algorithms are trained on various integrated datasets to avoid distortion and simultaneously address issues related to the privacy, consent, and impact of content from AI on social norms. Developers, Political Decisions - Creators and creators must work together to create guidelines that protect against harmful manipulation and promote responsible narratives that respect creativity and truth.

CONCLUSION

AI changes digital stories by enabling more personalized, urgent, and dynamic stories. Through AI-controlled tools such as natural language processing, machine learning, and data analytics, content creators can adapt their stories to individual target groups and respond to their preferences, emotions, and behaviors in real-time. It opens up new opportunities for interactive, adaptive development experiences for storytelling on digital platforms. AI also improves creativity by supporting content from scripts to visual design, allowing for more efficient production processes while maintaining high-quality results. Instead of exchanging it, it is important to integrate AI as a complementary tool to human creativity. Experts need to prioritize ethical narratives and ensure that the content generated by AI is diverse, integrated, and unbiased. Educators should focus on equipping students with the navigation skills of AI tools and promoting critical thinking about the effects of AI on media consumption and production. Investigating the emotional impact of AI-controlled narratives, improving algorithms for cultural representation, and understanding AI's role in social narrative design is important to driving technology and its ethical applications in digital stories.

REFERENCES

Alqahtani, M. M., Alanazi, A. M., Algarni, S. S., Aljohani, H., Alenezi, F. K., Alotaibi, T. F., & Ismaeil, T. T. (2024). Unveiling the Influence of AI on Advancements in Respiratory Care: Narrative Review. *Interactive Journal of Medical Research*, *13*(1), e57271. DOI: 10.2196/57271 PMID: 39705080

Avello Martínez, R., Gajderowicz, T., & Gómez Rodríguez, V. G. (2024). Is ChatGPT helpful for graduate students in acquiring knowledge about digital storytelling and reducing their cognitive load? An experiment.

Bansal, G., Nawal, A., Chamola, V., & Herencsar, N. (2024). Revolutionizing visuals: The role of generative AI in modern image generation. *ACM Transactions on Multimedia Computing Communications and Applications*, *20*(11), 1–22. DOI: 10.1145/3689641

Beguš, N. (2024). Experimental narratives: A comparison of human crowdsourced storytelling and ai storytelling. *Humanities & Social Sciences Communications*, *11*(1), 1–22. DOI: 10.1057/s41599-024-03868-8

Belda-Medina, J., & Goddard, M. (2024). AI-driven digital storytelling: A strategy for creating English as a foreign language (EFL) materials.

Bilici, S., & Yilmaz, R. M. (2024). The effects of using collaborative digital storytelling on academic achievement and skill development in biology education. *Education and Information Technologies*, *29*(15), 20243–20266. DOI: 10.1007/s10639-024-12638-7

Chubb, J., Reed, D., & Cowling, P. (2024). Expert views about missing AI narratives: Is there an AI story crisis? *AI & Society*, *39*(3), 1107–1126. DOI: 10.1007/s00146-022-01548-2 PMID: 36039046

Ciğerci, F. M., & Yıldırım, M. (2024). From Freytag pyramid story structure to digital storytelling: Adventures of pre-service teachers as story writers and digital story tellers. *Education and Information Technologies*, *29*(5), 5697–5720. DOI: 10.1007/s10639-023-12042-7

Dai, Y., Lee, J., & Kim, J. W. (2024). AI vs. human voices: How delivery source and narrative format influence the effectiveness of persuasion messages. *International Journal of Human-Computer Interaction*, *40*(24), 8735–8749. DOI: 10.1080/10447318.2023.2288734

de Lima, E. S., Casanova, M. A., & Furtado, A. L. (2024). Imagining from images with an AI storytelling tool. *arXiv preprint arXiv:2408.11517*.

Fan, M., Cui, X., Hao, J., Ye, R., Ma, W., Tong, X., & Li, M. (2024, May). StoryPrompt: Exploring the Design Space of an AI-Empowered Creative Storytelling System for Elementary Children. In *Extended Abstracts of the CHI Conference on Human Factors in Computing Systems* (pp. 1-8).

Febriandy, R. K., & Revolusi, P. (2024). Digital storytelling as political image construction in the 2024 presidential election campaign: Case study of the tiktok account@ gibran_rakabuming. *The International Journal of Social Sciences (Islamabad)*, *4*(2), 191–204.

Gourlet, P., Ricci, D., & Crépel, M. (2024). Reclaiming artificial intelligence accounts: A plea for a participatory turn in artificial intelligence inquiries. *Big Data & Society*, *11*(2), 20539517241248093. DOI: 10.1177/20539517241248093

Habib, M. Y., & ElTarabishi, M. (2024). The role of Artificial Intelligence in shaping the future of Media production and the application of Algorithm bias theory in Storytelling. *Journal of Media and Interdisciplinary Studies*, *3*(8), 1–28. DOI: 10.21608/jmis.2024.299137.1033

Hernandez-Martinez, P., & Keane, T. (2024). Learning mathematics and its relevance through a digital storytelling assessment task at university. *International Journal of Mathematical Education in Science and Technology*, •••, 1–17.

Jao, C. Y., Chen, C. H., & Yeh, H. C. (2024). Exploring the effects of cross-cultural collaborating on bilingual digital storytelling on students' intercultural learning. *Interactive Learning Environments*, *32*(10), 6815–6832. DOI: 10.1080/10494820.2023.2286386

Jiang, J. (2024). "Emotions are what will draw people in": A study of critical affective literacy through digital storytelling. *Journal of Adolescent & Adult Literacy*, *67*(4), 253–263. DOI: 10.1002/jaal.1322

Jiang, X., Liu, L., Wu-Ouyang, B., Chen, L., & Lin, H. (2024). Which storytelling people prefer? Mapping news topic and news engagement in social media. *Computers in Human Behavior*, *158*, 108248. DOI: 10.1016/j.chb.2024.108248

Kasemsarn, K., Sawadsri, A., Harrison, D., & Nickpour, F. (2024). Museums for Older Adults and Mobility-Impaired People: Applying Inclusive Design Principles and Digital Storytelling Guidelines—A Review. *Heritage*, *7*(4), 1893–1916. DOI: 10.3390/heritage7040090

Kendrick, M., & Early, M. (2025). Digital storytelling and intersectional identities: Youth with refugee experiences (re) claiming life stories. *International Multilingual Research Journal*, *19*(2), 99–115. DOI: 10.1080/19313152.2024.2332119

Kholifah, W., & Hamzah, H. (2025). Harnessing AI for Writing Excellence: Exploring ToolBaz. com and Gender Differences in Enhancing Twelfth Graders' Narrative Skills. *AL-ISHLAH: Jurnal Pendidikan*, *17*(1), 524–534. DOI: 10.35445/alishlah.v17i1.6563

Kurian, N., & Saad, C. (2024). Where technology meets empathy: Using digital storytelling, gaming, and AI to teach about peace and human rights. *Communication and education: Promoting peace and democracy in times of crisis and conflict*, 148-163.

Nader, K., Toprac, P., Scott, S., & Baker, S. (2024). Public understanding of artificial intelligence through entertainment media. *AI & Society*, *39*(2), 713–726. DOI: 10.1007/s00146-022-01427-w PMID: 35400854

Ngoi, S., Tan, K. H., Alias, J., & Mat, N. (2024). Digital storytelling to improve english narrative writing skills. *International Journal of Academic Research in Business & Social Sciences*, *14*(4), 546–560. DOI: 10.6007/IJARBSS/v14-i4/21249

Pierosara, S. (2024). Narrative autonomy and artificial storytelling. *AI & Society*, *39*(4), 1785–1794. DOI: 10.1007/s00146-022-01595-9

Rachman, R., Hamid, M. A., Wijaya, B. K., Wibowo, S. E., & Intan, D. N. (2024). Brand storytelling in the digital age: Challenges and opportunities in online marketing. *Jurnal Ekonomi*, *13*(01), 355–364.

Sanabria Zepeda, J. C., Olivo Montaño, P. G., Artemova, I., & Argüelles Cruz, A. J. (2024). Prospective narratives on global issues: An AI-based pedagogical model for assessing complex thinking. *JOTSE: Journal of Technology and Science Education*, *14*(1), 184–199. DOI: 10.3926/jotse.2445

Singh, A., Sethu, S. G., & Chaudhary, R. (2024). Artificial Intelligence in Storytelling: A Critical Analysis of Narrative Authenticity, Cultural Impact, and the Future of Creative Industries. *Library of Progress-Library Science, Information Technology & Computer, 44*(3).

Tariq, M. U. (2025). *AI-Driven Learning and Engagement in Higher Education.* IGI Global., DOI: 10.4018/979-8-3693-4074-5

Tariq, M. U. (2025). AI-Driven Personalized Learning: Revolutionizing Student Engagement and Teacher Efficiency in Education 5.0. In Mobo, F. (Ed.), *AI and Emerging Technologies for Emergency Response and Smart Cities* (pp. 75–96). IGI Global Scientific Publishing., DOI: 10.4018/979-8-3693-9770-1.ch004

Tariq, M. U. (2025). Co-Living With Augmented Digital Beings-Navigating the Intersection of AI and Everyday Life. In Moutinho, L., & Martins, L. (Eds.), *Impacts of Sensetech on Society* (pp. 187–206). IGI Global Scientific Publishing., DOI: 10.4018/979-8-3693-7147-3.ch009

Tariq, M. U. (2025). Unlocking Competitive Edge: Harnessing the Power of Collaborative Innovation. In Martínez-Falcó, J., Sánchez-García, E., & Marco-Lajara, B. (Eds.), *Open Innovation Strategies for Effective Competitive Advantage* (pp. 315–344). IGI Global Scientific Publishing., DOI: 10.4018/979-8-3693-9266-9.ch011

Tariq, M. U. (2025). Bridging Generations: Digital Transformation and Its Multifaceted Impact Across Societal Sectors. In Anshari, M., Almunawar, M., & Ordóñez de Pablos, P. (Eds.), *Impacts of Digital Technologies Across Generations* (pp. 1–22). IGI Global Scientific Publishing., DOI: 10.4018/979-8-3693-6366-9.ch001

Thakkar, A., Gupta, A., & De Sousa, A. (2024). Artificial intelligence in positive mental health: A narrative review. *Frontiers in Digital Health*, *6*, 1280235. DOI: 10.3389/fdgth.2024.1280235 PMID: 38562663

Thomas, S. (2024). AI and actors: Ethical challenges, cultural narratives and industry pathways in synthetic media performance. *Emerging Media*, *2*(3), 523–546. DOI: 10.1177/27523543241289108

Tosun, P., Uslu, A., & Erul, E. (2025). Connecting through chatbots: Residents' insights on digital storytelling, place attachment, and value co-creation. *Current Issues in Tourism*, *28*(4), 561–584. DOI: 10.1080/13683500.2024.2316857

Woodruff, A., Shelby, R., Kelley, P. G., Rousso-Schindler, S., Smith-Loud, J., & Wilcox, L. (2024, May). How knowledge workers think generative ai will (not) transform their industries. In *Proceedings of the 2024 CHI Conference on Human Factors in Computing Systems* (pp. 1-26). DOI: 10.1145/3613904.3642700

Zhao, X., Ma, Z., & Ma, R. (2024). Analyzing narrative contagion through digital storytelling in social media conversations: An AI-powered computational approach. *New Media & Society*, •••, 14614448241285445. DOI: 10.1177/14614448241285445

KEY TERMS AND DEFINITIONS

AI-Driven Personalization: Customizing content based on individual user preferences and behavior.

Generative Content: AI-generated media such as text, images, videos

Interactive Narratives: Stories shaped by user input and AI responses

Chapter 2
Audience Interactive Storytelling Anchors' Narrative Techniques in Opposition Television Channels in Turkey

Beril Sarılar
https://orcid.org/0000-0001-6181-9093
Istanbul Aydin University, Turkey

ABSTRACT

This study analyzes the evolving news narratives and audience engagements of anchors delivering primary news bulletins on Turkey's most viewed opposition television stations (NOW TV, Sözcü TV, Halk TV) regarding the development of news presentations. The study employed a mixed-methods approach, analyzing the primary news bulletins from four distinct days aired on three different networks (NOW TV, Sözcü TV, Halk TV) during January and February 2025. The purposive sample strategy was employed to identify days unaffected by special agendas that could accurately depict the routine broadcast flow.

INTRODUCTION

Television news displays, influenced by classical journalism, have experienced a significant transition due to the digital age. Traditional news anchors functioned as actors who only transmitted information, portrayed events impartially, and facilitated one-way engagement with the public; however, digitalization has fostered

DOI: 10.4018/979-8-3373-2023-6.ch002

the emergence of a two-way, interactive type of journalism. The main news anchors of opposition television networks in Turkey have emerged as influential characters who not only report news but also express their emotions, thoughts, and personal viewpoints, directly addressing the audience in the first person. These anchors are distinguished as individuals who influence the news setting, interpret its content, and cultivate personal connections with the audience.

This shift in Turkey commenced with the implementation of neoliberal policies in the 1980s, coinciding with global media dynamics. The policies enacted under former Prime Minister Turgut Özal disrupted TRT's monopoly and facilitated the emergence of private television networks (such as ATV, Kanal D, Show TV), so initiating the age of media privatization. In the 1990s, heightened competition for ratings prompted significant alterations in news presentation patterns; the anchor transitioned from the periphery to a central role in the news narrative. This transition reflects the anchor model pioneered by Walter Cronkite in the USA throughout the 1960s, as observed in Turkey.

Following the ascension of the Justice and Development Party (AKP) to power in 2002, the prevailing rivalry for ratings in the media sector was supplanted by ideological polarization. Over time, the AK Party established its own media network, resulting in a division of Turkish media between ro-government and opposition outlets. In the current political climate, the main news anchors of opposition television stations have adopted a more critical, emotive, and commentary-driven rhetoric, engaging directly with the audience. This alteration revolutionized both the modes of news presentation and the media consumption behaviors of the audience. The degree to which this new organization aligns with the principle of impartiality in journalism has been a subject of contention. This study seeks to analyze the narrative evolution evident in the primary news bulletins aired on opposition television channels in Turkey, the linguistic and interpretative strategies employed by news anchors, the frequency of commentary within the bulletins, and the influence of audience interaction through Twitter (X) on the news narrative.

The primary news bulletins from four distinct days, chosen from the three most-viewed opposition channels—NOW TV, Halk TV, and Sözcü TV—were evaluated, focusing on broadcasts from January and February 2025. The purposive selection strategy identified dates that were not indicative of special agendas, facilitating the observation of daily broadcast trends. The final day of the year, December 31, 2024, was incorporated into the January analysis.

In the study, these individuals were categorized as anchors due to the distinct separation between traditional presenters and anchors in Turkey, as the primary news presenters of favored stations are recognized as anchors by the public. The subsequent inquiries will be addressed within the parameters of the research. Have opposition presenters evolved from just news reporters to pundits and narrators?

Has the significance of comments in news material escalated? Have social media interactions influenced the development of news narratives.

THE EVOLUTION OF TELEVISION JOURNALISM AND ANCHORING PRACTICES IN TURKEY VIA THE LENS OF NEOLIBERAL POLICIES

Right-wing policies that proliferated globally from the 1970s, becoming increasingly pronounced in the 1980s, have facilitated a significant transition worldwide, similar to that observed in the West. The innovative economic framework initiated by Prime Minister Margaret Thatcher in the UK and President Ronald Reagan in the US manifested its influence in Turkey during Prime Minister Turgut Özal's administration, wherein privatization policies facilitated the state's withdrawal from the market, allowing it to operate autonomously. The process initiated by the January 24 Decisions advanced the narrative of "less state, less society" (Tanilli, 2009, p.72). This alteration in Turkey's economic infrastructure has concurrently changed the conventional media framework.

In the early 1990s, the Karacan and Simavi families, rooted in journalism, retreated from the media landscape, supplanted by media magnates like Aydın Doğan, Dinç Bilgin, and Korkmaz Yiğit, who were distinguished by their business affiliations. Since the 1980s, newspapers have primarily generated their revenue from advertising (Sarılar, 2021). Conversely, global economic transformations significantly influenced broadcasting. Notably, Prime Minister Turgut Özal and liberal factions criticized the public service broadcaster TRT (Turkish Radio and Television Corporation) for its political susceptibility stemming from its monopolistic status and for insufficiently accommodating pluralism. They consistently advocated for the emergence of commercial television funded by advertising revenue. The television channel "Star 1," established in 1989 and owned by "Magic Box," in which Ahmet Özal, son of then-Prime Minister Turgut Özal, was a partner, commenced broadcasting in 1990 without legal authorization. Its operations were overlooked despite contravening legislation until the legalization of private television and radio was enacted in 1993 (Sarılar, 2020, pp. 41-64). During the 1990s, media proprietors evolved from mere owners of news-producing outlets to active participants in tenders, seeking expansion through diversification into several sectors.

Since the Justice and Development Party (AKP) assumed power in Turkey in 2002, the media has evolved into an ideological domain rather than remaining solely an economic one, as it was during the 1990s. Despite Article 5 of the Turkish Radio and Television Law No. 2954 explicitly stipulating that TRT broadcasting must conform to the principle of "impartiality" (TBMM, 1983), it is evident that this principle has not been upheld: Over time, TRT has evolved into a propaganda instrument for disseminating the government's political narratives and policies to the public, while opposition parties have been inadequately represented. Consequently, the identity of public broadcasting has diminished, and the tenets of unbiased and pluralistic broadcasting have been significantly undermined. The ideological shift in broadcasting has transpired not only at TRT but also inside commercial media enterprises.

The AKP has marginalized critical publishing and established a proprietary framework for media ownership relations. Since 2007, heightened political pressures have precipitated a significant transformation in media ownership structures during the 2010s. Organizations like the Doğan Media Group, which once maintained more independent publishing policies, were compelled to exit the system and divest their publishing entities to government-aligned business figures due to substantial tax penalties and political coercion. The Demirören Group, aligned with the government and having acquired the Doğan Media Group, has secured a significant position in Turkish publishing history following this ownership transition; it has incorporated prominent media entities including the Hürriyet newspaper, CNN Türk, and Kanal D into its portfolio (NTV, 2018). Subsequent to the acquisition, these organizations promptly adopted a pro-government publication strategy. Currently, the majority of mainstream media in Turkey is controlled by business individuals sanctioned by the government, transforming the media into a hegemonic instrument that propagates governmental narratives and employs a monolithic, prescriptive approach, rather than adhering to the principles of pluralism, independence, and impartiality.

Currently, according to Antonio Gramsci's (1971) notion of hegemony, the state has influenced society not solely through Repressive State Apparatuses (Althusser, 2003) like the police and military, but also through cultural and ideological instruments in an unprecedented manner in the history of the Turkish press (Güngör, 2011, p. 294). Both the commercial broadcasting sector, a component of the Ideological State Apparatuses as articulated by French theorist Louis Althusser (2003), and the public sector have actively contributed to the intellectual and cultural development of society. Consequently, the predominant segment of the media has commenced operating through a process of suggestion and public pressure. This process has resulted in a transfer of ownership among media outlets in Turkey, leading to the unemployment and dismissal of long-standing journalists in mainstream media, who have been supplanted by those aligned with the government. Although the majority of the terminated journalists struggled to secure new employment, a subset persisted in their publishing endeavors through personal projects in alternative media, particularly on YouTube, while others transitioned to internet journalism (Kısa Dalga, 2022).

Broadcasting entities are required to secure authorization from the Radio and Television Supreme Council (RTÜK) for broadcasting licenses and frequency allocation; the quantity of television channels with oppositional broadcasting perspectives in Turkey has markedly diminished due to their inability to obtain this authorization and the preference of advertisers for mainstream television channels aligned with the government. NOW TV, previously referred to as TGRT, is one of the three channels analyzed in this study and operates within Turkey's mainstream media. In 2006, Rupert Murdoch's media conglomerate News Corporation acquired it from Ihlas Holding, a local conservative media entity, except TGRT NEWS. In 2007, the station was rebranded as FOX TV and took a more secular, oppositional broadcasting stance. In 2019, The Walt Disney Company acquired FOX TV, and upon discontinuing the use of the term "FOX" globally, the channel was rebranded as NOW TV in 2024. NOW TV maintains its opposition broadcasting by predominantly retaining its programming and personnel (Dünya, 2024).

The study also analyzed Halk TV. Halk TV is a news channel that commenced broadcasting in 2005, initiated by business associates of Deniz Baykal, the then-chairman of the Republican People's Party (CHP), Turkey's main opposition party. The channel garnered public recognition through its coverage of the Gezi Park Protests in 2013, an environmental civil resistance movement that originated in Istanbul's Taksim district and rapidly proliferated across Turkey. This movement evolved into a widespread social dissent against the government's authoritarian policies, as many mainstream media outlets overlooked this civil society initiative, while Halk TV prominently aired the street protests. In 2020, entrepreneur Cafer Mahiroğlu acquired Halk TV. Publicly available material indicates that there were disputes between CHP and Halk TV during Mahiroğlu's tenure; yet, Halk TV maintains its secular and oppositional broadcasting stance unchanged (10Haber, 2023). Sözcü TV, another station chosen as a sample in the study, is a news outlet characterized by a secular, nationalist, and oppositional broadcasting stance. The channel functions under Estetik Yayıncılık A.Ş., which also publishes a newspaper of the same name. The proprietor of the channel is entrepreneur Murat Akbay. The channel commenced broadcasting in March 2023 (Sözcü, 2023).

EVOLUTION OF PRIMARY NEWS FORMATS: TRANSITION FROM ANCHOR TO NARRATOR

The preparation of news is a collaborative effort involving reporters, cameramen, editors, broadcast managers, news directors, and ultimately, the anchorman. The term "anchor" utilized for anchors in Turkey derives from the English word "speaker," signifying speaker. In England, the public broadcaster BBC refers to the traditional news anchor as a newsreader, while the term presenter is employed to denote a general television presenter and occasionally an anchor in overseas broadcasts. In the United States, the term news anchor is favored. Anchor derives from the Latin term anchora, signifying "ship anchor" (Etymology Turkish). The term "anchor" refers to the individual who carries the flag last in a race, bringing it to the finish line as the team's most proficient runner; consequently, the most skilled and authoritative person who positions the flag at the finish line during the subsequent race is designated as the "anchorman" (Kars, 2015, p. 158). The evolution of journalism globally commenced in the 1940s, with CBS television broadcasting the inaugural evening news on August 15, 1948. Initially, television journalism was not essential for broadcasting; it only constituted a form of general programming (Kars, 2015, p.112). The emergence of announcers occurred in the 1950s and rapidly evolved (Atik, 2006, p.50).

The emergence of private television broadcasting, influenced by neoliberal policies, rendered the presence of the announcer and the requisite expertise and technical proficiency for delivering news essential. Turkey participated in the same procedure, and not only was the emphasis on accurate and effective news presentation, derived from the TRT school, insufficient, but registered beauty queens were also favored for news reading (Sarılar, 2018, p. 64). Neil Postman articulated this circumstance as follows: "While the Federal Communications Act contains no provision to this effect, it is virtually impossible for individuals who do not possess conventional beauty before the camera to communicate with the public in the 'news of the day'." Consequently, the majority of journalists allocate more time to their barbers than to news articles" (Postman, 2004, p.13). Turkish sociologist Emre Kongar articulated this predicament by stating, "Regrettably, some of these individuals are attractive children who have been selected from stages and competitions due to the emphasis placed on appearance; however, they are not only unable to articulate proper Turkish but also incapable of comprehending the significance of the texts they encounter" (Kongar, 2004).

In the 1980s, the implementation of neoliberal policies in Turkey, mirroring global trends, initiated a process of depoliticization. During the 1990s, television journalism evolved into a production hub for celebrities, including writers, beauty queens, models, and television actors. Corporations sponsored the attire of news anchors and commenced the transference of their branding from hairstyles to accessories such as watches and ties. During this age, the burgeoning consumer culture was accompanied by the marketing of popular culture approaches within news material to the audience. The advent of private television broadcasting significantly transformed news presentations. In this process, the objective, unbiased journalistic methodology was supplanted by a ratings-driven strategy. Neoliberalism characterizes the media as a business entity, thereby transforming news into a market "product" and positioning the viewer as a "consumer" within this framework. Amidst escalating rivalry, news narratives have evolved into dramatic accounts interlaced with personal stories designed to evoke emotional responses and enhance audience engagement for rating purposes (Sarılar, 2018, pp. 65-66). In the context of globalization, a prevalent term has emerged: "Returning home each evening as a guest," whereby anchors have become guests in the residences of viewers through their newly adapted formats. Mehmet Ali Birand's wife remarked following his demise, "Returning home every evening at 7 o'clock as a guest endeared him to many" (Sarılar, 2018, p.79).

The anchor notion originated in America, with news anchor Walter Cronkite being the first to embody this role, commencing his tenure at CBS television in 1950. Cronkite was designated "America's Most Trusted Man" due to his news reporting on the CBS Evening News from 1962 to 1981 (Schudson, 2001). Although possessing an objective reporting style, Cronkite expressed his opinions in extraordinary instances, such as the Kennedy assassination and the Vietnam War. On February 27, 1968, he asserted that the Vietnam War would not culminate in a definitive victory, stating, "But it is increasingly clear to this reporter that the only rational way out then will be to negotiate, not as victors, but as an honorable people who lived up to their pledge to defend democracy, and did the best they could." YouTube, 2012, is recognized as a pivotal milestone in media history. It has been asserted that US President Lyndon B. Johnson, upon hearing Cronkite's remarks, stated: "If I've lost Cronkite, I've lost Middle America" (Wicker, 1997). Cronkite's example illustrates that anchors have emerged as the predominant figures in news on major national channels like NBC, CBS, and ABC in America, embodying a national function and identity akin to heroes. Morse asserted that anchors are as crucial as the news they deliver (Morse, 1998, pp. 87-88).

Cronkite concluded his newscast with his famous phrase: "...And that's the way it is," followed by the date of the day. Cronkite's lucid and comprehensible language in news presentation enabled the viewers to effortlessly track events, and his avoidance of using his name as a news presenter for personal gain enhanced the credibility of his narratives. The American populace observed the Vietnam War, the Iran hostage crisis, the assassination of President Kennedy, and NASA's endeavors to land a man on the moon through him. Journalist anchors in Turkey, emulating Cronkite, crafted distinctive discourses for the openings and closings of newscasts, so establishing their own narrative structures. For instance, Mehmet Ali Birand would commence the newscast by stating, "We have initiated a new week." I am here with the most significant developments of the day, providing all the information," and for years, he would reiterate the phrase "That's it for tonight, do not schedule any appointments for tomorrow!" "Let us reunite" after the conclusion of the news. Reha Muhtar, a prominent figure of the era, is recalled for his frequent recitation of the words "Good evening Türkiye, wherever you live and are made to live!" during his tenure as an anchor on Show TV. Turkish sociologist Nurdan Gürbilek underscores the concept of anchoring, stating, "We encounter individuals who do not merely report news but actively shape the agenda, expressing their emotions and concerns regarding this agenda to the audience. They offer narratives intended for dissemination rather than merely conveying events, articulating their perspectives rather than representing an institution, and they themselves possess newsworthiness equivalent to the news they deliver." "These figures are more accessible, more genuine, and more relatable" (Gürbilek, 2001, p.114).

Communications academic Haluk Şahin described the British and American anchor traditions in the early 2000s as follows: *"The concept of newsreader, that is, a newsreader, was a concept that began to be used in England for news readers coming from the radio and continued to be used in this way until very recently. In the British tradition, these professional personalities are not stars themselves. Their main task is to read the news given to them well. In reality, they are people with no journalistic experience; their skills are usually related to reading, tone of voice and diction. In contrast, in American television, after such a transition period, a model emerged that was very competitive, in which there was a great competition and ratings were very important. And this process is also at the root of the 'anchor' professional personality. NBC featured a news team in the 1950s of two anchors, Huntley and Brinkley. This pair dominated the ratings for numerous years. Beginning in the 1960s, CBS introduced the seasoned journalist Walter Cronkite to the television audience. Crontike ultimately emerged as an opinion leader for a significant portion of the American populace. Crontike engaged individuals' psychology, asserting that the world was not as adverse as perceived. His announcements consistently concluded in this manner. "That is the way... this is how it is," signifying that life is not as adverse as it may seem"* (Vural, 2003).

Ali Kırca, regarded as Turkey's inaugural television reporter embodying the anchor archetype, hosted ATV Main News for numerous years. Walter Cronkite designated the evening news on CBS television as "CBS Evening News with Walter Cronkite," while Ali Kırca labeled the primary news segment as "Ali Kırca ile ATV News." In this context, Halk TV's evening news is identified as "Ece Üner ile Halk Main News"; Sözcü TV's evening news is referred to as "Fatih Portakal ile Sözcü Main News"; and NOW TV's evening news is designated as "Selçuk Tepeli ile NOW TV Main News" by associating them with their respective names. The identification of primary news bulletins with certain identities has also resulted in certain issues. Two of them are to presenters who were also part of this study: Fatih Portakal, the anchor of Sözcü TV's Main News, expressed his frustration during the broadcast regarding the "voice-over," or technically, the "individual who narrates the news text." He criticized this unnamed individual, whom the audience could neither see nor identify, for poorly delivering the news text, stating: "What is your opinion of the voice-over? Did you find it enjoyable? I found it unsatisfactory. I am accountable for every content in this news bulletin as I am associating my name with it. I provided my name for this news bulletin. I desire to witness the same application, compassion, and dedication in the substance and voice-over of the news. I am present before you. Because I am associating my name with this story. All aspects, from editing to voice-over, fall under my purview. Regrettably, I am assuming this obligation myself. I extend my apologies to you for this voice-over. (Gazete Duvar, 2023). Portakal's statement, "I am giving my name to this news bulletin," faced significant criticism on social media: "Walking ego, dot."; "Your inner voice is worse, Portakal"; "I believe you should apologize for that"; "They have ascribed so much significance to themselves that they have become symbols of arrogance"; "Monument of arrogance..."; "Come on, you are impressive again." You have crafted bread to satisfy your ego. (Gazete Duvar, 2023).

Fox TV Main News anchor Selçuk Tepeli expressed indignation regarding the government's policies, stating that villagers cultivating public lands perceive the current prices set for obtaining title deeds as exorbitant. He remarked, "Sir, half of the farmers in this country have abandoned their occupations now." "Proceed, proceed, proceed, proceed, proceed!" and hurled the paper, pen, and glass of water during the live show. Despite this approach aligning with public sentiment, the aggressive portrayal he exhibited faced criticism from certain individuals on social media (NOW News, 2021).

LITERATURE REVIEW

This research is grounded in Walter Fisher's Narrative Paradigm, Stuart Hall's Representation Theory, and Henry Jenkins' Participatory Culture. Stuart Hall's Representation Theory posits that the media does not mirror reality; rather, it reconstructs it through specific ideological frames. In Turkey, leading opposition news presenters deliver innovative representations with a critical viewpoint, articulating these narratives to the public through a dramatic and emotive style. Stuart Hall emerged as a significant figure in British intellectual life following World War II. Hall collaborated with Richard Hoggart and Raymond Williams at the British School of Cultural Studies in Birmingham. Jamaican thinker Hall characterizes the policies of Margaret Thatcher, the progenitor of neoliberalism in England, as authoritarian populism. Hall, who coined the term Thatcherism, assessed it as a regression of modernity (Hall, 1988). Hall concentrated on the emerging consumer society, the manifestations of popular culture, and the associated lifestyles. Following Hoggart's employment at UNESCO, he assumed leadership of Contemporary Cultural Studies, which evolved as a discipline from 1969 until 1980. "Under Hall's leadership, the studies at the center concentrated on mass media, examining their ideological functions and effects on daily life practices" (Chavez, 2009, p. 269). Cultural Studies focused on media discourses and sought to examine how these discourses rendered the ideologies of the powerful predominant. Hall employed the notion of hegemony, as articulated by Italian Marxist theorist Antonio Gramsci, in his examinations of media and ideology.

In this sense, Hall perceives the consumption of mass media as a domain of conflict. Hall asserts that media texts serve not merely as vessels of information but also as arenas of ideological conflict. In the study entitled Encoding / Decoding, Hall analyzes the simultaneous interpretation of media texts in oppositional, negotiated, and hegemonic modalities (Holmes, 2013, p. 187). Hall contends that media messages are not invariably interpreted by audiences as intended by the sender, and that audiences may perceive the same content in divergent manners—specifically in dominating, negotiated, or oppositional forms—contingent upon their social positions (Holmes, 2013). In this context, representation pertains not only to the composition of media content but also to the manner in which this content is perceived. The intersection of media representations with gender, class, ethnicity, and identity politics has emerged as a major research domain within cultural studies.

Procter (2004) states that Hall contests three elements of all mass communication models: Meaning is not solely defined or determined by the sender's simplicity. The message is consistently ambiguous and opaque. The audience is not a passive recipient of significance. Hall asserts that representation facilitates the connection between meaning, language, and culture. Representation is the creation of meaning for concepts in our minds via language. "Concepts and languages serve as a conduit for referencing objects, individuals, and events in both the 'real' world and the realm of fiction" (Hall, 2017, p. 23). Hall (2017) posits that meaning is constructed through the representation system. Representation serves as an intermediary layer in the construction of meaning maps; thus, one may conceptualize 'culture' as the codes that regulate the translation relationships inside these shared linguistic systems and instruments. "Codes establish the connections between concepts and signs" (Hall, 2017:31). In Representation Theory (2017), Stuart Hall contends that a book often fails to authentically depict individuals, events, locations, and history. Representation theory posits that the portrayals of images, characters, groups, and events in media and cultural discourses do not directly reflect reality; rather, they are formed within certain ideological, cultural, and historical frameworks. Stuart Hall asserts that television news does not convey events in a straightforward manner. The public agent converts the raw material incident into newsworthy content. Invisible elements, along with ideological and professional systems, determine what constitutes newsworthiness" (Kars, 2015, 112).

Walter Fisher's Narrative Paradigm posits that interpersonal communication is not solely grounded in rationality, but is also influenced by individual stories and narratives. The persuasion process of "Homo narrans," the storytelling entity, advances through narrative frameworks (Fisher, 1987). The study employed Fisher's Narrative Paradigm to illustrate that the examined anchors are not merely information transmitters, but also present the information through their own narrative frameworks; to uncover how the content of news texts is structured with a personal narrative for the audience, and to comprehend the emotional impacts they generate.

Fisher contested alternative paradigms by asserting that narrative constitutes the essence of an individual. Facebook's concept for storytelling is rooted in the aspiration to communicate human narratives and experiences. The platform's popularity is partially attributed to its capacity to facilitate the creation and distribution of personal tales. The core of the Narrative Paradigm is founded on narrative rationality. This paradigm posits that individuals not only subscribe to narratives based on logical reasoning but also emphasize the manner in which the narrative is conveyed. Two concepts arise in this context: coherence and faithfulness. The concept of coherence pertains to the consistency and integrity of a story's internal structure, whereas fidelity relates to the extent to which the narrative aligns with the individual's life experiences and beliefs, allowing for personal identification within the story. If these can be located, the narrative may be deemed trustworthy, hence facilitating an emotional connection. Fisher posits that the essence of effective communication lies in well-crafted narratives. The theory's emphasis on subjective interpretation over rationality and its questionable cross-cultural applicability are contentious aspects of the narrative paradigm (Media Theory, 2024). The Narrative Paradigm posits that the emotional impact of a narrative on the viewer or listener, achieved through eliciting responses from their emotional memory and fostering empathy, generates emotional resonance. The greater this emotional resonance, the more meaningful the viewer perceives the narrative, resulting in increased attachment. American media theorist and cultural studies scholar Henry Jenkins posits that in digital media platforms characterized as alternative and democratic, audiences transition from passive consumers to active participants, not only consuming information within a shared cultural context but also generating it themselves. Jenkins defines new media as a democratic arena in which media users interact and propagate their own concepts through the principles of convergence, participatory culture, and transmedia. Jenkins asserts that conventional media creators and contemporary media consumers together constitute a collective intelligence. According to Jenkins, participatory culture encourages individuals to engage actively online as watchers or readers (Jenkins, 2009, pp. 3-7). In participatory culture, users disseminate their own cultural expressions, ideas, and aspirations more than traditional media consumers, and they regard their engagement as a crucial component of the process.

Turner (2010), in elucidating Jenkins' notion of collective intelligence, references the emergence of dynamic, interactive mobile groups. Nomadic communities denote digital users unbound by a static media environment; they disseminate ideas, beliefs, and information—essentially narratives—across many media, contributing to the creation of collective intelligence while transcending temporal and spatial limitations. Jenkins' notion of Participatory Culture posits that audiences transition from passive consumers to active participants, engaging in the production and interpretation of content, while functioning as nomadic communities traversing various media platforms (Turner, 2010).

This approach elucidates that the television news narrative is influenced not only by the presenter but also by the audience, which actively participates through social media platforms (e.g., hashtag usage, survey responses, comments). The study reveals that primary news presentations, particularly on opposition television channels, transform into a pluralistic narrative that is interactive and enriched by collective intelligence, collaboratively constructed with the audience.

METHODOLOGY AND RESULTS

Owing to Turkey's intense and tumultuous news landscape, identifying days that can be deemed entirely "normal" is rather challenging. Consequently, the study employed purposive sampling to select days that are not extreme, devoid of extraordinary disasters, coups, or wars that significantly impact society, yet still facilitate ongoing political and social discourse, and possess a relatively high degree of representativeness. In this context, four days were analyzed: January 13 and February 24 to February 27 of 2025. The study for January included December 31, 2024, as part of the sample due to its news content and representativeness.

The qualitative aspect of the research involved a comprehensive analysis of news bulletin presentations from two distinct days for each anchor, focusing on narrative motifs, vocative discourses, audience interaction styles, and the presenters' personal narrative strategies. This qualitative research included thematic coding, focusing specifically on body language, mimicry, emphasis, gestures, and personal remarks made by the presenter within the news setting. In the quantitative analysis aspect, news bulletins from four distinct days featuring the same anchors were utilized; criteria included bulletin durations, the number of news items, and the presenter's speaking rate. Audience interactions with social media tags and mini surveys were also displayed in a table. A comprehensive analytical model integrating story structures and quantitative data was developed.

The narratives delivered by the anchors of the primary news bulletins on Sözcü TV, Halk TV, and NOW TV from January 13 to February 27, 2025, were assessed according to three fundamental theoretical frameworks: Walter Fisher's Narrative Paradigm, Stuart Hall's Theory of Representation, Participatory Culture by Henry Jenkins.

The presenter's narrative features in news presentation were analyzed through variables including audience engagement, political representation language, body language, and emotional conveyance.

Fatih Portakal (Sözcü TV)- January 13 and February 27, 2025

Walter Fisher- Narrative Paradigm

Fisher posits that individuals comprehend the world through narratives rather than by logical deductions. In this setting, Fatih Portakal conveys the news not merely as factual information, but in a narrative style imbued with passion and supplemented by personal testimony.

- "I did not become ensnared, allow me to clarify that as well" (February 27), he asserts, suggesting that, in contrast to others, he holds a divergent perspective. This viewpoint may invite criticism, yet he remains unreserved in articulating it, thereby disclosing his emotional and intellectual stance in the discourse. This indicates that the news is not merely delivered as facts, but is also interwoven with a personal narrative.
- In recounting the imprisonment, he cultivates a dramatic ambiance through temporal specificity, stating, "The clock was showing 4 in the morning…" and generates a door sound effect by knocking twice on the table where his documents are positioned (knock knock) (February 27). This movement engages the spectator in an emotional experience. Both the verbal and bodily narratives are engaged. He underscores the emotional fervor of the account by stating, "I am not composing a poem, I am conveying the truth" (February 27).
- He critiques this condition by asserting that the voices of individuals who lost relatives in the Kartalkaya disaster, one of Turkey's most significant fire calamities resulting in 78 fatalities, have become inaudible. Seventy-eight individuals perished, including infants, women, children, and men. Do the families not voice their grievances, or has no one initiated legal action against the minister, the hotel management, the governorship, the Provincial Special Administration, or those accountable? For instance, if such an event were to occur to me, I would annihilate the globe! In other terms, I would endeavor to the fullest extent possible! (February 27). He forges an empathetic connection with the tragedy victims using sentiments such as:

- "Let me tell you something" (January 13) offers intimate anecdotes that captivate the audience and foster direct engagement with them.
- The tale is enhanced by metaphors, such "How far can politics extend, my friend…" Collecting stamps, I am uncertain... Fatih Portakal's incorporation of emotional aspects, including anger, rebuke, sarcasm, comedy, and empathy, in his news broadcasts fosters an emotional connection with the viewer. Thus, the audience not only acquires knowledge; they also forge an emotional connection with the news and become integral to it.

Stuart Hall- Theory of Representation

Hall posits that the media does not objectively mirror reality; rather, it reconstructs it within specific ideological frameworks. Fatih Portakal redefines news through a contrarian mode of depiction.

- "Mr. President asserts, 'If we reduce the cost of water, consumption will increase; we sell it at a premium,' thus implying savings. Mr. President, do you believe the populace is naïve?" (January 13). He assumes a position adjacent to the crowd and articulates their perspective.
- In his publicly presented text, Öcalan, currently incarcerated, establishes a framework reflecting his composed demeanor in anticipation of potential public backlash, questioning, "Why wasn't this text read in Turkish?" It is inconsequential to me; ultimately, the flag remained aloft, the nation was not compromised, nor was it invaded... (February 27).
- He employs amusing yet critical representational language, exemplified by lines such as: "What will these individuals do, fish?" (February 27). it was suggested that one of the parties involved in the initiative process held no expectations; nonetheless, this assertion lacked realism.
- He articulates the dissenting perspective by questioning, "Did Devlet Bahçeli utter these words in a political context?" (February 27).
- He departs from the conventional function of a mere reporter by stating, "Today was a day to be noted in history" (February 27) at the outset of the broadcast, thereby establishing an ideological framework from the beginning.
- Statements like, "Öcalan passed the responsibility to the government," and "Will a provision be incorporated into the constitution?" (February 27) indicates that the news was not presented in impartial language; rather, Portakal underscores his attempt to interpret the government's intentions.
- When Portakal states, "I don't believe this government possesses a viable project," he does not merely convey information; he provides a significant commentary on the matter.

According to Hall's theory of representation, these examples highlight the media's guiding nature rather than its neutrality.

Henry Jenkins- Participatory Culture

Portakal redefines the news bulletin as a collaborative content creation process with the audience, rather than a traditional "broadcast." He creates a dynamic media network utilizing YouTube, X (Twitter), and street interviews across the country.

- He opens the show by posing the question, "Question of the day: Are you viewing the news?" (February 27). This introductory question positions the audience as active stakeholders, producers, and subjects of the content rather than passive consumers.
- He engages in a discourse by referencing the audience's tweets, stating, "Ms. Mine says… Derman Bey wrote…" (February 27). It represents the manifestation of a voice emerging from the grassroots within the media, transforming the audience's voice into a public discourse.
- By stating, "They wrote it on YouTube, let me share it too…" (January 13), he integrates cross-platform contact.

Nonverbal Communication and Symbols

While perusing tweets, he modulates his tone, occasionally elevating it and at times directly addressing individuals ("Ms. Mine, do not be concerned"). He transforms the audience from mere consumers into participants in the tale, demonstrating empathy.

- At the conclusion of each day, he concludes the announcements by forming a heart gesture and stating, "Take care of yourself, and remain with love and respect" (on both days). He forges a personal and emotional bond with the audience by surpassing his formal persona.

He highlights the texts on the table with a highlighter pen. In accordance with Hall's concept of reinterpretation, he constructs a story that gets reconfigured in the field through this action.

He does not utilize a prompter; instead, numerous pages are spread across the wide table before him, indicating that the news has not undergone a "editorial filter" and is presented in his own voice. This perspective aligns with Fisher's narrative paradigm. He fosters connection and allegiance with the audience through his personal narrative rather than an institutional one.

When employing sardonic statements, he elevates his eyebrows, reinforcing the emphasis with his brows, eyes, and verbal expression. Fisher's narrative coherence is evident, with consistency exhibited not only in the content but also in his nonverbal communication.

Upon hearing the phrase “Eagles fly alone” (February 27), he emulates the eagle by extending his arms to resemble wings. He transforms into a storyteller and endeavors to etch his narrative more deeply in memory.

He occasionally laughs, resorts to colloquial expressions such as “God willing, God willing,” and engages with the audience in a manner akin to a common individual (February 27). He incorporates his identity as a member of the community into his narrative.

Occasionally, he engages in conversation with a studio officer (cameraman, director), posing a question; the public hears Portakal but not the officer's response. Portakal remains indifferent to this and addresses the audience, relaying the discourse. This also fosters trust, as it conveys to the audience that no clandestine events are occurring.

Fatih Portakal transcends traditional journalism with his narratives and body language, exhibiting an ideologically encoded framework that generates counter-representations and engages the audience directly via both nonverbal and vocal communication. This scenario illustrates that the connection formed by opposition media channels with the audience transcends beyond passive information dissemination; representation constitutes an emotional, ideological, and political process.

Table 1. Fatih Portakal (Sözcü TV Main News) Interaction Methods with the Audience

Date	Hasthag – Number of Interactions	Poll of the Day (from X)-Participation rate-Top voted answer	Poll of the Day YouTubeParticipation rate-Top voted answer	Quote of the day
31st December 2024	#365 days ago 103 Tweets	-365 days ago, what kind of country did you dream of? What is the reality today? -11.439 votes -I had no hope, I was right (67.2%)	Bahçeli and Erdoğan gave both optimistic and harsh messages to İmralı. What do you think? -4949 votes -Might be an armored combat (%41)	Immanuel Kant "Be brave enough to use your own mind"
13rd January 2025	#I refuse -133 Tweets	- The government will give 150,000 lira interest-free loans to newlyweds, will you get married? -10.821 votes -No, of course (%57)	- Why is it always AKP that shows the red card? -8363 votes -Because voters did not learn their lesson (62%)	Charles Bukowski "Society is full of idiots who fervently defend idiots. The world is an idiot's paradise".
24nd January 2025	#I bet -340 Tweets	Erdoğan again asked for patience at the congress. What could he mean by patience? -11.417 votes - Bear with me (%36,6)	- If a person has no photos with friends from their university years, how can this be explained? -5953 votes -He is not a university graduate	Şems-i Tebrizi "Speak the word in the strainer and it will not muddy the lake; speak the word in the knee and it will be a pearl in the ear; speak the word to the face and it will not be backbiting and embarrassing."
7nd February 2025	#youhavetheball -199 Tweets		Öcalan said "PKK should dissolve itself". He wanted the way for democratic politics to be opened. What does AKP do? -7246 votes - Apo throws the ball to Erdoğan and Bahçeli (%55)	Ömer Hayyam "The darkness flees from the light and the lie from the truth; the sun shines even if it is alone; do not worry, loneliness is the fate of the righteous; crows fly in flocks, eagles fly alone".

Table 2. Fatih Portakal- Sözcü TV Main News Bulletin

Date	Channel	Anchor	Number of News	Duration (minute)	Anchor (%)
31st December 2024	Sözcü TV	Fatih Portakal	11	59	63,73
13rd January2025	Sözcü TV	Fatih Portakal	12	59	67,8
24nd February 2025	Sözcü TV	Fatih Portakal	11	58,55	68,35
27nd February 2025	Sözcü TV	Fatih Portakal	10	58	66,15

Fatih Portakal's speaking rate on Sözcü TV's Main News remains consistent over a four-day period, accounting for 63.73%-68.35% of the speaking duration within the approximately one-hour broadcast (excluding advertisements and including news teasers) (Table 2). The bulletin presents an average of 11 news items. Portakal's narrative and commentary beyond the duration of the news narrative. This scenario aligns with Sözcü TV's overarching programming ethos, as the network employs an opposition-focused, critical, and populist broadcasting strategy in Turkey. Fatih Portakal serves as an opinion leader, both with the news duration he addresses and his commentary on current events. He cultivates a connection with the audience through an emotive, populist, humorous, and occasionally critical tone, thereby constructing an alternative media paradigm. Fatih Portakal consistently endeavors to engage with the audience throughout the broadcast. He employs various techniques for this purpose, including street interviews, a daily question on YouTube, a hashtag initiated on X (Twitter), and a daily poll. Through continuous feedback inside the bulletin flow, he communicates audience interactions, positioning the audience as the focal point of the narrative and even shaping his narratives based on their remarks (Table 1).

Fatih Portakal's audience engagement with the hashtags he initiated on X surpasses that of Selçuk Tepeli and Ece Üner, attributable to his more vigorous utilization of social media.

Selçuk Tepeli (NOW TV)- January 13, 2025, until February 27, 2025

Walter Fisher- Narrative Paradigm

In both briefings, Selçuk Tepeli not only conveys the news while recounting events; he also constructs a meaningful universe with the viewer through his narration. For instance:

- "The stones that have been dropping from these skirts over the week will transform into a five-star necklace" (January 13).

- "Remember to utilize this healing menu nightly until it is fully consumed." (February 27).

These discourses enable the presenter to forge an emotional connection with the audience through the "persuasive power of narratives," as highlighted by Fisher. The viewer experiences narrative coherence and perception of reality. Expressions like "we will understand the shape of it" concerning Öcalan's remark on February 27 highlight the historical significance of the incident and elevate the narrative to a symbolic dimension.

Stuart Hall- Theory of Representation

Tepeli's lectures predominantly exhibit a "public speaking" demeanor. He assumes the role of the public's representative:

- "We informed you..." (January 13).
- "What does this signify now? I suppose someone will need to elucidate this as well." (February 27).
- Tepeli's phrases like 'İmamoğlu's leaving' or 'matters overlooked by TRT' transition from a neutral conveyance of news to a framework that incorporates interpretations and establishes representational relationships. This reinforces Hall's assertion that the presentation of news influences its meaning as significantly as its veracity.

Henry Jenkins- Participatory Culture

Tepeli's utilization of hashtags and his prompt replies to comments on social media position him as a content creator who engages with the audience in accordance with Jenkins' definition.

"A valued viewer remarked, Mr. Selçuk..." (January 13).

"You are in charge." One of our viewers states, " (February 27).

Furthermore, in the "One Minute" segment, he converts the news bulletin into a platform that not only disseminates information but also provides commentary, adopts a stance, and formulates political positions.

Nonverbal Communication and Signaling

In both broadcasts, Tepeli exhibits the following behaviors: throwing a pen on the table (anger, disappointment), raising his hands and leaning on the table (reactivity), emphasizing his speech with continuous gestures (emotional involvement), and standing beside the audience while discussing the team behind the camera (representation of sincerity), thereby reinforcing his vocative narrative through these movements. These movements indicate that he has developed a narrative pattern that embodies his emotive, pro-people, critical, humorous, and direct traits.

Table 3. Selçuk Tepeli – NOW TV Main News Bulletin

Date	Channel	Anchor	Number of news	Duration (dk)	Anchor (%)
31st December 2024	NOW TV	Selçuk Tepeli	12	46,33	36,6
13rd January 2025	TV	Selçuk Tepeli	11	46,28	35,58
24nd February 2025	NOW TV	Selçuk Tepeli	12	46,55	24,7
27nd February 2025	NOW TV	Selçuk Tepeli	14	46,07	30,54

Table 4. Audience Interaction Selçuk Tepeli (NOW TV Main News Bulletin)

Date	Hasthag – Number of Interaction
31st December 2024	#itisover 49 Tweets
13rd January 2025	#thisisthesituation 90 Tweets
24nd February 2025	#whatsmore 160 Tweets
27nd February 2025	#whataboutit 149 Tweets

In the examined NOW TV Main News bulletins hosted by Selçuk Tepeli, it was found that an average of 12-13 news items were aired during a segment lasting roughly 46 minutes, excluding commercials and including teasers. The speaking durations in the bulletin did not demonstrate a consistent flow; rather, Tepeli's speaking time fluctuated between 24.7% and 36.6% (Table-3). This rate is significantly lower than that of Fatih Portakal and more accurately represents the balance between video presenters. Selçuk Tepeli's approach, while critical, populist, and oppositional, is predominantly institutional. He engages with the public via the hashtag shared at the commencement of the bulletin and communicates directly under the section "1 minute" at the conclusion of the news segment, maintaining an engaged yet measured approach.

Ece Üner (Halk TV) – (January 13, 2025- February 27, 2025)

Walter Fisher- Narrative Paradigm

Fisher posits that individuals do not trust knowledge itself, but rather meaningful and cohesive tales. Ece Üner's presentation alters the impartial narrative style of traditional journalism by incorporating emotive tones, facial expressions, and personal commentary.

- For instance: "What is the state of life?" "If you were not apprehended during the dawn operation and did not have to endure freezing conditions to traverse the Bosphorus, it is not so dire," she beckons the audience into the narrative with a sarcastic introduction. Beginning with the inquiry "How is life?" (January 13) constitutes not a conventional broadcast, but rather the commencement of a tale. This inquiry serves as both an appeal to the audience and a collective expression of shared sentiment.
- "What will occur subsequently?" Upon reviewing the February 27 bulletin, the frequently employed interrogative phrase links two significant agenda items: Öcalan's letter and the political action begun by İmamoğlu. This guarantees the continuation of the tale and the narrative coherence referenced by Fisher. Fisher posits that the more the alignment of a narrative with the audience's life experiences, the higher the credibility becomes. Ece Üner operates by concentrating on individuals' personal testimonies and experiences. In the January 13, 2025 broadcast, her comparison of the phrase "either you are mine or your land" to the relationship between political authority and the populace serves as a narrative that emphasizes the audience's social awareness. In the February 27, 2025 bulletin, she articulates the ideals reflected in social memory by expressing widespread skepticism about Öcalan's message, posing the question, "Will peace come this way?"
- "I believe that the relationship formed with politics has evolved into a marital dynamic." (January 13) introduces personal narratives to the agenda.
- "Although it appears to be a minor note, its substance is highly significant." (February 27) enhances the dramatic framework with ironic undertones.
- If the world operates in this manner, the countenances of idealists reflect reverence. Emotional outbursts underscore the ethical aspect of the narrative.

According to Walter Fisher's notion of emotional resonance, individuals consider the emotional impact of narratives when making decisions; hence, Ece Üner's body language, facial expressions, and remarks convey emotionally charged narratives. For instance, The news bulletin from January 13, 2025, presents the story "A teacher warms her classroom by walking 23 km in the morning," which instills hope and motivation; conversely, the statement "He assures a 5-month pregnant woman that nothing will occur just once" elicits horror and pity. February 27, 2025: "Will peace manifest in this manner?", "Although it appears to be a trivial remark, its substance is profoundly significant," and similar statements serve to captivate the audience's attention while enhancing emotional impact.

Ece Üner's language seeks to construct a narrative that resonates with emotions, moral sensibilities, and empathy. This aligns with Fisher's assertion that "a compelling narrative is more convincing than empirical data."

Stuart Hall- Representation Theory

- "What are the objectives or offerings of the AK Party..." The Turkish populace seeks enlightenment. On February 27, she advocates for the populace.
- "You are either my jurisdiction or your territory." (January 13) —— paradoxically reveals the repressive nature of the regime.
- "The administration can no longer demonstrate its virtue"; it seeks to persuade the opposition of its malevolence, explicit critique of dominant representation (January 13).
- "We are a secular nation, are we not... we believe so." (February 27) generates a pluralistic viewpoint encompassing discourses of both representation and ambivalence. Ece Üner characterizes news as a domain of "representational struggle." She constructs an ironic, detached yet candid counter-representation to the government's narrative. Nonetheless, the adversarial stance he embodies is disclosed through diction and tone rather than analysis.
- "Öcalan's letter was recited; therefore, what was the purpose of Ahmet Türk reading this text?" A mayor who has been nominated as a trustee on three occasions..." The account presented by Ece Üner here
- This depiction reinterprets the state's position on Kurdish issues. The terms "trustee" and "elected but dismissed" establish a representative duality between democracy and law.

Hall posits that the media not only passively transmits social reality but also depicts and reproduces it. Ece Üner's journalistic language presents an alternate "dissident reality" within this framework.

Jenkins- Participatory Culture

Jenkins characterizes contemporary media as an arena in which the viewer is active rather than passive, engaging in content creation. Ece Üner offers a concise yet impactful introduction to this culture. Illustrations:

- She commences engagement on social media with the hashtag "How is life?" (January 13).

She chooses and examines 3 tweets from the X shares segment of the day. This serves to render the audience apparent in the bulletin. She explicitly identifies the tweeters by their full names, indicating her earnestness in engaging with them. Fatih Portakal use casual terms like "Ahmet abi," whilst Üner adopts a more formal approach.

- "A remark was made suggesting that if we were excessively joyful, insecticide would be applied to us" she fosters an emotional connection through her commentary on participation.

Ece Üner, although not directly engaging the audience on stage, creates an editorial platform for their voices. This largely aligns with Jenkins's assertion that "the audience becomes a producer."

Nonverbal Communication and Sign Systems

Ece Üner's vocal delivery is not as high-pitched as that of Fatih Portakal; yet, it is grounded in a robust narrative augmented by gestures and facial expressions. Eye motions and vocal intonation occasionally convey irony and at other times provide emotional intensity.

Her desk in the studio is diminutive, in contrast to the larger desks of others; it lacks a presentation style amidst numerous papers, exhibiting a more organized and content-focused arrangement. Üner delivers a less aggressive screen presentation compared to Fatih Portakal, approaching the news with a more measured style and little interventions.

She stands while maintaining eye contact with the camera, although she does not exhibit authoritative control over the studio; for instance, she refrains from striking the table like Fatih Portakal and does not engage in discourse with the staff.

Table 5. Ece Üner- Halk TV Main News Bulletin

Date	Channel	Anchor	Number of News	Duration (minute)	Anchor (%)
31st December 2024	Halk TV	Ece Üner	17	53,55	37,41
13rd January 2025	Halk TV	Ece Üner	36	105	34,17
24nd January 2025	Halk TV	Ece Üner	34	100	36
27nd February 2025	Halk TV	Ece Üner	19	47,75	19,1

Table 6. Audience Engagement Ece Üner (Halk TV Main News Bulletin)

Date	Hasthag – Number of Interactions
31st December 2024	#endurewithpatience -103 Tweets
13rd January 2025	#howislife -81 Tweets
24nd January 2025	#onhold --146 Tweets
27nd February 2025	#fromnowon -99 Tweets

In the primary news broadcasts of Halk TV, hosted by Ece Üner, the presenter's speaking rate fluctuates between 19.1% and 37.4%. This rate is far more balanced than Fatih Portakal's presentation time, allowing the news to occupy more space without interference, unlike Fatih Portakal's approach. Üner incorporates 3-4 tweets of the day that he appreciates at the conclusion of the news briefing. However, his narrative lacks the spontaneous remarks, hilarious satire, or vocative shock that characterize Fatih Portakal's style. A sensible emotionality interlaced with more significant phrases predominate.

Table 7. Comparative Analysis of Three Presenters (Fatih Portakal, Selçuk Tepeli, Ece Üner)

Criteria	Fatih Portakal	Selçuk Tepeli	Ece Üner
Discourse	Humor, colloquial, emotional, critical, oppositional	Critical, angry, populist intellectual dissident	Serious, sometimes ironic, emotionally empathetic, oppositional
Narration	Active subject - self-centered	Active subject-Critically	An interpreting but more subject
Vocative Discourse	Very high - "big brother", "big sister", "do you think?", "in my opinion..."	Very loud- direct address, reinforced with gestures and voice	Medium Level
Social Media Integration	Poll and hashtag of the day on X (Twitter), YouTube engagement- reading poll results from Wall	Hashtag of the day on X (Twitter)	Hashtag of the day on X (Twitter)- reading tweets from Wall
Audience	Talks to the audience, reads tweets	Talks to the audience, reads tweets sometimes in the bulletin, sometimes in the 'one minute' section at the end of the bulletin	Reads selected tweets at the end of the newsletter
Representation Style	Standing, dynamic, gesticulating, working at a big table full of papers, reading independently from the prompter, making the presence of the studio audience felt, talking to them	Standing, dynamic, intense facial expressions, working at a large table full of papers, reading independently from a prompter	Uses a small standing, prompter-supported, less mobile, paperless table
Emotional Depth	High- intensity of irony, angry, critical	High- critical, more anger and frustration	High- especially noticeable in women's/ children's news
Representation	Comment	Comment	It conveys the news, but breaks the frame from time to time

The research findings indicate that primary news anchors on opposition television stations employ a customized presentation style that engages the viewer directly, authentically, and in an informal manner. The anchors are seen as influential individuals trusted by the opposition. The predominant content of the news broadcasts include political news, which the anchors present with commentary. In several instances, the volume of comments surpasses that of the main news articles. Hashtags and surveys initiated on Twitter elicit varying degrees of engagement. Furthermore, the incorporation of street interviews demonstrates the intention to integrate public opinions into the program.

CONCLUSIONS AND RECOMMENDATIONS

This study demonstrates the absence of a singular anchor profile in primary news broadcasts in Turkey. Main news anchors have a uniform approach in their critical discourse, however they pursue distinct methods in creating these new forms of representation. Due to the neoliberal policies initiated in the 1980s in Turkey, the state retreated from production and service sectors, allowing the private sector to eradicate public broadcasting and dominate the media landscape. News transformed into a commodity for purchase and sale, with viewers seen as consumers. The rating competitions that commenced in the 1990s following the establishment of private television networks transitioned into a new phase after the Justice and Development Party assumed power in 2002. Over time, the government became increasingly involved in the media and exerted control over a significant portion of it. A multitude of unemployed journalists, hindered by the lack of communication avenues for their dissenting perspectives, created their own broadcasting platforms on social media. Meanwhile, the few journalists who retained their positions endeavored to sustain their careers through a limited number of opposition television channels that garnered minimal advertising revenue. This predicament has compelled opposition media, primarily focused on news, to adopt other presentation methods. Television news anchors, having established themselves as an institution, have transcended the duty of mere news reporting to assume the position of interpreters, functioning as "wise men" or "opinion leaders." Due to the prolonged governance of the AK Party and its influence on the media, opposition television's primary news broadcasts have increasingly fostered a more empathetic and communal connection with the viewers. The subjective remarks and theatrical narratives of anchors have transcended the confines of traditional, objective journalism, introducing a novel journalism paradigm. This narrative approach, along with the utilization of #hashtags, social media polls, and street interviews, establishes a domain of resistance for audiences in a context where freedom of expression has been constrained. Every news report delivered by anchors generates a counteractive echo chamber on social media. The transition of the audience from passive consumers of news to active participants, influenced by the digital era, directly impacts the construction of news narratives via social media. The audience is no longer merely a passive listener of news; they have become interpreters, shapers, and co-narrators of the bulletin. This new model illustrates that, in the digital era, anchors have adopted a bidirectional narrative creation approach. This scenario illustrates the evolution of the traditional "anchor" character from an objective and composed presenter to a "participatory narrator" who engages in thought and dialogue with the audience. This new presentation format has emerged in opposition media, and this is not coincidental. Political tensions and media polarization have compelled opposition channels to forge a more robust, emotional connection with their viewers. Consequently, participatory culture must be assessed not merely as a consequence of technical evolution but also as a political imperative. This novel narrative style obscures the distinction between news and commentary, prompting inquiries into the objectivity of journalism. Mehmet Ali Birand's approach of presenting a separate commentary column from the news, which he applied for a while, has now been replaced by personal comments that continue from the beginning of the news. This circumstance may cause viewers to engage with the news primarily on an emotional basis, complicating rational assessment and exacerbating social polarization.

The primary objective of the study is to elucidate the changes seen in the news reporting of opposition news anchors. Nonetheless, a thorough analysis of the correlation between this transition and political pressures will establish a significant foundation for future research. Research examining the impact of this novel storytelling style on public opinion and audience behavior will enhance our comprehension of structural transformations within the media sector.

REFERENCES

Althusser, L. (2003). *İdeoloji ve devletin ideolojik aygıtları*. İthaki Publishing.

Atik, A. (2006). *Türkiye'de özel televizyon haberciliğinde eğlendiren bilgi süreci ve örnek program Show TV Ana Haber Kuşağı* (Unpublished Doctoral Dissertation). Istanbul University Social Sciences Institute. DÜNYA. (2024, January 25). *FOX TV'den NOW TV'ye geçişin nedeni 71,3 milyar dolarlık anlaşma*. https://www.dunya.com/gundem/fox-tvden-now-tvye-gecisin-nedeni-713-milyar-dolarlik-anlasma-haberi-717941

Ekşioğlu Sarılar, N. B. (2018). 1950'lerden bugüne haber perspektifinde dönüşen haber sunucusu profili: Spiker–anchor. *Yeni Medya Electronic Journal*, *2*(2), 63–72.

Ekşioğlu Sarılar, N. B. (2020). Neo-liberal politikaların medya ve kamu hizmeti yayıncılığına etkisi. *İnsan ve İnsan*, 7(26), 41–64. https://doi.org/DOI: 10.29224/insanveinsan.791980

Ekşioğlu Sarılar, N. B. (2021). *Medya, iktidar, demokrasi: Sansür ve otosansür*. Kriter Publishing.

Gazete Duvar. (2023, June 27). Fatih Portakal'ın iç sesinden öfke çıktı: Canlı yayında 'dış ses'i azarladı. https://www.gazeteduvar.com.tr/fatih-portakalin-ic-sesinden-ofke-cikti-canli-yayinda-dis-sesi-azarladi-haber-1625687

Gramsci, A. (1971). *Selections from the prison notebooks* (Hoare, Q., & Nowell Smith, G., Eds. & Trans.). International Publishers.

Güngör, N. (2011). *İletişim Kuramlar Yaklaşımlar*. Siyasal Publishing.

10Haber. (2023, July 23). CHP yönetimi ile Halk TV'nin kavgası büyüyor. https://10haber.net/siyaset/chp-ile-halk-tv-arasindaki-gerilim-buyuyor-program-iptal-edildi-223265/

Hall, S. (1988). *The hard road to renewal: Thatcherism and the crisis of the left*. Verso.

Hall, S. (2017). *Temsil: Kültürel temsiller ve anlamlandırma uygulamaları (S. İrvan* (Güner, İ. Ed. & Trans.). Pinhan Publishing.

Holmes, D. (2013). *Communication theory: Media, technology and society* (2nd ed.). SAGE Publications.

Jenkins, H. (2006). *Convergence culture: Where old and new media collide*. New York University Press.

Jenkins, H. (2009). *Confronting the challenges of participatory culture: Media education for the 21st century*. MIT Press. DOI: 10.7551/mitpress/8435.001.0001

Kars, N. (2015). *Radyo-televizyon haberciliği*. Der Publishing.

Kısa Dalga. (2022, November 27). AKP'nin daveti üzerinden Türkiye'de gazeteciliğin güncel fotoğrafı. https://kisadalga.net/haber/detay/akpnin-daveti-uzerinden-turkiyede-gazeteciligin-guncel-fotografi_47878

Kongar, E. (2004, May 3). Üç güzeller. https://www.kongar.org/medyanotu/101_Uc_Guzeller.php

Morse, M. (1998). Televizyonda haberci kişiliği ve inandırıcılık / Geçiş sürecindeki haberler üzerine düşünceler. In Modleski, T. (Ed.), *Eğlence incelemeleri* (Gürbilek, N., Trans.; pp. 87–88). Metis Publishing.

NTV. (2018, March 22). Hürriyet, Kanal D, CNN Türk ve Posta'yı Demirören Grubu alıyor (Erdoğan Demirören kimdir?). https://www.ntv.com.tr/ekonomi/hurriyet-kanal-d-cnn-turk-ve-postayi-demiroren-grubu-aliyor-erdogan-demiroren-kimdir%2CXg4DGSoZoUCH5YNVwt8dCg

Procter, J. (2004). *Stuart Hall*. Routledge. Schudson, M. (2001). The objectivity norm in American journalism. *Journalism, 2*(2), 149–170. DOI: 10.1177/146488490100200201

Sözcü. (2023, March 1). SÖZCÜ televizyonu yayın hayatına başladı. https://www.sozcu.com.tr/sozcu-televizyonu-yayin-hayatina-basladi-wp7610389

Tanilli, S. (2009). *Nasıl bir demokrasi istiyoruz*. Cumhuriyet Publishing.

Turkish Grand National Assembly (1983). *2954 sayılı Türkiye Radyo ve Televizyon Kanunu*. https://www.tcmevzuat.com/normlar/2954-sayili-turkiye-radyo-ve-televizyon-kanunu/

Turner, G. (2010). *Ordinary people and the media: The demotic turn*. SAGE Publications. DOI: 10.4135/9781446269565

Vural, İ. (2003). *"Anchor" as a professional persona in television journalism – An evaluation in terms of source characteristics and a situational analysis of its practice in Turkey* (Unpublished doctoral dissertation). Anadolu University, Institute of Social Sciences, Eskişehir.

YouTube. (2012). *Report from Vietnam (1968)* [Video]. YouTube. https://web.archive.org/web/20120227183438/http://www.youtube.com/watch?v=Nn4w-ud-TyE&gl=US&hl

Chapter 3
Storytelling in Digital Games

Ayşe Nesrin Akören
https://orcid.org/0000-0002-7748-8783
Doğuş University, Turkey

ABSTRACT

In digital games, storytelling is an important element that enables the player to adapt more easily to the game world, ensures continuous follow-up, and enriches the gaming experience. These scenarios sometimes serve as entertainment and provide players with an emotional journey. Storytelling is the most crucial factor determining the structure of games. Therefore, it would be appropriate to distinctly separate and define the types of narratives in this section through examples. In digital games, storytelling develops in traditional follow-ups, which we can describe as linear narratives consisting of beginning, development, and conclusion sections. In this 'Linear' narrative style, players progress through a written script and witness pre-determined events of the story. Such scenarios are usually written for action, adventure, and role-playing (RPG) games. In conclusion, this book chapter will pay careful attention to addressing the deepening methods of interactions that digital games establish with individuals through the diversity of storytelling.

INTRODUCTION

Fairy tales, myths, and epics passed down from generation to generation have played an important role in the formation of storytelling. As these narratives developed and took on various forms, they helped people acquire habits such as following or reading stories with great interest. Over time, people were introduced to narrative forms such as novels and similar genres, and with the advancement of

DOI: 10.4018/979-8-3373-2023-6.ch003

technology, they gained advantages such as increased access and a wider variety of content. The emergence of digital games added a new dimension to this diversity, offering experiences where stories come to life through visuals and animations flowing before the eyes of players.

The most fundamental difference between digital games and other forms of storytelling is interactivity. Players can now find themselves immersed in games in various ways. When they take on the role of the main character, the concepts of time and space inevitably begin to change. Beyond this distinction, video games also offer differences in many aspects such as narrative structure, character development, and use of time.

The reader or viewer usually plays a passive role in fairy tales, novels, or movies. They can only follow the story as it unfolds, guided by the decisions of the author or the vision of the director. In contrast, digital games place the player in the story and allow them to actively participate in and directly influence events.

For example, Red Dead Redemption 2 has a narrative structure in which the fate of the main character and even Arthur Morgan's ending can change according to the player's choices. This is fundamentally different from narratives such as those in novels, where character development is predetermined and unchangeable. The game includes a mechanic called the "Honor System", where Arthur's moral or immoral behaviour directly affects the ending and character development. This marks one of the most important differences between digital games and traditional storytelling formats.

With the rapid advancement of technology and the miniaturization of digital screens on mobile devices, games have become more widespread and accessible. At the same time, the rise of the internet, especially since Web 3.0, has redefined the concept of culture. Cultural elements have become global, giving rise to a new symbolic language, often referred to as "Meta".

Digital game narratives can be seen as a modern representation of traditional storytelling. Players bring these games to life with narrative techniques enriched with symbols taken from shared cultural memory. Game worlds are fictional, but they are successful when they create an emotional impact that feels real. The game shapes the interaction between the story and the player; in other words, the way the story is played out is influenced by the mechanics of the game. Symbolic representations help convey messages to the player's perceptual world, increasing emotional resonance. Since the player is active in this process, a strong connection can be established between the player and the narrative. Therefore, this section will examine how the ancient method of storytelling evolved into its modern forms and what techniques are most effective in today's context.

STORYTELLING METHODS IN GAMES

The narrative is the representational expression of a sequence of events meaningfully connected in temporal and causal dimensions (Bostan, 2022, p.35). The story is one of the essential elements that allows a player to connect with the game world. Games are not solely composed of mechanics. While offering a narrative experience, they also strive to preserve emotional communication. A strong story makes it easier for players to form emotional bonds with characters and the game world. The characters' backgrounds, motivations, and developments enable the player to empathize with them. Therefore, games should be rich not only in terms of mechanics but also in narrative content. Visuals, sounds, and various NPC (Non-Player Character) dialogues in the concept design contribute deeper meaning to the game world through environmental storytelling.

Level or mission-based structures also provide essential narrative goals for players. Completing a level is not only about reaching an objective but also about progressing through a larger story. As players move through multiple levels, the sequential completion of objectives creates narrative consistency. Game levels offer players access to specific areas of the narrative world, each filled with unique events, objects, and characters that establish a distinct narrative tone and texture (Salen & Zimmerman, 2004, p.10).

In this context, categorizing storytelling methods by narrative type will help provide a broader perspective. For instance, in games like Red Dead Redemption 2, missions are not merely mechanical objectives but parts of the narrative that deepen player immersion in the game world.

Linear Narrative

Linear narrative is a storytelling method where the story in the game progresses in a fixed sequence, leaving no room for the player to alter the plot. Game designers offer a pre-written story that players are expected to follow. This structure closely resembles traditional storytelling formats like films or novels. The predetermined, unchangeable narrative is typically planned and scripted by game writers and developers along a fixed plotline.

In this type of narrative, levels and missions are written sequentially. While the player's path is predetermined, the ending is singular, with a clear beginning and a defined conclusion. Cutscenes are frequently used to increase player engagement. These may be cinematic presentations of animated or visual sequences.

According to Salen & Zimmerman, cutscenes may “interrupt” player interaction, but they support narrative gameplay on many levels. Cutscenes can foreshadow future events, function as flashbacks, or provide transitions between settings. They can also demonstrate how to interact with objects and give the players information about in-game resources (2004, p.31).

In digital games with a linear narrative structure, player choices are significantly limited, and the story progresses along a predetermined path. Within this structure, the player's control over the avatar is often an illusion. Rune Klevjer defines the avatar not just as a figure of representation but as an interface through which the player is physically integrated into the game world. However, this representation is shaped within the boundaries of the linear structure:

> *"The avatar might be the player's representative in the game world, but it is not the player. The player's agency is constrained by the rules and narrative design of the game." (Klevjer, 2006, p.67)*

According to Klevjer, even though the player affects the game world through the avatar, a linear narrative restricts those effects, leaving the narrative's direction in the hands of the designer. In this structure, the avatar primarily functions as an embodied witness and an executor of a pre-written script.

One of the most compelling examples of linear narrative in recent years is *The Last of Us. The Last of Us Part II* is a post-apocalyptic action-adventure game developed by Naughty Dog and published by Sony Interactive Entertainment for PlayStation 4 in 2020. The story takes place in the United States in the year 2033, twenty years after the outbreak of a fungus that transforms humans into aggressive creatures. Since its release, the game has won over 200 awards in various categories, including best narrative, music, acting, voice-over, and graphics. Most notably, it was awarded "Best Game of the Year" in 2020 for its storytelling, which makes it a prime example of a well-executed linear narrative structure. (The Game Awards, 2020).

Figure 1. The opening scene of The Last of Us.

Source: Naughty Dog (2013). Screenshot captured from the game.

The story of the characters Joel and Ellie in the game is scripted from start to finish, with no opportunity for players to alter their choices. For example, Joel's decision to save Ellie is entirely up to the writers. Players cannot choose a different option.

Other examples of linear games include:

- *Uncharted Series* (2007, Naughty Dog): Cinematic linear narrative in the action-adventure genre.
- *God of War* (2018, Santa Monica Studio): An emotional and fixed narrative structure focusing on the father-son relationship.
- *Inside* (2016, Playdead): Creates a linear narrative even without using dialogue.

In these games, the combination of graphic, audio, and textual content forms a cohesive structure that shapes the gaming experience. Visual and auditory content, while variable depending on cultural differences, remains understandable by the player. In other words, a player can stay immersed in the created universe of the game, even if they are unfamiliar with a particular landscape or music genre from their cultural context (Yılmaz & Canbaz, 2019, p.80).

Branching Narrative Structures

Branching narrative structures are a type of storytelling in which the player's decisions directly affect the flow and outcome of the story. In this type of structure, the story does not adhere to a fixed plotline but instead shapes itself according to the player's choices. Each decision can lead to different events, character relationships, and even endings.

In branching narratives, the player is an active agent who determines the direction of the story. Factors such as dialogue choices, action preferences, and timing can alter the story, giving the player a freedom that goes beyond a fixed narrative. There is no correct path in this type of structure, and multiple storylines may exist. Moral dilemmas, uncertainties, and emotional tensions are often used, enhancing the game's replayability because each playthrough can provide a different experience.

While some games progress with a single narrative, others offer multiple endings or different paths, leading to the same conclusion. For instance, *Star Trek*: 25th Anniversary (1992) has multiple characters, and the story continues to unfold continuously. Also, in games like *Facade* (2005), *Storyteller* (2008), *The Majesty of Colors* (2008), *Monkey Island* (1990), and *Mass Effect* (2007) feature various branching paths.

In games that follow branching structures, the background of the story should also be considered to provide the player with a sense of freedom. Players feel more liberated when they are guided towards different endings or pathways. This type of interactive storytelling allows players to engage with and shape the outcome of the narrative. Creating a compelling and engaging narrative is often done through a combination of text, images, and sometimes sound and video.

When analysing the structure of interactive narratives, Ryan explains branching structures with models such as "trees" and "mazes." These models discuss how the player's choices shape dynamic narratives. Branching narratives are not truly "storytelling" in the traditional sense but are instead "story construction" methods, where the player's actions actively shape the narrative (Ryan, 2003, p.247-254). Janet Murray also emphasizes these structures as "conceptual mazes." In this approach, the player navigates between different paths, yet the sense of narrative coherence is maintained, and the integrity of the story is preserved (Murray, 2017, p.35).

One of the strongest examples of branching narratives is the game *Detroit: Become Human*. Released in 2018, the game was developed by Quantic Dream. The story follows the lives of three android characters (Connor, Kara, Markus). The players' decisions shape their destinies.

In the announcement of the game's release on PC, Quantic Dream stated: "By placing the fate of humanity and androids in your hands, the game takes you to a near-future where machines are more intelligent than humans, a future that is not far from being realized. Every choice you make affects the outcome of the game, and you are facing one of the most complex branching narratives ever created. Each decision made in every chapter affects what happens next in the story. The game has more than 40 possible endings. You will face moral dilemmas and decide who lives and who dies. With thousands of choices and dozens of possible endings, how will you affect the future of *Detroit* and the fate of humanity? Shape an ambitious, branching narrative where your choices will determine the fates of the three main characters and the entire city of Detroit. How you control Kara, Connor, and Markus can mean life or death, and if one of them pays the ultimate price, the story continues. (Quanticdream, 2018) At the end of each chapter, the player is presented with a graphical representation of the decision tree; this makes it an essential example of this narrative type, both for showing the branching to the player and monetizing it.

Figure 2. Detroit: Become Human

Source: Gamebravers, (2018).

To be alive in the twentieth century is to be aware of our alternative possible selves, of alternative possible worlds, and of the limitless intersecting stories of the actual world. To capture such a constantly bifurcating plotline, however, one would need more than a thick labyrinthine novel or a sequence of films. To truly capture such cascading permutations, one would need a computer (Murray, 2017, p.44).

Examples of branching story structures can be found in the following other games:

- Until Dawn (2015, Supermassive Games): The survival or death of characters depends entirely on the player's choices. Released for PlayStation 5,

PlayStation 4, and Microsoft Windows, this interactive drama survival-horror game was nominated for the Best Story Award in 2015.

- The Witcher 3: Wild Hunt (2015, CD Projekt Red): The game's story, written by Marcin Blacha, celebrates its 10th anniversary in 2025. A part of the open-world genre, The Witcher 3: Wild Hunt follows The Witcher 2: Assassins of Kings. The game's website states: "You are a Witcher, a mutant. The sooner you accept this, the better. People will seek your abilities, but you must know how to disappear when your presence is no longer wanted. You are unique, different. This puts you in the same dangerous position as those who find themselves skewered (The Witcher, 2015)
- Life is Strange (2015, Dontnod Entertainment): Built around the mechanic of rewinding time to explore alternative decisions, this game was designed and developed by Dontnod Entertainment and published by Square Enix. It won the BAFTA Games Award for Story in 2016. Life is Strange is a cinematic game played from a third-person perspective. The time rewind mechanic allows the player to revisit actions taken at specific times. The player can interact with objects that will enable them to solve puzzles by examining, taking tasks, and changing the environment. The game has many things to do, such as reviewing every visible poster, watering plants, talking to any character, playing guitar, and so on. This allows the branching story structure of the game to incorporate various elements.

Open World and Environmental Storytelling in the Narrative

Open world games allow players to explore, interact, and experience the story in a much more interactive and in-depth manner. Unlike traditional linear narratives, open-world games typically present the story through environmental elements rather than a fixed path and narrator. In these types of games, environmental storytelling is enriched with objects, characters, and details that the player can interact with at every corner of the world. Common environmental elements embedded in the player's perception help support the story design.

Open world games generally include two different types of events: major events that advance the main storyline of the game and smaller events known as side missions, which depict the stories of secondary characters and contribute to the overall experience. Furthermore, they complete the story of the game world (Farca, 2010, p.75).

Environmental Storytelling places narrative elements directly into the environment using visual and auditory cues. In this way, game developers can reflect the historical and cultural context of the game world more easily.

Whether game designers aim for historical accuracy or completely new environments, the creative process cannot be separated from the field of architecture. As a result, developers have started collaborating with experts in video game design, such as architects and architectural historians. Moreover, renowned game design companies have begun spending significant financial resources to establish partnerships with universities for in-depth academic research consultancy (Güntan, & Ar, 2014, p.8).

Open-world games offer players the opportunity for in-depth exploration of the world. This exploration process presents the story to the player in small, interactive pieces. The player might gain information about the townspeople by walking around a village or try to understand past events by exploring an abandoned building (Newman, 2013, p.89). This exploration allows the story to become more personal and based on the player's choices.

In open-world games, the vast freedom given to players can sometimes lead to missing parts of the story. Therefore, environmental storytelling plays an important role as a tool to guide the player's interest and interaction with the story. Environmental elements draw the player into the story naturally while not restricting their freedom (Jenkins, 2002, p.10). Thus, the more immersion the player experiences in the story, the more details they uncover.

Open World and Environmental Storytelling in *Red Dead Redemption II*

Red Dead Redemption II (2018, Rockstar Games): By combining open-world design and environmental storytelling, the game offers the player a story not only through quests but also through the world itself. The game is set during the collapse of the western frontier in late 19th century America, allowing the player to explore the story in different ways. *Red Dead Redemption II* is an action-adventure game.

The game is presented from both first and third-person perspectives, and the player is free to roam the interactive open world. Game elements include conflicts, robberies, hunting, horseback riding, interactions with non-player characters, and maintaining the character's honor through moral choices and actions. A reward system manages the response of law enforcement and bounty hunters to the crimes committed by the player (en.wikipedia, 2018).

Figure 3. Red Dead Redemption II

Source: mmorpg.com. (2018).

The vast map of the game includes cities, towns, wilderness areas, abandoned houses, isolated farms, and hidden locations. Each region has its own unique atmosphere, social structure, and history. The player gains information about the themes of the game not only through quests but also through the atmosphere of these places.

Red Dead Redemption II addresses environmental storytelling in various ways. For example:

- Abandoned Camps and Houses: Many structures the player encounters on the map, through the objects inside (old letters, newspaper clippings, diaries), architectural style, and location, hint at past events. For instance, a diary found in a cabin tells the story of a family's disappearance due to illness, and unless the player discovers this place, the story might be completely missed (Vara, 2019, p.124).
- NPC Routines and Micro Narratives: NPCs (Non-player characters) in the game are not just decorative elements. Their daily routines, dialogues, and reactions make the game world feel alive. For example, if the townsfolk avoid a particular area out of fear, the player may be motivated to investigate what is

happening there. By engaging emotionally with the player, the game triggers curiosity, encouraging the player to explore further.

- Natural Indicators: The weather conditions, lighting, and animal behavior in the game are also part of the environmental storytelling. A foggy swamp creates the feeling of danger or mystery, while a sunny plain can evoke a sense of safety and tranquility. These emotions influence how the player approaches the narrative (Calleja, 2011, p.123).

These elements show that environmental storytelling is not just background but an active carrier of the narrative. Many different arguments can be made from various perspectives about what makes games more or less "story-like." For example, it's easy to say that Checkers is not narrative (in the adjective sense) and that *Dungeons & Dragons* is, but most games exist in a fuzzy realm where narrative often plays a role, even if abstract, allegorical, or metaphorical (Pearce, 2005, p. 2).

Emergent Narrative

The interactive structures offered by games allow for the creation of multi-layered and player-specific stories. Games like The Sims and Minecraft are perfect examples of this narrative type. This is because both games offer stories that constantly evolve and change based on the player's choices and interactions. In such games, the narrative is shaped by the player's creative power and interaction with the game world. Therefore, I specifically wanted to include them in this chapter.

Emergent Narrative refers to a dynamic narrative structure that arises from the player's actions and decisions. Unlike traditional linear narrative models, in these types of games, the story naturally takes shape through environmental elements, character interactions, and the player's decisions. This narrative type allows events within the game to develop without a predetermined roadmap, enabling a unique story for each player.

This freedom results in a process where the player decides how to construct the story. Of course, the environmental and character interactions provided by the game allow each player's experience to be different from one another.

The concept of emergence is truly useful in understanding many of the qualities that set a video game apart as both an environment and a specific example of a game. However, it is important to note that progressive game styles can be found across the entire spectrum of video games (Pablos, 2015, p.3).

In an emergent narrative, the story is not designed by developers. Instead, it is built by the player through their interactions and explorations, often influenced by the random factors inherent to each game. As the name suggests, the story emerges as the player continues to play. Sounds abstract, right? (Emergent Narratives, 2015).

Tinsley Galyean says:

"We all construct stories to help us recall, understand, categorize, and share our experiences. This is a skill used by many interactive systems. They present us with environments to explore. We allow a story to emerge by combining elements with our goals (user goals). If any story structure (or story) emerges, it is a product of our interactions and goals while navigating the experience" (Galyean, 1995, p.27).

Galyean positions emergent narratives as resulting from interactions between a user and a simulated environment (Barkman, 2024, p.200).

With the digital age and the transformation of narrative paradigms, user experience has become the focal point. Users, by utilizing the interactivity feature provided by new communication technologies, have gained the ability to guide the narrative through story-building. This, in turn, has made the audience more active, providing different experiences (oyunlastirma.co, 2023).

The Sims (2000, Maxis) as an Example of Emergent Narrative

The Sims is a strategic life simulation video game developed by Maxis and published by Electronic Arts in 2000 (tr.wikipedia (nd)).

In fact, The Sims followed the SimCity series that began in 1989. Games in the Sims series are sandbox games. The player creates virtual people called "Sims" and places them in houses, managing their lives, fulfilling their needs, and achieving their goals. Players can also build homes for the Sims or choose from the pre-existing houses available in the game. With every expansion pack and game pack, the Sims can engage in various activities (tr.wikipedia (nd)).

The Sims series offers players the opportunity to create individual characters and guide their lives. Here, the player's decisions directly affect the characters' lives and relationships. Thus, combined with the environmental factors the game provides, different stories can emerge with every playthrough.

One of the key features of The Sims is the emergence of micro-narratives in the daily lives of characters. Players can intervene in the daily routines of characters, shaping their crises, successes, or tragedies. A significant debate in digital games is often about what we do not do in real life or the irony of succeeding by doing similar things in the virtual world. Interestingly, while most players shout for the conservation of nature, it's a strange irony that they try to earn points by destroying trees/forests in the game. In this context, The Sims allows us to do many things we wouldn't attempt in real life, enabling us to accomplish tasks as meticulously as possible. There is no written story; in fact, only graphic designs, produced models, and various options are presented, leaving the story for you, the player, to create.

The problem is that simulating relationships, as described by Chekhov, is currently impossible because, unlike The Sims, they don't just rely on actions but also heavily depend on dialogue. Nevertheless, The Sims still works well enough, and someone should create a game where players can alter variables like age, number of children, economic status, or reasons for divorce, creating millions of different divorces. I bet that such a game would teach you more about human nature than all of Ingmar Bergman's films combined (Gonzalo, 2001.p. 3).

In The Sims, the player may not initially set a specific goal, but through the combination of environmental and personal interactions, unexpected stories emerge.

Figure 4. The Sims

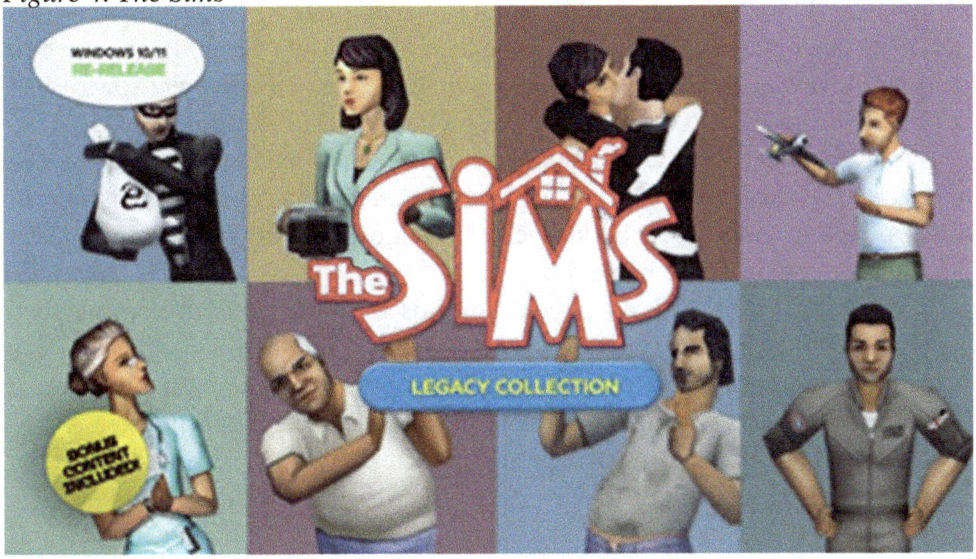

Source: ea.com

The ability to design our own "skins" encourages players to create characters emotionally important to themselves, rehearse their relationships with friends, family, or coworkers, or pair characters from other fictional universes with The Sims (Jenkins, 2002, p.13).

Minecraft (Mojang Studios, 2011)

It all started on May 16, 2009. Inspired by games like Infiniminer and Dungeon Keeper, Markus "Notch" Persson began working on a game initially known only as "Cave Game" a week prior and then decided on a more memorable name: Minecraft: Order of the Stone. Later, he chose an even more memorable name: Minecraft. The game, known as Java Classic Edition, lacked most of the things we associate with the game today, but the building blocks (pun intended) were already there (xbox wire, 2024)

Minecraft is a sandbox game based on player creativity and the shaping of the world. The freedom Minecraft offers allows players not only to build the environment but also to create their own stories.

Minecraft is a sandbox game, meaning there is no specific endpoint. Players can choose to play as one of nine official block-like characters, including Steve and Alex, who were introduced as the first and second characters in the game and are also the most famous faces of Minecraft. The player determines the in-game path through activities such as mining resources, crafting tools, brewing potions, and exploring the environment. Players can play in Minecraft's own proprietary "world" or in worlds created by other players, or they can create their own worlds. Each Minecraft world has three dimensions: the Overworld (the main game area), the Nether (a lava-filled underground world), and the End (a space-like area) (Thestraitstimes, 2025).

One of the most significant features of Minecraft is the emergence of worlds and characters that are entirely shaped by the player. Players can establish their own villages, explore dungeons, or build diverse structures. Naturally, this process results in each player's experience being different.

In Minecraft, the player is not directed towards a specific goal, but elements such as survival, building, and exploration generate new narratives based on the player's interaction with the world. The "emergent" element here is the continuous shaping of the world created by the player, both in physical and social structures.

Video games represent processes in the material world, such as war, urban planning, and sports, and create new spaces of possibility to explore these topics. This representation consists of the rules themselves. We encounter the meaning of games by exploring the space of possibilities, and we explore these spaces through the game (Bogost, 2008, p.121).

The now-iconic art style of Minecraft has become its defining feature. It is characterized by block-like textures and pixelated drawings that resemble the original video games from the 1980s and 1990s, such as Super Mario Bros (1985) and Pac-Man (1980).

These types of games allow the player to create their own stories through their decisions and actions. The environmental and character interactions offered by the game make each player's experience unique.

Figure 5. Minecraft

Source:Xbox Wire, (2024).

Reddit user AtmosphericBeats described the process of using this map and refining the city from start to finish. Many players on Reddit were impressed by the accuracy of this creation and the creator's ability to integrate OpenStreetMap data into the game. The maps used on this site come from publicly available sources, meaning they are quite accurate (Dot Esports, 2024). These passion projects make Minecraft one of the most adaptable sandbox games.

Character and Dialogue Development in Games through Narrative Types

Digital games use character and dialogue elements not only as carriers of narrative but also as one of the most fundamental forms of interaction that allow the player to engage with the world. Unlike traditional narrative forms, in digital games, characters are often shaped by the player's decisions. Dialogues, too, cease to be mere informational texts and enable the player to intervene in the narrative world. In this context, character and dialogue design not only adds narrative depth but also becomes central to playability, emotional interaction, and meaning making. The narrative expressed by non-playable characters (NPCs) differs slightly from that of the protagonist. In reality, emotions can broadly be divided into two types:

those directed towards ourselves and those directed towards other beings (Ryan, 2003, p.247-254).

Through game narrative, the player is given a certain identity or role, and when interacting with the video game, the player (or the player's virtual avatar) can actively move on screen. In this case, role activity can be seen not as the result of the player's observation but as a reflection of the player's consciousness (Jin, 2021, p.12). The emotional interaction gained by the player, regardless of the type of narrative in the game, can drive the narrative. Even in a linear structure, the emotional interaction the writers intend to create can be included.

Therefore, the narrative conveyed by NPCs, on one hand, serves as a carrier of information to the player in video games, and on the other hand, encourages players to change their identities in order to achieve emotional immersion and interactive storytelling effects. As the game progresses, relationships between characters will also change, sometimes requiring redefinition when the player engages with the game. The thoughts and adjustments based on the current situation of the player also become part of the game's narrative creation (Jin, 2021, p.12-13).

Each narrative type presents different strategies for how characters and dialogues are processed. In linear narratives, characters mostly develop according to pre-written scripts, while in open-world structures, the player's choices directly influence the development process.

This section will examine how different narrative types, such as linear, open-world, and emergent narratives, approach character development and dialogue systems through example games. In doing so, it will become clearer how the character in the game narrative is positioned not only as a literary figure but also as a dynamic and interactive structure.

At this stage, it would be useful to examine the contribution to narrative through the following subheadings:

1. Character and Dialogue in Linear Narrative
2. Character and Dialogue Development in Branching Narrative
3. Character and Dialogue in Open World Narrative
4. Character and Dialogue in Emergent Narrative

Character and Dialogue in Linear Narrative

Linear narrative is typically found in games that progress within a defined story framework and have fixed beginnings and endings. In such games, as players follow a specific storyline, character development and dialogue usually align with the narrative's structure. The defining feature of the linear narrative is that it guides the story along a predetermined path; thus, characters and dialogues stand out as elements that carry the themes and emotional weight of the story.

In linear narratives, characters often undergo a specific development arc. This arc progresses through the challenges they face, evolving relationships, and shifting goals throughout the story. In this type of game, dialogue is generally used as a tool to reveal the emotional states, thoughts, and relationships of the characters. For example, there is a transition between a character's initial and final states, made apparent through dialogue and interactions.

Dialogues are important both for reflecting the inner world of a character and for enabling the player to establish an emotional connection with the story.

Example Games: The Last of Us (2013) and the Uncharted Series (2007)

Naughty Dog's The Last of Us and the Uncharted series are prime examples of how linear narrative deepens character development and dialogue. In The Last of Us, the relationship between Joel and Ellie is one of the central focal points of the game, and this relationship is shaped by the events they encounter. Dialogues reflect the intimacy and tension of this bond while also offering the player insight into the characters' inner conflicts and emotional evolution. Each conversation provides important clues about their personal journeys.

Another strong example is the Uncharted series. In Nathan Drake's adventures, dialogue often serves as a source of humor and a tool for deepening character. In-game conversations not only draw the player into the story but also reveal key aspects of Drake's personality. In Uncharted, the dialogue goes beyond merely providing information. It also creates emotional opportunities for the player to connect with the characters.

It is also important to recall the limitations that come with character and dialogue systems in linear narratives. The fixed structure of linear storytelling can sometimes hinder the natural flow of character development and dialogue. Because everything is confined to a predetermined story arc, the player can only follow the characters' growth in one direction. However, The Last of Us stands out as a successful exception to this limitation. Even though the game is strong enough to stand on its own and could potentially support a multiplayer component, the narrative is entirely driven by the story being told. It is the game itself not the cutscenes that develops Joel and Ellie as characters. It is the game that explores the evolution of their relationship. It is the game that reveals their mutual dependence. It is the game that binds the player emotionally to these characters. It is the game that details their world and the risks it entails. The game is what transforms the characters, the story, and the world and is, in turn, transformed by them (reddit, 2019).

Dialogue generation is the production of speech acts involving characters within a context created by the storytelling system. Such a system allows players to steer the narrative based on their own preferences. Because this kind of system exists, it must be both understood and generated. First, it involves interpreting what the user says and identifying the conceptual meaning of their expressions. Second, it combines these expressions to generate appropriate responses according to the current discourse context (Fadak & Khozium, 2020, p. 4453).

Character and Dialogue Development in Branching Narrative Structures

The branching narrative is a type of storytelling in which the plot diverges in various directions based on the choices made by the player, leading to multiple alternative outcomes. In such games, as the story progresses, the player makes decisions that affect the fate of the characters. These choices directly shape character development, dialogues, and ultimately the narrative constructed within the game world. Unlike linear narratives, the branching type allows for an unpredictable and variable player experience. In literature, narratives are usually presented from a third-person perspective: events are conveyed to the reader through words carefully crafted by the author, and the reader visualizes these events in their mind. In films, on the other hand, viewers directly observe the events being portrayed but cannot go beyond witnessing what is shown. In games, a first-person perspective is often utilized. Events are not merely described; instead, the player experiences them through their own eyes. These narrative dimensions cause the player to perceive the virtual world as if they are truly a part of it (Güregen, 2020, p.47).

Figure 6. Narrative from the Audience's Perspective According to the Medium Used

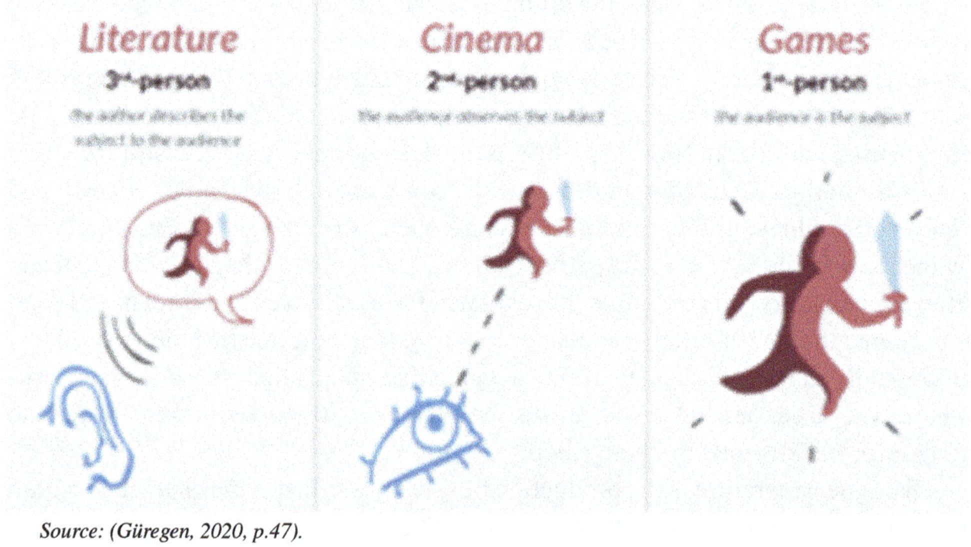

Source: (Güregen, 2020, p.47).

In terms of the impact of choices on character development, in branching narrative games, the evolution of characters often progresses in parallel with the decisions made by the player. These decisions can steer the characters' personalities and relationships in various directions. For instance, a character's moral values may shift based on how the player guides them; they may become loyal or treacherous. Such interaction strengthens the player's connection with the character, as the transformations experienced throughout the story depend on the player's active involvement.

In this context, dialogue also plays a critical role. In branching narrative games, dialogues not only advance the story but also reflect the characters' inner worlds and relationships. Regardless of which dialogue options players choose, these choices can influence characters' behaviours and even their relationships with others. Particularly in branching RPGs, dialogues allow the player to construct the identity of their character, and every choice leads to different outcomes.

Character dialogue may be depicted through cutscenes or simulated directly within the game, between the player-character (PC) and non-player characters (NPCs), or even just among NPCs. In such scenarios, the PC may remain silent while listening to what NPCs have to say and, as a result, function more as a passive listener than an active participant in the dialogue. This is commonly used in first-person shooter games (FPS). Alternatively, developers may choose to give the PC a voice, allowing them to engage with NPCs, often during cutscenes or during gameplay when accompanied by a companion (Smith & Moore, 2011, p.28).

Branching narrative games enable the story to take shape according to the player's decisions flexibly. Each choice leads the player down a different narrative path, resulting in a multi-layered storytelling experience. For example, whether a character survives or not, the punishment of another's crime, or how relationships evolve all are determined by the player's choices. This flexibility of narrative structure stands out as a significant element that shapes both character development and dialogue.

Example Games: The Witcher 3: Wild Hunt (2015), Mass Effect Series (2011, BioWare)

Many popular games successfully implement the branching narrative model, giving players the opportunity to exert meaningful influence over the story. Games like The Witcher 3: Wild Hunt (CD Projekt Red, 2015) and the Mass Effect series (BioWare, 2011) offer players direct interaction with character development and dialogue decisions. These games allow players to shape their characters through the choices they make, leading to profound changes within the game world. Players impact the lives of characters through their decisions, experiencing firsthand how each new choice leads to a different narrative flow. The branching narrative enriches storytelling and intertwines character evolution with player interaction, making the gameplay experience more personal and customized.

Character and Dialogue in Open World Narratives

The impact of character and dialogue in open-world narratives provides players with a broader range of freedom, allowing them to create diverse experiences within the story. In such games, characters typically possess greater depth and flexibility. The non-linear structure of the narrative plays a significant role in character development, as players' choices and actions directly shape the lives of the characters. This freedom also makes the dialogues and interactions between characters unique.

For BioWare's writers and developers, bringing a sense of cohesion and finality to Mass Effect's overarching, player-driven narrative was a great challenge in itself. The original Mass Effect allowed Shepard's gender, appearance, and core personality traits to be customized. Across that game and its sequel, players charted the course of the story through a series of pivotal choices influencing everything from race relations to the fates of entire civilizations. Mass Effect 3 had to incorporate this branching decision matrix and account for each player's unique journey, all while delivering a definitive ultimate conclusion (Upthrust, 2024).

In open-world narratives, a simple way to indirectly control the player is through computer-controlled characters in the game. If you can make the player truly care about the characters by using storytelling techniques whether it's making the player want to obey, protect, help, or even destroy them you suddenly have a perfect tool for controlling what the player does and does not do. Characters can be a great way to manipulate the player's decisions or feelings about those decisions. However, you must first make the player care about how those fictional characters feel (Schell, 2008, p.292).

In open-world games, dialogues are generally not used to direct a particular storyline but rather to add depth to characters and provide players with the opportunity to explore the story through environmental interactions. Therefore, dialogues are not just a tool for storytelling but also serve as a means for players to understand their relationships with the characters and the environment more deeply (Dreamertalin, 2023).

Much of the gameplay in open-world games involves interacting with other characters, particularly through conversation. An immersive, dramatic experience requires us to empathize with the characters in the story, and one of the best ways to learn about their struggles is by talking to them. Many game engines feature game-specific conversation modes. Players can choose the conversation option if they wish, and by doing so, they accept the additional mobility that can come from those dialogues. Of course, it is also important to keep the option to exit open and allow the player to continue the game outside of that mode.

Character and Dialogue in Open World Narratives

Character design in open-world games plays a crucial role in storytelling. Compared to linear narratives, characters in open-world games are much more layered. This allows players to explore the personal history, values, and motivations of characters more freely. For example, in games like The Witcher 3: Wild Hunt, characters' identities and backgrounds change according to the players' choices. In this way, the dialogues of characters can follow different paths depending on the decisions made by the player. This allows for the evolution of the character's personal story and creates a unique experience for each player.

Additionally, in terms of environmental dialogue and interaction with the game world, open world games are those in which characters' interactions with their environment play a significant role. Players engage in dialogues with NPCs (Non-Player Characters) they encounter while exploring the environment, and these dialogues hold an important place both in character development and in the narrative. For instance, in *Red Dead Redemption 2*, characters' daily lives, their reactions to the environment, and their interactions with other characters are constantly changing. This offers players the opportunity to explore not only the story of a character but also the game world itself.

In terms of the immersion and character connections within open-world games, dialogues encourage players to bond both with the characters and the game world. In these games, dialogues can lead in different directions based on the player's personal choices. This causes players to invest more emotionally in their characters. Another example would be The Elder Scrolls V: Skyrim, where players face dialogue options to determine the fate of a character. The results of each option directly affect the player's story experience and the evolution of the character. This helps players feel a deeper connection to their characters.

Under the heading of Character and Dialogue in Open World Narratives, it was essential to discuss how character design and dialogues are shaped interactively and how they evolve with the player's decisions. This is because games offer a unique experience to each player while liberating the development of characters and their dialogues.

Character and Dialogue in Emergent Narrative

To remind you briefly, an emergent narrative is a storytelling form in which the player's actions and choices directly shape the story. Unlike a predetermined narrative, the story naturally emerges through the player's interactions. This type of narrative is particularly prominent in games like The Sims and Minecraft. These games grant players the freedom to create their own stories within the game world.

In emergent narrative games, character development and dialogue often have a looser structure and are not strictly tied to a fixed narrative path. As the player interacts with the game world, characters and their relationships evolve, and the dialogues also change in the process. Each player's experience is different because the game creates its own story based on the player's choices. In other words, the emerging story pieces guide the progress of the game. At this stage, the impact of character development options through player interaction becomes unavoidable.

Concept design refers to the process of designing characters, assets, environments, materials, and all objects in the game universe. Sound design involves curating all content, from music to object sounds, to convey the in-game ambiance effectively. Finally, games are prototyped and tested, allowing players to experience them and identify flaws and errors. Based on this feedback, necessary improvements and updates are made, and the game reaches its final form (Sakman, 2021, p.329).

In emergent narrative games, the evolution of characters is typically based on the player's actions. For example, in The Sims, the player's interventions in a Sim's life shape the character's personality, relationships, and life events. This game creates a dynamic narrative shaped by the characters' daily routines and social interactions. In these games, characters can change based on the player's decisions. A character's career, relationships, even the colour of their skin or personality is shaped by the player's choices, allowing for the evolution of their dialogues.

In emergent narrative games, dialogues are often more dynamic and reactive to the player's actions. In games like Minecraft, while dialogues are typically not present in written form, the player's actions and interactions with the environment create an indirect narrative. However, in games like The Sims, dialogues play a significant role as an instrument for social interactions between characters. These dialogues shape based on the player's choices, making each player's experience unique.

In emergent narrative games, the evolution of relationships between characters and dialogues can develop through the player's interactions. These games allow relationships to evolve based on characters' backgrounds, values, and preferences. For example, in The Sims, a character's friendships, emotional bonds, and career goals are shaped by dialogues. These dialogues are among the key elements that determine how relationships will progress.

While the game may provide limited control over the story's progression, the freedom given to the player makes the narrative unique. However, this freedom can also be balanced with some limitations. In The Sims, players can manage their characters' lives, but the general framework of the story is based on the characters' personalities and their roles in society.

On the other hand, digital games, unlike traditional narrative media, include interactive and participatory elements. Thanks to these elements, the player plays an active role in shaping the game's narrative. Digital game narratives are not formed from a predefined set of events; the player's choices and actions can affect the course of the narrative. Therefore, the narrative in digital games is often referred to as "emergent narrative" (Murray, 1997, p. 97-126).

Among the most important reasons for the limitations in this area are the technical unpreparedness of game development technology for such complex interactivity and the developers' desire to avoid potential legal issues by defining all boundaries of their games. Offering the player complete freedom in an open world, with no technical or narrative restrictions, could trigger the enactment of criminal acts within the game world, which may even spill over into real life (Evren, 2024, p.165).

This freedom allows for the shaping of characters' choices and dialogues in previously unthought-of ways. In these games, dialogues are not just a narrative tool; they also become a part of the reality the player creates within the game world.

The Relationship Between Game Mechanics and Narrative

Digital games are a form of media in which the narrative is not only constructed through written texts or cinematic scenes but also through the gameplay itself. The player's choices, failures, repetitions, and interactions with the game world become an integral part of the narrative. This shows that, unlike traditional narrative mediums, in games, the story is shaped not only by 'what is told' but also by 'how it is experienced'. In this context, game mechanics, i.e., the system structures that enable the playability of the game, can serve as both the carrier and the transformer of the narrative. The choices, obstacles, rewards, and strategic necessities presented to the player through mechanics play a critical role in both character development and the narrative connection with the world. For instance, in order for a character to develop a certain ability, the player might need to perform a repetitive action, which is not just a game mechanic but also a carrier of the character's transformation within the narrative. Therefore, understanding the relationship between game mechanics and the narrative is not only a technical issue of game design but also an important way to grasp how digital narrative forms work. Some games create a Ludonarrative harmony by combining the narrative and mechanics in a compatible way, while others generate Ludonarrative dissonance by creating tension between the two elements. This duality deeply affects the player's perception of the game, their relationship with characters, and ultimately the narrative experience (Hocking, 2007). The relationship between narrative and mechanics in games can be examined through the following points:

1. Narrative Setup Through Mechanics
2. The Effect of Game Mechanics on Character Development
3. The Interaction Between Player Actions and Narrative Dynamics
4. Narrative Structures That Become Personalized Through Player Experience

Through this structure, we can better understand why digital games not only offer something to be played but also deliver "experienced" narratives.

Narrative Setup Through Mechanics

In digital games, narrative is often shaped not directly by text, dialogue, or cinematic scenes, but by the player's actions and their guidance through the rules. In this context, game mechanics not only build gameplay but also construct the fundamental framework of the narrative. The obstacles, choices, and reward systems encountered by the player should not merely be viewed as game design elements but as narrative tools that reveal the character's motivations, the world's rules, and the plot. Each document check or small decision might seem insignificant, but over time, it can evolve from a mechanical action to ethical dilemmas, emotional challenges, and critiques of the system. For example, in the game BioShock (Irrational Games, 2007), the player's use of genetic modifications not only facilitates progression within the game but also constructs the ideological critique of the game itself. Similarly, in Journey (Thatgamecompany, 2012), there are no traditional narrative devices like communication, conflict, or task lists. The player interacts with the environment using basic mechanics like movement and jumping. Yet, these limited interactions create a powerful narrative space for establishing emotional connections between players, making sense of the world, and experiencing the character's internal journey. The minimalist mechanics of the game allow the narrative to be constructed intuitively. On the other hand, many decisions that appear to offer choice in the game are, in fact, manipulated by pre-programmed systems, which directly support the narrative's exploration of "freedom." The concept of Ludonarrative dissonance is used to describe these types of situations. While the mechanics claim to offer freedom, there is an argument that at the narrative level, this is a mere illusion. Therefore, it might not be wrong to say that mechanics are not just tools but direct parts of the narrative.

The Effect of Game Mechanics on Character Development

In games, character development is shaped not only by written narrative, dialogues, or cinematic scenes but also through the actions the player performs, the decisions they make, and the outcomes of those decisions. In this respect, game mechanics become not just a reflection of the character's development process but a direct element in constructing it. Mechanics like level-ups, skill trees, or equipment systems commonly found in role-playing games are tangible tools that help the player feel the development of the character. However, these mechanics do not merely facilitate progress within the game. They also deepen the personal transformation of the character and the player's bond with the character.

For example, in The Witcher 3: Wild Hunt (CD Projekt Red, 2015), Geralt's development of various skills not only improves his ability to fight enemies but also influences how the player chooses to build the character. The selected skills impact the gameplay style and therefore the perception of Geralt's personality. Mechanics shape the player's decisions and reveal the character's personality. Undertale (Toby Fox, 2015) serves as a striking example in this regard. Instead of killing enemies in battle, the player can choose to empathize with them. Even the core battle mechanic is designed to support this approach. The decision of whether to kill or spare reveals the inner world of the character.

Interaction Between Player Actions and Narrative Dynamics

Ian Bogost's (2007) concept of Procedural Rhetoric suggests that game mechanics can be used not only for gameplay but also to argue ideas and develop characters. That is, mechanics become a way of defending an idea or constructing a character.

Ludonarrative Harmony and Ludonarrative Dissonance

For a narrative to be effective in games, it is not only the texts, characters, or cinematics that matter but also the harmony with the game mechanics. When inconsistency arises between mechanics and narrative, the player's experience may end poorly. This inconsistency is often explained by the term Ludonarrative dissonance. Thus, predefined objectives must be carefully placed in the game to align with the narrative.

What is Ludonarrative Dissonance?

This concept was first introduced by Clint Hocking (2007) to describe a conflict between narrative and game mechanics. As Hocking found, Ludonarrative dissonance occurs when the entertaining and thematic elements of a game are inconsistent with the narrative themes presented in the game. For instance, in BioShock, this arises when players are allowed to interact with actions that conflict with the narrative themes, disrupting the enjoyment.

The Power of Narrative and Mechanic Harmony

Ludonarrative dissonance is not always a problem. Some games consciously use this conflict or emphasize harmony to strengthen the narrative.

- Papers, Please (Lucas Pope, 2013): The dull, bureaucratic nature of the mechanics helps the player immerse themselves in the character's mental state. The passport control and decisions the player makes reflect the ethical dilemmas and the character's position within the system. Here, the game mechanics and narrative are intertwined; one complements the other.
- Hellblade: Senua's Sacrifice (Ninja Theory, 2017): The game's mechanics use visual and auditory illusions, in-game disorientation, and inner dialogues to express Senua's psychosis. This narrative harmony allows the player to feel the character's mental condition deeply.

CONCLUSION

Digital games, while evolving storytelling, have also been shaped by player demands and the development of game worlds, which are crucial factors in this process. In future games, storytelling will deepen even further, influenced by technology and player expectations, and interactive forms of narration will appeal to a wider audience. Players' increasing expectations are evolving in a rapidly changing era. While storytelling was once seen as a passive experience, today, players seek a more active and personal narrative experience. This shift has become even more pronounced as players now expect not only entertainment but also emotional and intellectual fulfillment from games. In this context, games are no longer just a form of entertainment but a cultural expression. Players' narrative choices and interactions are creating more meaning in the game world, with deeper character development, dialogues, and interactive narratives being demanded (Jenkins, 2002, p.222).

In the future, players' intense interest in storytelling will encourage games to feature richer and more dynamic narrative structures. This will require developers to create more sophisticated narrative techniques and provide players with more personal, unique, and interactive experiences.

Game design is evolving toward a deeper integration with storytelling alongside technical and visual elements. The game world is now being designed not only as a set of game mechanics and quests but also as a story world. The relationship between game mechanics and narrative is establishing a deeper connection, ensuring that the player becomes a part of the story with each step. In this context, open-world games, branching narratives, and emergent narrative types strengthen the player's interaction with the game and their connection to the story.

At the same time, the increasing diversity of narratives across games will encourage designers to develop more creative and innovative approaches to storytelling. Game mechanics, shaped in parallel with players' actions, will make storytelling richer and more meaningful, enhancing the player experience (Murray, 1997, p. 97-126). Game designers will place more emphasis not only on the visual and auditory elements of the game but also on the progression of the story and the player's influence on it.

In the future, the direction of interactive storytelling will remain one of the most important elements in digital games. The use of artificial intelligence and advanced interaction systems will allow players to form more natural and profound interactions with the game world. Future games will offer more options and possibilities, providing players with a narrative and a dynamic storytelling experience shaped by their actions.

Moreover, with the advancement of next-generation virtual reality (VR) and augmented reality (AR) technologies, the physical boundaries of storytelling in games will expand, and players' interactions with the environment will become an integral part of the narrative. This will allow players to feel more immersed in the story and strengthen their connection with the game (Ryan, 2003, p.247-254).

In the future, the direction of interactive storytelling will be shaped by technological innovations and cultural and societal changes. Games that offer in-depth narratives on social issues will allow players to experience more diverse and empathetic experiences.

In conclusion, the future of storytelling in digital games will be shaped by players' increasing demands, the deepening role of game design, and innovative developments in interactive storytelling. Stories will no longer be something to be told but rather an interactive experience in which the player actively exists. This marks an era where games will gain even greater significance, not only as a form of entertainment but also as a cultural, artistic, and intellectual expression. In future games, storytelling will become a process that players watch and a dynamic they shape.

REFERENCES

Barkman, C. (2024). *Narrative complexity in videogames* [Doctoral dissertation, Swinburne University of Technology]. Swinburne Research Bank.

Bogost, I. (2008). The rhetoric of video games. In Salen, K. (Ed.), *The ecology of games: Connecting youth, games, and learning* (pp. 117–140). MIT Press.

Bostan, B. (2022). Dijital oyunlar ve interaktif anlatı (Digital games and interactive narrative). Press and Publishing Industry and Trade Inc.

Calleja, G. (2011). *In-game: From immersion to incorporation.* MIT Press. DOI: 10.7551/mitpress/8429.001.0001

Dreamertalin. (2023). https://dreamertalin.medium.com/storytelling-in-open-world-games-part-2-c1409fee2606

Ea.com. (n.d.). https://www.ea.com/games/the-sims?isLocalized=true

Emergent Narratives. (2015). https://multiverse-narratives.com/2015/05/07/emergent-narratives-in-games/

Esports, D. O. T. (2024). https://dotesports.com/minecraft/news/minecraft-player-brings-stunning-real-world-creations-to-game-using-actual-map-data

Evren, F. B. (2024). *Açık dünya oyunlarında oyuncu odaklı hikaye anlatımı: The Witcher 3: Wild Hunt örneği* [Player-focused storytelling in open-world games: The case of The Witcher 3: Wild Hunt]. Sanat & Tasarım Dergisi.

Fadak, A. S., & Khozium, M. O. (2020). Dialogue generation for digital interactive storytelling. *International Journal of Future Generation Communication and Networking*, *13*(4), 4451–4460.

Farca, G. (2010). *Narratives in video games* [Unpublished manuscript]. Augsburg Phil. Hist University, Englische Literaturwissenschaft.

Güntan, S., & Ar, B. (2014). Recreating the past: Historical narratives and virtual environments of video games. Journal of Spatial Research, Istanbul Technical University.

Güregen, E. S. (2020). *Mobil oyunlarda hikaye anlatımının oyun deneyimine etkisi* [The impact of storytelling on the gaming experience in mobile games] [Master's thesis, Istanbul University Institute of Social Sciences]. Istanbul University Institutional Repository.

Hocking, C. (2007). Ludonarrative dissonance in BioShock: The problem of what the game is about. *Click Nothing*. https://clicknothing.typepad.com/click_nothing/2007/10/ludonarrative_d.html

Jenkins, H. (2002). Game design as narrative architecture. In Wardrip-Fruin, N., & Harrigan, P. (Eds.), *First person: New media as story, performance, and game* (pp. 118–130). MIT Press.

Jin, C. (2021). Game narrative conveyed through visual elements in digital games [Master's thesis, University of Skövde]. University of Skövde Digital Repository.

Klevjer, R. (2006). *What is the avatar? Fiction and embodiment in avatar-based singleplayer computer games* [Doctoral dissertation, University of Bergen]. University of Bergen Open Research Archive.

Murray, J. H. (2017). *Hamlet on the holodeck: The future of narrative in cyberspace* (Updated ed.). MIT Press.

Naughty Dog. (2013). *The Last of Us* [Video game]. Sony Computer Entertainment.

Newman, J. (2013). *Videogames* (2nd ed.). Routledge.

Oyunlastirma.co. (2023). https://oyunlastirma.co/makale/gamfed-turkiye-kaptanlari-karya-kortel-ve-sule-kucuk-yaziyor-dijital-oyun-ve-oyunlastirmada-hikaye-tasarimi-narrative-design-for-gamification

Pablos, T. G. (2015). Game design and emergent storytelling: The construction of new narrative models in early Japanese videogames. *KYOTO Conference.*

Pearce, C. (2005). Theory wars: An argument against arguments in the so-called ludology/narratology debate. In *DiGRA Conference Proceedings*. Digital Games Research Association.

Red Dead Redemption II. (2018). https://www.mmorpg.com/videos/not-so-mmo-red-dead-redemption-2-official-gameplay-video-2000113375

Reddit.(2019). https://www.reddit.com/r/truegaming/comments/dsqy4z/a_masterpiece_in_interactive_storytelling_how_the/

Ryan, M. L. (2003). *Narrative as virtual reality: Immersion and interactivity in literature and electronic media*. Johns Hopkins University Press.

Sakman, S. (2021). *Dijital oyun tasarımında görsel retorik* [Visual rhetoric in digital game design]. International Social Mentality and Researcher Thinkers Journal.

Salen, K., & Zimmerman, E. (2004). *Rules of play: Game design fundamentals*. MIT Press.

Schell, J. (2008). *The art of game design: A book of lenses.* Morgan Kaufmann. DOI: 10.1201/9780080919171

Smith, D. M., & Moore, A. W. (2011). *Narrative in video games: Theories and case studies.* Game Studies.

The Game Awards. (2020). Game of the year winners. https://thegameawards.com/

The Witcher. (2015). The Witcher 3: Wild Hunt, [Video game]. https://www.thewitcher.com/en/witcher2

Thestraitstimes. (2025). https://www.straitstimes.com/life/entertainment/how-minecraft-became-the-biggest-video-game-in-the-world

Upthrust. (2024). https://upthrust.co/2025/01/mass-effect-trilogy-retrospective-how-it-redefined-storytelling-for-sci-fi-rpgs

Vara, C. F. (2019). *Introduction to game analysis* (2nd ed.). Routledge. DOI: 10.4324/9781351140089

Wikipedia. (2018). https://en.wikipedia.org/wiki/Red_Dead_Redemption_2

Yılmaz, T., & Canbaz, E. (2019). Hikâye odaklı video oyunlarda çevirinin rolü: The Last of Us üzerine bir değerlendirme [The role of translation in story-driven video games: An evaluation of The Last of Us]. Journal of Translation Studies and Applications, *27*, 35–55.

Chapter 4
Shadows in the Stream: Turkish Horror, Gothic Storytelling, and Digital Narrative

Aman Deep Singh
https://orcid.org/0000-0002-4923-4137
Nirma University, India

ABSTRACT

This paper explores the convergence of Turkish horror cinema with Gothic storytelling and the transformative impact of new media. It examines how digital platforms have reshaped the production, distribution, and reception of horror narratives in Turkey, focusing on adapting Gothic elements for contemporary audiences. Key themes, such as the supernatural and the uncanny, are analysed within a Turkish cultural context, alongside the influence of Islamic motifs like the concept of jinn. The role of streaming platforms in shaping viewing habits and promoting active audience engagement is also highlighted. Additionally, the portrayal of women in Turkish horror films is scrutinised, linking societal anxieties to gender representation. The chapter concludes by reflecting on the future of Turkish horror in the digital landscape, emphasising innovative narrative experiences and the genre's adaptation challenges. It integrates scholarly and cinematic sources to address significant themes related to this evolving genre.

DOI: 10.4018/979-8-3373-2023-6.ch004

ECHOES OF TERROR: AN EXAMINATION OF TURKISH HORROR AND GOTHIC NARRATIVES IN THE DIGITAL ERA/AUTEURISM

The horror genre has been a vital element of global cinematic history, continually captivating audiences by delving into anxieties and the unknown. In Turkish cinema, although there has been a longstanding involvement with several genres, a notable surge in the production of specialised horror films became apparent in the post-millennium period, attempting "to overcome Eurocentrism and to bring into modernity the voices, experiences and cultural legacies of others" (Dirlik, 2003, p. 276). Initial occurrences of horror in Turkish cinema can be identified in films like *Çığlık* (Scream, 1949) and *Drakula İstanbul'da* (Dracula in Istanbul, 1953). The 2000s were a crucial period for Turkish horror, distinguished by the recurrent integration of Islamic motifs, Anatolian folklore, and a pronounced emphasis on local cultural surroundings (Gjinali & Tunca, 2020; Kazaz & Kartal, 2013). The transition to culturally unique themes, especially the notable portrayal of jinn as supernatural beings, profoundly connected with Turkish audiences, thereby setting a new direction for the genre. It suggested Gothic as "a process, not an essence; a rhetoric rather than a store of universal symbols" (Mighall, 1999, p. xxv).

Turkish horror, while influenced by Western film traditions, has effectively established a unique niche by addressing profound cultural and religious issues. The Gothic narrative, fundamental to the overarching horror genre, perpetuates its impact through the supernatural, the weird, and the examination of fear—components that seamlessly correspond with cinematic portrayal. Emerging from the shadows of nineteenth-century literary traditions, this genre has historically transformed Gothic fiction into early cinema. Throughout the years, Gothic aspects have infiltrated other film genres, such as horror, science fiction, and thrillers. The principal characteristics of Gothic narratives—such as apparitions, supernatural occurrences, psychological turmoil, and the disconcerting fusion of reality and fiction—offer a robust foundation for eliciting fear and suspense in film horror (Kaye, 2012). The motifs of the uncanny and the return of the repressed, frequently pivotal in Gothic storytelling, easily thrive in horror cinema's examination of concealed anxieties and cultural taboos.

Digital auteurism offers a robust theoretical framework for evaluating Turkish horror cinema and its narrative techniques in modern media. This method facilitates an examination of how directors, as auteurs, manoeuvre through the opportunities and limitations presented by digital platforms to express their unique artistic ideas within the Turkish horror genre. The advent of digital platforms in Turkey, like BluTV (established in 2015) and GAIN (launched in 2020), with international competitors such as Netflix, offers alternative distribution avenues that differ from conventional cinema and television (Atalay, 2022; Eminçe, 2022). These platforms provide directors with creative autonomy and an “unblemished space”, free from the constraints typically associated with traditional filmmaking settings. As a result, horror filmmakers can develop unique techniques and investigate specific issues that might otherwise go unexamined. Auteur philosophy fundamentally acknowledges the director as the primary creative force possessing a distinctive artistic vision. In Turkish horror on digital platforms, it is crucial to investigate whether filmmakers demonstrate constant artistic or thematic elements that differentiate their work. One may note a director's persistent involvement with Islamic folklore and jinn mythology, resulting in a distinctive visual and narrative style that defines their contributions to the genre.

Digital auteurism underscores the crucial influence of platform attributes on the formation of an auteur's oeuvre. Each platform has distinct editorial policies and user demographics that can influence storytelling and aesthetic decisions. For example, GAIN's dedication to assisting independent video makers may foster a distinct form of auteur-driven horror compared to Netflix's broad content strategy (Atalay, 2022; Eminçe, 2022; Jeong, 2016). Researchers can evaluate how these platform contexts influence the artistic choices of Turkish horror films. Furthermore, the digital landscape promotes narrative and formal innovation. Turkish horror filmmakers may utilise the serial format of series, integrate interactive components, or adopt unconventional narrative strategies that enhance the horror experience in ways distinct from cinematic releases (Alexander, 2011). BluTV's horror series, *Sahipli*, was created in response to a platform-driven need for serialised storytelling within the genre.

It is essential to analyse conventional tropes in Turkish horror cinema, which often derive from Islamic motifs, regional folklore, and cultural apprehensions. Digital auteurs may interact with these tropes by subverting, reinterpreting, or broadening their parameters within the digital medium. Examining a director's approach to themes like jinn possession, curses, or familial secrets via an auteurist lens can reveal their interpretations of these cultural myths. The audience involvement modes enabled by digital platforms introduce novel dynamics in contrast to traditional cinema. The capacity to pause, rewind, and binge-watch can significantly transform viewer involvement with horror material. Consequently, digital auteurism can function as a mechanism to examine how Turkish horror filmmakers modify their narrative strategies to align with the changing viewing preferences of their audience. However, apprehensions remain about the possible compulsion to sustain continuous audience interaction in the digital landscape, which may unwittingly obstruct the evolution of slow-burn, atmospheric terror.

The evolution of the Turkish movie landscape, especially in the horror genre, has been significantly shaped by digital media and emerging platforms. The shift from analogue to digital systems has profoundly affected all mass media, with digital technology being pivotal in cinema, particularly in Turkish filmmaking (Orkan, 2022). Digital visual effects have created new opportunities for storytelling; however, their efficacy depends on their seamless integration into the narrative. The advent and prevalence of digital streaming platforms (SVODs) in Turkey since the mid-2010s have transformed cinema creation, distribution, and consumption. Platforms like BluTV and Netflix Turkey expand audience access and promote the development of varied material, including horror themes that were previously less common in conventional television. These channels have transformed viewing habits, enabling filmmakers to investigate novel narrative techniques and connect with both national and worldwide audiences.

Cultural elements, as transferred to the digital medium, offer new features to the cultural field with the features of the digital medium. In this interaction, cultural elements are reproduced and appear in different forms.... The cinema, which is a cultural transporter, shows a tendency from conventional communication channels to digital communication channels in terms of promotion and marketing.... Social media, which is an important part of digital communication, also provides important data in terms of showing the change and tendency of cultural policies. (Aytekin & Akar, 2018, p. 2)

The notion of "genre" in film is intricate and contentious, with genre theory offering a framework for examining the conventions, forms, historical progressions, and interconnections of diverse genres. Genres, such as the Gothic, are dynamic; they develop over time, frequently overlapping and intermingling. This mobility is especially apparent within the realm of digital narrative theory, which includes formats such as digital storytelling and transmedia storytelling. These methods utilise digital technologies to disseminate narrative components across several media channels, enhancing audience engagement and interactivity. The interplay between digital narrative and genre is complex, as digital platforms facilitate the research of genres by revealing new forms such as Gothic elements in hypertext, video games, and online communities. Subscription Video on Demand (SVOD) platforms such as Netflix provide a wider variety of genres, facilitating exploration of storytelling techniques that are under-represented in conventional television. This expansion motivates producers to embrace creative risks, yielding a varied array of storytelling methodologies that include both mainstream and independent techniques.

Digital narrative practices significantly transform the expression and experience of genres. Transmedia storytelling disseminates narratives across several platforms, affecting consumer behaviours and questioning conventional concepts of plot and structure. This progress also influences aesthetic decisions within genres, since digital technology provide creative storytelling methods, particularly evident in horror, especially within Turkish cinema. Furthermore, audience interaction has transitioned from passive consumption to active participation, with digital platforms cultivating communities centred around genre material, so influencing the genre landscape. Theoretical frameworks, including psychoanalysis and feminist theory, are being utilised to examine the functioning of genres within new media contexts, emphasising how digital platforms contest traditional definitions of authorship and genre borders. The evolving characteristics of digital media result in a reorganisation of genres, as audience inclinations and technological progress perpetually alter the genre landscape. The interaction between genre theory and digital narrative theory demonstrates how narratives are manifested through both traditional and modern formats, altering the creation, dissemination, and analysis of genre content.

This article analyses the convergence of Turkish horror cinema with the tenets of Gothic narrative in the modern digital era. This will examine how digital platforms have altered the creation, distribution, and reception of horror fiction in Turkey. This paper will examine significant Gothic themes, including the supernatural and the uncanny, in Turkish cinema, utilising scholarly analyses and examples of horror films from these platforms, while highlighting the impact of Islamic motifs, particularly the concept of jinn. Furthermore, the study will emphasise the influence of streaming platforms on audience viewing behaviours and the promotion of active participation with horror material. This study will critically analyse the depiction of women in Turkish horror films, investigating how societal fears and patriarchal frameworks are manifested in gender representations within the genre. This study will examine the future of Turkish horror in the digital realm, addressing both the potential for unique narrative experiences and the obstacles the genre encounters in adapting to this changing world. The economic and industrial circumstances of digital platforms substantially impact digital auteurism. Examining the partnerships between Turkish horror directors and particular platforms, such as Alper Çağlar's relationship with BluTV, reveals how economic influences and strategic platform concerns influence the creative opportunities for auteurs in this genre. Given these reasons, it is essential to alter classic auteurist critique to maintain its relevance in the digital era. Applying the concept of digital auteurism to Turkish horror requires an analysis of how a solitary authorial voice functions within a collaborative digital production context. This entails evaluating a director's body of work across diverse digital initiatives and traditional films to discern consistent auteurial fingerprints that characterise their oeuvre. Digital auteurism provides a significant foundation for comprehending the intricacies of Turkish horror cinema in the digital age. This method surpasses simple genre classification, emphasising the creative agency and unique perspectives of filmmakers who actively influence the genre in digital media and streaming platforms. By examining the stylistic decisions, thematic issues, and cultural interactions of horror directors in this context, scholars can acquire significant insights into the development of Turkish horror narratives in the 21st century.

FROM SHADOWS TO SCREENS: UNVEILING TURKISH HORROR THROUGH GOTHIC NARRATIVES

Historically, Turkish cinema's involvement with the horror genre has been significantly limited, especially prior to the early 2000s. Throughout the Yeşilçam period, spanning the 1950s to the 1980s, melodrama and comedy prevailed in the Turkish cinematic domain, allowing minimal space for horror. As a result, the genre was predominantly overlooked, with only sporadic efforts at investigation. The inaugural recognised horror film in Turkish cinema, *Çığlık* (Scream), directed by Aydın Arakon in 1949, has regrettably not endured for examination, resulting in *Drakula İstanbul'da* (Dracula in Istanbul), produced by Mehmet Muhtar in 1953, being regarded as the first Turkish horror film, which was subsequently remade as *Dracula Untold* (2014). This version was inspired by Ali Riza Seyfi's 1928 novel, Kazıklı Voyvoda (The Voivode with the Stakes), successfully integrating the famous vampire archetype into Turkish culture.

Turkish horror integrates significant aspects of Anatolian folklore, intertwining local mythology and ancient customs with Islamic themes, featuring tales of demonic entities, pre-Islamic rituals, and components of witchcraft and sorcery. Revenge and familial discord are significant themes in numerous narratives, mirroring societal issues like honour crimes, which modern cinema has started to scrutinise. The novels frequently contrast psychological horror with supernatural components, highlighting themes of madness, solitude, and the fear of the unknown. Family dynamics are essential, as the family unit is often portrayed as the principal victim of curses or supernatural disturbances, underscoring the vulnerabilities intrinsic to familial connections. Turkish film, encompassing the horror genre, has endeavoured to establish its influence globally through historical exports and enhanced international recognition. In the Yeşilçam era, Turkish cinema gained popularity in adjacent Middle Eastern nations, and more recently, Turkey has been a prominent exporter of television programs globally. Turkish horror has interactively engaged with Western cinematic traditions; previous films frequently adapted Western horror, exemplified by "Drakula İstanbul'da" and "Şeytan." The contemporary Turkish horror cinema differentiates itself by emphasising culturally specific anxieties, particularly those associated with djinns, while utilising sophisticated special effects. This regional focus assists in addressing previous criticisms about uniqueness. Moreover, involvement in international film festivals has enhanced the prominence and critical acclaim of Turkish cinema, solidifying its significance in the worldwide cinematic arena.

Films like Yavuz Yalınkılıç's *Ölüler Konuşmaz ki* (The Dead Can't Speak, 1970) and Metin Erksan's *Şeytan* (The Devil, 1974), the latter being a version of William Friedkin's The Exorcist (1973), exemplified singular ventures into the horror genre. Kutluğ Ataman's *Karanlık Sular* (Dark Waters, 1993) was a significant endeavour in the horror genre prior to 2000. Multiple constraints impeded the genre's advancement, including insufficient technical infrastructure for special effects, production firms' hesitance to invest in perceived less profitable projects, and a constrained tradition of horror writing in Turkey (Kirişci, 2015; Koçer, 2019; Özkantar, 2022). Preliminary assumptions indicated a lack of interest among Turkish audiences in horror, and early works frequently clumsily emulated Hollywood standards without integrating culturally pertinent themes. The Turkish horror environment experienced a notable transition in the 2000s, especially post-2004, characterised by a surge in horror film production. Orhan Oğuz's *Büyü* (Magic, 2004) is often regarded as a pivotal work, interweaving religious elements that profoundly resonated with audiences. This period witnessed a tendency to integrate Islamic motifs and Anatolian folklore, adeptly responding to local cultural and theological concerns (Kazaz & Kartal, 2013). Prominent directors like Hasan Karacadağ, with his *Dabbe* series, Alper Mestçi's *Musallat*, and Özgür Bakar have significantly shaped this emerging trend of Turkish horror. Moreover, developments in digital technology and visual effects have empowered filmmakers to construct more complex storylines, signifying a shift from past simplistic efforts.

Modern Turkish horror cinema has been intricately connected with traditional mythology and Islamic ideas, profoundly influencing its themes and plots. The revival of horror production post-2000 led to the significant incorporation of Anatolian folklore, reflecting local culture and anchoring narrative anxieties in the Islamic faith, especially concerning the supernatural (Görgülü, 2015). The belief in jinn, malevolent beings from Islamic mythology, is fundamental to Turkish horror narratives, frequently addressing themes of possession, hauntings, and the repercussions of disturbing the supernatural. The Epic of Dede Korkut exemplifies the fusion of pre-Islamic and Islamic traditions, demonstrating the evolution of communal fears over centuries (Koçer, 2019; Laughlin, 2015). Post-2000 Turkish horror, in contrast, primarily incorporates indigenous cultural and religious motifs, diverging from traditional Gothic conventions, and emphasises jinn, familial curses, and the psychological distress experienced by humans fighting unfathomable powers. This unique storytelling approach effectively situates themes of the uncanny and the otherworldly within an Islamic environment.

The current environment of Turkish horror cinema is defined by various interrelated aspects, including representation, cultural authenticity, digital change, gender politics, the emergence of goblin-centric horror narratives, and the impact of digital auteurism. Each of these factors contributes to the genre's development and its appeal to viewers both domestically and globally. Representation entails the depiction of many characters and tales that mirror the intricacies of Turkish culture; modern films progressively emphasise marginalised voices and perspectives, providing nuanced portrayals of horror that align with current sociocultural concerns. This transition has resulted in enhanced representation across gender, race, and socioeconomic status, departing from conventional stereotypes and facilitating a more profound connection with audience identities. Cultural authenticity has emerged as a defining trait of the genre, with filmmakers highlighting local folklore, mythology, and religious beliefs. By using region-specific features like djinns and goblins, filmmakers cultivate a feeling of regional identity that enables audiences to engage deeply with the narratives, mirroring the cultural and historical background essential for comprehending Turkish fears and anxieties.

The emergence of digital technology has profoundly influenced Turkish horror cinema, providing filmmakers with enhanced special effects and post-production tools that facilitate more visually engaging and intricate storytelling. This digital change expands opportunities within the genre, enticing new audiences and facilitating a variety of storytelling strategies and styles. Simultaneously, gender politics have become more significant, as filmmakers increasingly explore themes of patriarchal oppression and women's agency. Female characters frequently traverse male-dominated environments, challenging society's expectations, and norms, hence critiquing conventional gender roles and empowering women to assert their agency within horror narratives.

Additionally, recent Turkish horror films have introduced goblin-centric tales that amalgamate tradition with modern concerns. These narratives often centre on individual and collective phobias, employing goblins as symbols for profound worries related to identity, morality, and history, so illustrating a cultural intrigue with the supernatural in a swiftly evolving society. The notion of digital auteurism has significantly impacted the genre, enabling filmmakers to utilise digital platforms for enhanced creative autonomy, hence facilitating distinctive stylistic expressions and personal narratives that contest traditional storytelling conventions. This trend allows directors to develop unique voices, heralding a new era of Turkish horror that harmonises individual vision with wider cultural concerns. These trends are intrinsically interconnected, converging and developing in reaction to each other. The emphasis on cultural authenticity might influence the portrayal of female characters, but digital transformation may augment the narrative possibilities of goblin-centric stories. Turkish horror evolves, showcasing a dynamic interaction between tradition and modernity, addressing changing cultural contexts while creating a vast array of themes that appeal to many audiences.

The advent of "New Turkish Cinema" in conjunction with globalisation and the proliferation of digital media underscores the dynamic interaction between cinematic expressions and the evolving landscape of Turkish identity, as "its role in the emergence of digital publics have made it a need to explore the effect of digital communication on communication applications with multiple perspectives…ordinary target audiences are transforming into digital publics as people are getting more and more interested in digital ways of communication" (Taşkıran, 2018, p. 145). In modern cinema, the heightened representation of religious and marginalised identities mirrors wider societal transformations as filmmakers address the intricacies of faith, cultural legacy, and the realities of varied communities in Turkey. This dynamic landscape illustrates the adaptability of Turkish cinema in addressing its historical and cultural circumstances, so enhancing our comprehension of national identity.

CONVERGENCE OF TURKISH HORROR AND GOTHIC STORYTELLING

The examination of Gothic components in Turkish horror cinema uncovers a complex interaction between conventional Gothic narratives and indigenous cultural subtleties. Gothic storytelling originated in the late eighteenth century and is characterised by prominent features, including distant and formidable settings—usually castles or manors—that elicit feelings of threat and seclusion. This genre is characterised by the inclusion of the supernatural or uncanny, creating an atmosphere rich in mystery, anxiety, and dread (McEvoy, 2007). The narratives frequently revolve around historical tragedies, hereditary curses, and familial secrets that disrupt the present, encapsulating themes of transgression and decay. Moreover, Gothic literature often explores the psychological distress of its protagonists, who contend with paranoia, loneliness, and internal strife intensified by fear of the unknown. Dramatic narratives featuring violence against vulnerable individuals, especially women, constitute a persistent pattern, alongside the examination of the thresholds between life and death, sanity and insanity, and the natural and supernatural realms.

Turkish horror films are mostly shaped by unique identities grounded in Islamic ideas and Anatolian folklore; however, they also exhibit adaptations and echoes of traditional Gothic elements. Turkish horror frequently employs claustrophobic and secluded locales—such as antiquated mansions, derelict structures, and remote villages—mirroring the atmospheric isolation typical of traditional Gothic environments. The omnipresent nature of the supernatural, primarily exemplified by jinn and other nefarious entities, corresponds with the Gothic thematic focus on otherworldly forces that disturb the natural order and provoke fear (Kızılca, 2015; Tutar, 2015). Moreover, numerous narratives are driven by historical transgressions, curses, or the consequences of breaching cultural and religious norms, reflecting Gothic themes of the past's inescapable influence on the present, frequently appearing as vengeful supernatural entities. These aspects reflect overarching Gothic themes regarding familial connections, inheritance, and the anxiety surrounding dynastic disruptions. (McEvoy, 2007). The psychological disintegration of protagonists facing unimaginable calamities is a common theme in Turkish horror. The interaction of paranoia, solitude, and the conflation of reality and nightmare reflects the psychological intensity characteristic of numerous Gothic fictions. The themes of transgression and taboo, particularly concerning violations of religious or cultural norms, just engage with the Gothic heritage of forbidden knowledge and the repercussions of transcending societal bounds. The apprehension over the "Other" is obvious in Turkish horror's portrayal of malicious spiritual beings, where the familiar and the unfamiliar converge to evoke a sensation of uncanny terror.

Numerous Turkish horror films illustrate the amalgamation of Gothic themes tailored to indigenous cultural and theological frameworks. *Drakula İstanbul'da* (1953), a direct adaptation of Bram Stoker's "Dracula," localises the setting while preserving essential Gothic themes, including the transgression of life and death via vampirism, encapsulating the terror elicited by the incursion of a foreign supernatural being into the familiar terrain of Istanbul. *Büyü* (2004), acknowledged as a pivotal work, intertwines themes of curses and sinister familial secrets with the destructive encroachment of otherworldly entities, paralleling classic Gothic narratives through its remote rural backdrop and the incremental unveiling of a horrifying history. *Musallat* (2007) further illustrates this fusion by exploring the Islamic notion of jinn as a spectral influence linked to historical misdeeds. The character's psychological turmoil and the feeling of being hunted by invisible forces reflect Gothic themes of guilt and vengeance. The haunted home scenario simultaneously reinforces associations with conventional Gothic environments. The *Siccin* series (2014-present) examines themes of dark sorcery and curses stemming from deep familial discord, vengeance, and treachery. The enduring haunting and psychological distress depicted in ostensibly mundane residential environments that transform into scenes of horror strongly reflect Gothic themes of eerie domesticity and the haunting repercussions of historical injustices. Turkish horror cinema intricately incorporates local beliefs and cultural anxieties into Gothic storytelling, thereby establishing a distinctive narrative identity while adapting and reinterpreting fundamental Gothic elements—such as atmospheric isolation, the supernatural encroachment of history, psychological turmoil, and transgressive motifs—into a culturally significant manifestation of horror. This synthesis offers a sophisticated and intricate analysis of terror, utilising ancient Gothic elements and modern Turkish cultural contexts.

Moreover, Turkish horror cinema reflects wider global Gothic traditions. The Gothic genre, entrenched in gloom, has traditionally derived its inspiration from Gothic literature, encompassing key themes such as dynastic turmoil, harsh environments, susceptible female protagonists, supernatural phenomena, and the revelation of antagonists. Turkish horror embodies Gothic themes by examining patriarchy and power dynamics, while also addressing societal anxieties and historical traumas, including experiences of political instability. Both cultures extensively incorporate supernatural aspects and the uncanny—where the familiar transforms into the strange—to provoke fear; nevertheless, Turkish horror uniquely draws upon local folklore, with djinns and curses shaped by Islamic and Anatolian beliefs. Gothic critique concepts, like the "monstrous-feminine" and Julia Kristeva's abjection theory, elucidate the depiction of gender and possession in Turkish storytelling, exposing the cultural concerns embedded in these horror archetypes.

The discussion on the "Globalisation of Gothic" emphasises the necessity of acknowledging many historical, social, and cultural settings in the genre's development. Turkish horror incorporates local folklore, religious beliefs, and socioeconomic tensions that contrast Eastern and Western influences, enhancing the global Gothic environment and demonstrating how universal anxieties are expressed through localised storylines. Turkish horror cinema has a unique history and cultural basis, notably reflected in its incorporation of Islamic and Anatolian mythology, yet it aligns thematically with international Gothic traditions, especially concerning gender, power dynamics, and societal worries. This gendered approach elucidates the integration of patriarchal anxieties and societal tensions into narratives and character portrayals, providing a culturally unique perspective on universal themes of fear and otherness as examined within the wider realm of Gothic and horror movies.

THE ROLE OF STREAMING PLATFORMS IN SHAPING TURKISH HORROR NARRATIVES

The emergence of new media has profoundly altered the terrain of horror narratives in Turkish cinema, especially regarding production and dissemination dynamics. The shift from analogue to digital technologies has significantly impacted the global landscape, including Turkish cinema. Digital technology has transformed filmmaking methods, offering novel tools and opportunities for directors and producers. This change is shown in various phases within Turkish horror. Integrating digital visual effects has proven essential in storytelling across all genres, including horror. An analysis of prominent Turkish films from 2004 to 2017 underscores the significant employment of digital effects to capture complex situations, generate atmospheric tension, and perform feats that would be challenging or unfeasible in real-world environments. The efficacy of these visual upgrades differs; some films adeptly incorporate them to enrich the story, while others may experience detriment from artificial or overdone implementations. Economic factors regarding access to advanced technology significantly influence the quality and execution of digital effects (Atam, 2009; Orkan, 2022; Yüksel, 2009). The rise of digital platforms has transformed filmmaking paradigms, as audience access to media directly impacts narrative and formal techniques in filmmaking. Digital platforms offer filmmakers the opportunity to explore a diverse range of film formats, from short films to feature-length projects, enabling experimentation with novel styles and narrative strategies.

Streaming platforms have significantly improved the accessibility of Turkish horror content both domestically and potentially on an international scale. The Turkish television industry has experienced significant expansion, mainly because of the advent of Netflix originals and various local streaming platforms, like BluTV, GAIN, and Disney+. These sites feature a variety of content and are progressively allocating resources to local projects, encompassing horror programs and films. In 2017, BluTV created Turkey's inaugural horror series for a subscription video-on-demand (SVOD) network, entitled Sahipli (Owner). This genre diversity demonstrates a tendency towards avant-garde filmmaking approaches, setting these platforms apart from conventional mainstream television, which may have been less open to such experimental storylines (Atalay, 2022; Simaku, 2022). Digital platforms possess the capacity to extend the awareness and consumption of Turkish horror films beyond traditional theatrical releases to a global audience. Advanced functionalities, including subtitles and dubbing in many languages, on platforms such as Netflix, facilitate this broadened market penetration. The digital era has provided novel methods of audience connection and participation in horror fiction. The evolution of viewing habits has fostered a more engaged audience that has greater control over what, when, and how they consume content, especially in genres such as horror.

The landscape of Turkish horror is increasingly influenced by sector dynamics, notably censorship and platform algorithms, which greatly affect the development, distribution, and reception of films in the genre. The history of censorship in Turkey is extensive and continues to impact the creative expression of filmmakers. Governmental restrictions frequently constrain the representation of sensitive subjects, including religious beliefs, political matters, and gender dynamics. Filmmakers must adeptly manage these limits, employing a dual method that utilises symbolism and metaphorical storytelling to express profound ideas while complying with governmental regulations. The requirement to conceal or alter content may foster inventive storytelling methods, although it can also limit the thematic depth and diversity of the genre.

The emergence of internet channels, alongside censorship, has altered the distribution and visibility dynamics of Turkish horror cinema. The algorithms utilised by these platforms are crucial in ascertaining which pictures attain more audiences. Content recommendation systems frequently emphasise interaction metrics at the expense of cultural relevance, potentially restricting the visibility of niche horror films that may confront traditional narratives or highlight marginalised perspectives. Consequently, filmmakers are becoming increasingly cognisant of the necessity to produce economically viable work that conforms to algorithmic preferences, occasionally compromising artistic integrity for marketability. This dependence on algorithms may unintentionally reinforce conventional themes while diminishing the significance of new or culturally distinct creations that diverge from established norms.

Furthermore, the interplay between censorship and platform algorithms establishes a multifaceted landscape in which filmmakers must reconcile artistic aspirations with commercial exigencies. As Turkish horror cinema progresses, filmmakers may utilise internet platforms to circumvent conventional gatekeepers, so enhancing creative autonomy and public accessibility. Nonetheless, this prospect for emancipation is mitigated by the actuality of algorithmic curation, which preferentially promotes content that aligns with recognised popular genres. Consequently, although the digital realm presents novel avenues for visibility and creativity, it simultaneously perpetuates established inequalities within the film business, since algorithmic content filtering may mask more varied or culturally pertinent narratives.

The interaction between censorship and platform algorithms influences the dynamics of Turkish horror cinema, affecting the construction, distribution, and reception of storylines. Filmmakers encounter the difficulty of manoeuvring between these limitations while striving to produce engaging and culturally authentic horror narratives. The industry's adaptation to these factors signifies the genre's growth, mirroring extensive cultural discussions over representation, authenticity, and technology's place in modern narrative.

The existing discourse inadequately addresses interactive narratives in Turkish horror films; nonetheless, a basic technological framework is available for examining non-linear and interactive storytelling. Moreover, the influence of social media and online communities is significant, as these platforms have enabled discourse, critiques, and fan engagement with horror films. This connection enhances the collective reception and understanding of horror storylines in Turkish cinema. New media have significantly transformed the creation, dissemination, and consumption of horror narratives in Turkish cinema. Digital production tools have enabled filmmakers to investigate visual effects and implement cost-effective production approaches. Streaming services have democratised access to Turkish horror content, fostering genre variety and expanding potential foreign audiences. While direct audience engagement via interactive media is currently underexamined, the developing digital landscape indicates potential future opportunities for more captivating and immersive horror encounters. (Whittaker, 2007).

DIGITAL TRANSFORMATIONS IN TURKISH HORROR: ENGAGING THE UNCANNY

This section explores the pervasive themes of the supernatural and the uncanny in Turkish horror narratives. It examines their deep roots in the country's cultural context, the significant influence of Islamic motifs—particularly the concept of jinn—and the uncanny representation in contemporary storytelling. Turkish horror storytelling is characterised by its distinct core elements, derived from cultural, religious, and folkloric traditions. These narratives often intertwine supernatural elements with psychological horror and dark psychological drama, forming a rich tapestry of beliefs that incorporate spirits and curses as foundational aspects of their plots. The Turkish cultural landscape reveals a strong animistic connection, wherein the earthly and spiritual realms coexist, making spiritual encounters a routine part of daily life, especially in certain regions. In contrast to some Western horror traditions that may emphasise explicit gore, Turkish horror cultivates fear through the unseen and the incompletely understood. Family dynamics and traditional values are central to these narratives, with familial bonds usually serving as both a source of support and a catalyst for supernatural disturbances that arise from their breakdown. Furthermore, Turkish horror films frequently incorporate social or cultural commentary, utilising the paranormal as a lens to explore themes of guilt, moral decay, and societal pressures. The fusion of traditional supernatural entities with modern settings and contemporary anxieties enables these films to resonate with both older and younger audiences, thereby bridging generational gaps.

A dominant influence within Turkish horror is the integration of Islamic and pre-Islamic mythology, particularly the concept of jinn or genies. Jinn are malevolent supernatural beings central to many horror narratives, underpinning the thematic core of possession, hauntings, and the consequences of disturbing the supernatural. Films such as *Dabbe, Siccin,* and "Gen" prominently feature jinn, exploring spirituality, the afterlife, and the conflict between good and evil, with jinn serving as manifestations of malevolent forces in these narratives (Koçer, 2019). The presence of jinn in the Holy Qur'an solidifies the belief in their existence within the Muslim faith, thus contributing to the fear they instil in Turkish audiences. Jinn is perceived as possessing powers more significant than those of humans—capable of traversing vast distances, remaining unseen while observing humans, and possessing knowledge beyond human comprehension. This results in standard practices in Turkey, where individuals carry protective verses from the Qur'an, such as Felak and Nas, to guard against these creatures (Erdağı, 2024). The prominence of jinn in Turkish horror has led to the genre being designated as "Islamic horror", with films often revolving around these ethereal beings to create heightened fear and tension. Following the release of *Büyü* (Magic) in 2004, which employed religious themes, a new era emerged in Turkish horror cinema characterised by an increased focus on jinn. This fascination distinctively sets jinn apart from Western horror monsters; their roots in Turkish society's cultural and religious foundations render them a potent source of fear. While jinn are frequent protagonists in Turkish Islamic horror, other films such as *Semum* employ devils, who personify evil and tap into more universal fears. Nonetheless, most Turkish Islamic horror films concentrate on jinn, depicting their interactions with humans—such as possession and other sinister encounters—as reflections of human actions like summoning these entities for selfish reasons, thus highlighting themes of social misconduct rather than solely metaphysical evil.

The concept of the uncanny, which involves rendering the familiar strange, plays a prominent role in contemporary Turkish horror narratives. Drawing on Gothic conventions, it literalises Freud's idea of the Unheimlich, presenting the utterly familiar in an inexplicably disconcerting manner. Several aspects of Turkish horror embody the uncanny. While not explicitly detailed in source materials, the motif of repetition and doubles aligns with classic Gothic tropes, manifesting interpretations that challenge established meanings. The nation's strong animistic beliefs, wherein the environment is perceived as animated by spirits, contribute directly to uncanny shape-changing narratives. Additionally, disturbing familiarity arises when established cultural and religious contexts are introduced alongside unsettling supernatural elements, transforming the known into something strange and threatening. The fear of jinn exemplifies this, as their existence within the Islamic framework represents a hidden, potentially malevolent aspect of known reality. By integrating elements deeply ingrained in the Turkish psyche and distorting them through supernatural narratives, contemporary Turkish horror films leverage a unique form of unsettling familiarity.

GENDER REPRESENTATION AND SOCIETAL ANXIETIES IN TURKISH HORROR FILMS

Since the 2000s, Turkish horror films have attained considerable reputation, serving as a medium to examine societal worries and shifting gender dynamics within Turkish society. Rooted in local customs, Islamic imagery, and folklore, these films mirror and frequently perpetuate prevailing patriarchal institutions and the fears associated with gender. The representation of women in Turkish horror serves as a medium for articulating wider societal anxieties, often constructed via a patriarchal perspective that diminishes their identities. Studies reveal that numerous modern Turkish horror films depict women as the "other," frequently linking them to negativity or deformity. Semiotic examinations of 2021 movie posters indicate a notable prevalence of negative images, notwithstanding the persistence of feminist movements in cinema (Özer Özkantar, 2022). This reflects a wider trend in the horror genre, where masculine anxieties are frequently imposed upon female characters, so reinforcing conventional gender stereotypes. In these films, religious beliefs and cultural narratives frequently associate female characters with spiritual malevolence or depict them as susceptible to possession by supernatural beings, such as jinn. These narratives profoundly connect with entrenched worries within a predominantly superstitious and conservative society. This persistent motif not only reinforces patriarchal norms but also portrays women as feeble or exclusively characterised by their sexuality and reproductive abilities (Kazaz & Kartal, 2013; Koçer, 2019). Even traditionally affirmative notions like as motherhood can be recontextualised within horror, depicting women birthing horrific entities, so reinforcing constricted roles akin to those observed in older cinematic traditions, such as Yeşilçam flicks.

The depiction of gender in Turkish horror cinema is notably evident when analysed semiotically in the context of film releases from 2021, such as *Enna: Karabüyü, Azamet, Lübbey'in Laneti: İfritler*, and *Defin Ecin Zulman*. This analytical method uncovers a concerning consistency in the portrayal of women as either victims or threats, underscoring a problematic persistence of patriarchal notions despite progress in feminist discourse. For example, *Enna: Karabüyü* depicts a malevolent, eyeless woman shrieking, personifying hideous characteristics beside a sanguine countenance. The lack of masculine figures underscores femininity as a source of dread, portraying the woman as both possessed by malevolence and defenceless against sinister powers. The inclusion of Arabic calligraphy indicates an Islamic backdrop that merges spirituality with terror, further marginalising the female image as a demonised "other." Likewise, *Azamet* depicts a rural girl whose envy compels her to adopt malevolent wizardry. The billboard, showcasing her visage merged with the silhouette of a snake—a powerful emblem of sin associated with femininity—portrays her as a vessel for malevolence and perpetuates a patriarchal viewpoint that perceives womanhood as a societal menace. The ominous imagery, intertwined with themes of pride and envy, reinforces negative perceptions about the inherent dangers of women. In Lübbey'in *Laneti: İfritler*, a female character is depicted in profound fear among a setting of jinn incursions. Her expression and the accompanying Arabic inscriptions utilise Quranic themes that highlight cultural anxieties around women's spiritual potency and their susceptibility to malevolent forces. This dichotomy demonstrates a societal trepidation over feminism, like the idea that women's acts may incite disorder, echoing the myth of Pandora. Ultimately,

Defin Ecin Zulman centres on a jinn narrative that depicts a woman lacking an eye, eliciting terror, and implying ominous connotations. The poster's visuals and hues place women at the centre of fear and peril, perpetually reinforcing a patriarchal perspective that depicts women unfavourably. Moreover, female ugliness in these narratives frequently represents a challenge to entrenched patriarchal conventions (Erdağı, 2024; Koçer, 2019). The "monstrous-feminine" serves as a medium for examining issues about female agency and potential transgression. Victimisation is a common motif, with female characters being portrayed as victims of supernatural attacks, possessions, or curses. This depiction underscores their perceived vulnerability and impotence, closely coinciding with patriarchal notions that require male safeguarding.

Turkish horror cinema's analysis of masculine representations and narrative structures uncovers critical perspectives on male victimisation and the changing dynamics of familial relationships. Historically, male protagonists in horror novels have been shown as embodiments of strength and authority, frequently reflecting cultural notions of masculinity. Contemporary films are increasingly challenging these clichés by depicting male characters who exhibit vulnerability and victimisation. This transition opposes the traditional depiction of males as solely guardians or aggressors, instead examining the intricacies of masculinity when confronted with supernatural and psychological dangers. The absence of masculine figures in these tough circumstances highlights a societal apprehension regarding women, perpetuating legacies of fear and inferiority.

Furthermore, the transformation of familial roles in Turkish horror narratives significantly influences the representation of masculinity. Numerous contemporary films depict male characters contending with the disintegration of conventional family systems, mirroring societal conflicts around gender roles and expectations. The narratives often emphasise the challenges faced by dads who are unable to safeguard their families against supernatural entities, resulting in sentiments of inadequacy and hopelessness. This depiction not only encourages a reassessment of masculine identity but also highlights the vulnerability of familial relationships in the face of external adversities. The contrast between male victimisation and the representation of women asserting agency in these narratives confuses the picture of masculinity. Female characters are frequently depicted as not just survivors but also as proactive individuals who fight the terror within their familial environments. This dynamic encourages a more profound examination of gender politics, as male characters confront their flaws while female characters demonstrate their resilience under hardship.

A Turkish horror movie illustrates a complex interaction among masculine representations, narrative structures, and transforming familial roles. Contemporary films depict men as victims and examine the intricacies of masculinity, thereby challenging conventional gender standards and providing a more nuanced comprehension of male identity. This progression reflects wider societal shifts, inciting essential discussions regarding gender, power, and familial interactions in a swiftly changing cultural environment.

Women are predominantly restricted to clichéd portrayals as virtuous victims or malicious threats, with limited storylines examining substantial female agency or identity. A prevalent feature in these films is the male saviour archetype, frequently depicted as a pious elderly hoca (religious teacher) conducting exorcisms to liberate female victims, so reinforcing a gender dynamic entrenched in patriarchal authority. Although several Turkish horror films, like Haunted (*Musallat*), have challenged conventions by exploring male possession, the foundational structure often reflects conventional anxieties, particularly apprehensions around male homosexuality. The emergence of Islamic horror in Turkish cinema increasingly incorporates religious themes with the depiction of gendered dangers. Despite a significant rise in horror film output post-2000, the diversification of female representation has been constrained since numerous films perpetuate analogous themes and tropes, thereby impeding the genre's thematic evolution concerning gender representation. Clover (2015) posits that the victimisation of women in Turkish horror embodies masculine worries around the decline of male power, with "female cover" serving as a projection surface for male fears and crises.

In modern Turkish horror cinema, female protagonists often serve as pivotal characters confronting the intricacies of otherworldly terrors, as demonstrated in films like Siccin and *Dabbe*. These narratives frequently examine the challenges encountered by women, exemplified as Hacer's anguish in *Siccin*, where she is pursued by the malevolent spirit of her husband's former wife. This narrative embodies themes of jealousy and cultural expectations around marriage, successfully reflecting bigger fears concerning women's roles and the widespread apprehension of female autonomy. Furthermore, the notion of the "monstrous feminine" is extensively featured, linking female characters to themes of terror and retribution. In *Dabbe: The Curse of the Jinn*, Yasemin's horrifying metamorphosis as she yields to the spell of a jinn epitomises societal anxieties around the unleashing of women's wrath and strength. This characterisation aligns with Gothic themes, portraying female figures as representations of society's anxieties over sexuality, agency, and conventional conventions. Furthermore, these novels frequently examine familial relationships and themes of treachery. Films like *Beddua: The Curse* exemplify how familial lineages are imbued with betrayal and curses, mirroring both individual and collective suffering. This dynamic situates women between victimhood and empowerment, highlighting the interaction between societal expectations and supernatural components within conventional family arrangements. The horror narratives embody fundamental worries around gender roles, sexuality, and the quest for women's autonomy. The ethereal characters in these films often represent the enduring impact of societal tragedies on women. In *Musallat*, Yeliz faces the fury of a spirit intimately connected to themes of betrayal and sorrow, highlighting the significant repercussions of unaddressed societal concerns that persistently influence women's experiences inside patriarchal structures. Turkish horror films, via their diverse representations, offer insight into the supernatural and critically examine the societal challenges confronting women.

THE FUTURE OF TURKISH HORROR: INNOVATIVE NARRATIVES IN A DIGITAL LANDSCAPE

The digital era offers distinct problems and promising opportunities for the future of Turkish horror cinema. A major problem is the necessity for thematic creativity beyond the predominant dependence on Islamic motifs and the Jinn image. Although these features have supported the genre's early popularity since the 2000s, the filmmakers' propensity to replicate similar themes threatens to impede the long-term development and wider appeal of Turkish horror. To prevent stagnation, future productions must expand their reach to investigate a broader spectrum of concerns and storylines, potentially incorporating elements of Turkish folklore, societal worries, and current issues. Furthermore, the Turkish film business encounters difficulties in advancing special effects makeup techniques, which are considerably inferior to those of established industries like Hollywood. This disparity frequently compels filmmakers to depend significantly on computer-generated imagery (CGI). While CGI presents creative opportunities, its excessive or unrealistic application may undermine narrative effectiveness. Turkish horror must attain a seamless integration of digital effects that amplifies the narrative instead of eclipsing it. Investing in the cultivation of practical special effects expertise could enhance the genre and distinguish it on a global level.

Historically, originality and cultural adaptation have posed considerable obstacles for Turkish horror cinema, with early productions frequently failing as insufficient approximations of Western horror conventions. Recent achievements have arisen from a more profound integration of local cultural and religious components. The future necessitates a more sophisticated adaptation that transcends the mere inclusion of religious characters, demanding a comprehensive examination of wider cultural anxieties and modern phobias. Furthermore, the emergence of digital platforms is expected to result in an increased emphasis on low-budget projects. This accessibility may enable more filmmakers to engage with the genre, but it could also foster a dependence on uncomplicated and perhaps uninspired horror that is devoid of engaging narratives and efficient resource utilisation. Conversely, the digital era presents unparalleled chances for Turkish horror films to resonate with international audiences via diverse streaming platforms. The success of Turkish programmes on international platforms, such as Netflix, underscores the potential for Turkish narratives and production quality to connect globally. This prominence may foster specialised audiences interested in culturally specific and diverse horror encounters. The distinctive cultural and religious aspects inherent in modern Turkish horror may appeal to worldwide audiences in search of alternatives to conventional Western horror. By examining Islamic cosmology, ideas on Jinn, and traditional Turkish folklore, filmmakers can craft scenarios that distinguish themselves in the international horror genre.

Digital platforms have transformed production methodologies, artistic decisions, and audience interaction in Turkey. Digital platforms are frequently seen as "fertile grounds" that provide filmmakers considerable autonomy, greatly enhancing their audience reach and evading some censorship constraints characteristic of conventional film and television industries. These sites offer "alternative pathways" for independent and art-house films, facilitating significant public visibility. Industry experts see a "promising impact" of these platforms since they obscure the distinctions between mainstream and independent filmmaking, enabling producers to transcend the limitations of prevailing American and Anglo-Saxon storylines. This transition provides filmmakers with access to a wider audience, promoting different and inventive narrative techniques. Furthermore, the working circumstances on digital platforms are frequently perceived as superior to those on traditional television, hence fostering creativity. The adaptability of these platforms facilitates experimentation with other genres and formats, including science fiction shows and shorter content durations.

Nonetheless, apprehensions remain over the ramifications of these alterations. The fierce rivalry for viewer engagement, exacerbated by the simplicity of transitioning between various information, compels filmmakers to emphasise rapid storytelling, often sacrificing narrative depth and aesthetic excellence. This focus on participation may result in the "standardisation" of material and the emergence of a "blockbuster genre system", thereby undermining the original diversity that platforms pledged to provide. Moreover, audiences frequently favour established filmmakers within the extensive selection available, hindering the opportunities for emerging or avant-garde directors to attract recognition.

Filmmakers must consider the "medium-specific characteristics" intrinsic to digital platforms, especially the dominance of smaller screens such as mobile phones, which might affect content consumption. This prompts a crucial discussion on whether filmmakers ought to prioritise storytelling universally or tailor their narratives to accommodate digital streaming requirements and viewer tendencies. Certain industry experts think that adaptation may lead to a "lethal compromise" in storytelling quality. While other sources examine Netflix and digital platforms primarily from the audience's perspective—focusing on viewing habits, genre preferences, and subscription motivations (such as evading advertisements and appreciating on-demand access)—these insights deviate from the fundamental concerns of filmmaking practices, including the representation of masculine roles and victimisation within narratives. Thus, the most relevant insights regarding the impact of digital platforms on Turkish cinema and filmmaking techniques emerge from discussions with industry professionals, highlighting both the newly acquired creative liberties and the commercial pressures and obstacles they face.

Moreover, some Turkish horror films that integrate classic supernatural motifs with contemporary locations, technology, and urban deterioration may appeal to viewers who value the fusion of ancient fears and current worries. This contrast may provide a universally relatable sort of dread that surpasses cultural limitations. The emergence of "New Turkish Cinema" and its increasing visibility at international film festivals may offer essential venues for presenting innovative Turkish horror films to a global audience, where acknowledgement can result in expanded distribution agreements and critical recognition, thereby augmenting the genre's international impact. Digital platforms are acknowledged for facilitating independent and niche filmmaking, enabling rising and diverse voices in the Turkish horror genre to investigate various styles and themes. This may result in innovative films that garner international acclaim, as the ease of online distribution allows filmmakers to engage directly with global horror enthusiasts, circumventing conventional gatekeepers. Turkish horror cinema in the internet era has problems with thematic and technical innovation; yet, the extensive potential provided by digital platforms creates considerable prospects for its global impact.

CONCLUSION

This chapter provides a comprehensive analysis of the evolution of Turkish horror cinema, contextualised within Gothic narrative frameworks, while also considering the significant impact of the digital streaming era. However, it does not present specific examples or discussions of interactive Turkish horror content, which constitutes a limitation of this study and may be explored by future researchers. Principal findings indicate that Turkish horror exhibits unique traits intricately linked to cultural, religious, and mythological traditions, frequently amalgamating supernatural components like djinns, demons, and curses with psychological horror and dark drama. The apprehension of the unknown persists as a continual source of anxiety in these narratives. Since the 2000s, there has been a significant rise in the production of horror films in Turkey, especially those including Islamic motifs, which mirror the region's distinctive cultural and religious context.

The examination of Gothic narrative illustrates it as a debated and dynamic genre marked by recurring themes such as the supernatural, paranoia, and the interrogation of boundaries. This genre possesses a profound history spanning diverse media, such as literature, theatre, film, graphic novels, and television, continually evolving in response to emerging societal anxieties and aspirations. Moreover, digital streaming platforms have profoundly influenced the production of Turkish series by augmenting both the quantity and diversity, providing enhanced creative autonomy, and facilitating the exploration of new genres, such as horror and science fiction, while broadening potential global audience engagement. Platforms such as BluTV have innovated the creation of horror shows in Turkey.

The advent of the digital narrative landscape in the mid-2010s has profoundly influenced Turkish horror cinema. The emergence of local streaming services such as BluTV, PuhuTV, and GAIN, in conjunction with the introduction of foreign platforms like Netflix, has enabled the production of original Turkish content. The digital transition has generated new chances for the horror genre by broadening thematic diversity and facilitating the investigation of psychological thrillers, science fiction, and fantasy, which were previously under-represented on conventional television. This enhanced visibility enables Turkish horror, characterised by its distinctive cultural worries, to engage both domestic and worldwide audiences, so contributing to the phenomenon termed “Global Gothic”, wherein many cultural anxieties converge with universal Gothic motifs.

The study underscores the persistent significance and evolution of Gothic aspects in modern media, as demonstrated in graphic novels and film. Notwithstanding the growing fame of Turkish horror, there persists a necessity for advancement in domains such as special effects makeup, which can enhance the genre's production quality. The depiction of women in Turkish horror has been analysed through a semiotic framework, uncovering potentially detrimental and stereotypical representations that correspond with wider discourses on gender within the horror genre. The internet environment significantly affects viewer engagement, especially among Turkish Generation Z consumers, as services such as Netflix offer escape and amusement, perhaps influencing their consumption of horror content. The interaction between Turkish horror, Gothic motifs, and digital storytelling constitutes a vibrant cultural phenomenon. Turkish horror intrinsically corresponds with fundamental Gothic motifs, invoking the otherworldly and examining apprehensions related to cultural and religious prohibitions. Entities such as the jinn serve as localised embodiments of the Gothic “Other”, functioning as catalysts of terror that contest the set limits of the known realm. The expansion of digital streaming fosters innovation, enabling filmmakers to go into darker subjects and tales that old media platforms may have restricted. This progression offers potential for renewed Turkish horror to include sophisticated Gothic elements while tackling modern societal issues within the existing framework.

The blending of traditional motifs with modern storytelling techniques not only enhances the genre's appeal but also allows for a more nuanced exploration of contemporary anxieties. As Turkish Gothic Horror continues to evolve in the digital landscape, it addresses both aesthetic and thematic challenges, positioning itself within a global context while retaining its unique cultural identity. Addressing the representation of marginalised groups, particularly women, is crucial for the development and engagement with current social issues. Moreover, incorporating novel digital narrative techniques, such as interactive storytelling or transmedia extensions, could augment the immersive experiences of Turkish horror. Enhancing the special effects makeup industry in Turkey could substantially improve the visual impact and overall quality of horror productions.

REFERENCES

Alexander, B. (2011). *The New Digital Storytelling: Creating Narratives with New Media*. Praeger. DOI: 10.5040/9798216979456

Atalay, D. G. (2022). Insider Conversations: Film Making in the Age of Digital Media. In Tetik, T., Atalay, D. G., & Ulusoy, N. (Eds.), *Turkish Cinema and Television Industry in the Digital Streaming Era* (pp. 63–72). Peter Lang.

Atam, Z. (2009). Critical Thoughts on the New Turkish Cinema. In Bayrakdar, D., Kotaman, A., & Uğursoy, A. S. (Eds.), *Cinema and Politics: Turkish Cinema and The New Europe* (pp. 202–220). Cambridge Scholars Publishing.

Aytekin, M., & Akar, D. (2018). Cinema and Social Media: Role of Media in Movie Publicities in Turkish Cinema Industry. In Dogan, B. Ö., & Ünlü, D. G. (Eds.), *Handbook of Research on Examining Cultural Policies Through Digital Communication* (pp. 1–30). IGI Global., DOI: 10.4018/978-1-5225-6998-5.ch001

Clover, J. C. (2015). *Men, Women and Chain Saws: Gender in the modern horror film*. Princeton University Press. DOI: 10.1515/9781400866113

Dirlik, A. (2003). Global modernity? Modernity in an age of global capitalism. *European Journal of Social Theory*, *6*(3), 275–292. DOI: 10.1177/13684310030063001

Eminçe, D. T. (2022). Gaining Digital Auteur: Digital Auteurism on the Turkish SVODs, GAIN. In Tetik, T., Atalay, D. G., & Ulusoy, N. (Eds.), *Turkish Cinema and Television Industry in the Digital Streaming Era* (pp. 105–120). Peter Lang.

Erdağı, D. Ö. (2024). Evil in Turkish Muslim horror film: The demonic in "Semum.". *SN Social Sciences*, *4*(27), 1–22. DOI: 10.1007/s43545-024-00832-w

Gjinali, V., & Tunca, E. A. (2020). A General Look on the Impact of Turkish Horror Movies: An Exploratory Study on the Opinions of Youth on Horror Movies. *SAGE Open*, *10*(4), 1–11. DOI: 10.1177/2158244020979701

Görgülü, T. (2015). *Islamic Motifs in Turkish Horror Films* [M.A Thesis]. Bahçeşehir University.

Jeong, S. (2016). Digital Auteurism in Film Criticism. *Film Criticism*, *40*(1), 1–2. DOI: 10.3998/fc.13761232.0040.116

Kaye, H. (2012). Gothic Film. In *A New Companion to The Gothic* (First, pp. 239–251). Wiley-Blackwell. DOI: 10.1002/9781444354959.ch17

Kazaz, M., & Kartal, H. (2013). "Turkish Cinema vs. Religion" Religious Elements Used in Post-Millennium Turkish Horror Films. *Book of Proceedings: International Symposium on Language and Communication: Exploring Novelties*, 1289–1301.

Kirişci, M. (2015). Korkusuz Türk Sineması [Com]. *Oteki Sinema [Fearless Turkish Cinema. Oteki Cinema].* https://www.otekisinema.com/korkusuz-turk-sinemasi/

Kızılca, M. (2015). Türk Korku Sineması'na Genel Bir Bakış. Oteki Sinema [An Overview of Turkish Horror Cinema. Oteki Cinema] [Com]. *otekisinema.* https://www.otekisinema.com/turk-korku-sinemasina-genel-bir-bakis/

Koçer, Z. (2019). The Monstrous-feminine and Masculinity as Abjection in Turkish Horror Cinema: An Analysis of Haunted (Musallat, Alper Mestçi, 2007). In S. Holland, R. Shail, & S. Gerrard (Eds.), *Gender and Contemporary Horror in Film* (pp. 151–165). Emerald Publishing Limited. DOI: 10.1108/978-1-78769-897-020191011

Laughlin, V. A. (2015). A Brief Overview of al-Jinn within Islamic Cosmology and Religiosity. *Journal of Adventist Mission Studies, 11*(1), 67–78. DOI: 10.32597/jams/vol11/iss1/9/

McEvoy, E. (2007). Gothic Traditions. In Spooner, C., & McEvoy, E. (Eds.), *The Routledge Companion to Gothic* (pp. 7–9). Routledge.

Mighall, R. (1999). *A Geography of Victorian Gothic Fiction.* Oxford University Press.

Orkan, S. (2022). The Use of Digital Effects on Storytelling in Turkish Cinema. *MEDIAJ, 5*(2), 356–369. DOI: 10.33464/mediaj.1162233

Özkantar, M. Ö. (2022). Woman Depiction in Turkish Horror Films: A Semiotic Analysis as Part of the Concept of "Alterity.". *Intermedia International E-Journal, 9*(17), 154–169. DOI: 10.56133/intermedia.1099340

Simaku, X. (2022). Netflix and Chill: An analysis of Turkish Generation Z viewers on The New Hedonistic Product. *İletişim Kuram Ve Araştırma Dergisi, 58*, 170–184. DOI: 10.47998/ikad.1004162

Taşkıran, H. B. (2018). Digitalization of Culture and Arts Communication: A Study on Digital Databases and Digital Publics. In Dogan, B. Ö., & Ünlü, D. G. (Eds.), *Handbook of Research on Examining Cultural Policies Through Digital Communication* (pp. 144–160). IGI Global., DOI: 10.4018/978-1-5225-6998-5.ch007

Tutar, C. (2015). Türk Korku Sinemasının Yapısal Engelleri: Sosyo-Kültürel Bir Bakış. Gümuşhane University [Structural Barriers of Turkish Horror Cinema: A Socio-Cultural Perspective. Gumushane University]. *E-Journal of Faculty of Communication, 3*(2), 247–274. DOI: 10.19145/guifd.33671

Whittaker, J. (2007). Gothic and new media. In Spooner, C., & McEvoy, E. (Eds.), *The Routledge Companion to Gothic* (pp. 270–279). Routledge.

Yüksel, M. (2009). Film as the Media and the 'Mediator' in Conflict Transformation. In Bayrakdar, D., Kotaman, A., & Uğursoy, A. S. (Eds.), *Cinema and Politics: Turkish Cinema and The New Europe* (pp. 172–187). Cambridge Scholars Publishing.

ADDITIONAL READING

Atakav, E. (2013). *Women and Turkish Cinema: Gender Politics, Cultural Identity and Representation*. Routledge.

Kiran, A. (2023). Between global and local: Translation and localization in Netflix Turkey's media paratexts. *Translation Studies, 16*(3), 361–378. DOI: 10.1080/14781700.2023.2201282

Özyürek, E., Özpınar, G., & Altındiş, E. (Eds.). (2019). *Authoritarianism and Resistance in Turkey: Conversations on Democratic and Social Challenges*. Springer. DOI: 10.1007/978-3-319-76705-5

KEY TERMS AND DEFINITIONS

Digital auteurism: applies auteur theory to the digital realm, where creators, such as directors and critics, establish a personal artistic vision through online platforms and technologies, influencing storytelling and audience engagement.

Digital storytelling: involves telling stories using digital technologies, with narratives often incorporating diverse media and ranging from personal accounts to broader applications. It leverages digital platforms for creation and distribution.

Genre evolution: describes how narrative categories change over time and how Genres adapt to new cultural contexts, hybridizing with others to lead to new forms and interpretations.

Gothic: Gothic literature, emerging in the 18th century, highlights supernatural elements, decay, and terror, exploring transgression and the uncanny to challenge societal norms and reveal historical anxieties regarding the human condition.

New media: These are digital technologies that emerged in the latter part of the 20th century, characterized by multimodality, interactivity, accessibility for both creators and consumers, interconnection, and diverse uses, primarily encompassing the internet and related platforms.

Turkish Cinema: It encompasses films produced in Turkey, reflecting the intersection of European and Middle Eastern cultures, identities, and religious values, and engages with Western cinematic traditions while asserting its own national and cultural identity.

Chapter 5
Analyzing Sahmaran as an Example of Transmedia Storytelling

Nur Emine Koç
https://orcid.org/0000-0002-3477-8019
İstanbul Aydın University, Turkey

Mine Demirtaş
Istanbul Beykent University, Turkey

ABSTRACT

Storytelling is a social and cultural activity. Transmedia storytelling, whose main elements include story, technology, and consumers, ensures that the previous plot is remembered by continuing the existing story and makes the audience experience the stories by identifying them with their period. An effective transmedia storytelling strategy interacts with popular culture. It produces a new perspective on the original meaning. The Sahmaran story, the subject of the study, is not only famous in Anatolia but also in many parts of the world. These legends have been known among the people from ancient times to the present day and are based on universal cultural foundations. The event patterns are continued with transmedia narration. As an example of transmedia storytelling, the Legend of Sahmaran and the Sahmaran series streamed on the Netflix platform in 2023, are analyzed by the content analysis method. It is revealed how the story fed from oral culture has changed on digital platforms and how it has moved away from its cultural story by incorporating Western elements.

DOI: 10.4018/979-8-3373-2023-6.ch005

INTRODUCTION

Societies have gone through various processes from the period they were formed until today. The era until the invention of writing was oral culture, visual with the invention of the printing press, verbal, auditory, and visual with the introduction of electronic media, and digital with the advent of the Internet and Web 2.0 in the 2000s. Each period has brought innovations with it, from oral culture to written culture, from written culture to printed culture, electronic culture, and finally to the period of digital culture in which tools that digitize and transfer audio-visual content are used. From those times to these days, stories that bear the technological and cultural traces of the period they are in have become processed in various media and digital platforms. In this context, transmedia storytelling, which is the subject of the study and a popular technique used to tell a story differently on more than one platform, was compared with oral storytelling. In this context, since there are many Sahmaran stories, the most widely told Sahmaran story in our country, the Sahmaran story set in the Tarsus region, and the Sahmaran story processed on the Netflix digital platform are compared and analyzed in terms of their content. It is compared in the context of similarities and differences.

Storytelling is a magical interaction tool that has been going on for centuries and has the power to distract, relax, and make humanity think. It has been a powerful tool for communication between cultures throughout history. Beyond being just a form of entertainment, it has played an important role in conveying the values, beliefs, and history of societies. People wanted to maintain their lives, the elements they considered important, and the situations they found dangerous to the next generation. From the most primitive communities to the most modern ones, they have expressed themselves through drawing, writing, and word of mouth. The story contents, strengthened by the oral and then written transmission of cultural elements, were passed down from generation to generation. With digital culture, people from all over the world gather in a single culture. Everybody consumes the same kind of film and music content, wears the same kind of clothes, and has the same style of eating and drinking, so it has become the most dominant culture compared to other cultures. The formation of popularity now flows from digital culture. Therefore, storytelling has also shifted to digital. New media platforms have assumed the storytelling role of this culture, and their impact is much stronger and lasting.

Storytelling, which refers to the process of creating, communicating, and sharing a story, is a powerful tool that has kept people entertained, relaxed, and simultaneously thought-provoking for centuries and has provided communication between cultures throughout history. The story is not only a form of entertainment but also plays an important role in transferring the values and beliefs of societies.

The concept of 'storytelling', which existed long before the invention of writing, has been carried to quite different dimensions with the effect of technological developments in our age. It is seen that it has transformed formally and contextually from animal pictures and hunting stories drawn on cave walls to folk tales on digital platforms (Mutlugün, Topuz, 2020: 37). People want to convey the life they live, the situations they consider important and dangerous to the generations that come after them, and to express themselves in a way that will spread from the most primitive communities to the most modern ones through drawing, writing, and word of mouth. The story contents, which are strengthened by the oral and then written transmission of cultural elements, are transferred from generation to generation through storytelling.

Within the digital culture, where people from all cultures gather in a single popular one, consume the same kind of film and music content, wear the same kind of clothes, and have the same style of eating and drinking. It is seen as the most dominant culture compared to other cultures. New media platforms undertake the storytelling of this culture, and their effects are much stronger and more permanent. The formation of popularity is now realized through the interactivity of digital culture, so storytelling takes place in digital media by evolving into another form.

In this study, as an example of transmedia storytelling, the widespread narration of the story of Sahmaran in the Tarsus region and the new Western-oriented form of the Sahmaran story on the Netflix platform, which has evolved into digital, have been examined by content analysis. It is a qualitative research method that analyses the transcriptions of the text or mass media systematically and objectively and investigates their similarities and differences.

1. STORYTELLING AS A CONCEPT

In storytelling, the process of creating, communicating, and sharing a story, characters, events, and emotions are brought together in a certain order. It takes place on many different platforms such as books, films, theatres, video games, and other digital media. One of the most basic elements of storytelling is character. Stories usually revolve around certain characters and the characteristics, motivations, and development of these characters form an important part of the story. The second important element is the plot, and stories are shaped around a specific plot.

The story is shaped around a specific plot, and these events usually include an introduction, rising action, climax, falling action, and conclusion. Another important element is the message and theme of the story. Stories are usually centered around a certain theme, which represents the intended message or meaning of the story. Another element is emotion. Stories aim to evoke various emotional reactions in the audience, and this emotional connection enables the audience to be more deeply involved in the story. In addition to emotion, narrative style is also very important, and storytelling determines the way a story is told. This includes whether it is told from a first-person or a third-person point of view, in a specific time frame, or in an asynchronous way. If it is told in the first person, the story is told from that person's point of view and has a more subjective structure. Sometimes this subjective structure can be realized through three different narratives. In this way, the story is presented to the audience from a more objective point of view.

It is possible to recognize storytelling as a means of communication and emotional connection. A good story makes the audience think, evokes an emotional response in them, and sometimes contributes to a deeper understanding of life. For this reason, storytelling is recognized as an important artistic and communicative tool in many cultures.

In stories with important elements such as introduction, rising action, climax, falling action, and conclusion, the plot is conveyed through mimesis or digesis. Mimetic narrative, which is based on image and visuality, is narration through animation (imitation). Cinema and television films correspond to the definition of mimesis, while digesis narrative is defined as narration through a narrator (Ersümer, 2013:10; Mutlugün, Topuz, 2020: 39). Television has caused the emergence of a different field of dramatic narrative, taking its place as the main storyteller of societies. The programs we watch on television have emerged as a different example of the story type that appeals to all segments of society, while on the one hand being the culture produced, on the other hand (Mutlu, 1991:79).

Digital storytelling has many features that traditional storytelling has, such as having a specific sequence of events and effectively conveying the point of view that carries a certain integrity of meaning in the characters who play a role in this sequence of events. By combining these features with technology, it also enables the creation of stories that can reach wider audiences (Bahadır, Tüfekçi, Çakır, 2021). It is known that digital storytelling started to emerge in the 1980s and began to be institutionalized in the 1990s. Especially with the concept of 'transmedia' used by Marsha Kinder, platforms with various features were used synchronously. The content created, started in traditional media and was applied to this field through various applications in new media (Ökmen, 2021: 74). With the advent of Web 2.0 in internet technologies, digital storytelling has become widespread, stories have reached global dimensions, and each message has become instantly shared with millions of people. This change has enabled the production and dissemination of stories very quickly (Küngerü, 2016: 41).

2. TRANSMEDIA STORYTELLING

Transmedia storytelling is a popular technique used to tell a story differently on multiple platforms. In this technique, the story is told differently according to the medium used. Each platform has its audience, a special storytelling method, and a transmedia strategy (Shahbazi, 2024). Stories that can be told as if they are the story of a single plot told in multiple media while preserving the characteristics and language of each, can have a special narrative structure that expands across various languages and different channels.

In the most general definition, the circulation of a story on multiple platforms such as radio, television, cinema, comics, and mobile platforms can be defined as 'Transmedia Storytelling' (Sarı, 2017:71). According to Henry Jenkins, transmedia storytelling is a new phenomenon born as a response to media convergence that creates new demands on consumers and depends on the active participation of information communities. Jenkins thinks that transmedia storytelling is the art of world creation. In transmedia storytelling, which emerges with new texts on various media platforms, a story is introduced in a film, expanded through television, novels, and comics, and finally on digital platforms. Each content can remain independent in itself (Jenkins, 2016, cited in Sarı: 73).

As storytelling began to take its place in the digital universe, the development of the entertainment, electronic industries and the discovery of interactive fiction enabled the audience to take part in the story in a more active and interactive position (Murray, 1997: 66, Ersümer, 2013:10, Mutlugün, Topuz, 2020).

The 2000s, on the other hand, have been the years when visual and auditory possibilities as well as verbal ones have started to be used within the visual possibilities of the digital world in which technology has developed. In such an environment, stories have also started to evolve in a different direction through digitalization, and what is at the forefront of the digitalized narrative is no longer the narrator but the narrator itself (Bouchardon, 2014:123; Ersümer, 2013:10; Mutlugün, Topuz, 2020).

Transmedia storytelling, defined as 'transmedia storytelling' in English, is a form of storytelling created in line with today's social and cultural structure and consumption-oriented acts of entertainment industries. In Jenkins' definition (Jenkins, 2007), transmedia storytelling is defined as "a structure in which the integral elements of a fiction are systematically spread across many distribution channels to create a holistic and coordinated entertainment experience" (Uzun, 2016: 79).

3. DIFFERENCES BETWEEN TRADITIONAL STORYTELLING AND TRANSMEDIA STORYTELLING

The most important difference between traditional storytelling and transmedia storytelling is the number of media that tell the story. In traditional storytelling, only one platform and medium is used to tell the story, while in transmedia storytelling, multiple media and platforms such as books, films, TV shows, animations, video games, social media, and new media are used. Transmedia storytelling is a more challenging form of storytelling that allows the audience to connect with the story in a variety of ways. However, traditional storytelling is limited to a single medium (Shahbazi, 2024). In traditional storytelling, audiences view a story through a single medium such as a book or a film, whereas in transmedia storytelling, each audience member can interact with a world of stories that cross platforms.

The feature that makes a story transmedia is that it has depth in each aspect, allowing each part of it to be analyzed from a different perspective with different characters created (Naghdi, 2024). Another difference is that in a traditional story, the whole is less than the sum of the parts, which can lead to dissatisfaction when consuming media. In a transmedia story series, on the other hand, the whole is more than the sum of the parts, and the combination of different parts in the story creates excitement in the audience.

An important feature of transmedia storytelling is that it is possible to create a story that develops the entire plot and the backgrounds of the characters. The world around them on every platform is where the story is processed, and a more immersive and engaging story is presented to the audience.

Netflix As A Digital Platform:

Netflix Platform is an American new media tool established in California in 1997. When it was first established, it served as a DVD sales and rental company. In 2007, Netflix, which started broadcasting over the Internet as it is now, started to serve as an unlimited broadcasting platform, first limited to hours, and then with the increase in competitors. In 2010, the platform was opened for IOS phones 2010 and Android phones in 2011, and because it is as close as a phone, it has shown a significant increase in viewing rates. In 2012, when the feature that all episodes can be watched as binge-watching was added, the audience rate increased even more.

Netflix is a streaming platform, and as of 2012, content planning was made with the idea that it would create a Hollywood effect. By changing the form of storytelling in terms of content, it was able to reach many more people than cinemas and television in a short time. Since it could not be used as an application on the phone at first, its interaction was slow.

However, in 2013, the first original series, 'House of Cards', was broadcast with all episodes of the season. This series, which was specially prepared and captivated the digital audience, made a lot of noise with its binge-watching feature and the fact that it was planned more freely than the censorship and stereotyped structure of television, and was an ad-free platform. With the activation of the feature of creating up to five profiles at once, the content, image quality, and original productions have also increased. In 2013, the first film 'Beasts of No Nation' was also released, and it was revealed that the content strategy varied greatly compared to television and traditional cinema. In 2016, Netflix, which also included special content for children, added the 'Narcos' series, a Spanish production, to its content as the first non-US content. Thus, it enabled foreign users to be included in the platform. In the same year, it added an offline feature to the platform, allowing content to be downloaded to phones or computers when there is no Internet and then watched in an Internet-free environment. In 2017, the like feature was introduced, and in 2018, the parental protection system and pin code feature were introduced for individual use. Although it was previously thought to remain at high levels, its transition to the IOS and Android systems has become indispensable with its timeless, ad-free viewing feature everywhere.

Turkey was included on Netflix in 2016 along with 130 other countries. The 'Hakan Muhafız' series is the first series filmed for the Netflix platform in 2018. The series, starring famous actors such as Çağatay Ulusoy, Okan Yalabık, Ayça Ayşin Turan, and Hazar Ergüçlü, was directed by Can Evrenol, Umut Aral, and Gönenç Uyanık. The series, which can also be called a story of heroism, has been a successful serial that synthesizes Western symbolism and Turkish history with chosen norms, Ottoman and Istanbul motifs.

The first season of the eight-episode Turkish-produced Netflix original television series Sahmaran aired in 2023. The book "Sah-ı Mar- The Children of the Sahmaran," written and directed by Pınar Bulut and published by Emine Buzkan Kaynak in 2023, as well as the original Sahmaran story, served as inspiration for this series. The series is now considered a modern adaptation of the Sahmaran tale, viewed via a Western synthesis and directed by Umur Turagay. As such, it was chosen as an example of transmedia storytelling and analyzed in detail as the subject of the research.

4. SNAKE STORIES AND SAHMARAN:

The serpent is an important character from the Creation of the world and is also present in the Garden of Eden. The animal, Satan, chooses to disguise himself as an important role in "The Creation Story". The snake, which talks to Eve, persuades her to eat the apple and deceives Adam, is also known as the character that causes humanity to fall from paradise. The use of the phrase 'Woman is evil, evil is woman' also comes from this story. Evil is the snake here. Only Eve understands its language, and only the two of them speak. The serpent never speaks to Adam, just as Yahweh never speaks to Eve. Manipulatively whispering in Eve's ear that the reason why they do not eat the fruits of the Tree of Knowledge is a challenge for them, he knows that he can deceive her, not Adam, and he achieves his goal. The serpent's crawling is the punishment it received from God for falling to the Earth. As can be understood from the Genesis story, the connection between the serpent and the woman goes back to the Garden of Eden. On the one hand, the snake turns into a positive figure in terms of the woman giving birth. The snake is considered a reward for the act of giving birth, which is given as a punishment, in terms of ensuring the continuation of the lineage, rather than a curse and punishment in terms of the continuation of humanity (Carr, 2020).

The snake, which exists in the underworld and on the earth, is the protagonist not only in "The Creation Story" but also in many other stories. The snake, which is attributed as sacred due to religious books and stories, is a universal symbol and has taken on a sacred being in many cultures in positive or negative, frightening or fascinating ways. The snake, which is also taken as an important animal in mythology, is thought to be both immortal and a sacred being because it is associated with the same moment of its molting, the underground, and the earth (Carr, 2020). Especially in Egypt, the snake, which is a strong example of the belief in its sanctity, is found in the remains of many figures and motifs in the Isis culture. In addition, pharaohs and queens are depicted with snake crowns (Harva, 1933). According to Egyptian beliefs, it was believed that people bitten by snakes actually stepped into immortality, and snake venom was also used in suicides (Hooke, 2004). In Balil and Hittite mythology, the snake is known as the symbol of life, immortality, and health. In Indian mythology, the snake is both feared and deified. In Indian mythology, the snake, which is thought not to harm them when the snake is worshipped, also appears as a God figure in the form of a half-human and half-snake (Currid, 1997). In Chinese mythology, the snake is identified with the dragon figure, some of which represent the good spirit and the evil spirit (Werner, 1994:252).

The snake, the subject of many legends, tales, and myths, has taken its place, especially in Anatolian stories. Since it is known as an important figure that helps people in their spiritual journeys in Shamanism, it is seen that snake figures are used in many Shaman drums and folkloric clothes (Warrell, 2010). In Altai, Erlik is the evil god and the lord of the underworld in Tengrism. Yerlik is the earth, Erlik is the underworld. In Mongols, the same symbols are used as Erleg and Yerleg (Işık, 2018:178). Erlik Khan has a snake in his hand instead of a sword. He is even famous for the snake figure wrapped around his whole body. He gets his power from snakes. Contrary to the belief of the cursed animal in the Bible, the snake is considered sacred in Shamanism and Islam (Schimmel, 1996:70). Another belief is that the snake is protective. Believing that the snake pictures hung in the houses would protect them from enemies and evil, people believed that they would be protected from evil by having tattoos with snake figures on their arms and legs and wearing jewelry (Işık, 2018:190). In the Göktuğ inscriptions, there are two intertwined snake figures in the name of famous heads of state, such as Bilge Kagan and Kül Tigin (Caferoğlu, 1988:96). According to another belief, the intertwined snake is a symbol of reproduction (Salt, 2006). In The Story of Prophet Moses, the staff in the hand of Prophet Moses turns into a snake, swallows the staff of Pharaoh's magicians, and then returns to its original form (Beydavi, 2013:3).

In the story of the snake, also mentioned in "The Epic of Gilgamesh", Gilgamesh, who is looking for the formula of immortality, sees the snake eating the herb of immortality (Cassuto, 1997:37). In the Epic of Gilgamesh, the snake is a character who plays an important role during Gilgamesh's adventures and informs Gilgamesh about the plant of immortality (George, 2003:38). When he finds the plant and realizes that he has no immortality, he realizes that the snake has deceived him, just as Eve was deceived by Satan in the form of a snake.

Humankind's quest for immortality has been the subject of many stories since its existence. Both religious books and many Western and Eastern masterpieces deal with the quest for immortality. Humanity's desire to attain the attributes of God has given birth to many mythological legends and characters. The fact that it changes its skin every year, its rebirth, its mysterious connection with the underworld, and its being the only animal chosen by Satan in the Garden of Eden have made it one of the symbols of immortality (Çoruhlu, 1994:96).

From a Freudian point of view, the snake as a phallic symbol is considered a masculine power, while it is said to symbolize feminine power with its twisted circular movements (Freud, 2007(1915): 275). Sahmaran, known as half man/woman, half snake, is an important figure in Mesopotamian culture, especially in Mesopotamian culture, dating back to the origins of Middle Eastern mythology. The story of Sahmaran, who is believed to be wise, is a legend that has been passed down from generation to generation and is told in Southeastern Anatolia, especially in Mardin, Tarsus, Adana, and Şanlıurfa regions. The figure of Sahmaran in the same depiction appears in Indian and Greek mythology under different names and stories and is also mentioned as a fairy in the Thousand and One Nights Tales and in European folkloric stories in the Middle Ages (Özdemir, 1998:252).

Sahmaran, known as the queen of snakes in Anatolian culture, is always taken as a woman in the stories since she is associated with women due to the common consciousness in religious books. She is a female figure symbolizing fertility in terms of her physical structure, and wisdom is attributed to her. She is a being depicted as half human and half snake. There are stories in which she is described as a woman on top and a man on the bottom, or a woman on top and a snake on the bottom. 'Fool is fare, fare is fool' (Shakespeare, 1993), which is believed to contain contrasting elements such as good and evil, yin, yang, white and black, and with these contrasts, like the world or like human beings. In other words, it reminds humanity that there can be a good in every evil, an evil in every good, and that only a certain trigger is needed for this to occur. For this reason, it symbolizes the sacred as it reflects the dark, magical, or sinful side of humanity.

When we look at its name, its origin is Persian. Shah means ruler, mar means snake, and maran means snakes. Since it is referred to as the head and ruler of snakes, it has always been identified with the devil. The half-human, also known as Erbüke and Erböke, or İşbüke and Sahmaran in Turkish culture, is generally characterized by beauty, handsomeness, and wisdom. In the stories, she is mentioned not only as a woman but also as a being whose male and female aspects are named separately. She is believed to live in a cave or a special place (Çıblak, 2007:16) . There are many different versions of the story of Sahmaran, which was first mentioned in the Camasbname in the 15th century. It is known that Sahmaran, whose similar story is also found in the Thousand and One Nights Tales, is of Tarsus origin. In the research, the story of Tarsus's origin is discussed.

5. ANALYSES OF SAHMARAN IN THE CONTEXT OF TRANSMEDIA STORYTELLING

5.1. Purpose

This research aims to examine the transformation and changes in the story of Sahmaran from Anatolian cultural norms to digital platforms, its similarities, and the ways it is influenced by Western norms in the context of transmedia storytelling. The effort of Anatolian stories, which have changed with digital platforms, to keep up with digital platforms and to resemble Western stories with the desire to gain appreciation, is investigated in terms of story, character, symbols, theme, plot, emotion and narrative style of the story, and the Netflix example of the story of Sahmaran in Tarsus are examined.

5.2. Universe, Sample, and Limitations

The research universe of this study, based on qualitative research methods, was determined as Netflix and the Tarsus origin story of Sahraman in the context of the Anatolian story. In the research, 8 episodes of the first season of the Sahmaran series, filmed in 2023 in the context of the Netflix platform, and the story of Sahmaran originating from Tarsus were discussed.

5.3. Method

Van Dijk's qualitative content analysis was chosen as the research method. This method was used to analyze the deep structure and content of texts and communication materials. Van Dijk has developed various analytical tools to understand the structural features and contents of texts in the field of linguistic and social sciences. In the context of story analysis, Van Dijk's content analysis aims to examine what themes, concepts, characters, and events a story or text contains. The content analysis method used in this study was categorized by the characteristics of storytelling, and the stories were structured by examining their content, symbols, and themes.

In the story analysis conducted in the research, with the help of Van Dijk's content analysis, the way the story was formed, the symbols used in the story, the main characters, relationships, and the values represented were analyzed. In addition, the place, time, and social contexts in which the story takes place are portrayed. The effect of the story on the audience, whether a certain social problem or element is addressed or not, is also analyzed in parallel with this, and the bond established with the audience is revealed.

5.4.Findings

Table 1. An Analysis of the Comparison of the Sahmaran series broadcast on the Netflix platform and the Sahmaran story originating from Tarsus

Legend of Sahmaran Tarsus	Sahmaran Netflix
The time of the story is unknown. It is mentioned in the story as thousands of years ago. The stories of the serpent and the Sahmaran vary according to the region. The story based on this article is the most popular story in Tarsus: According to the legend of Sahmaran in Tarsus, many years ago, there used to live snakes in the seven layers below the ground. These snakes were called Maran. Sahmaran was called the queen of these intelligent, merciful, and peaceful Marans. The upper part of Sahmaran was a young and beautiful woman, and the lower part was a snake. According to the legend, Jamshab was the first person to see Sahmaran. She was also very wise. Jamshab was the son of a poor family who sold firewood for a living. One day, Jamshab and his friends discovered a cave full of honey. His friends took Jamsab down to get the honey out, but they left Jamsab in the cave and ran away. Jamshab saw a hole in the cave and noticed that there was light coming out of it. In this garden, there were unique flowers, beauties, pools, and many snakes. He lived here for many years and won the love and trust of Sahmaran. As the years passed, he said he missed his family very much and asked Sahmaran to see them. Sahmaran released Jamshab on the condition	The Sahmaran series, published on Netflix, is set in 2023. It draws upon the Tarsus legend, exploring the concept of immortality and the consequences of suicide. The series opens with a youthful image of Camsap, who has been doomed to immortality for centuries, and his suicide from the cliff. Throughout the series, the snake, snake figures, and symbols effectively refer to the origin of the Sahmaran story, creating a visual feast. The protagonist, Shahsu, a research assistant, travels to Adana to deliver a seminar and oversee a project. Her primary motivation for undertaking this journey is to exact revenge on her grandfather for abandoning her mother years ago. During this expedition, Shahsu engages in introspection, questioning her own beliefs, her grandfather's actions, her mother's role in her life, and her overall perspective on life. She ultimately realizes that the facts she has been led to believe are not entirely accurate. In the course of these events, she encounters Maran, with whom she is destined to be united, and learns, following the interpretation of enigmatic prophecies, that she is a member of an extraordinary and enigmatic community called Mar, a descendant of Sahmaran. The Mar race adheres to the legend of Sahmaran, the symbol of love and wisdom, and with the arrival of Shahsu, they await the

continued on following page

Table 1. Continued

Legend of Sahmaran Tarsus	Sahmaran Netflix
that he would not tell anyone where he was or go to the hammam. Jamshab kept his promise for years, telling no one where Sahmaran was. One day, when the Sultan fell ill, the Vizier announced to everyone that the cure was to eat the meat of Sahmaran. Jamsab was forcibly taken to the bathhouse, and it became clear that he knew where Sahmaran was when he shed snake scales from his body. Jamshab, who was being tortured to reveal the location of the well, was forced to show the location of the well, which was the entrance to Sahmaran's garden. Sahmaran was captured, but the man he loved made a plan for Jamshab's sake. When he was dying, he sacrificed himself for Jamshab and told him to boil him in an earthen pot. He made the vizier drink the water and feed the meat to the sultan. The vizier died, and when the sultan's life was saved, he made Cemşab his vizier. According to the legend, from that day on, the serpents did not know that Sahmaran had been killed. When we look at the prophecy in the Tarsus legend, the phrase "Ceyhan from the wind, Adana from the flood, Tarsus from the snake" has been adopted by the local people.	fulfillment of the historical prophecy. As Shahsu encounters Maran on his quest to resolve the past, he learns that he and Maran are the chosen ones and that his grandfather is Jamsap simultaneously with the fulfillment of the prophecies. The narrative, which is a sequel to the prophecies and Tarsus, is situated in the West. The viewer is left to decide whether the love between the snake and the human is a curse or a gift that persists for centuries, as the fate of both is left to the viewer. The love between the snake and the human does not occur by chance. There are 8 episodes of the serial. All the episodes are released on the same date: 20th January 2023. Episode Names: 1. "Throes of the Earth" 2."Things Rain Says" 3."Unstable Equilibrium" 4."Unbearable Lightness of Believing" 5."Future Changes" 6."The Turmoil That Is Life" 7. "The Recurrence of Love" 8."The Snake Inside Me"

Table 2. An Analysis on the comparison of the characters of the Sahmaran series broadcast on the Netflix platform and the Sahmaran story of Tarsus origin

Legend of Sahmaran Tarsus	Sahmaran Netflix
Sahmaran: She is a wise, strong, motherly, sacrificing female character who is loved and respected by everyone. She also has supernatural features. This power, which comes from the superior characteristics of snakes, includes features such as hypnotizing the other person, making them do what they say, and performing magic. Even though she is the head of snakes, she gives up her own life and race for the man she loves. In fact, she can be defined as a typical Anatolian woman. **Cemsap:** In the story, she is seen as not betraying Sahmaran and not spending her. She is forcibly taken to the bathhouse, and it is revealed that she has a relationship with Sahmaran. Despite this, she does not want to tell the location of Sahmaran. As soon as the hero realizes that he is being tortured and tells his location in order not to die, he forgives him. He even dies for her. 'Would you die for a snake? But he died for a human being is a quote from this story. Between the two characters, although Sahmaran chooses to die for her beloved, Cemsap tells the location of the well where Sahmaran is located, even though he will regret it all his life. Although this situation was ignored at the time, the character who is valued and remembered centuries later, and whose paintings are found in houses, is Sahmaran. **Snakes**: In the Tarsus legend, snakes are peaceful,	**Shahsu**: The character of Shahsu is treated as a strong, wise, and intelligent character, just like Sahmaran. She is a graduate of Boğaziçi University Psychology and a good research assistant in her job. She studied psychology to escape her and her mother's psychological traumas, and as a woman who has lived as a witness to her mother's years of her father's trauma and psychological collapse, she decided not to live as her mother lived. She is the granddaughter of Camsab and is an important human character of the prophecy. Throughout the series, she goes through a journey in which she realizes that it is her destiny to be with Maran. It is only in the last episode that he realizes why he and his grandfather are sleepwalkers and their spirits are disturbed, and as soon as he accepts his own existence, he becomes the chosen one, and his latent powers are revealed. **Camsap:** He is called Camsap in the series and is condemned to live with regret throughout his life. Since Sahmaran makes him immortal when he dies, he has to live with his regret forever, even if he wants to. Unlike the story in Tarsus, Camsap is a character in the series who wants to die but cannot die, has psychological problems, sleepwalks, and is doomed to live as a restless spirit. The beginning of the series starts with Camsap trying to commit suicide but not
wise, and supernatural creatures.	being able to die. In the continuation of the story, the viewer realises that not only he but also his entire lineage is cursed with the same curse. Thus, it is understood that in the series, Sahmaran is not only a character who sacrifices herself, but also a powerful figure who cursed Camsab centuries ago. Jamsab and his descendants also have superior qualities inherited from Sahmaran. Immortality is only Camsap's curse, but the dreams or nightmares seen serve as a harbinger of the future. **Camsap's Daughter Gül:** The character Gül is a
	dead character who is mentioned a lot in the series but does not appear in the series. She died because of not being able to bear the curse and psychological delusions imposed on her. She waited for her father, who had abandoned her since she was a little girl, to make rose gardens by multiplying the rose seed her father gave her when he left, and kept the rose seed that she would plant with her father in the palm of her hand when she died. At the same time, when her daughter Shahsu learnt that she knew where her father was but never dared to go to him, she decided not to be like her mother.

continued on following page

Table 2. Continued

Legend of Sahmaran Tarsus	Sahmaran Netflix
	Lilith: There are many different versions of Lilith's story. According to one legend, she is a female figure created for Adam before Eve, but she was destroyed because she was too questioning and headstrong. In another story, Lilith is the serpent who encourages Eve to eat the fruit of the Tree of Knowledge with Adam and Eve. She acts together with Samael. Rebellious and strong female characters are always identified with her. Lilith, who is taken as a very strong woman in the story, is shown as cursed throughout the series, sleeping naked and locked up in a bathhouse. It is seen that she becomes active every time a prophecy is fulfilled (Buzkan, 2023:133). It is seen that she wakes up in the last episode when Shahsu learns the meaning of her existence and her reason for living. In the last episode of the series, her existence and reason are explained to the audience. She is referred to as Sahmaran's sister. When Camsap, the vizier and the sultan's soldiers come to take Sahmaran, she wants to kill them all, but Sahmaran locks her in a place and seals her there. Thus, the character is created for Season 2 as a supernatural being waiting for centuries for revenge.
	Maran: One of the most important characters of the series. He is the marked person and is a descendant of Sahmaran. All other snakes care for and respect him. Although he denies his destiny, as soon as he sees Shahsu, he realises that he cannot escape his destiny and experiences a skin change during his first intimacy with Shahsu. Since it is said that the reason for the immortality of snakes is that they change their skin, the skin change scenes take place in the baths on the bottom floor of the mansion where the Marans live with their father and 3 sisters. Since the skin change in the bath is also in the Tarsus Sahmaran story, it has become one of the scenes that ensures the continuity of the story. Maran, who is repeated many times in the series, is thought to be the savior of snakes. Snakes are also divided into two as: those who obey and those who rebel. The rebellious snakes say that Maran can never fulfill the prophecy and are seen as beings who sell their souls to Satan, do evil, can take over people's bodies, and whose pupils return to the land when they are in the human body, just like the Western Satan characters.

continued on following page

Table 2. Continued

Legend of Sahmaran Tarsus	Sahmaran Netflix
	Ural the father: He appears as Maran's father and the head of the snakes. Like Maran, he was also born marked. Being marked is also referred to as the chosen one in the series. He is a moderate and wise snake character who respects Maran's decisions and tries to calm both the snakes and his son, knowing that the prophecy will come true. Cihan: This character is seen as a character placed in the university as the protector of snakes and Shahsu. But then he is manipulated by the most malevolent snake, the character who appears as a Satan type, and he questions why he is not the chosen snake and wants to revolt and take Shahsu to Anavarza Castle to give her to the malevolent snake. The prophecy will be fulfilled there. But Maran prevents this, and the two snakes fight for the first time over a human. This is a harbinger of the fulfillment of the prophecy. **Diba, Hare, and Bike:** They are Maran's sisters. They have supernatural powers because they are from a family of snakes. Maran, her sisters, and their father, who are similar to the family in Twilight, are considered strange by people. The chosen snake family, which is known as a rich and strange family, gives the impression of a new era vampire family. **Lakmu:** The spokesperson of the snakes is Cihan's
	father. He is a snake who spends his life in hiding, waiting for his shah to come back and provide communication between the snakes and the chosen family. In the end, he will act for his son and give up his duty and move to the dark side. **Miraç**: It is one of the snakes that thinks that humans are unnecessary and evil creatures. Since it can be easily manipulated, it wants to kill the chosen ones of humans, namely Shahsu and Camsap. At the last moment, he gives up killing Shahsu with Cihan's manipulation and wants to kill Camsap, but Camsap does not let him do it and takes the knife from his hand and stabs himself. **Arun:** He is a mysterious snake dressed in black with a face that is not easily recognisable, but fits the representation of the character of Satan in Western TV series. It is clear as soon as the series starts that he is the head of the malevolent characters. He tries to reach Shahshu from the beginning of the series. It has superior features compared to other snakes. It does its best to prevent the realisation of the prophecy. **Chavgeesh:** He communicates with Shahsu by appearing deaf and dumb. As the soothsayer in the series, he is the character who predicts the omens.

Table 3. An Analysis on the Comparison of the Symbols of the Sahmaran series broadcast on the Netflix platform and the Tarsus-originated Sahmaran story

Legend of Sahmaran Tarsus	Sahmaran Netflix
The most important symbolic figure in the Tarsus Sahmaran story is the picture of Sahmaran, which is used as a symbol of fertility in many houses in Anatolia. In the story, Sahmaran's self-sacrifice for the person she loves has circulated by word of mouth in oral culture, and the picture of Sahmaran in the painting is not only the symbol of the story, but also the symbol of fertility and abundance. In the vicinity of Tarsus, the belief that Sahmaran still lives and helps those in distress continues. The reason why snakes in Anatolia are not regarded as evil beings, but as helpful and sacred to people, comes from this legend.	**Snake:** At the beginning of the first episode, we see a train carrying Shahsu to the place where her grandfather lives. With the visual, we see the train moving like a snake. It symbolizes the snake going to the place where the prophecy is going to be fulfilled. In Episode 1, the audience is introduced to the snake sisters (Diba, Hare, and Bike). The first time we see them, we see the image of one of them resembling the ubiquitous posture of Sahmaran. In Figure 5, it is seen that Shahsu goes back to Maran's house, where there is a cactus in a pot at the entrance of the house. Its figure is also in the shape of a snake. **Rose seed:** the flower and rose seed planted by her mother, T., Gudin S. Encyclopedia of Rose Science. The rose
	parable reference brings the rose seed to Shahsu Daoud in Episode 1. He told his grandfather that he grew up in a rose garden, that his mother kept only this seed, that when his father came he waited to sow it with him, and that when he died he had it in the palm of his hand. We learn in Episode 2 that David planted that seed in the garden. It is at this point that the rose sprouts take root in the garden and begin to multiply. The rose can symbolize many things. Love and the fact that the rose seed is planted, takes root and envelops the whole garden symbolizes that the rose has found its place and its fertility has returned to the region (Debener, 2003:45). In Episode 4, Maran tells Shahsu that the rose is a different flower that loves to belong and feels lonely where it does not belong and that it needs only one thing, and that is contact (Epi 4, 18:37). **Water:** We see the water lust of Shahsu from the
	beginning of the serial. She has a reservation for a hotel close to her grandfather's house. She insists on a room with a bath. When she cannot rent that room, she goes to a lake and sees Shahsu with water in harmony. When she is inside the water, she feels herself safe and sound, but when the exterior shooting of the lake is shown, we see the storm outside the lake. There, Shahsu and Maran meet each other. For the third time, they meet each other, but this time on purpose, there starts a heavy rain which symbolises abundance, and it is understood by the house workers that the rain is unusual but expected for a long period. In Episode 4, Maran and Shahsu realize that they cannot resist each other in the botanical garden they enter. This garden represents the Garden of Eden. Later, when they

continued on following page

Table 3. Continued

Legend of Sahmaran Tarsus	Sahmaran Netflix
	start kissing, the snakes watch them as a whole. A scene has been created like a bunch of snakes wrapped around a branch, watching the inevitable end of Adam and Eve, who committed the first sin of humanity. This kiss, which also symbolizes the fall from the earth, emphasizes once again that an irreversible path has been taken and that the snakes have a great share in the fulfillment of this prophecy. **Chosen One**: From the very beginning of the series, it is emphasized that Shahsu and Maran are the chosen ones. The fact that they cannot resist their fate and that they are attracted to each other as soon as they see each other is proof that they are the chosen ones for each other in their destiny. Maran knows that he is the chosen one when he saves
	Shahsu from Cihan and talks to the snakes. Shahsu, on the other hand, goes through phases just like Neo's belief that he is the chosen one in The Matrix. There is a moment like Neo's first encounter with Agent Smith's character in The Matrix when he realizes his power and stops the bullets. In the last episode of the series, after hearing the prophecy from Maran, Shahsu encounters the character of Arun and realizes his own power when Arun moves to kill him. Shahsu, who has the power to prevent Arun, realizes his power and defeats Arun, just like Neo's unwitting hand gesture.

Table 4. An Analysis of the Comparison of the Narrators of the Sahmaran Series Broadcast on the Netflix platform and the Tarsus-originated Sahmaran Story

Legend of Sahmaran Tarsus	Sahmaran Netflix
The legendary story of Sahmaran is a folk tale that circulates by word of mouth. For this reason, the narrator is taken as the 3rd person singular. In some sources, although Sahmaran's speeches are taken, there is no story told by the characters.	The first episode starts with a curse that a human has. First, we do not know who he is, but later we will realize. As the readiness of the audience, the voice-over recalls the legend of the Sahmaran story and from the beginning of the serial, the voice-over refers to the creation story of humanity betraying God and the curse after that. At the beginning and throughout the series, we see the voice-over disrupting the sequence of the events. Sometimes they are words from the novel written by Emine Buzkan, "Şah-ı Mar- The Children of the Sahmaran". It gives a better understanding to the audience of the legendary story adapted to the serial.

Table 5. An Analysis of the Comparison of the Sahmaran Series Streamed On the Netflix Platform and The Prophecies of The Tarsus Origin Sahmaran Story

Legend of Sahmaran Tarsus	Sahmaran Netflix
On the Day of Judgement, the snakes will learn that humans killed Sahmaran and will attack humans. In the legend, Sahmaran says, 'I am going to marry my beloved. Don't trust people. Never travel alone and never leave each other. After that day, snakes never travel alone. Since the snakes, which are seven floors below the ground, perceive every drum sound they hear above as Sahmaran's wedding, they say that when the wedding starts, they first hit the drum with all their might. There is a group of people in and around Tarsus who believe that this omen of doom will be like this in the world. For this reason, people also believe that Sahmaran came and stopped the apocalypse. It is rumored that Tarsus will one day be invaded by snakes who learned that Sahmaran was killed. Folk belief is that Sahmaran is alive and comes to the aid of those in distress. In Tarsus, the Sahmaran figures are still hung in people's houses to bring prosperity.	**Prophecy in the series:** The prophecy in the series is handled differently than the prophecy in Tarsus. Sahmaran, which is more Western-oriented in the series broadcast on the Netflix platform, has paired the snake with the devil and evil. The prophecy begins with Shahsu and Maran loving each other. Man's betrayal of God is identified with the betrayal of Sahmaran, and it has a structure that shows that man always clings to a power arising from deception. Betrayal makes people strong. The signs that need to happen for the prophecy to be fulfilled take place in the order written, step by step, throughout the series. Fire, cattle perishing, a mar attacking a mar, snakes (mars) being able to get inside a human, and the last omen is a human giving birth to a snake.

Figure 1. Popular Sahmaran figure

Figure 2. Episode 1: 4.21 The snake figure

Figure 3. Episode 1, 15:44 Snake Figure

Figure 4. Episode 3, 45:30 Snake Figure

Figure 5. Episode 6, 15:24 Snake Figure

Figure 6. Episode 4, 21:19-21:20 Garden of Eden

CONCLUSION AND DISCUSSION

Societies have gone through various processes from the period in which they were formed until today, from oral culture to written culture, from written culture to printed culture, electronic culture, and finally to the period of digital culture, where tools that digitise and transfer audio-visual content are used. From those times to these days, stories that bear the technological and cultural traces of the period they are in have become processed in various media and digital platforms.

In storytelling, which consists of the processes of creating, communicating, and sharing a story, characters, events, and emotions are brought together in a certain order and take place in many different media types such as books, films, theatres, radio plays, video games, and other digital media. Transmedia storytelling is a popular technique used to tell a story differently on more than one platform, and the content of the stories can be told in different ways according to the media used.

The 2000s have been the years when visual and auditory qualities have started to be used in addition to the verbal within the visual possibilities of the digital world, where technology has developed. In such an environment, the story has also started to evolve in a different direction by digitalisation, and in the digitalised narrative, it is no longer the narrator who is at the forefront, but the narrated itself. In digital narrative, literariness has decreased, and visuality has come to the fore. Traditional stories have been a source of inspiration for television series and cinema films, inspiring the scripts written and determining the subjects of the content created in the next medium. In this respect, it is possible to say that traditional stories have continued to exist until the last period, albeit in different forms, and that their content has turned into a technology-centered structure with the effect of recently developing technologies, and that there have been changes in the main elements such as narrator, content, and audience.

In our age, it is seen that storytelling has started to take its place in the digital universe, with the development of game industries and the discovery of interactive fiction, the audience has started to take a more active and interactive position in the story. The story of Sahmaran, which is the subject of the research and fits the concept of Transmedia storytelling, which is a popular technique used to tell a story differently on more than one platform, was analyzed by content analysis method in terms of its plot and content in terms of its first and last release channels.

REFERENCES

Bahadır, H., Tüfekci, A., & Çakır, H. (2021). Dijital hikâye anlatımının disiplinlerarası öğretim bağlamında kullanım durumları. *Muğla Sıtkı Koçman Üniversitesi Eğitim Faculty Journal*, *8*(2), 635–654.

Beydâvî. (2013). Beydavî Interpretatşon: Envâru't-Tenzîl ve Esrâru't-Te'vîl. Trans. Abdülvehhab Öztürk. 3. Volume. İstanbul: Kahraman Publishing.

Bouchardon, S. (2014). *La Valeur Heuristique De La Littérature Numérique*. Hermann.

Buzkan, E. (2023). *Şah-ı Mar- The Children of the Şahmaran* (1st ed.). Destek Publishing.

Caferoğlu, A. (1988). *Türk Kavimleri*. Enderun Publishing.

Carr, D. M. (2020, May 4). The Formation of Genesis 1-11. Oxford University Press. http://books.google.ie/books?id=FcDgDwAAQBAJ&printsec=frontcover&dq=genesis&hl=&cd=10&source=gbs_api

Cassuto, U. (1997). *A Commentary on the Book of Exodus*. The Hebrew University Magnes Press.

Çıblak, N. (2007). *Tarsus Kültürünün Tanıtımında Şahmaran Efsanelerinin Önemi*. Ç.Ü. Social Sciences Institute Journal.

Çoruhlu, Y. (1994). *Türk Sanatında Görülen Yılan Tasvirlerinin Sembolizmi*. Turkish World History Journal.

Currid, J. D. (1997). *Ancient Egypt and the Old Testament*. Baker Books.

Debener, T., & Gudin, S. (2003). Encyclopedia Of Rose Science. Three-Volume Set, Burlington, Elsevier Science, sect.2 45.

Ersümer, A. (2013). *Klasik Anlatı Sineması*. Hayalperest Publishing.

Freud, S. (2007). *(1915). Thoughts For The Times On War And Death, The Standart Edition of the Complete Psychological Works of Sigmund Freud* (Vol. XIV). The Hogarth Press.

George, A., Sandars, N. K., & Pasco, R. (2003). The epic of Gilgamesh (A. George, Trans.). Penguin Classics.

Harva, U. (1933,January1). Altain suvun uskonto. http://books.google.ie/books?id=P8ssHQAACAAJ&dq=Altain+Suvun+Uskonto&hl=&cd=1&source=g s_api.

Hooke, S. H. (2004, January 1). *Middle Eastern Mythology*. Courier Corporation. http://books.google.ie/books?id=YSUnmTKWhtkC&printsec=frontcover&dq=Hooke,+Samuel+Henry&hl=&cd=3&source=gbs_api

Işık, S.Y (2018). "Yılan, Su, Söz: Kadın Düşmanlığı ile Belirsizlik Korkusu Arasındaki İlişikiye Dair Bir Yorum Denemesi". Folklor Edebiyat Journal. Volume: 24. No: 93. ss. 177-196.)

Jenkins, H. (2007). Official Weblog of Henry Jenkins. 11. 12.2015. *TransmediaStorytelling*101:http://henryjenkins.org/2007/03/transmedia_storytelling_101.html

Jenkins, H. (2016). *Cesur Yeni Medya: Teknolojiler ve Hayran Kültürü* (Yeğengil, N., Trans.). Communication Publishing.

Küngerü, A. (2016). "Bir İfade Aracı Olarak Dijital Öykü Anlatımı", *Abant Cultural Researches Journal (AKAR)*, Volume 1, Number 2.

Murray, J. H. (1997). *Hamlet On The Holodeck: The Future Of Narrative in Cyberspace*. MIT Press.

Mutlu, E. (1991). *Televizyonu Anlamak*. Gündoğan.

Mutlugün, A., & Topuz, M.Y.(2020). New Position of Storytelling in the Context of Digital Narration. *International Journal of Humanities and Research*, February, Year 4, Issue:4, Volume 3.

Naghdi, A. (2024). https://dreamfarmstudios.com/blog/what-is-transmedia/, E.T.

Ökmen, Y. E. (2021). *Gelenekselden Dijitale Hikâye Anlatıcılığı: Youtube Örneği,* İstanbul University Social Science Institute, Radio, TV and Cinema Department, Unpublished Doctoral Dissertation. Sarı, Gülşah. (2017). "Transmedya Hikâye Anlatıcılığı Kötü Çocuk Örneği", *Abant Cultural Researhes Journal (AKAR)*. Volume 2, No. 4.

Özdemir., H. (1998). "Geleneksel Kültürümüzde Şahmaran", V. *International Folk Culture Congress Folk Literature Section Papers*, v.2.Ankara. p.252.

Salt, A. (2006). *Ansiklopedi Semboller*. Ruh ve Madde Publishing.

Schimmel, A. (1996). Deciphering The Signs of God: A Phenomenological Approach to Islam. Oxford University Press. Vol 7. No. 1 January. p. 70-72.

Shahbazi, N. (2024). https://pixune.com/blog/transmedia-storytelling/, E.T.

Shakespeare, W. (1993). *Macbeth*. Dover Publications.

Uzun, Ö. (2016). *Canlandırma Sinemasında Transmedya Hikâye Anlatım Örneği Olarak Shrek Serisi,* Marmara University Social Sciences, Unpublished Doctoral Dissertation. https://www.chip.com.tr/makale/sahmaran-dizisi-konusu-ne-oyunculari-kimler-netflixin-yeni-yerli-dizisi-mercek-altinda_155606.html, E.T.10.04.2024

Warrell, D. A. (2010). *Guidelines of the Management of Snake Bites.* World Health Organization.

Werner, E. T. (1994). Edward T. Chalmers, Myths and Legends of China. Courier Corporation. p. 252.

Chapter 6
Exploring the Influence of Long-Form Narrative in Digital Journalism: The Model of "Scrolli.co"

Ahmet Serkan Okay
https://orcid.org/0000-0002-3190-5895
İstanbul Medipol University, Turkey

ABSTRACT

Digital journalism has progressed in a dynamic structure from Web 2.0 to the present, thanks to new communication and artificial intelligence technologies. In journalism, which has transformed into a dynamic structure, content has become enriched, and production is carried out with different narratives. Digital storytelling has also brought with it new narrative structures for news. Among these narrative structures, long-scroll news narratives have become a preferred type in digital news production. The aim of this study is to reveal the AI-supported structure of long-scroll narratives used in digital journalism in Turkey within the framework of story flow designs, as shaped by new communication technologies. The study also aims to demonstrate the impact of long-scroll narratives on digital news production under the umbrella of new communication and artificial intelligence technologies. Furthermore, the importance of this research lies in its potential to lead the way in examining long-scroll narrative structures in the field of digital journalism in Turkey.

DOI: 10.4018/979-8-3373-2023-6.ch006

DIGITAL JOURNALISM: A DYNAMIC EVOLUTION FROM WEB 2.0 TO THE PRESENT

News is a concept as old as human history. Communication processes between individuals or societies were initially carried out through oral communication or written correspondence, such as news letters. In the 15th century, the emergence of significant social transformations and the invention of the printing press brought about a substantial change in the notion of news and journalism. With the transition of news into the pages of newspapers—a mass communication tool—it assumed a public function and acquired a different structure.

Journalism, seen both as a profession and a public service, began to professionalize by the 18th century, and news reporting evolved into an institutionalized sector. As journalism became a sectoral field, it incorporated fundamental professional principles and responsibilities such as accuracy, public interest, timeliness, reliability, and fact-checking (Girgin, 2008). Based on these principles, various stages of news production—such as investigation, news writing, editing, and distribution—were developed and refined.

In the second half of the 19th century, advancements in electronic technology led to a shift in journalism from printed media tools to electronic media tools such as the telegraph and radio. Electronic devices such as radio and television, where audio and visual technologies were transformed into mass communication tools, initiated both a technical and structural transformation in journalism. Within this transformation, a new understanding of journalism emerged—one that went beyond the design of news through text and photographs to include sound and video elements.

Journalism has thus transformed into a field conducted by large corporations under the umbrella of the media sector, forming its own ecosystem. Alongside print publications such as newspapers and magazines, broadcasting activities are carried out via mass media tools like radio and television, which have significant social impact. These traditional forms of media continue to maintain their presence today.

The emergence of computer and internet technologies has profoundly influenced various aspects of our lives. This technological advancement, often referred to as the digital age, marks the beginning of a process that continues to shape contemporary society. Evolving from large-scale machines to microcomputers suitable for home use, computer technologies have now become an integral part of everyday life through portable smart devices (Barger, 2008). Alongside computer technologies, the advancement of internet technologies constitutes the foundation of the current digital era. Initially characterized by a one-way and static structure, internet systems have evolved into dynamic platforms in accordance with their purposes of use. The interactive features introduced during the Web 2.0 era have enabled individuals to communicate with one another (Törenli, 2005). Particularly with the development of wireless internet technologies, individuals have established a continuous online presence in the digital world. This communication among users has led to the emergence of social media applications. Internet systems have integrated with cloud computing and artificial intelligence tools, culminating in their current form.

Digitalization is a concept that emerged through computer and internet technologies and has come to influence all spheres of life through new communication technologies and artificial intelligence tools. The concepts of news and journalism have found a place in the digital realm to fulfill individuals' need for information. In digital platforms where the phenomenon of information holds significant importance, journalism plays a crucial role. The journalism sector progresses in a technology-oriented manner and in parallel with technological advancements. The emergence and evolution of digitalization have been accompanied by the development of news and journalistic practices (Timisi, 2003).

New communication technologies have profoundly impacted journalism, as they have influenced many other fields. In the last quarter of the 20th century, journalism transitioned to digital systems during the Web 1.0 era, widely regarded as the inception of the first digital age. any newspapers have approached digitalization by simply digitizing their print pages, offering news to users in a one-way, non-interactive manner (Marconi, 2024). This digitalization process, which began with traditional media content appearing on the internet, has undergone significant change and transformation, driven by the evolving features of new media. Within this evolution, media organizations now deliver content and interact with users through internet-based technologies (Anadolu Ajansı, 2024). In the Web 2.0 era, online news platforms began to engage with users and started producing news content in an interactive and multi-dimensional manner. However, with the emergence of social media applications, user interaction with news websites has declined. This is because users have reduced their news consumption via websites and increasingly turned to social media platforms for accessing news. Consequently, news outlets have found it necessary not only to produce content for their websites but also to create content specifically tailored for social media platforms (Kaya, 2019).

Today, digital journalism produces and delivers content within a structure that incorporates new communication technologies as well as artificial intelligence systems. Media organizations now generate news not only for their websites but also for social media platforms, mobile applications, and portable smart devices. This diversification of content has led to the emergence of new journalistic practices within the field of journalism.

The new media environment is defined by characteristic features of digitalization, such as digitization, interactivity, hypertextuality, user-generated content production, and convergence (Binark, 2007). These features also constitute the structure of the new media environment. Scholars such as Lev Manovich, Everett Rogers, and

Teun Van Dijk, who have examined new media from a technological perspective, have identified its defining characteristics. Lev Manovich outlined the principles of new media as numerical representation, modularity, automation, variability, and transcoding, thereby delineating the fundamental features of new media (Manovich, 2001). Rogers, on the other hand, highlighted interaction, asynchronicity, and de-massification as key characteristics of digital technologies within a framework of historical transformation (Rogers & Picot, 1986). Teun Van Dijk emphasized that the new media environment—defined as interactive media, multimedia, or digital media—is built upon the characteristics of interactivity, integration, and a digital structure (Dijk, 2006). These features form the basis for defining new media and simultaneously differentiate it from traditional media.

The attributes of new communication technologies have played a pivotal role in the transformation of digital journalism. During the transition from traditional to online journalism, these features have been harnessed to reach target audiences more effectively. They have also influenced the news production process, enabling a dynamic structure that integrates users into the creation and dissemination of news.

In today's digital environment, a dynamic structure continues to emerge. Particularly in social media applications, individuals act as both producers and consumers, fostering a uniquely interactive ecosystem (Özdemir & Çetinkaya, 2019). This development has prompted professional content creators to design content catering to both producing and consuming audiences.

News content in digital journalism is now crafted following professional production standards, tailored to engage users within the digital ecosystem. This evolution, which began with the digitization of traditional newspapers, has developed into a multifaceted framework shaped by advances in communication technologies and diverse production channels (Kalsın, 2017).

NEWS PRODUCTION IN DIGITAL JOURNALISM

The concept of journalism encompasses the investigation of events, data collection, the structuring and writing of news in accordance with specific techniques, its processing through editorial procedures, and finally its distribution. Any event that concerns the public and holds news value can find its place within media platforms.

The digital world has transformed the production stages of journalism. Individuals who live in the digital realm play a significant role in shaping digital journalism. The change in news consumption habits among individuals guides the practice of contemporary journalism. Just as the habit of consuming news through print newspapers in the 1990s shifted to online environments, today's news consumption patterns have transitioned from websites to social media applications, and further to portable and wearable technologies. This transformation in news consumption habits also affects the news production process in digital journalism. Newsrooms have adapted to the digital age by embracing technology and integrating technological innovations into the editorial workflow.

When examining the stages of news production in digital journalism, they can be categorized as research, data collection, production, editorial processing, and distribution (Marconi, 2024, p.36). Although these stages are similar in structure to those in traditional media, they differ significantly in terms of operation. Pavlik likens the digital journalism production process to a "digital cauldron." He emphasizes the selection of multimedia elements (audio, visuals, video, text, GIFs, vectors, etc.) in alignment with the narrative structure of the news content. The inclusion of multimedia components and their dissemination on interactive digital platforms underscore the fundamental distinctions between traditional and digital news production processes. However, among these differences, the most critical development is the incorporation of artificial intelligence (AI) tools into the journalist's workload (Diakopoulos, 2019). AI technologies, which are software systems developed through algorithms to meet needs in various domains, are also actively used in journalism (Koski & Murphy, 2021).

The initial stage of news production involves research and topic development. In digital journalism, this process is increasingly supported by AI tools capable of collecting and analyzing large volumes of data (Diakopoulos, 2019). These tools, with broader and faster research capabilities than human journalists, are frequently utilized for efficient data gathering. Moreover, by scanning trending topics and current discussions, AI assists journalists in determining which issues are newsworthy. This significantly facilitates the journalist's task.

Following the research phase, the next step in news production is writing and structuring the news. Unlike traditional journalism, digital journalism not only relies on text and photography but also utilizes a wide range of multimedia elements. Pavlik highlights the use of non-linear narrative structures in digital news production (Pavlik, 2013). Non-linear storytelling emerges through the digital representation of multimedia elements and the hypertextual nature of texts (Gürcan, 2002). With non-linear narrative forms, digitally researched topics are transformed into news pieces on digital platforms. News writing, supported by visuals, video, audio, and graphics, is approved by an editor before being presented to the audience.

Today, news production is not limited to journalists or editors alone; AI-supported software also contributes by generating text, visuals, and video content. A key practice in digital journalism, robotic journalism, uses Natural Language Generation (NLG) to automatically generate news content. NLG is a software process that transforms data-driven analysis results into natural language understandable to humans (Dale & Reiter, 2000). With NLG, financial reports, sports news, and weather forecasts can be produced and published in an automated manner. Furthermore, there are AI tools capable of generating not only text but also visual and graphic content. As a result, visual and video components for news stories can be obtained more easily and efficiently. Among the most notable visual content generated by AI in journalism are infographic charts. The involvement of AI in news writing and visual production enables journalists to focus on more creative tasks rather than repetitive and time-consuming ones.

Before distribution, news content undergoes editorial review. The compatibility of the content with institutional guidelines and the appropriateness of its message are evaluated by the editor prior to publication (Girgin, 2008). After passing through the editorial stage, the news enters the final phase—distribution. During distribution, news is delivered to users via websites, social media platforms, or mobile applications. AI software personalizes the content for distribution based on users' data profiles. AI systems prioritize and foreground the news items that align with individual user preferences.

The digitization of news production processes has introduced numerous changes to journalism. These transformations have led to the emergence of new narrative structures shaped by different dynamics. With the incorporation of multimedia systems into journalism, news production formats have diversified significantly. This diversification stems from journalism's adaptation to new communication technologies and the integration of artificial intelligence applications in contemporary news production. Examining this adaptation process reveals a consistent evolution in news production. Initially characterized by static replication of print newspapers, it now reflects the dynamic progression of web and computer technologies. Digital journalism increasingly benefits from variable digital platform infrastructures, and the unique characteristics of social media applications have introduced novel styles of news production processes.

News production in digital journalism represents an ongoing evolution shaped by technological advancements. This evolution enables journalists to create faster, more diverse content while offering readers a more interactive and personalized news experience. Moreover, the sources, target audiences, and working methods of journalists have undergone substantial transformation. As part of this shift, news production has adopted a more formalized approach, integrating diverse data formats such as audio, video, graphics, images, and maps. This multimedia integration has transformed traditional news formats into storytelling-driven content, leveraging the interactive potential of communication technologies to redefine the news production process.

Discussing the transformation of journalism in the electronic environment, Pavlik observes that online systems, referred to as contextual journalism, have introduced a new form of news storytelling within the field. Pavlik characterizes contextual journalism by its broad communication methods, hypermedia, high levels of readership participation, dynamic content, and adaptability (Pavlik, 2013). Evaluating the news production process through the lens of contextualized journalism suggests that the dynamic structure of new media platforms allows for the creation of a news production process that is both dynamic and interactive, facilitating direct engagement with users.

Technological convergence has further enriched journalism content, transitioning it from a traditional framework to a more dynamic structure within new media. Unlike traditional journalism, where the news language follows a linear narrative structure and adheres to a fixed format, new media platforms enable news production in diverse channels using non-linear narrative structures. This shift demands the transformation of the language and content production processes, leading to the development of news narratives in varied formats that align with the structural characteristics of new media (Kaya, 2019).

DIGITAL STORYTELLING IN NEWS PRODUCTION

Digital storytelling has become a prominent production style in digital news production today, widely adopted not only in journalism but also in various areas of content production on digital platforms. This narrative style combines the concepts of digitalization and storytelling, as described by Robin (2016). Storytelling, a literary genre with deep historical roots, began in oral cultures and evolved alongside traditional communication tools, serving as a key element in cultural transmission and literary traditions (Şimşek, 2018). Over time, storytelling became an industrial and mass-produced process during the development of traditional media.

The concept of digital storytelling emerged in California in the mid-1990s (Bal & Onay, 2018). Its development advanced digital content production, allowing for story-formatted narratives in diverse styles. The growing significance of storytelling in content production paved the way for the rise of digital storytelling. Defined by Alexander (2011) as a narrative created using multimedia tools, digital storytelling incorporates elements such as text, video, audio, and graphics to engage users interactively in digital content production. This approach leverages various digital elements to create an immersive experience that fosters user interaction.

With the advent of new media platforms, users have taken on the role of content creators, further driving the development of digital storytelling and enabling the emergence of diverse narrative formats. These advancements continue to broaden the definition of digital storytelling. Miller emphasizes the creation of interactive, participatory content, while Qiongli highlights its versatility across various fields, particularly in digital games, where hypertextual and interactive narratives play a significant role (Jenkins & Gravestock, 2009).

Jenkins defines digital storytelling as story content created through digital tools, distributed via digital platforms with networked participatory elements, and consumed by users. He further identifies three models of digital storytelling: multimedia, transmedia, and cross-media. Multimedia stories combine text, video, audio, and interactive media within a single platform. Transmedia stories unfold across multiple platforms, with each contributing to the overall narrative, allowing users to piece together the story from dispersed content. Cross-media stories can be accessed from one digital platform while being produced in varied formats on other media platforms. These models have demonstrated that digital storytelling is not merely the creation of digital content but a narrative form that fosters interactive consumption and engagement across multiple platforms, as highlighted by Jenkins, Lashley, and Creech (2017).

Digital story narratives used in news production are created both within the framework of traditional journalism principles and in alignment with the storytelling styles emerging on digital platforms. This dual orientation necessitates the production of digital storytelling in varied ways within journalism. Media organizations, fulfilling their public duty, adapt story narratives to fit their institutional frameworks. Simultaneously, news formats are crafted in digital processes to align with the interactive storytelling preferences of users on new media platforms.

Pavlik's narrative model in journalism exemplifies contemporary digital storytelling styles. Pavlik likens digital narratives to content that is "poured into a container" for journalism, which carries a public responsibility (Pavlik & Pavlik, 2017). For journalists, these narratives represent structures built with digital components—such as text, audio, vector graphics, video, and photographs—that present factual and accurate information, tailored for dissemination across various digital platforms. Additionally, artificial intelligence technologies are increasingly being integrated into the creation of these narratives. However, the integration of AI in journalism is guided by the principles and ethical responsibilities of the profession. Notably, many media organizations in Turkey have established principles and guidelines governing the use of AI in journalism.

In digital journalism, a variety of digital storytelling structures are widely utilized in both national and international media today. These narratives, which have evolved since the Web 2.0 era, continue to be updated and newly developed in line with technological advancements. The "Print Plus" digital print narrative, introduced by Jonathan Dube during the Web 2.0 era, remains prevalent today. This narrative structure is considered the closest to the traditional media's news narrative style. Dube also highlights the emergence of news narrative structures such as slideshows, audio stories (now commonly referred to as podcasts), live chats, and dynamic stories (Dube, 2000).

Reflecting on the current landscape of digital storytelling, the journo.com team identifies various narrative structures frequently employed by media organizations. These include infographics, graphics, interactive stories, animations, virtual reality narratives, social media narratives, news games, and long scrolling narratives. These formats illustrate the diverse digital storytelling structures used by media organizations today to engage audiences and adapt to the evolving digital media environment (journo.com.tr, 2016).

LONG SCROLLING NEWS STORYTELLING

The long scrolling news story narrative is a digital production strategy in journalism that integrates multimedia resources—such as text, photographs, videos, dynamic maps, and data visualizations—to effectively convey news messages to users across online news sites, social media applications, and mobile platforms (Garreton et al., 2023). This narrative style, characterized by a non-linear and hybrid form, merges various elements like numbers, words, photos, videos, and GIFs. Its interactive nature engages users, offering an immersive storytelling experience. Moreover, this format is often employed for stories rooted in detailed research, where the temporal value of the news is less significant. The goal is to retain user attention for an extended duration, guiding them seamlessly through the narrative, much like a story.

The long scrolling narrative stands against the dominance of "fast, small-sized news" by promoting a more in-depth and comprehensive approach to news production, with the potential to reshape the landscape of online journalism. It is particularly well-suited for topics requiring comprehensive coverage, such as war, climate change, politics, global health, the economy, and election results. Unlike typical "breaking news," long-form storytelling requires a greater depth of analysis and a detailed exploration of the subject matter. As a result, it demands a distinct approach and differentiation from shorter news formats, establishing itself as a critical tool in modern journalism.

This narrative format is widely used, especially by international media organizations. A pioneering example of the long scrolling narrative is the Pulitzer Prize-winning "Snow Fall," created by *The New York Times*. This groundbreaking piece holds a significant place in the professional production of digital storytelling. The story was crafted using advanced technical features such as HTML5, custom JavaScript, parallax scrolling effects, transparent overlays that scroll on hover, fading and disappearing images during scrolling, a progress bar, and a lightbox for pictures. As the first example of a long scrolling narrative, "Snow Fall" set a new standard in journalism and led to the development and widespread adoption of the long scrolling narrative structure in the digital media landscape (Michel & Ladd, 2015).

The long scrolling narrative is also referred to as "Scrollytelling." Scrollytelling is a storytelling method that combines the concepts of storytelling and scrolling, making it inherently compatible with the long scrolling format (Tjärnhage, et. al,, 2023). This approach uses cinematic storytelling, enhanced with data visualizations, to narrate in-depth, researched topics, forming the foundation of the long scrolling news story narrative.

The long scrolling format can be analyzed through three primary narrative styles: scrollytelling, selective multimedia stories, and web documentaries (Wolf & Godulla, 2016). These three narrative types are built using a range of multimedia elements.

In a scrolling narrative, users navigate through web or mobile pages, often vertically, using parallax effects—an approach shaped by technological advances and user consumption habits. This format integrates various multimedia elements, including text, photos, videos, interactive graphics, audio files, and data visualizations, creating a rich and engaging storytelling experience.

Selective multimedia stories, on the other hand, are developed for web-based platforms and mobile applications. Unlike scrolling narratives, these stories often require users to click through the content. Text is typically the central component of the story but is supplemented with visual elements. Examples of selective multimedia stories often take the form of slideshows within a narrative structure.

Web documentaries rely on video-based content production and are often presented in a documentary format. Leveraging asynchrony, a core feature of digital platforms, these documentaries are crafted as narrative-driven stories and published on dedicated websites and social media platforms. Professionally edited with techniques similar to film or television series production, web documentaries are enriched with video, audio, and text to enhance storytelling. In journalism, examples of this narrative style are frequently seen in videos produced for YouTube channels (Wolf & Godulla, 2016).

CHARACTERISTICS AND LAYOUT OF LONG SCROLLING STORYTELLING

Nowadays, due to the inherent features of websites and the evolving media consumption habits of users, online content is frequently presented in a scroll-based format. Instead of encountering click-through content, users increasingly come across scrollable structures while browsing web pages. Scrolling not only simplifies navigation for users but also enables content producers to create more engaging and interactive narratives. In the context of digital journalism, especially when examining news content on websites, one can observe the widespread use of long-form scrolling story formats as a method of news production.

Long scrolling storytelling emerged as a news production style with the introduction of the "Snow Fall" format in 2012 (Michel & Ladd, 2015). Since then, this storytelling approach has evolved into various formats, shaped by technological advancements. The ease and speed of productivity offered by new communication technologies, combined with their integration with artificial intelligence, have further facilitated the creation of long scrolling stories in diverse styles.

To explore the diversity and organizational structure of long scrolling narratives, it is essential to examine the story flow designs described by McKenna et al. These flow designs outline the key characteristics of long-scrolling narratives, the organizational framework of the stories, and how they diversify. McKenna et al. provide visual narrative flow designs that illustrate how users interact with the story, the feedback they receive during the experience, and the visual components embedded in the narrative. Additionally, they identify processes addressing significant factors such as story entry points, navigation types, and user interaction mechanisms. McKenna et al. categorize story flow design components into the following elements: control level, navigation input, navigation progression, story layout, role of visualization, story progression, and navigation feedback (McKenna, et al 2017).

Figure 1. Level of Story Control Source: McKenna, Riche, Lee, Boy, Meyer, 2017.

The level of control refers to how much autonomy users have over the movement of story elements or animated transitions, as depicted in Figure 1. This control is categorized into three types: intermittent, continuous, and hybrid (McKenna, Riche, Lee, Boy, & Meyer, 2017). At the intermittent control level, users are required to make specific transitions, progressing through the story in a step-by-step manner. Intermittent control refers to a mode of user interaction in which the user intervenes in the narrative at predetermined intervals, with the progression of the content being entirely subject to the user's discretion. The continuous control level provides an uninterrupted flow, allowing users to experience seamless transitions through animations, text, and visuals. In a manner akin to video content streams, the narrative progresses in a continuous fashion, without any active intervention from the user. The hybrid control level combines these two approaches, offering a mixed progression. In this format, users are expected to actively move the story forward at certain points while enjoying continuous transitions in others. The level of narrative control is determined by the editor based on the format of the content and the design of the storytelling framework.

These components not only enhance the storytelling experience but also define how users interact with and perceive long scrolling narratives, thereby enriching the overall effectiveness and diversity of this storytelling method.

Figure 2. Story Navigation Source: McKenna, Riche, Lee, Boy, Meyer, 2017.

The navigation input defines how users engage with and enter the long scrolling narrative, directly influencing the way the story unfolds. If the story design involves a downward movement, a scrolling input is utilized, allowing users to navigate through the content by scrolling. In cases where the story incorporates click-oriented elements alongside downward movement, a button-click input is employed, enabling users to interact through clicks for specific transitions. Additionally, some narratives adopt a mixed input method, combining both scrolling and clicking progression to create a more dynamic and versatile navigation experience.

Figure 3. Story Progress Indicators Source: McKenna, Riche, Lee, Boy, Meyer, 2017.

The navigation progression within the story can be implemented in a variety of ways, utilizing elements such as dots, numbers, text, or visualizations. McKenna et al. identify these progression designs, as shown in Figure 3, as integral components of long scrolling narratives. Progress markers within the story help users track their position and progression through the narrative. Similar to scroll bars commonly found on the right side of websites, these markers provide users with a sense of orientation within the content.

In long scrolling narratives, progression indicators often extend beyond traditional scroll bars. Depending on the narrative format, they may include dots, descriptive text, or visualized images, adding an interactive and aesthetic dimension to the storytelling experience. These diverse designs not only guide users through the story but also enhance engagement by visually connecting users to the narrative structure.

Figure 4. Story Layout Source: McKenna, Riche, Lee, Boy, Meyer, 2017.

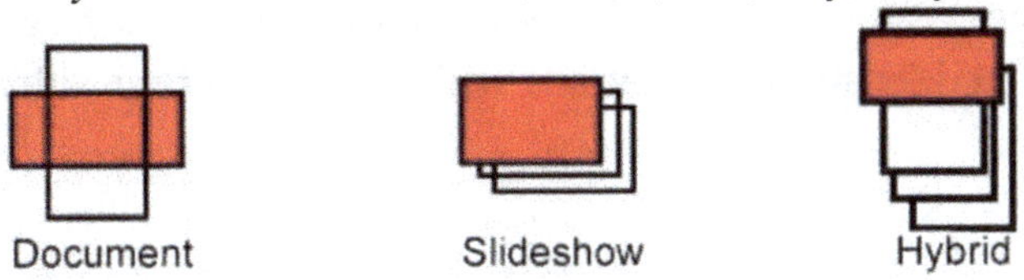

The story layout both shows the order in which the story is organized and is used to determine the number of pages of the story. As seen in Figure 4, there are three types of story layout: document, slide layout and hybrid. The document style layout can be seen as a layout created in news entries on websites. In the slide layout, there is a layout with page transitions that integrate the story. Formats in which mixed story layouts are created in these two layouts are also produced.

Figure 5. The Role of Visualisation in Story Source: McKenna, Riche, Lee, Boy, Meyer, 2017.

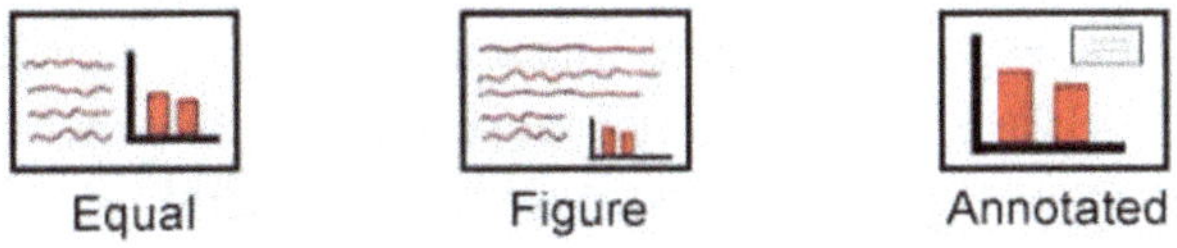

The role of visualization component measures the impact of visualizations on the story as a whole. This component identifies the direction of the visual narrative flow by analyzing how visual elements (such as photos, videos, GIFs, vectors, animations, etc.) and text interact. It also determines the degree of relationship between the visuals and the text. In storytelling, visuals and text can be equally distributed, visuals may support predominantly text-based stories, or explanatory text may be used to enhance narratives where visuals are the primary focus.

Figure 6. Story Progression Source: McKenna, Riche, Lee, Boy, Meyer, 2017.

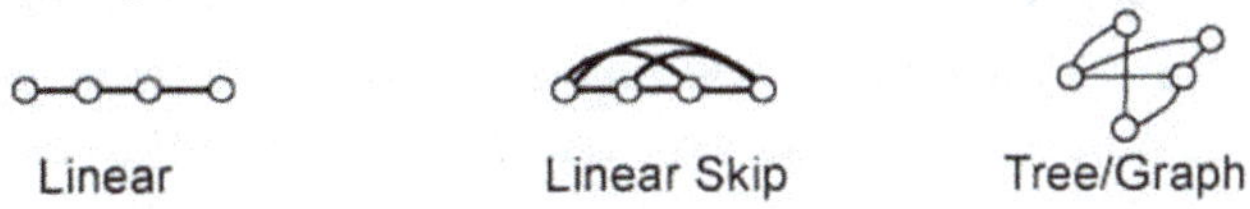

Story progression is categorized into storytelling paths with linear progression, progression with linear jumps, or more complex progressions, as shown in Figure 6. While narratives are typically produced with linear progression, the story can also be told with linear jumps, allowing for different transitions within the narrative based on how the creator structures the story. Additionally, tree or graphic progression can be utilized, enabling transitions within different topics that deviate from the linear plane.

Figure 7. Types of Story Transition Source: McKenna, Riche, Lee, Boy, Meyer, 2017.

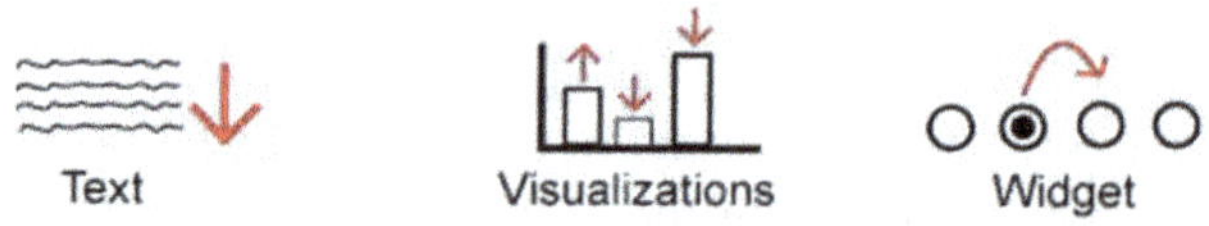

The story transition type is a criterion that guides how transitions are to be structured within the overall narrative design. In text-heavy narratives, scrolling downward can be accompanied by visual cues such as fading animations to enhance transitions and maintain the story's flow. Alternatively, feedback can be provided through visual elements like dots, numbers or other markers that indicate the user's position and progress in the story.

McKenna et al. categorized long scrolling narratives into seven distinct categories (McKenna, et al., 2017). These categories represent variations within the narratives produced. By using these categories in storytelling, McKenna et al. highlighted both the defining characteristics of the narratives and the patterns that can be constructed within the story.

METHOD

In the study, the content analysis method commonly used in qualitative research was employed. Content analysis is a qualitative research technique used for the objective, systematic, and quantitative description of content (Türkdoğan & Gökçe, 2015). It is a method widely applied in disciplines such as sociology, politics, and communication within the social sciences and has gained greater importance with the proliferation of mass media. Particularly, content analysis is extensively used in research focusing on the content and messages conveyed by mass media (Aziz, 2013). In this study, the content analysis method was utilized to examine the narrative structures of long scrolling news stories, which represent new practices in digital news production.

The research was conducted in Turkey, and the sample included only the news stories published by the *scrolli.co* news website, which adopts a long scrolling story narrative in digital news production in Turkey (scrolli.co, 2025). Among the digital news platforms within the research universe, *scrolli.co* was selected using purposive sampling due to its alignment with the research focus. This news platform has been selected for analysis in this study due to its pioneering role in digital journalism through the use of long-scroll narrative formats. Founded on the principles of next-generation journalism, Scrolli.co produces technology-driven and AI-supported news content, which justifies the study's specific focus on this organization. The inclusion of this site in the sample was justified by its pioneering role in implementing long scrolling storytelling in Turkey.

MAXQDA is a data analysis software used for qualitative, quantitative, and mixed methods research, allowing for focus group analysis, online surveys, content analysis, frequency analysis, and code comparisons (Maxqda.com, 2025). In the study, frequency analyses of the news on the *scrolli.co* site were conducted using the MAXQDA program, along with code relationship analyses between categories. Frequency analysis was used to assess the characteristics and organization of the news stories, while code relationship analysis was employed to compare the content of the data. The research data were categorized based on Pavlik's digital storytelling process and McKenna et al.'s visual story flow design models. These categorizations included 41 subcategories across 11 main categories. The categories identified in the research are as follows: navigation entry, control level of the story, navigation within the story, story layout, distribution of visualization in the story, story progression, story transition, use of artificial intelligence technology, type of research, subject of the story, and use of data in the story.

The study aimed to address the following research questions in its analysis of long scrolling news narratives:

– How do long scrolling news narratives interact with users?
– How do the types of data used in the news affect the narrative structure?
– What is the role of artificial intelligence technologies in the long scrolling news story?

OBJECTIVE AND IMPORTANCE OF THE STUDY

Today, journalism has continuously been evolving, driven by advancements in new communication technologies and artificial intelligence systems. As part of this evolution, the news production process is being reshaped within a digitalized framework aligned with technological progress. Digital news content is now delivered to users through diverse narrative structures, with digital storytelling gaining prominence on various digital platforms and significantly influencing the field of journalism. This shift has facilitated the transformation of news production formats, steering them toward storytelling and introducing innovative narrative structures.

Among these, long scrolling news narratives have emerged as a preferred format in digital news production.

The purpose of this study is to explore the structure of long scrolling narratives supported by new communication technologies and artificial intelligence, as utilized in digital journalism in Turkey, within the context of story flow designs. The study further aims to examine the impact of long scrolling narratives on digital news production, considering their integration with new communication and artificial intelligence technologies. Notably, the study holds significance as it serves as a pioneering effort in analyzing long scrolling narrative structures within the domain of digital journalism in Turkey.

There is a substantial body of research in the literature focusing on digital news production. Among the topics addressed in these studies, long-scroll narrative structures within the framework of digital storytelling have also been explored. For instance, the news story *"Snow Fall"-ing Special Collections and Archives* has been examined in terms of its content and design process (Michel & Ladd, 2015). Other articles investigate long-scroll news content within the context of media organizations. One such study, *Cultural Translation, Long-form Journalism, and Readers' Responses to the Muslim Veil* by Kyle Conway, analyzes the impact of long-form journalism on readers (Conway, 2012). Another study titled *The Impact of Scrollytelling on the Reading Experience of Long-Form Journalism*, conducted by Anja Tjärnhage et al., investigates the effects of long-scroll narratives on reader experiences, concluding that such narratives are generally preferred over static news structures (Tjärnhage et al., 2023). Similarly, the article *Scrollytelling – An Analysis of Visual Storytelling in Online Journalism* finds that long-scroll narratives enhance users' emotional engagement through their interactive features. Within the scope of the existing literature, this study is original in that it focuses on long-scroll news content produced by a media organization in Turkey, and analyzes these contents in relation to their design elements.

LIMITATIONS

For the purpose of the study, the long scrolling news story narrative produced as new news content in Turkey was analyzed. Accordingly, the study was limited to the digital news website *scrolli.co*, which produces news using the long scrolling news story narrative among digital news platforms in Turkey. The news content included in the data analysis was confined to long scrolling news story narratives produced during May and July, in alignment with the study's objectives.

RESULTS

In the study, a frequency analysis was conducted on 20 long scrolling news stories from *scrolli.co* within the defined research limitations. Using the codes created as part of the research, the frequency analysis was performed in the MAXQDA program, and the research questions were examined based on the findings obtained from this analysis.

Figure 8. Type of Research Used in the News Story

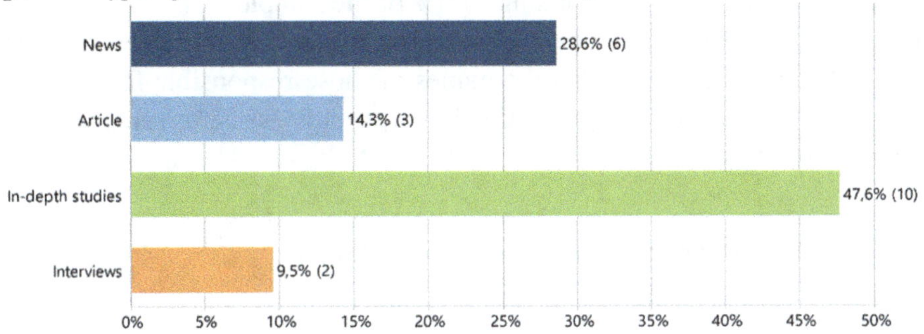

When the research types of the news included in the sample were examined, it was found that the content comprised a combination of news articles, in-depth studies, articles, and interviews. Among these, in-depth analysis emerged as the most frequently used research type, accounting for 47.6% of the sample. Additionally, 28.6% of the content focused on specific topics. Articles, a research type where opinions are presented by expert researchers, journalists, and writers, constituted 14.3% of the sample. Interviews, another research type identified in the findings, represented 9.5% of the news items analyzed.

Figure 9. Subject of News Story Content

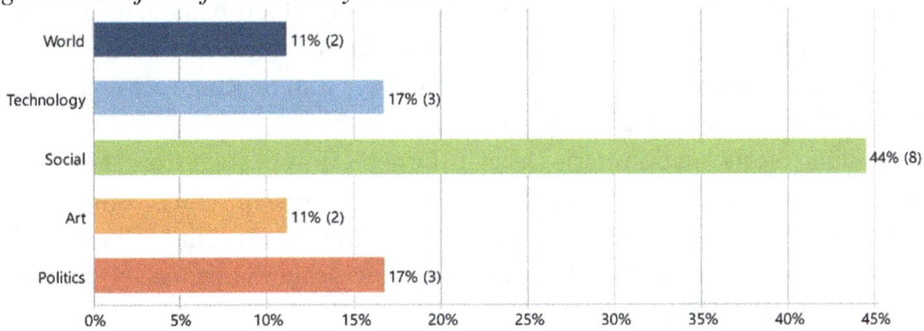

The subject of a news item determines what readers are informed about and which event or situation is covered, serving as a key factor in shaping the flow of the news. Topics such as politics, law, or the economy are characteristic of serious news, while subjects like social issues, art, or entertainment represent softer news that is less constrained by time. In this context, the subject of the news significantly influences the direction of long scrolling news flow designs.

Analyzing the news topics in the study reveals that social issues are the most frequently covered, accounting for 44.4% of the news content. Other topics, including politics and technology, are equally represented at 16.7%, while art and world news are equally distributed, each comprising 11.1% of the sample.

The subject and the research behind the news report have not been specified. However, it has been observed that the names of those responsible for designing the long-scroll news format and presenting it in a narrative structure are mentioned during the design stage.

Figure 10. Navigation Entry in News Story Flow Design

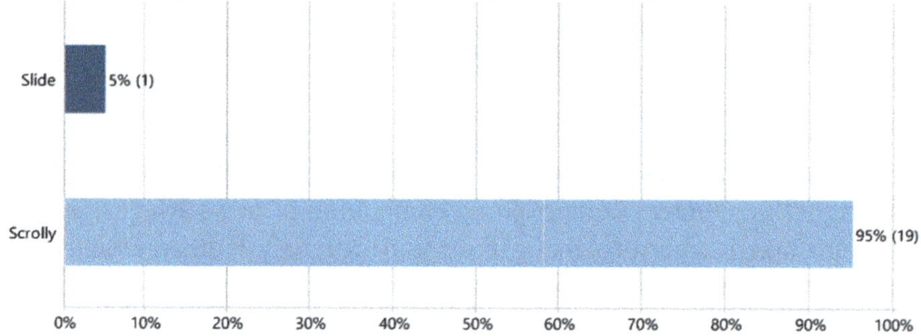

In long scrolling news feed designs, the navigation entry is a crucial element that indicates the type of story users will encounter within the story's design framework. In traditional journalism, the introduction of the news is designed to engage readers and keep them immersed in the story. Similarly, in digital journalism, the introduction is crafted to capture users' attention through both content and design. In long scrolling news narratives, the navigation entry plays a significant role in attracting users' attention and encouraging interaction.

Examining the navigation entries used in the news flow designs from the research findings, it is observed that 95% of the news flow is initiated with scrolling, while only one news story begins with a button. The predominant reliance on scrolling as the input method highlights that the news flow design is primarily structured around the scrolling flow.

Figure 11. Story Layout in News Story Flow Design

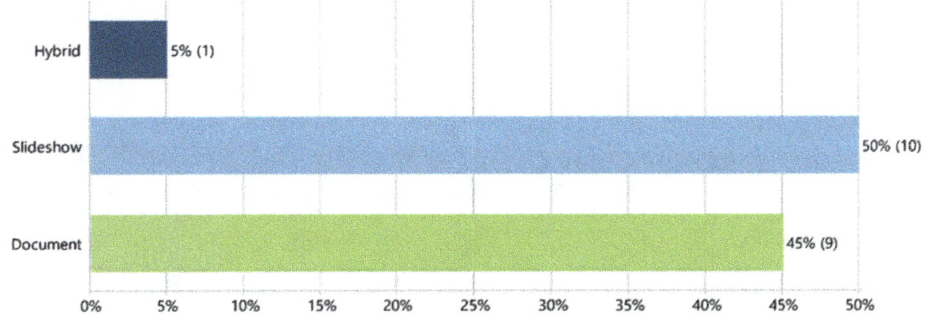

The flow designs used in story production play a significant role in organizing the structure of the story. The design elements utilized in the story determine its layout and the type of flow it follows. In the slideshow story layout, influenced by advancements in web technologies, design variations such as scrolling, bot progression, and visual progression have emerged. Although there are different styles within slide designs, they are categorized under slideshows. With technological developments, slideshows are typically created within the framework of the scrolling layout on web-based sites.

As shown in Table-4, the slideshow story layout is employed in 50% of long scrolling narratives. Additionally, it was observed that diverse types of data were incorporated into news articles utilizing slideshows as the story layout within long scrolling narratives.

In the context of contemporary internet journalism, the digital print narrative style is extensively used for news published on websites. In the document-style story layout, the structure closely resembles the digital print narrative seen on websites. However, this layout is also applied in long scrolling story narratives. According to Table-4, document-style storytelling is used in 45% of long scrolling story layouts, underscoring its significance in this narrative format.

Figure 12.. Transition Type in News Story Flow Design

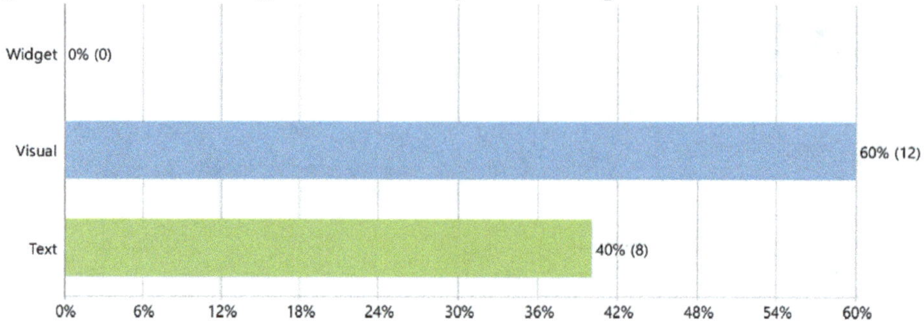

In long scrolling news stories, page transitions, i.e. navigation within the website, are made in the form of scrolling or scrolling created with visual elements, as seen in Figure 12. The navigation entry in news story flow designs is analyzed and interpreted in Table-3. When we look at the development and conclusion sections of the news after the introduction in the news design, it is seen that 60% of the news in the sample create a transition based on visuals, while 40% of the transition is provided through the news text. This situation was also observed to vary according to the design type of the long scrolling narrative.

Figure 13. Distribution of Visualisation in News Story Flow Design

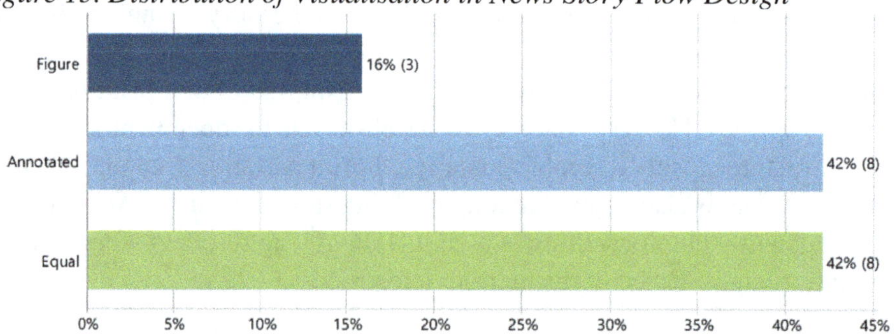

In the production of long scrolling news stories, visual elements take precedence due to the narrative's inherent structure. As illustrated in Figure 13, this format—designed to complement news texts with visual components—reveals that exclusively visual elements are employed in 16% of news stories, while text-dominated stories account for 42%. Similarly, the proportion of news items that integrate both visual and text-based elements is also 42%. These findings highlight that, although long scrolling narrative structures are inherently visual-centric, textual content remains a critical component of the overall design.

Figure 14. Data Type Used in the News Story

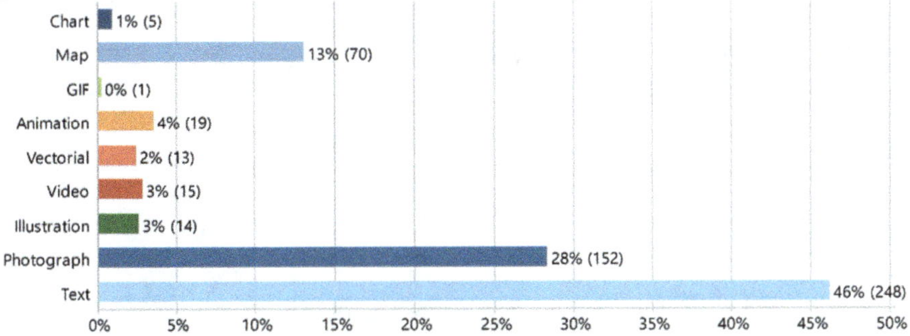

In digital journalism, news production across web, mobile, and social media platforms extends beyond traditional text, pictures, and photographs by incorporating various data types enabled by technological advancements. Particularly in long scrolling narratives, which have emerged through the integration of new communication technologies and artificial intelligence tools, diverse data formats are utilized.

As indicated in Figure 14, the analysis of data usage in news stories reveals that text constitutes the most frequently employed data type, accounting for 46.2%, followed by photographs at 28.3%. Additionally, the analysis shows that other data types, such as animated maps, animation graphics, vectors, videos, GIFs, graphics, and illustrations, are also integrated into news production. The selection and use of these varied data types are closely tied to their alignment with the story's flow design. This relationship was further assessed through a cross-analysis of data type usage and visualization within the narrative structure.

Figure 15. Navigating Within the Story in News Story Flow Design

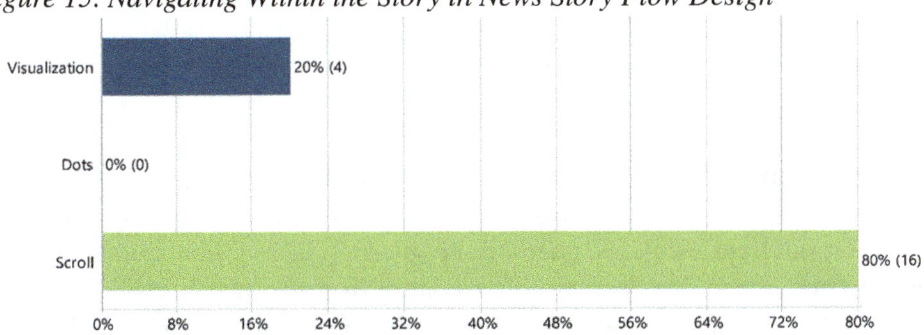

An analysis of navigation rates within the news stories reveals that 80% of the sampled news items provide navigation services to users through scrolling. While point navigation is absent in other navigation types, it is observed that visualization methods incorporating animation and graphic data are utilized in 20% of the cases.

Figure 16. Progression Layout in News Story Flow Design

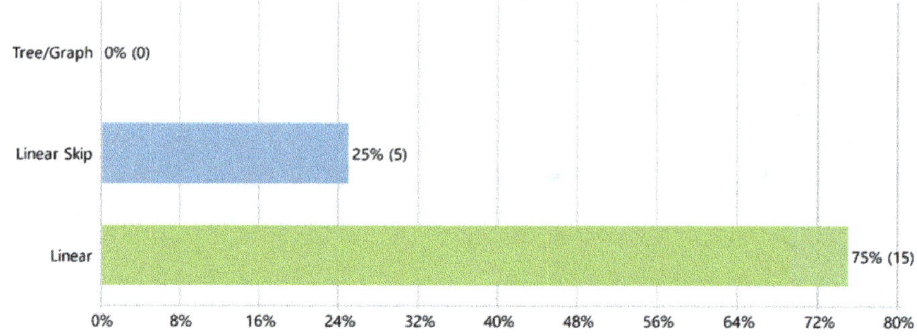

The flow of the news stories analyzed in the research was structured either with a linear progression, maintaining the design trajectory of the story, or with a non-linear skipping progression enabled by various navigation types. Notably, 75% of the news stories were crafted as long scrolling narratives employing a linear progression.

Figure 17. Level of Story Control in News Story Flow Design

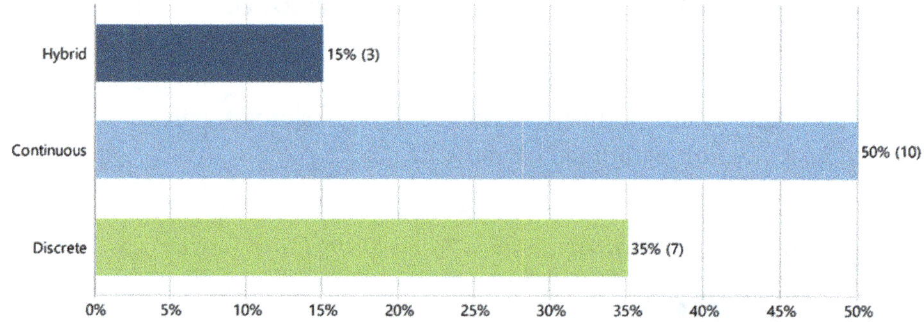

When designing the flow of news stories, users may be prompted to interact in various ways. Some stories require only scrolling control, while others allow users to click on different elements, enabling progression in a discontinuous manner. This variation affects the degree of user control over the narrative. As shown in Figure 17, 50% of the news stories are designed with continuous control, 35% with discontinuous control, and 15% with a mixed control structure.

Long scrolling news narratives are designed with an interactive structure. The frequency analysis shows that scrolling serves as the primary navigation method and acts as the entry point for user interaction. Continuity is a dominant feature in the control levels of the stories, with scrolling being the preferred navigation mechanism. Visual and text-based content play significant roles in the design of the news stories, with some narratives exhibiting an equal distribution of these elements. A variety of data types is utilized, and artificial intelligence technology is integrated into most of the analyzed news stories. These findings suggest that long scrolling news narratives are developed to enhance user interaction by incorporating advanced technologies and diverse content formats.

Figure 18. Use of Artificial Intelligence Technologies in News

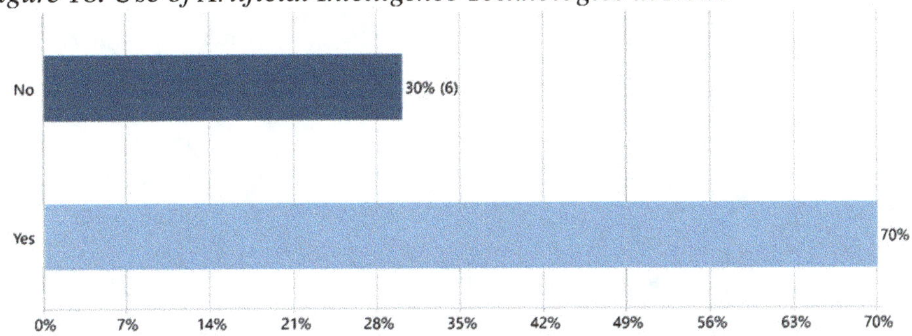

In the modern era, artificial intelligence tools have become integral across various fields, including journalism. Media organizations now employ artificial intelligence technologies in news production, adhering to the principles of professional journalism and ethics. An analysis of the news included in the research reveals that artificial intelligence tools are explicitly referenced in 70% of the cases, as shown in Figure 18. This demonstrates the increasing adoption of artificial intelligence technologies within the journalism sector.

Regarding the question, *"What is the role of artificial intelligence technologies in long scrolling news stories?"*, the findings indicate that artificial intelligence plays a significant role in creating many story designs. This highlights its integration into news production processes and its critical role in digital storytelling. Artificial intelligence technologies not only streamline news production but also contribute to the evolution of storytelling methods in the digital age. In contemporary news production processes, artificial intelligence technologies are increasingly being utilized. This study focuses specifically on the use of AI in the news production phase, rather than its role in distribution. Within the scope of the research, it has been observed that artificial intelligence is employed in various aspects of news creation, such as summarizing content, generating graphics, and producing visuals.

Figure 19. Cross Table Analysis Exhibiting the Distribution of Data Used in Stories to Story Visualisation

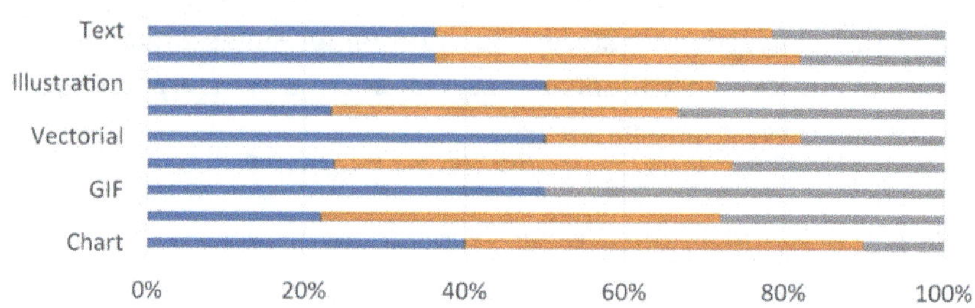

	Chart	Map	GIF	Animation	Vectorial	Video	Illustration	Photograph	Text
Figure =	4	31	1	9	14	7	14	111	181
Annotated =	5	70	0	19	9	13	6	140	211
Equal=	1	39	1	10	5	10	8	55	107

■ Figure = ■ Annotated = ■ Equal=

Figure 19 provides a cross-tabular analysis of the data types used in news stories in relation to the distribution of visuals, text, and visualizations in equally categorized narratives. The analysis reveals that news items are produced using various data types across different visual distributions. Text and photo elements emerge as the most frequently used data types across all categories. When examining other data types, despite variations based on the visual production of the news, a range of data formats is employed in all visual distribution categories. This indicates that long scrolling narratives incorporate multiple data types in their visual distributions, even in text-dominated productions. The frequent and varied use of data underscores that these narratives are constructed with rich data content.

The selection of data types aligns with the flow of digital story designs. To enhance user engagement through visual intelligence, stories are formatted with diverse data content, including animations, vectors, maps, and graphics. The flow design—whether visually or text-oriented—significantly influences the choice of data types. Long scrolling narratives inherently demand design-rich data types, necessitating the use of varied data for both visually and text-weighted content, as reflected in Figure 19.

When analyzing the question, *"How do the data types used in the news affect the narrative structure?"*, it is evident that different data types are utilized regardless of the story design. The design richness of long scrolling stories facilitates the inclusion of diverse data types, contributing to a narrative structure characterized by varied and enriched content.

Figure 20. Cross Table Analysis of Story Order and Story Progression

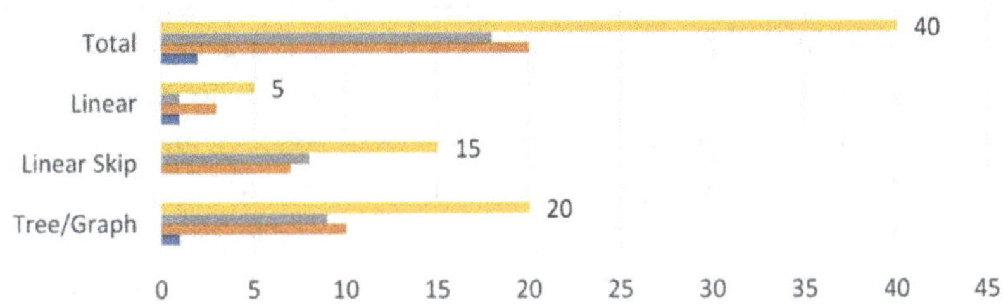

	Tree/Graph	Linear Skip	Linear	Total
Total	20	15	5	40
Document	9	8	1	18
Slideshow	10	7	3	20
Hybrid	1	0	1	2

Total Document Slideshow Hybrid

In story flow design, the sequence and progression of the narrative provide insights into how the flow unfolds. Figure 20 presents a cross-tabular analysis of story progression and layout, highlighting that the progression style results from various design layouts. Document-style layouts and slideshow formats are predominantly produced with graphic-oriented and non-linear progression structures. Interactive designs, which guide users through the story, also adopt a graphic and non-linear progression style.

The interactive nature of long scrolling stories has transformed digital news production by introducing dynamic progression styles, contrasting with the linear progression characteristic of traditional narratives. This evolution underscores how interactive and visually enriched designs have redefined the storytelling experience, offering greater flexibility and engagement in story flow.

CONCLUSION

The long scrolling narrative is a powerful storytelling structure that enhances the immersiveness and interactivity of digital journalism. This narrative approach provides users with a rich experience while simplifying the communication of complex topics. The creation of long scrolling news stories requires the integration of digital design elements alongside the fundamental stages of news production, demanding meticulous planning and execution for optimal effectiveness.

Since the publication of *Snow Fall* in 2012, the long scrolling narrative structure has offered a more interactive news experience, leveraging new communication technologies integrated with artificial intelligence. As a component of digital storytelling, this narrative format enables users to navigate within the story while delivering diverse news experiences across various formats.

The diversity in long scrolling news story designs reflects differences in their structural composition. To explore this diversity, the structures of long scrolling narratives were analyzed based on the story flow designs proposed by McKenna et al. This study examined the narratives produced by the news website *scrolli.co*, categorizing them according to story flow elements and presenting the findings.

The news samples were coded using the Maxqda data analysis program, creating a dataset for evaluation. Frequency analysis was conducted on the long scrolling news from *scrolli.co* based on categories from the story flow design. Cross-tabular analysis further revealed relationships between categories relevant to the research questions.

The findings indicate that long scrolling news stories establish interactive engagement with users. Through these experiences, the preferred features in news flow elements and interaction structures became evident. News stories based on scrolling provide users with rich content by incorporating diverse data types.

Long scrolling narratives employ various data types to construct their stories. The research revealed that these stories utilize a wide range of data types, demonstrating that, despite the diversity of narrative structures, content production consistently integrates multiple forms of data.

The continuous development of digital technologies, coupled with artificial intelligence applications, has profoundly influenced journalism. Artificial intelligence tools, with their multifaceted functions, are increasingly employed in news production, elevating the design and functionality of news content to new dimensions. The analysis showed that artificial intelligence tools were prominently used in the majority of the news studied. The design-rich nature of long scrolling narratives, particularly their visual components, necessitates the integration of artificial intelligence tools, further reinforcing their role in modern digital journalism.

REFERENCES

Alexander, B. (2011). *The New Digital Stroytelling*. Praeger. DOI: 10.5040/9798216979456

Anadolu Ajansı, A. (2024). *Muhabir*. Anadolu Ajansı.

Aziz, A. (2013). *Sosyal Bilimlerde Araştırma Yöntemleri ve Teknikleri*. Nobel.

Bal, D., & Onay, A. (2018). Yeni Medya ve Dijital Hikaye Anlatıcılığının Geleceği. *International Symposium Communication in the Millennium*, 863-875.

Barger, R. N. (2008). Introduction. In *Computer Ethics: A Case-based Approach* (pp. 1–15). Cambridge University Press.

Binark, M. (2007). *Yeni Medya Çalışmaları. M. Binark içinde, Yeni Medya Çalışmaları*. Dipnot.

Conway, K. (2012). Cultural Translation, Long-form Journalism, and Readers' Responses to the Muslim Veil. *Meta: Translators'. Journal*, (57), 997–1012.

Dale, R., & Reiter, E. (2000). *Building Applied Natural Language Generation*. Cambridge University Press.

Diakopoulos, N. (2019). *Automating the News: How Algorithms Are Rewriting the Media*. Harvard University Press. DOI: 10.4159/9780674239302

Dijk, T. A. (2006). *The Network Society Social Aspect Of New Media*. Sega.

Dube, J. (2000). *Online Storytelling Forms*. cyberjournalist.net: Retrieved from cyberjournalist.net/online-storytelling-forms

Garreton, M., Morini, F., Moyano, D., Grün, G.-C., Parra, D., & Dörk, M. (2023). Data Stories of Water: Studying the Communicative Role of Data Visualizations within Long-form Journalism. *Eurographics Conference on Visualization (EuroVis) 2023*, 99-110. DOI: 10.1111/cgf.14815

Girgin, A. (2008). *Gazeteciliğin Temel İlkeleri*. İstanbul: Der.

Jenkins, H., Lashley, M., & Creech, B. (2017). Voices for a New Vernacular: A Forum on Digital Storytelling Interview with Henry Jenkins. *International Journal of Communication*, 1061-1068.

Jenkins, M., & Gravestock, P. (2009). *Digital Storytelling Synthesis*. (Çevrim İçi): digitalstorytellingsynthesis.journo.com.tr. (2016, 04 26). journo.com.tr. journo.com.tr: Retrieved from journo.com.tr/yeni-medya-caginda-haberi-anlatabilmenin-9-yolu

Kalsın, B. (2017). *Tüm Boyutlarıyla İnternet Haberciliği.* Gece.

Kaya, Z. (2019). *Yeni Medyada Haber Anadolu Ajansında Haberin Yapısal Dönüşümü.* Gece Akademi.

Manovich, L. (2001). *The Language of New Media.* MIT Press.

Marconi, F. (2024). Yapay Zekâ ve Gazeteciliği Geleceği. (A. Açıkgöz, Çev.) Ankara: AA Kitap.

Maxqda.com. (2025). *Maxqda.com.* Retrieved from https://www.maxqda.com/tr

McKenna, S., Riche, N., Lee, B., Boy, J., & Meyer, M. (2017). Visual Narrative Flow: Exploring Factors Shaping Data Visualization Story Reading Experiences. *Computer Graphics Forum, 36*(3), 377–387. DOI: 10.1111/cgf.13195

Michel, J. P., & Ladd, M. (2015). "Snow Fall"-ing Special Collections and Archives. *Journal of Web Librarianship, 9*(2-3), 212–131. DOI: 10.1080/19322909.2015.1044689

Özdemir, Z., & Çetinkaya, A. (2019). *Dijital Çağda Habercilik Kuram ve Uygulamada Yeni Yönelimler.* İstanbul: Der.

Pavlik, J. V. (2013). Yeni Medya ve Gazetecilik. Ankara: Phoenix.

Pavlik, J. V., & Pavlik, J. (2017). Understanding Quality in Digital Storytelling: A Theoretically Based Analysis of the Interactive Documentary. *Springer International Publishing*, 381-396.

Robin, B. R. (2016). The Power of Digital Storytelling to Support Teaching and Learning. *Digital Education Review*, 17-29. scrolli.co. (2025). Scrolli.co: Retrieved from www.scrolli.co

Rogers, E. M., & Picot, A. (1986). *Impact Of New Communication Technologies. E. M. Rogers, & F. Belle içinde, The Media Revolution in America and Europe.* Ablex Publishing Corporation Norwood.

Şimşek, B. (2018). *Dijital Hikâye Anlatımı Kavramlar ve Türkiye Deneyimi.* Alternatif Bilişim.

Timisi, N. (2003). *Yeni İletişim Teknolojileri ve Demokrasi.* Dost.

Tjärnhage, A., Söderström, U., Norberg, O., Andersson, M., & Mejtoft, T. (2023). The Impact of Scrollytelling on the Reading Experience of Long-Form Journalism. *European Conference in Cognitive Ergonomics.* DOI: 10.1145/3605655.3605683

Törenli, N. (2005). *Yeni Medya, Yeni İletişim Ortamı.* Bilim ve Sanat.

Türkdoğan, O., & Gökçe, O. (2015). *Sosyal Bilimlerde Araştırma Yöntemleri.* Çizgi.

Wolf, C., & Godulla, A. (2016). Potentials of digital longforms in journalism. A survey among mobile Internet users about the relevance of online devices, Internet-specific qualities, and modes of payment. *Journal of Media Business Studies*, *13*(4), 199–221. DOI: 10.1080/16522354.2016.1184922

Chapter 7
An Exploration on Rousseau and Arendt's Accounts About Communication Listening, Voice, and Self

Tuğba Gülal
https://orcid.org/0000-0001-8991-1334
Istanbul Aydin University, Turkey

ABSTRACT

In Rousseau's key works, including Émile or Treatise on Education (1918), and Reveries of a Solitary Walker (1992),the author examines the dimensions of communication, emphasizing engagement with oneself, others, and nature through silence.This paper utilizes Laverty's (2011) analysis of Rousseau's philosophy, which categorizes communication into three voices:articulate, melodic, and accentuated, representing different listening modalities,particularly in education.A central question emerges regarding the relationship between the self and the external world.I will compare Rousseau's model with Hannah Arendt's views on thinking and selfhood from The Human Condition, ultimately grouping their communication models into two categories: (i) the listening self (Rousseau) and (ii) the performative self (Arendt).Both authors contribute unique insights into communication and the role of silence.In conclusion, I propose the term "tacet sui," or "soundless self," to describe a form of storytelling relevant to both models,drawing on Moskalewicz's (2024) interpretation of Arendt's storytelling.

DOI: 10.4018/979-8-3373-2023-6.ch007

1.INTRODUCTION

Rousseau, in *Émile or Treatise on Education* (1918), posits that "children hear spoken language from their birth; we speak to them not only before they comprehend what is said to them but before they can reproduce the tones they hear" (Rousseau ibid, p.36). This observation serves as the foundation for understanding the significance of listening within Rousseau's first communication model. My interpretation of Rousseau's insights suggests that listening to oneself constitutes a crucial initial step in the educational journey. The listening self acts as a primary mechanism for human communication with the external world, a concept elaborated upon in *Reveries of a Solitary Walker.* In this reflective text, Rousseau grapples with various themes—fear, societal interactions, the beauty of nature, interpersonal relationships, and his intimate observations during solitary walks outdoors. In the Sixth Walk, Rousseau recounts a significant encounter with a young boy, expressing his delight in listening to the child's exuberant chatter: "At first I was charmed to see him; I gave to him very goodheartedly and for some time continued to do so with the same pleasure, quite frequently even prompting and listening to his little prattle which I found enjoyable" (Rousseau, 1992, pp.74). He further contemplates, "Why, then, should not the education of a child begin before he speaks and understands since a mere choice in the objects presented to him is sufficient to render him timid or courageous?" (Rousseau, 1918, pp.27). Thus, for Rousseau, the act of listening embodies a critical function in communication, serving as an essential precursor for making sense of the external world and facilitating speech. Without the listening self, effective communication remains elusive. Silence, as Rousseau suggests, plays a crucial role in allowing individuals to gather their thoughts free from distraction. It is particularly significant in the context of nature and the countryside, where human beings often find a greater capacity to reflect and listen to their inner selves. This concept of listening to oneself is foundational to the listening self as the first principal group of communication. Based on Rousseau's philosophy of humane interaction, Laverty observes that there are profound implications for understanding the role of listening within educational settings. By engaging with Rousseau's ideas, Laverty elaborates on the triad of voices—articulate, melodic, and accentuated—which each represent unique facets of human understanding in interactive contexts. The significance of these three voices is multifaceted in Rousseau's philosophy, as they each carry distinct meanings for humane interaction and underscore the role of listening in education, particularly in the upbringing of children.This triangular interaction includes both successful and unsuccessful attempts at achieving comprehension, with each aspect uniquely contributing to our overall understanding of humane interaction and educational practices. In *Emile: Or, On Education*, Rousseau articulates a transformative model of communication based on listening and highlights its profound significance in education. He also helps reconstruct our broader conception of communication as a form of action. This will be touched upon again later.

The second principal form of communication is associated with the concept of performative action, which I will refer to as the "performative self," drawing on Arendt's relevant accounts of communication. This model emphasizes the role of an agent who conveys meaning through speech. This interpretative framework is enhanced through Arendt's ideas, where communication transcends mere spoken words and embodies a performative engagement with the surrounding world. Arendt's conceptualization of communication is grounded in three interconnected dimensions: thought, action, and speech. These elements are not just individual concepts; they form an intricate web of interdependence that is essential for understanding her notions of agency and communication. While this chapter does not primarily focus on Arendt's views on political action, it aims to explore the relationship between thought and action as a foundation for examining the performative self within a communication framework. Drawing from the Ancient Greek tradition, Arendt argues that to fully understand the relationship between action (praxis) and speech (lexis), it is crucial to recognize that "thought was secondary to speech, but speech and action were considered to be coeval and coequal, of the same rank and the same kind..." (Arendt, 1998, pp.25-26). This assertion underscores Arendt's acknowledgment of the importance of rhetoric in Ancient Greek society, highlighting the profound connection between speech and thought. According to her perspective, thinking is actualized through the act of speech, revealing the essence of rhetoric during the era of the polis, where action and speech were perceived as distinct yet related categories. Arendt further notes that as time progressed, "the emphasis shifted from action to speech, and speech as a means of persuasion rather than the specifically human way of answering, talking back and measuring up to whatever happened or was done" (Arendt,1998, pp. 24). Here, Arendt illustrates a transition in focus from the immediacy of action to the nuances of speech, positioning speech as an essential conduit for communication. In her framework, the connection from action to speech signifies the journey from thoughtful consideration to effective communication, suggesting that the self finds expression through speech. The communication aspect emphasized by Arendt draws a profound relationship between thinking, action, and speech, suggesting that communication is not just an exchange of words but a directed act linking thought to expression. Speech serves as the communicative embodiment of action and a manifestation of the self. To broaden Arendt's accounts about communication and performative self, Luhmann's term "second-order observation" will also be helpful.

One might wonder how Arendt's conception of the self integrates with her theories on communication. Her exploration of communication can be viewed as an analytical endeavor that examines how identity is revealed through speech.

This process aligns with phenomenological approaches and connects to the notion of storytelling, a concept that will be elaborated on later in the chapter with the example of Adolf Eichmann's trial. According to Arendt, "thinking... in contrast to cognitive activities... needs speech not only to sound out... it needs it to be activated at all" (Moskalewicz, 2024, pp.44). Expanding on this idea, Moskalewicz argues that "thinking and consciousness do not exist alongside each other; rather, thinking extracts the duality present in consciousness and thus actualizes the pre-reflective sense of the self into the form of an inner dialogue. A silent, passive, and pre-reflective self transforms into soundless speech reflection. It is a process of self-presentation—a crucial concept for understanding the link between thinking and action" (Moskalewicz, 2024, pp.43-44). Here, Moskalewicz explains how Arendt views thinking as a reflective process that engages in an inner dialogue, ultimately transforming the self when expressed through speech. For Arendt, the idea that "speechless action would no longer be action" (Arendt, 1998, pp.178) reinforces the necessity of a listener in the communication process. This means that action, as Arendt delineates, is inherently performative and interactive.

The concept of the performative self suggests that an individual becomes a distinct entity through speech; prior to this articulation, the self exists only as a passive thought process. Authenticity is achieved through the act of speaking, which reinforces the notion that speech and action are interlinked and that the self unfolds through this communicative performance. Both Rousseau and Arendt make significant contributions to a phenomenological framework of communication. Their models highlight the dynamic interaction between speaker and listener, wherein communication becomes a performance aimed at understanding oneself and others. In this discussion, I categorize Rousseau's understanding of communication as the i) listening self, while Arendt's is referred to as the ii) performative self. These frameworks introduce various dimensions to the concept of communication, and this chapter seeks to articulate a third principle—iii) the silent self. The silent self represents a unique form of storytelling that embodies performative action, through which the self is realized. This prompts an essential inquiry: what does the silent self, as a performative mode of communication, signify? This chapter continues rigorously exploring this question. The first section will examine Laverty's analysis of Rousseau's listening model and his philosophy of communication. The second section will explore Arendt's ideas surrounding storytelling and her communication model. Finally, the third section will propose the term tacet sui (the silent self), synthesizing insights from both Rousseau and Arendt to deepen our understanding of communication.

The following aspect must be considered: the aim of this chapter is not to directly address the nature of digital communication within contemporary communication theories, but to explore the idea of communication or different narrations through a specific ontology that phenomenological investigation profoundly examines. This chapter also includes a critical perspective on how communication theorists may engage with the subjects being investigated. Notably, some significant contemporary communication theories are not the primary focus of this chapter; instead, it highlights the views of philosophers and thinkers such as Rousseau and Arendt, whose perspectives are often overlooked in contemporary communication research. Within the scope of this chapter, they will be regarded as philosophers of communication. To achieve the chapter's goal, I propose three principles of communication: i) the listening self, ii) the performative self, and iii) the tacit self (silent self). As previously defined, these three principles elucidate different ontological aspects of communication: i) education and tranquility, ii) action and thought, and iii) the soundless aspect of the authentic self. Although there is no hierarchical relationship among them, these principles suggest that we can seek a deeper understanding of communication or humane interaction grounded in philosophical thought.

2.ON J.J. ROUSSEAU'S ACCOUNTS ON PHILOSOPHY OF COMMUNICATION AND THE CONCEPT OF *LISTENING SELF*

Jean-Jacques Rousseau was an influential philosopher who lived from 1712 to 1778. He was deeply engaged with numerous philosophical questions in political philosophy and moral psychology, profoundly impacting the thinkers who followed him. This chapter focuses on Rousseau's philosophy of communication, which has two main aspects: educational and ontological. The educational aspect of Rousseau's philosophy of communication is based on the concept of listening, which holds a special significance in his educational philosophy through a taxonomy of voices for humane interaction. To explore this concept, Laverty identifies three distinctive voices that Rousseau examines: i) articulate, ii) melodic, and iii) accentuated. Before delving into these three distinctive characteristics, it is important to briefly introduce Rousseau's perspectives on listening. According to Rousseau, "the first law of speech" is that individuals speak to be understood and listen to grasp the speaker's intended meaning (Rousseau, 1979, pp.72). Rousseau's communication model encompasses two dimensions: listening and speaking. What makes listening particularly significant in Rousseau's accounts of communication and education is its involuntary aspect. Speaking is a voluntary activity, while listening is involuntary. As Laverty notes, "Rousseau stressed that listening is involuntary: we cannot choose whether or not to listen, nor can we decide when we do so" (Laverty, 2011, pp.157). This involuntary nature of listening makes it vital for human interaction and psychology, as it requires pure attention to different levels and types of voices in communication. In contrast, speaking is a much more voluntary and intentional component of communication. As Laverty states, "humans intend to speak; they both choose to do so and decide when to do so. Speech is a message sent from one person to another, a signal of the speaker's meaning or reason for speaking" (Laverty, ibid, pp.157). Both dimensions—listening and speaking—play essential roles in understanding human interaction; however, the concept of listening occupies a unique position in Rousseau's educational philosophy. Rousseau articulates, "Man has three kinds of voice: namely, the speaking or articulated voice; a singing or melodious voice; and the impassioned or modulated voice, which serves as a language for the passions, and which gives animation to song and speech. The child, like the man, has these three kinds of voice without knowing how to combine them as he does" (Rousseau, 1918, pp.115). For Rousseau, each kind of voice has a specific function in communication, operating in harmony to create a robust concept of interaction. In this regard, both the speaker and listener play essential roles in communication. To further elaborate on the three kinds of voices Rousseau emphasizes, we can refer to Laverty's relevant reformulation.

Laverty notes that "the articulate voice denotes the actual words. It is consonant with the subject matter or substance of what the speaker says. In the case of the articulate voice, the listener's primary concerns are truth and sincerity; they consider whether the speaker believes what they are saying and if it is true. The melodic voice, on the other hand, refers to the harmonious sequence of sounds produced when words are said or sung and is less of a focus. The accentuated voice adds sentiment and truth to speech (EOE, 72) (Laverty, 2011, pp. 158). Rousseau describes three kinds of voices that serve as a function of humane interaction, leading to harmony." (Rousseau, 1918, pp. 115) For this reason, Rousseau states that "perfect music is that which best unites these three voices." Consider a person who speaks like a singer; such a person articulates harmoniously or recites rhythmically and automatically, which makes listeners more inclined to pay attention for a longer duration than they might expect. This example aligns closely with what Rousseau means by perfect music. Additionally, one might think of a skilled singer who employs various tones with a harmonious structure, or someone with exceptional rhetorical talent. These instances can be multiplied to deepen our understanding of the relationship between speech and listening, which is crucial to exploring Rousseau's philosophy of communication. Rousseau elaborates on his account of communication by discussing the concept of accent, claiming that "accent is the soul of discourse; it gives to it feeling and truth." (Rousseau, 1918, pp. 38). Consequently, the speaker's accent introduces an additional dimension for the listener, aiding in comprehension and engagement. Through Rousseau's perspectives, it can be established that the nature of communication involves the inseparable relationship between speech and listening, which encompasses various categories. Listening is significant in Rousseau's views on education from early childhood. Infants do not immediately develop their speech abilities; instead, they are directed toward listening. Rousseau states, "The child, like the man, has these three kinds of voice without knowing how to combine them as adults do. Like us, he resorts to laughter, cries, wails, exclamations, and groans, but he does not know how to blend their inflections with the two other voices." (Rousseau, 1918, pp. 115).

The "articulated voice, melodious voice, and modulated voice" that Rousseau emphasizes are three types of voice present in children, but they lack the systematic organization and harmony to use them effectively. However, actively listening to a child and teaching them "to speak simply and clearly, to articulate correctly" is essential for understanding Rousseau's philosophy regarding education and communication (Rousseau ibid, p. 116). Therefore, attentively listening to a child's voices is the first step toward robust communication and humane interaction. The practice of transforming unexpressed thoughts into audible expression is aptly described by Laverty who states, "Adults must listen, perpetually seeking to understand the mystery of children's motivation." (Laverty, 2011, pp.169)

The second aspect of Rousseau's philosophy of communication is ontological and significantly more complex than listening. In this chapter, the ontological dimension of Rousseau's philosophy of communication is linked to the concept of darkness. How does darkness function in Rousseau's discussions of communication? The concept of darkness is tied to the existential character of communication, interrelated with the listening self, which serves as the primary model in this chapter. The listening self signifies the existential dimension of communication, through which fear operates in the dark, according to Rousseau. He contends that, similar to humane interaction, fear develops early in human life and is relevant to both infants and adults. Rousseau perceives darkness as a source of horror for individuals. Reflecting on a frightening experience while walking in the hills, he expresses, "I have always hated the dark; it naturally fills me with a dread which the darkness they have surrounded me with for so many years could not have diminished. (Rousseau, 1992, pp. 17). Additionally, Rousseau argues that the fear of darkness originates in infancy when an infant differentiates only between pleasure and pain. At this early stage, "affective sensation" caused by light is pleasurable because it allows the infant to perceive objects in their immediate surroundings that would otherwise be hidden (cited in English & Stengel, 2010, pp. 424-525; EOE, 62f). Thus, an infant's inclination toward light reflects a persistent desire to avoid the darkness that obscures accessible knowledge. Rousseau makes significant contributions to the understanding of listening and speaking in "Emile," emphasizing the crucial role that fear plays in a child's education and the politics surrounding it. He connects the concept of fear in children to a new object, indicating the complex layers of communication interconnected with listening and the inherent responses to fear.

Accordingly, listening self means the character of humane interaction within his or her own being. In other words, the listening self comes to the stage in many ways but one of those main ways is darkness based on Rousseau's accounts. Listening to self signifies that humane interaction with self and the external world continues substantively even though there is no direct human voice surrounding us. Probably, when there is no human voice around, the listening self is much denser compared to other situations and external possibilities such as the places where there is a concert of dense communicative activities. The relation between the listening self and its relation with dark and fear as emphasized in Rousseau's accounts is caused by the ontological character of human beings. The ontological character of human beings in terms of communication is difficult to explain. Since it is not directly in the scope of this chapter, it will not be elaborated. To briefly put it, the ontological character of human being is based on the idea that human can talk and listen to him or herself and this is about our ontological aspect. Our interaction within ourselves appears ontologically since we come into the world, maybe before it, this character already exists, nevertheless, it will not be discussed for now.

Then, the listening self is linked to the concept of authenticity and its relation communication. Charles Taylor defines authenticity as follows:

> *[By "authenticity"] I mean the understanding of life which emerges with the Romantic expressivism of the late-eighteenth century, that each one of us has his/her own way of realizing our humanity, and that it is important to find and live out one's own, as against surrendering to conformity with a model imposed on us from outside, by society, or the previous generation, or religious or political authority. (Taylor, 2007, pp.475)*

The notion of the listening self intricately reveals a deeper layer of our authentic identities, particularly in the rich tapestry of human interactions. We can vividly illustrate this concept through various examples, such as the solitary joy of a person hiking through breathtaking landscapes or the evocative painting *Wanderer Above the Sea of Fog* (1818) by Caspar David Friedrich which captures the essence of introspection and inner exploration. The tranquility and contemplation that the listening self experiences are not merely abstract concepts; they embody a heartfelt resistance against the norms imposed by society and prevailing religious or political authorities. Yet, the idea of authenticity is complex and multifaceted. On one hand, it presents the authentic self as an ontological presence—an entity that simply exists. On the other hand, it illustrates authenticity as a social construction, shaped by the environment we navigate. In today's rapidly changing world, our understanding of authenticity becomes increasingly intricate and paradoxical, as explored by Moeller and D'Ambrosio in their insightful paper titled "Orientation to Profiles: Identity in a Digitized World." Authenticity can embody both the idea of being original and the concept of being unoriginal; it is dynamic, evolving within a digital landscape where it can be influenced by engaging with literature, films, or narratives that portray what it means to be an authentic person. (Moeller and D'Ambrosio, 2023) In other words, "we learn how to be authentic by reading novels, watching movies, or hearing stories about authentic people." (Moeller & D'Ambrosio, 2023, pp. 40). This paradoxical dimension of authenticity deserves careful consideration. Recognizing authenticity often transcends simply unveiling one's true self or embarking on a journey of self-discovery; it involves the thoughtful process of curating a relevant self through meaningful interactions with others. Furthermore, one can distinguish between the broader concept of authenticity and the realm of Romantic expressivism. The latter emphasizes the profound connection to one's own autonomy, a creation—the ability to articulate and realize personal values and humanity, a point that resonates strongly with Taylor's insights.

3.ON HANNAH ARENDT'S ACCOUNTS ON HUMANE INTERACTION AND *PERFORMATIVE SELF*

The second prominent thinker is Hannah Arendt. Hannah Arendt was a German-American historian and philosopher of the twentieth century who is well known for her thoughts about history, totalitarianism, and human conditions. Hannah Arendt's views on thinking, selfhood, and communication are articulated in her work in *The Human Condition* (1998) with very insightful thoughts. In order to explore Arendt's relevant thoughts, three concepts become relevant and these are speech, thinking and action. Three concepts are intertwined and they are connected based on Arendt's thoughts. Arendt posits that speech constitutes a form of action—a meaningful engagement through which individuals perform and assert their identities. She articulates this interconnection by stating: "Speechless action would no longer be action because there would no longer be an actor, and the actor, the doer of deeds, is possible only if he is at the same time the speaker of words" (Arendt, 1998, pp. 178-179) Based on Arendt's relevant statement, one of the possible of interpretation of the thought might be as follows: Action and speech is interconnected and the speech is an action through which speaker performs and appears as an actor of the words. This interaction with the external world is caused by the appearance of the speaker as performer of the words. In other words, the speaker turns into a performer of an action of interaction. Nevertheless, the speechless action is not the same.

For Arendt, speechless actions do not have the same function as speech because speech is the action that individuals perform with their thoughts. Arendt extends her conception of action and speech based on the Aristotelian conceptualization of action (praxis) and speech (lexis) that is grounded on logos (logic). Relevantly, Arendt states "of all the activities necessary and present in human communities, only two were deemed to be political and to constitute what Aristotle called the bois politikos, namely action (praxis) and speech (lexis), out of which rises the realm of human affairs (ta ton anthropon pragmata, as Plato used to call it) from which everything merely necessary or useful is strictly excluded." (Arendt, 1998, pp.24-25) Praxis and Lexis are two basic political dimensions of human life, and based on Aristotelian biopolitics, Arendt expands the concepst. Action, speech, and thinking are intertwined through Arendt's formulation of humane interaction. Arendt's communication model, therefore, is directed to the concept of performance. Performance is the action of speech through which thinking is activated and this happens through writing, doing philosophy, etc. Arendt refers to this as follows:

"Since Plato, and probably since Socrates, the thinking was understood as the inner dialogue in which one speaks with himself *(erne auto,* to recall the idiom current in Plato's dialogues); and although this dialogue lacks all outward manifestation and even requires a more or less complete cessation of all other activities, it constitutes in itself a highly active state." (Arendt, 1998, pp.291)

Based on the history of philosophy within Ancient terms, thinking was regarded as an inner dialogue that manifests itself through different activities such as rhetoric, philosophy, and writing. Besides, this process of thinking is directly linked to speech as an action. Speech is motivated by thinking and in other words, this creates an inevitable relation between thinking and speech and action which creates a performative self. Aligned with Arendt's accounts of consciousness, Moskalewicz states "thinking and consciousness do not exist alongside each other for thinking extracts the duality present in consciousness and thus actualizes the pre-reflective sense of the self into the form of an inner dialogue." (Moskalewicz, 2024, pp.43-44) This is where Arendt's storytelling begins and it is linked to the performative self. Arendt's storytelling is not limited to inner dialogue or soundless speech but mainly perforation. What does this mean? By interpreting Arendt's relevant thoughts; soundless speech is not what creates the storytelling but the speech itself and speech is a performance in which the self appears.This process is inevitable and "silent, passive and pre-reflective sense transforms into the soundless speech reflection." (Moskalewicz, 2024, pp.44) Nevertheless, it seems that soundless speech is still not performative and it does not create real storytelling for human communication.

Arendt states "Speechless action would no longer be action." (Arendt, 1998, pp.178) Accordingly, Moskalewicz adds "and since the spoken word requires a listener-it is a communicative interaction." (Moskalewicz, ibid, pp.69) Communicative interaction is a process between speaker and listener and the question of self is ambiguous. Moskalewicz, aligned with Arendt's thoughts, asks "What is the who?"It is not tangible for the actor and appears solely and fleetingly to others in the discontinuities of language." For the question of self, Arendt applies Heidegger's account of the self from *Being and Time,* nevertheless this will not be elaborated within the scope of the chapter. Returning to the function of communication for self, for Arendt, "the unique distinctiveness of the who is also an achievement, but it appears through communicative action with others." (Moskalewicz, ibid, pp.70) Though the communication or linguistic aspects do not uncover the package of the self completely, it shows its unique character.

The concept of the performative self has a unique place considering Arendt's storytelling. "The difference between the who and physical identity is that unlike the latter, it is mediated by language. Its linguistic character makes revelatory action exceptionally transient—"as futile as life itself." Language itself is the process where the self enters into being and without speech, this performative aspect of communication is never complete. The reason why speech has a significant foundation for the performative self is naturally grounded on the character of humane interaction with others and the external world. This humane interaction goes with the concept of orientation hand in hand and speaking can be defined as "a means of gaining and losing orientation." (Stegmaier, 2019, pp. 125) What is the self or who of orientation through humane interaction? Stegmaier states "An orientation does not distinguish such a self within itself....it experiences itself as an orientation in all its orientation processes." (Stegmaier, 2019, pp.83) The concept of orientation discussed by Steigmaier is complex, nevertheless what matters is to expand its meaning through communication and can be overlapped with Arendt's accounts of self, speech and thought as "activity of thought, which goes on within one's self by means of words..." (Arendt, 1998, pp.20)

We direct ourselves to the external world and we deal with difficulties and problems through interaction. Our capacity for interaction is also our capacity of orientation with situations and as soon as orienting ourselves starts, we see our oriented self is not identical to whom we think we are. This sounds a bit difficult. One example to clarify the function of interaction for orientation can be about people who change their workplaces or houses. Firstly, it can be a bit challenging to get accustomed to a new situation or a new place but slowly, since people's routines change or can be modified, new situations may not be the same. People mainly can orient themselves according to a new situation if they are genuinely prepared for it. For example, if someone else starts studying or working in another country, the sounds and language become much more familiar than someone else who does not live in the same context and does not have any idea about that language. S/he may not have the same tea s/he has each day in the morning, nevertheless, there are some possibilities to orient oneself according to that new situation though this can be tough. Day by day, s/he may learn the language and find the possibility to communicate in a given domain. Here, speech plays a crucial role in humane interaction and this role is significant for both Arendt and Stegmaier. Speech is a way to reveal our orientation toward new challenges. Based on Kant's relevant accounts

(Kant, 1914) Stegmaier says "According to Kant, the 'I' itself is otherwise empty. It is at first only a pronoun, but it has a special grammatical function." (Stegmaier, 2019, pp. 79) Here, the pronoun "I" has a different grammatical function for Kant. Steigmeaier adds "In communication, it indicates who speaks; and it thus indicates that a consciousness speaks to other consciousnesses – in the terms of orientation, it refers to the standpoint of a speaker. However, Kant does not refer to such communication with the term 'I,' but rather wants to justify the objectivity of objects with it." (Stegmaier, ibid, pp.79) Kant's usage of "I" has a grammatical function except it is solely being pronoun and it is about the objectivity of objects. Since it is not the main angle of the chapter, the objectivity of objects shall not be discussed but this is important to understand Kant's usage of "I" is different from orienting self.

Speech is orienting the self within different situations of disorientation. To clarify the "performative self", Stegmaier's concept of "communication disorientation" can be helpful. Stegmaier writes about the "communication disorientations" as follows:

"If you ask others for directions, you cannot always rely on them to give you correct and helpful information. If the problems persist when communicating with others, you can try to solve them in more intensive conversations; but this can also lead to new and worse disorientations, which cause distrust, anger, and disappointment. If relationships, friendships, work teams, or political relations enter a state of crisis, crisis talks may help – but they may also worsen the crisis." (Steigmaier, 2019, pp.90-91)

Speech serves a dual purpose in orientation. It can either function as a medium for our understanding or complicate our surroundings, leading to disorientation. For example, one might imagine being a tourist in a foreign country where you don't understand the language. Navigating unfamiliar streets can be challenging, as you may struggle to orient yourself amid strange directions, shops, landmarks, and interactions, each with its own unique social and cultural dynamics. When you seek directions from a local, the response may not always be reliable, as their way of communicating could be more intricate than you expect. In a challenging political climate or crisis, dense communication can be beneficial, but it might also contribute to confusion, a phenomenon termed "communicative disorientation." Disorientation arises from various factors, such as a lack of reliable reference points, misleading signs, disrupted routines, inadequate understanding, fragmented memories, or poor decision-making regarding orientation. This concept highlights the potential for finding your way in new situations. As stated by Stegmaier, "Disorientations are always possible due to a lack of footholds, misleading clues, disrupted or failing routines, untenable plausibilities, fragmentary memories, or infelicitous orientation decisions" (Stegmaier, 2019, pp.90). Ultimately, speech can either help or hinder our ability to navigate new circumstances. This duality of speech ties into the concept of the "performative self," which refers to how individuals orient themselves in new situations through communication, particularly speech.

The performative self is based on Hannah Arendt's ideas about humane interaction, which relate to human orientation in the face of social, political, and cultural challenges. When revisiting the main theme of this chapter—storytelling in the works of Rousseau and Arendt—one common thread emerges: both philosophers are deeply interested in the transformative power of communication. Rousseau, as an early modern thinker, and Arendt, a twentieth-century political philosopher, both recognize humane interaction as a cornerstone of human progress and cultivation. They have redefined concepts of speech, language, and interaction from different perspectives. The two key approaches to communication in Rousseau's and Arendt's works are as follows: Rousseau's "listening self" and Arendt's "performative self." These concepts underscore the transformative power of communication. The transformative power of communication transcends mere listening; it encompasses our ability to engage with ourselves, with others, and with the world around us. Daily interactions occur in various contexts, but our engagement with ourselves is often limited due to distractions, demanding work hours, and additional responsibilities. This limitation is particularly evident for those living in metropolitan areas characterized by heavy traffic, noise, and a bustling environment. In contrast, tranquil settings, such as the countryside or a forest, enhance our interaction with ourselves and our surroundings. Rousseau's long walks exemplify how tranquility can facilitate deeper listening and engagement.

Arendt's concept of the performative self can be linked to various subsets of communication theories, such as Habermas's idea of power of communicative action (1977) or Luhmann's observations regarding systems theory.The particular relevance here is Luhmann's theory of observation. Arendt traveled to Jerusalem to report on the trial of Adolf Eichmann, a German-Austrian official of the Nazi Party during the Holocaust. Through her observations of the trial, Arendt developed the idea of the "banality of evil," which raises important questions about moral philosophy and Arendt wrote the book titled *Eichmann in Jerusalem: A Report on the Banality of Evil* (1963) What makes these trials particularly significant is their observatory nature regarding human communication; specifically, the way people in the courtroom, except Arendt observed Eichmann and his interactions. While Arendt was observing Eichmann and his statements, the entire court was also spontaneously observing him. This recalls Luhmann's discussions of observation. For Luhmann, observation indicates a framework based on differences.This suggests that observation has multiple layers, with each observation possessing its own distinct characteristics. For example, people can observe the sea in various ways: for some, it may symbolize eternity, while for others, it could represent an end or evoke fear. Each observation can give rise to further observations, leading to what Luhmann terms second-order observation. Luhmann's concept of observation, especially second-order observation, connects to Arendt's views on speech and its relationship to the performative self. Second-order observation refers to the observation of observers, or describing what others say or do not say. Luhmann defines it as follows:

"The observation of the observers—that is a shift from a consciousness of reality to a description of descriptions, or the perception of what others say or do not say—has become the advanced mode of perceiving the world in modern society. This is true in all major functional domains, in academia no less than in the economy, in art as much as in politics" (Luhmann, 2012, pp. 100).

Second-order observation can be considered with many exampled in digitzed world such as selfies in social media, or someone else taking the photo of others observing a football match. For the chatper, the second-order observation ties directly to Arendt's concept of the performative self, as it expands on the idea of observation in relation to speech. In Eichmann's case, the court interprets his narration as evidence of evil intentions paired with monstrous actions. In contrast, Arendt perceives Eichmann's narrative primarily as that of a man lacking the capacity for thought or consciousness; for Arendt, court's main motivations to explain his actions based on intentionality and evil might suffice to explain the real foundation of his actions. This philosophical investigation will not be elaborated more within the scope of chapter, but what matters for now we encounter two layers of observation, which can be considered as second-order observations. The first layer pertains to how Arendt observes Eichmann's situation and narration, while the second layer involves how Eichmann is observed and his narration interpreted by the court. These layers of observation can be further expanded; nonetheless, the Eichmann trials illustrate the significant nature of the performative self through action and thought.

In summary, Arendt's perspective emphasizes that communication primarily involves speech directed toward thought processes. It is an utterance and action that can reveal moral and political considerations. Thus, speechless actions differ significantly from speech itself. For Arendt, speech represents a fundamental aspect of humanity, as she asserts, "Wherever the relevance of speech is at stake, matters become political by definition, for speech is what makes man a political being" (Arendt, 1998, pp.3). She views speech as a potent tool for political action and personal expression. Both Rousseau and Arendt offer valuable insights into communication, linking it to storytelling. Arendt's interpretation of storytelling connects it with historical and political contexts, emphasizing the profound impact of human interaction.

What matters for the motivation of the chapter is that both philosophers endorse a substantive concept of humane interaction. The discussion does not end here; it will also explore the third principal group of communication: the soundless self. Two specific principal groups of communication discussed earlier are significant in examining the concept of the soundless self. Rousseau's listening self helps illustrate the function of listening as it pertains to the self directed toward soundless activity. Furthermore, Arendt's performative self guides us in viewing soundless action as a form of performative action for the self, aside from the context of speechless beings, which plays a crucial role in this chapter. The listening self and performative self intersect with the soundless self, emphasizing the importance of silence within each category. The primary aim of this concept is to expand the understanding of communication to include soundless activity and to question whether soundless actions can also be considered a form of storytelling.

The soundless self serves as the third principal group of communication, for which the term "tacet sui" will be introduced. Tacet sui, derived from the Latin term "tacet" (meaning silent) and "sui" (the genitive reflexive pronoun meaning himself, herself, itself, themselves, one another, each other, etc.), refers to the soundless self. To explore this concept and address the related question of storytelling, one critical question arises: What does it mean for communication to be speechless? Does it imply being without sound or being in silence? These questions will be followed through the next section.

4. ON SOUNDLESS SELF

The concept of the soundless self is challenging to articulate; however, some philosophical discussions exist regarding it. The notion of silence is not commonly examined within communication studies and is often overlooked in philosophical discussions. Nevertheless, the concept of silence will briefly be articulated in the context of the soundless self by creating a connection between philosophy and communication studies. Before proceeding with the theoretical aspects, some examples may be helpful. In our daily lives, we often experience moments of silence. For instance, when we are alone in our rooms, gazing into a mirror and engaging in deep reflection, we find ourselves in silence. Similarly, when we hike through deep forests, we can also experience profound silence probably except the sounds of birds and some grass.

During a car trip, we often find ourselves gazing at the mountains, lost in deep thought, or standing in silence while observing a painting or an artwork in a museum. These moments highlight the significance of silence, which can be pluralized and explored from various perspectives. The concept of silence is crucial for understanding the term "tacet sui." The philosophy of silence is a relatively new branch of study that investigates its meaning. While silence is not commonly discussed in the Western philosophical tradition, it holds profound significance in Eastern thought. In this chapter, the connection between silence and the philosophy of communication shall be examined. Silence acts as a bridge between communication and philosophy, serving as a powerful tool. In both political and social contexts, silence can wield considerable influence. For instance, politicians may silence certain groups or individuals, denying them their right to speak. Furthermore, in traumatic situations, such as the loss of a loved one, silence often prevails. Here, silence is viewed as a process rather than merely a tool; it operates as an action rather than an end-oriented motivation for humane interaction. Thus, the nature of silence as a process or action warrants further exploration. Wittgenstein famously stated, "What we cannot speak about we must pass over in silence." (Wittgenstein, 1961, pp.74). This statement reflects a process-oriented view of humane interaction. Wardley expands on this notion by suggesting that silence is an act with many different possibilities, akin to speech. Silence, then, is not simply the absence of speech but rather a deliberate and intentional state. This form of muteness can create an opportunity for listening that respects the integrity of matter, the individual, and the Other. Silence is rich and multifaceted; "being silent" may communicate transcendence most profoundly. It can also represent an act of asceticism, removing attitudes, mental images, and ideas while bridging notions of radical immanence and transcendence—moving beyond purely textual reality into nonlinguistic forms of culture (Wardley, 2010, pp.1). Silence, in all its forms, carries philosophical meanings and can be linked to speech. In the absence of speech, silence takes center stage as an intentional action. Silence can serve not only to halt speech but also to open space for listening to the Other. This reflects its ontological meaning, which often lies hidden within its transcendental aspects. This form of silence transcends mere absence of sound and becomes a form of inner communication with the Self. Wardley adds, "Silence indicates the concealment of self and the individual's withdrawal from society; yet, in a religious or liturgical setting, one often—paradoxically—maintains silence in company, reinforcing human solidarity" (Wardley, 2010, pp.1). To better understand the notion of silence as an act of human solidarity, consider Buddhist monks who live on top of mountains. Often, they join in deep silence for prayer or individual meditation, seeking human peace and solidarity. These examples do not only highlight the religious aspects of silence but also its ontological connections. Therefore, the ontological meaning of silence as related to the soundless self needs to be further explored.

4.1.Ontological Meaning of Silence

To advance the discussion of silence, it is essential to remember that silence exists alongside sound and music. Without sounds or voices, the role of silence in humane interaction cannot be fully grasped. This principle applies even to animals and plants; for example, pigeons communicate with one another, and plants whisper to each other, filling the air with their voices. This is the music of nature, bringing us joy, peace, and various emotions. When they cease their communication, we begin to appreciate silence more deeply. However, the concept of silence in humane interaction differs significantly from that among animals and plants. In human contexts, silence can be both a passive and active form of communication. A person may remain silent because they are tired and lack the energy to engage, which represents passive silence. Conversely, a child might be silent because of fear speaking the truth, exemplifying active silence.

Max Scheler, writing in 1913, noted that while individuals can choose to remain silent and keep their thoughts to themselves, this is distinctly different from simply not saying anything. "It is an active attitude" (cited from Wardley, 2010, pp.5). Active silence is a robust form of silence, allowing for continuous humane interaction with both the internal and external worlds. This type of silence can occur when someone travels by bus, gazing at mountains and rivers while engaged in deep thought. The thinking process does not cease when silence emerges, as silence—much like speech, according to Arendt—serves as a mode of communication. Through silence, the traveler can engage in imagination, reflection, dreaming, and analysis. Therefore, the concept of silence has multi-strong functions for humane interaction and it is as substantive as speech for humane interaction.

Relevant to this discussion, Wardley states, "Bernard Dauenhauer (1980:7) summarizes the thesis of Max Picard's *The World of Silence* (1952) thus: silence is an ontological principle; it belongs to almost every dimension of human activity and the world it inhabits. It is one of the 'forces' that constitute the human world, a principle distinct from (though associated with) other forces such as spirit and word" (Wardley 2010, pp. 5). Silence serves as an ontological foundation for human activity, existing beyond mere words. Furthermore, silence opens new horizons for human experiences and existence itself. The concept of silence as an ontological principle relates to the idea of the "soundless self," which signifies a unique form of storytelling. In moments of silence, this soundless self operates as a means of communication, conveying meaning even in the absence of speech. The soundless self communicates from within one's being, embodying an existentialist perspective. Consequently, certain types of human interaction, such as those featuring the soundless self, can hold a more profound ontological significance than others. What makes the soundless self ontological in the realm of communication? The answer lies in the notion of authentic consciousness, which allows individuals to discover their true selves. While this concept may appear complex, one can experience the soundless self through everyday activities. For instance, when a person looks into a mirror and sees their reflection, they may be engaging with their soundless self. Similarly, before falling asleep, when one gazes at the walls or emptiness of the room, they might be in a process of deconstructing their soundless self. Despite the absence of verbal communication, this process still indicates an active interaction. To illustrate this form of communication, we can look at examples from history and art, including the works of Van Gogh and Monet. One notable example is Casper David Friedrich's painting, *Wanderer Above the Sea of Fog*, created in 1818. As a remarkable representation of Romanticism, this painting depicts a man gazing into the distance through a misty atmosphere. It evokes contemplation and self-reflection, while also highlighting the concept of the soundless self discussed in this chapter. Edward Hopper is another great artist who effectively captures characters embodying the soundless self in his paintings. Hopper, an American realist painter, often portrays characters who are profoundly alone. One prominent example is his 1972 oil painting titled *Automat.*

Figure 1. Edward Hopper's Automat

In *Automat,* Hopper depicts a solitary woman seated in front of a cup of coffee in an automat. The well-dressed woman holds her cup of coffee, and her expression is ambiguous—viewers cannot be certain if she is sad or happy. Nevertheless, her presence suggests a state of contemplation. The painting conveys a sense of tranquility and a soundless state of being. The woman's portrayal invites us to consider whether her soundless self represents a distinct type of human interaction. Likely, the answer is yes, as it reveals an authentic expression of self. Thus, we arrive at an important conclusion: the soundless self offers the potential for creating an authentic self through self-referential communication. In other words, *tacet sui* serves as a form of storytelling that fosters autonomous consciousness and facilitates the discovery of the true self, albeit through a complex process. The soundless self expands the spectrum of thoughts on human interaction. It suggests that there is a possibility for meaningful engagement beyond speech; in essence, silence can itself become a means of communicating with the authentic self and the external world.

4.2.Applied Reflections on *Tacet Sui* (Silent Self)

In this section, some philosophical debates relevant to the concept of the soundless self will be explored. How does silence function within the framework of the soundless self? To address this question, we must consider what differentiates soundless interaction from conversation. While communication and interaction are related, the soundless self can be considered a unique domain of communication. The soundless self is more closely linked to interaction, whereas conversation is more aligned with verbal communication. We rely on communication to socialize and connect with others, which can evoke various states of being, such as peace, joy, or conflict. As Stegmaier notes, "In the medium of language, you can create a shared community; at first, it is only the medium you share with others" (Stegmaier, 2019, pp. 114).

Although words and signs can be powerful tools in communication, soundless communication possesses a profound strength of its own. Meditative practices serve as a strong example of the relationship between silence and the soundless self. As previously mentioned, Eastern practices can help expand our understanding of silence in relation to the soundless self. In Zen Buddhism, specific rituals guide individuals into a state of mindful isolation from the distractions of the outside world, desires, and pleasures. These meditative and silent practices open new avenues for self-discovery.

I refer to this process as "tacet sui," which I propose as a third primary form of communication, following i) the listening self and ii) the performative self, which have been discussed earlier. *Tacet sui* is inherently connected to Zen Buddhism. To create a bridge between communication studies and Eastern philosophical thought, we can link *tacet sui* to Zen Buddhism, which emphasizes meditative practices and rituals aimed at purifying consciousness through silence. Silence operates in relation to sound, raising questions about how silence functions within sound and how we find balance between the two in human thought and consciousness. We can also consider whether animals and plants communicate and interact with each other and the external world. Some research in the natural sciences suggests that plants and animals have ways of communication, though not in the same manner as humans. Understanding the differences in communication among animals, plants, and humans requires us to reflect on the nature of thinking. This discussion aligns with Arendt's ideas about how communication and thinking are interwoven with speech.

However, the thinking process associated with human interaction changes when we consider the soundless self, and this is where Zen Buddhism plays a crucial role in deepening our understanding of the concept. Zen Buddhism is a discipline rooted in the constant pursuit of mindfulness and a state of being. It encompasses philosophical teachings that originated in Eastern contexts, particularly in India, China, and Japan. Zen Buddhism emphasizes the philosophy of silence, which is also linked to Chan-ism. The Chinese term "Ch'an" (Japanese: Zen) is a phonetic adaptation of the Sanskrit word "Dhyana," typically translated as meditation, contemplation, and mental concentration. For examples of meditation and contemplation, we might recall the painting *The Wanderer Above the Sea of Fog* (1818) by Caspar David Friedrich, or for mental concentration, we can refer to the artwork *Automat*. These examples further illustrate Zen Buddhism and its characteristic features, such as silence. Zen Buddhism relies on teachings passed down through disciples, one notable Chan master being Hui-chung. Buddhist masters have employed various communication techniques to convey the meanings and teachings of Zen Buddhism, with silence being a significant method. However, silence is not isolated from sound; it is a part of our everyday experiences. For instance, while stuck in traffic, we may hear raindrops falling on our car window. Simultaneously, the sounds of honking horns can be distracting. The soothing sound of raindrops can evoke feelings of being alive, peace, and calm, while car horns create disturbance. This illustrates two modes of operating within silence: one occurs "by interference," and the other is "to sound." Zen practitioners highlight these two ways of relating to silence. The horns represent interference, while the raindrops exemplify sound that contributes to inner and outer experiences of silence. Thus, silence and sound are intertwined.

Zen priest and teacher Seiso Paul Cooper (2023) cites the writings of Zen teacher Dainin Katagiri, who authored books titled *Returning to Silence* (1988) and *You Have to Say Something* (1998) Cooper emphasizes that both sound and silence hold significance. Cooper follows the question about silence as a kind of matrix that contains all through psychoanalytical thinking in Zen Buddhism. He elaborates how silence connects all sound. Consciousness has a specific fucntion to understand the way how silence and sound operate. Silence serves as the background while sounds occupy the foreground. (Cooper, 2023) The relationship between sound and silence can be understood as a dual aspect of human perception and experience, both internal and external. One can still find peace and calm amidst sounds by discovering silence within their internal world. Conversely, while some might feel distracted by noise, relinquishing judgment can lead to the discovery of a more peaceful state of being. This concept is at the heart of contemplation.

A great illustration of the dual relationship between silence and sound is found in the movie *Perfect Days* (2023), directed by Wim Wenders. The main character, Hirayama, cleans public toilets in Tokyo and leads a simple life. His routine can be related to Zen Buddhism, as he views daily activities—such as witnessing a crying child or listening to the trees while sitting on a bench—as acts of contemplation.

Hirayama wishes to soothe the crying child who has lost their mother. This dilemma echoes teachings from Zen Buddhism. For example, Ma-tsu, a disciple of Hui-Neng, was once asked, "Why do you say that the very mind is Buddha?" Ma-tsu replied, "I simply want to stop the crying of the children." When the questioner responded, "What if they do stop crying?" Ma-tsu answered, "Then not-mind, not-Buddha" (Nazari, 2015, pp. 6). The tranquility and simplicity that Hirayama experiences can also be connected to the concept of the soundless self, which represents the third principal group of communication. Without using words, Hirayama, the main character of *Perfect Days*, is connected to both his internal and external worlds. His internal perception of life is intertwined with a soundless self that pursues genuine contemplation, even while he cleans public toilets in Tokyo. Hirayama's story aligns with the following statement: "If we let go of judgment, we can experience a balance between silence and sound and feel a sense of ease in just noticing what is happening." (Zen priest and teacher Seiso Paul Cooper, InsightTimerblog, date is not determined).

The concept of a soundless self, or Tacet sui, is deeply interwoven with Zen Buddhism, creating a connection between the fields of communication and philosophy in this discussion. The philosophy of silence is a subset of the philosophy of communication, revealed through the practice of Zen Buddhism or Ch'anism. Silence serves as a means to uncover a soundless self through humane interaction with both the internal and external world, as it represents a path toward enlightenment. Nazari states: "There were Ch'an Masters who used silence to convey the idea of Wu, or the First Principle. It is said, for example, that when Hui-chung (who died in 775) was to debate with another monk, he simply mounted his chair and remained silent. The other monk then said: 'Please propose your thesis so I can argue.' Hui-chung replied: 'I have already proposed my thesis.' The monk asked: 'What is it?' Hui-chung responded: 'I know it is beyond your understanding,' and with that, he left his chair. The thesis Hui-chung proposed was that of silence. Since the First Principle of Wu is beyond verbal expression, remaining silent is the best way to convey it." (Nazari, 2015, pp. 6) Wu carries significant meaning in Chinese philosophical thought, dating back to the third century. It embodies a kind of spirituality and mindfulness, with the Oxford Dictionary defining it as "a Chinese term meaning 'non-being' or 'to lack." Initially, Chinese Buddhists used Wu to translate concepts of 'emptiness' (śūnyatā) from Indian Buddhist thought, but it was later replaced by the term k'ung. Wu can be interpreted as a process of awakening the mind through self-reflection and plays a crucial role in the Chinese philosophical system and Buddhism, linking the concept of the soundless self to silence.

Silence is an essential method for reaching the soundless self, representing the process of selflessness or mental emptiness. Shizuteru Ueda investigates the concept of the selfless self within the context of language. He suggests that the movement of the selfless self toward itself occurs as a liberation from language toward language. Ultimately, he posits, "The selfless, the true self says at this moment: I am myself by not being myself (Ich bin, indem ich nicht ich bin, ich). To gain a better understanding, we now start from the problem of language." (Ueda, 1995, pp.1) One interpretation of Ueda's perspective might be that this movement reflects a transition from words to silence in Zen Buddhism.

Furthermore, the selfless self can also denote a process of unselfing, as described by Murdoch. This concept resonates with the soundless self in communication. Murdoch explores counseling from various angles in *The Sovereignty of Good* (1970) and *Metaphysics as a Guide to Morals* (1993), linking it to the notion of "no-self" (Maden, 2024) in Zen Buddhism or Simone Weil's concept of décréation. (Weil, 1952) Murdoch explains, "a similar counseling, or 'décréation,' to use Simone Weil's vocabulary, involves attending 'without thinking about' it. This is 'good for us.' It emphasizes respect and serves as an exercise in cleansing the mind of selfish preoccupations, as it provides an experience of what truth is like." (Murdoch, 1993, pp. 337) The notions of unselfing or a selfless mind are closely related to the soundless self. The soundless self symbolizes a cleansed mind, free from ego, achieved through contemplation, tranquility, and silence. The earlier examples from art history, film, or daily life illustrate how the soundless self forms a bridge between philosophy and communication, where Eastern and contemporary Western thoughts converge through humane interaction. Two subsets of soundless self or tacet sui deserve attention. First, tacet sui represents a third grouping of principles for humane interaction with both the internal and external worlds, encompassing communication. Second, it emerges through silence and contemplation, devoid of sound, where the true self or unselfing exists. These two subsets of the soundless self—relating to humane interaction and the true self—contribute to communication through i) the listening self and ii) the performative self articulated earlier.

CONCLUDING REMARKS

In this essay, I present the concept of the soundless self as a critical framework for understanding communication. By synthesizing the philosophies of Jean-Jacques Rousseau and Hannah Arendt, I aim to illuminate their shared inquiries into the complex nature of selfhood and relationality—a theme that resonates throughout their respective works. Rousseau's insights on communication are most prominently articulated in his seminal texts, *Émile, or Treatise on Education* and *Reveries of the Solitary Walker*. These works, while distinct, offer complementary perspectives on the communicative process, allowing for a nuanced classification of the diverse voices that permeate both listening and educational paradigms. In particular, the interpretations offered by Laverty on Rousseau prove invaluable, reformulating his ideas in ways that enrich contemporary discourse on these themes. In *Reveries of the Solitary Walker*, Rousseau engages profoundly with the interplay between inner reflection and the external world, leading to a significant exploration of the fundamental principle of communication: the significance of self-listening. This introspective dimension draws heavily upon Charles Taylor's philosophical explorations of authenticity.

Taylor proposes that the listening self approaches a more genuine state of being through authentic dialogue and humane interaction with others. Such contributions underscore the importance of internal dialogue, emphasizing that it is through self-reflection that individuals can achieve personal realization and deeper understanding of their place within a broader social context. Shifting the focus, the second part of this discussion examines Hannah Arendt's *The Human Condition*, which serves as an essential foundation for scrutinizing the intricate connections between thought, speech, and the broader spectrum of communication. In her work, Arendt asserts that speech transcends being merely a communicative act; it is, in fact, an essential mechanism for self-disclosure, a concept I term the performative self. This depiction constitutes the second principle of communication, emphasizing that our verbal expressions reveal not just information but also layers of identity and intention. Furthermore, the theoretical scaffolding offered by Niklas Luhmann regarding observation—particularly his notion of second-order observation—illuminates the dynamics inherent in interpersonal communication.

Arendt's analysis of the Eichmann trials serves as a profound example that illustrates the banality of evil while offering critical insights into the ethical dimensions of communicative practices. Through this lens, we grasp not only what is spoken but also the moral weight of our speech. The third principle of communication, introduced through Eastern philosophical traditions, particularly Zen Buddhism, is encapsulated in the notion of the soundless self, or *tacet sui*. This construct emphasizes the often-overlooked relationship between philosophical contemplation and effective communication, positing that silence can facilitate deeper, more humane interactions. Through *tacet sui*, we encounter the selfless self, which emerges from practices of contemplation, tranquility, and silence. Everyday experiences, such as quietly gazing into a mirror, hiking through nature, or simply observing the contours of one's private space, exemplify this principle and highlight the richness inherent in non-verbal awareness. Art history provides compelling illustrations of the soundless self; for instance, Caspar David Friedrich's *The Wanderer Above the Sea of Fog* captures themes of solitude and introspection, which are characteristic of Romanticism, while Edward Hopper's painting *Automat* poignantly conveys a sense of isolation in modernity. These artworks invite us to reflect on how moments of contemplation can serve as gateways to a more profound understanding of the self.

Additionally, the character of Hirayama in the film *Perfect Days*, who finds solace in quietly observing trees from a bench, embodies this principle by illustrating how serene moments can lead to profound insights and self-revelation.

Ultimately, *tacet sui* functions not only as a conduit for humane interaction but also as a transformative process through which the self is elucidated and redefined via selflessness and silence. This exploration invites broader contemplation on how we can cultivate meaningful relationships and more profound understandings of ourselves within an increasingly noisy and fast-paced world. In a society where voice surrounds us, the ontological aspects of soundless speech are often overlooked. However, this does not diminish the significance of the listening self and the performative self, as both remain substantive principles of communication. One of the motivation of this chapter has been to demonstrate that these three principles, including the concept of *tacet sui*, possess an organic structure, operating spontaneously within the rhythm of our daily lives and interactions. Moreover, this investigation underscores the critical importance of establishing a solid philosophical foundation for future communication research—one that transcends the limits of mainstream communication theorists. In this vein, philosophers such as Charles Taylor, Werner Stegmaier, Paul J. D'Ambrosio, and Hans-Georg Moeller have been woven into the discussion. Their insights concerning authenticity, selfhood, and communication serve to bolster the central motivation of this paper: to explore the intricate nature of communication from a deeply philosophical perspective. One of the humble aspects of this investigation is this: Through this synthesis, we can better understand the essential dynamics of how we communicate, relate, and ultimately, connect with both ourselves and others in meaningful ways. By combining Western and Eastern philosophy, subject matters in communication can be interpreted within different angles and new insights.

REFERENCES

Arendt, H. (1963). *Eichmann in Jerusalem: A Report on the Banality of Evil.* Viking Press.

Arendt, H. (1998). *The Human Condition.* University of Chicago Press. DOI: 10.7208/chicago/9780226924571.001.0001

Cooper, S. P. (2023). *Psychoanalysis and Zen Buddhism: A Realizational Perspective.* Routledge. DOI: 10.4324/9781003289821

Cooper, S. P. (1988). "Zen's Two Silences." *InsightTimer Blog.* https://insighttimer.com/blog/zens-two-silences

Dauenhauer, B. P. (1980). *Silence: The Phenomenon and Its Ontological Significance.* Indiana University Press.

English, A., & Stengel, B. (2010). Exploring fear: Rousseau, Dewey, and Freire on fear and learning. *Educational Theory, 60*(5), 521–542. DOI: 10.1111/j.1741-5446.2010.00375.x

Friedrich, C. D. (1818). *The Wanderer Above the Sea of Fog.* Oil Painting.

Habermas, J. (1977). Hannah Arendt's Communications Concept of Power. *Social Research, 44*(1), 3–24. https://insighttimer.com/blog/zens-two-silences/

Hopper.E. (1972). "Automat." Oil painting.

Kant, I., & Bernard, J. H. (1914). *Kant's Critique of judgement* (2nd ed., rev). Macmillan.

Laverty, M. J. (2011). Can you hear me now? Jean-Jacques Rousseau on listening education. *Educational Theory, 61*(2), 155–169. DOI: 10.1111/j.1741-5446.2011.00397.x

Luhmann, N. (2012). *Introduction to Systems Theory.* Polity Press.

Maden, J. (2024). Iris Murdoch: "Unselfing" is Crucial for Living a Good Life". *Philosophy Break.* https://philosophybreak.com/articles/iris-murdoch-unselfing-is-crucial-for-living-a-good-life/. Access: 10.02.2025.

D'Ambrosio. (2023). *"Orientation to Profiles: Identity in a Digitized World." How Does the Digitization of Our World Change Our Orientation.R.G. Mueller& W.Stegmaier (edt).* Orientation Press.

Moskalewicz, M. (2024). *Hannah Arendt's Ambiguous Storytelling. Temporality, Judgment and the Philosophy of History*. Bloomsbury.

Murdoch, I. (1993). *Metaphysics as a Guide to Morals*. Allen Lane, Penguin Press.

Nazari, M. (2015). "Zen Buddhism." *Philosophy of Religion*. https://www.academia.edu/19495154/Zen_Buddhism

Picard, M. (1952).*The World of Silence*. H.Regnery. Original from University of California.

Rousseau, J. J. (1918). Émile or Treatise on Education. (W.H.Payne,Trans) New York and London. D.Appleton Company.

Rousseau, J. J. (1979). *Emile: Or, On Education* (Bloom, A., Trans.). Basic Books.

Rousseau, J. J. (1992). *The Reveries of the Solitary Walker* (Charles, E., Trans.). Hackett Publishing Company., https://www.scribd.com/document/555838753/Rousseau-Reveries-of-the-Solitary-Walker-Butterworth

Stegmaier, W. (2019). *What is Orientation:A Philosophical Investigation* (Mueller, R. G., Trans.). De Gruyter. DOI: 10.1515/9783110575149

Taylor, C. (2007). *A Secular Age*. Harvard University Press.

Ueda, S. (1995). Silence and Words in Zen Buddhism. *Diogenes*, *43*(170), 1–21. DOI: 10.1177/039219219504317001

Wardley, K. J. (2010). "Learning to be silent: theological and philosophical reflections on silence and transcendence." *Culture and Transcendence: Shifting Religion and Spirituality in Philosophy Theology, Art and Politics*. VU Amsterdam, 28-29th October, pp.1-23.

Weil, S. (1952). *The need for roots: prelude to a declaration of duties towards mankind*. Routledge.

Wenders, W. (2023). *Perfect Days*. Master Mind Limited and Spoon Inc.

Wittgenstein, L. (1961). *Tractatus logico-philosophicus*. (D.F.Pears-B.F.McGuinness, Çev.). London: Routledge-Kegan Paul. "Wu". *Oxford Reference*. https://www.oxfordreference.com/display/10.1093/oi/authority.20110803125126659.Access: 15.02.2025.

Chapter 8

An Essay on Digital Storytelling in the Art of Refik Anadol

Nazan Alioğlu
https://orcid.org/0000-0002-5143-0348
Istanbul Beykent University, Turkey

ABSTRACT

In this article, digital storytelling will be interpreted through the works of Refik Anadol, which are mainly "Machine Hallucination" (2019), Machine Memories (2021) and other works when necessary, in which he transforms machine learning into stories with algorithms, by relating it to technological determinism and Marshall McLuhan's motto "the medium is the message". As a philosophical essay on generative art, the article will analyze Refik Anadol's art in the context of concepts such as digital culture, digital storytelling, generative art, artificial intelligence and its aesthetics, technological sublime, technological determinism, using a qualitative method based on descriptive narration through the mentioned works.

INTRODUCTION

The empire of man in this world has always been intertwined with the empire of technology. Technological artifacts have been transformed along with human brainpower (Shinkle, 2013). The first information technology realized by humans in this direction is stories. Since the Stone Age, people have been connected to each other through stories and intersubjective realities. In other words, people's identities are

DOI: 10.4018/979-8-3373-2023-6.ch008

determined by stories, and today artificial intelligence is almost better at developing stories than most humans.

The invention of artificial intelligence is potentially more important than the invention of the telegraph and the printing press, or even the invention of writing, because it is the first technology that can make its own decisions and generate its own thoughts. Digital storytelling with artificial intelligence algorithms is, in the broadest sense, the creation of short, personal narratives that combine image, sound and content on a computer-based system. Digital storytelling came into circulation in the late 1980s when digital technologies became cheap and easy to use, allowing people to easily produce digital stories. Digital stories were first defined as still or moving images, short, personal stories created using simple digital video editing software.

The interaction with new digital systems through networked computers has paved the way for the development of human knowledge, which has accelerated social change in all areas, including cultural, political, and economic. This process of change has also affected art. Generative art, an important part of digital storytelling, with its latest version constantly changing depending on the technology used in the historical process, reshapes the concept of art and highlights the technological aspects of contemporary art production, exhibition and consumption. Every work of art is different and special, but in generative art, which started with computer scientists and means the system producing artworks, the system works and the results are unpredictable. In other words, in generative art, the final shape of the work is given automatically by the machine without the influence of the artist.

Many recent generative practices take place in contemporary technology-based cultural production areas such as design, cinema, and music, without falling within the scope of elitist art. Again, many artists work in different fields and contexts such as science, technology, and social sciences, which makes it inadequate to look at generative art only from the perspective of classical art. Initially, the art community showed less interest in generative art, which was between art, technology, and popular culture. However, today, the use of algorithms in generative art has become decisive, opening up a new area of artistic and aesthetic expression to the mainstream art world and making it a part of contemporary art.

The art of the digital age, in which the traces left on the digital network are processed as data, is influenced by the scientific developments, technological features and socio-political structure of the cultural environment in which it is located; it presents a "post-digital" tendency that changes the perception of reality and is a continuation of the digital age in which human-machine interaction intertwines in a way that pushes the boundaries. In this process, all traditional media have been recontextualized. Artists can now use computers to create, store, modify, transfer, exhibit and reproduce their works much more easily than in the past. Artistic production based on computer technology refers to the idea that the medium is the message by Marshall McLuhan, who was both the first thinker to consider the media in terms of its power to shape humanity and the first thinker to state that modern societies will be shaped by media technologies with his medium theory and that the media has a strong influence on societies.

The projects of world-renowned artist Refik Anadol, who performs generative art as an important sub-branch of contemporary art, offers new perspectives on data storytelling and machine intelligence, and creates digital art projects by formulating these perspectives within an aesthetic framework, will be discussed within the scope of the article, in terms of philosophical issues such as the characteristics of the data used, the techniques and technologies used in data processing, the characteristics of his works, the cooperation between machine intelligence and human creativity, the interaction between the viewer and the work of art, the technological sublime as an aesthetic experience provided through the work, the transformation caused by artificial intelligence algorithms in art, and the aesthetic connection of algorithmic art with the postmodern era. The article will be a philosophical essay on generative art and aesthetics through digital storytelling in Refik Anadol's art.

From this point of view, the article will interpret the phenomenon of storytelling, which has a long history, in its current version as digital storytelling, in relation to technological determinism and Marshall McLuhan's motto ‘the medium is the message’, through Refik Anadol's works, mainly ‘Machine Hallucination’ (2019), ‘Machine Memories’ (2021) and other works, where Refik Anadol transforms machine learning into narrative/story with algorithms. In this direction, as a philosophical essay on generative art, the article will analyse Refik Anadol's art within the framework of concepts such as digital-post digital culture and digital storytelling, generative art, data art, artificial intelligence and its aesthetics, technological sublime, technological determinism, within the scope of the mentioned works with a qualitative method based on descriptive narrative.

In this study, the existence of some problems that arise in the encounter between computer technologies and art will be discussed within the scope of the titles of storytelling in post-digital culture, generative art: the system's production of works/stories, generative art and creativity, generative art and aesthetics, generative art and technological sublime, technological determinism and technological aesthetics, and the art and aesthetics of Refik Anadol as a digital storyteller.

Storytelling in Post Digital Culture

Each era is reshaped under the influence of its own cultural characteristics, and thought systems and perceptions change from individuals to societies. It is computer technologies that shape the cultural climate of the digital age and the dominance of algorithms, especially in today's post-digital culture where human and machine interaction is intertwined. Although the prefix "post" means "after/after", the concept of post digital does not mean after the digital age, but rather its continuation and beyond (Güney & Uysal, 2021). From this perspective, more and more examples of "generative art" created through digital technologies can be found on the internet, in galleries, art fairs, biannels and museums.

In the digital age, where the traces left by users on the digital network are processed as data, culture and ways of perceiving the world are directed and managed by states and companies with the information produced from the mass of data. The art of algorithms as the new storytelling is realized through the interpretation of big data by algorithms. An algorithm, in its simplest definition, is a set of detailed and complementary instructions for solving a problem or carrying out a task. In other words, it is the mathematical or geometric expression of the propositions that define the execution of the process. Therefore, numbers drive algorithms. The concept of "Algorismus" is the Indo-Arabic way of calculating numbers" and the term 'algorithm' is derived from the name of the 9th century mathematician Muhammad bin Musa al-Khwarizmi. The first algorithms date back to ancient Greece, the birth of mathematics (Artun, 2021).

Considering that humans are reasoning, calculating creatures, all contemporary life is algorithmic in a sense. In the digital age, social life is governed by algorithms. Google, which indexes information, is the source of all kinds of information and directs and manages thoughts and interpersonal relations. Algorithms and computability are literally the foundation of post-digital culture. Algorithms control and manage the world of finance-industry-trade, wars, as well as the world of communication and culture-art (Artun, 2021).

Algorithms are fed by data. The more and more detailed the data, the stronger the power of the algorithms. That is why one of the most influential research fields of our time is data science. Today, data science drives decision-making processes in almost every component of modern societies. As a result, people's ideologies, biologies, psychologies, psychologies, physiologies, neurologies, etc. are reduced to data, translated into numbers and handed over to algorithms in order to control and direct their behavior as much as possible. In order to deepen their surveillance and control networks, governments and companies such as Facebook, Amazon, Google, Microsoft have embarked on a massive data collection race in order to take our existence in their hands and increase their data-based capital and profits (Artun, 2021).

While post-digital culture is shaped with the support of science, technology and ideology, it creates the perception that artificial intelligence technologies can imitate the human brain, its ability to establish context and consciousness. This way of thinking, which is designed to take place between man and machine, has also infiltrated the field of art, restructuring its definition, form and content, and the identity of the artist. In an environment dominated by digital culture, artworks with various classifications such as computation-based, process-oriented, participatory, collaborative, performance-based, video, digital installation are created with new media technologies with interdisciplinary approaches. In the post-digital process, artificial intelligence technologies such as machine learning, data learning, algorithm-based deep learning are used as "tools" in the artistic production process, and sometimes these tools have evolved into a "content creator" (Güney & Uysal, 2021).

The main starting point of artificial intelligence is related to computer automation. Today, the role of artificial intelligence in culture and art is very important. The aim of the original artificial intelligence design in the 1950s and 1960s was to train the computer to perform given tasks. In this way, the computer would be able to do many things that the brain can do, such as recognizing images, playing chess, and solving equations. (Manovich, 2018). With the increasing use of artificial intelligence in cultural and artistic production, the concept of artificial intelligence itself has continued to evolve and change. In this process, artificial intelligence shapes daily life, behaviors and automates aesthetic-artistic creations and preferences. All relationships between human communities are shaped by stories, because all identities that people belong to are defined by stories themselves. Today, artificial intelligence is becoming better storytellers than most humans, and stories are created digitally through AI algorithms and big data.

Harari (2024) uses the term computer to refer to software and hardware that have a physical existence. Computers are material, consume energy and have volume. A huge amount of electricity, fuel, water, soil, precious minerals, countless resources are used to produce and operate computers. For software, he uses the term "algorithm", but algorithms also run on a computer. "Artificial intelligence" emphasizes the ability of algorithms to learn and transform themselves. He states that artificial intelligence is compared to human intelligence, but that artificial intelligence is not progressing towards human-level intelligence, but is developing a completely different type of intelligence. The most important difference between artificial intelligence technology and telegraph, writing or other technologies is that artificial intelligence is the first technology that can make decisions and generate its own thoughts on its own.

Digital storytelling is the creation of personal narratives that combine images, sound, and content in a multimedia computer-based environment. Digital stories can be briefly defined as "participatory and immersive experiences". Digital storytelling is often associated with short autobiographical multimedia narratives produced during collaborative workshops, a methodology developed for digital storytelling at the University of California (High, 2010).

On the scale of popular culture or mass culture, digital storytelling started in the 1980s as a democratic entity that encouraged production and a medium for people to publish their personal stories, as mentioned above. At that time, digital technologies were easy to use and inexpensive, and even with a little training, people could easily create multimedia digital stories. Digital stories were initially referred to as short, personal stories that included still or moving images, words and text, created using simple digital video editing software. Again, in popular usage, digital storytelling refers to the sharing of individually created stories in a way that can be published on the internet, so that people anywhere can broadcast to people all over the world. In this direction, digital storytelling has become extremely widespread due to the decreasing cost and increasing power of multimedia authoring tools and has become an important part of digital and post-digital culture. At this point, digital storytelling has become a mode of engagement in which individuals create, publish, share, respond, criticize, and engage in other interactive activities.

In fact, to put it briefly, digital storytelling has moved beyond its importance in education, computer game narratives and its popular, widespread use, and has been enthusiastically welcomed in the artistic context as a term referring to various forms of narrative presentation directed by artists using multimedia and the internet, that is, through computer technologies (High, 2010). However, in the context of the subject matter that the article addresses and discusses, the following chapters will focus on new generation digital storytelling within the framework of generative art, which is one of the main sub-branches of art: can a machine make artistic production, can there be an aesthetic understanding valid for all humans, what are the innovations that the computer has brought to the history of art? to what extent can generative art be mimetic, what is the place of randomness in generative art, how should the concept of creativity be contextualized in computational generative art, what are the criteria of beauty in generative art, what does generative art teach about art (McCormack et. al., 2014).

Generative Art: The System's Production of Work/Story

There are many names that may cause confusion about making art through computer technology or classifying and naming this kind of art. Although this new form of artistic expression is called new media art, network art, data art, algorithm art, generative art, cyber arts, digital art, etc., what is common and necessary in all of them is the presence of computer and information technologies. Today, however, the term 'digital art' is more commonly used in relation to computer-based visual practices than other terms (Crowther, 2008). In this article, the theme of digital storytelling in the field of art will be discussed in the context of Refik Anadol's works through the concept of generative art. However, before moving on to the topic of generative art, it would be useful to briefly touch upon the concept of digital art, considering the concept's reference to computer technology.

"Since the 20th century, with the further development of technology and digital transformation, human life has changed and every field related to it has been deeply affected. This situation, which is also observed in the field of art and design, emerges as the digitalization of art, that is, digital art. Digital art is a form of art in which non-physical works are produced with computer support" (Doğan, Ersöz & Şahin). Digital art is realized with electronic-based technology that works with mathematical algorithms. In other words, digital art is a sub-branch of art created based on algorithms (Crowther, 2008). The most important factor that distinguishes digital art from traditional artistic experience is that it is open to interaction. The viewer is active in the reception and interpretation of traditional artworks. The viewer is not allowed to interact with the work of art in a way to reorganize it. Some avant-garde art movements such as Dadaism, surrealism and conceptual art are open to interactivity, but it is not common. When it comes to interactivity, the situation is different in digital art or visuals. The viewer of digital visuals is not a passive viewer, but is active in the production of the work, even in its recreation over and over again. The reason why the viewer is active in digital visuals is that the software, by its very nature, allows them to modify or improve the visuals. The defining feature that differentiates digital art from traditional visual arts is the use of algorithms to create autonomous digital works. This has led to the development of many different styles of artistic expression (Crowther, 2008). This emphasis on the contribution of algorithms to artistic production paves the way to generative art.

As a style of artistic production within the scope of new media art, generative art refers to the technology used in the creation of the work. On the other hand, from the cave art of thousands of years ago to the fractal works realized with coding through today's digital technologies, to the artistic productions created with artificial intelligence, machine learning and deep learning algorithms, each period has made artistic production with its own technology. Generative art, which can be classified as a subset of art, is a form of artistic production in which the artist contributes to the creation of the work by using a computer program, software, a machine or a system that acts autonomously to some extent. In other words, the artist designs a system that is partially or completely autonomous, that is, self-generating. This system design is created by hand, with instructions, codes, software or algorithms. While the works produced by hand and with instructions are associated with the artist's personal talent and skill, the works structured with algorithms produce unique and countless variations within the limits defined by the designer. From this point of view, it becomes clear that generative art cannot be limited to the technology of a certain period and is as old as art (Güney & Uysal, 2021). While artists and tools can be clearly separated in traditional visual arts, in the context of the interactive symbiosis between humans and machines, generative art in its latest version has eliminated these boundaries. In fact, the machine, that is, the tool, has almost put its signature on the work, has become the determinant of the work, and has overtaken the artist.

In the 21st century, with an interdisciplinary approach in the collaboration of science, technology and art, generative art productions, which started with computer engineers and emphasized the ability to use technology, in the context of projects that combine real and virtual experiences, have moved from computer laboratories to art institutions and then to professional design agencies and commercial production studios. Studios such as Field in London, Studio Wrigler and Waltz Binaire in Berlin, Nervous System in New York and Refik Anadol Studio in Los Angeles are design studios that use artificial intelligence, traditional and digital environments, and combine digital and physical realities with human and autonomous system interactions (Güney & Uysal, 2021).

It will be useful to briefly present the development of generative art in a historical context in order to make sense of storytelling with technology. In early generative works using new media technologies, small-scale fractal structures could be created on the computer based on mathematical equations and repetition of simple geometric forms. In this sense, the use of computers for artistic purposes is based on early programmable computers. The Z3 computer, produced by Konrad Zuse in 1941, is considered the first programmable computer (García & Whittinghill, 2011).

Later, Aldo Giorgini, who made computer-based art, made art by blending mathematical models, computer graphics and landscape thanks to his scientific studies as a civil engineer. As both an artist and a scientist, Giorgini brought techniques that provided a new aesthetic understanding to digital arts (García & Whittinghill, 2011).

Like Aldo Giorgini, Georg Nees worked as an industrial mathematician at Siemens for many years, both as an artist and scientist, and his academic background in mathematics paved the way for him to create computer programs. While working at Siemens, Nees used randomness to create computer graphics. In 1965, he became the first generative computer graphics artist. Georg Nees combined mathematics, physics and philosophy with computer art. He completed his doctorate in philosophy as a student of Max Bense at the University of Stuttgart. Bense's main aim, which came to the fore in the context of information aesthetics, was to combine philosophy and mathematics in a way that would complement each other. For Nees, who was influenced by his teacher's information aesthetics, objective reality lay at the basis of things such as language, beauty, aesthetics and psychology. (AB 101: Historical Figures in Generative Art - Georg Nees, 2021).

Like Georg Nees' career at Siemens, Herbert W. Franke's career as a pioneer of early computer art began with experimental photography at Siemens. While lecturing on cybernetics, aesthetics and computer art, he continued to develop his work on experimental aesthetics (AB 101: Historical Figures in Generative Art - Herbert W.

Franke, 2022). Again, in the context of generative art in the 1960s, A. Michael Noll is among the pioneers of computer-based digital art. (AB 101: Historical Figures in Generative Art - A. Michael Noll, 2022).

Based on these examples, which can be further multiplied, it is observed that the performers of computer-based artistic practice have appeared with the identity of scientist-artist since their early periods. In the early examples that found machines incredible, these pioneering names realized their artistic productions by combining disciplines such as mathematics, physics, engineering, computer, software, programming, philosophy with the help of coincidence. These scientist-artists started their artistic journey by being influenced by the machine's ability to produce visuals, that is, technology-mediated visual production. Today, in a collective production process, artistic production is realized in studios such as Refik Anadol Studio, which consists of teams from different disciplines.

In sum, in the field of generative art, which is a part of contemporary art production, each work of art is different and unique, yet it is produced automatically, almost without human intervention. In generative art, which means that the system produces artworks, the system works and the results are unpredictable. It is always possible to innovate in the field of visual arts, but the continuous development of digital arts in our age should be evaluated in relation to more traditional visual art styles. Because despite the exaggerated claims made for digital art, this type of digital art will never replace old artistic production styles. The digital "aura" of generative art has its own unique atmosphere or power of influence; however, humans have a body and will always need to touch, to rediscover something of their own identity through the beauties of individual physical presence. Drawing, painting and sculpture, namely traditional artistic production styles, have always been interested in responding to these needs and will certainly not give up on this task (Lavander, 2010, p.170).

Art is traditionally a creative process full of unknowns specific to the artist. Making art is a special expression of the artist's talent and vision of the planet in which he lives. In this context, the increasing number of artists adopting and preferring generative methods can be interpreted as an indicator of the powerful impact of technology on art and creativity.

Generative Art and Creativity

When it comes to the concept of creativity in digital storytelling, what can generative art or computational generative art tell us about creativity? Creativity is always desirable. Brains, societies and evolution are creative, but how do all of these things produce new, surprising and valuable works and ideas? Creativity can be divided into two: creativity, where different elements are combined to form new structures, and creativity, where new symbolic structures emerge from nothing. The first type of creativity is carried out by generative systems, because symbolic structures with new meanings are created by a self-executing program. Perhaps the most exciting question of our time is whether storytelling machines (algorithms) can be creative. Of course, computers have played a role in creating a work of art, a new idea, and many other things, but how much of the creativity belongs to the program and how much to the programmer? (McCormack et. al., 2014) is still a question that has not been answered clearly.

These early computers, which were run by writing a program, were developed as tools for mathematical, logical, and scientific purposes. However, researchers such as Georg Nees, who is described in the article as one of the pioneers of generative art, saw the potential of these machines for more than just printing graphs and charts. Nees explained his early understanding of algorithmic art as follows: "The great attraction for me was to represent, for once, not something technical with this machine, but rather something 'useless'—geometric patterns" (Xu, 2020). With geometric algorithms, programmers were able to draw complex patterns with lines as an experimental form of creativity. Thus, plotter printing created a unique style of art that could be achieved by people who had more technical skill than manual dexterity and who would not otherwise be considered artists in the traditional sense (Xu, 2020). Similarly, today, the term algorithmic art mainly describes works of art produced by computers.

To emphasize again, from the 1960s and even earlier to the present day, computer engineers and software developers have believed that machines are creative. Accordingly, the human brain is similar to a computer, and a computer is similar to a human brain. The brain's operating system is similar to that of a computer, and artificial intelligence has been created using the brain as a model. Both store information and activate this information through algorithms. In fact, such ideas go back to the philosophies of Thomas Hobbes (1588-1679) and La Mettrie (1709-1751), who argued that humans are machines, and even earlier, to Democritus (460-370 BC) (Artun, 2021).

Deep Dream, one of the first software used in the analysis and classification of visual data that works with big data, was created by Aleksander Mordvintsev in 2015. The algorithms of "Google engineer" Mordvintsev classify millions of images and create patterns between them, and these algorithms create a new set of cats and dogs, for example, from the cat and dog data loaded into the system. Of course, the important point here is that the machine does not see cats and dogs like humans. The machine operates with a set of numbers. In other words, it digitizes the data. In other words, numbers actually create algorithmic art. The DeepDream software has proven that machines offer a new way of seeing by creating images that abstract reality in ways that humans cannot think of (Ferenczi, 2024). Mordvintsev and Deep

Dream later became known for hallucinations. This spread so much that in 2017, a "Hallucination Machine" was built at the University of Sussex. Another "algorithmic structure" widely used to produce images is GANs, which Refik Anadol also uses. GANs were developed by Goodfellow and his team in 2014, who started working at Google. They work by having two neural networks compete or compete with each other to produce new artificial data (Artun, 2021). Artists such as Nathalie Miebach, Moritz Stefaner, Paolo Cirio, Aaron Koblin, Ryoji Ikeda or studios such as Ouchhh work with artificial intelligence and data. Today, for example, thanks to programs such as GAN, invented by Ian Goodfellow and his colleagues in 2014, it is possible to make sculptures of any dataset, from tweets about a city to landscape photos on social media (Yılmaz, 2021).

After Deep Dream and GANs, new algorithms such as Elgammal's CANs, which claim to create art that transcends art history, Colton's emotional portrait painter The Painting Fool, Cohen's AARON, and Philip Isola's Pix2Pix have continued to be developed. In fact, new algorithms are being added to these algorithms day by day. International competitions, which are becoming increasingly common, play an important role in the development of new algorithms. The Code Jam, which Google has been organizing since 2003, is at the forefront of these competitions. The number of people who registered for this competition in 2020 was 96,000. When the "coding" or "programming" Olympics are added to the competitions, it becomes clearer why Google art and artists are important actors of generative, algorithmic art. At the same time, this situation is effective in terms of Google organizing its own staff (Artun, 2021). Referring to Refik Anadol's relationship with Google in this sense, Artun (2021) critically commented that 'there is no need for special creativity, genius or anything like that to make art with algorithms. But Anadol's skills in entrepreneurship and communication are certainly rare' (para. 9).

It can be said that narratives in which originality and creativity are attributed to deep learning algorithms are produced with the operations performed by the designer/artist with these autonomous systems designed by generative artists who create original works of art using Generative Adversarial Networks (GANs) (Güney & Uysal, 2021, 2021). The same applies to the images produced by Google engineers using the DeepDream neural network and later by others using the same technology. In the DeepDream example, artificial intelligence can create artistically plausible images that refer to the human world because these images can be interpreted as modern art, abstract art, non-figurative art, as seen in the Nees example (Manovich, 2018).

From this point of view, it can be thought that in computational generative art, the creativity dimension is mainly realized in the design phase of the programs and the aesthetic dimension is of secondary importance. The aesthetic dimension depends on the program used and it is not possible to predict where the creation will end up or what the work will look like. According to Crowther (2008), design problems go far beyond questions of mathematical or technological competence and the artist must strive to go beyond what the programs provide and make more fundamental innovations (p. 167).

The question of whether a computer program can create something that it is not programmed for can be answered in two ways. The first is related to knowing all the behavior of any program in advance. The program behavior created by the programmer can sometimes occur in a single executable path, sometimes in multiple executable paths. This makes it impossible for the programmer to completely control the results of all but the simplest programs. The second emphasizes the ability of a program to change itself. This means that computer programs can learn and thus initiate new and potentially creative behaviors (McCormack et. al., 2014). However, many computer engineers are working to make the behavior of neural networks more transparent and to develop methods to control them (Manovich, 2018). On the other hand philosophers such as Anthony O'Hear have argued that machines cannot create works of art because art is "thoroughly based on human experience." Because computer-generated works derive their meaning from the analysis of existing art objects, not from the direct experience of the artist (McCormack et. al., 2014).

We can expand the topic to ask about the role of consciousness in a machine becoming an artist. People often confuse intelligence with consciousness, leading them to conclude that nonconscious beings cannot be intelligent. But intelligence and consciousness are very different things. Intelligence is the ability to achieve goals, such as maximizing user engagement on a social media platform. Consciousness is the ability to experience personal emotions such as pain, pleasure, love, and hate. In humans and other mammals, intelligence and consciousness are generally equal. For example, business executives and engineers rely on their emotions to make decisions, solve problems, and achieve their goals. Computers do not have emotions such as pain, love, or fear.

There are two different artistic perspectives here. If the art object is merely an aesthetically pleasing form, then consciousness seems unnecessary. Many natural and human-designed systems can produce aesthetically appealing patterns and compositions without the need for a mental process. A machine can create an image of some kind from a mass of data by collage, and this image is usually an abstraction and usually has some degree of appeal. But can such systems be considered "artists"? On the other hand, if a social or cultural context is required to perform artistic activity, this probably also requires a conscious intention and action on the part of the artist. Although computers and robots cannot currently socialize as artists or participate in culture, perhaps in the future they will be able to do all these things. But since a computer does not currently have consciousness, it does not know what it is like to be a computer that creates its own art or to be an artist.

Generative systems are relatively simple mechanisms that produce effective results but cannot be compared to the creative systems possessed by humans. Most of these systems operate through the clever use of randomness. Of course, original, creative works can be produced with generative art. So, does creativity reside in the algorithm that gives form to the work or in the artist's intervention? The important point here is to clarify where the creative act is attributed. In generative art, the process is decisive. This points to the advantages and disadvantages of using the process brought about by creative software or programs designed by others in the artist's productive practice.

The understanding of art in the West has undergone a radical transformation from the classical understanding of antiquity to the complex aesthetics of today. During this time, the content of concepts such as "creation," "production," and "reveal" has remained far from being fixed; it has undergone constant change. In short, if the future is to host automatic machines that can participate in society as artists, it is not known what form these will take at present, because it will depend on how technology and art affect people.

Generative Art and Aesthetics

Another problem that arises in the encounter between computer technologies and art is the issue of artificial intelligence and aesthetics. Although measuring aesthetics is a problematic issue since it changes according to taste, time and culture, it is observed that attempts to formalize aesthetics using quantitative measurements or algorithmic techniques are almost as old as the concept of aesthetics itself. Current studies aimed at formalizing aesthetics direct the subject of aesthetics to the Kantian terms of beauty and pleasure. When viewed from the formalist perspective, which is an art historical concept that excludes all elements other than the form of the work, generative art generally emphasizes the aesthetics of the surface that is pleasing. From this, it can be said that as generative art matures, there is a shift from a mimetic, imitation-based style of expression to a non-mimetic style of expression, similar to the emergence of modernism in painting.

Starting in the 1960s, artists, composers, and architects used algorithms to produce images, animations, music, and three-dimensional designs. These works are magnificent examples of aesthetic creativity and sophistication. These works are often abstract compositions with interesting and complex patterns and do not directly refer to reality, in other words, they are formalist (Manovich, 2018).

When it comes to the aesthetic understanding of the artist during the production phase of machine-based digital stories and the emotional impact these stories leave on the recipient/viewer, the post-digital age aesthetics based on technology influence and admiration come to the fore. In the post-digital culture where human and machine interaction are intertwined, machine aesthetics emphasize the concepts of digital elevation, coincidence and chance, erasure, repetition, error aesthetics and glitch aesthetics. If the subject of art is simply an aesthetically appealing form, a multitude of natural and human-designed systems can create interesting and aesthetically pleasing patterns.

Digital technologies are radically transforming artistic production and the reception of art, as they do in every aspect of life. The use of algorithms and artificial intelligence technologies in this area raises questions about the position of the artist as an artistic subject, while also highlighting the possibilities of technological and audience participation. Digital art, which requires the collaboration of various fields of expertise such as engineering, physics and mathematics, complicates the discussion of what art is with its convergent and hybrid appearance and raises new questions about artistic production and aesthetics (Okan & Okan, 2024).

For example, in Refik Anadol's Quantum Memories (2020), which includes audience participation, he uses publicly available quantum computing data and algorithms from Google AI in the creation process where he processes 200 million images of nature and landscapes through artificial intelligence. The resulting product is an aesthetic object. In the project, the movements of the audience are simultaneously tracked by artificial intelligence while the performance takes place. In this way, an interactive aesthetic experience is created in which the audience becomes a part of the performance. This experience brings to mind the questions of who performs the artistic act and what is performed in this act (Okan & Okan, 2024).

It is problematic to measure aesthetic knowledge at any point, which is the domain of sensory, subjective knowledge. Although many theorists argue that it is wrong to even ask this question, attempts to fix aesthetics using quantitative criteria or procedural (algorithmic) techniques have a history almost as old as the concept of aesthetics itself. This situation is most clearly observed in the thought system and works of German cyberneticist and philosopher Max Bense, who is among the influential figures in the history of generative art, and who tried to quantify the aesthetic experience and computerize the creation and evaluation of art. When Max Bense began writing about aesthetics in the 1950s, his aim was to calculate and measure this obvious, non-objective information. While developing his understanding of art and aesthetics, Max Bense was influenced by mathematician George David Birkhoff's concept of aesthetic measurement. In addition, Claude Shannon's information theory and Norbert Wiener's cybernetics, who contributed to the creation of modern computers and conceived of humans as information-processing machines, also had an important place in Bense's theory (Caplan, 2020).

According to German cyberneticist and philosopher Max Bense, who explains the basic mechanisms and principles of beauty and stands out with his studies on quantitatively formalizing aesthetics, the purpose of aesthetic knowledge is to measure the formal innovation of a work, and the subjectivity and vagueness related to aesthetics should be eliminated by mathematical formulas. Bense's understanding of productive art argues that aesthetic experience can not only be measured, but also produced in a rational and predictable way (Caplan, 2020).

Bense's theory proposed a series of formulas for evaluating aesthetic situations by combining irregular or random elements with regular ones. For Bense, artistic production took precedence over the reception of the work; it was indeed a generative theory of art rather than aesthetics. Nees, Bense's doctoral student and a pioneer of generative art, used a simple algorithm to instruct the machine to distribute eight dots, for example, inside a square and connect them with a closed line. This work, called 8-corner (1964), was a composition of simple geometric line drawings. Again, this artistic experiment demonstrated not only the creativity of the algorithms, but also the logical basis for aesthetically balanced forms that were considered beautiful. Bense's generative theory of aesthetics aimed to remove subjectivity and verbal fallacy from art and aesthetic judgment and to bring the transparency of science to aesthetics. In short, Bense aimed to "transform aesthetics, a metaphysical discipline, into a technological discipline" (Caplan, 2020). With its extreme clarity, that is, its formalism and complexity, the digital image emphasizes the high-tech and information aspects characteristic of today's post-digital age.

When the subject of artificial intelligence and aesthetics is addressed from the perspective of the artist, a number of important questions are encountered. These are; who is the artist who created the work, is it a machine or a human? If the work is created jointly by a machine and a human, how will the contribution of these two to the creation of the work be calculated? Who is dominant when the story of the work is created, the artist or the machine? Or is the story the technology used in generative art? When the work is created, does the artist's taste or the taste of the algorithm, neural networks, GANs emerge? What is the impact of technology on aesthetic taste? When algorithms create a collage of data, they cannot collate the data using their senses, emotions, or tastes as a human artist does. Yet, sensuality lies at the core of aesthetic knowledge. Than how will the problem of aesthetic taste be explained in artificial intelligence/algorithm art? How should the problem of taste, which is one of the fundamental problems of classical aesthetics for both the artist and the viewer/receiver, be explained?

When it comes to aesthetic pleasure experienced by both the artist and the viewer/receiver, that is, experienced in different ways by these two parties, what kind of pleasure does the "artist/machine" experience? In addition, making art has a psychological function such as being good for the human soul and repairing the soul. Does a computer have a soul or will it have a soul, will making art be good for the computer's soul as well? What is the purpose of a computer in making art?

Performing art is a conscious act and choice of a person, and under normal circumstances, the work is filtered out of the artist's subjective world of meaning.

Since the aesthetics of chance is mentioned for generative artworks, how should the concept of chance be explained? How does knowledge of what chance is affect the comprehension and interpretation of a work? Chance is often used to "humanize" generative artworks, that is, to give the works the effect of a human/artist touch, to add flaws to the work as in human production. So when questioned by the artist, if the artist is fully in control of the art-making process, why would he resort to chance? (McCormack et. al. 2014). Or is the existence of chance necessary due to the nature of generative art, which requires collaboration with the machine in the formation of composition or content?

Generative work of art "codes" human aesthetic judgments. Although at the end point, a human designer determines the criteria and conditions of the artistic object produced by the machine, is the aim of artistic production with neural network model or deep learning algorithms to exclude humans from the artistic production process and to emphasize the tool/technology? Maybe, understanding the originality of an algorithm allows a better understanding of the content and expression of a generative work, but this is a significant problem for most casual viewers, and the focus is on the surface aesthetics, i.e. the appearance, of the artwork, as is often the case in computational generative art, where the computational process, i.e. the technical side, is rarely directly understood (McCormack et. al., 2014).

In the article, which is mainly a philosophical essay on digital storytelling, important questions on generative art and aesthetics are put forward, while artificial intelligence is observed to be an important actor with a very important role in this new global culture atmosphere. Digital technologies raise big questions about the future of culture. Will such powerful, effective automation lead to a decrease in aesthetic diversity over time? What does this mean for image culture? Does this kind of aesthetic judgment refer to popular culture, popular arts and popular/easy/non-elitist taste? In short, it can be stated that the aesthetic reception of popular and distinguished examples of digital storytelling is realized through both easy taste and the entertaining geometric-abstract narratives of popular formalism.

Generative Art and Technological Sublime

In this section, the relationship between the aesthetic feeling created in the subject by digital storytelling and the feeling of the sublime and what the contemporary technological sublime might mean in the context of contemporary digital technologies will be briefly discussed.

Digitally narrated generative art is an aesthetic form that includes software and hardware. The category of the sublime as an aesthetic emotion is quite complex.

For the Enlightenment, the affect of the sublime was defined as 'negative pleasure', a mixture of positive and negative emotion, pleasure and anxiety. This bipolar interpretation of the sublime is also typical of its contemporary manifestations. In the case of digital storytelling, the affect of the sublime, as a combination of anxiety and boredom, high emotion and ordinariness, is also expressed in an affective complex specific to modernity and postmodernity.

The first thinker to think about the concept of the sublime is Pseudo-Longinus, who is thought to have lived in the 1st century AD. Although his work appeared in the 17th century, the concept of the sublime did not come to the fore until the mid-18th century. According to Longinus, the sublime is an artistic effect. It aims to delight, creates astonishment, enchants, and is superior to what is merely pleasing (Eco, 2006). Kant divided the experience of the sublime into two: mathematical and dynamic. Both sublime experiences occur in the presence of natural objects; the first is related to greatness, the second to power and strength (Tunalı, 2010). In Kant's understanding of aesthetics, sublime greatness is based on force and is grounded in the subject, while N. Hartmann, who emphasizes that technological objects can also be beautiful, is grounded in the object. The sublime is evaluated as a superiority and greatness value found in the object (Tunalı, 2010). In the post-digital age, in other words in today's world, it is difficult to talk about a unity of meaning regarding the concept of the sublime, since it is addressed from different perspectives such as techno-sublime, eco-sublime, gothic-sublime, suburban-sublime in the literature of art and literary theory. The sublime has become fashionable again with postmodern contemporary art; because the sublime is always related to a break from or a differentiation in aesthetics (Cunningham, 2004).

Within the theoretical framework of the sublime, as it manifests itself in the present, are the differences between the "aesthetic" concerns of philosophers and critical theorists and the work of contemporary artists. This is problematic for both philosophers and artists, and gives rise to what Nicolas Bourriard calls "a situation in which artists, happy to make an inventory of yesterday's concerns, regret not receiving an answer" (as cited in Cunningham, 2004).

Since modernity, art is fragmented, open-ended and incomplete, beyond any inherited framework, because it is specifically defined by not being identical with what it has been and opening up to what it could be (Cunningham, 2004). Since Kant, it has carried the experience of the sublime within meanings such as "formless", "boundless", "infinite". Typically, the focus has been on "the sensory achievements of modernist painting from 1850 to 1950", and subsequently its "changes and transformations" after conceptualism have come to the fore (Cunningham, 2004).

The contemporary technological sublime is a different interpretation of the sense of the sublime, particularly as set out in Kant's 1790 Critique of Judgment (Shinkle, 2013). According to Kant, judgments of the sublime do not take into account the functions of objects and arise when the imagination is incapable of fully analyzing certain sense presentations. The sublime, as Kant frames it, is a question of the subject, and the sublime object or situation transcends the limits of comprehension and the senses, just like the aesthetic experience experienced by the aesthetic subject in Refik Anadol's Machine Hallucination. Here, the effect of the technological sublime stems from intelligence or machine intelligence, coding, pure measurement and pure power without human characteristics. The sense of the technological sublime is experienced through machines interacting with human beings.

The technological sublime combined both the mathematical and dynamic registers of its Kantian forebears, while also eliminating some of the subtle distinctions between the two. The sense of the sublime has become identified with heightened emotions such as awe. The visual presentation of awe-inspiring magnitude or complexity has become the most important dimension of the sublime experience (Shinkle, 2013).

In contrast to the Kantian, classical sublime, contemporary sublime formations are associated with the idea and appearance of technology. Technology is therefore placed in the context of the posthuman, a non-organic form of being that has no relation to nature and the natural. The contemporary digital sublime is characterized not only by its relationship to technology, but also by its proximity to an equally powerful twentieth-century type of affect. This type of affect is called banality. Banality is historically and semantically linked to boredom. If boredo is among the symbols of early modernity, characterized by changing patterns of work and leisure, the banal is both an engine and a consequence of post-industrial culture, fueled by the endless cycle of unsatisfied desires. Mediocrity and the banal are ways of satisfying unsatisfied desires (Shinkle, 2013). The sublime and the banal merge in the feeling of 'stupor'. The experience of the contemporary technological sublime depends on merging with an artifact that can be described as 'posthuman' (Shinkle, 2013).

Aesthetic discourse first emerged in the eighteenth century as an investigation into the subject and its sensory world experience. Since Baumgarten, the founder of aesthetics as a philosophical discipline, aesthetics has focused on the knowledge of the sensory (Tunalı, 2010). Aesthetics is a cognitive category that is concerned not only with the formal properties of objects but also with the effects of these objects on the subject. From this point on, contemporary interpretations of generative art have become the primary expression of digital storytelling, while in the aesthetic context, the technological sublime can be linked to electronic entertainment.

In terms of aesthetics, that is, in terms of the emotional impact that the work of art leaves on the recipient/viewer, art made with algorithms or art created by algorithms from a large amount of data that pushes the boundaries of reason can leave an effect of mathematical/technological sublimity that can be considered an interpretation of the modern sublime. An aesthetic experience has emerged where the powerful impact of the medium and the medium on the viewer/receiver comes to the fore through digital storytelling, where the mathematical sublime and the technological sublime are experienced. The fact that viewers who want to experience a digital-techno show consisting of a large budget, a collage of data that exceeds the limits of reason, who want to surrender themselves to the magic of audiovisual effects, form queues in front of the opening exhibitions is important indicator that information aesthetic has evolved into the banal.

Art movements that shared the Bauhaus principle of rationalisation of art were numerous in the early 20th century: Arts and Crafts (London), De Stijl (Amsterdam), purism (Paris), Jugendstil and Bauhaus (Berlin), kinetism (Vienna), constructivism (Moscow). All these movements are formalist and this formalism is based on geometric abstraction. Their aesthetics are based on the admiration for machines, engineering and Taylorism (Artun, 2011). The love of machines that dominates these movements goes to such extremes that the arts are identified with machines. According to Artun (2011), ideal beauty is now identified with machines. The result of this machine admiration is the sanctification of the engineer for designing machines. In short, machine aesthetics is an aesthetic based on geometry, which is the basis of design. Engineers, machines, numbers and forms are the dynamics of the new order both in the power of the working class and the power of the bourgeoisie. Every kind of modernity is geometrical. From now on, the most impressive of revolutions is the scientific and technological revolution.

Technological Determinism and the Aesthetics of Technology

The model known as the information model or mathematical communication model addresses the functioning of communication from a purely technical perspective. It evaluates the flow of information, that is, communication, with numerical measurement. Claude Shannon emphasizes the medium. In this model, the emphasis is on the channel that receives the message from the sender and transmits it to the receiver, that is, the medium, and therefore technology. This model will form the basis of the technological determinism approach that will be developed later, and it is also important in terms of being the first clear emphasis on the medium (Güngör, 2011).

However, Marshall McLuhan is one of the first to take technology as a starting point in evaluating social processes. One of the leading media theorists of technological determinism, Marshall McLuhan's criticism of modern society and his theory are based on his criticisms of mass communication technologies and their historical and social effects. Since his first courses in literary criticism, McLuhan has been interested in the stages of the formation and spread of dominant cultural patterns and the characteristics of the environments in which this culture is transmitted. In this context, McLuhan's statement "the medium is the message", which refers to the medium, emphasizes the effects of new technologies rather than the use of communication tools. McLuhan tried to understand the technological environment created by the electronic age, which would reshape Western history, and the social transformations experienced in this environment, based on the changes caused by writing and then printing technology (Altun, 2006).

In the 1960s, McLuhan defended the view that the medium, not the message or content, was important. The medium was an extension and transformer of the human body, and technological determinism expresses exactly this (Güngör, 2011). "The medium is the message itself" is probably the most famous phrase in the history of media studies. The owner of this saying, Canadian Marshall McLuhan, is the most famous media theorist of all time. What makes him so famous is that he is the first thinker to seriously consider the power of media to shape human history. McLuhan's medium theory indicates that modern societies will be shaped by various media technologies. Accordingly, media or technology has a strong effect on societies. This effect is experienced by the individuals who make up the society in line with their interests and needs (Laughey, 2021). From this perspective, what is important is not the content and quality of media technologies, but the technology itself (Laughey, 2021). For example, taking an action in a network environment for our social media accounts or any other purpose is not important, the medium is important, not the message. Because as McLuhan stated in his book *Understanding Media* (1964), "the message of a medium or technology is a scale, step or attitude change that is embedded in human relations" (as cited in Laughey, 2021). The relevance of the motto 'the medium is the message' to the subject of this study stems from this point of view. The connection of generative art in general, and in the case of Refik Anadol in particular, computer-based, i.e. tool-based digital storytelling with this premise is that it causes a change of scale, step or attitude regarding art and aesthetics. This is reflected in Anadol's own or other people's enthusiastic comments about his works in the press and other media (the prominent theme in the speeches about the works is mostly about the technology in which the works were made, the emphasis on machine creativity, the astonishment created by the use of a mind-boggling amount of data, large-scale production, large-scale public relations and publicity).

McLuhan was much more critical in the early 1950s when he started thinking about technology. In fact, it is even possible to feel the influence of the Frankfurt School's pessimism in his thoughts on technology in his book *The Mechanical Bride* (1951). In the book, he argues that mass media massify society and make people passive. It is observed that the book is influenced by mass culture and, in connection with this, consumer culture ideas. However, after a short period of 10 years, McLuhan's admiration for technology reached its peak and he began to put technology at the center. *The Gutenberg Galaxy* (1962), published in the early 1960s, brought the McLuhan wind to the world. In this book, McLuhan considers the printing press as the beginning of modernization and sees it as the basis of the process of change that has taken place in the world in recent centuries. With the printing press and subsequent industrialization, the world has shrunk, become smaller and turned towards the old village culture (Güngör, 2011).

The world is being transformed into a single cultural marketplace or global village where certain images, ideas, values, narratives, products and styles are marketed to everyone and are available everywhere, reducing diversity (Manovich, 2018). At this point, McLuhan's motto of "the medium is the message", considering the many developments affecting global aesthetic diversity (Manovich, 2018), the role played by cultural artificial intelligence once again highlights the strong popular aesthetic impact of technology. In other words, according to McLuhan, the prophet of media, the personal, political, economic, aesthetic, psychological, moral and social consequences of the media penetrate us to such an extent that it has left us untouched (Artun, 2011).

Claude Shannon, the pioneer of information theory, redefined knowledge to exclude the need for a conscious subject. All languages consist of two basic elements: syntax (the structure or form of the language) and semantics (the content or meaning of the language). Shannon made information purely mathematical – defined by patterns and probabilities – by excluding semantic meaning, which is not amenable to measurement. Information is created when a message is selected from a possible sequence of messages. Shannon stated in 1948 that messages have meaning, but these semantic aspects of communication are outside the scope of engineering (O'Gieblyn, 2023).

Cybernetics, which deals with controlling and designing people's communication with other people and machines, has turned into a cyberculture today. Numbers, letters, signs, images, information, money, commodities, art, emotions circulate in the cyberspace of the internet (Artun, 2011). The "machine human" project that emerged immediately after World War II is related to artificial intelligence. According to Artun (2011), artificial intelligence is a design field that deals with people's cognitive and perceptive skills. In artificial intelligence design, human intelligence and technological intelligence, the individual and the computer are intertwined. However, as Baudrillard said, as a person designs her own reproduction, eventually all her naturalness and humanity will turn into an artifact (Artun, 2011).

In the early studies in the field of cybernetics, Shannon had kept the concept of knowledge independent of the thinking mind. McCulloch, on the other hand, applied the logic of information processing to the mind, paving the way for a model of the mind in which thinking could be explained in a purely abstract, mathematical way. If thinking were just information processing, computers could be said to learn, reason and understand - words that were initially metaphors. But as cybernetics developed and computational analogy was applied to a wide variety of biological and artificial systems, the boundaries of metaphor blurred. It became difficult to distinguish between matter and form, medium and message, metaphor and reality. Even more difficult was to understand aspects of the mind that could not be explained by these metaphors (O'Gieblyn, 2023).

In fact, the semantic or meaning problem, which Shannon, one of the important names in mathematical communication, said did not concern his engineering, is still a problematic and questionable part of artistic digital storytelling. On the other hand, it can be said that Marshall McLuhan, while excluding the meaning/content that is not suitable for measurement on the path opened by the pioneers of cybernetics, brought technology, that is, the tool, to the forefront of the measurable effect.

Refik Anadol establishes a kind of analogy between humans and machines, asking the question "If machines can learn, can they dream?". In fact, Refik Anadol likens the way machines work to the human mind, in other words, he makes a metaphor. Anadol considers human experiences and memories as inputs and dreams and hallucinations as outputs. The process of reinterpreting these inputs corresponds to a learning process for machines as well as for humans. In the context of the examples discussed in the article, Refik Anadol's projects mostly consist of artificial intelligence-based abstract moving or still images and forms that are the result of uncontrolled machine learning, similar to modern abstract art, by processing or, metaphorically speaking, interpreting the uploaded ready-made data with algorithms or neural networks.

All traditional media have been recontextualized. This refers to the idea that the medium is the message, both the first thinker to consider media in its capacity to shape human history and the medium theory of Marshall McLuhan, who stated that modern societies will be shaped by media technologies and that media has a strong effect on societies. Artists can now create, store, change, transmit, exhibit and reproduce their works much more easily than in the past using computers. In fact, when computers and art first met, they brought out the worst in each other. As Negroponte (1995) points out, another problem is that the signature of the machine can be very strong. As is often the case in holographic art and 3-D movies, the intended purpose can override the expression" (Lin, 2005). The signature of the machine or algorithm may override that of the artist, or it may remain a question mark whether the signature belongs to the machine or the artist. Another option in this regard may be the emergence of works with two signatures.

The Art and Aesthetics of Refik Anadol as a Digital Storyteller

Refik Anadol is a Turkish new media artist and designer as a digital storyteller in the post-digital age. In this section, the phenomenon of storytelling, which has a long history, will be interpreted in its current version in the form of digital storytelling, mainly 'Machine Memories' (2021), Machine Hallucination (2019) and other works of Refik Anadol, in which he transforms machine learning into narrative/ story with algorithms.

Refik Anadol's projects consist of data-driven machine learning algorithms that create abstract, colorful environments. His areas of interest include media arts, neuroscience, architecture, machine intelligence, and GAN algorithms. The artist uses a data pool and algorithms when designing and telling the story of his works, and has the algorithms interpret a large amount of data. For this reason, it is not possible to do the same exhibition twice. Many issues such as training the algorithm, what it will forget and remember or learn too much, where it will take the data, how much it will use, how it will show it, and how it will be given in integrity depend on coincidences. Computer technology, artificial intelligence, algorithm emphasis, experience, and coincidence aesthetics are at the forefront in his works. Anadol's answer to the question of the share of coincidence in his works is, in his own words, "There are many. It is not possible to do the same exhibition twice. Where will I take the data, how much will I use it, how will I show it, and how it will be given in integrity. There is a lot of coincidence here" (Akbay, 2021).

New media artist Refik Anadol created the exhibition 'Machine Memories: Space' over the course of five years, based on the question 'Can a machine dream if it learns?' and as a result of his NASA-supported research. The theme of the exhibition is to present the place of space exploration in human history through an artistic perspective. The works in the exhibition consist of more than 2 million space-themed datasets recorded by space telescopes, the largest space-themed dataset ever used in an art installation (Yılmaz, 2021). In his work Machine Hallucinations: Mars Landscapes, Anadol created an example of cognitive cartography using neural networks trained on the 1.5 million-photo archive obtained by the HiRISE telescope of the MRO (Mars Reconnaissance Orbiter). The work is a depiction of a poetic journey in the mind of a machine (Doğan, Ersöz & Şahin, 2022).

Refik Anadol is able to make the artificial intelligence, which has filmed the surface of Mars for 11 years and recorded every point of the planet, dream. In the exhibition, an artificial intelligence that has learned all the colours of the planet, Mars and the Earth will dream. The viewer will experience the technological sublime as an aesthetic feeling while being entertained by this story that exceeds the limits of reason. Refik Anadol has prepared a comprehensive work by visualising NASA's 60-year archives. He was inspired by many science fiction writers and thinkers such as Carl Sagan, who thought about space, or Philip K. Dick and William Gibson. With an anthropomorphic, i.e. human-centred way of thinking, he realised a project that suggests that a machine can also have a memory based on the concept of memories with the question 'Can a machine dream if it learns?', and tells the story of the poetic journey of a machine in space, a dreaming artificial intelligence (Yılmaz, 2021).

Refik Anadol, while defining the storytelling with data about the Machine Memories exhibition, says that data is a language that machines create within themselves and that data is not just a number but also a memory. Artificial intelligence turns into a metaphor for a thinking brush. In other words, at this point, data is not just a boring number, but a thinking brush together with artificial intelligence (Uygur, 2021). Whether these confectionery colorful, fun moving visuals are imagined and designed in advance or randomly emerged as a result of written codes, both situations are possible and emphasize human-machine cooperation in this regard. We have gone through the works of new algorithms that have emerged in the last four months in the exhibition. Refik Anadol, who uses computer technologies in a fun, enjoyable style, has pursued experiences that can create a poetic effect on the audience (Uygur, 2021). There were queues at the door of the Machine Memories: Space exhibition, and the exhibition was met with great interest from visitors (Yılmaz, 2021).

In Refik Anadol's works, numerical data is made accessible to the audience's senses through various software and machine learning techniques, in other words, it is made tangible. In Machine Hallucination (2019), another work by Refik Anadol and his studio, a neural network and various modifications were used to process 300 million photographs and 113 million other raw data consisting of public images of New York City. A specialized algorithm scoured the internet to find images of New York on social media, search engines, digital maps and library sites. Due to data privacy requirements, all photos were taken from publicly accessible areas. Once the images were collected, an image recognition algorithm identified the context of the original images, while another algorithm removed all people, faces, body parts from the images.

After processing a large amount of visual and auditory data, the StyleGAN algorithm is programmed to "dream", that is, to speak back the visual associations it has learned while studying the images. The dream state in Machine Hallucination is abstract; colors and forms come and go in waves and patterns. In Refik Anadol's method, data comes in, memory is formed, dreams come out. In this setup, dreams and memory are not exactly interchangeable, but as millions of processed and stored data, memory directly generates dream images. This reflects the metaphorical nature of the title, as the machine does not have human qualities, i.e. it does not misperceive or hallucinate, but rather processes existing data. Witnessing how computer technologies have enabled software to transcend the limits of storytelling and imagination, Anadol's work visualizes algorithmic processes and their extensions, revealing the enormous potential of machines to process images.

As discussed throughout the article, the issue of art produced by AI raises deep philosophical questions such as the nature of creativity and being human in a digitally networked world. Returning to the subject of art, Refik Anadol defines his own art as collaboration and companionship with machines. Such an art-making practice, which involves the autonomous functioning of the machine or vehicle and has the potential to transcend the artist's individual preferences, can be considered as a kind of partial attempt at "subjectless creativity" (Okan & Okan, 2024).

In general, Refik Anadol's works can be interpreted in the light of the following questions: What is the position of the artist in an age dominated by computer technologies? What does art say about the intertwined virtuality and reality? What does it mean to experience a memory composed of a mass of data in the digital age? If machines can learn, can they also dream? With this perspective, Refik Anadol and his team visualize vast amounts of data and use artificial intelligence software to create their stories. They transform data based on the collective memories of places, nature and cities into multidimensional visual artworks. Data aesthetics based on collective visual and auditory memories, images from nature, space, winds and radar data are materialized and presented to the audience in different ways in different modes of expression such as installations, NFT collections, "AI Data Painting" and "AI Data Sculpture" using tools such as archives, machine learning and neuroscience (Okan & Okan, 2024).

Refik Anadol offers dreams/hallucinations to his viewers by transforming data, which he thinks constitutes collective memory, into images inspired by the dynamics of fluids. As emphasized on the studio's website, he uses algorithms such as DCGAN, PGAN and StyleGAN developed with large data sets to make data the material of his works. For example, for WDCH Dreams (2018), the studio utilized the 100-year digital archive of the Los Angeles Philharmonic Orchestra (Okan & Okan, 2024).

Undoubtedly, Refik Anadol and his art have been criticized from different perspectives. For example, in Lossin (2023), Refik Anadol used the MoMA collection as a dataset, reducing this collection from being an archive of art history and symbol production practices with social meanings to a random pile of visual pieces that can be replaced. The name of the work is "Unattended" and this work represents the control and colonization of the museum as a public space, the usurpation of forms of human creativity, and turns this into an entertaining spectacle.

The visuals are not less valuable because there is no human skill in Refik Anadol's works. The problem is the cultural function of the flashy artificial intelligence to normalize surveillance systems. It transforms computer technologies that have a destructive effect on the environment into something pleasant, even comforting (Lossin, 2023). According to Lossin, technology is not neutral. In order for Refik Anadol to believe that the technology he uses in his craft is neutral, he has to suppress much information that everyone is aware of (2023, para.11). Here, Lossin reminds us that technology cannot be independent and innocent from the dominant ideology, and that is why this context should not be overlooked because Refik Anadol's works are so heavily technology-based that they overshadow the artist, the work, and the content.

It reminds us that this context should not be overlooked because it is fundamental. Like everyone who knows how artificial intelligence works, Anadol is undoubtedly aware that machines cannot dream. However, humans think in metaphors. "All forms of perception are metaphors, in Wittgenstein's words, we never see directly, we always "see as something." Whenever we encounter an object, we immediately compare it to models in our repertoire and try to draw conclusions about what it is like. And after all, one of our oldest and most reliable models is the human being. Anthropologist Stewart Guthrie argues that our anthropomorphic tendency is an evolutionary strategy. All perceptual predictions have consequences in the context of survival; this is evolution's method of positive and negative reinforcement" (O'Gieblyn, 2023).

As O'Gieblyn (2023) points out, as soon as computers appeared, we saw our own image in them or projected our own image onto them. We even saw them as a metaphor for the brain. In the early 1940s, Warren McCulloch and Walter Pitts, the cybernetics experts who came up with the "computational theory of mind", argued that the human mind functions at the neural level in a similar way to the Turing Machine, one of the first digital computers. In 1943, the pair presented for the first time a computational model for an artificial neural network based on the idea that mental functions could be realized by mathematical operations. McCulloch was aware of the flaws of this metaphor. He acknowledged that the fact that the brain processes thought in the same way that electronic computers compute numbers - in other words, that computing is an idealization of the mind - does not reflect physical reality. While machines fulfill many of the characteristics of how the brain works, such as prediction, pattern recognition, solving equations, they do so with commands, algorithms, and no emotional agency. The computer uses only symbols, obeying only commands without understanding the content or the concepts those symbols are intended to represent (O'Gieblyn, 2023). For this reason, many generative artists have recognized that programming a computer to produce something other than what is encoded in the design of the software is difficult but desirable.

Lossin's (2023) interpretation of Refik Anadol's metaphor of dream and hallucination is revealing: Accordingly, it is claimed that a 7-square-meter carbon-dense screensaver on display in MoMA's courtyard "dreams" and discovers hallucinations. The full title of the work referred to above as Unattended reads: "Unattended-Machine Hallucinations-MoMA-Fluid Dreams". The subconscious mobilities mentioned here emerge from a consciousness that consists of publicly available data from MoMA's permanent collection. Contrary to what is stated in the press release and what the viewer assumes, AI does not see images, because artificial intelligence is incapable of sensation. It only knows that Vincent Van Gogh's Starry Night is composed of the colors blue and yellow, just as a calculator knows how to subtract one number from another. Refik Anadol takes this information and combines it with weather data and data collected from devices that monitor the movements of museum-goers without their consent to produce ice cream confections that flow in waves of color (para. 3).

Artificial intelligence-supported digital art or algorithmic art, exemplified by the works of Refik Anadol, has a visuality that is dominated by technology in which it repeats an aesthetic form consisting of visual elements such as abstract, fluid, moving animations, and has a commercial, fascinating appearance. As such, it is subject to criticism that it can be considered as a new, attractive and marketable derivative of abstract expressionism. Such criticisms may also include the claim that these works lack depth or meaning, are shallow, superficial and even contribute to a loss of meaning characteristic of the postmodern era (Okan & Okan, 2024)

Indeed, the extent to which the utopian content implied by these big-budget projects is shared or understood by those perceiving the art is an important question. It can be difficult to analyze the superposition of elusive elements, the repetition and speed of flow, and the uncanny images of colored liquids. Understanding the data on which some of these works are based, or the subject matter they are attempting to narrate, requires knowledge of the background of the work, as does the expected communication with many other contemporary artworks, in which the technology of the work can often substitute for the story of the work. In this context, it is very difficult to determine to what extent Anadol's artistic works resonate with the viewer/receiver and how they evaluate the ways of seeing, perceiving and interpreting his works and the philosophy he presents through his art (Okan & Okan, 2024).

So, what is the place and role of generative art in contemporary culture? Is it limited to academic research or is it a commercial art tool? Is its role only to produce new techniques to be applied in the design and culture industries? Is it closer to craft than art? (McCormack et al., 2014). The questions listed here remind us of the fact that the elites and elitist high art have created their own culture industry, as entertainment culture has infiltrated high art and in contrast to Adorno's concept of the culture industry developed for the masses.

CONCLUSION

Generative art, which was initially between technology and mass culture, has taken its place in contemporary art with its emphasis on algorithmic technology, artificial intelligence, machine learning and deep learning in today's art world, its interdisciplinary characteristic, and the many questions it contains.

In general, computer-based generative works do not derive their meaning directly from the artist's experience, but by feeding a large number of already existing, ready-made images into algorithms. The unconscious machine cannot create the concept of the work, choose the theme, make a metaphor, or influence which data to collect. In the case of Refik Anadol, he and his team decide all these things. It is the human-artist who narrates the theoretical-conceptual framework of the work such as peace, drawing attention to rainforests, planets, dreams, hallucinations, and manages the public relations dimension. As Refik Anadol states, the beginning and the end of the work, that is, the creation process, is realized through the collaboration of human-artist and machine-artist, but under the direction of the human-artist.

At the intersection of art, science and technology, Refik Anadol has made data, which are valuable assets for companies in various sectors, the raw material of his installations, data sculptures and NFTs. When expressed through Refik Anadol and his aforementioned works, it can be stated that algorithms are the prominent actors of storytelling in its current form. The artist has the freedom to choose the algorithms and the data groups he will use when trying to tell some stories with some tools, when applying data as paint on digital canvas, but due to the nature of generative art, he does not have the authority to decide where the work will evolve or what the final aesthetic form will be.

On the other hand, the new possibilities offered by technology, which exemplifies the typical high-tech and information aspects of the postmodern age, are considered exciting by both the artist and the receiving subject. In the section of the article where the concept of the sublime is discussed, N. Hartmann defines the sublime as the value of superiority and greatness in the object. Here, the visual presentation that stands out as awe-inspiring magnitude or complexity is the most important reason for the sublime feeling realized in the viewer. In other words, the sublime and the banal are united in the feeling of 'stupor'. Similarly, as observed in the case of Refik Anadol, one of the reasons why the artist's exhibitions attract a large number of viewers is the aesthetic feeling experienced as a kind of vertigo in the face of generative works consisting of a mass of data exceeding the limits of reason, created with huge budgets, with the support of world giant sponsors, appealing to the easy taste of popular culture, completely surrounding and burying the viewer in.

One of the reasons for the contemporary experience of technological sublime is the fascination with technology. In this sense, in the context of technological determinism, similar to McLuhan's emphasis on the medium with the proposition “the medium is the message”, in generative art, the medium/technology both overrides the work and the artist and becomes the determinant of aesthetic experience. The strong effect caused by the collage of technology used in the works is almost perceived as the story of the work.

Aesthetic discourse first emerged in the eighteenth century as an inquiry into the subject and its sensory experience. When Refik Anadol's works referred to in the article as Machine Memories and Machine Hallucinations are evaluated, the exhilarating effect of abstract, fun, fluid images and easy penetration of the viewer into these images evokes the concept of digital entertainment. Again, through these works, it can be said that digital storytelling has turned into a visual feast or show.

While Refik Anadol, on the one hand, explains his works by using GANs or by taking advantage of the storytelling feature and power of technology, on the other hand, in terms of public relations and promotion, he uses literary language, metaphors and anthropomorphism such as "pigments transformed into a poetic visual aesthetic, data not only as numbers but also as memories, trying to create collective dreams and consciousness from the accumulation of knowledge that constitutes collective memory". Stories consisting of words accompany the works, but the awe-inspiring effect of the technology used exceeds these stories. Therefore, the effect of the poetic information notes created to explain the works and make them meaningful on the audience lost in the entertainment feast remains open to discussion.

Stories are the oldest form of information exchange between people. Storytelling has been a part of our daily lives since we started communicating with each other. The new name of traditional storytelling is digital storytelling, with digital technology permeating every field today, with the visualization of raw data. Digital storytelling is based on the idea of using computer-based tools and applications to create stories. Algorithms are capable of creating an infinite variety of formalist stories. Other forms, other stories can emerge with the same algorithms, and different interpretations can be obtained with similar algorithms. The problems centered on the technology discussed in the article within the scope of Refik Anadol's works are all existential features inherent in the new storytelling method based on digital technology. The article has discussed these issues and philosophically interpreted digital storytelling through the works created by Refik Anadol and his team within the framework of the concepts of art and aesthetics.

REFERENCES

AB 101: Historical figures in generative art — A. Michael Noll (2022, January 8). https://medium.com/the-link-art-blocks/ab-101-historical-figures-in-generative-art-a-michael-noll-5a23ea78ac41

AB 101: Historical figures in generative art — Georg Nees (2021, December 5). https://medium.com/the-link-art-blocks/ab-101-historical-figures-in-generative-art-georg-nees-6b006e62126a

AB 101: Historical figures in generative art — Herbert W. Franke (2022, January 30). https://medium.com/the-link-art-blocks/ab-101-historical-figures-in-generative-art-herbert-w-franke-48911e977096

Akbay, B. (2021-present). Refik Anadol'la makine hatıraları sergi turu [machine memories with Refik Anadol exhibition tour]. YouTube. https://www.youtube.com/watch?v=-_gTYr_zFT4 (In Turkish)

Altun, F. (2006). *M. McLuhan ve J. Baudrillard'ın medya kuramlarının karşılaştırmalı çözümlemesi* [Comparative analysis of the media theories of M. McLuhan and J. Baudrillard] [Doctoral thesis] Istanbul University Social Sciences Enstitute, İstanbul. https://nek.istanbul.edu.tr/ekos/TEZ/41475.pdf

Artun, A. (2011). *Çağdaş Sanatın Örgütlenmesi: Estetik ve Modernizmin Tasfiyesi* [The Organization of Contemporary Art: Aesthetics and the Liquidation of Modernism]. İletişim Publishing.

Artun, A. (2021, March 29). Refik Anadol ve algoritma sanatı [Refik Anadol and the art of algorithm]. *Skopbülten.* https://www.e-skop.com/skopbulten/refik-anadol-ve-algoritma-sanati/6111

Caplan, L. (2020, January 3). The social conscience of generative art, *Art in Amerika.* https://www.artnews.com/art-in-america/features/max-bense-gustav-metzger-generative-art-1202674265/

Crowther, P. (2008). Ontology and aesthetics of digital art. *The Journal of Aesthetics and Art Criticism, 66*(2), 161–170. https://www.jstor.org/stable/40206323. DOI: 10.1111/j.1540-6245.2008.00296.x

Cunningham, D. (2004). How the sublime became "now": Time, modernity and aesthetics in Lyotard's rewriting of Kant. *Canadian Journal of Continental Philosophy, 8*(3), 549–571. https://westminsterresearch.westminster.ac.uk/download/d2a7f877f0f5c20d11e1fffe409dfd3655db9d8223db312f2c562a265ff689b6/875498/Cunningham_2004_final.pdf. DOI: 10.5840/symposium20048341

Doğan, B., Ersöz, S. Ş., & Şahin, C. (2022). Kripto sanatı ve NFT [Crypto Art and NFT]. *Tarih Kültür ve Sanat Arastirmalari Journal, 11*(1), 1–12. DOI: 10.7596/taksad.v10i4.3127

Eco, U. (2006). *Güzelliğin Tarihi* [History of Beauty]. (Akkoyunlu, A. C., Trans.). Doğan Publishing. (Original work published 2004)

Ferenczi, A. (2024, Jun 9). The art and science of Alexander Mordvintsev. https://www.katevassgalerie.com/blog/the-art-and-science-of-alexander-mordvintsev

García, E., & Whittinghill, D. (2011). The Aesthetic Legacy of Aldo Giorgini. *Leonardo, 44*(4), 309–316. https://www.jstor.org/stable/20869493. DOI: 10.1162/LEON_a_00207

Güney, E., & Uysal, S. (2021). Jeneratif sanat: Nöroplastisite ve derin öğrenme ilişkisinde post dijital dönüşümler [Generative art: Post-digital transformations in the relationship between neuroplasticity and deep learning. *Yıldız Journal Art and Design*, 8(2), 62-74. https://yjad.yildiz.edu.tr

Güngör, N. (2011). *İletişim Kuramlar Yaklaşımlar* [Communication theories approaches]. Siyasal Publishing.

Harari, Y. N. (2024). *Neksus, taş devri'nden yapay zekaya bilgi ağlarının kısa tarihi* [Nexus: a brief history of information networks from the stone age to AI]. (Şentuğ, Ç., Trans.). Kolektif Publishing. (Original work published 2024)

High, S. (2010). Telling stories: A reflection on oral history and new media. *Power and Protest*, 38(1), 101-112. https://www.jstor.org/stable/40650320

Laughey, D. (2021). *Medya çalışmaları teoriler ve yaklaşımlar* [Media studies theories and approaches]. Kalkedon yayınları. (Original work published 2009)

Lavander, A. (2010). Digital culture. In S. Bay-Cheng, C. Kattenbelt, A. Lavander, R. Nelson (Eds.), *Mapping intermediality in performance* (pp. 125-134). Amsterdam University Press. http://www.jstore.org/stable/j.ctt46mwjd.23

Lin, P. H. (2005). A dream of digital art: Beyond the myth of contemporary computer technology in visual arts. *Visual Arts Research, 31*(1), 4–12. https://www.jstor.org/stable/20715364

Lossin, R. H. (2023, March 17). Refik Anadol'un MoMA Sergisi Üzerine: Teknoloji, Sanat, Propaganda [On Refik Anadol's MoMA exhibition: technology, art, propaganda] (E. Gen Trans.). *Skopbülten*. https://www.e-skop.com/skopbulten/refik-anadolun-moma-sergisi-uzerine-teknoloji-sanat-propaganda/6558

Manovich, L. (2018). *AI Aesthetics*. https://monoskop.org/images/6/66/Manovich_Lev_AI_Aesthetics_2018.pdf

McCormack, J., Bown, O., Dorin, A., McCabe, J., Monro, G., & Whitelaw, M. (2014). Ten questions concerning generative computer art. *Leonardo*, *47*(2), 135–141. https://www.jstor.org/stable/43834149. DOI: 10.1162/LEON_a_00533

Monro, G. (2009). Emergence and generative art. *Leonardo*, *5*(42), 476–477. https://www.jstor.org/stable/40540082. DOI: 10.1162/leon.2009.42.5.476

O'Gieblyn, M. (2023). *Tanrı insan hayvan makine: Teknoloji, metafor ve anlam arayışı* [God, human, animal, machine: Technology, metaphor, and the search for meaning]. (Sarıalioğlu, F., Trans.). Altın Kitaplar Publishing. (Original work published 2021)

Shinkle, E. (2013). Video games and the technological sublime. In N. Llewellyn, C. Riding (Eds.). *The art of the sublime*, Tate Research Publication. https://www.tate.org.uk/art/research-publications/the-sublime/eugenie-shinkle-video-games-and-the-technological-sublime-r1136830

Tunalı, İ. (2010). *Estetik* [Aesthetics]. Remzi Publishing. (Original work published 1989)

Uygur, T. (2021, March 13). Refik Anadol NASA'nın 60 yıllık arşivlerini görselleştirip sergi açtı... uzaya sanatsal bakış [Refik Anadol visualized 60 years of NASA archives and opened an exhibition... an artistic view of space]. *Hürriyet Cumartesi.* https://www.hurriyet.com.tr/kelebek/hurriyet-cumartesi/refik-anadol-nasanin-60-yillik-arsivlerini-gorsellestirip-sergi-acti-uzaya-sanatsal-bakis-41761577

Xu, C. (2020, Nowember 10). *Algorithmic Art: Beyond the Artist. Illumine Magazine.* https://illumin.usc.edu/algorithmic-art-beyond-the-artist/

Yılmaz, İ. (2021, April 05). Yeni medya sanatı ve anten tartışması [New media art and antenna discussion]. *Hürriyet.* (https://www.hurriyet.com.tr/yazarlar/ihsan-yilmaz/yeni-medya-sanati-ve-anten-tartismasi-41780110

Chapter 9
Reading The Concept of Storytelling Within the Framework of Fashion Marketing Through Luxury Brands

Erdem Varol
https://orcid.org/0000-0003-3940-2122
Marmara Üniversitesi, Turkey

Merve Çelik-Varol
https://orcid.org/0000-0002-0698-929X
Istanbul Beykent University, Turkey

ABSTRACT

This study is based on the analysis of how five luxury brands utilize the concept of storytelling in their fashion marketing strategies, employing the content analysis method. The concept of storytelling, a popular marketing strategy today, manifests as brand-specific narratives that convey the brands' histories, unique values, cultural heritage, and quality principles. In the current digital age, it is known that luxury brands frequently leverage storytelling in fashion marketing to establish a strong brand image. In this study, the stories in the campaigns of Louis Vuitton, Gucci, Rolex, Dior, and Prada are analyzed using the content analysis method within the fields of luxury branding, fashion marketing, and storytelling. The campaign analyses reveal that luxury brands not only offer expensive, high-quality, and rare goods and services but also present their consumers with stories that attribute a lifestyle, exclusivity, prestige, and emotional connection.

DOI: 10.4018/979-8-3373-2023-6.ch009

INTRODUCTION

Today, luxury brands effectively employ the concept of storytelling in their marketing strategies. Luxury brands, which can be associated with high price, quality, and rarity, narrate unique stories to convey their historical heritage, distinct cultural contexts, and long-term emotional connections established with consumers. Storytelling, a concept increasingly emphasized by institutions and brands in recent years, refers to the process of conveying a brand's value, history, and vision to its target audience through various narratives. In this context, these narratives are communicated to customers to establish an emotional bond between the brand and its customers, to instill belief in the brand's identity, and to gain their loyalty. It is known that luxury brands utilize the concept of fashion marketing in conjunction with storytelling to accurately express themselves to their customers and connect with their target audience.

The concept of fashion marketing, which has emerged as a significant marketing type, operates within the current consumer society characterized by rapid production and a highly competitive industry. Consequently, the concept of fashion marketing is defined as a set of strategies encompassing efforts to produce, promote, and increase the sales of fashion products. In this context, fashion marketing not only refers to the clothing sector but also includes the production of many more goods and services such as accessories, shoes, personal care, and beauty products. As understanding today's consumers and responding to their needs and desires has become more critical than ever, implementing dynamics such as a strong brand identity, sustainability, social media marketing, digital content creation, e-commerce optimization, and ethical marketing, which are significant components of fashion marketing, holds vital value for brands. For instance, for fashion marketing, fashion blogs, videos, storytelling, and personalized e-mail campaigns attract consumers' attention and contribute to the creation of an emotional bond between them and the brand. Similarly, in order to reach fashion consumers, the ability of fashion brands to exist on platforms such as Instagram, TikTok, and Pinterest, which have seen a steady increase in user numbers in recent years, as well as collaborations with engaging visuals and influencers seen as new-generation opinion leaders, significantly increases brand visibility. Furthermore, the adoption of ethical and fair trade practices by fashion consumers who are sensitive to the ecosystem and social sustainability in the fashion brands they purchase can become an essential reason for preference. Especially in a society where the “buy-use-dispose” mentality prevails and conspicuous consumption has become dominant, digital fashion and cyber showrooms, influencer partnerships, augmented reality applications, diversity, and inclusivity can be considered as the driving forces of fashion marketing.

The rise of digital fashion, consumers' openness to digital innovations, the increasing number of visits to cyber showrooms contribute to brands presenting their collections to consumers in more contemporary ways, especially in events where their physical presence is limited. Additionally, ethical collaborations carried out by fashion brands in line with their mission, vision, and quality principles, and telling stories to consumers in the digital environment also increase access to and trust in the brand. The contributions of augmented reality technology to fashion marketing have also been noteworthy in recent years. Reasons such as consumers virtually wearing and trying on fashion products in a virtual environment and having access to detailed information about the product enable them to improve their shopping experience. Moreover, inclusive representation in visuals and advertising messages used in fashion marketing campaigns, the emotional messages and stories conveyed strengthen the connection with different consumer groups. This situation is not only valid for fast fashion brands but also for luxury brands that promise quality and rarity to their consumers. In this context, it can be stated that luxury brands, from past to present, not only provide high-quality goods and services but also build a lifestyle, prestige, value, and emotional loyalty for their customers. Therefore, storytelling holds a significant place in the marketing strategies of luxury brands. In the storytelling process of luxury brands, the brand's value, vision, mission, and quality principle meet with customers within a narrative pattern. In this context, storytelling in the context of fashion marketing holds an essential place for luxury brands compared to other brands. Since the concept of luxury is associated not only with a product but also with keywords such as aesthetics, lifestyle, and prestige, these narrative patterns are also significant in terms of transforming into customers' individual experiences. Especially in the consumption age we live in, where consumers are subjected to a bombardment of messages, storytelling emerges as an essentail strategy for brands that want to connect with their consumers on a deeper level. Effective storytelling can transform a brand from merely a provider of goods and services into an appealing character in the eyes of the consumer.

Today, it is of great importance for luxury brands to establish an emotional bond with their consumers, differentiate themselves from other competing luxury brands, remain memorable, and create brand loyalty. Since the stories told with the brand directly appeal to consumers' emotions and create a bond with them, it also leads to the personalization of the brand in the eyes of consumers and its association with positive keywords. Considering that there are a large number of luxury fashion brands in a saturated market, original and creative brand stories, unique narratives, and a transparent explanation of what makes a brand special will affect consumers and make this brand a reason for preference. Therefore, brand stories created transparently and consistently will create an impact on consumers and build brand loyalty. Well-told brand stories will be memorable for consumers and will become recallable in the process of purchasing goods and services. Authentic stories told, narratives that reflect the experiences and desires of the target audience, can enable consumers to see themselves within that story, thus contributing to the creation of an emotional bond between their own identity and the brand. Especially when brands are sincere with their consumers about their missions, values, and the challenges they have faced, it can be easier to establish a bond of trust and loyalty.

Therefore, it can be stated that the concept of storytelling is not only a marketing tool for luxury brands but also a fundamental element that helps to preserve the identity and value of luxury products. In other words, effective storytelling emerges as a significant dynamic for luxury brands to convey their heritage, tradition, and uniqueness to consumers. Consequently, since luxury brands possess a rich history, heritage, and originality, they benefit from the concept of storytelling both to preserve these values and to convey them to their consumers with an effective language. Narratives that highlight the unique values of luxury brands such as exclusivity, rarity, limited production, special craftsmanship, and the original design processes of these brands contribute to making the brand more attractive and more desirable in the eyes of consumers. Furthermore, the association of luxury brands with emotional desires and experiences enables consumers to identify with the brands they admire and also creates purchase motivation. Especially sharing the stories of artisans who will emphasize the unique designs of luxury brands through social media differentiates luxury brands among their competitors and makes them valuable. In addition, using customer stories, experience narratives, and references about luxury brands also attracts luxury brand consumers who refer to essential life events. Indeed, storytelling emerges as a powerful strategy that increases positive emotions for luxury brands. Impressive and original stories that express the heritage, history, and originality of luxury brands and involve customer experiences essentialy contribute to the development of brands. In this study, how luxury brands use the concept of storytelling in their marketing strategies within the framework of fashion marketing has been compiled for informational purposes. Although there are numerous individual studies on "luxury branding" and "storytelling" in the literature, this study differs from other studies in the literature both because it is structured within the axis of "fashion marketing" and because it presents significant examples of the stories of world-renowned luxury brands.

The Facet of High Quality and Rarity in the Realm of Fashion Marketing: Luxury Branding

With the proliferation of product variety and the initiation of manufacturers reaching extensive target audiences, each producer embarked on a quest for distinctiveness for their produced goods and services. This pursuit led to the emergence of the brand concept. Tracing the history of the brand concept reveals roots extending back to the Middle Ages and even earlier periods. The English term "brand" is suggested to have originated from the North European language word "brandr," entering the English lexicon. In regions where animal husbandry held significant importance, "brandr" signified the act of individuals marking their livestock to differentiate them from others (Blackett, 2003). Following interactions resulting from frequent invasions by North European tribes in Britain, the word "brand" became established in both the English language and England itself. For instance, in 1266, the Assize of Bread and Ale was enacted in England. This regulation mandated that bakers attach a label indicating the place of production to the bread they produced. Consequently, it became easier to identify the producer of the bread, and in case of an issue with the product, the responsible party could be readily located (Perry & Wisnom, 2003, p. 17). By the Middle Ages, the concept of the brand began to spread to Continental Europe, and with trade becoming a significant source of livelihood alongside animal husbandry, merchants resorted to marking their products to achieve distinctiveness, thus initiating branding (Lee, et al., 2015).

The increasing prevalence of industry and mechanization, coupled with the growth in both the volume and variety of production, gave rise to a need for international brand and intellectual property rights. In 1883, the Paris Convention for the Protection of Industrial Property was signed in Paris, the capital of France, with the participation of 11 commercially developed countries of the time (Yılmaz, 2020). Thus, the brand concept, particularly with the surge in mass production and consumption following the Industrial Revolution, attained its contemporary meaning. To provide a general definition of a brand, David Aaker (1996), a prominent figure in marketing theories, defined a brand as follows: "A brand is a name, term, sign, symbol, design, or a combination of these, intended to identify the goods or services of one seller or group of sellers and to differentiate them from those of competitors."

With the Industrial Revolution, the brand concept became a significant marketing element. From that era to the present day, the brand has gained increasing importance. Especially after the competitive conditions that emerged with the rise in production volume, the brand concept has been central to marketing communication. A brand is a concept that goes beyond a product's usage, benefits, or price, bestowing upon it an identity and image, offering symbolic meanings, and engaging in communication with the consumer. Consumers, when making a purchase, consider the brand before the product's features (Aaker, 1996). The American Marketing Association (AMA) defines a brand as a name, term, design, symbol, or any other feature that identifies one seller's goods or services as distinct from those of other sellers (AMA, 2025).

A brand can be defined both abstractly and concretely. While the positioning and identity creation of a brand by businesses reflect its concrete aspect, the perception of this positioning and identity by consumers, leading to the formation of brand image, reflects its abstract aspect. It is possible to discuss the brand as a phenomenon. A brand is a phenomenon through which the promises of the owning institution are conveyed to consumers. This phenomenon consists of consumers' perceptions of the product or institution. The brand phenomenon is always present in the consumer's mind, from past experiences to future anticipated experiences. A brand is a phenomenon that creates distinctiveness and recognizability among dozens or hundreds of products, accelerating the consumer's purchasing process (Kotler & Pfoertsche, 2006).

Brand Types

The concept of a brand is generally defined as the distinguishing feature of one organization's goods or services from those of other organizations. However, following the diversification of goods and services, various types of brands have emerged.

Product Brands: Products are categorized into services and goods. The service sector represents an intangible concept that is not physically touched or seen, whereas a good is a tangible, physical product. However, it is not possible to define every tangible or intangible product as a brand. For a product to be defined as a brand, it must possess a distinctive logo or name by an organization and must be communicated to customers through advertising and other communication processes. Product brands are defined as brands identified through goods that are bought and sold. These types of brands can also be described as tangible product brands (Lee, et al., 2015). For instance, it is the most common type of brand that defines a specific good. Examples include Coca-Cola in the carbonated beverage category and Apple in the mobile phone and computer categories (Keller, 2013). Product brands focus on the features, benefits, and quality of the product.

Service Brands: Service brands represent intangible products. They are brands that represent services of an intangible nature. It is their intangible qualities that transform an abstract product into a brand, unlike a tangible product (Hermansson, 2005). While the evaluation of a tangible product by consumers is proportional to the pleasure and benefit it provides, the evaluation of a service, being an intangible product, can be proportional to customer experiences and post-purchase processes. Banking products, insurance products, and telecommunication products can be given as examples of service products. Brands such as Garanti BBVA and Vodafone can be cited as examples of service brands (Zeithaml, Bitner & Gremler, 2018). In service brands, reliability, customer service, and experience take precedence over benefit or pleasure.

Corporate Brands (Company Brands): These are brands that represent an entire company, business, or institution, generally reflecting the company's values, culture, reputation, and image (Aaker, 2004). Holdings and large enterprises can be given as examples of corporate brands. While institutions like Beko and Samsung use their corporate names as brand names for the products they manufacture, businesses like Apple and Microsoft offer their products to consumers by adding sub-brands (iPhone, Teams, etc.). Nevertheless, these institutions also align their image and values with the values of their sub-brands (Aaker, 2004, p. 8). Corporate brands serve as an umbrella for all business units and products and focus on building trust among stakeholders.

Personal Brands: With the widespread adoption of the brand concept, goods and services initially came to mind when branding was mentioned. However, with evolving marketing strategies, personal brands have also emerged. Individuals targeting and communicating with a specific audience have also created their own brands. According to the personal brand concept, an individual's physical attributes, appearance, hairstyle, personality, clothing style, area of expertise, and other characteristics enable them to be positioned differently within society (Clark, 2012). Thus, individuals position themselves as brands, much like the products produced by an institution. For example, the famous English footballer David Beckham has become a brand personality with his physical features, appearance, football style, clothing style, and family life. Especially well-known individuals, experts, or influencers aim to create reputation, credibility, and influence by building their personal brands (Montoya, 2002). The proliferation of social media and the concentration of shopping in the virtual environment have highlighted the concept of the influencer, and individuals have become both advertising faces for brands and creators of their personal brands through their product promotions.

Retailer Brands (Private Labels): Retail chains not only feature branded products manufactured by institutions on their shelves but also sell products they themselves produce or have produced. These types of brands are called private labels. For instance, milk or cleaning products sold under the supermarket chain's own name are private labels (Ailawadi & Keller, 2004). These types of brands generally offer more affordable alternatives compared to other brands.

Geographic Brands (Place Brands): These are brands that represent a specific geographic region or city and aim to promote that region's image, tourism, or products. Examples of this brand type, also known as brand cities, include Istanbul, Paris, or Tuscany as geographic brands (Anholt, 2006).

Nation Brands: Following the fall of the Berlin Wall, not only Germany but all of Europe began to integrate, and the European Economic Community evolved into the European Union. The concept of globalization emerged during this period, and it was suggested that borders would disappear (Zurn, 2010). With globalization in the 2000s, tourism and travel marketing gained prominence. Countries resorted to practices that would create a difference in terms of tourism revenue, and the concept of nation branding emerged. Countries positioned their prominent features, almost like a product, as a brand, creating identity and image (Nas, 2017). In addition to their own nation brands, countries also construct significant tourism centers or goods and services produced uniquely to the country as sub-brands. For instance, the Aegean and Mediterranean coasts alone are not sufficient to be positioned as a brand; they are positioned as a sub-brand of the Turkey brand.

Generic Brands: Certain brands stand out among similar products either because they were the first on the market when they were produced or because they are preferred by a large number of consumers. These types of brands can become synonymous with the product name. These types of brands are called generic brands (Akın, 2014). Examples of such brands include Nescafe, Kleenex (Selpak), Gillette, Always (Orkid), and Vileda (Öncel, 2004).

Luxury Brands: Consumers desire the products they purchase to be special and unique to them. Especially for consumers belonging to the high-income group, the uniqueness and exclusivity of the goods and services they purchase stand out as the foremost criterion in their purchasing behavior. Luxury products, which focus on hedonistic and symbolic consumption rather than utility, are also called luxury brands. Certain factors need to come together for a brand to be defined in the luxury status. First and foremost, the brand's positioning, values, image, and identity must be suitable for luxury. Luxury brands create a persona and structure their marketing strategy accordingly. The pricing policy of luxury brands is also in a position that not everyone can afford. The image of being difficult to reach further attracts consumers who want to buy luxury brands (Çelik Varol, 2022). This situation can be explained by the principle of rarity and scarcity, which are prominent features of luxury (Nueno & Quelch, 1998). According to Kapferer and Bastien (2015), luxury brands aim to create a high brand value through elements such as scarcity and uniqueness, focusing not only on the quality and price of the products but also on ensuring that the brand image and perception are special and unique.

The marketing strategies of luxury brands can be summarized as follows:

1. **Limited Access and Exclusivity:** Luxury brands offer their consumers a privileged experience by producing in limited quantities and offering their products for sale at high prices. This strategy contributes to increasing the brand's value and prestige (Chevalier & Mazzalovo, 2008).
2. **Storytelling and Exclusive Experience:** Luxury brands construct a strong storytelling strategy based on elements such as historical heritage and handcrafted production processes by artisans. This creates the image that the brand offers the consumer not just a product but a lifestyle and a cultural meaning (Lachance et al., 2003). Additionally, luxury brands place customer experience at the center. Elements such as the designs of luxury stores, limited-edition collections,

and personalized services reinforce the value of the luxury brand (Dubois & Paternault, 1995).

Fashion Marketing Strategies of Luxury Brands

Fashion marketing is a strategy inspired by fashion, a concept that continuously encourages consumers to purchase. Predominantly used in the clothing, accessories, and jewelry sectors, fashion marketing is a dynamic field shaped by brands with creative and cultural values. From this perspective, luxury branding is seen as one of the crucial elements for fashion marketing. While brands emerge for consumers to distinguish products from one another and possess an identity geared towards pleasure and utility, luxury brands have an identity strategy focused on quality, prestige, exclusivity, and high prices.

For the fashion industry, the brand concept extends beyond just a name or logo; it is a concept that establishes emotional connections with consumers, enables consumers to identify with the brand's identity, and carries a meaning of social status. Establishing a brand story, which is one of the fundamental features of fashion marketing, is necessary for this emotional bond and social status. Fashion brands build their brand values by using cultural codes and symbolic meanings that determine how consumers express themselves (Kapferer, 2012).

Within the scope of their marketing strategies, luxury brands create a perception of a certain status and authenticity, in addition to offering a product to their customers. To create this perception, luxury brands utilize elements such as the quality of goods and services, customer relations, store atmosphere, and communication strategies (Ko & Megehee, 2012).

In this context, fashion marketing and luxury branding aim not only to create economic value through mere production and consumption but also to construct cultural and social meanings.

Brands' New Strategy for Building Emotional Connections: Storytelling

It is known that institutions or brands today are turning to various strategies to attract consumers' attention under global competitive conditions. Storytelling, as a significant strategy that can establish emotional bonds between brands, institutions, and their target audiences, can be defined as the sum of ideas, beliefs, personal experiences, and life lessons through narratives that evoke strong emotions and insights (Serrat, 2008). In this context, storytelling, which can also be defined as the way a brand expresses itself in different forms, contributes to the transfer of experience by enabling listeners and viewers to use their imagination (Duran & Topbaşoğlu,

2017). Consequently, storytelling today not only serves to promote brands' goods and services but also aims to influence consumers by creating narratives that align with their values, beliefs, and lifestyles (Paquette, et al., 2017). In this regard, the concept of storytelling encompasses three basic elements for brands to establish a strong bond with their target audiences. These are expressed in the form of character usage, conflict, and resolution (Mills & John, 2021). Within this framework, stories in narrative form describe a real or fictional event in the logical order in question. These types of stories are subject to the construction of realism, carefully chosen to sound real using descriptive language (Hopkinson & Hogarth-Scott, 2001). Considered one of the oldest arts, storytelling today frequently takes place through personality-focused brand narratives by institutions or brands. Strong storytelling is realized through well-established brand personalities, appealing to consumers' emotions, desires, and fantasies (Herskovitz & Crystal, 2010). Furthermore, brands that have established a strong brand personality can position themselves differently from others through interesting storytelling, attract customers' attention, present word-of-mouth messages organically, and also offer their consumers an emotional added value (Mucundorfeanu, 2018). Wala (2015) states that brands can create successful stories based on their founding history and story, how they manage risks and crises, the production stages of goods and services, brand positioning strategies, employees they can be proud of, and having consumers who trust them even in risky situations. For instance, the world-renowned technology brand Apple constructs its narrative not only on the quality and originality of its products but also on a digital world where consumers can have a unique experience (Medium, 2017). Similarly, Tesla, one of the global brands, has implemented a brand positioning that advocates for a sustainable future to make electric vehicles more accessible and appealing. Led by Elon Musk, Tesla's brand story focuses on being a leader in environmentally friendly practices and reshaping the future. In this context, Tesla is not only perceived as a car brand but also as a symbol of innovative technologies and sustainability (Ryder, 2021). Consequently, the place of brand storytelling in marketing and branding has become increasingly significant in recent years. Today, storytelling is considered highly essential in terms of being able to establish emotional bonds with consumers by drawing on branding stories from around the world and in Turkey, enabling consumers to give emotional responses to brands, connecting with the story of the good or service rather than just the good or service itself, and ultimately achieving brand loyalty (Kosakarika, 2023). Stories told rationally and emotionally, utilizing the power of social media, influence consumers' emotions and preferences, thereby affecting brand-consumer communication (Rosenthal & Brito, 2017).

The concept of storytelling is created not only for brands to establish an emotional bond with consumers but also to gain a place in their memories. Consumers can better recall information about brands or products when they listen to it accompanied by stories, and this situation paves the way for creating a good brand story to be more permanent in consumers' minds (Teraiya, et al., 2023). In this context, brands aim to gain a more lasting place in consumers' minds by presenting their narratives effectively. In the communication age we live in, the creation of impressive narratives by brands through advertisements is also a highly credible and memorable situation for consumers (Kang, et al., 2020). For instance, the world-renowned personal care brand Dove, in its campaign called "Real Beauty Sketches," tells a story in which women question their own perceptions of beauty. Within the said advertising message, an emotionally charged story is created based on women's perceptions of beauty, revealing their lack of confidence and their real beauty as they describe themselves (Dove, 2024). Spotify is another brand that tells stories to consumers through advertisements. With its "2023 Wrapped" campaign, Spotify offers a personalized experience that highlights the songs, artists, and music genres that users listened to throughout the year. The emotional aspect of the campaign is strengthened by stories that emphasize the personal moments people experienced with music and the meanings of these musics in their lives. Especially in the "Wrapped" advertisement of 2023, it allows users to establish nostalgic and emotional connections through their musical journeys. In this context, this campaign makes the impact of music on people and how Spotify has become a part of its users' lives more memorable through an emotional narrative (Romero, 2024).

Brands frequently prefer storytelling not only to establish an emotional connection with consumers and become more memorable in their minds but also to be more distinguishable and desirable than their competitors in the market. According to Kaufman (2003), brand narratives are also used as a differentiation strategy in today's environment where global competitive conditions have increased in the sector or market. In this context, while every brand can have its own story, storytelling can be done through advertisements and various communication efforts, especially via digital channels. In particular, brands can move away from being distant entities with purely commercial purposes and gain their own personality. Stories, by making brands act like humans, can enable consumers to have more trust in them. Creating personality stories tied to archetypes also facilitates consumers in forming stronger bonds with brands. For example, George Lucas developed the Star Wars screenplay by conducting research on various subjects and examining fairy tales (Herskovitz & Crystal, 2010). Furthermore, the Glossier brand tells powerful stories, especially by using social media, and gains brand personality by drawing inspiration from the beauty and personal care experiences of its founder, Emily Weiss. Moreover, the storytelling of these experiences and their presentation to the brand's target audience highlight its unique approach in the beauty sector. Glossier has abandoned the traditional "perfect" and "flawless" images in the beauty sector, adopting a more natural and authentic approach. It promotes its products by centering the stories of real people to its consumers. The Glossier brand especially shares these sincere stories through customer reviews, user experiences, and influencers (referred to as new-generation opinion leaders) via digital channels, which strengthens the brand's connections with consumers. Indeed, behind Glossier's success lies its identity as a brand that created its own story while also establishing a brand personality. In this way, the brand has not only become a beauty or personal care brand but has also formed a community and lifestyle, possessing a loyal customer base (Medium, 2019).

Storytelling is not only used to build brand personality but also enables brands to convey their existing values, mission, vision, quality principles, and goals more effectively (Fog, et al., 2005). Consequently, in the digital age we live in, brands can convey their messages to consumers more organically through various stories instead of direct advertising messages. In this framework, it is also significant for the consumer to gain an experience. For instance, users can add their own experiences to the story or interact on social media through these stories (Pereira, 2019). In this context, storytelling has become central to marketing strategies and a way for brands to express themselves. A well-told, original story enables a brand to do much more than just sell products; it contributes to establishing an emotional bond between the brand and consumers, while also fostering the creation of a brand community and generating customer loyalty for the brand in the long term (Woodside, et al., 2008). Mandung's 2024 research, titled "The Influence of Storytelling Techniques in Digital Marketing on Brand Loyalty: A Consumer Psychology Perspective," analyzed the emphasis on the transformative power of storytelling techniques in digital marketing through brand loyalty. The research concluded that storytelling satisfies consumers' psychological needs such as attachment and trust, and increases brand loyalty (Mandung, 2024). For example, the Airbnb brand has gone beyond being just an accommodation platform and has created a powerful storytelling strategy that transforms the way people travel. The brand's story is based on creating a platform where hosts and guests connect with each other, and trust and sincerity are prioritized. In this context, the brand promises its users more than just renting a room or a house. The story offered by Airbnb conveys the message that homes are not just physical spaces but also a warm environment where local cultures, memories, and experiences are shared. It can be stated that Airbnb's "Belong Anywhere" campaign strongly supports this philosophy. Airbnb offers stories that enable travel enthusiasts to discover new places all over the world while also making them feel at home. Today, many of Airbnb's communication efforts narrate how people discover local experiences in different cultures and communicate with different people in this process. This story created by Airbnb has been quite effective in building brand loyalty, conveying the message that this brand is not just a travel platform but also a significant experiential space that brings people together. At this point, consumers have felt not only like consumers or customers but also as part of a community, which has strengthened their loyalty to the brand (Brandhopper, 2024).

Ben & Jerry's ice cream is also seen as one of the brands that achieves brand loyalty through storytelling. Beyond being just an ice cream seller, Ben & Jerry's stands out as a brand that also undertakes efforts in social sustainability, such as environmental and social justice, and societal equality. This brand creates a sense of belonging by presenting stories through the themes of transparency, honesty, and social responsibility. The brand's "Save Our Swirld" campaign clearly demonstrates Ben & Jerry's stance on environmental sustainability. Consequently, this campaign aims to create awareness through storytelling by blending the fight against climate change and environmental disasters with the brand's high-quality and delicious ice creams. The "Save Our Swirld" campaign emerges not only as an ice cream promotion but also as a story that narrates the environmental values advocated by the brand. With the stories it tells, Ben & Jerry's aims to be not just a taste but also a symbol that embraces its values and the environment for its target audience. In this way, it also aims to ensure the loyalty of its target audience. Indeed, consumers purchase not just the flavors offered by Ben & Jerry's but also the story and values behind the brand. This allows consumers to establish an emotional bond with the brand. In this context, similar to the Airbnb example, it can be stated that Ben & Jerry's, by combining storytelling with being a good corporate citizen and activism, has built an identity aimed at creating not just ice cream but also societal change (Bamford, 2015). Consequently, brands place importance on creating an image and using characters in their stories to influence their target audiences and convey their messages accurately. Brands create characters to draw consumers into the story and enable them to empathize. The characters used by brands represent the values and cultures offered by the brand (Escalas, 2004). For instance, in the advertisements for M&M's chocolates, there are chocolate characters, each with different personalities. These characters are designed to draw consumers into the fun and colorful world of the M&M's brand. Therefore, it can be stated that these character uses narrate the brand's energetic and dynamic structure. The humorous aspects of the characters are emphasized in the stories that M&M's chocolates tell their consumers (Bredava, 2021). One of the fundamental components of storytelling is fiction. Brands take the consumer on a journey through a story. The fiction of the story consists of the beginning, development, and conclusion sections. Brands that present a problem and a need at the beginning provide a narrative about the solution to this problem or the solution offered by the brand in the development section. In the conclusion, the relationship between the brand and the consumer is strengthened, and the brand image is clearly conveyed to the consumer (Fog, et al., 2005).

In its "Dream Crazier" campaign, world-renowned sportswear brand Nike tells a story about how female athletes overcome these obstacles and how strong they are, emphasizing that women can achieve extraordinary goals and transcend the boundaries imposed by society. Furthermore, in the story of this campaign, Nike highlights that despite social norms and challenges, sports and achievements are not limited by gender. Consequently, this story ensures that Nike's products are presented not only as tools for performance but also as instruments of freedom and equality. With this narrative, the brand aims not only to sell its products but also to raise awareness about a social issue and contribute to finding solutions (Soodo, 2025). One of the fundamental elements that ensures the progression of the story and captures consumers' attention is conflict. Brands use conflict to enable consumers to establish an emotional bond with the brand. In this context, conflict can be narrated to consumers in a context where the goods and services offered by the brand provide solutions to problems in the consumer's life. Therefore, conflict also creates an opportunity to establish a relationship between the brand and the consumer (Schmitt, 2012). For example, Red Bull's advertisements often feature athletes and ordinary people struggling to push their physical and mental limits. The brand's slogan, "Gives You Wings," presents a conflict and resolution where characters facing difficulties and limitations can overcome these obstacles thanks to Red Bull (Howell, 2025). Not only conflict and resolution but also the values and messages conveyed in brands' stories reflect the brands' identity and vision (Feng, et al., 2024). These messages reinforce the meaning of the brand's story, establishing an emotional bond with consumers. In this context, consumers may want to identify with the values conveyed by the brand. The values offered by brands stand out as one of the most significant elements that differentiate them from their other competitors. The values and messages presented in brands' stories can help increase brand loyalty (Keller, 2013).

The Allbirds brand, as a manufacturer of sustainable and eco-friendly shoes, presents a storytelling approach centered on environmental awareness and respect for nature. The brand's mission is to produce the world's most comfortable shoes while also protecting the environment (Allbirds, 2025). Allbirds strives to minimize its carbon footprint by using entirely organic materials (e.g., wool, sugarcane, trees) in its production processes. The brand's storytelling features a narrative that highlights not only aesthetics and comfort but also an environmentally conscious lifestyle. The "Better for the Planet" themed campaign, in particular, places Allbirds' eco-friendly approach and sustainability mission at the heart of its storytelling. This brand presents environmental responsibility not just as a marketing strategy but also as an integral part of the brand's identity. By offering a visionary brand story that strongly emphasizes its values and mission, Allbirds encourages its consumers to shop not only for high-quality products but also with consideration for the planet's future (Zamora, 2025). The values and messages used in the stories offered by brands not only win consumers' loyalty but also ensure their emotional belonging to the brand. This emotional attachment can increase the brand's perceived value and help develop long-term customer relationships.

When consumers connect with brands through stories, this connection usually occurs at an emotional rather than a rational level (Thomson, et al., 2005). Lego's 2019 "Rebuild the World" campaign can be shown as an example of the creative strategy the brand used to establish an emotional bond with its target audience. Lego has successfully gained a strong place in the hearts of its viewers with a message that unites children and young people and highlights imagination. Lego aimed to establish an emotional bond with its target audience through themes such as imagination and creativity, social change and progress, and inclusivity and diversity. In this context, starting from the idea of creating a boundless world of imagination, Lego offers consumers not only toys but also the opportunity to think freely, create, and rebuild. With its "Rebuild the World" campaign, Lego addresses the theme of rebuilding social structures and values. This strategy is significant not only for the child target audience but also for the adult, family, and collective target audiences. Furthermore, by presenting multicultural characters and stories throughout the campaign, Lego aims to establish an emotional bond with its audience by adopting an approach that encompasses people of all ages and cultures. It is known that content expressing diversity also appeals to a broad target audience (Lego Education, 2025). Lego strives to leave lasting messages in the minds of its consumers by telling both emotional and consistent stories. In this context, the power of a brand's story is shaped by the brand's identity and consistency (Lundqvist, 2013).

When brands explicitly reveal their identity in their stories and consistently maintain this identity, they can become more sincere in the eyes of consumers. When storytelling is carried out consistently, it can increase trust in the brand and ensure brand loyalty (Aaker, 1996). For instance, Warby Parker, an eyewear brand, stands out as a brand that employs a strategy of consistency and trust in its storytelling. Warby Parker has established a social responsibility strategy with its promise to donate a pair of glasses for every pair sold, thus portraying a brand image that promises trust. In this context, the eyewear brand, which has created the image of a "benevolent brand," has also conveyed messages of consistency and empathy. Warby Parker's digital experience also forms a strong storytelling element. Its service of sending free glasses for at-home try-on provides customers with a sense of trust and makes the glasses shopping experience easier and more transparent. The importance the brand places on customer experience increases trust, while also creating a story that successfully reflects digital transformation. In addition to the stories narrated through Warby Parker's experience and digital service offerings, its design and pricing policy also stand out as a remarkable narrative element. While bringing stylish, high-quality, and affordable glasses together with its target audience, the brand also presents stories that convey its value-oriented and customer-friendly approach

(Grow, 2018). Furthermore, a solution-oriented and results-oriented approach is also significant in brands' storytelling. It is crucial for the conflict and problems narrated in stories to find a resolution and a satisfactory conclusion. Brands generally offer a solution in their stories, and this solution is related to the service offered by the brand. The solution provides the consumer with a concrete indicator of the brand's value and impact.

The end of the story demonstrates how the goods and services offered by the brand improve the consumer's life or provide value (Cohen, 2013). IKEA is at the forefront of brands that frequently use the problem-solving and results strategy in their stories. IKEA's "Everyday Heroes" campaign focuses on creative and functional products designed to improve the lives of ordinary people. In this campaign, IKEA takes on a kind of "hero" role by showcasing its products that offer solutions to the challenges of people's daily lives. This storytelling emphasizes not only the functionality of the products but also their ability to make life easier, more efficient, and more meaningful (Murphy, 2015). Another example is IKEA's "The Wonderful Everyday" campaign, which narrates how the brand's products can make people happy in their daily lives and improve their lives. In this campaign, IKEA adopted a solution-oriented approach that enables transformation and personal development in living spaces, and it established an emotional connection with its customers through this narrative (Effie, 2018). Furthermore, world-renowned brands such as Amazon build their stories on speed and time. Amazon uses speed and timing perfectly in events such as "Prime Day," creating effective storytelling. Additionally, Amazon's fast delivery time is highlighted during these events. This attracts consumers not only to buy products quickly but also with the promise that they will usually receive the products within a few hours. Moreover, Amazon combines speed and timing in such campaigns not only with physical delivery but also with the digital experience (Ukeni, 2022: 6). During events like Prime Day, the opportunities offered by brands and Amazon change instantly, and new opportunities are added rapidly, which reinforces the feeling that consumers need to act quickly. Furthermore, it can be stated that a similar speed strategy exists in Amazon's campaigns such as "Black Friday" and "Cyber Monday." On these days, when sales increase, Amazon appeals to its target audience by presenting a narrative based on timing and speed. As can be understood from the Amazon example, brands attract consumers' attention by using the right timing in storytelling. The tempo and good timing of a story increase its impact, ensuring that the brand's message is conveyed more effectively (Pulizzi, 2012). Today, not only cargo, furniture, and food brands but also fashion brands frequently use one or more of the storytelling strategies for marketing purposes. For instance, Patagonia adopts a strong storytelling strategy that focuses on environmental sustainability and ethical production processes. The brand has narrated its mission to be in harmony with nature and environmentally conscious through striking campaigns such as "Don't Buy This Jacket." In such campaigns, it encourages consumers not only to buy products but also to make decisions by considering their environmental impact. Patagonia's story not only creates a non-profit brand image but also directs consumers to establish an emotional bond with the brand. This bond is strengthened through content, documentaries, and brand stories that emphasize environmentally friendly production and recycling processes (Brownell & Kurtz, 2022). In addition to outdoor fashion clothing brands like Patagonia, luxury brands also frequently adopt the storytelling strategy. Luxury brands, which are structured on the basis of high price, quality, and rarity principles, have increasingly benefited from storytelling in recent years to strengthen their prestigious image (Hughes et al., 2016, p. 357). Therefore, it is stated that luxury brands, especially within fashion marketing, need to take advantage of new trends such as storytelling, narratives, and marketing strategies (Ko & Megehee, 2012). The main features of luxury brands also include limited production, craftsmanship, heritage, elegance, innovation, and high demand. However, these elements are nourished not only by the product but also by the brand's story (Andrade, 2021). Hughes, et al. (2016) state that the stories that luxury brands tell their target audiences are based on the brand's unique history and that these stories help consumers better understand the characteristics of the brands. For example, Cartier, a world-renowned luxury accessory brand, appeals to the emotions of its target audience with its "Love Collection," offering romantic narratives to its consumers through key words such as love, affection, and romance conveyed through its communication campaigns. This narrative both contributes to the prestige of a luxury accessory brand like Cartier and reminds consumers of the brand's elegant image (Saifa, 2023). Kapferer and Bastien (2009) emphasize that the main focus of luxury brands is to draw consumers into the brand's fantasy world, which increases sales by captivating customers' desires. Through storytelling, luxury brands convey a message that will enhance consumers' perception of the brand. In addition, the spiritual aspect of a brand is of great importance, and as an epic tale consisting of stories, a luxury brand becomes a form of expression (Donzé & Wubs, 2019). It is known that luxury brands are brands that possess not only high prices and quality but also a history and prestigious past that make them unique (Çelik Varol, 2022). In this context, as Kapferer and Bastien (2015) also states, it can be said that luxury brands, which establish emotional and psychological bonds with their consumers by offering special experiences, do not only sell goods and services to their consumers. Consequently, these luxury brands promise sensory pleasures rather than functional values to their consumers by offering them stories of lifestyle, identity, and prestige (Ciulu, 2024). For example, the narratives of a brand with a deep heritage like Patek Philippe regarding prestige, and the storytelling of a Rolls Royce car being more than just a vehicle can be shown as examples. Furthermore, the stories told by luxury brands also stand out as an element that strengthens brand identity.

As Aaker (1996) also states, since brand identity represents the meaning and values offered by a brand, luxury brands frequently utilize storytelling to create the desired perception and image in consumers' minds. Brands like Rolex emphasize the idea of timeless quality and excellence in their storytelling, promising their consumers more than just a watch (Rolex, 2025). In this context, the brand's positioning is seen as related to its historical significance and the perception of luxury, beyond just the products themselves (Beverland, 2006). Authentic narratives are a crucial strategy for luxury brands to build trust with consumers. In other words, a genuine and deep-rooted narrative can have a significant impact on consumers (Ciulu, 2024). For example, luxury brands like Chanel and Dior meet this tradition of authentic storytelling with their long-standing cultural heritage and histories. These luxury brands emphasize their mastery and craftsmanship passed down from generation to generation, demonstrating that their products are not just a luxury but also carry cultural value (Silva, 2024). Indeed, authentic narratives strengthen the respected image of luxury brands while also helping them establish a deeper and more meaningful connection with consumers. Brands provide their consumers with trust and emotional bonds through narratives that make them feel special and unique, emphasizing their long history. Escalas (2004) states that consumers value not only the functional aspects of products but also the emotional connection they form with these products.

Luxury brands reinforce brand loyalty by offering emotional and cultural messages that can be associated with the consumer's sense of identity. Consumers not only purchase a product but also feel like a part of this story. For instance, when Hermès offers its customers a story based on the brand's history and artisan approach, it provides them not just a product but also an identity, prestige, and social status. This strategy increases the emotional bond and loyalty to the brand and allows consumers to identify with the brand's story (Srisan, 2024). Another element that allows luxury brands to bring their stories together with a broad target audience is digitalization. In other words, digitalization has become a significant tool for luxury brands to deliver their storytelling quickly and organically to wider audiences. Hudders, et al. (2013) state that digital marketing tools enable luxury brands to interact with their target audiences, making brand storytelling more effective. Gucci, a well-established global brand, establishes an emotional bond with its target audience by sharing creative and original content that emphasizes the brand's historical and cultural heritage on platforms such as Instagram and YouTube. Thanks to digital platforms, brands can reach a global audience with their stories and interact with young consumer groups (Rawal, 2018). Furthermore, luxury brands create a feeling of “limited production” and “exclusivity” by offering their consumers a limited number of products (Çelik

Varol, 2022). This strategy ensures that luxury brands maintain a prestigious and rare position (Kapferer & Bastain, 2009). Consequently, luxury brands in their own stories often focus on an "exclusive audience" or "offering a special experience." For example, luxury brands like Patek Philippe emphasize that each of their watches is produced in limited quantities and frequently highlight the story that each one is a special, handcrafted product (Chuo, 2017). As in the Patek Philippe example, these stories not only show that the products are valuable and rare but also bestow symbolic meanings on their owners. At the same time, luxury brands appeal to a wide audience by incorporating cultural and social meanings into their stories (Ekebring & Mellqvist, 2019). For instance, Hermès enriches its designs and stories with different cultural references, drawing inspiration from Asian cultures. Such stories enable brands to appeal to broader markets as well. Indeed, the storytelling strategies of luxury brands are not just a marketing tool but play a fundamental role in the construction of brand identity, prestige, and loyalty. The fashion stories used by brands enable consumers to establish emotional bonds and see the brand as a part of themselves. Modern strategies such as digital channels and limited access strategies ensure that these stories reach the targeted audiences, helping brands gain a competitive advantage in the global market in terms of both fashion marketing and content production. The next section of the study will analyze the storytelling strategies of selected luxury brands.

Statement of the Problem

Within the contemporary understanding of marketing, luxury fashion brands can resort to various communication strategies to effectively convey their brand values, prestige, and image to consumers, going beyond merely offering goods and services. The success of these luxury brands in the fashion world lies not only in providing their target audiences with high-quality, stylish, and expensive products but also in communicating a strong brand identity and story. In this way, the communication strategies of luxury brands transcend a product promotion based on symbolism and pleasure, enabling them to establish emotional bonds with their consumers and convey narratives about the tangible and intangible values of the brand.

In recent years, it has been observed that storytelling has gained increasing importance in the marketing communication strategies of brands. Storytelling allows brands to differentiate themselves, emphasize their values, and establish a deep connection with their consumers. However, looking at the literature, research on how luxury brands create stories and the role of these stories in their marketing strategies is quite limited. In other words, the scarcity of academic studies on how luxury brands use storytelling and branding strategies within the framework of fashion marketing, how these brands appeal to their target audiences, and how these strategies shape brand perception is noteworthy. Furthermore, when looking at studies on similar topics in the literature, it can be said that most of these studies remain at a theoretical level, and content analyses based on concrete examples of practical applications are not included. In this context, content analysis-based studies on luxury fashion brands are quite limited. It is thought that this research, which aims to examine the role of storytelling in the fashion marketing or communication efforts of luxury brands in depth, can contribute to this area, which is quite open to research. The research will examine how five prestigious luxury fashion brands structure their stories and how these stories align with the brands' marketing strategies, using the content analysis method. It is believed that this study will contribute to the literature and constitute a significant step in understanding the impact and role of storytelling in fashion marketing, both due to the selected research method and the fact that the communication efforts of the luxury brands included in the study have not been previously addressed in this context.

Aim and Significance of the Research

The aim of this academic study is to conduct an analysis of how luxury brands utilize storytelling in their communication efforts within the framework of luxury branding, fashion marketing, and storytelling. It has been observed that in today's fashion world, luxury brands are making a difference not only with the goods and services they offer but also with the narratives they convey to their consumers. In this context, the storytelling strategies of luxury brands stand out as a significant tool that enables consumers to identify with the brand identity. This study aims to contribute to the advertising and marketing literature by analyzing the role of storytelling in the communication strategies of luxury brands and fashion brands using the content analysis method. At the same time, it aims to shed light on new consumer trends in fashion marketing by understanding how luxury brands use the concept of storytelling in the context of communication strategy and by investigating how the communication strategies of these brands are shaped. The significance of the study lies in its potential to allow us to understand how brand image and value can be reinforced not only by product quality but also by effective storytelling in the fashion industry. In this context, information will be provided on how storytelling can be used more efficiently as a tool for brands to differentiate themselves and gain a competitive advantage. Thus, a new perspective will be gained in the academic field on fashion marketing and luxury branding strategies.

Universe and Sample of the Research, Limitations

The luxury fashion brands and their stories examined in this study are part of a universe where the number of elements is not limited or countable. In this context, the universe of the study has been evaluated as an "infinite universe." This research is structured on the basis of the stories told in the campaigns of well-established luxury fashion brands, and the sampling frame was created through concepts such as "storytelling," "luxury fashion brands," and "fashion marketing." The sample consists of campaigns selected through simple random sampling. An academic study will be conducted using content analysis related to luxury branding, fashion marketing, and storytelling. The reasons for selecting the stories in the Louis Vuitton (Spirit of Travel), Gucci (Gucci Garden), Rolex (Perpetual Spirit), Dior (Dior and I), and Prada (Prada Paradoxe) campaigns to be examined within the scope of the study lie in the strategic goals pursued by the effective storytelling of these brands in the field of luxury branding and fashion marketing. The main reasons for selecting prestigious brands such as Louis Vuitton, Gucci, Rolex, Dior, and Prada are their leading positions in the luxury segment and their symbolic meanings in the fashion industry. Furthermore, these brands not only focus on product sales but also build a strong brand identity by interacting with in-depth cultural, artistic, and social contexts. These campaigns, on the other hand, are seen as content strategies that highlight the cultural, historical, and aesthetic values of each brand and aim to establish an emotional connection with the consumer, and therefore, they are considered worthy of academic examination. It can also be stated that the mentioned brands were included in the research part of the study due to reasons such as having at least 10 million followers on social media despite their target audiences being niche, their fashion campaigns frequently being reflected in the media, and having deep-rooted histories and cultures.

Method of the Research

This research aims to analyze the stories in the Louis Vuitton (Spirit of Travel), Gucci (Gucci Garden), Rolex (Perpetual Spirit), Dior (Dior and I), and Prada (Prada Paradoxe) campaigns using the content analysis method in the fields of luxury branding, fashion marketing, and storytelling. Content analysis is a research method used in the social sciences for the detailed and systematic analysis of written or visual images or different content. This method allows for the organization and interpretation of the data to be examined in order to provide a more in-depth analysis of a particular phenomenon or event (Metin & Ünal, 2022). The descriptive content analysis method, which is one of the content analysis methods in this study and is used, involves the comprehensive examination and systematic arrangement of qualitative and quantitative studies that are independent of each other in a specific topic or field. In this way, the general trends in the relevant field are revealed. In other words, Descriptive content analysis involves the systematic analysis of independent research on a topic; the findings obtained become a guide for future studies (Ültay, et al., 2021). The main purpose of the research is to qualitatively analyze how the stories presented in the communication campaigns of 5 luxury fashion brands are utilized from perspectives such as brand strategies and what they offer to the consumer.

Analysis of Luxury Brands' Stories with Content Analysis Method

"Storytelling," which stands out as one of the most significant communication strategies of luxury brands, provides a number of advantages for brands both in terms of establishing emotional bonds with consumers and strengthening brand image. The different stories told through the communication efforts and campaigns of the well-established luxury brands listed below will be analyzed using the content analysis method in terms of the campaign theme, campaign story, campaign message, and the symbolic meanings conveyed by the campaign.

1. Rolex: Perpetual Spirit

Rolex, established in London in 1905 by Hans Wilsdorf, is a luxury watch brand. Renowned for the quality of its mechanisms, chronometric precision, and Class A accuracy certification, Rolex has consistently symbolized elegance, quality, luxury, and prestige from its inception to the present day (Rolex, 2025). Rolex's "Perpetual Spirit" communication campaign, planned in three-month or six-month periods, has designed a communication strategy based on periodicals that detail watch models, design stories, and aspects highlighting the lifestyles of its target audience. This communication campaign features well-written stories and offers enchanting glimpses into the lifestyles of the brand's target demographic. It can be stated that Rolex's Perpetual Spirit campaign is designed to emphasize the brand's commitment to timelessness, excellence, and passion. With this campaign, Rolex aims to convey the story that it goes beyond just manufacturing watches, with each timepiece embodying a passion and a spirit of continuous innovation. This campaign stands out as a narrative that celebrates the most significant elements in Rolex's history—elegance, durability, and excellence. The expression "Perpetual Spirit" symbolizes Rolex's dedication to constant innovation, the pursuit of excellence, and transcending time. By presenting the brand's unique designs and engineering genius in harmony with time, this campaign narrates that Rolex offers not just a watch but a lifestyle and a spirit. The driving force behind Rolex's time-honored and continuously evolving structure is the concept of "Perpetual," meaning "Endless."

Rolex's Perpetual Spirit campaign tells a story that offers a journey beyond time. The campaign traces the excellence and passion involved in every stage of a Rolex watch, from its production to its design and engineering details. Each gear within the watch's mechanism is inspired by the brand's past achievements while also laying a foundation for future innovations. The story reflects not only the passion and lifestyles of the watches themselves but also of the individuals who live in harmony with these timepieces. Rolex watches do not just show people the time; they also elevate them to high goals, success, and timeless excellence. In this context, the campaign emphasizes that Rolex is not just a watch brand but also a symbol of a philosophy of life, perseverance, and determination. The Perpetual Spirit campaign is a celebration of the quality, passion, and excellence that Rolex offers with each of its watches. The brand aims to provide its users with a tool that will enable them to push boundaries in their respective fields. These watches are seen not as timepieces but as symbols of a life lived beyond time. The campaign narrates that Rolex is not only a watch brand but also represents a lifestyle and a philosophy. The campaign not only celebrates Rolex's timeless values and the power of the human spirit but also highlights the brand's evolution and continuous pursuit of innovation.

2. Louis Vuitton: Spirit of Travel

Founded in Paris in 1854, Louis Vuitton has emerged from the past to the present as a symbol of quality, timelessness, and excellence in the art of travel (Sortiraparis, 2023). Jean Lariviere spent 40 years photographing products in awe-inspiring locations such as Burma, Yemen, Greenland, Nepal, and Thailand to narrate the story of the Louis Vuitton brand (Louis Vuitton, 2025). Louis Vuitton's Spirit of Travel campaign is interpreted as an aesthetic expression of the brand's deep-rooted heritage and its relationship with travel. This campaign has generally emerged to highlight Louis Vuitton's luxury travel bags and accessories. Both the visual language and the intended message of the campaign also provide consumers with information about the brand's history, target audience, and contemporary understanding of luxury.

As a brand established on the principles of durable and long-term transport of leather travel goods such as bags and suitcases, Louis Vuitton has reflected the theme of Spirit of Travel to its consumers within the framework of "naturalness." The brand gained recognition in its early days by producing sturdy, lightweight, and stylish trunks for train journeys. The Spirit of Travel campaign alludes to these rich roots, attempting to convey the luxury, freedom, and sense of discovery associated with travel. Louis Vuitton tells a story that aims to revive the elegant journeys of the past in the modern world. Spirit of Travel presents travel not just as a means of transportation but also as luxury, freedom, a contemporary lifestyle, modernity, and personal discovery. The campaign is not just a product promotion but also states that travel is a modern form of individual expression. In this campaign story, Louis Vuitton tries to convey that traveling is not just a physical movement but also a lifestyle, an aesthetic, and a way to discover individual experience. It is known that Louis Vuitton generally uses an impressive and striking visual style in its campaigns. The Spirit of Travel campaign also stands out as a visually powerful campaign, creatively reflecting the magic of travel. The campaign usually features grand landscape photographs, exotic locations, and luxurious settings. These visuals present travel not just as going from one place to another but as a way to explore the world and create a new story with each journey.

The campaign often features famous photographers and significant artists with whom the brand collaborates. For example, the Spirit of Travel campaign bears the signature of world-renowned photographer Jean Lariviere. Lariviere's photographic style highlights the emotional depth of the characters and the magic of the locations, which emphasizes the campaign's themes of luxury and discovery. Louis Vuitton goes beyond just being a travel brand in its campaign. This campaign shows that the brand appeals to a select and sophisticated customer base. The Spirit of Travel message represents wealth, freedom, and a desire to live life "successfully." Through this campaign, Louis Vuitton offers not just a travel bag but also a representation of freedom and the desire for exploration. This makes the brand attractive to the global elite. The campaign also states that travel holds an essentail place in a socio-cultural context. While travel was previously accessible only to the wealthy classes, it has become possible for wider audiences today. Louis Vuitton both celebrates this transformation and associates it with high socio-economic status. The campaign presents traveling as a way of life but also conveys the message that this way of life is an "exclusive" experience. However, considering Louis Vuitton's sustainability efforts in recent years, the Spirit of Travel campaign has begun to carry a touch of an understanding of travel in harmony with nature and the environment, beyond just luxury and visual appeal. While travel is often made to different parts of the planet or natural wonders, adopting an environmentally responsible approach aligns with the brand's modern sensibilities. Indeed, Louis Vuitton's Spirit of Travel campaign contains a message based on the brand's rich history, cultural context, and understanding of luxury. The association of travel with freedom, discovery, and the process of finding meaning in life transforms Louis Vuitton from merely a bag brand into a lifestyle, a culture, and a "luxury way of life." The campaign presents the brand's classic and modern values together, both respecting the past and revealing its vision for the future.

3. Gucci: Gucci Garden

Gucci, one of the well-established luxury Italian fashion brands, was founded in Florence in 1921 by Guccio Gucci. This brand, established by Guccio Gucci, is particularly known in the fashion world for its quality-promising products, aesthetic designs, and elegant iconic logo and patterns. The brand stands out especially with its bags, shoes, clothing products, accessories, and perfumes (Berksü, 2021). While the Gucci Museum, opened in Florence in 2011, showcases the tangible and intangible heritage of the brand passed down from the past to the present, Alessandro Michele aimed to transform the classic museum concept into an interactive experience by launching the Gucci Garden project (Vogue, 2018). The Gucci Garden campaign story stands out as a significant step where the brand offers an innovative experience by bringing together luxury and art. This campaign is noteworthy as a project that explores Gucci's creative vision, aesthetic understanding, and cultural influences in the fashion world. Gucci Garden is a story designed not just as a shopping experience but also as an art gallery and experiential space. Gucci Garden offers a journey into the brand's history and cultural heritage. It encompasses a broad narrative from the first steps of Gucci's founder, Guccio Gucci, to the unique and bold designs of the brand's recent creative director, Alessandro Michele. This provides an aesthetic and deep-rooted storytelling that emphasizes the connections between the brand's past and present. Gucci Garden exhibits a multi-layered approach in terms of aesthetics. The space design, colors, and graphics create an experience that blends fashion and art. As in every campaign, Gucci blends different art forms, popular culture elements, and historical images with a modern perspective in this project. The visuals and videos featured in the campaign are also intertwined with art and equipped with visually striking elements. This is an essentail in terms of offering consumers an experience. Gucci Garden goes beyond traditional advertising, setting a significant example in terms of experiential marketing. It not only offers visitors fashion products but also tells a story. This world created by Gucci becomes a “discovery space” for the brand's loyal customers. This campaign also allows the brand to create a brand identity enriched with cultural and artistic values. Furthermore, although Gucci Garden started as a physical space project, it also demonstrates a strong presence in the digital realm. Promotions made through social media platforms and the brand's website have ensured that the campaign reaches a wider audience. In this context, it can be stated that an attempt is made to create unity in both the physical and digital worlds with this narrative. The Gucci Garden campaign, by adopting a storytelling-based approach, enables us to explore the brand's identity and values more deeply. Indicators from Gucci's history and modern interpretations emerge as an aesthetic experience. This helps Gucci express its brand identity in a more comprehensive and in-depth manner. Indeed, the Gucci Garden campaign is not just a store opening or a collection launch but rather a significant example of experiential storytelling that shows how the brand has evolved culturally. Gucci highlights art and design not only in its products but also in the brand's overall experience. This campaign establishes a strong connection both visually and emotionally because it presents the brand's respect for its past and its vision for the future in a modern way. In this context, the Gucci Garden campaign enables the brand to establish a deeper connection with its loyal audience as well as a more meaningful relationship with new generation consumers.

4. Dior: Dior and I

Christian Dior was established as a fashion house in 1905 in the Normandy region of France (Vsco Works, 2023). Seen as a representative of luxury and elegance in the fashion world, Dior brought numerous narratives to its audience in the fashion documentary titled "Dior and I," ranging from the brand's establishment to its designs, fashion designers, and fabrics (Ergen, 2015). Dior's "Dior and I" campaign, while emphasizing the brand's history, elegance, and luxury, has also managed to impress the audience with a modern storytelling approach. The campaign addresses the period that began with designer Raf Simons's joining Christian Dior and conveys the brand's founder Christian Dior's struggle to create an aesthetic revolution in the design world with a contemporary perspective. This campaign not only promotes a fashion brand but also shares an emotional and dramatic story, encompassing the concept of fashion marketing. At the heart of the campaign lies the process of Raf Simons joining the Dior brand and preparing his first collection. At this point, the Dior brand is treated almost like a character. How Raf Simons will approach this legacy and how he will reflect his own vision narrates a process of change to the audience. The elegance and graceful lines created by Dior's founder are being attempted to be reshaped in a fashion world that changes over time. This process actually symbolizes a kind of innovation and revolution that every brand harbors within itself. Furthermore, from a storytelling perspective, the campaign also reveals the challenges faced by Raf Simons. Each new collection carries the responsibility of confronting the previous legacy, adapting it to the modern world, and keeping the brand's identity current. In Dior's creative process, elements such as the technical dimensions of the work, the balance between designs, and collaborations with artists and teams come to the forefront. This conflict can be seen as the most exciting and dramatic part of the campaign because it shows the audience what an artist in the "real" fashion world has to do to overcome these challenges. However, in the "Dior and I" campaign, Raf Simons's personal journey and his connection with the brand can be considered one of the most significant elements of storytelling. Simons's commitment to his designs and the responsibility assigned to him present to the audience how his relationship with the brand transforms into a personal bond. The campaign shows the audience the inner workings of the design process; it narrates how the emotional, creative, and technical obstacles encountered in the creation of the collection are overcome. This story connects the audience to the brand not only aesthetically but also emotionally by showing the designer behind the brand. Moreover, the focus of this narrative is also the introduction of Raf Simons's first collection. This collection exalts the past of the Dior brand while also presenting Simons's own aesthetic vision. The modern touches blended with Dior's elegance and luxury create a kind of evolution for the brand. This point can be described as a kind of "victory" because the rebirth and adaptation of a symbolic brand to the modern world are presented to the audience. At the end of the story, the relationship between Dior and Raf Simons provides the audience with a deep meaning. The campaign not only promotes the products of a brand but also tells the story behind the design process, the challenges, the successes, and the personal struggles. In this context, the Dior brand opens the doors to a world of art and creativity, going beyond just being a luxury brand. Indeed, Dior's "Dior and I" campaign offers a multi-layered and impressive approach in terms of storytelling. The campaign tells a story that blends the past, present, and future of the Dior brand, involving the audience not only with a fashion brand but also with the creative process of a design house. This can be expressed as a narrative that highlights the human aspect of the brand, its creative struggles, and its innovative vision.

5. Prada: Prada Paradoxe

Prada, founded in Milan in 1913 by Mario Prada, stands out as a luxury brand that delicately offers high-quality and aesthetically blended bags, shoes, watches, eyewear, and travel products (Prada, 2025). The communication campaign for the brand's Paradoxe perfume is structured around a story that references the brand's deep-rooted history, aesthetic understanding, and innovative perspective. This campaign was created within the framework of modern touches, with a strategy that takes Prada's traditional luxury image a step further. Prada Paradoxe emerges in the luxury perfume category as a form of expression that combines pleasure and elegance. As can be understood from the brand name, Prada Paradoxe reveals the brand's sophisticated structure with a romantic language. The concrete value conveyed by the product, being composed of fruit and flower scents, and the abstract value, being a blend of classic and modern lines, are narrated through storytelling within the advertising campaign message. The narrative, which gives the target audience a "sense of experience," also conveys information to consumers about the brand's story, elegance, and deep-rooted history. Starting from the perfume's name and theme, Prada Paradoxe, the campaign is shaped by the idea that contradictions can coexist. "Paradoxe," on the one hand, carries a deep meaning, while on the other hand, it symbolizes the brand's modern female identity and lifestyle. In the campaign, contrasts such as strong and fragile, free and connected, natural and sophisticated are presented together. This can be interpreted as a metaphor for the perfume's structure, which is both simple and complex. The visual language used in the campaign stands out as one of the basic tools that tell the story. With a simple yet elegant aesthetic understanding, the viewer is offered a "spiritual journey." Visuals generally hold a large place in the fashion world, and Prada, in this campaign, focuses on the viewer's sensory experience by using the power of visual narration. An impression of the perfume's abstractness is created through the play of light and shadow, deep color palettes, and different figures. The emotional transitions of the woman become distinct, just like the different notes of the perfume. The campaign visuals narrate a kind of inner conflict and the process of self-discovery that comes at the end of this conflict. Critical moments and instantaneous emotional outbursts form the essence of the perfume. It is observed that abstract elements are used intensively in the storytelling of this campaign. The viewer is enabled to identify with the perfume through symbolism and abstract images. The campaign conveys a narrative that aims to create an emotional experience rather than a direct product description. Abstractly conveying the contradictions of the perfume and the inner journey of the character also allows the viewer to include their personal experiences in the campaign. For example, through the visual representation of the perfume and the music used, the viewer can experience a feeling of emotional "pleasure." The dream-focused sequences in the campaign can be interpreted as reflections of the perfume's abstract structure. In this context, it can be stated that the main elements of storytelling in the fashion brand's message are character, conflict, problem, and solution. Indeed, it can be said that the Prada Paradoxe campaign is a very powerful communication effort in terms of visual language and storytelling. This campaign, built on contrasts and expressive contradictions, presents the perfume itself not just as a product but as a story of emotional experience and inner discovery. The abstract and symbolic language used in the storytelling not only makes the viewer watch but also takes them on a deep inner journey. This campaign elevates the brand's perception of luxury to a deeper narrative level, offering individuals not just a perfume but an experience through a luxurious lifestyle and identity.

CONCLUSION

Storytelling, which stands out as an essential communication strategy today, is significant not only for personal and corporate brands but also for luxury fashion brands. The stories created to establish brand identity, build long-term relationships with consumers, form emotional bonds, and create impressive narratives about the brand's deep-rooted heritage and fashion marketing appeal to consumers' emotions, also enabling them to communicate with brands. In this context, luxury brands tell stories to their consumers through various communication campaigns both within the framework of fashion marketing and to establish long-term relationships with consumers. This research aims to examine the stories in the Louis Vuitton (Spirit of Travel), Gucci (Gucci Garden), Rolex (Perpetual Spirit), Dior (Dior and I), and Prada (Prada Paradoxe) campaigns using the content analysis method within the context of luxury branding, fashion marketing, and storytelling. It can be stated that in the advertising messages, documentaries, and communication campaigns prepared for consumers by the 5 luxury fashion brands – Rolex, Louis Vuitton, Prada, Dior, Gucci – examined with the content analysis method within the scope of the study, the deep-rooted history, design history, quality and originality, and principles of rarity of the brands are particularly emphasized. Furthermore, the heritage that these luxury brands possess from the past to the present, and the symbolic meanings such as prestige, status, and wealth that they convey to consumers have been blended within the framework of narratives and communicated to the target audience. From this point of view, it shows that the narrative elements of each campaign are designed in strong harmony with the historical identities, values, and target audiences of the brands. Louis Vuitton's Spirit of Travel campaign creates a narrative where travel and discovery are combined with luxury, while Gucci's Gucci Garden campaign offers the consumer an aesthetic and intellectual experience by emphasizing the brand's connection with art. Rolex's Perpetual Spirit campaign, as a symbol of time and excellence, has a narrative that reinforces the brand's prestige. Dior's Dior and I campaign offers a perspective on the brand's design process, conveying the brand's creative identity to the consumer, while Prada's Prada Paradoxe campaign presents the brand's contemporary and bold image by combining it with a commitment to modernism. The content analysis method used within the scope of this research has revealed that the design and narrative elements in each of these campaigns are carefully selected and developed in line with the strategic goals of the brands. Brands manage to strengthen their brand identities and prestige while establishing a narrative that appeals to the values and expectations of their consumers. Each campaign is built in harmony with the brand's cultural codes, historical background, and the emotional and aesthetic needs of its target audience. As a result, this research demonstrates the crucial role that storytelling plays in the fashion marketing strategies of luxury brands and that the experiences that brands offer to consumers carry not only product value but also cultural and emotional significance. The content analysis method provides significant information about how the narratives of these campaigns are shaped both aesthetically and strategically by ensuring their in-depth understanding. Therefore, it is believed that this research will contribute to both the marketing literature and communication studies. Although a large number of studies on "luxury branding," "fashion marketing," and "storytelling" attract attention in the literature, no study analyzing these three concepts through current communication campaigns has been found. In this context, it can be stated that this research will provide an original contribution to the relevant literature. Similarly, a study titled *"Luxury Brands' Storytelling on Social Media"* published in 2019, one of the studies included in the literature, revealed that luxury brands effectively communicate luxury values through storytelling on social media platforms. While storytelling makes it possible to build emotional connection and build a collective brand meaning with followers, social media serves as a tool that strengthens this interaction. The findings show that luxury values have remained stable, but the forms of transmission of these values have been reconstructed in the context of social media (Ekebring & Mellqvist, 2019). According to the findings of Andrade's study titled *"Luxury Brand Communication on Social Media"* conducted in 2021, luxury brands reflect brand values through social media in four basic ways: (1) to ensure consistency, (2) to maintain originality, (3) to maintain desirability, and (4) to offer interesting and educational content. The study contributes to the literature on social media-based brand communication in the luxury sector and largely coincides with the results of this research. according to the study titled *"Storytelling and Social Networking as Tools for Digital and Mobile Marketing of Luxury Fashion Brands"*, which was conducted in 2017 and examined the increase in the value of the fashion industry within the framework of globalization, digital marketing, brand strategies and generational differences; globalization and digitalization have reshaped the strategies of luxury brands and enabled them to reach new consumer profiles. While brand identity has become the basic element of luxury products, digital marketing and influencer collaborations increase interaction, especially with younger generations. The consumption habits of the millennium generation are of critical importance in determining the future of the sector (González Romo, et al., 2017). When similar studies in the literature are evaluated, it can be stated that they largely coincide with the results of this research, but the study in question differs from other studies due to the analysis of stories told by both fashion marketing and luxury branding and luxury brands through different campaigns. Our recommendations for future studies are as follows: research can be conducted that analyzes more campaigns or communication efforts, quantitative research can be carried out using the survey method on different sample groups, or field research can be included.

REFERENCES

Aaker, D. A. (1991). *Managing Brand Equity: Capitalizing on the Value of a Brand Name*. Free Press.

Aaker, D. A. (1996). Measuring Brand Equity across Products and Markets. *California Management Review, 38*(3).

Aaker, D. A. (1996). *Building strong brands*. Free Press.

Aaker, D. A. (2004). *Brand portfolio strategy: Creating relevance, differentiation, energy, leverage, and clarity*. Simon and Schuster.

Ailawadi, K. L., & Keller, K. L. (2004). Understanding retail branding: Conceptual insights and research priorities. *Journal of Retailing, 80*(4), 331–342.

Akın, L. (2014). Jenerik Marka İsimlerin Oluşumu ve TDK Sözlüğüne Giriş Şekilleri, Uluslararası Sosyal Araştırmalar Dergisi, Cilt: 7, Sayı: 31.

Allbirds. (2025). Mother nature made us do it. https://www.allbirds.com/pages/our-story

AMA. (2025). Branding. https://www.ama.org/topics/brand-and-branding/

Andrade, R. F. C. (2021). *Luxury brand communication on social media. Management with Specialization in Marketing, at the Universidade Católica*. Portuguesa.

Anholt, S. (2006). *Competitive identity: The new brand management for nations, cities and regions*. Palgrave Macmillan.

Bamford. (2015). Ben & Jerry's pushing green message with Save Our Swirled. https://www.thegrocer.co.uk/news/ben-and-jerrys-pushing-green-message-with-save-our-swirled/523992.article

Berksü, Ö. Z. (2021). Gucci: Bir marka hikayesi. https://www.oggusto.com/moda/markalar-ve-tasarimcilar/gucci-bir-marka-hikayesi

Beverland, M. (2006). The Freal thing: Branding authenticity in the luxury wine trade. *Journal of Business Research, 59*, 251–258.

Blackett, T. (2003). What is a Brand? In R. Clifton, & J. Simmons (Ed.), Brands and Branding (ss. 13-26). London: Profile Books.

Hopper, B. (2024). A case study on airbnb's belong anywhere campaign. https://thebrandhopper.com/2024/07/29/a-case-study-on-airbnb-belong-anywhere-campaign/

Bredava, A. (2021). Why everybody loves M&Ms: A marketing success story of a brand mascot. https://awario.com/blog/mms-marketing-mascot/

Brownell, J., & Kurtz, Z. (2022). The power of storytelling at patagonia. https://blog.uvm.edu/si-mba/2022/05/27/the-power-of-storytelling-at-patagonia/

Chevalier, M., & Mazzalovo, G. (2008). *Luxury Brand Management: A World of Privilege*. Wiley.

Chuo, F. (2017). History at a glance: the story of patek philippe. https://deployant.com/history-at-a-glance-the-story-of-patek-philippe/

Ciulu, A. (2024). Luxury brand storytelling: crafting narratives that resonate. https://www.sublimio.com/luxury-brand-storytelling/

Clark, C. (2012). *Personal Branding*. http://illinois.edu/2059/personal_branding_2012.pdf

Cohen, H. (2013). 5 Image storytelling tips brands need. https://heidicohen.com/images-how-to-tell-your-brand-story-examples/

Çelik Varol, M. (2022). *Lüks tüketimde ikinci el*. Orion Yayınevi.

Donzé, P. Y., & Wubs, B. (2019). Storytelling and the making of a global luxury fashion brand: Christian Dior. *International Journal of Fashion Studies*, *6*, 83–102.

Dove. (2024). Dove real beauty sketches. https://www.dove.com/us/en/campaigns/purpose/real-beauty-sketches.html

Dubois, B., & Paternault, C. (1995). Understanding the World of Luxurious Brands. *Journal of Marketing*, *59*(4), 75–91.

Duran, E., & Topbaşoğlu, N. (2017). Hikaye anlatıcılığı ve eğitimde kullanımı. *IJLA*, *14*, 109–124.

Effie. (2018). IKEA & Mother London, The wonderful everyday. https://www.effie.org/insights/ikea-mother-london-the-wonderful-everyday/

Ekebring, K., & Mellqvist, C. (2019). *Luxury brands' storytelling on social media*. Department of Business Studies, Uppsala University.

Ergen, R. C. (2015). Dior and I filminde bilmeniz gereken 8 gerçek. https://vogue.com.tr/moda-haber/dior-and-i-filminde-bilmeniz-gereken-8-gerce

Escalas, J. E. (2004). Imagine yourself in the product: Mental simulation, narrative transportation, and persuasion. *The Journal of Consumer Research*, *30*(2), 249–269.

Escalas, J. E. (2004). Narrative processing: Building consumer connections to brands. *Journal of Consumer Psychology, 14*(1-2), 168–180.

Feng, X., Wang, P., Wang, S., & Zhang, K. (2024). *A study on the construction of brand storytelling and the emotional connection of generation z.* Dean & Francis.

Fog, K., Budtz, C., & Yakaboylu, B. (2005). *Branding through storytelling. Storytelling.* Branding in Practice.

González Romo, Z., Garcia Medina, I., & Plaza Romero, N. (2017). Storytelling and social networking as tools for digital and mobile marketing of luxury fashion brands. *International Journal of Interactive Mobile Technologies., 11*(6), 136–149. DOI: 10.3991/ijim.v11i6.7511

Grow, P. (2018). Power of Storytelling I Warby Parker knows that storytelling is vital to their identity. https://www.pamelagrow.com/10335/power-storytelling-warby-parker-knows-storytelling-vital-identity/

Hermansson, F. (2005). *The Service Branding Model: Small Service Firms' Approach to Building Brand Equity* (Yayınlanmamış Yüksek Lisans Tezi). Jönköping University, İsveç.

Herskovitz, S., & Crystal, M. (2010). The essential brand persona: Storytelling and branding. *The Journal of Business Strategy, 31*(3), 21–22.

Hopkinson, G. C., & Hogarth-Scott, S. (2001). What happened was... broadening the agenda for storied research. *Journal of Marketing Management, 17*(1-2), 27–47.

Howell, P. (2025). Brand storytelling is not about what you make, but what you make happen. https://businessofstory.com/brand-storytelling-not-make-make-happen/

Hudders, L., Pandelaere, M., & Vyncke, P. (2013). Consumer meaning making: The meaning of luxury brands in a democratised luxury world. *International Journal of Market Research, 55*(3), 391–412.

Hughes, M., Bendoni, W. K., & Pehlivan, E. (2016). Storygiving as a co-creation tool for luxury brands in the age ofthe internet: A love story by Tiffany and thousands of lovers. *Journal of Product and Brand Management, 25*(4), 357–364.

Kang, J. A., Hong, S., & Hubbard, G. T. (2020). The role of storytelling in advertising: Consumer emotion, narrative engagement level, and word-of-mouth intention. *Journal of Consumer Behaviour, 19*(1), 47–56. https://doi.org/10.1002/cb.1793

Kapferer, J. N. (2012). *The New Strategic Brand Management: Advanced Insights and Strategic Thinking.* Kogan Page Publishers.

Kapferer, J. N., & Bastien, V. (2009). *The luxury strategy: break the rules of marketing to build luxury brands*. Kogan Page Publishers.

Kapferer, J. N., & Bastien, V. (2015). *The luxury strategy: Break the rules of marketing to build luxury brands* (2nd ed.). Kogan Page Publishers.

Kaufman, B. (2003). Stories that sell, stories that tell. *The Journal of Business Strategy, 24*(2), 11–15. http://dx.doi.org/10.1108/02756660310508155

Keller, K. L. (2013). *Strategic brand management: Building, measuring, and managing brand equity*. Pearson Education.

Keller, K. L. (2013). Strategic brand management: Building, measuring and managing brand equity. *Pearson Education.*4.th Edition. ISBN: 978-0-13-266425-7.

Ko, E., & Megehee, C. M. (2012). Fashion Marketing of Luxury Brands: Recent Research Issues and Contributions. *Journal of Business Research, 65*, 1395–1398. DOI: 10.1016/j.jbusres.2011.10.004

Ko, E., & Megehee, C. M. (2012). Fashion marketing of luxury brands: Recent research issues and contribution. *Journal of Business Research, 65*(10), 1395–1398.

Kosakarika, S. (2023). Brand storytelling techniques arousing emotional bonds in different customer groups based on cluster analysis. *Kasetsart Journal of Social Sciences, 44*, 281–292.

Kotler, P., & Pfoertsch, W. (2006). *B2B Brand Management*. Springer.

Lachance, M. J., Beaudoin, P., & Robitaille, J. (2003). Adolescents' brand sensitivity in apparel: Influence of three socialization agents. *International Journal of Consumer Studies, 27*(1), 47–57.

Lee, A., Yang, J., Mizerski, R., & Lambert, C. (2015). *The Strategy of Global Branding and Brand Equity*. Routledge.

Lego Education. (2025). Rebuild the world with storytelling. https://education.lego.com/en-us/rebuild-the-world-with-storytelling-/

Vuitton, L. (2025). The spirit of travel by jean lariviere. https://hk.louisvuitton.com/eng-hk/magazine/articles/louis-vuitton-jean-lariviere

Lundqvist, A., Liljander, V., Gummerus, J., & Van Riel, A. (2013). The Impact of storytelling on the consumer brand experience: The case of a firm-originated story. *Journal of Brand Management, 20*, 283–297. DOI: 10.1057/bm.2012.15

Mandung, F. (2024). The influence of storytelling techniques in digital marketing on brand loyalty: A consumer psychology perspective. *Golden Ratio of Marketing and Applied Psychology of Business*, *5*, 66–78.

Medium. (2017). Apple's art of storytelling. https://medium.com/@absofx/apple-and-the-art-of-storytelling-fd782af8596f

Medium. (2019). Glossier's brand storytelling and the democratization of beauty. https://medium.com/@itmovesit/glossiers-brand-storytelling-and-the-democratization-of-beauty-fc5cab75716c

Metin, O., & Ünal, Ş. (2022). İçerik analizi tekniği: Iletişim bilimlerinde ve sosyolojide doktora tezlerinde kullanımı. *Anadolu Üniversitesi Sosyal Bilimler Dergisi*, *22*(2), 273–294.

Mills, A. J., & John, J. (2021). Brand stories: Bringing narrativetheory to brand management. *Journal of Strategic Marketing*, *28*, 1–9.

Montoya, P. (2002). *The brand called you: Make your business stand out in today's competitive marketplace*. McGraw-Hill.

Mucundorfeanu, M. (2018). The key role of storytelling in the branding process. *Journal of Media Research*. Vol. 11, Issue 1(30). p. 42-54.

Murphy, P. I. (2015). New Ikea campaign focuses on everyday heroes. https://www.retaildive.com/news/new-ikea-campaign-focuses-on-everyday-heroes/374081/

Nueno, J. L., & Quelch, J. A. (1998). The Mass Marketing of Luxury. *Business Horizons*, *39*(6), 61–68.

Öncel, Ş. (2004, Eylül 1). Jenerik Markanın Sonu mu Geliyor? *Capital* http://www.capital.com.tr/yonetim/pazarlama/jenerik-markanin-sonu-mu-geliyor-haberdetay-1614 sayfasından alınmıştır.

Paquette, A. A., Yang, B., & Long, Y. (2017). *How is storytelling used to strengthen a brand? Strategic Brand Management* (3rd ed.). Student Papers.

Pereira, G. (2019). Brand storytelling: A three-dimensional perspective. *Henry Stewart Publications 2045-855x. Journal of Brand Strategy*, *8*(2), 146–159.

Perry, A., & Wisnom, D. (2003). *Markanın DNA'sı, Çev. Zeynep Yılmaz*. Media Cat Yayınları.

Prada. (2025). Galleria 1913. https://www.prada.com/tr/tr/pradasphere/places/galleria-1913.html

Pulizzi, J. (2012). The rise of storytelling as the new marketing. *Journal of Publishing Research Quarterly*, *28*(2), 116–123. DOI: 10.1007/s12109-012-9264-5

Rawal, A. (2018). Gucci's art of storytelling. https://medium.com/@anahatrawal/guccis-art-of-storytelling-e5451cc9d976

Rolex. (2015). About rolex. https://www.rolex.com/tr/about-rolex/history/1905-1919

Rolex. (2025). Making history with rolex. https://www.rolex.org/perpetual/making-history-with-rolex

Romero, A. (2024). How Spotify Wrapped Turns Your Year of Music into a Viral Sensation. https://medium.com/we-are-storytellers/how-spotify-wrapped-turns-your-year-of-music-into-a-viral-sensation-8ee33da89d5d

Rosenthal, B., & Brito, E. P. (2017). The brand meaning co-creation process on Facebook. *Marketing Intelligence & Planning*, *35*(7), 923–936. https://doi.org/10.1108/MIP-09-2016-0171

Ryder, B. (2021). The magical realism of Tesla. *The Economist.* https://www.economist.com/business/2021/04/29/the-magical-realism-of-tesla

Saifa, S. (2023). *The use of storytelling in luxury brands on social media. Bachelor of Arts Program in Journalism (Media Studies) International Program Faculty of Journalism and Mass Communication.* Thammasat University.

Schmitt, B. (2012). The consumer psychology of brands. *Journal of Consumer Psychology*, *22*, 7–17.

Serrat, O. (2008). Storrytelling. *Knowledge Solutions.* October, 10. p. 1-4.

Silva. (2024). Christian dior and coco chanel's ınfamous rift. https://www.elledecor.com/life-culture/a46583225/dior-chanel-rivalry-history/

Soodo. (2025). Nike: The masters of storytelling. https://soodo.co/the-power-of-storytelling-how-nike-inspires-action-with-every-ad/

Sortiraparis. (2023). Louis Vuitton: modaevinin tarihçesi ve Paris'teki haberler. https://www.sortiraparis.com/tr/hobiler/alisveris/articles/306728-louis-vuitton-modaevinin-tarihcesi-ve-paris-teki-haberler

Srisan, K. (2024). The art of storytelling with hermes. https://www.hashtaglegend.com/th-en/the-art-of-storytelling-with-hermes

Teraiya, V., Namboodiri, S., & Jayswal, R. (2023). The impact of storytelling advertising on consumer advertising experiences and brand equity. *Journal of Management Review and Transformation.* Volume 2, Issue 1. e-ISSN: 2583-5076.

Thomson, M., Maclnnis, D. J., & Park, C. W. (2005). The ties that bind: Measuring the strength of consumers' emotional attachments to brands. *Journal of Consumer Psychology*, *15*(1), 77–91.

Ukeni, S. C. (2022). Strategy behind the business success of amazon: a case study. *Texila International Journal of Management.* p.1-16. ISSN: 2520-310X.

Ültay, E., Akyurt, H., & Ültay, N. (2021). Sosyal bilimlerde betimsel içerik analizi. *IBAD Sosyal Bilimler Dergisi*, (10), 188–201. DOI: 10.21733/ibad.871703

Vogue. (2018). Gucci Garden hakkında. https://vogue.com.tr/metropol/gucci-garden-hakkinda

Works, V. (2023). Dior marka hikayesi. https://www.vscoworks.com/blog/dior-marka-hikayesi

Wala, H. H. (2015). *Meine Marke. Was Unternehmen authentisch, unverwechselbar und lagfristig erfolgreich macht, 7.th updated edition.* Redline Verlag.

Woodside, A. G., Sood, S., & Miller, K. E. (2008). When consumers and brands talk: Storytelling theory and research in psychology and marketing. *Psychology and Marketing*, *25*(2), 97–145. https://doi.org/10.1002/mar.20203

Yılmaz, B. F. (2020). Lüks Markalamada Sanatın Kullanılmasının Sosyal Medyada Yansımaları. Istanbul University Social Sciences Institute, Unpublished Master's Thesis.

Zamora. (2025). Unraveling allbirds' strategic narrative. https://zamora.design/unraveling-allbirds-strategic-narrative/

Zeithaml, V. A., Bitner, M. J., & Gremler, D. D. (2018). *Services marketing: Integrating customer focus across the firm.* McGraw-Hill Education.

Zurn, M. (2010). "Fall of the Berlin Wall": Globalisation and the Future of Europe. New Zealand International Review, 35(3), 2–7. https://search.informit.org/doi/10.3316/informit.062924525552962

Chapter 10

The Role of Digital Storytelling in Transforming Consumption Motivations:

"Not an Advertisement, Dubai Chocolate"

Başak Gezmen
Istanbul Medipol Universıty, Turkey

Asena Temelli Coşgun
https://orcid.org/0000-0002-8736-6229
Istanbul Medipol Universıty, Turkey

ABSTRACT

In the digital world we live in today, the meanings produced by advertisements have changed and transformed with representations and discourses, and the functional stories about the product have been replaced by storytelling that emphasises emotional benefit and focuses on creating desire. Consumption motivations are reconstructed around these stories, meaning worlds and symbols. The current study aims to examine the role of storytelling in digital media in the transformation of consumption motivations. For this purpose, in-depth interviews will be conducted with 16 participants from the digital native generation, the most common users of

DOI: 10.4018/979-8-3373-2023-6.ch010

digital media in Turkey. The findings to be obtained through in-depth interviews, one of the qualitative research methods frequently used in social sciences, will be analysed through descriptive analysis.

INTRODUCTION

Since the earliest periods of history, humans have tried to preserve their culture and keep their communities together by transferring information through images, oral narratives, epics, legends, and mythological stories drawn on cave walls. Storytelling has been used as a very important tool in this process. The history of storytelling dates back to ancient times as one of humanity's oldest forms of communication. Theatrical activities in Ancient Greece, folk poets in the Middle Ages, messengers who provided news and information, and storytellers continued this tradition. These stories, which did not reach many people in the past, reached a wider audience as written stories with the invention of the printing press. With the introduction of mass media such as newspapers, radio and television into our lives, storytelling has become much more powerful and effective. The emergence of the internet, developments in new communication technologies and the increased interactivity of social media platforms have enabled everyone from institutions to brands to individual content producers to share their stories.

Digital storytelling, which brings together visual, auditory and interactive elements, has begun to be used as an effective tool for brands, individuals, political parties, leaders, and audiences to attract attention and establish emotional connections. Especially with the proliferation of social media and digital platforms, brands have begun to prefer digital storytelling to develop new strategic communication and persuasion techniques and to introduce themselves in a more sincere and human-focused way. Creating stories is of great importance in terms of attracting the attention of consumers who are constantly bombarded with information and advertising content in the digital world and increasing the memorability of messages. Digital storytelling is an effective tool in creating a world based on users' experiences as well as promoting products and services, thus creating loyalty and trust.

Today, consumer purchasing motivations are changing. Now, consumers' purchasing motivations are also based on the value, meaning and emotional connection offered by brands. Campaigns and communication efforts based solely on the functionality of products and services have begun to lose their effectiveness. In the post-turth world, individuals now live in a world based on the senses presented to them through algorithms. Digital storytelling plays an important role in this world. Consumers find brands that understand them, appeal to their emotions and appeal to their lifestyles attractive. Digital storytelling allows them to effectively convey product or service values through the eyes of those who have previously experienced the product or service. The ultimate goal of institutions is to positively influence consumers' purchasing decisions, and at this point, they benefit from the power of digital storytelling in order to establish a stronger emotional bond and build loyalty and trust.

This study aims to reveal the role of digital storytelling in the changing consumption motivations of the digital native generation, who are the young generation that actively uses social media. For this purpose, the content of Dubai Chocolates, which has recently gone viral on social media, has been taken as an example and the ways young people evaluate the content have been analyzed. In-depth interviews conducted with students selected from Istanbul Medipol University students with the convenience sampling method were examined with the descriptive analysis method and divided into themes. In the study, the role of digital storytelling and narrative techniques as an effective tool in viral content and the role of the stories told on social media platforms, products and consumption styles that become popular through stories on the consumption tendencies of young individuals are evaluated.

Literature

The first attempts to define consumption were made within the economic field, and the concept was considered as an action that takes place in direct proportion to needs and income levels. Accordingly, consumption is a situation that occurs in the simplest form, depending on the income level, in order to meet needs. However, while economic-based developments have transformed societies in the deepest sense, they have also changed the meaning of consumption. At the point we are at today, the concept of need that gives rise to consumption, the level of income that governs it, and the impact and importance of a host of variables in the consumption process are being questioned. According to Raymond Williams (1985), consumption means "spending, destroying, squandering". Williams emphasizes the act of consumption as destroying rather than acquiring something. It is an undeniable fact that the Industrial Revolution is the reference point of the capitalist system and consumption. The perspective brought by Williams is shaped within this point and emphasizes that industrial capitalism has transformed the meaning of consumption. According to him, consumption is a necessity to ensure the expansion of the capitalist system. This necessity puts individuals in a constant cycle, often independent of their needs (Featherstone, 1991).

Within the capitalist system, the act of consumption is more than just meeting needs; it is an element that feeds and develops the system. For the continuity of capitalism, the production and consumption leg must be ensured to function magnificently. The improved production leg of the capitalist system after the Industrial

Revolution will only be achieved by creating a successful consumption network. Therefore, consumption is seen as an action that is powerful enough to ensure and sustain the functioning of a system far beyond the definitions made by classical economists. Baudrillard considers consumption as a concept that develops within the economy as well as a process that reflects the social system. Accordingly, consumption is an action shaped by artificial needs rather than real needs, by signs and symbols, by desires and identity construction (2004). Baudrillard's definition explains the changing role of consumption within capitalist society. As Williams states, consumption, as an action that feeds the field of production, brings about destruction rather than acquisition. Almost every perspective on consumption in social theory is positioned on a similar basis. Consumption is seen as a source that is disconnected from real needs and has an important role in creating values and meanings (Elliot, 1997). In modern capitalist society, individuals who are aware of the power that commodities have, or more accurately, the power that is attributed to commodities through media and advertisements, want to benefit from this power through consumption. In modern society, the individual aims to build an identity for himself through the act of consumption. Archaeologists claim that sharing stories as a social and cultural activity in various human cultures predates the emergence of writing. Stories now exist in a variety of ways, in different forms, offering unprecedented opportunities for multimodality, semiotic reinterpretation of well-known stories, and the creation of new narratives. An engaging and original story makes the message easily understandable, convincing, and memorable (Belova, 2021). Since the earliest times of history, people who enjoy both telling and listening to stories have found that stories make it easier to connect and remember information. Storytelling, which is not a new concept, has become a more effective, accessible and widespread tool for brands in the digital age. Serrat (2017) defines storytelling as follows: It is the effective sharing of ideas, beliefs and personal experiences through stories that evoke strong emotions and insights. Storytelling is a communication method that people use to share, evaluate and benefit from their knowledge. Serrat, who reveals some of the advantages of digital storytelling, states that it conveys informative content as well as emotional aspects, makes it easier to express implicit knowledge that is particularly difficult to express, increases meaningful knowledge sharing by providing that information is presented in a broader context and increases the possibility of learning and transferring knowledge. New communication technologies make sharing stories easier for everyone. In the digital world, social media platforms make it easier for brands to communicate with consumers, but the intense flow of messages and content on these platforms can make it difficult for brands to effectively convey their messages. Storytelling stands out as an important strategy to increase the effectiveness of communication and encourage consumers to interact with brands. Especially on social media, it can help overcome obstacles such as information overload and negative attitudes towards advertisements (Barbosa et al., 2022). Storytelling has become a popular strategy in marketing and brand development today. Using storytelling to strengthen brand messages and increase customer interest is now seen as an indispensable method. One of the prominent approaches in this field, Donald Miller's StoryBrand, is based on the idea that stories can be used as a powerful persuasion tool in brands' sales and marketing messages. The approach suggests that brands position themselves as a guiding guide. The ultimate goal of brands should be to establish an emotional connection and build trust by focusing on customers' needs and problems (Pereira, 2019).

With storytelling, which can be seen as a more memorable promotional technique, marketers can promote messages that can create new perspectives, reinforce certain beliefs or behaviors, and help customers make sense of the world around them, as well as create connections and identification between the brand and customers. Storytelling can be perceived as a more natural and engaging form of communication and can be applied to a more diverse audience, as a method that helps customers make sense of the world around them, as well as forming new or strengthening existing connections at an emotional level between customers and brands. Within this perspective, storytelling can be defined as a message creation process that generates new perspectives, helping to increase opinions or behaviors through narration about the company's features, products/services, and mission and vision statements (Nesser, 2019). By telling a persuasive story, brand storytelling advertising can strengthen a brand and influence customers' advertising experience and other brand-related outcomes. Video storytelling advertising defines brand meanings using a compelling story and brand benefits that are personally relevant to the viewer. Based on the argument that all mental processes and capacities converge in narrative events, storytelling assumes that viewers become fully immersed in a brand's video storytelling initiative and feel like the characters in the advertisement (Teraiya et al., 2023). Digital storytelling, which acts as a bridge between brands and customers and potential customers, is also an effective tool for transforming experiences and developing advocacy. While the literature on branding has long acknowledged the power of storytelling to provide brand meaning, practitioners are increasingly using storytelling to enhance consumers' connection to brands. To help practitioners develop effective digital storytelling strategies, research is providing a better understanding of the impact of digital storytelling campaigns, particularly on attitudes and perceptions toward brands and the behavior of consumers in general and especially young consumers. Generations can be categorized differently. The generation born into technology, also known as digital natives, that is, the generations that use SNS more intensively are younger. Generation Y (born between 1978-1994) is known as the Facebook generation and Generation Z (born after 1995) is called the "Net Gen", this generation has fully integrated the Internet into their daily lives.

The impact of communication campaigns on SNS is widely accepted on the millennial generation. Members of these two generations were born and grew up in the digital age, where the Internet and SNS are an integral part of their lives (Barbosa et al., 2022). The media ecosystem has been reshaped by changing technologies. The emergence of Web 2.0 and the use of social media and new mobile devices (tablets and smartphones) are promoting a new ecology of participation. This new ecology allows any individual to be part of an audience in a participatory and active way while creating, sharing and interacting with content. At this point, young people are taking on roles not only as consumers but also as content producers and creators. This idea is based on the fact that media products and networks are part of our daily lives and therefore all the events of our daily lives are worth recording and sharing. In contrast, individuals always act to be observed; they are the center of attention in all the events of their daily lives, in terms of where they are, what they do, and who they are with. Young people already construct stories on social networks and enjoy doing so for different reasons. However, this process can be further strengthened in the formal educational environment, giving greater importance to reflection and helping students construct digital stories as new forms of learning, reflection, and social participation as citizens (Rubio-Hurtado et al., 2022). Although this framework is based on theoretical foundations, researchers can develop an assessment system to identify brand story archetypes using quantitative methods in the future. In addition, examining how prevalent these archetypes are in the literature of different cultures can help understand which narrative types are more effective in which markets. Although this framework provides a solid foundation, both quantitative and qualitative research is needed to better understand the impact of storytelling on marketing (Pereira, 2019). **Method** This study examines the role of stories told in digital media on current consumption motivations. The study seeks answers to two questions: What is the role of digital media on consumption motivations? What kind of a mission do stories told in digital media undertake in the consumption preferences of young individuals studying in the field of communication? In line with the determined purpose, the experiences of university students who use social media platforms intensively in Turkey were examined. In-depth interview technique, which is a qualitative research method frequently preferred in the field of social sciences, was used in the study. Qualitative research methods allow for a broad perspective on a situation or phenomenon and access to deep information on the reasons (Gürbüz & Şahin, 2018). Within the scope of the current study, it is aimed to examine in detail the role of the stories that young individuals (no pre-criterion has been determined in terms of age) who use social media intensively in Turkey are exposed to on social media platforms, in terms of products and brands, on their consumption preferences. The universe of the research consists of young individuals living in Turkey and continuing their education at the Faculty of Communication. In this context, the students of the Faculty of Communication at Istanbul Medipol University, who are considered to represent the universe of the research, were determined as the sample group of the research using the convenience sampling method. The main reason why students of the Faculty of Communication were preferred in the semi-structured in-depth interviews conducted is the assumption that, in addition to being potential communication professionals, they have theoretical knowledge about the nature of social media and consumption, the effects of popular culture and advertising. The relevant assumption enables a specific assessment by reaching conclusions about the current role of storytelling in digital environments on the consumption motivations of young individuals who have even basic knowledge. In this context, 8 semi-structured questions prepared on the axis of consumption motivations, social media and storytelling were asked to the participants in the in-depth interviews, in addition to demographic questions. The interview questions were designed by examining the literature within the scope of the purpose of the study. Within the scope of the study, 16 students, 8 male and 8 female, were interviewed and the interviews of 2 students were not included in the analysis due to insufficient data. The interviews conducted via online platforms and face-to-face lasted an average of 20 minutes. The data obtained from the interviews were converted into written texts, subjected to descriptive analysis and categorized under various themes. Depending on the course of the interview, different questions were asked to the participants, beyond the questions included in the questionnaire designed before the research. In-depth interviews were completed within an average of 25 days. **Findings**

The responses given by the students of the Faculty of Communication who participated in the in-depth interview conducted within the scope of the current study were examined by descriptive analysis, categorized under various themes. The names of the interviewed participants were kept confidential in accordance with the "Personal Data Protection Law" and ethical rules, and in the direct quotes, codes consisting of nicknames were used to indicate the participant to whom the relevant response belonged: (Cemrenur). The researchers determined the nicknames to be given to the participants based on phonetic tendency. Thanks to the nicknames, the confidentiality of the interview participants is protected and multiple data are classified under the same name (The University of British Columbia, 2018).

Table 1. In-Depth Interview Participant List

Participant	Name	Gender	Age	Income Level
1	Cemrenur	Female	19	Not specified
2	Mehmet	Male	21	Medium
3	Semih	Male	22	Medium

continued on following page

Table 1. Continued

Participant	Name	Gender	Age	Income Level
4	Alara	Female	23	Medium
5	Özer	Male	21	Medium
6	Beyhan	Female	26	High
7	Serhat	Male	20	High
8	Ceren	Female	22	Not specified
9	Beren	Female	19	Medium
10	Zehra	Female	21	Medium
11	Berra	Female	20	Medium
12	Ayla	Female	21	Not specified
13	Özge	Female	21	Low
14	Berk	Male	23	Low

Social Media Usage Habits in the Digital World: Which Platforms, How Long?

According to the data in the Digital 2024 Türkiye report prepared by We Are Social and Meltwater:

''Internet users have reached 5.35 billion worldwide and the usage rate is 66.2% of the population. In Turkey, internet users are 74.41 million users, making up 86.5% of the population. This rate is well above the average when looking at the world.

The number of social media users worldwide is 5.04 billion, while the ratio of this number to the population is 62.3%. In Türkiye, there are 57.50 million active social media users. While the ratio of active social media users to the population in Turkey is 66.8%, the vast majority of internet users use social media.'' (İnternet Araştırmaları Koordinatörlüğü, 2024)

Internet and social media usage rates in Turkey are well above the world average. While the ratio of internet users to the population is 66.2% worldwide, this ratio has reached 86.5% in Turkey, indicating widespread use of the internet. Similarly, while the ratio of social media users to the population is 62.3% worldwide, this ratio is higher in Turkey at 66.8%. This data shows that internet access has become widespread in Turkey and that a significant portion of users actively use social media platforms. The fact that a large portion of internet users are also active on social media indicates that digital communication, information sharing and entertainment consumption are concentrated on social media. This situation proves that Turkey is making rapid progress in the digitalization process.

When internet usage habits in Turkey are examined, it is seen that users spend an average of 6 hours and 57 minutes on the internet daily. This time shows that the internet has become an inseparable part of daily life and is used intensively. While the main reason for internet use is to obtain information with a rate of 73.5%, this situation reveals that users actively use the internet not only for entertainment or social media, but also for learning and research purposes. When looking at social media usage, it is striking that users in Turkey actively use an average of 7.4 different social media platforms. The most preferred platform is Instagram with a rate of 91.8%, followed by WhatsApp, Facebook and X (Twitter). In addition, users spend the most time on Instagram with an average of 32 hours and 41 minutes per month. This data shows that social media has an important place in daily life in Turkey, that users spend a large part of their daily lives intertwined with the internet and that Instagram in particular has become one of the most powerful platforms in the digital world (İnternet Araştırmaları Koordinatörlüğü, 2024).

Individuals consciously use various media tools to meet and satisfy their specific needs. The fact that the most basic reason for internet users in Turkey is to obtain information (73.5%) shows that individuals actively use the internet to meet their cognitive needs. At the same time, the intensive use of social media platforms shows that people prefer digital platforms by seeking different gratifications such as social interaction, entertainment and identity construction. According to the "Uses and Gratifications Theory", which is based on the idea that the viewer is active and makes motivated choices based on their previous experiences, individuals use media to meet their basic needs in their daily lives (Mcquail & Windahl, 2005).

In the study, it is observed that the participants use social media platforms intensively and spend the most time on Instagram. Cemrenur, one of the participants who uses social media intensively, uses applications such as Instagram, Whatssapp and X, and spends approximately 7-8 hours of screen time per day, and this time includes arbitrary virtual chats, reels, news reading and blogging.

Mehmet also uses Instagram and Twitter (X) the most, and the time can be more than 10-15 hours. Semih, who spends approximately 35 hours a week on social media, uses many social media platforms such as Instagram, Facebook, Twitter (X), Youtube, Linkedin and Reddit. Alara, on the other hand, uses Instagram and Tik Tok for approximately 6-7 hours per week. Another user who uses social media 14 hours a week, Özer, actively uses Twitter(X), Instagram and Youtube platforms, Beyhan, who stated that he spends a lot of time on social media, uses the platforms he uses most frequently are Instagram, Twitter(X), You tube, Linkedin, Facebook, Pinterest and TikTok. While he generally expresses his social media time as 10-12 hours, he emphasizes that this time can sometimes increase to 2-3 times because he works as a social media content producer. Serhat uses Instagram and Youtube the most, 15-16 hours a week.

Ceren uses Tik Tok, Instagram, X and You Tube for more than 20 hours per week, Beren uses Twitter (X), Instagram, TikTok and Whatsapp for 20-25 hours, Zehra spends 5 hours per week on social media, mostly using Instagram and Tik Tok. Berra spends four hours per day on social media, frequently uses Instagram, Tik Tok and Twitter (X) platform. Ayla uses Instagram, TikTok, Snapchat and Whatsapp platforms for 11 hours per week. Özge states that she has 9-10 hours of screen time per week due to working in a social media-focused job. She spends most of her day looking at the screen and browsing Instagram, TikTok and X. Berk spends approximately 4 hours and 43 minutes per day on Twitter, Instagram, Whatsapp and TikTok.

When the participants' statements are evaluated, it is seen that the person who uses social media at least weekly uses social media for 5 hours a week and up to 35 hours at most. The average usage time is 10-15 hours. At this point, it is seen that social media is used intensively. The most used platforms are Instagram, TikTok, Twitter X and You tube, but Linkedin, Facebook, Whatssapp are also among the frequently used platforms. Some of the participants also stated that they spend time on Pinterest, Snapchat and Reddit applications.

What content and posts on social media attract our attention?

In the past, the consumption culture, which was aimed at meeting basic needs, aims to reach psychological satisfaction in today's digital world. In this area, everyone is encouraged to consume whether they need it or not. In this context, the way has also been opened for unnecessary consumption. Advertisements and content on the internet encourage users to consume, and consumption has become a means of expressing and showing oneself on social media. Many shopping applications have become popular among young people and encourage them to purchase products and services (Tiryaki & Kaya, 2019). Thanks to augmented reality and artificial intelligence-supported content, social media allows the creation of visually and auditorily powerful, emotionally bonding stories. Consumers and viewers can consume more when they find these narratives compatible with their own identities and beliefs.

Corporate storytelling can be seen as a more memorable promotional technique, creating new perspectives and encouraging messages that can strengthen certain beliefs and behaviors. Storytelling, which allows customers to make sense of the world around them, strengthens the bond between the brand and the customer and intensifies identification. Perceived as a more natural, sincere and engaging form of communication, storytelling shapes opinions and behaviors about the company's product or service through narration. In this sense, digital storytelling is a message creation process that produces new perspectives (Nesser, 2019).

Social media has become an indispensable area for adolescents and young people who are defined as digital natives. In the digital world, young people are greatly affected by direct visual and interactive storytelling. Adolescents and young people, who also spend a significant amount of time publishing content on social media and social networking sites, have become part of the new participation ecology (Rubio-Hurtado 2022. et al). Especially social media content, short video formats (TikpTok, Instagram Reels) and gamified narratives are quite effective in attracting the attention of young people and establishing an emotional connection with them. Digital natives prefer hypertextual access and communication, and like parallel processing and multitasking. Digital natives, who are accustomed to disseminating information quickly, prefer graphics before texts. They tend to learn visually, auditorily and by experience rather than written texts (Prensky, 2001). Therefore, brands and content producers can influence young people more by offering interactive, participatory and emotionally bonding stories. Brands, interactive social media campaigns It can attract the interest and attention of this audience to digital stories.

The connection and interactivity feature of digital storytelling is quite effective on the young generation. Young people who spend a lot of time on social media can express themselves more easily by interacting with these srenstories. Storytelling also plays an active role in creating a sense of community. Especially the most used social media platforms such as TikTok, Instagram and YouTube provide young people with the opportunity to comment, share, like and produce content. In this way, young people are included in the narrative. The way individuals communicate with each other reflects their own cultural backgrounds and contexts. In some cultures, people tend to convey messages clearly and directly; in some cultures, messages are conveyed in more indirect and non-verbal ways. Basic information is conveyed through context. It is the listener's responsibility to understand the meaning by reading between the lines. In the context of communication, this approach emphasizes that the meaning of messages is shaped not only by the content, but also by the interaction with the environment, cultural context and the audience (Nam, 2015). What makes digital storytelling effective is that young people create content that aligns with their own experiences and that they can relate to personally. Interactive stories such as surveys organized on social media, interactive games, and user-driven narratives increase the participation of the young generation. In this way, young people who experience the powerful storytelling can see themselves as a part of the stories.

The first participant, Cemrenur, claims that pages that are considered reliable primarily attract attention in posts, while user comments under products and aesthetic photos are also impressive. Another participant, Mehmet, is interested in aesthetic, eye-catching storytelling and sincere collaborations, as well as posts where influencers reveal their personal experiences and provide detailed information about products. Advertisements of brands that produce computer hardware on YouTube,

Sleepy, Dyson etc. cleaning and cosmetic products given via reels on Instagram, products marketed by influencers, clothing brands, Burcu brand leaf rolling machine, chocolate etc. products attract attention, as in the example of Dubai chocolate that has gone viral recently, and another participant, Semih, states that these contents go viral. While Alara finds posts about cosmetics and travel content, and sometimes interesting information and food posts, attractive, Özer says that applications that will make her life easier attract her attention.

''For example, I am interested in advertisements for foreign language learning sites, advertisements for applications that correct grammatical errors for my academic life, and advertisements for platforms where I can read various articles and books..''. he uses the espressions. Beyhan, on the other hand, states that sincere and informative content based on real user experiences attracts her attention, and says, ''In the food sector, the sections where consumers share their instant taste and pleasure feelings or explain the content and benefits of the product are more appealing to me,'' and adds that advertising content that goes beyond marketing strategy and aims to tell a story or inform can be more impressive, and emphasizes that these contents attract like a worm trap. A student named Serhat finds the posts of viral people remarkable, but he also states that he does not buy these products except for Dubai chocolate. Ceren finds the posts that highlight both the positive and negative aspects of the products more sincere and interesting, while Beren does not find the content that smells like advertising sincere and

''Frankly, any product that smells like advertising does not appeal to me or is worth buying. For this reason, they do not attract my attention. I quickly move past those contents. Especially when I see the same type of advertising collaboration content everywhere about that product, I get turned off by the product. I feel like something of poor quality is being marketed to me.'' she said. She also states that influencers with many followers do cheap marketing and that since they have to write ads everywhere, they quickly pass over the content that includes the advertising collaboration tag

Zehra finds content that is mostly in the makeup category interesting and says that content that is viral by the community and is not made for advertising purposes is remarkable. Berra states that advertisements and collaborations do not attract her attention as much as they used to and are not effective in purchasing these products, and that she finds cosmetic clothing and places attractive. Ayla states that content related to makeup products and clothing-based collaborations attract her attention. Özge likes product promotion videos that are not commercialized more and emphasizes that makeup content comes to her attention more. Berk also states that makeup products and personal care products generally attract her attention.

According to the general statements of the participants, the most interesting content on social media can be categorized as aesthetics, emotional connection, sincerity, personal experience sharing, promotion and information content. Most of the participants do not find advertising and collaborations sincere. Especially clothing, cosmetics and food-themed content are found more interesting.

The Role of Storytelling in Effective Content Strategies on Social Media

The interactive connection that storytelling establishes with the young generation can be interpreted as a parallel transition between messages and codes when evaluated in the context of Stuart Hall's Cultural Coding and Decoding Theory. The interpreter implied in Hall's model is the key to understanding how interpreters interpret and respond to signs in relation to the discursive contexts in which they are produced. At this point, messages are not only a system of sign tools, but also a system of meanings (Tomaselli, 2016). Within the framework of the approach that states that media messages are coded within a certain ideology and cultural context and that audiences decode these messages in different ways according to their own experiences, identities and cultural backgrounds, young people can be seen as a mass that not only consumes stories on social media platforms, but also reinterprets, shares and even reproduces them. Content produced in the digital world transforms the way young people interact with stories. Brands and content creators can establish a stronger bond with young people by offering them stories that appeal to their cultural references, are open to their participation, and are reproducible. In this way, the narrative is transformed into a collective experience.

Digital storytelling presents idealized lives and reconstructed identities on social media. In this context, the life practices, clothing styles, and eating and drinking habits produced by the system are constructed through stories. According to Adorno and Horkheimer, the culture industry provides functionality to the system by creating standardized consumption habits that render individuals passive. According to the fundamental thesis of the Frankfurt School theorists, capitalist society is definitely trying to transform culture into a real industry. This industry produces standardized and inherently homogeneous consumer products in the name of cultural products. The culture industry maintains the illusion of escape by providing easy entertainment. In this way, the masses are drawn into an imaginary world (Roy, 2023).

Although digital storytelling on social media is a tool that encourages individuals to discover their unique identities, it also produces the ideal lifestyles imposed by the capitalist system. In social media stories, different extraordinary lives, perfect extraordinaryxury consumption, constant happiness, and success-oriented posts are told daily. Individuals must align their identities with these norms. Thus, social media has become a significant force in the viticulture of consumption as a space where the culture of consumption is internalized, and individuals are transformed from subjects into consumers. Digital storytelling, as the key to this process, imposes certain images and lifestyles on specific people. Individuals consume and consume these images, creating a space of need that sometimes does not exist. By rec, sometimes, sing life practices, stories encourage individuals to define themselves through these narratives.

The results of the interviews with young people in the study support these approaches. According to Cemrenur, if there is no liking at first sight in purchasing the product, there should be psychological closeness; the closer the story is, the more buyable the product is, while the participant states that the themes of family, love, and love are effective, Mehme,t states that the products given with stories that offer sections from emotional life increase his interest and that he is influenced by the story of the Yves Rocher brand, one of the products that contribute to the protection of nature in cosmetics. Semih:

"I think it is more sincere and interesting for people to place the product in a story instead of a direct promotion. It arouses curiosity. We all feed on stor becausean throughout our lives and in our existence. Therefore, of course, this is also preferred very often in advertisements. We see them a lot in reels in the same way.

As far as I remember, if I have to answer the question of whether there is a product or advertising story that I remember, I remember a story in the reels of a make-up promotion product that I saw recently. For example, a son was getting ready for a date and was chasing his phone, the time of the ise is this and that, ; or example, 10.30, for example, there ist there are about one, two, three minutes left to it, and the wheel is spinning like this. The countdown sign is spinning on the phone and that person starts to get ready even faster, of course, in order to catch up". At that point, an advertisingtohat the make-up materials used are products that are much faster fixing, much faster drying, can be applieddand andnot waste time, anmore rapidpractical is integrated into the storytelling.

Alara states that the stories first influenced her and then focused on the product and that influencer Şeyda Erdoğan's exam. That own make-up bag, which is her own brand, was initial in telling her own life story, that this was her biggest dream, and talking about the difficulties she experienced while establishing the brand. Özer states that realistic storytelling can be one of the important conditions for the success of advertisements in the eyes of consumers. He also states that

"Especially during my university entrance exam year, when I used social media to study, I was interested in Doping Hafıza advertisements. Doping Hafıza was an application that included systematic lectures, question solutions and sample essays for all central exams. Unlike classical learning and study methods, here, education was given with narrative and symbolic memorable elements. In the advertisements of this application, the narratives of the students who passed the exam, thanks to this application, were presented in an effective way, as the product-advertisement relationship was effectively presented as a realistic result in the eyes of the consumer.

Beyhan states that storytelling increases the sincerity and memorability of the advertisement and that the storytelling in Tesla's Robot Taxi project and Barış Özcanın's Northern VPn advertisement are interesting, apart from that, he likes the way the food sector, where he can find himself more, storytells the flavors and product promotions of different cultures. Serhat emphasizes that the story of the product to be sold adds meaning to the product and eliminates the feeling of just spending money and buying a product, while Ceren says that storytelling strengthens the bond with the influencer or creator, and that she follows content that creates an emotional bond between her and the product that gives the feeling that similar situations can happen in her own life.

Beren explains that "stories that are too scripted do not attract my attention, while stories that are sincere, where I find something from myself and give me the feeling that I have the same problems as me attract my attention." She states that the reason why she was influenced by the stories of the Biotin & Caffeine hair tonic of the popular rate Urban Care brand against hair loss is the stories of people on TikTok who have the same problem rather than influencers with many followers on Instagram, who do not have many followers and who I am convinced are not really an advertisement.

Zehra, one of the students, stated that she was influenced by the story of Jalepeno pickles and the advertisements of the NYX brand in the make-up category; Berra stated that the story increases product loyalty and makes it more realistic. Ayla states that the stories make her feel emotional towards the brand and increase brand loyalty if it is a brand she uses, and arouse a sense of curiosity if it is a brand she does not use. Two participants stated that they could not remember any sample advertisement content. Another participant Özge, who stated that storytelling is more sincere and memorable, finds it impressive that examples from their own lives are given in make-up videos and experiences are shared; Berk said, "There are a lot of promotions that are lynched on social media and then understood to be advertisements, these attract more attention. For example, Şeyma Subaşı's Airfryer advertisement has been quite popular." and draws attention to the 'lynch culture' in the stories.

Considering the common points of the discourses in in-depth interviews, they can be categorized as memorability, experiences and slices of life, sincerity, creating a lynch culture, and viral user posts. It is also emphasized by the participants that digital storytelling has effects such as increasing brand addiction, arousing curiosity, memorability and bonding.

Determinants of Consumption from Aesthetics to Uniqueness in the Age of Social Media

The most fundamental determinant of consumption is undoubtedly need. This is a claim that traditional economic theorists agree on. Global changes in economic policies, developments in communication technologies and capitalism's efforts to maximize its efficiency have transformed the meaning of the concept of consumption. In fact, the concept of need itself has undergone a profound change. Real needs have been replaced by artificial needs, while the expectation of functional benefits from the product has been replaced by emotional benefits, symbolic meanings, images and indicators in which identities are constructed.

We live in an age of consumption in which everything is aestheticized. It is clear that a "pressure" has been created that this should be the normal flow of life with the perfected content from conventional and social media, perfect life presentations, filter bubbles, healing applications and many other examples that we can multiply. The claim that the media shapes lives with each element of content is one that has dominated social sciences and more specifically communication studies for decades. (Horkheimer & Adorno 2002; Althusser, 2019; Gramsci, 1971; Hall, 1980). The digital transformation of communication technologies in recent years and the intensive use of platforms such as Facebook, Pinterest, Instagram and Tiktok increase visual presentations and aesthetic components as a necessity of the existence of platforms. Here, in direct proportion to the increase in content, there is an increase in the aesthetic concerns and expectations of the affected audience, as well as their attention to aestheticized content.

The concept of aesthetics, which has been in the field of discussion of many disciplines for many years, has an increasing interest in the field of marketing, especially in the consumer perception of product design aesthetics. Many studies show that the design aesthetics and visual appeal of the product increase the perceived value of the product for consumers and significantly affect consumer behavior (Chartes, 2006; Cai & Xu, 2011; Hoyer & Stokburger-Sauer, 2012). Studies match consumers' interest in aesthetic designs with hedonic consumption (Holbrook & Hirschman, 1982). Here, the hedonic context draws attention to the emotional and sensory aspects of the consumption process, linking the main purpose of consumption to the feeling of pleasure that demands immediate gratification. In order to satisfy this emotional arousal, the consumer is in a position of constantly seeking and consuming products and thus experiencing pleasure. Aesthetics appears as a field that feeds emotional arousal and therefore pleasure. While an aesthetic design triggers the consumer emotionally, it also creates a behavioral response (Wiecek et al., 2019).

Research on consumption and aesthetics has shifted to a new field of discussion with the increasing intensity of use of social media. In the age of social media, where digital developments are developing at a great pace, we are surrounded by social networks at every moment, everywhere. In the light of these developments, social commerce emerges as a popular business model of e-commerce. Social commerce, where social media environments are integrated into e-commerce, is also called the referral economy (Chen et al., 2015; Wang & Zhang, 2012). The main medium of social commerce is visual-oriented social media platforms such as Facebook, Instagram, Tiktok. These platforms present the functional or symbolic features of the product and information about the brand in a visual communication format (Wang & Zhang, 2012).

Today, when it is not possible to stand out from its competitors with its functional features, it is clear that each content and presentation prepared with attention to visual aesthetic elements gives the product a distinctive quality. Social commerce is especially characterized by the visual aesthetics of the content creator, which is often an influencer, shaped by individual presentations, interesting lifestyles and unique tastes (Marwick, 2015). Product and service experiences conveyed by an influencer or micro-celebrity through the social commerce channel can also provide an aesthetic experience. When it is accepted that social media platforms are environments where information about products and services is sought in addition to being used for many purposes, the combination of these two points will explain the progress of social commerce on the basis of visual aesthetics. The rise of visual-oriented platforms increases the impact of social commerce environments and micro-celebrities aesthetically designing their content (Djafarova & Trofimenko, 2019). In the research conducted by Yang et al. in 2021, the relationship between visual aesthetics and consumers' social commerce intention is measured. The results show that visual aesthetics is a direct determinant of online consumers' decision-making mechanisms.

The in-depth interviews conducted within the scope of this study reveal results that support the research data and theoretical claims put forth in the field of marketing related to aesthetics. While explaining their consumption tendencies, the interviewed members of Generation Z, who are digital natives, brought up various motivations. Almost all participants agree that social media determines consumption habits. However, interviewees made different emphases regarding the specific characteristics of the content on social media.

Cemrenur, one of the in-depth interview participants, stated that the content coming from social media determines consumption behaviors either deliberately or unintentionally, drawing particular attention to the visual aesthetic elements of a product's presentation:

"... I think that constantly seeing a product on any platform affects us after a while, even if we don't admit it... when a product is continuously in front of our

eyes through aesthetically pleasing photos or videos, we start to feel closer to it and eventually take steps to buy it."

A similar reason was put forward by Mehmet. Expressing that social media plays a major role in consumption habits, the participant also emphasized the impact of social media on consumption tendencies with the words, "I am particularly interested in aesthetically appealing collaboration content," highlighting the aesthetic elements of the content.

The expressions used by Beyhan, another in-depth interview participant, while explaining her consumption habits, dramatically reveal the transformation of actual needs into visual aesthetic desires:

"I can't say that social media has a big impact on my consumption habits. I actually see these platforms as a glittery world full of exaggeration and perception management. However, it would not be realistic to say that I am not influenced at all. There have been times I chose certain services or products through sponsored ads or collaborations. For instance, I have visited a cafe or restaurant just because the ambiance and the food looked visually appealing to me."

A similar assessment about the changing face of consumption was made by Ayla. The participant expressed the factors determining her consumption habits as "... color, quality, texture, and tastes that appeal to my personality," with the last criterion being particularly notable. The concept of gusto, which means taste or preference, is a key term in explaining changing consumption motivations. The consumption journey, which entered a deep transformation in the 1980s, not only labeled cultures and societies with the same concept but also transformed individual habits. At the same time, this transformation was reflected in notable changes in newspaper columns. Pages titled "Life," "Gusto," and "Lifestyle" directed readers toward a broad spectrum of consumption, from fashion to trending restaurants, motivated by the desire to "live better" (Bali, 2002). Gusto, as a subject of aesthetic understanding, is a concept that defines individuals' tastes and preferences. Its emergence as a criterion that determines consumption stems from it being an expectation shaped through media channels.

In addition to the interviewees who accepted that social media influences consumption habits, there were also a few participants who stated that they usually do not accept messages coming from there without filtering them through their own evaluations. However, even in these cases, it should be noted that the aesthetic elements of either the product or the content were put forward as significant criteria in the decision-making process. Semih, one of the participants, stated that content from social media alone cannot be a decisive factor in determining consumption preferences with the following words:

"The advertisements created by influencers don't really attract my attention. I think they have become too repetitive and they don't feel very sincere to me.

That's why I can say I consume more products from brands that feature more appealing, big-budget, and aesthetic advertisements... Products that appeal to my interests and visual taste—especially those that stand out with their design—are among the factors that influence my consumption habits..."

In the social media era we live in, it is possible to say that every aspect of life—from "basic needs" to "directed needs"—has been aestheticized. The influence of visually driven digital platforms and applications in this process is undeniable. Research and the current study reveal results that support the idea that aesthetics is an important factor in consumption tendencies. For the modern consumer, for whom even the meaning of the concept of "need" (long accepted as the primary determinant of consumption) has become vague, many other criteria now come into play when choosing a product or brand.

These influencing factors, beginning with aesthetics, can be extended to include expectations of feeling unique and special. These are criteria that cannot be directly equated with the concept of need, but they reflect the changing nature of consumption. One of the participants, Semih, expresses his consumption tendencies with the following statement:

"It's important for me that the products make the person feel special, that they make me feel special." The most straightforward conclusion we can draw from this is that feeling unique is an important factor in modern consumer behavior.

There are numerous studies on the role of feeling different and unique in consumption tendencies (Snyder, 1992; Gierl & Huettl, 2010; Kauppinen-Räisänen et al., 2018; Wang et al., 2022). In the current study, which aims to determine how messages from digital platforms shape consumption habits—especially in specific contexts—the feeling these messages create of uniqueness or distinctiveness among consumers stands out as a defining feature.

Another response that strengthens this claim comes from participant Serhat. While stating that social media content has a direct impact on his consumption behavior, he emphasizes a specific point:

"Instagram definitely influences my purchasing behavior. Since I accept cookies from websites, I frequently encounter the same ads, and this encourages me to buy. But frankly, I'm more influenced by ads that feel personalized to me than by those sent to everyone."

Serhat's words lead us to conclude that—even though the message's source has drastically changed due to technological developments—the desire to feel different remains a significant and effective determinant in consumption preferences.

Understanding, analyzing, and identifying the reasons behind consumption behavior is a highly complex task. Among the factors that make this process so challenging are, of course, changes in economic policies and developments in communication technologies. It is important to give special attention to the need or expectation for aesthetics among the elements that shape new consumer behavior. Recent research in the field of marketing, as well as the responses from participants in this study, once again highlight the influence of social media in determining consumption habits, and show that the desire for aesthetics—or in other words, the expectation of visual appeal—is a significant factor in guiding consumption behavior.

Another variable, which we cannot categorize under "actual need," is the desire to feel "special" or "unique." The participants' responses clearly demonstrate that the feeling of uniqueness is a major factor shaping consumption motivations.

Social Reference Groups: Comment and Recommendation and the Axis of Trust

The social reference group includes friends, family members, celebrities and opinion leaders. Studies conducted in different branches of social disciplines have revealed that the attitudes, behaviors, and directions of the social reference group affect almost all individuals in society. When we evaluate this interaction in marketing, it is possible to say that consumers are influenced by their reference groups in their product and brand preferences and often perform their purchasing behavior with this effect (Yadav et al., 2022). It would not be a wrong statement to say that social media content producers, more commonly known as influencers, are new members of the social reference group. Many studies have shown that social media, which is the companion of our lives in almost every moment of our lives, and social media influencers have a direct or indirect impact on today's consumption habits (Subitha et al., 2024; Leung et al., 2022; Lang & Armstrong, 2018).

Participants who conducted in-depth interviews referred to reference groups when explaining their consumption preferences. Cemrenur, one of the participants, stated that her consumption is more need- and price-oriented, and explained the importance of reference groups in her consumption preferences by saying that the suggestions of my family and friends are also important to me. Another participant, Alara, states the importance of reference groups by saying "I am influenced by what a person I like and follow shares, and my consumption habits are actually shaped accordingly". A similar statement is made by Beren: "I keep the suggestions and experiences of my social circle in mind when I buy things, especially if that product has recently found its place on social media and a friend of mine has tried it, I will definitely get their opinion and according to the product, it will be certain whether I will buy it or not." Beren's statement emphasizes the intersection of social media and the reference group. Acknowledging the impact of recommendations from social media on consumption preferences, the participant states that the last variable that activates the purchasing mechanism is the immediate environment. Berk, another participant who responded to the intersectional effect of social media and the immediate environment, points to a similar situation with the words ".... I am more willing to buy the products I see on social media, and since my circle of friends also see and shop on social media, a cycle is formed in this way." In the same way, Berra, one of the participants, emphasizes the influence of the reference group like the other participants, saying that in addition to the influence of social media, suggestions from my friends and social environment also affect my consumption habits.

Within the scope of the current research, it is seen that the participants especially emphasized the concepts of recommendation and comments in their evaluations about the reference group. Beyhan, while explaining his consumption habits, says "....It is based on factors such as real user experiences and comments, and being offered by reliable brands. At the same time, the suggestions of people around me are also effective in my preferences." Here, it is explained that the experiences conveyed by real users are as effective as professional advertising content or influencer posts. A similar emphasis is made by Özge: "Of course, I am also influenced by my close environment. But on social media, especially Tiktok, I have the opportunity to listen to more people's personal experiences. Especially if the content is not an advertisement or a collaboration, I hear transparent comments and this definitely directly affects whether I buy something or not." The influence of the reference group in shaping consumption trends is clear. Here, we see a concrete reflection of the sincerity or credibility questioning about social media content and influencer recommendations that we have frequently encountered in recent years. The participants' search for "real" user comments is essentially a consequence of this question of trust.

Within the scope of the current study, the responses of young individuals regarding their consumption habits once again reveal the determining effect of reference groups on consumption trends. Reference groups include a wide range of people, from influencers who produce new content on social media channels almost every day, every moment, recommend products and brands, and tell stories, to the social circle including family and friends. The responses of the participants show that real users and individuals as well as social media influencers, family and close friends play a decisive role in consumption habits.

Popular Culture vs Viral: Dubai Chocolate

As the foundations of a heterogeneous mass society were laid with the development of production techniques after the Industrial Revolution, the establishment of factories, and the increasing migration from villages to factories in big cities, mass culture and popular culture were preparing the ground to dominate the whole world. Mass culture refers to a mechanical and constructed culture in which consumption is conditioned as much as production in order to maximize the efficiency of capitalism. It would not be a misnomer to describe modern societies as societies of mass culture, and even one step further as societies of consumer culture. Popular culture, on the other hand, is used to describe the rising elements of the consumption-indexed culture conditioned by the system in certain periods. Mass culture societies are a culture that deprives the individuals within them of the power to resist the capitalist system, destroys differences and polyphony, and has the ability to build harmonious and unquestioning individuals. Popular culture, on the other hand, refers to the short-term forms of widespread consumption and products that develop within mass culture (Erdoğan, 1999).

Mass media and social media can be defined as important mechanisms in shaping and transmitting popular culture to societies. This argument, which has been defended by Gramsci, Althusser, Adorno and Horkheimer, Habermas, and many other theorists of critical communication studies, is today reasserted with the same results through research on social media (Dahlan, 2024; Rafique et al., 2022; Asur et al., 2021; Nouri, 2018).

Within the scope of the current research, it is aimed to reach results that will enable the analysis of the consumption tendencies of the students of the Faculty of Communication, the factors determining their consumption habits, and the role of digital platforms and digital stories in the consumption process. Within the scope of the research, a separate parenthesis was opened for the products that went viral and the trending consumption trends through social media channels and the stories told through them. In order to analyze popular consumption trends, Dubai chocolate, which has recently g,one viral all over the world, was chosen as an example item, and while the participants were asked about their habits of consuming products and brand content recommended on social media and from there, it was aimed to measure the general trend from the specific Dubai chocolate example. Based on the responses we obtained from the in-depth interview participants, we can clearly say that social media content, and the professional or user stories told therein, often confront consumers with an effect that they are not aware of or do not want to accept. In other words, consumers are frequently influenced by content and popular culture elements on digital platforms, even if they are often unaware of it. It is possible to concretize this claim with the statements of Beyhan, one of the participants:

> *"To be honest, the content on social media did not make me want to try Dubai chocolate. On the contrary, I even laughed. However, I had the opportunity to try it twice. I was saying these things and becoming a regular. Just like the story of the product's origin, where a pregnant woman had this chocolate made to meet her sweet need for dessert, my brother's pregnant wife is craving it now that she sees it everywhere. On this occasion, we go to the Marie Antoinette chocolate shop in Beşiktaş. We have the opportunity to try it as a family. We were also near Vadi Istanbul and I had the opportunity to taste it once again while having coffee with my friend at Paradox Lounge."*

Beyhan says in two consecutive sentences that she finds these contents funny, and then she states that she has tried Dubai chocolate twice. A similar conclusion can be drawn from Beren's responses. Stating that the Dubai chocolate trend has grown much bigger than she expected, the participant continues her words as follows:

> *"I think it was a very pointless trend and not very interesting. I saw a lot of videos especially on the Tiktok platform. I was not convinced enough to buy it, but I was also wondering "what was so exaggerated?" The fact that it was so viral created antipathy in me rather than sympathy. One user in particular had a dubai chocolate makeover that was not successful at all, and I can't get the absurdity of it out of my mind."*

Beren expresses that she tried the Dubai chocolate, which she says she is more antipathized than impressed, with the words "yes, it made me want to eat it". Here, similar to the previous example, it is possible to say that the trends that go viral on social media create a motivation for consumers to buy or at least try, even if they do not welcome the content.

The fear of the elements of popular culture not being known or missed by the general public creates a pressure on individuals, as stated in Adorno and Horkheimer's ideas theorized with the concept of culture industry. The concept of FoMO (Fear of Missing Out), which has emerged in recent years in the field of communication, especially in studies on social media, and the "Spiral of Silence" put forward by Elizabeth Neulle Neumann decades ago, reveal that people tend to conform to their surroundings with the fear of being excluded, and that they are afraid of missing out on the developments around them, especially due to social media platforms where information flow is intense and fast. The current research reveals results that confirm these claims. Özge, one of the participants, uses the following statements about products that go viral on social media through the example of Dubai chocolate: "There is a perception that everyone must try it and not miss it." Similarly, Ceren, one of the participants, states that the fear of being ostracized or missing out are important variables that feed the viral culture:

> *"The viral culture on social media is getting bigger every day. It goes from being local to global. I think people like the perception of doing something in common. They include themselves in a group; the bigger the viral thing, the more they exclude those who don't know. Although I don't have this state of exclusion, there are products that I am inevitably influenced by."*

With the data we have obtained, we can claim that consuming popular culture products is shaped by belonging to a group or, to put it mildly, not missing out on what is common or at least having an opinion. While the popularity is shaped by the content from mass media and social media, it keeps individuals under pressure to follow and prefer. While this pressure creates the need to consume popular products and brands and to follow trendy consumption patterns, it also creates the fear of being the same as the "other" for some individuals. This situation creates a deliberate tendency among consumers not to consume what is popular. The words of Beyhan, one of the participants, reveal this situation strikingly:

"I have preferred some services and products through sponsored advertisements or collaborations... Still, I prefer to consume even products I am very curious about after their popularity has waned. This preference is a bit psychological and related to my fear of being the same as everyone else. When the shine of such sparkling fairy dust blowing over us fades and is replaced by a cloud of real dust, it creates a more realistic and satisfying feeling of preference for me."

Özer's comment against the consumption of popular products also shows a conservative opposition. The participant, who we understand does not even question the need for viral products on social media, evaluates popular culture products and such content on social media in a very critical manner:

"The consumption of viral products on various social media platforms, especially with cultural imperialism, is quite high in the "Z generation" to which I belong. The young people who use TikTok and Instagram applications actively show their existence worldwide by consuming these viral products. I only bought a viral fidget spinner product 7-8 years ago. I don't remember buying any other viral product. I have never tried viral products such as bubble tea, Dubai chocolate, or chocolate donut, which my friends also recommended, and I don't plan to try them because they are not suitable for my taste. I don't want to "consume for the sake of consuming" when something is popular."

The data obtained from the participants within the scope of the current research reveal the power of social media to create virality while also indicating that participants who admit to consuming what is popular tend to justify this consumption with functional reasons. In other words, statements that begin with "I consume what is popular, but..." are often completed with a functional explanation.

For example, Alara states, "If the viral product interests me, I want to try it," implying that the content itself does not directly lead to consumption behavior unless it resonates with her interests. Ayla shares a similar perspective: "If it interests me, I'll try it. I'm personally open to such things. Yes, I have purchased a product that went viral on social media. And if something interests me again, I will continue buying or trying it." Likewise, Berk expresses a similar view by saying, "Yes, I might buy a viral product on social media... but not just because it's viral. I also do my research, and if it makes sense, I buy and try it," thereby attempting to rationalize his tendency to consume popular items through functional reasoning.

When the participants' responses regarding social media's role in shaping popular culture, setting trend tendencies, and influencing consumption behaviors are evaluated, the findings appear to confirm results presented by numerous previous studies. The data reveal that there are varying tendencies among young individuals: those who accept and purchase popular culture products without resistance, those who resist them, and those who purchase them but justify their actions with functional reasons.

CONCLUSION

Unlike what traditional economic theorists claim, today, need-based consumption has been replaced by the desire to consume in all circumstances and situations. The variables that make societies consumption-centered are the changes in production patterns since the Industrial Revolution, all kinds of political and social developments aimed at maintaining capitalism most effectively, and undoubtedly, the developments in communication technologies. Consumption, which it would not be wrong to state that it has reached its peak with digitalization, has created a new order that affects the whole world.

Human beings have endeavored to explain themselves or what they have experienced since their existence. Storytelling is a reflection of this endeavor. Stories are told through oral, written, and mass media with the development of technology and digital media with the development of internet-based technologies. Digital stories, which are used in different sectors, from education to cinema and health to psychology, are frequently used in communication activities carried out by brands in the marketing sector. In the new world, where order is dominated by consumption, reaching consumers with the functional features of the product and service is impossible.

Because brands with almost the same technical facilities cannot make their products preferable only with functional features, providing consumers with stories in which they can find emotional benefits and establish a common bond with the brand is an essential element that can distinguish the brand from other brands.

With digitalization, social media platforms accompany every moment of our lives. Social platforms, which have an intense usage rate and duration, have become the environments brands use to reach their consumers and tell their marketing and advertising stories. Aiming to reach consumers with much more complicated consumption motivations than real needs and with many more options, brands do not refrain from trying any and chance while using social media environments intensively for the same purpose, telling stories to consumers, sometimes directly or sometimes through an influencer. The undisputed power of stories can make brands different from other brands, such that a successful product, service, brand, or advertisement story can turn the story's subject into a ‘qualified’ element of popular culture.

Within the scope of the current study, the aim is to determine the role of digital stories on the motivations for consumption by young individuals who actively use social media. In line with the stated purpose, in-depth interviews were conducted with 14 undergraduate students at Istanbul Medipol University Faculty of Communication. The students were determined by convenience sampling, and the data obtained from the interviews were subjected to descriptive analysis and analyzed under six themes.

Research results show that young people living in Turkey use social media intensively. In-depth interviews conducted within the scope of the current research reveal results that confirm previous studies. Accordingly, university students' average weekly social media usage time is 10 to 15 hours. On the other hand, the data obtained from the interviews show that social media plays an essential role in the consumption tendencies of young individuals. Undoubtedly, the intensive use of platforms is the main factor in this importance. However, apart from this, qualities such as aesthetics, sincerity, and reliability of the content shared through digital platforms, as well as the fact that they contain experiences, are factors that increase the impact of the content. Another theme discussed within the scope of the research is the role of storytelling in content strategies shared on social media. The data obtained from the interviews show that storytelling is an essential determinant of young individuals' consumption motivations. Memorable stories convey experience, contain sincerity, and arouse curiosity. They also stand out as highly effective in influencing consumption preferences. The changing face of young individuals' general consumption tendencies draws attention as another theme reached as a result of the data obtained from the research.

The intensive use of visual-oriented platforms such as Facebook, Instagram, and TikTok also includes the aesthetic components that the environments have to have as a result of their existential characteristics into the consumer's expectations. In other words, while visual-oriented social platforms that diversify with digitalization increase the aesthetic qualities of the content, they also increase the expectations and desires of the consumer in the same direction. For the modern consumer, it is seen that the product and service are evaluated with their aesthetic qualities, both design and content, rather than being recognized at the point of need. Another variable that is effective in consumption tendencies is social reference groups. The answers given to the questions by the young individuals participating in the research show that the experiences conveyed by real users are as effective in their consumption preferences as the content shared by social media influencers and the product and brand recommendations they make, and even more so for some individuals. Again, as previous studies on consumption have shown, family and friend recommendations appear as essential variables in the preference for products and brands. Here, what is more effective than the source of the recommendation is that it is reliable, sincere, and real. The last theme discussed within the scope of the research is the ability of social media to determine popular culture, products and services, consumption patterns, and the ability to make brands viral.

Dubai Chocolate, which has recently occupied social media content and consumer agenda intensively, has been determined as a sample item to carry out the related discussion. The responses obtained from the participants show a tendency to try, buy, or at least know about the product and brand content that is shared intensively on social media. However, it is not possible to comprehend whether they are voluntary or involuntary. Young individuals often express curiosity about popular culture products or, in other words, viral products. However, an important detail that draws attention here allows us to understand the changing nature of consumption. In the new world order, consumption sometimes takes place with the motivation of feeling different. In this context, the widespread consumption of popular culture products shows that some individuals are resistant to consuming these products. In other words, the consumer does not prefer a product or brand only because it is popular. Yet another detail is that the preference for popular culture elements is generally desired to be supported by a functional situation.

The current research was conducted to determine the changing motivations of young individuals, Generation Z digital natives, and the role of stories told through digital platforms in their consumption preferences. Within the scope of the research, interviews were conducted with undergraduate students studying at the Faculty of Communication. Specifically, the subject of the analysis is the current situation of students who have received education on consumption, economic models, digitalization, storytelling, and the manipulative effect of advertising, albeit at different intensity levels. This is because it is a crucial problem whether the current level of knowledge of students who know specifically on these topics creates consciousness in their consumption preferences and hampers their preferences. From the data we obtained, we can clearly say that the existing knowledge does not create any awareness of the preferences of young communication students. Among the 14-person interview team, only two participants made statements referring to the current situation. While Semih says that marketing something so intensely and insincerely, only in a capitalist-oriented way, does not seem sincere to me, Özer says that I generally spend to meet my basic needs in the consumer society created by today's capitalist system and evaluates the act of consumption conditioned by the capitalist system with all its mechanisms in this context.

Of course, this discourse and claim is a result we encounter when we discuss the issue from a critical perspective. The following statements made by Cemrenur, one of the in-depth interview participants, in her answers to the questions, reveal our starting point, the results we have reached, and the relationship between consumption and communication activities in a striking way:

> *"I think it tastes good, but it's not something spectacular enough to be the cause of this craze. I don't think it's about beauty, though. However, it is also true that Dubai Chocolate should remain a label when it comes to the impact of*

the media world on consumption habits. When its name is mentioned, everyone should understand that they are discussing the relationship between media and consumption..."

REFERENCES

Althusser, L. (2019). *Devletin ideolojik aygıtları* (Tümertekin, A., Trans.). İthaki Publications.

Asur, S. A., Huberman, B., Szabo, G., & Wang, C. (2021). Trends in social media: persistence and decay. *Proceedings of the International AAAI Conference on Web and Social Media*, 5(1), 434-437. https://doi.org/DOI: 10.1609/icwsm.v5i1.14167

Bali, R. (2002). *Tarzı-ı hayattan life style'a yeni seçkinler, yeni mekanlar, yeni yaşamlar*. İletişim Publications.

Barbosa, B., Simões, D., & Leal, F. (2022). Young adults' views on digital story-telling campaigns. *Innovar (Universidad Nacional de Colombia)*, *32*(83), 63–74.

Baudrillard, J. (2004). *Tüketim toplumu. (Trans. H. Deliçaylı ve F.Keskin)*. Ayrıntı Puclications.

Belova, A. (2021). Storytelling in advertising and branding. *Cognition, Communication. Discourse (Berkeley, Calif.)*, (22), 13–26.

Cai, S., & Xu, Y. C. (2011). Designing not just for pleasure: Effects of web site aesthetics on consumer shopping value. *International Journal of Electronic Commerce, 15*(4), 159–188. DOI: 10.2753/JEC1086-4415150405

Chen, F., Wyer, R. S., & Shen, H. (2015). The interactive effects of affect and shopping goal on information search and product evaluations. *Journal of Experimental Psychology. Applied, 21*(4), 429–442. DOI: 10.1037/xap0000059 PMID: 26460676

Dahlan, N. F. (2024). Media and Culture: The role of media and social media in the formation and dissemination of popular, local, global and international culture. *Journal of Studies on Art, Culture and Society*, 1(1), 13–17. Retrieved from https://jacs.professorline.com/index.php/journal/article/view/3

Djafarova, E., & Trofimenko, O. (2019). 'Instafamous'–credibility and self-presentation of micro-celebrities on social media. *Information Communication and Society, 22*(10), 1432–1446. DOI: 10.1080/1369118X.2018.1438491

Erdoğan, İ. (1999). Popüler kültür, kültür alanında egemenlik ve mücadele. Güngör, N (Eds.) Popüler Kültür ve İktidar (pp. 18-53). Ankara: Vadi Publications.

Featherstone, M. (1991). *Consumer culture and postmodernism*. Sage Publications.

Gierl, H., & Huettl, V. (2010). Are scarce products always more attractive? The interaction of different types of scarcity signals with products' suitability for conspicuous consumption. *International Journal of Research in Marketing, 27*(3), 225–235. DOI: 10.1016/j.ijresmar.2010.02.002

Gramsci, A. (1971). *Selections from the prison notebooks* (Hoare, Q., & Smith, G. N., Eds. & Trans.). International Publishers.

Gürbüz, S., & Şahin, F. (2018). *Sosyal Bilimlerde Araştırma Yöntemleri*. Seçkin Publishing.

Hall, S. (1980). Encoding/decoding. In Hall, S., Hobson, D., Lowe, A., & Willis, P. (Eds.), *Culture, media, language* (pp. 128–138). Routledge.

Holbrook, M. B., & Hirschman, E. C. (1982). The experiential aspects of consumption: Consumer fantasies, feelings, and fun. *The Journal of Consumer Research, 9*(2), 132–140. https://www.jstor.org/stable/2489122. DOI: 10.1086/208906

Horkheimer, M., & Adorno, T. W. (2002). *Dialectic of enlightenment: Philosophical fragments (G. S. Noerr* (Jephcott, E. Ed. & Trans.). Stanford University Press.

Hoyer, W. D., & Stokburger-Sauer, N. E. (2012). The role of aesthetic taste in consumer behavior. *Journal of the Academy of Marketing Science, 40*(1), 167–180. DOI: 10.1007/s11747-011-0269-y

İnternet Araştırmaları Koordinatörlüğü. (2024, February). Türkiye Dijital 2024: Türkiye'nin nüfus, internet, sosyal medya, mobil, e-ticaret ve dijital pazarlama göstergeleri. https://www.guvenliweb.org.tr/dosya/3degJ.pdf

Kauppinen-Raisanen, H., Bjork, P., Lonnstrom, A., & Jauffret, M. N. (2018). How consumers' need for uniqueness, self-monitoring, and social ıdentity affect their choices when luxury brands visually shout versus whisper. *Journal of Business Research, 84*, 72–81. DOI: 10.1016/j.jbusres.2017.11.012

Lang, C., & Armstrong, C. M. J. (2018). Collaborative consumption: The influence of fashion leadership, need for uniqueness, and materialism on female consumers' adoption of clothing renting and swapping. *Sustainable Production and Consumption, 13*, 37–47. DOI: 10.1016/j.spc.2017.11.005

Leung, F. F., Gu, F. F., & Palmatier, R. W. (2022). Online influencer marketing. *Journal of the Academy of Marketing Science, 50*(2), 226–251. DOI: 10.1007/s11747-021-00829-4

Marwick, A. E. (2015). Instafame: Luxury selfies in the attention economy. *Public Culture, 27*(1), 137–160. DOI: 10.1215/08992363-2798379

McQuail, D., & Windahl, S. (2005). *Kitle iletişim çalışmalarında iletişim modelleri. Trans. Konca Kumlu.* İmge Publishing.

Nam, K. A. (2015). High-context and low-context communication. The SAGE encyclopedia of intercultural competence, 377-381.

Nesser, C. (2019). Characteristics of visual storytelling advertisement-*From a Millennial & Communication Professional point of view,* Bachelor Thesis, Faculty of Behavioral. Management and Science.

Nouri, M. (2018). *The power of influence: Traditional celebrity vs social media influencer* (Student thesis, Santa Clara University). *Pop Culture Intersections*, 32. https://scholarcommons.scu.edu/engl_176/32

Pereira, G. (2019). Brand storytelling: A three-dimensional perspective. *Journal of Brand Strategy*, *8*(2), 146–159. DOI: 10.69554/CEWY2163

Prensky, M. (2001). Digital Natives, Digital Immigrants, Part 1. *On the Horizon*, *9*(5), 1–6. DOI: 10.1108/10748120110424816

Rafique, S., Khan, M. H., & Bilal, H. (2022). A critical analysis of pop culture and media. *Global Regional Review*, *VII*(I), 173–184. DOI: 10.31703/grr.2022(VII-I).17

Roy, B. (2023). Standardization of Culture: A Constructed Ideology for Dominion and Power Maintenance.

Rubio-Hurtado, M. J., Fuertes-Alpiste, M., Martínez-Olmo, F., & Quintana, J. (2022). Youths' posting practices on social media for digital storytelling. Journal of new approaches in educational research, 11(1), 97-113.

Serrat, O. (2017). Storytelling. In Knowledge Solutions (pp. 839-842). Springer. DOI: 10.1007/978-981-10-0983-9_91

Snyder, C. R. (1992). Product scarcity by need for uniqueness interaction: A consumer Catch-22 carousel? *Basic and Applied Social Psychology*, *13*(1), 9–24. DOI: 10.1207/s15324834basp1301_3

Subitha N.., G., M. S., & C., T. (2024). Influence of social media ınfluencers on buying behavior of college students in ernakulam district. *Journal of Lifestyle and SDGs Review*, 4(4), e03539. https://doi.org/DOI: 10.47172/2965-730X.SDGsReview.v4.n04.pe03539

Teraiya, V., Namboodiri, S., & Jayswal, R. (2023, May).. . *First Published*, *5*, 231160591. DOI: 10.1177/jmrt

The University of British Columbia. (2018). Data pseudonymization. Retrieved from: https://researchdata.library.ubc.ca/share/anonymize-and-de-identify/data-pseudonymization/

Tiryaki, S., & Kaya, E. (2019). Sosyal medyanın gri yüzü. In Livberber, T., & Tiryaki, S. (Eds.), *Sosyal medya çalışmaları: Kuram, söylem, pratik* (pp. 239–262). Literaturk Academia.

Tomaselli, K. (2016). Encoding/decoding, the transmission model and a court of law. *International Journal of Cultural Studies*, *19*(1), 59–70. DOI: 10.1177/1367877915599611

Wang, C., & Zhang, P. (2012). The evolution of social commerce: The people, management, technology, and information dimensions. *Communications of the Association for Information Systems*, *31*, 105–127. DOI: 10.17705/1CAIS.03105

Wang, Y., Kong, S., Li, M., & Liu, L. (2022). Need for uniqueness moderates the effectiveness of different types of scarcity appeals. *Frontiers in Psychology*, *13*, 890350. DOI: 10.3389/fpsyg.2022.890350 PMID: 36507003

Wiecek, A., Wentzel, D., & Landwehr, J. R. (2019). The aesthetic fidelity effect. *International Journal of Research in Marketing*, *36*(4), 580–597. DOI: 10.1016/j.ijresmar.2019.03.002

Williams, R. (1985). Keywords: A vocabulary of culture and society (Rev. and expanded ed.). Oxford University Press.

Yadav,P., Gupta P.K.,Upamannyu, N.Kr. (2022). Influence of social reference group and personality traits on automobile buying decision: a research on youth, ınspira-*Journal of Modern Management & Entrepreneurship (JMME)* 207, Impact Factor: 6.280, Volume 12, No. 01, January-March 2022, pp. 207-216

Yang, Y., Tang, Y., Zhang, Y., & Yang, R. (2021, September 6). Exploring the relationship between visual aesthetics and social commerce through visual ınformation adoption unimodel. *Frontiers in Psychology*, *12*, 700180. DOI: 10.3389/fpsyg.2021.700180 PMID: 34552529

Chapter 11
Digital Self-Help Culture: How Social Media is Reshaping Psychological Discourse

Eser Levi
https://orcid.org/0000-0003-3932-4216
Istanbul Bilgi University, Turkey

Eda Aylin Genç
Manchester Metropolitan University, UK

ABSTRACT

This chapter examines how social media has transformed psychological discourse from academic field to popular cultural phenomenon. Tracing the evolution from early self-help literature and TV psychotainment to digital platforms, it explores how psychological concepts migrated from clinical settings into everyday language through influencer culture and algorithmic amplification. Drawing on communication theories such as Framing, Parasocial Interaction, and Cultivation, the chapter analyzes how content creators package mental health content for viral reach. It examines the cultural impact of this shift, showing how terms like trauma or gaslighting enter mainstream use, while neoliberal values frame mental health as personal responsibility. Though social media democratizes access to psychological knowledge, it also spreads misinformation, simplification, and pseudoscience. The rise of conspirituality where wellness merges with conspiracy exemplifies these risks, pointing to the need for regulatory frameworks while preserving benefits in digital mental health discourse.

DOI: 10.4018/979-8-3373-2023-6.ch011

INTRODUCTION

Psychology has thoroughly permeated everyday life, a phenomenon that may be referred to as psychologization (De Vos, 2011). The field gained a prominent position and a central role in the public imagination and the daily discourse. The emergence of a "psychological society" is the product of the interaction between individualization, social management, and the expansion of psychology, a focus on the inner world of feelings (Jansz, 2004). We're constantly saturated with information about various psychological topics, such as brain function, memory, parenting, romantic relationships, sexuality, crime, drug use, mental health, therapy; through self-help books, popular media articles, TV shows, films, and the internet (Lilienfeld et al., 2009). More than ever before, psychologization has become a global phenomenon, shaping the way we interpret ourselves, other people, and our surroundings through the lens of psychological concepts. Psychological discourse increasingly influences companies, advertising, cultural practices, political narratives, and even social and family relationships (De Vos, 2012).

However, much of what is presented to the public as psychology is, in fact, not scientifically grounded. Popular media content often overshadows the genuine intellectual and scientific foundations of the field, and it's not always easy to recognize which elements are valuable and which are misleading, leading to common misconceptions (Cordón, 2005). Critical psychological phenomena, especially mental illnesses and their treatments, are frequently misrepresented in entertainment media (Beins, 2008). Moreover, popular psychology has extended the scope of the discipline beyond the examination of individual thoughts and emotions, it now also functions as a guide for navigating various aspects of daily life, such as life coaching, career coaching, and relationship coaching. In addition, self-help media not only serves for individual well-being but also contributes to the psychologization of intimate relationships through online social networks. Individuals often draw on popular psychology to make sense of everyday experiences, even those involving their most intimate lives (Nehring et al., 2016).

This increasing integration of psychology into everyday life is now being amplified by digital platforms, particularly social media, where storytelling has become a central vehicle for conveying psychological insights. Audiences increasingly turn to social media platforms for health-related content, just as they do for entertainment, education, and journalism. Within this context, mental health content has become increasingly widespread, reflecting the broader trend of popular psychology (Aschbrenner et al., 2019). Popular psychology aims to make psychological knowledge understandable and accessible to general audiences (Ussher, 2013), and it often addresses the needs of individuals who are unable to access psychotherapy due to time constraints, financial limitations, or social stigma. Professionals in the field of psychology, along with opinion leaders (i.e., mental health influencers), use platforms like Instagram, Twitter, YouTube, and TikTok to reach broad audiences, raise mental health awareness, and offer a form of therapeutic support through the resources and content they create (Roberts & David, 2023). Originally part of the private sphere, mental health issues now permeate a consumption-driven society, as the therapy space is transferred to entertainment platforms where superficial and short-lived content dominates. Shaped by the discourse of self-help culture, topics such as childhood trauma, intimate relationships, and attachment styles are widely marketed and popularized on social media (Brooks, 2023). This shift invites deeper theoretical reflection on the implications of commodifying psychological discourse. In light of this commercialization, drawing on Baudrillard (1998), we may question the implications of placing psychology alongside practices such as meditation, shamanism, and energy healing. Within a postmodern spiritual marketplace that commodifies nearly everything, psychology risks being perceived not as a scientific discipline but as one more symbolic product promising salvation. This convergence of psychological science with pseudo-scientific or spiritual practices diminishes its cultural value and scientific credibility, blurring the boundaries between empirical knowledge and commodified self-help. It also raises concerns that individuals seeking secular and evidence-based guidance may be redirected toward spiritual or pseudo-scientific alternatives under the illusion of equivalence. These concerns highlight the need for closer analysis of how psychological discourse is shaped and circulated within digital media environments.

Given the growing role of social media in shaping psychological discourse, it becomes essential to examine how psychological content is constructed and delivered in this environment. The way popular psychology is framed and communicated (often through emotionally resonant storytelling) in digital spaces influences the meaning attributed to incidents, experiences, and concepts related to the psychological discipline. Thus, focusing on the communicative methods used in disseminating popular psychology content on social media is essential to understanding how the medium reshapes psychological discourse. In this respect, the current chapter aims to examine how mental health issues, both problems and their proposed solutions, are represented in these posts. The strategies adopted by content creators mirror the transformation of the field from a scholarly discipline to a widely consumed cultural product. The visual, auditory, and textual elements that form the basis of the content can be seen as cognitive windows that reinforce meaning-making. Grounded in media and communication theories, the chapter investigates how content creators construct mental health narratives. The chapter also discusses the potential impact of this content on audiences. The authors address both the challenges and opportunities posed by popular psychology, asking whether it serves as a democratizing force for mental health or operates as a pseudoscientific trend that dilutes the field and generates unforeseeable risks.

FROM THE ACADEMY TO THE ALGORITHM: THE EVOLUTION OF POPULAR PSYCHOLOGY

Early Roots and the Rise of Self-Help Literature

Understanding the emergence of popular psychology requires a closer look at its early development and the foundational role of mass communication in shaping public engagement with psychological ideas. How did psychology evolve from an academic discipline into public knowledge, leading to the emergence of popular psychology? Examining the role of both traditional and digital media in this transformation offers valuable insight into this paradigmatic shift. Psychology is generally considered to have emerged as an independent discipline in 1879 (Jansz, 2004). Since then, psychological ideas have steadily moved beyond academic boundaries, contributing to the rise of popular psychology, broadly defined as any psychological approach or perspective that has achieved widespread public acceptance (Lilienfeld et al., 2009). This widespread appeal first began to take shape through traditional media, with the simplified dissemination of psychological content emerging in self-help books, popular magazine articles, and television specials (Cordón, 2005). However, its origins can be traced back much earlier (to the 17th century) when philosophers like Descartes and Locke drew on their understanding of human nature to support ideas that would later be recognized as scientific theories (Cuncic, 2023). In written material, self-help literature represents the earliest form of psychology in popular culture. Samuel Smiles, often regarded as an early advocate of the self-help movement, articulated a compelling ideological framework that emphasized the virtues of hard work, success, and personal development as essential pathways to social and economic success (Richards, 1982). His work *Self-Help* (published in 1859) is one of the most prominent examples of early self-help literature and laid the foundation for a genre that would grow significantly in the following decades (Murray, 2015). These early texts introduced storytelling as a persuasive tool, using personal anecdotes, success narratives, and moral tales to make psychological insights more accessible and emotionally resonant for the general public.

Psychology also began to appeal to the lay public through non-academic writings in newspapers and magazines that promised personal improvement and emotional insight. By the early 20th century, psychology had entered mainstream general-interest magazines and books. Popular materials related to psychology saw a significant rise in prominence around 1920, especially in general interest magazines (Rapp, 1988).

Even accredited psychologists contributed to daily psychological advice columns. Joseph Jastrow's column *Keeping Mentally Fit*, was syndicated and featured in over 150 newspapers during the 1920s. *Harpers*, *Forum*, *Atlantic Monthly*, and *Colliers* were among the magazines through which psychologists communicated their work to the general public. During the 1930s, three popular psychology magazines; *Modern Psychologist*, *Practical Psychology Monthly*, and *Psychology Digest* were launched but proved to be short-lived (Benjamin, 1986). Furthermore, advice columns in major newspapers, such as *Dear Abby* and *Ann Landers*, played a pivotal role in mainstreaming psychological discourse, offering a form of quick, simplified psychology that resembled moral guidance delivered with humor and wit (Weiner, 2002). In 1957, the widely read magazine *Life* ran a series of articles under the title *The Age of Psychology*, reflecting growing public interest in the field. A major milestone in the popularization of psychology occurred in 1967 with the launch of the American magazine *Psychology Today*, one of the most significant examples of this trend, which became a platform for leading psychologists to share their research with a general audience (Jansz, 2004). The content often distilled complex theories into digestible advice and reflected society's growing fascination with the self, motivation, and behavior. Popular forms of psychological knowledge also experienced significant growth through women's magazines. Advice columnists in the problem pages of these publications played a key role in shaping the intersection of permissive attitudes and the increasing psychologization of everyday life, as they adopted emerging psychological concepts and effectively translated them for an eager readership (Loughran, 2023). These early forms of psychological popularization laid the groundwork for future media formats, establishing a template where psychological advice could be repackaged for mass consumption.

Psychology Meets the Screen: Television and Cinema

With the advent of visual media, psychological discourse took on new forms and reached wider audiences, particularly through the emergence of psychotainment on television and in film. Following the era of print media, psychologists gained additional platforms to share their message, with television emerging as a particularly influential medium (Benjamin, 1986). This medium played a significant role in increasing psychology's visibility to the public, beginning from the 1950s and 1960s. Therapists began to appear on television as media personalities during this period. Psychologists like Dr. Joyce Brothers and later Dr. Phil McGraw became public figures, bringing therapy-related talk to daytime television. Their influence on popularizing psychological discourse was substantial (Jansz, 2004). These representations exemplified the blending of therapeutic discourse with entertainment formats. This incorporation of psychological themes into television for entertainment purposes is called the phenomenon of psychotainment. Television psychotainment programs clearly illustrate how the refusal to acknowledge fiction as fiction creates space for the imaginary to take hold. These reality shows appear to be a modern site where the psychology and subjectivity of the postmodern individual are fictionalized and performed (De Vos, 2011). Shows like Oprah featured therapy segments, blurring the lines between education, advice, and entertainment. A commonly echoed message among Oprah Winfrey and her network of guest psychologists, advice columnists, and spiritual mentors is the idea that adopting successful behaviors can lead to personal achievement (Lofton, 2011). In the early 2000s, Dr. Pamela Connolly was hosting a show called *Shrink Rap* in which she interviewed celebrities through a therapeutic lens (Nunn & Biressi, 2010). Confessional shows like these use a form of pseudo-therapy to frame personal struggles as public spectacle (Waddell, 2014). The "therapy culture" emerged, bringing healing and emotional expression into public discourse more prominently than before. These shows often dramatized psychological issues, contributing to both public awareness and the spread of simplified or stereotypical portrayals.

While psychology presents itself as capable of fully understanding every aspect of the human being, television creates the illusion of offering a complete account of events. In television shows, the therapist functions as a director, representing the authority of 'science' by offering 'effective strategies' to ensure that individuals deliver the appropriate behaviors. For instance, on television programs that address parenting challenges, therapists communicate with parents to offer real-time guidance and advice. Shows such as *Little Angels* feature therapists observing parent–child interactions on small monitors and coaching parents by discreetly suggesting appropriate responses. Advocates of educational television argue that these programs effectively equip parents with clear information and practical models to help them implement recommended strategies. Moreover, the slogans used by these reality TV shows are worth-considering: "*the human condition laid bare*" or "*life as it is*", both of which highlight the genre's claim to present raw, unfiltered human experiences (De Vos, 2011).

The theme of psychology emerged not only in television programs but also in cinematic works. Directors such as Alfred Hitchcock demonstrated a deep fascination with psychoanalysis, often weaving its concepts into their films (Jansz, 2004). His films have been cited as early examples of psychoanalytic psychotainment, blending psychological theory with popular narrative (De Vos, 2011). More broadly, cinema served as a key medium for dramatizing psychological concepts and making psychotherapy more accessible and engaging to the public, reflecting Hollywood's enduring fascination with the therapeutic process (Gabbard, 2001). Television and cinema not only helped expand public familiarity with psychological ideas but also contributed to their dramatization, simplifying complex concepts for entertainment and emotional appeal.

The Boom and Critique of Popular Psychology Books

The rise of mass-market psychology books in the late 20th century marked another pivotal moment in the popularization of psychological knowledge. The 1980s stood out with the emergence of popular psychology books again. In bookstores, shelves increasingly became stocked with popular psychology titles (Jansz, 2004). Books such as *Men Are from Mars, Women Are from Venus* by John Gray, which actually has quite stereotypical representations and generalizations over genders, made psychology-based insights highly marketable (Cameron, 2007). Moreover, some of these books offer overly simplistic or unrealistic assurances to individuals seeking relief from complex mental health challenges. For example, a self-help book by well-known psychologist Arnold Lazarus, titled *In the Mind's Eye*, promises that it can help readers enhance creativity, quit smoking, drinking, or overeating, overcome sadness and low mood, build self-esteem and competence, and reduce fear and anxiety (Rosen, 1987). From that point on, psychology was increasingly commodified, reduced to easy steps, quizzes, and personality types. After this booming effect, scholars began criticizing popular psychology for being scientifically shallow, therapeutically vague, or commercially driven. This has led scholars to label them with critical terms: Rosen (1977) described them as *psychobabble*, Morris (1977) characterized them as *airport books*, and Lilienfeld et al. (2017) referred to them as *psycho-mythologies* (Katz, 2022). While these books extended psychology's reach, their commercial orientation and oversimplified messages prompted criticism from scholars concerned with scientific rigor and ethical communication.

The Digital Turn: From Websites to Social Media Influencers

The emergence of digital platforms has profoundly altered how psychological content is created, shared, and consumed, ushering in a new era of influencer-driven mental health communication. Since the 2000s, the transition to digital platforms has significantly reshaped both the practice and profession of psychology. With the rise of the internet, blogs, forums, and online magazines emerged as new spaces for psychology-themed content. Psychologists began utilizing websites and digital technologies to connect, communicate, promote their services, and engage with broader audiences (Kolmes, 2012). In recent years, this digital presence has expanded further through social media platforms such as Instagram, TikTok, YouTube, and Twitter, which have become widely used channels for disseminating popular psychology content that is both visually engaging and emotionally resonant. These platforms have been flooded with bite-sized psychological narratives, often created by licensed professionals. For example, Dr. Julie Smith is recognized as one of the first accredited psychologists to successfully use TikTok to share mental health information on topics ranging from anxiety to suicidality. Her content has attracted millions of followers and generated widespread engagement by presenting professionally grounded, accessible insights in short-form videos (McCashin & Murphy, 2023). Alongside professionals, non-experts and life coaches have also entered the scene, positioning themselves as mental health influencers. These individuals often share personal stories, therapy tips, or motivational advice and have gained considerable attention, even in the absence of formal credentials. As a result, a new category of public figure has emerged, blending therapeutic discourse with entertainment and lifestyle branding. In parallel, the field of psychology has increasingly merged with wellness trends such as mindfulness and positive thinking (Shapiro, 2009). This convergence reflects a broader cultural shift in which "therapy talk" has become part of everyday language. However, it has also led to the decontextualization of complex psychological concepts, the erosion of scientific accuracy, and a risk of therapeutic overreach as nuanced ideas are simplified for mass consumption. This reflects a broader cultural shift from expert-driven, structured dissemination to the reframing, reshaping, and popularization of psychological knowledge in response to the emotional, aesthetic, and social needs of online audiences. In this new digital environment, psychology is no longer confined to clinical or academic spaces, but is continually reinterpreted through algorithmic trends, user expectations, and the aesthetics of everyday online interaction. Storytelling now serves as a central method for shaping how psychological knowledge is communicated and understood, as content creators craft emotionally engaging narratives that blend self-disclosure, advice, and social commentary.

COMMUNICATING PSYCHOLOGY ON SOCIAL MEDIA: NARRATIVES AND THEORETICAL PERSPECTIVES

Framing the Creator: Self-Presentation and Identity Construction

To understand how popular psychology circulates on social media, it is essential to begin with the role of the content creator and how they construct and manage their public persona. This section focuses on how online personas use social media as a channel for mental health advice. Content creators in the realm of popular psychology, much like those in other domains, adopt specific communication strategies that are perceived as effective and have become widely adopted as a result. These creators tailor their content by anticipating the needs and expectations of their target audience, developing their communication approach accordingly. Factors such as the characteristics of the medium, along with the language, tone, and visual aesthetics that audiences associate with this type of content, play a key role in guiding how creators brand themselves on social media. This raises important questions about how popular psychology is shaped as a content category in the digital environment, how it is framed communicatively, and what kinds of communication models creators employ. Exploring these dynamics may offer valuable insights into how the discipline is being reinterpreted by the public as well as how it is practiced by various actors.

To explore how creators manage these communicative dynamics, media and communication theories, many of which were originally developed for traditional media, provide valuable insight and frameworks for understanding how psychological content is framed and conveyed in today's digital environment. In this context, Self-Presentation Theory serves as a particularly relevant starting point, as it directly addresses the role of the content creator as a source and how they strategically manage their public image. Self-Presentation Theory (Goffman, 1959) suggests that in social settings, individuals behave in ways designed to control how others perceive them, much like actors performing on a stage (Fine & Manning, 2000). In this theatrical metaphor, the "back stage" is where individuals can be their authentic selves, free from audience expectations or judgment, while the "front stage" represents the space where people present a carefully curated image to others, performing the actions necessary to fulfill their roles (Miller, 1984). On social media, most content creators actively manage their self-presentation to appear credible, authentic, or expert-like in order to achieve desired outcomes (Özçelik & Levi, 2020). Mental health influencers may share personal struggles to seem relatable and trustworthy, while also using professional language or highlighting credentials to establish authority. Their success often depends not only on the quality of the content they produce, but also on how effectively they manage their image in the digital public sphere, something especially critical when dealing with psychology-related topics. Self-Presentation Theory, therefore, offers a valuable lens through which to understand how content creators manage their identity and shape audience perception in the context of popular psychology. This active curation of identity not only reinforces credibility in a competitive digital landscape but also shapes how audiences come to trust and engage with psychological content online.

Shaping the Message: Framing and Agenda-Setting

Beyond personal branding, creators also shape how psychological information is structured and prioritized, often relying on framing and agenda-setting strategies to influence audience interpretation and attention. While self-presentation focuses on identity and image management, The Framing Theory extends the analysis to how content itself is structured to shape audience interpretation. The Framing Theory, originally introduced by Goffman (1974) from a sociological perspective and later adapted to the field of mass communication, examines how individuals interpret experiences through mental structures or frames (Van Pinxteren et al., 2020). More specifically, framing refers to the process of selecting certain aspects of perceived reality and emphasizing them in communication in order to influence how audiences understand that reality (Entman, 1993). This theory is particularly relevant to popular psychology content on social media, where the presentation of information; especially through storytelling, language, and visuals; can significantly shape public perceptions of psychological concepts by embedding psychological ideas into compelling personal narratives and simplified explanations.

As a result, these representations often differ markedly from how psychological issues are understood and addressed within the scientific discipline of psychotherapy. Framing Theory, which explores how content creators design and craft their messages based on anticipated audience responses, has undergone significant development in the digital age, where social media platforms, user participation, and algorithmic curation play a central role in constructing and circulating meaning within public discourse (Almakaty, 2025). The way content is framed directly shapes broader processes of meaning-making. We are nearing a point where image culture, rising in both cultural and scientific fields; is overtaking our perception of reality, leaving limited space for approaches that value the discursive and symbolic aspects of human experience. Engaging with reality beyond visual representation remains essential (De Vos, 2011).

Beyond how content is presented, it is also important to consider how attention is directed toward particular psychological topics; this is where Agenda-Setting Theory becomes relevant. McCombs and Shaw proposed Agenda-Setting Theory, which highlights how media influences the topics that people perceive as important (Coleman et al., 2009). This occurs, in part, because individuals possess an inherent psychological need for orientation; a desire to understand and feel familiar with both their physical surroundings and cognitive environment. As a result, people often turn to the media to construct their own agendas and, consequently, their perceived realities (McCombs et al., 2018). The theory, traditionally focused on how mass media shapes public attention, is also highly relevant to popular psychology content on social media. Here, various content creators; including licensed therapists, life coaches, and self-proclaimed mental health influencers; direct public focus toward specific psychological themes such as trauma, narcissism, anxiety, and more. In this context, social media content creators function as micro-agenda setters, shaping discourse by emphasizing particular topics through compelling storytelling, relatable narratives, and engaging visual formats. Moreover, the findings suggest that social media enables individuals to actively participate in shaping agendas (Albalawi and Sixsmith, 2015). Consequently, it can be argued that agenda-setting processes in the context of popular psychology on social media involve not only content creators but also audiences who engage with and disseminate their content. Agenda setting may result in misconception since media's coverage of the outside world is often deceptive, causing us to overestimate how often dramatic events occur while underestimating more common, less dramatic ones. Additionally, the media tends to exaggerate straightforward psychological concepts and, at times, oversimplifies those that are actually quite complex (Lilienfeld et al., 2009). Together, Framing and Agenda-Setting Theories illuminate how creators selectively highlight psychological themes and format content to influence what audiences consider significant in mental health discourse.

The Long View: Cultivation and the Spread of Psychological Myths

While framing and agenda-setting shape short-term perceptions, Cultivation Theory helps explain the potential long-term effects of repeated exposure to digital psychology content. Agenda-setting addresses short-term attention focus, but Cultivation Theory offers insight into the consequences of media exposure over time. Cultivation Theory (Gerbner, 1998), which focuses on the long-term effects of television viewing, suggests that repeated exposure to media content gradually shapes viewers' beliefs, values, perceptions of reality, and, over time, their broader worldview (Koch et al., 2017). Although television content may initially appear highly diverse, with a wide range of themes, program types, and presenters, systematic analyses reveal a striking consistency in the underlying value systems conveyed (Shrum, 2017). While initially developed in the context of television, the core principles of the theory can also be applied to new media environments, including social media. This raises an important question: How might continuous exposure to simplified, emotionally charged, dramatized, or sensationalized portrayals of psychological concepts, such as trauma, mental illness, or toxic relationships, affect the ways social media users perceive psychological norms and realities? Over time, could this repeated exposure cultivate distorted or overly generalized understandings of complex psychological phenomena? Since prolonged and systematic exposure to media content influences the ways in which audiences construct meaning according to the Cultivation Theory, popular psychology content on social media may also contribute to the long-term shaping of users' perceptions of mental health issues.

These long-term effects also contribute to the construction and reinforcement of cultural myths, many of which are sustained and circulated through popular media portrayals. The most common psychology myths that people believe are often the ones most frequently featured in popular culture content in the media (Furnham & Hughes, 2014). Popular psychology contributes to the spread of several myths. Although these examples are widely recognized clichés, they become troubling upon closer examination, as they are not grounded in factual accuracy. In terms of brain and perception, people are often labeled as either left-brained or right-brained. When it comes to memory, it's widely believed that traumatic experiences are usually repressed. Regarding personality, some think handwriting reveals character traits. In the realm of emotion and motivation, many assume a positive mindset can prevent cancer. In interpersonal communication, it's claimed that men and women speak in entirely different ways. For development and aging, there's the belief that playing Mozart to babies boosts their intelligence. Concerning mental health, people often think only those with severe depression consider suicide. In psychological treatment, it's assumed that all effective therapies dig into childhood issues. And in matters of psychology and law, there's a stereotype that mentally ill individuals are violent. These are just a few among many misleading ideas (Lilienfeld et al., 2009). Cultivation Theory and the proliferation of psychology myths point to the risks of oversimplified or dramatized representations becoming normalized as mental health knowledge.

Encoding, Decoding, and the Power of Interpretation

Moving from content design to audience interpretation, Stuart Hall's Encoding/Decoding model emphasizes the dynamic relationship between creator intention and audience reception. Stuart Hall, in his both creator and audience focused model, presents a framework in which the concept of code is central, emphasizing the process of meaning-making; first through encoding, where the source constructs the meaning, and then through decoding, where the receiver interprets and reconstructs that meaning (Ross, 2011). If we examine popular psychology through the lens of this model called Encoding/Decoding; encoding refers to how popular psychology is constructed. In regard to the encoding phase of the communication process, media messages are encoded by producers with intended meanings, shaped by dominant ideologies and cultural assumptions (Pillai, 1992). In the case of popular psychology, content creators encode psychological messages with particular intentions such as simplifying complex theories into digestible, emotionally resonant formats; promoting certain norms like self-care, boundaries, trauma awareness; and aligning with dominant cultural values such as individualism, productivity, and emotional expression. These encodings often reflect dominant ideologies about mental health and selfhood in neoliberal, consumer-driven societies, for example, the idea that healing is a personal responsibility or that success stems from mindset alone. On the other hand, the decoding phase refers to how audiences interpret popular psychology. Hall claims that audiences are not passive recipients, but instead, they decode messages in different ways, depending on their cultural backgrounds, lived experiences, and social positions (Hall, 2010). When engaging with popular psychology, users may interpret content in different ways. According to Hall's classifications, dominant/hegemonic reading would result in a full acceptance of the message by the viewer. Negotiated reading, on the other hand, results in the viewer receiving the message partially, questioning or adapting others. Lastly, oppositional reading would result in the viewer's rejection of the dominant message, criticizing it as they consider it shallow or misleading for example. A receiver employing a negotiated reading recognizes that statements like "if you have these five traits, you may be a narcissist" represent a reductionist and overly generalized approach to complex psychological concepts. Hall's framework underscores that psychological content is not passively received but is actively decoded in ways that may reinforce, challenge, or reinterpret dominant mental health narratives. By foregrounding the interplay between media encoding and user decoding, Hall's framework reveals the diverse ways popular psychology is interpreted, ranging from acceptance to resistance, within digital culture.

Audience-Centered Design: Anticipating Needs and Emotions

Alongside top-down message construction, many content creators design material based on anticipated user motivations, emotional needs, and psychological tendencies, drawing on audience-centered theories. This study focuses on how creators of popular psychology content on social media frame their messages, present themselves, and select formats or styles in ways that reflect an implicit understanding of audience preferences and psychological tendencies. In this sense, audience-centered theories are used not as models of media effects, but as frameworks for interpreting the motivations behind creators' communicative choices. As a result, although many other foundational media theories such as Uses and Gratifications Theory, Elaboration Likelihood Model, Diffusion of Innovations, and Parasocial Interaction Theory primarily emphasize audience motivations and responses, they remain relevant in the context of this study by offering insight into how content creators anticipate and shape communication strategies to align with perceived audience needs.

Uses and Gratifications Theory (Blumler & Katz, 1974) focuses on the motivations behind audiences' engagement with specific media. According to the theory, audiences actively select and use media to fulfill particular needs and desires (Haridakis & Humphries, 2019). The relevance of this theory has been revitalized with the emergence of new media, as content is increasingly shaped by creators' anticipation of user needs. The theory has consistently offered a forward-looking framework during the early development of each major mass communication medium; from newspapers to radio, television, and now the Internet (Ruggiero, 2000). In the context of social media, it helps explain why users are drawn to psychology-related content, often seeking information for self-help or turning to such content for emotional relief. Content creators strategically design material to address common user motivations by offering bite-sized psychological advice, inspirational quotes, personal narratives, and therapeutic tips.

Another key aspect of audience engagement with popular psychology content involves the perception of personal connection with creators, as explained by Parasocial Interaction Theory. Parasocial Interaction Theory, suggested by Horton and Wohl (1956), describes a one-sided psychological relationship in which an audience member develops a sense of intimacy, friendship, or emotional connection with a media personality (Rojek, 2015). Originally applied to traditional mass media (particularly television) the theory explains how viewers may come to feel that they "know" a public figure personally, forming emotional bonds as though the person were part of their real social circle, despite the absence of actual interaction (Hartmann, 2016). In the age of social media, parasocial relationships have naturally evolved and become more intensified. Unlike traditional media, platforms such as Instagram, TikTok, and YouTube allow for likes, comments, and direct messages, creating the illusion of mutual interaction, even when the communication remains largely one-sided. Moreover, many mental health influencers share personal stories, adopt a relatable persona, and speak to their audiences in a casual and empathetic tone, which helps to foster trust and emotional closeness. As a result, followers may come to view these creators as credible sources of psychological insight (even when they lack formal training or professional credentials) and may even treat them as surrogate therapists. Online personas who are aware of their influence often design content to foster emotional connection with their followers, taking user psychology into account, whether consciously or subconsciously.

Understanding the persuasive impact of this content requires attention to how audiences cognitively process it, as framed by the Elaboration Likelihood Model. Petty and Cacioppo (1986) proposed this model that focuses on persuasion and explains how individuals process messages and form attitudes. It proposes two primary routes to persuasion: the central route and the peripheral route (O'Keefe, 2013). The central route is used when individuals are motivated and able to engage in careful thought about the message, focusing on the quality of arguments, logic, and supporting evidence. This pathway leads to more enduring and resistant attitude change (Cook et al., 2004). In contrast, the peripheral route is taken when individuals are less motivated or lack the ability to process information deeply. Instead, they rely on superficial cues, such as the speaker's appearance, emotional appeal, or the attractiveness and relatability of the content. Persuasion through this route often results in temporary attitude change, which is more susceptible to future influence

(Petty & Cacioppo, 1986). The Elaboration Likelihood Model helps explain why emotionally appealing or visually engaging popular psychology content often spreads rapidly on social media, even when it lacks depth or scientific grounding. Some users may process such content through the central route; especially when it is detailed, evidence-based, or encourages deeper reflection; while others may engage through the peripheral route, drawn primarily by its style, tone, or emotional resonance.

Finally, to examine how psychological terms and ideas spread across digital platforms and enter popular discourse, Diffusion of Innovations Theory provides a compelling framework. Diffusion of Innovations Theory by Rogers (1962) explains how new products, ideas, or practices spread through a population or social system over time (Goss, 1979). The adoption of an innovation depends on several factors, including its perceived benefits, ease of understanding and use, compatibility with social norms and values, and the extent to which its outcomes are visible or shareable (Wejnert, 2002). Applied to the context of social media, this theory offers insight into how psychological concepts –such as attachment styles, boundaries, or trauma responses– may become widely adopted in everyday language and even go viral, migrating from academic or clinical settings into popular discourse. These terms often gain momentum through social media content creators who present them in simplified, emotionally resonant formats. As early adopters engage with and share this content, the ideas may begin to diffuse across platforms, eventually becoming embedded in everyday language and social interactions. This process illustrates how complex psychological theories can evolve into widely accepted, and sometimes misunderstood, cultural references, as creators adopt strategies focused on virality and simplicity. They design content to be "diffusion-ready": easily shareable, emotionally engaging, and simplified for quick audience uptake. Together, these theories illuminate how creators, attuned to user psychology and platform dynamics, strategically design content that is emotionally resonant, visually engaging, and optimized for widespread appeal.

Platform-Specific Influences on Psychological Content

While this chapter addresses the broader theoretical and cultural dynamics shaping popular psychology on social media, it is important to note that different platforms exert unique influences on the form, reach, and perception of psychological content. These platform affordances like video length limits, algorithmic recommendation systems, and monetization structures shape not only what content gets produced but also how audiences engage with it and what types of narratives gain traction.

A comparative look at platforms like TikTok, Instagram, and YouTube reveals key differences in content style, audience interaction, and susceptibility to misinformation.

TikTok, with its short video format, encourages highly distilled, emotionally resonant, and often humorous content often lending itself to simplified messaging, such as "symptom checklists" or "quick mental health tips" (McCashin & Murphy, 2023). On the other side, Instagram emphasizes aesthetic appeal through its stories and reels, cultivating a space where psychological content merges with influencer culture and self-branding. YouTube, by enabling longer-form video content, allows for more in-depth exploration of psychological topics and offers greater space for nuance, expert commentary, and credentialed authority (Choi et al., 2021). While TikTok and Instagram are particularly susceptible to the spread of misinformation due to oversimplified and decontextualized advice, emotional appeal, and the presence of unverified creators (Milton et al., 2023; Pretorius et al., 2022); YouTube's format, though not without its own risks, offers comparatively more room for evidence-based content. Future research could expand on this discussion by systematically examining how platform affordances shape the stylistic, epistemological, and emotional contours of popular psychology in digital spaces.

A BENEFICIAL TOOL FOR SELF-HELP OR MISLEADING PSEUDOSCIENCE?

Social media has revolutionized how people access psychological information, creating a space of openness and connection. This digital transformation has democratized psychological knowledge in significant ways, breaking down traditional barriers (Bucci et al., 2019; Guntuku et al., 2020). Yet this accessibility brings forth fundamental dilemmas about the nature and quality of psychological content circulating in these digital spaces. The central tension lies in understanding whether social media serves as one of the essential tools for mental health empowerment or as a vehicle for the dissemination of pseudoscience masked as legitimate psychological support. While these platforms offer many opportunities for peer support, community building, education, and destigmatization of mental health issues. On the other hand, the same accessibility that enables helpful content also allows unverified claims, oversimplified solutions, and potentially harmful misinformation.

This ethical dilemma is complicated by the blurred boundaries between professional expertise and popular psychology in digital spaces. While democratization of knowledge has clear benefits, questions arise about content quality, misinformation risks, and the potential harmful stereotypes. As psychological discourse moves increasingly into digital spaces, understanding these dynamics becomes essential for leveraging the positive potential of social media while eliminating its risks and addressing the ethical implications of unregulated mental health content (Roshni Rehab Centre, 2024).

Current research demonstrates that social media platforms function as vital spaces where individuals experiencing mental health challenges can connect and support one another. Studies show that these online communities facilitate important exchanges of personal experiences and information about treatment options (Aschbrenner et al., 2019; Naslund et al., 2020). It is especially significant to highlight how these platforms enable peer-to-peer support among individuals who might otherwise remain isolated due to stigma or geographic limitations (Highton-Williamson et al., 2015; Bucci et al. 2019). Especially for marginalized groups, minorities, and those in low-resource settings, social media becomes a vital, accessible alternative to formal mental health services (De Choudhury & De, 2014; Keles et al., 2020). Some research also suggests that AI-driven interventions such as chatbots and automated peer-support systems can enhance accessibility for underserved populations (Fitzpatrick et al., 2017; Inkster et al., 2018). Recent research by Siddals et al. (2024) demonstrates that people are increasingly turning to generative AI chatbots like ChatGPT for mental health support, with most users reporting significant positive outcomes including improved mood, reduced anxiety, and healing from trauma. This user-based study found that users evaluated these spaces as an 'emotional sanctuary': a consistently available, non-judgmental space for processing feelings—and appreciated the personalized guidance they received, particularly for relationship issues. Emerging AI capabilities are transforming mental health support in the digital space. Research by Owen et al. 2024 demonstrates that machine learning systems are effective means to detect linguistic markers associated with psychological distress. These technological tools serve to detect, expand and respond via tailor made features. Rather than replacing human connections, they can work alongside peer communities to recognize vulnerable and self- help seeking individuals who have limited or no access to clinical care options. For example, the Woebot chatbot, a chat-based AI wellness tool, designed to deliver cognitive based therapy through conversational interactions, tested in a randomized controlled trial demonstrated reduction in depression levels (Fitzpatrick et al., 2017).

This accessibility and interactive nature of social media creates environments where individuals learn through observation and engagement with content creators and community members sharing their mental health journeys, often through emotionally resonant forms of storytelling that enhance relatability and foster a sense of shared experience (Fergie et al., 2016). The success of tools like Woebot chatbot suggest AI augmented platforms may further enhance this process by providing real-time, evidence-based coping strategies during these interactions. The findings from Siddals et al. (2024) also support this, showing that users experience therapeutic benefits from AI interactions, though they also highlight the need for better safety measures and more human-like conversational capabilities. This process can facilitate the development of new coping strategies and self-management skills through different forms of learning experiences that were previously unavailable to many people struggling with mental health challenges (Elmquist & McLaughlin, 2018).

Some studies highlight how mental health influencers on platforms like TikTok, Instagram, and YouTube contribute to psychoeducation by simplifying clinical concepts into digestible content, enabling ease of information access to content (Bauman & Rivers, 2015). These practices take psychological concepts and repackage them as solutions independent from their therapeutic origins, intervening into their clinical practices. The lexicon around ADHD serves as a good example; despite being known as a medical disorder, there is no clear medical diagnosis for testing it. Even though it is still not proved to be a medical disorder, due to all the uses around it, it became widely (socially) accepted as one, as most schools integrated in educational jargon (De Vos, 2011). However, this simplification is not without risks. Misinformation and oversimplification of complex disorders (e.g., self-diagnosis trends) remain significant concerns (Lilienfeld et al., 2009; Feucht, 2025).

While social media has enabled a more democratic space to access mental health information, it has also amplified the spread of oversimplified, misleading, and even content that might be harmful. The lack of scientific oversight, coupled with algorithmic amplification, creates significant risks for users that are unknowledgeable and vulnerable.

In addition, the mental health discourse on social media comes with significant privacy risks, particularly for individuals seeking support in digital spaces. Research highlights how platforms collect and exploit sensitive mental health data, often without users' full awareness (Naslund et al., 2020). For example, individuals engaging with depression-related content may be algorithmically targeted by unregulated mental health apps, happiness promising wellness products, or even harmful content with conspiracy theories (Moorhead et al., 2013). This raises ethical concerns about informed consent, as many users, especially adolescents and marginalized groups, unknowingly trade personal info and access to peer support.

Beyond the algorithmic-driven target, public disclosures of mental health struggles carry real-world consequences. Users who share their experiences risk discrimination, cyberbullying, or doxxing, particularly if the content they produce, are linked to stigmatized conditions (Hamm et al., 2015). While anonymity can mitigate some risks, privacy breaches remain a significant concern for people seeking help online. The paradox of social media, which serves as both a supportive community and a surveillance model presents a valid dilemma.

While social media can foster solidarity, it also reinforces harmful stereotypes and intensifies self-perception issues through distorted representations of mental illness. Studies show that these distorted representations online might lead to upward social comparison—measuring one's own mental health progress against the curated "recovery journeys" of influencers, which has the potential to increase depressive symptoms and diminished self-worth (Feinstein et al., 2013). This phenomenon is particularly seen among adolescents, who frequently encounter romanticized or normalized depictions of disorders further minimizing severe conditions (Best et al., 2014).

The social comparison processes that occur in digital mental health spaces can create unrealistic expectations about recovery timelines and outcomes. When individuals struggling with mental health challenges compare their experiences to highly curated social media narratives, they may develop feelings of inadequacy and hopelessness about their progress. In many cases, these narratives rely heavily on idealized storytelling techniques that dramatize personal recovery, subtly promoting unrealistic expectations about healing and resilience. These distorted comparisons are especially problematic when content creators present idealized versions of mental health journeys that overlook setbacks and ongoing difficulties, creating a false impression of improvement that rarely reflects clinical reality.

The absence of regulation in digital mental health spaces allows misinformation to co-exist with evidence-based content. As Bucher (2020) puts it, social media algorithms prioritize engagement over accuracy, amplifying controversial figures who blend pop psychology with outright pseudoscience. For example, people with no proper qualifications calling themselves "trauma coaches" promote treatments that haven't been scientifically tested. This trend is particularly dangerous when influencers encourage self-diagnosis through different social media games or preset checklist frames, practices that lack scientific validity and may lead to misguided self-treatment (Lack & Rousseau, 2022).

The proliferation of unregulated mental health content creates a marketplace where credentials and expertise are difficult for consumers to assess. In this environment, idealized online personas with large followings can gain authority that rivals or exceeds that of trained clinicians, despite lacking formal education. This phenomenon is strengthened by platform algorithms that reward controversial statements and simplified solutions to complex psychological problems, further blurring the lines between entertainment and mental healthcare.

Even well-intentioned creators often are not aware of ethical boundaries by offering therapeutic advice without credentials, risking potential harm through misapplied interventions. Naslund et al. (2020) emphasize that while social media platforms hold a peer support value, they must implement safeguards to distinguish between personal anecdotes and professional guidance. Without such measures, the line between empowerment and exploitation remains dangerously blurred.

CULTURAL IMPACT OF POP-PSYCHOLOGY: MEANING-MAKING IN THE DIGITAL AGE

Social media has fundamentally reconfigured psychological discourse into a pervasive cultural force, one that actively constructs new frameworks for self-understanding and social positioning. This change echoes Pierre Bourdieu's (1987) observation that psychology has long competed in a broader field of salvation goods where its scientific value is challenged by spiritual, commercial and now digital alternatives. This is a dynamic that Rey (2012) argues reflects psychology's gradual conversion into a commodified landscape of personal transformation, no longer standing as a distinct, professionally bounded discipline but instead appearing as one of many tools within a broader New Age spiritual "toolbox" alongside pseudo-scientific practices. This transformation operates through a dual-engine system: the micro-influencer industrial complex, where algorithmically privileged creators repackage clinical concepts as consumable lifestyle content, and the participatory remix culture, where audiences collaboratively reinterpret and often distort these ideas through comments, reshares and viral challenges (De Santo, 2024). The result is a self-reinforcing cycle where pop-psychology content transcends mere information dissemination, it rewires collective cognition. This transformation is deeply rooted in storytelling: creators package psychological ideas into compelling narratives that are easy to relate to, share, and internalize, turning therapeutic language into emotionally resonant content that circulates widely across platforms.

One of the most visible effects is the inclusion of clinical terms into everyday speech. Words like trauma, gaslighting, and narcissist have escaped the confines of therapy rooms and academia, now thriving in TikTok hashtags, Instagram stories, and YouTube commentary. Here Baudrillard's (1998) critique of cultural objects detached from their original meanings finds new relevance: these terms are stripped away from their clinical contexts and reorganized into thematic clusters of digital consumption; simplified to shareable symbols rather than tools for deeper insight. Popular Psychology terminology around self-actualization and stress has woven itself into the social fabric of how people express their challenges and problems (Madsen, 2015). While this shift has democratized mental health awareness, potentially reducing stigma (Naslund et al., 2020), it also risks misinterpreting and distorting complex concepts. What was once learned from clinical diagnosis may now be applied to everyday stress, and therapeutic tools.

This shift in lexicon isn't neutral. Scholars like Rodríguez-López (2023) and Adams et al. (2019) argue that digital self-help culture mirrors neoliberal ideologies, framing emotional struggles as personal failures rather than responses to systemic issues. The message is clear: your mental health is your responsibility. Bourdieu's (1987) marketplace of "salvation" now operates in the digital world, where commodification of psychology is like a trend; new age spirituality (Carette & King, 2004); a process which stripped away complexities and sensitivity of mental health into a simple transaction. Social media amplifies this narrative, promoting an idealized self via meditation apps, productivity boosting notifications, and pumped-up positivity; as solutions to structural problems like economic precarity or social isolation. The technological structures of digital platforms intensify these dynamics. An echo chamber is a closed information ecosystem in which individuals are repeatedly exposed to opinions, beliefs, and content that reinforce their preexisting views while excluding dissenting perspectives. This phenomenon is amplified by social media algorithms, which prioritize engagement by showing users content similar to what they have previously liked, shared, or interacted with (Zimmer et al., 2019).

The algorithmic design of most social media applications favors content that aligns with users' prior behaviors (likes, shares, comments) creating self-reinforcing informational environments. In the context of self-help and pop-psychology content, this means individuals are repeatedly exposed to ideologically consistent messaging, whether it's about attachment styles, trauma recovery, or toxic relationships. Echo chambers are not merely passive filters of information; they are dynamic spaces in which identity is co-constructed through belief (Begby, 2024). In self-help communities, these mechanisms are at work: users adopt psychological language and frameworks not just as knowledge but as a central part of their self-concept. This identification can lead to epistemic closure; where challenges to a favored model (e.g., inner child work or narcissist abuse cycles) are dismissed, and opposing viewpoints are treated as invalid or even harmful.

The consequences create two main challenges. First, users find themselves with limited exposure to diverse viewpoints, which reduces opportunities for critical reflection and professional intervention. Second, as Putri et al. (2024) note, ideological polarization increases when users are trapped in identity-based echo chambers. Within such environments, even well-meaning content may solidify limiting beliefs or overgeneralizations (e.g., labeling all emotional discomfort as trauma or all conflict as toxicity), ultimately discouraging the kind of contextual nuance that is essential to both mental health and societal well-being.

When examined together, the popularization of psychological language, the structure of algorithmic echo chambers, and the ideology of digital self-help form a unified cultural apparatus. Following Cosgrove and Karter (2018), neoliberalism here refers to the ideological project that recasts all aspects of social life; including mental health as domains of market logic, where individuals are rendered as entrepreneurial actors responsible for their own well-being, and structural problems are reframed as private challenges to be solved through consumption. In this light, self-help on social media is not just a tool for coping, it becomes a moral framework, one that is deeply embedded in these neoliberal values of individualization, self-surveillance, and privatized solutions to public problems. This ideology transforms emotional struggles into personal projects of optimization, where mental health becomes another domain of individual responsibility rather than a collective concern requiring social and structural interventions.

This raises a profound question: In these spaces where our most intimate emotional processes; our meaning-making struggles and quests for healthier selves, are emptied out and repackaged as consumable content, do they too become commodified; stripped of their authentic significance? The psychological lexicon serves not only as a mode of expression but also as a regulatory script: it instructs users on how to think, feel, and act in line with the "therapeutic self" (Illouz, 2008); a modern form of identity shaped by neoliberal being-well discourses; a self always under construction, always personally responsible for failures in emotional management. Yet this process underestimates a fundamental truth: the individual exists for and within society. When emotional processes are reduced to self-help products and trends, we risk losing sight of the collective dimensions of suffering and healing. As Cosgrove and Karter (2018) emphasize, this neoliberal life systematically hides how social factors; like economic instability and systemic exclusion create psychological distress, instead making personal resilience the only focus for solutions.

In this context, what emerges is a vicious loop in which culture not only shapes individual psychology, but psychology through its social media reframing, shapes culture in return. The very act of seeking meaning and healthier selfhood becomes part of the marketplace, where "working on yourself" is both the commodity and the ideology that sustains the system. In this process, storytelling serves as both a vehicle and a disguise; narratives of self-discovery, healing, and transformation become marketable scripts that frame personal growth as a linear, individualized journey, often masking the social complexities underneath.

CONCLUSION

In this chapter, the authors discuss the complex terrain of popular psychology on social media by tracing its historical evolution from academic origins to mass media dissemination, analyzing its communication mechanisms, evaluating its ethical implications, and discussing its broader cultural impact. The chapter first explores how psychological discourse entered popular culture through self-help books, magazines, and psychotainment. It then examines social media as a dominant space where digital aesthetics, influencers, and algorithms reshape mental health communication. Drawing on media and communication theories, the chapter analyzes how creators frame and circulate psychological knowledge to align with audience expectations and platform dynamics. Finally, the chapter critically reflects on the cultural consequences of digital pop-psychology, revealing how commodified therapeutic language can obscure structural issues, reinforce neoliberal values, and reshape selfhood through market-driven identity work. Our investigation reveals that what appears to be a straightforward democratization of mental health information is actually a multifaceted transformation that touches every aspect of how psychological knowledge is produced, circulated, and reconfigured in contemporary society.

The challenge moving forward is neither to uncritically celebrate nor to condemn this digital transformation of psychological discourse. Instead, we must develop more sophisticated frameworks for understanding how these platforms operate, implement ethical safeguards that protect vulnerable users while preserving beneficial aspects of peer support and democratized access, and enhance digital literacy that enables individuals to navigate these complex information ecosystems critically (Gooding, 2019). This requires collaboration between technology companies, mental health professionals, educators, and policymakers to create standards for mental health content that distinguish between peer support and professional guidance, protect user privacy, and promote accurate information while preserving the genuine benefits of digital community building.

Such collaboration should include platforms prioritizing verification systems (e.g., credential badges for clinicians) and algorithmic safeguards to promote accurate content while limiting harmful misleading information (Kennedy Krieger, 2024). Content creators must adopt ethical guidelines, such as citing reputable sources that have public confidence, avoiding diagnostic language, and disclosing conflicts of interest (e.g., sponsored "therapy" products). Educators and clinicians should promote digital literacy, teaching audiences to identify red flags (e.g., pseudoscientific claims, quick-fix, simple solutions to mental health issues) and prioritize seeking professional help when needed. Policymakers can incentivize transparency by requiring platforms to label AI-generated mental health content or enforce ad disclosures for wellness products.

This urgency becomes more apparent with the rise of *conspirituality*; a phenomenon Wiseman (2021) identifies as the merger of wellness culture with conspiracy theories. Influencers increasingly promote pseudoscientific remedies (e.g., essential oils as alternatives to vaccines or astrology as mental health guidance) while distorting trust in science. For instance, wellness figures now pair anti-vaccination rhetoric (e.g., "naturally boost immunity") with QAnon-adjacent claims about "energy attacks" from 5G networks. Such practices obscure the line between science and pseudoscience, leaving help-seekers vulnerable to misinformation. The packaging of mental health advice with spirituality ("feminine energy", "trauma coaching") and overt conspiracy theories demands protective measures akin to content filters for children or medical advertising regulations. Without intervention, the dilution of therapeutic rigor risks displacing science entirely, replacing it with a marketplace of unverified, often exploitative alternatives. Addressing this issue necessitates not just policy solutions but also a public awareness of how wellness rhetoric can inadvertently cause long lasting harm.

REFERENCES

Adams, G., Estrada-Villalta, S., Sullivan, D., & Markus, H. R. (2019). The psychology of neoliberalism and the neoliberalism of psychology. *The Journal of Social Issues, 75*(1), 189–216. https://psycnet.apa.org/doi/10.1111/josi.12305. DOI: 10.1111/josi.12305

Albalawi, Y., & Sixsmith, J. (2015). Agenda setting for health promotion: Exploring an adapted model for the social media era. *JMIR Public Health and Surveillance, 1*(2), e21. Advance online publication. DOI: 10.2196/publichealth.5014 PMID: 27227139

Almakaty, S. (2025). *A comprehensive and critical literature review on framing theory in the digital media age. Preprints.* https://www.preprints.org/manuscript/202504.1728/v1

Aschbrenner, K. A., Naslund, J. A., Tomlinson, E. F., Kinney, A., Pratt, S. I., & Brunette, M. F. (2019). Adolescents' use of digital technologies and preferences for mobile health coaching in public mental health settings. *Frontiers in Public Health, 7*, 178. DOI: 10.3389/fpubh.2019.00178 PMID: 31312629

Baudrillard, J. (1998). *The consumer society*. SAGE Publications Ltd, https://doi.org/, S., & Rivers, I. (2015). *Mental health in the digital age*. Palgrave Macmillan. DOI: 10.4135/9781526401502Bauman

Begby, E. (2024). From Belief Polarization to Echo Chambers: A Rationalizing Account. *Episteme (Edinburgh), 21*(2), 519–539. DOI: 10.1017/epi.2022.14

Beins, B. C. (2008). Why we believe: Fostering critical thought and scientific literacy in research methods. In Dunn, D. S., Halonen, J. S., & Smith, R. A. (Eds.), *Teaching critical thinking in psychology: A handbook of best practices* (pp. 199–210). Wiley Blackwell., DOI: 10.1002/9781444305173.ch17

Benjamin, L. T. (1986). Why don't they understand us? A history of psychology's public image. *The American Psychologist, 41*(9), 941–946. DOI: 10.1037/0003-066X.41.9.941 PMID: 17154720

Best, P., Manktelow, R., & Taylor, B. (2014). Online communication, social media and adolescent wellbeing: A systematic narrative review. *Children and Youth Services Review, 41*, 27–36. DOI: 10.1016/j.childyouth.2014.03.001

Blumler, J. G., & Katz, E. (1974). *The uses of mass communications*. Sage Publications., DOI: 10.1086/268277

Bourdieu, P. (1987). Legitimation and structured interests in Weber's sociology of religion. In Lash, S., & Whimster, S. (Eds.), *Max Weber, rationality and modernity* (Turner, C., Trans.; pp. 119–136). Allen & Unwin.

Brooks, A. (2023). Popular psychology. In *A suspicious science: The uses of psychology* (pp. 90–157). Academic.

Bucci, S., Schwannauer, M., & Berry, N. (2019). The digital revolution and its impact on mental health care. *Psychology and Psychotherapy: Theory, Research and Practice, 92*(2), 277–297. DOI: 10.1111/papt.12222 PMID: 30924316

Bucher, T. (2020). The right-time web: Theorizing the virologic of algorithmic media. *New Media & Society, 22*(9), 1699–1714. DOI: 10.1177/1461444820913560

Cameron, D. (2007). *The myth of Mars and Venus: Do men and women really speak different languages?* Oxford University Press.

Choi, B., Kim, H., & Huh-Yoo, J. (2021). Seeking mental health support among college students in video-based social media: Content and statistical analysis of YouTube videos. *JMIR Formative Research, 5*(11), e31944. Advance online publication. DOI: 10.2196/31944 PMID: 34762060

Coleman, R., McCombs, M., Shaw, D., & Weaver, D. (2009). Agenda setting. In Wahl-Jorgensen, K., & Hanitzsch, T. (Eds.), *The handbook of journalism studies* (pp. 167–180). Routledge.

Cook, A. J., Moore, K., & Steel, G. D. (2004). The Taking of a Position: A Reinterpretation of the Elaboration Likelihood Model. *Journal for the Theory of Social Behaviour, 34*(4), 315–331. DOI: 10.1111/j.1468-5914.2004.00252.x

Cordón, L. A. (2005). *Popular psychology: An encyclopedia.* Greenwood Press. DOI: 10.5040/9798400699191

Cosgrove, L., & Karter, J. M. (2018). The poison in the cure: Neoliberalism and contemporary movements in mental health. *Theory & Psychology, 28*(5), 669–683. DOI: 10.1177/0959354318796307

Cuncic, A. (2023) What Is Pop Psychology? *Very Well Mind.* https://www.verywellmind.com/what-is-pop-psychology-5195653

De Choudhury, M., & De, S. (2014, May). Mental health discourse on Reddit: Self-disclosure, social support, and anonymity. In *Proceedings of the International AAAI Conference on Web and Social Media, 8*(1), 71–80. DOI: 10.1609/icwsm.v8i1.14526

De Santo, M. (2024). Digital narratives of mental health: Investigating medical communication on TikTok. *Textus, 36*(3), 97–120. DOI: 10.7370/115625

De Vos, J. (2011). Psychologization or the discontents of psychoanalysis. *Psychoanalysis, Culture & Society*, *16*(4), 354–372. DOI: 10.1057/pcs.2010.29

De Vos, J. (2012). *Psychologisation in times of globalisation*. Routledge. DOI: 10.4324/9780203115459

Elmquist, D. L., & McLaughlin, C. L. (2018). Social media use among adolescents coping with mental health. *Contemporary School Psychology*, *22*(4), 503–511. DOI: 10.1007/s40688-017-0167-5

Entman, R. M. (1993). Framing: Toward clarification of a fractured paradigm. *Journal of Communication*, *43*(4), 51–58. DOI: 10.1111/j.1460-2466.1993.tb01304.x

Feinstein, B. A., Hershenberg, R., Bhatia, V., Latack, J. A., Meuwly, N., & Davila, J. (2013). Negative social comparison on Facebook and depressive symptoms: Rumination as a mechanism. *Psychology of Popular Media Culture*, *2*(3), 161–170. DOI: 10.1037/a0033111

Fergie, G., Hunt, K., & Hilton, S. (2016). Social media as a space for support: Young adults' perspectives on producing and consuming user-generated content about diabetes and mental health. *Social Science & Medicine*, *170*, 46–54. DOI: 10.1016/j.socscimed.2016.10.006 PMID: 27750067

Feucht, C. (2025). *Self-diagnosis goes viral: Exploring the impact of social media on women's mental health practices* [Doctoral dissertation, The Ohio State University].

Fine, G. A., & Manning, P. (2000). Erving Goffman. In Ritzer, G. (Ed.), *Blackwell Companion to Major Social Theorists* (pp. 457–485).

Fitzpatrick, K. K., Darcy, A., & Vierhile, M. (2017). Delivering cognitive behavior therapy to young adults with symptoms of depression and anxiety using a fully automated conversational agent (Woebot): A randomized controlled trial. *JMIR Mental Health*, *4*(2), e19. DOI: 10.2196/mental.7785 PMID: 28588005

Furnham, A., & Hughes, D. J. (2014). Myths and misconceptions in popular psychology: Comparing psychology students and the general public. *Teaching of Psychology*, *41*(3), 256–261. DOI: 10.1177/0098628314537984

Gabbard, G. (2001). Psychotherapy in Hollywood Cinema. *Australasian Psychiatry*, *9*(4), 365–369. DOI: 10.1046/j.1440-1665.2001.00365.x

Gerbner, G. (1998). Cultivation analysis: An overview. *Mass Communication & Society*, *1*(3–4), 175–194. DOI: 10.1080/15205436.1998.9677855

Goffman, E. (1959). *The presentation of self in everyday life*. Doubleday.

Goffman, E. (1974). *Frame analysis: An essay on the organization of experience.* Harper & Row.

Gooding, P. (2019). Mapping the rise of digital mental health technologies: Emerging issues for law and society. *International Journal of Law and Psychiatry*, *67*, 101498. Advance online publication. DOI: 10.1016/j.ijlp.2019.101498 PMID: 31785726

Goss, K. F. (1979). Consequences of diffusion of innovations. *Rural Sociology*, *44*(4), 754–772.

Guntuku, S. C., Sherman, G., Stokes, D. C., Agarwal, A. K., Seltzer, E., Merchant, R. M., & Ungar, L. H. (2020). Tracking mental health and symptom mentions on Twitter during COVID-19. *Journal of General Internal Medicine*, *35*(9), 2798–2800. DOI: 10.1007/s11606-020-05988-8 PMID: 32638321

Hall, S. (2010). Encoding, decoding 1. In Marris, P., & Thornham, S. (Eds.), *Media studies: A reader* (2nd ed., pp. 569–599). NYU Press.

Hamm, M. P., Newton, A. S., Chisholm, A., Shulhan, J., Milne, A., Sundar, P., Ennis, H., Scott, S. D., & Hartling, L. (2015). Prevalence and effect of cyberbullying on children and young people: A scoping review of social media studies. *JAMA Pediatrics*, *169*(8), 770–777. DOI: 10.1001/jamapediatrics.2015.0944 PMID: 26098362

Haridakis, P., & Humphries, Z. (2019). Uses and gratifications. In Stacks, D. W., Salwen, M. B., & Eichhorn, K. C. (Eds.), *An integrated approach to communication theory and research* (pp. 139–154). Routledge., DOI: 10.4324/9780203710753-13

Hartmann, T. (2016). Parasocial interaction, parasocial relationships, and well-being. In Reinecke, L., & Oliver, M. B. (Eds.), *The Routledge handbook of media use and well-being* (pp. 131–144). Routledge.

Highton-Williamson, E., Priebe, S., & Giacco, D. (2015). Online social networking in people with psychosis: A systematic review. *The International Journal of Social Psychiatry*, *61*(1), 92–101. DOI: 10.1177/0020764014556392 PMID: 25381145

Horton, D., & Richard Wohl, R. (1956). Mass communication and para-social interaction: Observations on intimacy at a distance. *psychiatry, 19*(3), 215-229. DOI: 10.1080/00332747.1956.11023049

Illouz, E. (2008). *Saving the modern soul: Therapy, emotions, and the culture of self-help*. Univ of California Press. DOI: 10.1525/9780520941311

Inkster, B., Sarda, S., & Subramanian, V. (2018). An empathy-driven, conversational artificial intelligence agent (Wysa) for digital mental well-being: Real-world data evaluation mixed-methods study. *JMIR mHealth and uHealth*, *6*(11), e12106. Advance online publication. DOI: 10.2196/12106 PMID: 30470676

Jansz, J. (2004). Psychology and society: An overview. In Brock, A. C. (Ed.), *A social history of psychology* (pp. 12–44). Wiley.

Katz, D. L.Academic Psychology Books. (2022). Don't judge a book by its cover: A case study and comparative analysis of popular vs. academy psychology books. *Journal of Scientific Exploration*, *36*(2), 233–250. Advance online publication. DOI: 10.31275/20222463

Keles, B., McCrae, N., & Grealish, A. (2020). A systematic review: The influence of social media on depression, anxiety and psychological distress in adolescents. *International Journal of Adolescence and Youth*, *25*(1), 79–93. DOI: 10.1080/02673843.2019.1590851

Kennedy Krieger Institute. (2024). Tips for navigating mental health content on social media. *Kennedy Krieger.* https://www.kennedykrieger.org/community/parent-education/tips-for-navigating-mental-health-content-on-social-media

Koch, T., Arendt, F., & Maximilian, L. (2017). Media effects: Cumulation and duration. *The international encyclopedia of media effects*, 1-11. DOI: 10.1002/9781118783764.wbieme0217

Kolmes, K. (2012). Social media in the future of professional psychology. *Professional Psychology, Research and Practice*, *43*(6), 606–612. DOI: 10.1037/a0028678

Lack, C. W., & Rousseau, J. (2022). Mental health, pop psychology, and the misunderstanding of clinical psychology. *Academic Questions*, *35*(4), 519–534. DOI: 10.1016/B978-0-12-818697-8.00052-2

Lilienfeld, S. O., Lynn, S. J., Ruscio, J., & Beyerstein, B. L. (2009). *50 great myths of popular psychology: Shattering widespread misconceptions about human behavior*. John Wiley & Sons.

Lilienfeld, S. O., Lynn, S. J., Ruscio, J., & Beyerstein, B. L. (2017). *From inquiry to understanding* (4th ed.). Pearson.

Lofton, K. (2011). *Oprah: The gospel of an icon*. University of California Press. DOI: 10.1525/9780520948242

Loughran, T. (2023). Sex, relationships and 'everyday psychology' on British magazine problem pages, c. 1960–1990. *Medical Humanities*, *49*(2), 203–213. DOI: 10.1136/medhum-2022-012497 PMID: 36549861

Madsen, O. J. (2015). Optimizing the self: Social representations of self-help. In Parker, I. (Ed.), *Handbook of critical psychology* (pp. 222–230). Routledge.

McCashin, D., & Murphy, C. M. (2023). Using TikTok for public and youth mental health: A systematic review and content analysis. *Clinical Child Psychology and Psychiatry*, *28*(1), 279–306. DOI: 10.1177/13591045221106608 PMID: 35689365

McCombs, M. E., Shaw, D. L., & Weaver, D. H. (2018). New directions in agenda-setting theory and research. In Fortner, R. S., & Fackler, P. M. (Eds.), *Advances in foundational mass communication theories* (pp. 131–152). Routledge. DOI: 10.4324/9781315164441-9

Miller, T. G. (1984). Goffman, social acting, and moral behavior. *Journal for the Theory of Social Behaviour*, *14*(2), 141–164. DOI: 10.1111/j.1468-5914.1984.tb00492.x

Milton, A., Ajmani, L., DeVito, M. A., & Chancellor, S. (2023, April). "I see me here": Mental health content, community, and algorithmic curation on TikTok. In *Proceedings of the 2023 CHI conference on human factors in computing systems* (pp. 1-17). DOI: 10.1145/3544548.3581489

Moorhead, S. A., Hazlett, D. E., Harrison, L., Carroll, J. K., Irwin, A., & Hoving, C. (2013). A new dimension of health care: Systematic review of the uses, benefits, and limitations of social media for health communication. *Journal of Medical Internet Research*, *15*(4), e85. Advance online publication. DOI: 10.2196/jmir.1933 PMID: 23615206

Morris, R. L. (1977). The Airport Project: A survey of the techniques for psychic development advocated by popular books. In J. D. Morris, W. G. Roll., & R. L. Morris (Eds.), *Research in parapsychology* (pp. 54–56). Scarecrow Press.

Murray, C. E. (2015). Self-help and the helpless subject: Samuel Smiles and biography's objects. *Nineteenth-Century Literature*, *69*(4), 481–508. DOI: 10.1525/ncl.2015.69.4.481

Naslund, J. A., Bondre, A., Torous, J., & Aschbrenner, K. A. (2020). Social media and mental health: Benefits, risks, and opportunities for research and practice. *Journal of Technology in Behavioral Science*, *5*(3), 245–257. DOI: 10.1007/s41347-020-00134-x PMID: 33415185

Nehring, D., Alvarado, E., Hendriks, E. C., & Kerrigan, D. (2016). *Transnational popular psychology and the global self-help industry: The politics of contemporary social change*. Palgrave Macmillan. DOI: 10.1057/9780230370869

Nunn, H., & Biressi, A. (2010). 'A trust betrayed': Celebrity and the work of emotion. *Celebrity Studies, 1*(1), 49–64. DOI: 10.1080/19392390903519065

O'Keefe, D. J. (2013). The elaboration likelihood model. In Dillard, J. P., & Shen, L. (Eds.), *The SAGE handbook of persuasion: Developments in theory and practice* (2nd ed., pp. 137–149). Sage Publications, Inc.

Owen, D., Lynham, A. J., Smart, S. E., Pardiñas, A. F., & Camacho Collados, J. (2024). AI for Analyzing Mental Health Disorders Among Social Media Users: Quarter-Century Narrative Review of Progress and Challenges. *Journal of Medical Internet Research, 26*, e59225. Advance online publication. DOI: 10.2196/59225 PMID: 39546783

Ozcelik, A. B., & Levi, E. (2020). Choosing the right influencer for your brand. In Yesiloglu, S., & Costello, J. (Eds.), *Influencer marketing* (pp. 79–97). Routledge. DOI: 10.4324/9780429322501-8

Petty, R. E., & Cacioppo, J. T. (1986). The elaboration likelihood model of persuasion. In Berkowitz, L. (Ed.), Vol. 19, pp. 123–205). Advances in experimental social psychology. Academic Press.

Pillai, P. (1992). Rereading Stuart Hall's encoding/decoding model. *Communication Theory, 2*(3), 221–233. DOI: 10.1111/j.1468-2885.1992.tb00040.x

Pretorius, C., McCashin, D., & Coyle, D. (2022). Mental health professionals as influencers on TikTok and Instagram: What role do they play in mental health literacy and help-seeking? *Internet Interventions : the Application of Information Technology in Mental and Behavioural Health, 30*, 100591. Advance online publication. DOI: 10.1016/j.invent.2022.100591 PMID: 36458161

Putri, S. D. G., Purnomo, E. P., & Khairunissa, T. (2024). Echo chambers and algorithmic bias: The homogenization of online culture in a smart society. In *SHS Web of Conferences* (Vol. 202, p. 05001). EDP Sciences. DOI: 10.1051/shsconf/202420205001

Rapp, D. (1988). The reception of Freud by the British press: General interest and literary magazines, 1920–1925. *Journal of the History of the Behavioral Sciences, 24*(2), 191–201. DOI: 10.1002/1520-6696(198804)24:2<191::AID-JHBS2300240206>3.0.CO;2-X PMID: 3286754

Rey, P. J. (2012). Alienation, exploitation, and social media. *The American Behavioral Scientist*, *56*(4), 399–420. DOI: 10.1177/0002764211429367

Richards, J. (1982). Spreading the gospel of self-help: G. A. Henty and Samuel Smiles. *Journal of Popular Culture*, *16*(2), 52–65. DOI: 10.1111/j.0022-3840.1982.00052.x

Roberts, J. A., & David, M. E. (2023). Instagram and TikTok flow states and their association with psychological well-being. *Cyberpsychology, Behavior, and Social Networking*, *26*(2), 80–89. DOI: 10.1089/cyber.2022.0117 PMID: 36716180

Rodríguez-López, R. (2023, July 18). Self-help or self-governance? The role of the psy-disciplines in neoliberalism. *Mad in America*. https://www.madinamerica.com/2023/07/self-help-or-self-governance-the-role-of-the-psy-disciplines-in-neoliberalism/

Rogers, E. M. (1962). *Diffusion of Innovations*. Free Press.

Rojek, C. (2015). *Presumed intimacy: Parasocial interaction in media, society and celebrity culture*. John Wiley & Sons.

Rosen, G. M. (1987). Self-help treatment books and the commercialization of psychotherapy. *The American Psychologist*, *42*(1), 46–51. DOI: 10.1037/0003-066X.42.1.46 PMID: 3565914

Rosen, R. D. (1977). *Psychobabble: Fast talk and quick cure in the era of feeling*. Atheneum.

Roshni Rehab Centre. (2024). The destructive impact of social media addiction on society. *Roshni Rehabilitation Centre*. https://www.roshnirehabilitationcentre.com/post/thedestructiveimpactofsocialmediaaddictiononsociety

Ross, S. (2011). The encoding/decoding model revisited. Paper presented at the *Annual Meeting of the International Communication Association*, Boston.

Ruggiero, T. E. (2000). Uses and Gratifications Theory in the 21st Century. *Mass Communication & Society*, *3*(1), 3–37. DOI: 10.1207/S15327825MCS0301_02

Shapiro, S. L. (2009). The integration of mindfulness and psychology. *Journal of Clinical Psychology*, *65*(6), 555–560. DOI: 10.1002/jclp.20602 PMID: 19340826

Shrum, L. J. (2017). Cultivation theory: Effects and underlying processes. In Rössler, P. (Ed.), *The international encyclopedia of media effects* (Vol. 1, pp. 1–12). Wiley. DOI: 10.1002/9781118783764.wbieme0040

Siddals, S., Coxon, A., & Torous, J. (2024). " It just happened to be the perfect thing": Real-life experiences of generative AI chatbots for mental health. *NPJ Mental Health Research*, 48. DOI: 10.21203/rs.3.rs-4612612/v1

Ussher, J. (2013). Media representations of psychology: Denigration and popularization, or worthy dissemination of knowledge? In Smart, B. (Ed.), *Social scientists meet the media* (pp. 123–137). Routledge.

Van Pinxteren, M. M., Pluymaekers, M., & Lemmink, J. G. (2020). Human-like communication in conversational agents: A literature review and research agenda. *Journal of Service Management, 31*(2), 203–225. DOI: 10.1108/JOSM-06-2019-0175

Waddell, T. (2014). Shrink-wrapped television: Simulated therapy, disclosure, and the lure of 'plausible doubt. In Hillis, K., Petit, M., & McCallum, K. D. (Eds.), *Eavesdropping* (pp. 129–143). Routledge. DOI: 10.4324/9781315739526-9

Weiner, R. (2002). An ode to Ann Landers and Dear Abby. *Public Relations Quarterly, 47*(3), 7.

Wejnert, B. (2002). Integrating models of diffusion of innovations: A conceptual framework. *Annual Review of Sociology, 28*(1), 297–326. DOI: 10.1146/annurev.soc.28.110601.141051

Wiseman, E. (2021, October 17). Conspirituality: The dark side of wellness – how it all got so toxic. *The Guardian*. https://www.theguardian.com/lifeandstyle/2021/oct/17/eva-wiseman-conspirituality-the-dark-side-of-wellness-how-it-all-got-so-toxic

Zimmer, F., Scheibe, K., Stock, M., & Stock, W. G. (2019). *Echo chambers and filter bubbles of fake news in social media: Man-made or produced by algorithms? In 8th Annual Arts*. Humanities, Social Sciences & Education Conference.

KEY TERMS AND DEFINITIONS

Conspirituality: The term coined by Charlotte Ward and David Voas refers to the dangerous mix of wellness, spiritual ideas and methods with conspiracy theories.

Echo Chamber: Coined by Cass Sunstein, the term refers to digital spaces where people only see information that resonates with their ideas and beliefs.

Popular Psychology: The term refers to use of psychological concepts, theories and insights simplified and adapted to be understood for general public understanding.

Pseudoscience: The term refers to the practices and claims that appear to be scientific but lacks solid scientific grounding and/or evidence.

Psychologization: The term refers to the pervasion of psychology in everyday life, influencing both the language and thinking mechanisms of individuals.

Psychotainment: The term refers to the blending of psychology with entertainment, blurring the boundaries between psychological insight and content designed for public engagement and consumption.

Self-Help: The term refers to the practice of improving oneself through personal effort aimed at solving problems without professional support; often guided by several different sources (books, programs, offline/digital).

Chapter 12
The Role of Storytelling in Creating a Country's Image on the Example of Eurovision Song Contest:
How the "Rim Tim Tagi Dim" Rhythm Contributed to the Global Promotion of Croatia

Tanja Grmuša
https://orcid.org/0000-0002-2675-0171
Zagreb School of Business, Croatia

ABSTRACT

The chapter explores the role of storytelling as a communication tool in the process of nation branding through music using the example of the Eurovision Song Contest. The motive for the above was Croatia's historic success at this popular music competition in 2024, where the performer Baby Lasagna won second place with his song "Rim Tim Tagi Dim". Recently, storytelling has been gaining more importance in the marketing context with the aim of better placing products and services, highlighting the strength of the brand and creating the soft power of states. In addition to focusing on the images and messages we want to send to others about ourselves, it is important to have an institutionalized approach to national branding, which Croatia as a country still needs in order to (re)maintain competitiveness. However, Croatia's image in the world is positively stable and is mainly associated with culture, natural beauty and lifestyle, which Baby Lasagna confirmed with his performance and contributed to the global promotion of Croatia in the world.

DOI: 10.4018/979-8-3373-2023-6.ch012

INTRODUCTION

The first association with storytelling refers to people and their everyday conversational patterns. Stories take us back to the past, to our childhood and to the people who shaped us, such as our parents, grandparents, and others in our narrow environment. Today, stories are told by the media, journalists, and politicians, and the images from those stories (un)consciously influence the perception of those who listen to them. In doing so, we often rely on stereotypes as mental constructs that serve us to classify things, objects and other phenomena. Stereotypes can be autostereotypes (what we think about ourselves) and heterostereotypes (what others think about us), and both categories can have positive and negative connotations. By repeating the same positive stereotypes, a positive picture (positive image) is created in the public, while placing negative ones contributes to the creation of prejudices and potentially socially harmful forms of communication (Labaš & Grmuša, 2011).

By consuming certain products (material and immaterial), by associating images with objects, states and nations, the identity and image of those countries is created. This has been recognized by the countries, which, by telling stories about themselves, contribute to the creation of communication and marketing strategies and long-term positive public opinion. This results in the creation of interest and the desire to visit the destination, to consume the products of a particular country, and this is a reflection of respect for that country. Branding the country, as well as local destinations, is a demanding activity that requires knowledge of the competition, but also a precise definition of the tourist product (Grmuša et al., 2020).

Storytelling requires understanding the value of national identity, a way of life that others recognize so that it can be presented in the right way. Countries that are not internationally recognizable must invest more effort and diplomatic activities in presenting themselves. The role of the media in the global recognition of a country is inevitable, and Croatia relied mainly on natural beauty (Skoko, 2009; Skoko & Kovačić, 2009; Skoko & Hlača, 2020; Skoko & Frka Petešić, 2023) and globally famous athletes (Leško, 2019; Skoko et. al., 2022; Tomić, 2022; Skoko & Frka Petešić, 2023) such as Luka Modrić and Joško Gvardiol. However, Croatia is not only the land of the sun and the sea as many recognize it, but also the land of numerous great people who have left a significant mark on the history of humanity with their inventions and certainly deserve respect. Strategic communication of countries as brands requires quality strategic planning and strategic management, which is what public relations deals with. In doing so, it is necessary to consider the diverse use of public relations communication tools and the synergy of digital and traditional media in order to achieve maximum message effectiveness.

Storytelling is experiencing a renaissance thanks to the power of social networks, where stories are created by ordinary people, and no longer by professionals. The importance of personal experience as well as the stories of locals are becoming more and more important. For content creators, creating and shaping the experience is becoming more and more important, as well as for marketers because they have common points: ensuring authenticity, stimulating emotions, offering a brand promise and sharing content online (Arsenault, 2019, p. 175).

Storytelling involves sharing the experiences we have gained throughout our lives: at a concert or other event, on vacation, in some specific situations that we fondly remember, but also those that we may want to forget. Creating an experience is a complex process that can be observed from a neurological, psychological and business perspective. Neurotransmitters transfer information about stimuli from our environment to our body, creating feelings and connecting them to people, objects and places. James Lang's theory talks about emotions and physiological reactions to them, whether it is a feeling of pleasure or a perception of threat (Reardon, 1986). In the process of creating an experience, we rely on various senses (taste, smell, touch, sight). The eyes, as visual channels, are the primary means, but they include and require an auditory component in order for the image to be complete. Music contributes to creating an atmosphere and emphasizing experiences, and its perception is influenced by the technology used (Jelinčić, 2019, p. 9). The cult of fun as one of the hallmarks of happiness and hedonism has become widespread in postmodern societies, which creates the need to be delighted and enchanted (Stasiak, 2019, p. 19).

It is precisely this mosaic of emotions and experiences that the Eurovision Song Contest, a unique music competition for the best song on the old continent, brings. By choosing the slogan 'United in Music' as the permanent motto of the competition, the cultural and political unity of Europe and its identity is symbolized. It is an important place for the positioning of each country (Milenković & Stamenković, 2013). The distribution of postcards about the country and the artist before their performances serves as a significant contribution to building the image of the country, but also for the purpose of tourism promotion through positive impressions. It is up to each country to decide how to use this opportunity and position itself in the eyes of a global audience.

The Eurovision Song Contest is a television spectacle that is eagerly awaited year after year. This is evidenced by the fact that the tickets (42,000 of them) for the spectacle, which took place in May 2025, were sold out in just seven minutes. Although it is accompanied by many controversies: from political pressures, controversial messages and outfits of performers, to the attitudes of the audience and the jury that are often not in agreement, the Eurovision Song Contest is a media spectacle that continues to gather viewers. It is a musical event that ensures a positive impression of the country, and although the buzz around the event itself is limited in duration, connecting with its identity is a long-term activity. In 2024, Croatia was represented at this competition by Marko Purišić alias Baby Lasagna, whose performance won the hearts of audiences around the world. Although he entered the Croatian Eurovision Song Contest as a substitute at the last minute after one of the performers withdrew, his winning song "Rim Tim Tagi Dim" won second place in a very tense finale at the European competition behind Swiss Nemo and his song about gender conformity.

A modest, introverted young man who bursts with energy on stage, publicly spoke about his own inner struggles, and soon after the release of the song and video, he captivated the entire country, which gave him immense support through gatherings and numerous choreographies in the famous infectious dance rhythm outdoors. Firefighters, police officers, students, ballerinas, majorettes, old and young, all of them accepted to be part of the virtual challenge on social networks, thus contributing to the creation of digital stories and digital postcards in order to ensure wider support for the national representative.

The aim of the chapter is to analyse the role of storytelling in creating a country's image using the example of a musical performance presented at the Eurovision Song Contest. The motive for choosing the topic was last year's best result of Croatia at this European competition and the fact that the self-effacing young man with a memorable identity, Baby Lasagna, won the world's music charts with his performance, as well as the attention of the world's media, and in a short time did more for the global promotion of the country than any athlete or politician ever before. The chapter will cover the process of branding a country and a destination and the role of public relations in the above. What techniques and tools can contribute to a better strategic positioning of a country in the world? How can musicians contribute to this? Can musical events such as the Eurovision Song Contest and the atmosphere of spectacle that accompanies it contribute to the creation of soft power of countries? How has Croatia's image changed over time? How did Baby Lasagna's performance at the Eurovision Song Contest 2024 contribute to global interest in Croatia? What elements of Croatian identity did Baby Lasagna promote in his video/performance? are just some of the questions that this chapter aims to answer. The paper will use a descriptive case study as one of the most popular qualitative methods in social science research. A case can be an object, a person or a phenomenon, and the aim is to provide a deeper insight and analysis of the case (Bryman, 2016). It is a method that includes single, as well as multiple cases. Its main advantages are that it provides a lot of detail, is used in the exploratory phase and can be used to collect descriptive data. On the other hand, its disadvantages are reflected in the lower scientific rigor, the fact that it is not prone to generalization, and can provide a lot of qualitative data that is sometimes difficult to summarize (Wimmer & Dominick, 2014, p. 141).

THE ROLE OF STORIES IN MODERN SOCIETY - FROM A TECHNIQUE FOR CONNECTING WITH THE AUDIENCE TO A MARKETING TOOL

Storytelling is as inherent to humans as breathing or sleeping, amplifying the impact of the message being conveyed, and contributing to the construction of (personal) identities, but sometimes also to an escape from harsh reality. Storytelling is a fundamental and enduring aspect of human culture that has evolved significantly over thousands of years, adapting to changing social, technological and cultural contexts (Hou, 2024). From its beginnings through visual communication in caves, to the development of storytelling in early civilizations, to the use of new media and new technologies in modern times. Despite dramatic changes in the media and techniques used, the essential human need to share, understand and preserve stories has remained constant, reflecting our innate desire to understand the world and our place in it, points out Hou (2024).

Story themes can be diverse – from family, friendship relationships, analysis of mystical events or phenomena to adventures and overcoming challenges. Speaking about mythological/archetypal stories, Zimand-Sheiner states that he accepts previous findings on the theme of the story and its structures. Namely, the themes of stories take place in different times (Berger, 1997 according to Zimand-Sheiner, 2024, p. 4), while the structure does not necessarily have to refer to a person, but can include a deity or an animal (Berger, 1997 according to Zimand-Sheiner, 2024, p. 4). In addition to the emotional aspect, stories contribute to strengthening trust and authenticity, connecting with values, better persuasion, strengthening the cognitive functions of the individual (McKean, 2024), socio-cultural connections, strengthening creativity and implementing changes (Prasetyo, 2017). Today, stories also serve as an important tool in the strategic communication of organizations, destinations and countries.

Lund et al. state that modern travel is actually a "balance between narrative identity and entitlement" (Noy, 2012 according to Lund et al., 2024, pp. 9-10). Social networks and digital media in general are meeting places of multiple identities and a form for negotiating a brand and its values, whether it is a corporation or a state. However, there is a difference. Corporate storytelling is telling the story of the brand to various stakeholders, and its strength depends on meaning, definition and rituals, and distribution through communication platforms. The author developed a model that includes 4 indicators: the story component (the transmedia component as a reflection of the social function of storytelling), the meaning component (symbolism in a certain group of people), the ritual component (the way the story is shared within the community) and the platform component (monitoring the story's compliance with the audience's needs) (Zimand-Sheiner, 2024, p. 2). The author starts from the definition of a myth as an important story expanded by the following dimensions: story content, meaning, and associated rituals (Zimand-Sheiner & Limor, 2017 according to Zimand-Sheiner, 2024, p. 4).

Transmedia storytelling involves using multiple media platforms to tell interconnected stories within a shared story world - it offers a powerful and engaging method for forecasters to shape perceptions, foster understanding, and inspire action about the future (Von Stackelberg & Jones, 2014). The authors further point out that everyday discourse has certain limitations, as presenting dry data does not call listeners to action, nor does it contribute to shaping their perceptions, especially in the complex world we live in. The power of storytelling lies in the power to influence people, in the context of strengthening their perceptions. Furthermore, relying on a transmedia approach (using different types of media) ensures that transmedia storytelling can build complex, immersive story worlds that engage diverse audiences and enable co-creation and participation. Relying on creative storytelling is essential for social change because it puts a human face on social problems and highlights local voices and solutions more effectively than reports or graphs (Von Stackelberg & Jones, 2014).

Stories do not only serve as communication mechanisms, but also actively influence the beliefs, values, and practices of organizational members, both proactively (before strategies are formulated) and retroactively (after strategies are implemented) (O'Neill, 2002). Stories in organizations help construct and reinforce shared realities, influencing how members perceive their environment, interpret events, and make sense of strategic decisions. Storytelling is not just a method of communication but a strategic tool that managers can use to influence organizational reality, foster engagement, and improve the effectiveness of the strategic management process. By understanding and using different types of stories, leaders can better shape organizational culture, especially in the context of organizational resilience (Kampann & Pedell, 2022), guide decision-making, and achieve long-term strategic goals.

The dimension of meaning in corporate branding involves connecting brand values with consumer desires and needs, thereby contributing to the creation of collective meaning. This is followed by the ritual dimension, which has an emotionally motivational component since it serves to achieve goals (in this context, mythological stories go hand in hand with rituals). At the organizational level, they contribute to the construction of values (Varlaj, Grmuša, Vuković, 2021), local identities and a sense of belonging. The author believes that the synergy of story, meaning and ritual has the best effect. Furthermore, the transmedia dimension requires the adaptation of the story to various channels, which offers the audience various opportunities for engagement with the narrative.

Social networks have strongly influenced online communication, but also marketing activities in managing the image of an organization, which shifts control to the position of the audience (Fisher and Smith, 2011 according to Lund et al., 2018, p. 2). Sharing the user/consumer experience through a brand narrative strengthens or disintegrates its identity, which shows brands that creating experiences and stories is not only in their hands, but the power is shifting to the audience. The paper presents an ethnographic case study of Facebook posts "Visit Denmark" and an analysis of the use of social networks in branding the country. Rather than focusing solely on the final digital stories or the technologies used, Hill (2023) emphasizes the importance of the (digital) story-making space—the rhetorical, dialogical, and co-productive environment in which stories are created. She situates digital storytelling as a process co-created by writers, storytellers, educators, institutions and audiences, then explores interrelationships within workshops and the dissemination of stories, emphasizing that authenticity and meaning are co-constructed, not individual (Hill, 2023).

Tourism as an area is very attractive for sharing stories as consumers search for vacation destinations online as well as read recommendations from others that influence their own, therefore data collection/mining is extremely important for creating a brand strategy (destinations, countries, etc.). Branding a destination is a particularly demanding activity that requires reliance on digital channels in creating a brand narrative or at least trying to influence it, and the winners are those with a high conversational value (Morgan and Pritchard, 2004 according to Lund et al., 2018, p. 7). Marketing activities play an important role, not only in trying to capture attention, but also in inviting dialogue with the audience. Effective storytelling is a key component of successful communication strategies for content creators on social media. Research conducted by Pertiwi & Sanusi (2023) highlights several key factors that contribute to the effectiveness of storytelling in a digital context: authenticity and connection, visual appeal, emotional engagement, conciseness and interactivity, and strategic use of platforms to increase audience reach and engagement.

Stories provide a connection between tourism, businesses and destinations, ensuring emotional connection. Storytelling is the foundation of content development, and the choice of media for story distribution becomes a key issue in storytelling – it is important to answer the following questions: "what is our story?", what is the experience, how to convey it to the world" (Arsenault, 2019, p. 176) We all have some stories, but not all stories are for everyone and are not worth telling (Johnson, 2006 according to Arsenault, 2019, p. 177). The key elements of the experience economy are reliance on "vision, innovation, value creation, decision-making and performance orientation" (Arsenault, 2019, p. 181) Encountering stories is something we are exposed to from birth, but the success of storytelling in the launch depends on the abilities of the storyteller (Solis, 2015 according to Arsenault, 2019, p. 187). Stories contribute to creating a direct connection between visitors, content and destination features, and can have long-lasting effects on the experience economy and visitors (Arsenault, 2019, p. 187), therefore it is important to better understand the country branding process.

NATION BRANDING: CHALLENGES AND OPPORTUNITIES

Branding Concept

The branding process was mainly observed through the marketing concept and the value of the product in the consumer's perception. Brand image is actually "brand perception that exists in the minds of consumers" (Skoko, 2009, p. 130). All countries have their own image that is shaped in the branding process (Han, 2001 according to Skoko, 2009, p. 131), which relies on advertising and public relations. Those countries that ignore this will become uncompetitive. However, states can also become a product or a brand, which is possible with thoughtful action. Branding a place differs from a product, as it encompasses numerous stakeholders (Skoko, 2009, p. 132). Brand management (including the country as a brand) is a multifaceted process that takes place on several levels; meaning, reputation, common goals (Skoko, 2009, p. 132), while at the same time one should be aware of the fact of possible controversies surrounding the branding of states and nations.

Many EU countries that are successful today by many criteria had a completely different past (e.g. Spain under Franco as a poor country, and today very rich) (Skoko, 2009, p. 134). The process of branding a state and nation is not too different from corporate branding when it comes to technique, believes Skoko, adding that the key to everything is motivating people to participate in the process (2009, p. 136). The branding process is a somewhat worn-out concept, so Simon Anholt offered a new one – competitive identity. "Many brands help create a sense of identity or belonging, just like some nations" (Skoko, 2009, p. 136). The research conceptualized by Anholt, attempting to explore people's real perception of a particular state/nation and analyze the global power index, is supplemented with additional categories every year (Skoko, 2009, p. 138). "Anholt's index confirms the assumption that citizens around the world positively perceive those countries that stand out with concrete advantages and quality communication with the world" (Skoko, 2009, p. 141). The image of the state is important in attracting tourists, as well as foreign investments. Simon Anholt's concept of competitive identity is a concept that is a kind of superstructure of the branding process. For Anholt, the first step is to strengthen positive nationalism, emphasizing that changing the image of a particular country begins with changing the perception of others about that country (Anholt, 2003 according to Skoko, 2009, p. 204). It is a good basis for selling the state on foreign markets. Marketing and branding form the basis of improving the country's image for Anholt

(2009, p. 205). According to Anholt, there are three steps of a competitive identity strategy: 1) analysis of the public's perception of the state and an attempt to change it, 2) research on how people should perceive the state, 3) create stages of brand transfer (Skoko, 2009, p. 205).

On the other hand, Mucundorfeanu (2018, p. 42) reminds that the branding process is no longer just a matter of marketing activities, selling products and services, but relies on communication, i.e. telling a story and offering a promise to the user about a new experience. Thus, the brand refers to the group, communities and individuals (Green, 2009: 32 according to Mucundorfeanu, 2018, p. 43). On the other hand, branding refers to the process of brand management, but the brand needs to be known and presented to the public. A brand is a promise of a positive experience, but also the result of interaction with the environment, which assumes that key stakeholders must communicate uniformly and with the same information. The branding process is not a one-time event, warns Sinčić Ćorić (2019), but must constantly include set goals and messages.

Destination branding is a process that began to be systematically analyzed in the late 90s by examining the impact of a country's image on the desire to visit it, whereby leading authors from the profession agreed that country branding can be similar to product and service branding (Telišman-Košuta, 2017, p. 69), so that this topic would become one of the leading ones when it comes to tourism marketing. Destination branding is an attempt to define the destination while leaving the freedom to independently create an image (Telišman-Košuta, 2017, p. 70). The author further states several prerequisites for successful branding: 1) understanding the concept, which starts from the research of the perception of the destination as guests and its characteristics, but also the analysis of the brand strategy (relationship between brands and sub-brands) (Telišman-Košuta, 2017, p. 72). The next factor is 2) understanding of meaning, since some authors believe that the image of a destination is not necessarily connected to the branding process (Telišman-Košuta, 2017, p. 72). Furthermore, 3) the issue of implementation is highlighted, 4) the perception of responsibility, since tourism organizations do not see their role in the branding process, but consider the government and other bodies responsible. This is followed by 5) the perception of barriers and the lack of so-called 'destination thinking' as well as the imposition of their own interests by individual tourism stakeholders (Telišman-Košuta, 2017, p. 73). Finally, an additional deficiency is the lack of leaders whose leadership would be oriented towards the organization (Telišman-Košuta, 2017, p. 74).

The branding process according to Sinčić Ćorić (2019) includes three phases: 1) defining the concept and adopting guidelines for its management (which is actually the brand and the essence of the brand), 2) creative and communication concept (clear definition of key messages) and 3) implementation (production, operationalization and long-term brand management). The goal of the project led by Sinčić Ćorić (2019) was to develop guidelines for the development of a national brand that would be based on national identity, bringing together a large proportion of diverse participants from different industries and sectors using a combined methodology.[1]

Country branding must be based on differentiation from others in the environment, but also encompass the national culture, history, economy, political and social context, and values shared by its inhabitants. When this is not the case, then the image of a particular country is left to the subjective (pr)estimations of individuals, which can result in unpleasant stereotyping. Therefore, according to Sinčić Ćorić (2019), national branding must be:

- "visionary, oriented to the present, but also to the future
- based on optimism and positive characteristics of the country
- liked by the country's inhabitants
- above daily politics
- a long-term national project
- considered as a unifying factor for the domestic population and
- a competitive tool in the international environment."

Storytelling has a long history, and it is interesting to many experts, especially cognitive psychologists, but also to neuroscientists, since storytelling encourages communication and speech, causes emotional reactions, contributes to the development of ideas, and stimulates imagination (Sammer, 2015, pp. 29-34 according to Mucundorfeanu, 2018, p. 45). The author states that a new sub-discipline has been developed - story branding, which encompasses the activities of the organization with the aim of strengthening the image, and this makes the difference between responsible and irresponsible brand management. Storytelling does not guarantee success in the branding process, states Mucundorfeanu (2018), but it is important to try. It relies on brand specifics that are transformed through narrative elements to make the audience identify with them. Most of the stories are focused on "the shape of product, family tradition and reference to historical events (Mucundorfeanu, 2017, pp. 35-39)" (Mucundorfeanu, 2018, p. 47).

It should be noted the differences in the concept of brand and branding; and while a brand is a product that has a name and a reputation, branding refers to the process of building a reputation (Anholt, 2007, p. 4 according to Felknerová, 2014, p. 20). She states that all countries of the world already have their own image and identity naturally. Building national identities is a multidimensional process according to many authors. Nevertheless, Felknerová makes a clear distinction between soft power and nation branding. Thus, the term soft power implies the ability to attract and the ability to achieve the desired persuasion outcomes, and that is why a good image and reputation are important (Felknerová, 2014, p. 22). On the other hand, nation branding has similarities with soft power because it means the possibility for people to believe in the qualities of the country. Thus, she sees nation branding as an instrument for achieving soft power and as a contribution to the creation of the country's brand (Felknerová, 2014, p. 22). The role of public diplomacy is also not negligible in building a country's brand, but it is limited to people/diplomats. States communicate through different channels, states Felknerová, referring to Anholt's brand hexagon, which encompasses tourism, exports, policy, culture and communication between people. For example, the French present themselves as old white Christians, which they are not at all (Felknerová, 2014, p. 32). The role of the government is crucial, although sometimes dissonant messages are sent.

Soft Power of States

The term soft power was first coined by Joseph Nye, referring to American dominance in the world that goes beyond economic and military power. It is a concept that implies the ability to influence others to act as we wish. However, Skoko & Kovačić state (2009, p. 30) that the term soft power should not be immediately equated with persuasion, given the fact that influence can be achieved through legitimate as well as illegal means.

> *"Soft power is the ability to seduce and attract, and attraction often leads to imitation. If a state manages to make its power legitimate in the eyes of others, its desires will encounter less resistance. In short, the universality of culture in a particular state and its ability to create institutions that govern various areas on the international scene represent key sources of power (Nye, 2002: 9)" (according to Skoko & Kovačić, 2009, p. 30).*

The use of the concept of soft power is implemented with the aim of strengthening its image in the international environment, and this is manifested in public and cultural diplomacy and public relations (Felknerová, 2014, p. 4). The author presents a special case study – an analysis of Germany through the theory of competitive identities, recalling the negative image of Germany, especially after the Second World War, which needed to be changed. Many countries therefore resort to the concept of soft power – so Germany decided to use this tool with the aim of ensuring recognition at the international level (Felknerová, 2014, p. 3). Germany was chosen to demonstrate the impact of national branding on the domestic and international environment. Germany's transformation path lasted almost two decades until the image of Germany as a modern, strong and desirable European country that it is today (Felknerová, 2014, p. 4). The concept of soft power was established by Joseph Nye in the 1990s, but the author warns that the concept originated in the 1960s in the work of Morgenthane, Knorr and Cline (Felknerová, 2014, p. 12), while Nye only re-established it in the era of globalization, showing that by framing topics and good persuasion we can achieve a lot (Nye, 2009, p. 38 according to Felknerová, 2014, p. 11).

The concept of soft power is therefore viewed through two dimensions: persuasive and ideological. While the first is based on the principle of outside-in, relying on communication channels and media such as film and television, the second dimension is directed outward through democratic processes (Nye, 2003, p. 9 according to Skoko & Kovačić, 2013, p. 31).

Reliance on elements of popular culture, more precisely on film, is becoming an important tool in ensuring the soft power of the state. The primarily ideological and promotional function has been replaced by a commercial one, promoting the values of the country, but also the way of life of its inhabitants (Skoko & Primorac, 2021, p. 7). Hollywood is slowly replacing Bollywood, and in addition to India, the power of film production has also been recognized by South Korea (mostly thanks to the popularity of K-drama and K-pop) and Turkey (through Turkish soap operas that are conquering Southeast Europe, but also the world in general by relying on propaganda narratives, Benković, 2011; Zgurić, 2021). The popularity of cinematography is reflected in the subtle promotion of life values, but also in the possibility of achieving parasocial interaction with the content or characters (Giles, 2003). The importance of film is reflected in its universality, and its use as a tool of soft power of the state differs from country to country, and most often it is about screen adaptations, biographies of great people who support the national identity and image of the country (Skoko & Primorac, 2021, p. 11).

Speaking about the relationship between hard and soft power, Skoko & Kovačić (2013) point out that a clear theoretical distinction between these two concepts is sometimes not visible in practice, but rather the opposite occurs – they intertwine and complement each other, and they explain this through the humanitarian actions of states (for example, the USA in Asia in 2024 after a devastating earthquake and tsunami) (Skoko & Kovačić, 2009, p. 34).

It is precisely soft power that contributed to the global image of the strength and dominance of the USA in the 20th and 21st centuries. The value of the American brand consists of American values such as: individualism, freedom, materialism and patriotism (Pandžić Skoko, 2023, p. 11). The author further states that myths about America have been created for a long time through the content of western films, the differences between East and West, as well as stories about the American dream and freedom that were so attractive to numerous immigrants, but she still considers citizens to be the best promoters of American values (Pandžić Skoko, 2023, p. 17). The emphasis on materialism, consumerism and individualism as integral parts of American culture (Bovée & Thil, 2012) contributes to the banalization and unification of life, which is increasingly repulsive to many people (Milišić, 1997 according to Pandžić Skoko, 2023). At the same time, he warns that America has begun to gain competition from other countries (Scandinavian countries, India) and their global soft power is growing), and the beginning of the military intervention in Iraq in 2001 in response to terrorist attacks led to the weakening of American soft power and a decline in trust in American institutions and diplomacy (Pandžić Skoko, 2023, p. 21).

However, soft power is also a reflection of citizens' perceptions, and a study from Spain in 2003 found that citizens first see "elements of hard power such as the economy, the military, and technology" (Noya, 2006, pp. 53-67 according to Skoko & Kovačić, 2009, p. 36). Furthermore, they believe that Nye's dualistic prism of power among citizens is not the only one, but that the influence of the media, the degree of democratization of society, the educational system, and the role of new technologies should also be emphasized (Noya, 2006, p. 66 according to Skoko & Kovačić, 2009, p. 37). They see culture as a key tool in strengthening the state's soft power and its promotion, mainly because "consumers are not as suspicious of it as they are of commercial messages" (Skoko & Kovačić, 2009, p. 39). Anholt (2007) shares the same opinion, considering culture to be key to strengthening national identities and awareness of the state. Skoko & Kovačić further describe the potential of Croatia's soft power in the context of culture and natural beauty, and it is worth mentioning the role of regional leader that Croatia assumed by joining NATO in 2009 and the EU in 2013 (Skoko, 2009, p. 40).

The wealth of cultural, material and intangible heritage, magnificent monuments from the era of ancient Greece and Rome, are only part of the country's cultural power and evidence of centuries-old belonging to the European cultural circle, which must be told and made available, Skoko & Kovačić (2009, p. 43) point out. This is also supported by research from 2021 and 2023 (Croatiaweek, 2023) which confirm that Croatia is among the most desirable countries to live in. Croatia's image in the world is mostly associated with natural beauty, and it should also be mentioned as "the image of an ecologically preserved country" (Skoko & Kovačić, 2009, p. 43). The potential of soft power is much more influential because it plays on emotional appeals, and thus is more long-lasting. However, Croatia must start taking systematic and institutional care of its image like other countries (the USA) in order to better capitalize on the achievements in modern history in less than three decades and the attention of the international public. Gotal (2015) recalls the initiative of former Croatian President Stjepan Mesić in 2000 to establish a working group for branding Croatia, which managed to produce one publication. Differences in opinions and the direction of strategic development have led to everything remaining only at the conceptual level. His initiative was continued by former Croatian president Kolinda Grabar Kitarović in 2018 (Filipović, 2018).

"We need to develop a brand that is different from the countries that are our competitors and attract similar investors. Croatia is already known for its knowledge, innovation, and natural beauty, but our lifestyle, way of thinking, and the character of our people are also something that makes us different from our competitors. Together with other institutions, we participated and generated joint content that was positively evaluated. In order for the image of Croatia to be synchronized considering the diversity of the messages we send, we still lack a body at the level of the Government of the Republic of Croatia," said Sinčić Ćorić. (Suvremena.hr, 2019).

The results of preliminary research presented by the head of the working group, Dubravka Sinčić Ćorić, a university professor at the Faculty of Economics, University of Zagreb, highlighted seven elements of Croatian identity: 1) people (open, warm-hearted, proud, hospitable, hardworking, ready to help, successful) 2) lifestyle (safe country, balance between ambition and pleasure, work and family), 3) natural beauty and diversity in a small territory, 4) preservation and innovation (as a basis for new investments), 5) social responsibility (healthcare and insurance for all), 6) cultural wealth (a link between East and West), 7) sweet and salty (a metaphor for flavorful food) (Sinčić Ćorić, 2019).

Finally, the working group developed seven guidelines for the development and management of national identity and brand: "1) establish an official government body for branding Croatia, 2) define the symbols of the identity of Croatia as a brand and synchronize them for all promotional materials for official bodies in Croatia, 3) continue to continuously research the perception of the brand and Croatian identity among different target groups, 4) define key activities for brand management in specific areas, 5) organize public debates and conferences on national values with the aim of raising awareness of national identity among Croatian citizens, 6) develop a medium-term plan of activities that will include the presentation of Croatia and 7) develop a central website with all relevant information about Croatian identity and brand with the help of social media and influencers" (Sinčić Ćorić, 2019).

Understanding the difference between hard and soft power is crucial in finding a balance (Fan, 2006, p. 22 according to Felknerová, 2014, p. 12). The concept of power is viewed differently in the prism of international relations through the concepts of idealism and liberalism, but it is a simple form of achieving goals (Nye, 2009, p. 170 according to Felknerová, 2014, p. 13). Tuđman also writes about the use of soft power in the context of international relations, considering diplomatic activities to be crucial in relation to the demonstration of hard power or "hard force" as he calls it (Tuđman, 2013, p. 1). The author believes that small countries are too exposed to a greater risk for soft power given the presence of large, global players that directly influence elements of soft power such as culture, sports, etc. The sources of soft power are culture, political values and foreign policy, which are interconnected.

The ways of promoting soft power are through government bodies (example Germany), through companies and brand distribution, security services and through the distribution of information. Measuring soft power is not easy, and is mainly done through surveys and public opinion polls. The limitation of soft power lies in the fact that some authors believe that this is not a type of power due to the coercion and command domain, and the fact that the attraction is not under the command/supervision of the authorities (Nye, 2004, pp. 17-18 according to Felknerová, 2014, p. 17), then it is not possible to influence the policy or the target group (Fon, 2008, pp. 11-12 according to Felknerová, 2014, p. 17), while others consider it a new form of imperialism (Ferguson, 2004, p. 24 according to Felknerová, 2014, p. 17).

Pandžić Skoko believes that the USA has lost a lot of its power in the 21st century due to the weakening of the ideal of the American dream, mainly due to the growing polarization in society and the erosion of democratic values. This opens up an opportunity for many European countries to strengthen their soft power (2023, p. 6). According to the global soft power index published by Brand Finance, headquartered in London, since 2020, America's vulnerability is visible in terms of its shift from the leading position; on the one hand, economic growth and investment, and on the other, racial conflicts and divisions due to political circumstances (Pandžić Skoko, 2023, p. 10). This is an online survey that includes participants from 100 countries around the world. According to data for 2025, Croatia ranks 48th, leaving its neighbors behind (Jagodzinski, 2025).

"Brand Finance believes that a country's soft power is based on three universal measures and seven specific dimensions (pillars). The universal measures are: familiarity (the more people know about a country, its talents, companies and potential, the greater its power), reputation (in order for a nation to be attractive and become a role model, its overall reputation must be strong and positive) and influence (the perceived global presence and influence that the country has on other countries, i.e. whether the reach of influence is local, regional or global). The seven pillars represent: business and trade (economic strength, ease of doing business, brands, taxes, trade, investment, infrastructure), governance (laws, human rights, crime rate, security, constitution, political elites), international relations (diplomatic relations, international organizations, conflicts, decisions, international aid, environmental protection), culture and heritage (sports, food, fine arts, literature, music, film, entertainment industry, fashion), media and communication (traditional media, social media, marketing), education and science (higher education, science, technology) and people and values (values, character, trust)" (Jugo et al., 2021, pp. 355-356)

Countries that know how to communicate better have a higher level of power, according to Jugo et al., 2021, who analyzed the communication strategies of countries during the Covid-19 crisis, which has strongly affected all spheres of life. Strategic communication is thus becoming crucial in shaping the identity and image of a country. Positive attitudes about Croatia as a safe and pleasant place to live form the foundation for a future communication strategy for national branding, since they highlight competitive advantages in the best possible way (Ivanković et al., 2024, p. 77). We will show what Croatia's image is in the world and who is promoting it best in the chapter below.

Identity and Image of Croatia in the World

The issue of identity is often the starting point in defining oneself in relation to others, but when considering identity, one should take into account its complexity and the fact that it is composed of many smaller identities and micro-entities (cultural, national, economic, religious), warns Skoko (2009, pp. 18-20). As an example of a successfully created identity, he singles out the American identity, which is recognizable throughout the world. Globalization and the consumerist way of life affect national identities that are in a kind of crisis, but not only that, but also by uniting into movements and communities, unification is emphasized in comparison with pluralism (Milardović, 2002, p. 132 according to Skoko, 2009, pp. 22-23). For Skoko, national identity is at the center of the process of branding and strengthening the image of an individual country, where he emphasizes that it is precisely pride and awareness of national identity that can strengthen its power in the public. Furthermore, he reminds us that the issue of Croatian national identity was revived with the creation of an independent state (2009, p. 35), when it needed to be rebuilt. It is certainly worth recalling the unfounded fear of losing it that prevailed on the eve of Croatia's accession to the EU. "It is precisely the management of competing identities, like any other factor, that determines which states will be strengthened by accession, which will be impoverished, and which may be completely destroyed" (Anholt, 2007, p. 119 according to Skoko, 2009, p. 25).

The concept of image is multidimensional and can be studied in different fields – political science, communication science, marketing, with Skoko citing elements from the latter manual that highlight three dimensions; perception, image and point of view (Rocco, 1993 according to Skoko, 2009, p. 27). "Image is the perception/experience that an individual has about a person or object, and is often based on their own (acquired) opinions, beliefs and attitudes" (Skoko, 2009, pp. 28-29). "The process of image creation is very complex, and it is influenced by categories and symbols such as memorability and persuasiveness in communication" (Skoko, 2009, p. 33).

The image of Croatia is most influenced by "tourism, natural beauty and Croatian athletes" (Klasnić & Rukavina, 2011, p. 131), while political ideology and media freedom are least influenced, the authors state, presenting a comparative overview of research results from 2004 and 2010. They believe that an important part of a country's image also includes "the opinion and mentality of the citizens of that country" (Klasnić & Rukavina 2011, p. 132), and here we are already entering the domain of stereotypes.

Stereotypes, as a related concept, are often associated with image and perception (Skoko, 2009), which is not surprising given that they are both linked by a subjective experience related to a person or an individual. Labaš and Grmuša warn of the ambiguity of the concept of stereotype, burdened by terminological inflation from various disciplines, most notably cultural studies and literature (2011, pp. 92-95). Skoko states that the distinction between the concepts is possible, and is reflected in the fact that "perception precedes the creation of an image" (2009, p. 35). Prejudices as a form of negative stereotyping arise from a simplified view of the environment or generalizations, often based on exclusion when it comes to others and those who are different. "Repeating and further transmitting bad stereotypes and prejudices is the same as transmitting untruths, because a lie repeated a hundred times becomes a "truth" that is very difficult to change later" (Labaš & Grmuša, 2011, p. 97). Furthermore, Grmuša & Mori (2022) in their work remind us of the transformation of the Croatian image - from negative images during the communist era and during World War II to positive ones with independence in the early 90s.

How Croatia's image has changed in comparison to other neighboring post-socialist countries?

Speaking about Croatia's image in relation to other countries of the former Yugoslavia, Šeremet reminds us (2024, p. 10) that the termination of state-legal relations was not enough as a political act, but the country still had to fight for international recognition. Croatia's transition from socialism to a market-oriented democracy was complex and full of challenges, states Jambrač (2020), and was often misunderstood or misrepresented. The author explains that the term "transition" is often used, but "transformation" is actually a better term since it implies much deeper structural, political and social changes. Finally, the author points out that the aforementioned process was "lost in translation" due to oversimplification, ideological biases and difficulties in adapting Western models to the Croatian context. The effects of the war's devastation were felt most strongly in the Croatian economy, which repelled many potential investors. Skoko states (2021, p. 113) that an additional challenge in the entire process was related to reducing the influence of propaganda activities from Belgrade. Šeremet adds that Croatia and Slovenia worked most on building their image after the war. The beginnings were predominantly related to building tourist recognition, in which the Croatian National Tourist Board (CNTB) played a major role in promoting the then young country. Although tourism and sport are key cards on which we rely, the author also states the untapped technological and innovative potential in foreign markets. The issue of national identity was again evoked on the eve of Croatia's entry into the EU, accompanied by euroscepticism (Kersan-Škabić & Tomić, 2009; Popović, Grmuša & Popović, 2013; Butković & Šelo Šabić, 2023) and reduced support for entry. This is a consequence of the different levels of media coverage of the topic and the different levels of information available to individual social groups (Popović, Grmuša & Prpić, 2011; Grubiša 2012). Twelve years later, this relationship is better, because according to Eurobarometer data, the majority of Croatian citizens state the benefits of EU membership (Šeremet, 2024, p. 18), as awareness of the benefits of accession is growing (HINA, N1, 2024).

With the collapse of the former state of Bosnia and Herzegovina, with which Croatia shares its longest land border, it faced the greatest challenge in the context of nation branding due to the difficult war legacy, but also the complex internal structure defined according to the ethnic key of the three constituent peoples. Each of them has its own vision of identity, which often represents an obstacle to a unified national branding. This is confirmed by regional research conducted by Skoko (2012) among citizens of Croatia and Serbia, for whom the first association with the neighboring country is the consequences of the war and political tensions that manifest themselves in the ubiquitous divisions related to certain areas, as well as commemorations. At the same time, positive associations relate to people, hospitality, openness, a relaxed lifestyle and natural beauty. Skoko (2017) sees additional aggravating circumstances in the disagreement of political actors on most issues, but also in the misunderstanding of the importance of this process. Bosnia and Herzegovina has focused its country branding process on tourism, but with significantly less success compared to Croatia and Slovenia. While the role of the international community has also sought to help establish the country by ensuring political and economic stability, this is only a small step towards a systematic branding process that would place the country more strongly on the European map.

Having experienced a brief conflict during its independence, Slovenia's visual national identity is less marked by war trauma and more by symbols of European integration and economic progress. Namely, Slovenia has always been closer to the Central European circle of countries than to the Balkans, and the branding of the country began while it was part of the former Yugoslavia (Ruzzier & Petek, 2012, p. 472). Its public spaces and cultural heritage emphasize stability and modernization, reflecting a collective identity focused on successful transition, rather than prolonged conflict. Ruzzier & Petek point out that when rebranding its identity, Slovenia became aware that it must first approach the local population as a prerequisite for the success of the process. Therefore, the first public opinion survey was conducted half a year after the introduction of the slogan 'I feel Slovenia' (Ruzzier & Petek, 2012, p. 466). Borko (2017, p. 2) states that the perception of Slovenia today is linked to natural beauty, without any problems (social or political), which shows that "nation branding is indeed a practice of selection and idealization, where certain images are chosen with the aim of commodification." However, frequent changes in slogans and their general character did not contribute to a stronger identification of the population with the newly created brand, and this is considered the most common mistake in the branding process. Therefore, in the next stage, everything that had previously been missed was done: setting a clear activity schedule, creating a clear and simple message, and supporting the government through an institutionalized body responsible for monitoring the implementation process (Ruzzier & Petek, 2012, pp. 473-474).

Novčić Korać et al (2012,2020) state that Serbia, as a transitional post-Yugoslav country, must make better use of the process of nation branding in order to reconstruct its national identity, which is still unclear. At the same time, it is necessary to change negative stereotypes (Perić, 2011) and create a better image of the country in the international environment, since negative images have long contributed to Serbia's low position on the world map of national brands (Domazet and Hanić, 2012). Earlier research (Novčić Korać et. al., 2012; Novčić Korać et. al., 2020) showed a difference in perception between internal and external stakeholders (the national body consisting of residents of the country and representatives of the diaspora), and this represents a challenge in shaping a unique brand.

Sports successes, innovations, creativity and the cultural industry as new tools of Croatia's soft power

The perception of Croatia's image differs depending on who you ask. The image of Croatia among expatriates mainly refers to Croatia being an attractive tourist destination, followed by the perception of Croatia as a European country. This is followed by sporting successes and tourism, and then famous people and the war past (Skoko et. al. 2022, p. 175). Expatriates outside Europe "perceive Croatia as a Central European country" (Skoko et. al. 2022, p. 176), a Mediterranean country, while expatriates in Europe see Croatia as a Balkan country and a former Yugoslav socialist republic. These results show twofold outcomes – the expected criticism, but also bring a view from the outside, according to Skoko et. al. (2022, pp. 177-184). Winning second place in the semi-finals of the 2022 World Cup in Qatar increased interest in Croatia on Internet search engines. This is proof that sporting successes are the greatest Croatian national promoters, despite the often insufficient infrastructure and modest conditions, and it is not surprising that Croatia is described as the "sportsiest" nation in the world (Skoko & Frka Petešić, 2023, p. 63). Skoko and Hlača emphasize the role of sport in Croatia's international recognition in the first half of the 1990s, mostly thanks to the successes of athletes, both in individual (Goran Ivanišević) and team sports (Dražen Petrović and the basketball team). The aforementioned trends continued in the second half of the 1990s, which also affected the image of the country - from a country associated with war to a country recognizable for its natural beauty and sporting successes (Skoko & Hlača, 2020). Tomić emphasizes partiality and reliance on it as an occasional activity as the main shortcoming of sports diplomacy (Tomić, 2022, p. 48). Although Croatia is a successful sports nation whose results in individual and team sports are admirable, the author states that football has brought the most happiness, since the national team brings the nation together like no one before in victory and defeat (Tomić, 2022, p. 53). Tomić mentions the following reasons for the implementation of sports diplomacy as an extended tool of the state's soft power: 1) ensuring the liveliness of diplomatic activities and influencing the active shaping of the country's image, 2) relying on numerous stakeholders, 3) sport as a test for risk and creating foreign policy, 4) sport has a positive perception among people in general (Murray, 2018; Hocking, 2013; Balci, 2015; Nye 2004 according to Tomić, 2022, p. 49). In addition to the potential of sport for strengthening national identity, Leško also cites the potential of business partnerships, strengthening social inclusion, reliance on knowledge in the organization with the aim of strengthening sports ecosystems, and the development of sports tourism (Leško, 2019, p. 99). Furthermore, there is also the possibility of relying on sports ambassadors, as well as the contribution of sports to "economic, demographic and tourist development" (Leško, 2019, p. 102).

The main associations at the mention of the name Croatia were related to natural beauty, the backdrops for blockbuster films such as Game of Thrones and Mamma Mia, but Skoko & Frka Petešić agree that apart from these general concepts, others know too little about Croatia (2023: pp. 5-6). Many do not know that Croats are one of the oldest European nations who were the first to have their own state (as early as the 7th century or their coat of arms in the 11th century (2023, p. 6). It is worth noting that 2025 is also the anniversary year in which we remember the 1100th anniversary of the Croatian Kingdom, and the decision to this effect was made by the Croatian Parliament in March 2024 (V.G., 2005). "With the coronation of the first Croatian king Tomislav as well as his mention in the letter of Pope John X which convened the First Split Church Council in 925, Croatia, the Ministry emphasizes, became independent and recognized kingdom, which played a key role in shaping Croatian national identity and sovereignty." (V. G., 2025).

Therefore, Skoko & Frka Petešić have brought 30 attractively told stories about Croats and Croatia that offer a kind of breakthrough in comparison to popular tourist guides. Thus, the book describes Croatia as a country at the meeting point of the Mediterranean and Central Europe and at the crossroads between East and West, which confirms the openness of Croats towards the cultures of Others. Furthermore, due to its natural beauty and biodiversity, Croatia is recognizable as a "European national park", a "Small country for a big vacation" and "Europe in miniature" (2023, pp. 15 -23). When it comes to the character of the people living in Croatia,

Skoko & Frka-Petešić emphasize the Slavic soul, love and affection for one's neighbor, as well as a sense of solidarity for others, which is often manifested through numerous community actions towards people in need (2023, pp. 27-35). Focusing on family and friends, and coffee drinking rituals are just some of the examples of achieving social cohesion that make Croatia attractive as a country to live in and to the increasing number of foreign workers.

"The country of top-quality olive oil and rich gastronomy", "the country of a thousand islands" are just some of the epithets with which Croatia is presented to the world (Skoko & Frka Petešić, 2023, pp. 43-47). At the same time, thanks to numerous emigrants and the diaspora, Croats contributed to the improvement of fishing in the Pacific, but also revealed the quality of good wine to Americans, according to Skoko & Frka-Petešić. However, the oldest European stereotype about Croats refers to us being a "country of warriors" (2023, p. 75) respected for their devotion to their homeland and exceptional courage, which is why even small children were afraid of Croats in oral traditions. On the other hand, Croats enjoy the status of one of the most tolerant peoples in Europe, according to Skoko & Frka-Petešić (2023, pp. 95-99), recalling how they were a civilizational and cultural bridge.

However, Croats stand out most for their rich legacy to the world in the context of inventions that have changed the way we live: from the invention of electricity (Nikola Tesla), dactyloscopy (Ivan Vučetić), the pen (Slavoljuv Eduard Penkala), the discontinuity of records (Andrija Mohorovičić), but which continue to change the world, such as the electric car Nevera (Mate Rimac) (Skoko & Frka-Petešić, 2023, pp. 99-107). Relying on innovation and creativity is the foundation of success in the field of cinematography and popular film culture, as well as the festival scene where Croatia is also a trendsetter. And how music can contribute to strengthening the country's visibility and national identity will be shown using the example of the oldest television competition in Europe - the Eurovision Song Contest, where Croatia achieved notable success with its representative in 2024.

EUROVISION SONG CONTEST - A TELEVISION SPECTACLE IN THE SERVICE OF BRANDING AND CULTURAL DIPLOMACY

History of Music Competition: Political, Cultural and Sociological aspects

The history of the Eurovision Song Contest can be traced back to 1956 as an attempt to unite the EU through music, and was inspired by the Italian Sanremo music festival. From a competition that initially brought together only a few performers to a global event with an audience of millions (Falck, 2024, p. 7). It is an important television spectacle that imposes musical and social trends (Fricker and Gluhovic, 2013, p. 4 according to Falck, 2024). It was conceived as a television format devoid of any bias and form of influence and as a platform for the exchange of cultural and artistic agendas and diversity (Falck, 2024, p. 8). It has managed to maintain a significant cultural and political role in the EU, reflecting the current political climate and contributing to the creation of soft power (winning songs with political messages or messages for vulnerable groups such as LGBTIQ communities), and allowing countries to promote their national identity.

The Eurovision Song Contest (ESC) is used as an excellent platform for promoting national identities by relying on brand ambassadors – influential figures in the world of music. Falck states (2024, p. 19) that this can be crucial for strengthening brand value and its reinforcement over time. Some countries have used their appearance for stronger branding and image transformation (e.g. Estonia, 2022). Falck mentions the role of strategic narrative in the field of international politics in the context of shaping impressions and behavior in domestic and international politics. Bolin and Ståhlberg (2010) identified four basic components in the analysis of strategic narratives; 1) the role of the actor, 2) the environment, 3) the conflict, 4) the proposed solution or outcome (according to Falck, 2024, p. 22). An analysis of strategic narratives in media reports on a sample of 16 articles covering the period 2016 and 2022 showed two different narratives – Ukrainian resistance to the invasion and support and solidarity of Europe. The 2000s saw the transformation of this competition in the context of format and EU policy. From a classic concert performance, the ESC has become a mega-event that is broadcast live and gathers thousands of people as an audience. Since the 2000s, victories by countries (Estonia, Latvia, Turkey, Ukraine) have shifted the public's focus away from Western countries (Baker et al., 2024, p. 32), and new member states have joined the competition.

Let us mention how Azerbaijan used its victory in the 2011 Eurovision Song Contest to build its image. It is a post-Soviet, Muslim country located in a special geographical position on the border of East and West, which makes it susceptible to various influences. The victory in this popular music competition and the organization of the host country a year later put this country at the center of Western media interest. This is evidenced by the increased interest in popular Internet search engines (Ismayilov, 2012, p. 834). The author analyzes four ways in which the victory affects nation-building: 1) the development of Western feelings within the national corpus, 2) as a connective tissue within civil society, 3) as a medium through which elements of Western culture and lifestyle are imported that could be considered a threat to the indigenous Azerbaijani culture, and 4) as an opportunity for the development of democratic values and a pluralistic society (Ismayilov, 2012, p. 834).

Analyzing the country's self-perception at the music competition, the author states that everything was permeated with Western influence – from the choice of song, its authors to the performance itself in English. It was a major transformation since Azerbaijan's first appearance at this competition in 2008, but also a well-designed marketing approach, the background of which is the process of Westernization, and according to some, the dissolution of indigenous culture (Ismayilov, 2012, p. 840). The victory enabled the organization of a previously unprecedented transnational event in that country, but also provided an opportunity for continuous questioning of its own identity in relation to European and Western in general, given the large number of participants (audience) coming from all over the world and thus meeting the local population. Although the country created potential for future tourism development, the author states that the dominant visitors were from neighboring countries that are culturally closer to Azerbaijan. Therefore, the ESC was perceived as an extraordinary opportunity to come into contact with Western values not only on the screen, but also in person, which for many Azerbaijanis was in the realm of the imaginary and fantasy, states the author (Ismayilov, 2012, p. 837). Furthermore, the ESC was perceived as an opportunity for the development of civil society, which in this country consists of two different groups: those who were educated abroad and those who completed their education in the local environment. This is interesting due to the observation of their socialization frameworks, as well as the effects on the political life of the country, since the ESC is perceived as an opportunity for the meeting and unification of these two groups and the establishment of public dialogue as a prerequisite for building a unified national identity (Ismayilov, 2012, p. 839).

Although the ESC is predominantly viewed as an event that can bring together the EU public sphere, the authors also mention concerns about the content of songs that should satisfy the tastes of a transnational audience (Baker et al., 2024, p. 23). At the same time, the transformation of the music industry and the rise of social networks have enabled better digital visibility of individual performers on a global level. Fricker and Gluhović emphasize the importance of the ESC in building national identities, especially in the context of a pan-European identity, but also in building the EU public sphere and bridging the differences between East and West (2013 according to Baker et al., 2024, p. 33). Georgiou mentions (2008, pp. 3-4) a two-dimensional reinforcement of stereotypes through the strengthening of a nation-centered ideology and through an attempt to give meaning to reality. Explaining the changing attitude towards the ESC in Britain, especially after losing its leading position among the winning countries, the author also highlights the presence of the ESC's transnationalism present from the top down, as well as the creation of myths about the superiority of certain nations and national identity. The role of stereotypes is, “to justify irrational bias and resistance to social change, and on the other hand, a method of information processing, especially necessary in diverse societies where attitudes and cultures may be unknown to its members” (Lippmann, 2007 according to Georgiu, 2008, pp. 7-8). Stereotypes are not a priori negative, but depend on the context of use of relations and power.

The question of performance in the context of similarity or nurturing diversity has also been raised – is it a threat to European unity? The return of Celtic and Balkan sounds in the late 1990s and early 2000s marked a return to ethnicity and contributed to the cultural promotion of individual countries. The decade that followed was marked by performances of amateurs from numerous reality shows and their performances in English, which opened the way for further musical careers for some, and closed the doors of the music scene for others. The digitalization of the music industry has enabled the performers of this competition to reach a transnational audience like no other festival so far, as evidenced by the success of the Armenian performer Rose Linn in 2022 on the social network TikTok, which won the public over with the song "Snap" (Baker et al., 2022, p. 33). The trend of platformization has also been reflected in the transformation of public media services (Dragomir & Túñez López, 2024).

Baker et al. they further point out that the ESC deals with the issue of inclusion, whether it is the rights of sexual, racial minorities, etc., imposing values such as unity, diversity and tolerance, placing them in a unique discourse (Baker et al., 2024, p. 34). A mega event like the ESC spectacle allowed host countries to focus more on national branding as well as strategic narratives. This is visible through the rights of the host country, which from the moment of victory can start using the opportunity for promotion (Baker et. al., 2024, p. 37). In the year of the competition, no significant infrastructure investments are expected from the host country, which leaves additional room for promotion for many. As a reminder, Estonia used the ESC to rebrand the country and move away from the Eastern narrative, but also the perception of a post-Soviet country (Jordan, 2015).This competition has followed numerous world conflicts since the beginning, and it is the same in the 21st century. The latest is certainly the monitoring of the Russian-Ukrainian conflict since the annexation of Crimea in 2014, as well as the monitoring of the political messages of the representatives throughout the years that followed. The victory of Russia in 2008 and the hosting of the same year later marked a turning point in the budget (the largest budget secured until then), but also ensured the communication of the Euro-Asian power (Baker et al., 2024, p. 39).

Host country producers influence the framing of cultural relations and the communication of strategic narratives (visual identity, scripts, etc.), country postcards before each performance. Public service media (PSM) play a major role in this, as they contribute to fulfilling their fundamental role by being involved in the distribution of this content – building national identity, diversity, providing a forum for all, respecting minority interests, and ensuring high quality standards (Miletić, 2003). The presentation of the host country's and contestants' culture is evidence of how they see the ESC as a whole. Host countries and their PSMs serve to highlight diversity, but also cultural specificities without losing their national perspective. Since 1970 and the addition of Turkey and Israel to the performances, debates have been opened about the participants and their belonging to Europe, and this was further intensified by the addition of Australia in 2014-2015, which raised questions about Australian multiculturalism versus Eurocentricity, but the event was perceived very pragmatically through opening up to the Australian market (Baker et al., 2024, p. 45).

Although the ESC is predominantly perceived as an event that brings people together and contributes to interculturalism, Baker et al. believe that the biggest promoters of countries are actually performers who, as the main actors of cultural diplomacy, participate in numerous pre-contest parties organized by Eurovision fan clubs (2024, p. 45). Some artists use the ESC to raise glocal issues. Supporting another country (other than one's own) can strengthen interest in that country in the context of language issues, culture, etc. Thus, the ESC acts as a true bearer of ''Internationalism'' (Baker et al., 2024, p. 46).

The ESC has contributed to the development of popular EU culture, which many consider important. What was perceived as something far away and foreign is currently accessible, and thanks to digital technologies, viewers can follow national competitions online via streaming platforms (Baker et. al., 2024, p. 47). It is also worth mentioning that since 2010, viewers have been able to actively participate online via social networks – tagging, hashtags, etc. which ensured greater reach, but also additional popularity of this mega spectacle.

The concept of voting at the ESC is marked by often emotional moments in which conflict boundaries are erased and minorities are supported. When it comes to voting, the EBU reformed the model from 1997 to 2003, excluding the role of national juries, often perceived as biased and manipulative, and decided to leave everything in the hands of the audience. This was an attempt to make the process more transparent and fair. Nevertheless, it was not possible to stop the neighborhood vote, and many interpret this as a new dimension of cultural diplomacy. This was seen at the competition in 2004, when the Croatian audience awarded the maximum 12 points to the representative of Serbia, Željko Joksimović, and the song "Lane moje". It was a symbolic gesture of progress in neighborly relations after bloody war conflicts in the early 90s (Baker et al., 2024, p. 48).

The idea of EU values and unity in an era of rising populism and extremism has never been more important in strengthening the political landscape. The impression of trust is undermined by the direct entry of the five countries that are also the largest financiers of the EBU, the so-called Big Five. The authors state that in addition to their privileged status, they also have less exposure, which protects them from potential failure, but that the voting system still functions fairly is proven by the fact that, apart from Italy, most of the so-called Big Five do not usually receive a large number of points. Bekcan & Uz recall that the competition has historically had a political connotation through controversies related to performances with political messages between warring parties in a conflict on the domestic or foreign political scene. They recall that Turkey participated for the first time in 1975, but was not selected due to the small number of points awarded by the jury and leftist elements in the song (Kuyucu, 2011, p. 41 according to Bekcan & Uz, 2021, p. 89).

With the fall of socialism in Eastern Europe in the 1990s, followed by bloody wars in the territory of Yugoslavia, there was a growing awareness of the strengthening and promotion of national identities (Bekcan & Uz, 2021, p. 90), and the ESC proved to be a great tool for this. The authors further provide a broader context for Turkey at the ESC competition – it was often ranked low, and many saw this as a reflection of fear towards identity-religious issues. The above resulted in resigned attitudes of the Turkish public towards the ESC until 2003 and the victory with the song "Every Way That I Can" (Bekcan & Uz, 2021, p. 93). Although Turkey cooperated with the EU on the political scene, it was excluded from the cultural scene. The author believes that the ESC is a dominantly political event with a musical side, which is seen through two dimensions: the use of the ESC as a political tool with a variable voting system and bloc voting (Güvendik, 2020, p. 98). Creating music with the aim of winning is an ambitious undertaking in the context of international relations, but also geographical specificities. The influence of mass media on the perception of the image of other countries is crucial. Host countries use the power of mass media to advertise the nation (Güvendik, 2020, p. 100), and this is visible in postcards before the broadcast of a performance by an individual candidate. However, the author states that by emphasizing positive stories for the purpose of marketing and tourism activities and strengthening interest in a particular country, socio-political circumstances and social problems such as human rights and autocratic regimes are often ignored. Furthermore, the increasingly present Anglo-Saxon influence is cited due to the dominance of victory songs in the English language (2000 – 2015) with the aim of connecting with the audience. Themes dedicated to life and happiness generally do best, while ballads and love themes are not as popular due to different understandings of love in national and cultural frameworks (Güvendik, 2020, p. 102). The paper examines the role of kitsch and queer as communication strategies of this music competition that opens up numerous taboo topics and which is why it has found its place in popular culture. The cancellation of the ESC in 2020 moved to the virtual sphere when a special program, "Eurovision: Shine a Light", was broadcast. The ESC is held every year in May, which is a symbolic overlap with the celebration of Europe Day on 9 May, which reflects the symbolic awakening of life after winter (Vuletic, 2018, p. 190 according to Rosenberg, 2020, p. 97). The symbolic exit from the ESC and the integration of queer people into the European public space were marked by the songs "Diva" in 1998 and "Molitva" in 2007, and this integration also opened up numerous discussions about the relationship between the so-called “high” and “low culture”. However, the performance at the ESC is preceded by national competitions and the selection of national representatives, which are important to present in order to understand the broader context of this musical event.

Dora - Selection of the Croatian Song for the Eurovision Song Contest

Croatia has been participating in the Eurovision Song Contest since 1993, when the group Putokazi won with the song "Don't Ever Cry". It was wartime in this region, and participation in this music competition was seen as an opportunity to promote the newly created European state and inform the world about the horrors of war and the suffering of people (Morić, 2025).

The primary competition in which the Croatian representative was selected was called the Croatian Television Festival, which evoked memories of the iconic Opatija Music Festival, which was held on the model of the Italian Sanremo. The competition has been held for many years in the city of Opatija in the Crystal Hall of the Kvarner Hotel, which is considered the cradle of Croatian tourism and a synonym for the successful year-round season that Croatia strives for in other destinations. The event brought together numerous Croatian pop stars whose performances were eagerly awaited (Šarčević, 2023).

Despite several unsuccessful moves to the capital Zagreb, the festival has finally found its permanent home in Opatija. In addition to the place, the name of the festival has also been changed – instead of the Croatian Television Festival, at the initiative of the project editor and respected television editor Ksenija Urličić (cf. Eurosong.hr) the event is renamed Dora. The choice of name is not accidental – it bears the name of the famous Croatian composer Dora Pejačević, who “contributed to the pluralism of musical and stylistic orientations in Croatia at the beginning of the 20th century” (enciklopedija.hr, 2025).

However, changes in the place and name of the festival are not the only things that have happened. Many years of searching for a good result and performers after numerous failures and eliminations already in the semi-final nights (from 2010 to 2013), forced the organizers to withdraw from participation, but also to subsequently try to change the situation by directly selecting representatives. Let us recall that Croatia's best placings in this competition were in 1998, when it won 5th place (Danijela Martinović with the song “Neka mi ne svane”), and in 1996, Maja Blagdan won 4th place (with the song “Sveta ljubav”) and in 1999, Doris Dragović (with the song “Marija Magdalena”) (Bebek, 2023; Šarčević, 2023). Since 2019, Dora has returned in a new, more modern outfit, and with a modern production worthy of European stages and Eurovision, attracting numerous viewers in front of the small screens, but also live. Baby Lasagna's performance at this popular music competition in 2024 and the 2nd place he won are Croatia's greatest success at this competition since independence.

BABY LASAGNA - THE ARTIST WHO WON THE HEART OF EUROPE IN 2024

About the artist

Marko Purišić, alias Baby Lasagna, was born in 1995. He is a singer, songwriter and producer who, before his worldwide success with the performance of "Rim Tim Tagi Dim", was previously awarded in Germany for songs he wrote for the local group Mondo Inc. This is the album that was the most listened to on the local music scene. However, Baby Lasagna's performance at the Croatian competition Eurovision Song Contest was not his first appearance in this musical format. In fact, he had performed there before with the group Mantra, but without significant success. The performance at Dora 2024 happened by chance after the musician Jelena Žnidarić, whose stage name is Zsa Zsa, withdrew at the last minute due to personal reasons. Baby Lasagna confirmed this in an interview on the show "Ususret Dori" broadcast on the public service media (HRT), which organizes and broadcasts the music event:

"It wasn't my plan to go to Dora, this song wasn't written for Dora, it wasn't even a "single" on the album. A friend told me to apply and I wondered if applying was complicated. When I saw that it wasn't, I said: "Why not?". I didn't believe I would get in, I thought it would be one of those things like when you send your resume to a job, then send it to 30 addresses and never get a response. But then I got in the reserve and that was already a shock. They called me after a couple of weeks and said: "Are you ready?", says Baby Lasagna." (A. D., 2024).

His performance in the second semi-final night of Dora held on February 23, 2024, delighted viewers and garnered 178 thousand views on YouTube, surpassing all other contestants and competitors. In addition, his video ranked eighth on the most viewed YouTube trending list that week (I. B., 2024). Furthermore, his performance at the Dora competition, which was available on the official Eurovision YouTube channel, was viewed as many as three million times (Index Magazin, 2024a). This resulted in numerous enthusiastic comments from Eurovision fans who predicted great success for Croatia with this candidate. This resulted in numerous enthusiastic comments from Eurovision fans who predicted great success for Croatia with this candidate. Some of them are included in the appendix at the end of the chapter.

United in the "Rim Tim Tagi Dim" Rhythm

The performance at the final night of Dora held on 25. 2. 2024 was a combination of dark style and folklore, as Baby Lasagna mentioned in numerous introductory interviews, and delighted the audience in the hall, but also in front of the small screens. The stage performance was designed by dancers Luana Klinčić and Sebastijan Žeželić, who also performed with him at Dora (A.D., 2024b).

"Rim Tim Tagi Dim" won a total of 321 points, of which 247 were audience votes, and officially became Croatia's representative for the Eurovision Song Contest 2024. Although the media hype was present for weeks before the song and video were released, it seems that the performer did not believe in such success until the very end, as evidenced by his first statement after the victory:

> *"Thank you! Thank you all for voting. I've always had the attitude that it's not over until it's over. It's only over when it's over, I didn't even think about winning. I don't know if I'll be able to sleep tonight. It was just always important to me that we did our best and that I could sleep later that night that I had done my best - he said in shock after the announcement." (Ćuk, 2024).*

Let us recall that 203 songs were submitted to the Eurovision Song Contest 2024, which a six-member jury had to select and choose the best ones. That year, changes were also recorded in the voting system; so, in addition to the national jury gathered in the regional centers of 4 large Croatian cities (Zagreb, Osijek, Split and Rijeka), an international jury also had the right to vote, namely four international juries – Iceland, Italy, Germany and Ukraine (Ćuk, 2024).

"Rim Tim Tagi Dim" soon became a virtual challenge on the popular social network Tik Tok, where users tried to dance a part of this dynamic and somewhat demanding choreography. From ordinary citizens, pupils, students, artists, members of the creative industries, members of emergency services (police, firefighters), to local politicians and Croatian MEPs – everyone published video content from the comfort of their homes, workplaces and beautiful destinations in Croatian cities, thus contributing to the creation of a large virtual postcard and support for the Croatian representative (A.D., 2024b).

The US Ambassador in Croatia in 2024, Nathalie Rayes, publicly supported Baby Lasagna by dancing to his song, which was shared on official social media, signaling diplomatic support for Croatian culture. Croatian embassies, such as the one in Ireland (mvep.gov.hr, 2024), promoted Baby Lasagna concerts and performances among the diplomatic corps and local audiences, using his popularity to enhance Croatia's cultural profile abroad and engage both the Croatian diaspora and the local population.

Additional euphoria was raised by announcements from media outlets such as the Daily Mail about the status of the favorite, as well as the fact that Baby Lasagna was named the best solo artist at the ESC (L.M.B., 2024), and according to fans, his song is the best. Although he was a step away from victory, it was won by the Swiss Nemo with the song “Code”. However, the second place he won did not disappoint Baby Lasagna, as evidenced by these statements:

> „- I'm surprised at how happy I am. I thought I would be sadder, like we lost, but I'm not sad at all, I'm really happy" (Rožman, 2024)
> „ - On the Eurovision stage it was great and I'm really glad that, after all, all of us in the team agreed that we really gave our best. We couldn't have done better at this moment. We didn't screw anything up, everything was done exactly as we imagined, as it should have been. We won't lie down now with thoughts 'maybe it would have been better if we had done it that way'. No, we did the best." (Rožman, 2024).

After the competition, Croatia organized a grand reception in the main city square, which was widely covered by the media and highlighted by diplomats as a symbol of national unity and pride. The event was used as a diplomatic event to showcase the Croatian cultural scene and the enthusiasm of its people for individuals who have achieved significant international achievements.

The audience's support for him is evidenced by the You're a Vision award for the most memorable Eurovision costume (Index Magazin, 2024c). The combination of lace and leather quickly became a new clothing trend, but also an indicator of the deeper story that the entire performance conveys.

What story does Baby Lasagna tell? - Promoting Croatia in the World

The role of the media in the global recognition of the country is unavoidable, and Croatia relied mainly on natural beauty and athletes such as Luka Modrić (40) and Joško Gvardiol (23). Many agree with the words of the famous Croatian music critic Aleksandar Dragaš that Baby Lasagna did more to promote the country than any politician so far (Furjan, 2024).

The Baby Lasagna effect and the second place at the Eurovision Song Contest were a great advertisement for Croatia, and the music event itself has an impact on the tourism of the countries from which the candidates come. Since this year's Croatian representative was born in Umag (Istria), the aforementioned resulted in the fact that the Croatian National Tourist board (CNTB) put Istrian cities at the center of the promotion, emphasizing ethno-gastronomy and active holidays, expecting an increase in the popularity of rural tourism in Croatia, and 33.3 million impressions were recorded (Furjan, 2024).

Baby Lasagna's success at the Eurovision Song Contest has resulted in increased interest in Croatia on internet search engines. Although this does not necessarily mean interest in visiting the country and does not guarantee success in the context of the tourist season, it can be a significant indicator for taking concrete actions in the context of communication and marketing activities.

"We noticed an increased interest in Croatia at that time, and our partners reported the same, which gives us great hope for the season. It isn't only Sweden, either, but also. Denmark is also interested, with an emphasis on the area around Copenhagen, which has been closely following all of this. We have the largest number of flights to different airports in Croatia from Copenhagen," says Staničić (TotalCroatiaNews.com, 2024).

The video for the song was shot in the rural areas of Istria, where the singer is from, which is just one way to attract fans to this destination. His first performance after the Eurovision Song Contest was in Umag at the SeaStar festival, which is held in partnership with the Croatian Tourist Board, and according to communication experts, there are too few such events that could contribute to the global visibility of Croatia.

The interest in Baby Lasagna is also confirmed by an analysis of Google trends on the day of the Eurovision Song Contest, which, according to the Digital News Report 2024, was conducted by one of the most read and visited Croatian news portals, Index.hr (Newman et al., 2024: 3), and showed that searches for the name of our artist were higher than searches for the music competition itself (ESC).

"His artistic name was searched for the most in the countries of the region, but interest was also great in Austria, Germany, Finland and even Russia, Switzerland and Sweden. As for "related" queries, Google recorded an increase in interest in Dejan Lovren (due to comments about Lasagna and demonism), Kaaria (due to accusations of copying), but also Severina (who appeared on Dora, along with Let 3)." (Indeks Magazin, 2024d)

Croatia's performance at Eurovision 2024 generated more media hype than the previous year, judging by discussions among Eurovision fans on platforms such as Reddit. His performance got people and the media talking about the contest, suggesting an increase in online attention during and after the contest. In addition, Croatia's strong performance and fan favorite status at Eurovision 2024, including winning the audience poll for the first semi-final (Eurovisonfun.com, 2024; Muir, 2024; Savage, 2024), further fueled online engagement and curiosity about Croatia. The rapid increase in fan interest and media coverage around the contest contributed to a rapid and significant increase in Croatia's online visibility (Furjan 2024).

Furthermore, Furjan (2024) confirms that Croatia was significantly more searched for in that period worldwide. This is supported by the claims of the Croatian National Tourist Board (CNTB), which recorded a 32% increase in reach on the social network

Instagram in one week. Specific indicators also refer to the number of arrivals and overnight stays from Scandinavian countries, which were 7% higher (arrivals) and 12% higher (overnight stays) than from Sweden. At the same time, the Croatian National Tourist Board was in continuous contact with the Croatian representative for the Scandinavian market, from which it received confirmation of the growing interest of citizens of Sweden and Denmark in Croatia (Furjan, 2024).

"Rim Tim Tagi Dim" is a song about a young man who is forced to leave his hometown, saying goodbye to his family and a pet cat, and the difficult emotions he deals with, such as anxiety. It is a relevant topic that represents a challenge for many countries in the world and their governments – how to prevent the emigration of young people and stop the extinction of nations. At the same time, there is also the anxiety that many, especially young people, feel due to the uncertain future, parents' and society's expectations of them, which helped to easily identify the national, but also global audience with the key message of the song. His video shows stylized life in the countryside in the interior of Istria, one of the most popular Croatian tourist destinations. He also promoted the cultural customs and gastronomy of the region to which he belongs, tablets as a form of fashion accessory, brought elements of folklore back into public performance (he wears Istrian folk costumes, promotes crocheting as a forgotten skill of our grandmothers), and showed an immense love for animals (cats), whose visual was dominant on the stage as well.

It was mentioned earlier that Croatia is mostly recognized in the world for its natural beauty, culture and sporting achievements, but this event and its result contributed to the integration of all these dimensions. Namely, Baby Lasagna connected music with tradition, heritage, culture and economy, believes Skoko (2024), using the power of social media and contributing to Croatia's recognition in the world. This is also proven by the previously mentioned award for the best Eurovision costume, which united the Croatian tradition of lace with modern fashion expression, creating a unique outfit that is not forgotten. For Skoko, Baby Lasagna is a new brand ambassador of the new generation who very successfully creates the image of Croatia in the world:

> *"Croatia has very few areas where we are number one in Europe or the world, so in addition to athletes, especially football, here is a young man who we can identify with because he is one of us. By chance, he got the opportunity and by doing so he shows this new face of Croatia," Skoko pointed out. (Dnevnik.hr, 2024).*

One of the most famous television reporters in Croatia, Andrija Jarak, thinks similarly, and summed up the Baby Lasagna phenomenon in the following statement:

> *"A guy who writes and composes himself, who is a decent, well-bred young man. With his pure soul and open heart, he has won over so many people. He is the best example of how someone without scandals and without a PR machine can*

succeed in life, and I am especially pleased with that and I think he is truly a phenomenon to whom I wish all the best in life." (Zavišić, 2024).

That Baby Lasagna's success is no coincidence and that this young man will still be talked about is proven by the awards he has received so far in 2025. That Baby Lasagna's success is no coincidence and that this young man will still be talked about is proven by the awards he has received so far in 2025. The first of these, awarded in March 2025, is the Porin discography award, which has been awarded since 1994. It is one of the most prestigious music awards, founded by the Croatian Music Union (HGU), Croatian Radio Television (HRT), and the Croatian Composers' Association (HDS) (Porin, org., 2025). Baby Lasagna won a total of four awards - for Song of the Year, New Artist of the Year, Best Male Vocal Performance for the song "Rim Tim Tagi Dim", as well as for Best Video Number for this song.

Furthermore, Baby Lasagna is also the winner of the Večernjak Rose 2025, awarded in April 2025 in the category of musician of the year. "The most prestigious and oldest media award in Croatia was awarded in eight categories this year, which were: "Digital Rose", "Musician of the Year", "Acting Achievement of the Year", "New Face of the Year", "Radio Show of the Year", "Radio Person of the Year", "Television Show of the Year" and "Television Person of the Year"." (Ćuk, 2024). In the same month, he also received the Pride of Croatia award, which is awarded for the honesty and humanity of individuals who have left their mark with their gestures and behavior in the past year. Baby Lasagna certainly did this by deciding to donate the 50,000 euros awarded by the Government of the Republic of Croatia for Croatia's historic success at the Eurovision Song Contest and the country's extraordinary promotion to those in need.

Baby Lasagna certainly did this by deciding to donate the 50,000 euros awarded by the Government of the Republic of Croatia for Croatia's historic success at the Eurovision Song Contest and the country's extraordinary promotion to those in need. As he wrote in his Instagram post, Baby Lasagna decided to donate the amount as follows: "25,000 euros to the Department of Pediatric Oncology and Hematology with the 'Mladen Ćepulić' Daily Hospital, and the remaining 25,000 to the Insititute of Pediatric Hematology, Oncology and Hematopoietic Stem Cell Transplantation at the Clinical Hospital Center Zagreb." (Grgić, 2025).

Finally, his simplicity and spontaneity in communication earned him the award for Communicator of the Year, as chosen by the Croatian Public Relations Association (HUOJ). Here is how the expert jury explained his nomination for this year's award:

"But he also won the hearts of his fans thanks to his authenticity, immediacy, honesty, simplicity, transparency and friendliness - key qualities that a Communicator of the Year must have. Baby Lasagna, also a public relations student, showed veterans how it's done. Despite his instant star status and sudden popularity,

he remained true to himself - humble, approachable and always available and patient with journalists, even when the pressure was too much." (Huoj.hr, 2025).

CONCLUSION

Storytelling has always been an important ritual in people's everyday lives and their interpersonal communication and socio-cultural connections (Prasetyo, 2017; McKean, 2024). In this, the structure of the story, as well as the communication skills of the storyteller, come to the fore (Arsenault, 2019). Namely, people are attracted to narratives, and this makes storytelling effective for identifying listeners with a story or characters, as well as for strengthening brand recognition. The development of new media and social networks has resulted in a change in the role of the communicator in the communication process, with the control of power on the side of the audience (Lund et al., 2018). At the same time, new technologies have accelerated the distribution of stories by emphasizing speed, interactivity and virality.

Storytelling is not only a marketing tactic, but also a strategic concept that can be applied in organizational communication with the aim of shaping organizational values and identity with the aim of strengthening organizational culture, but also a clearer reception of messages among internal and external stakeholders. In addition, storytelling stands out as a driver of social change and advocacy, helping to mobilize support and raise awareness of various social problems. Furthermore, the role of storytelling is increasingly used in the country branding process. It is a complex multi-stage process that must be well strategically thought out (Anholt, 2007; Skoko, 2009). Namely, country branding encompasses culture, history, socio-political order, as well as the values shared by its inhabitants. Some authors see the process of national branding as a tool for creating the soft power of the state (Felknerová, 2014), a concept that contributes to creating the image of the country in the international environment. Analyzing the reasons for American global dominance and the strength of the American brand, numerous authors highlight culture as one of the most important elements used in creating the soft power of a state (Skoko & Kovačić, 2013; Skoko & Primorac, 2021; Pandžić Skoko, 2023). On the other hand, the weakening of American influence in recent years as a result of growing social polarization and an unstable political climate opens the way for numerous smaller states to strengthen their own potential.

This is also an opportunity for Croatia, whose image is mainly associated with rich culture and natural beauty (Skoko, 2009), and recently with outstanding sporting successes (Leško, 2019; Skoko et al., 2022; Tomić, 2022; Skoko & Frka Petešić, 2023). The image of Croatia as a safe and desirable place to live (Ivanković et al., 2024), which has already been recognized by numerous foreign workers who contribute to the stability of the labor market and economic development, is just one of the competitive advantages that should be better used in the strategic communication of the country's image and identity. A better institutionalized approach (Gotal, 2015; Sinčić Ćorić, 2019) based on the model of other European countries (Germany, Estonia) which, thanks to the synergistic action of representatives of the academic community, branding experts and political actors, have successfully built or transformed national images.

One of the channels for promoting the national image that contributes to the branding of the country is the Eurovision Song Contest (ESC). The popular music competition founded with the symbolic intention of culturally unifying post-war Europe has grown into a global television spectacle that plays a significant political and cultural role in the EU (Falck, 2024). Accompanied by political messages, controversies, and even the occasional scandal, the ESC is primarily a gateway to the international music industry and an excellent promotional channel for most countries (Baker et. al., 2024). The slogan "United in Music" serves as a reminder of the idea of European unity and togetherness, which has never been more important in a world burdened by war conflicts and divisions. Performers who serve as the main actors of cultural diplomacy play a major role in this. In 2024, Croatia was represented at this competition by Baby Lasagna, who won with his song "Rim Tim Tagi Dim". His performance and the media attention he attracted was the motive for a case study analyzing the impact of using storytelling through music with the aim of promoting the country's image using the example of a global music competition such as the ESC. Although quantitative data on the time and extent of the increase in online searches is very limited due to insufficient research on the topic, qualitative data (statements from fan communities and analyses by individual experts in media reports) confirm the increase in online interest in Croatia immediately after the event, which opens new perspectives for future research on this topic.

From a bench player to a winner of the audience's hearts - that's how the Croatian representative's journey could be briefly summarized. The victory at the national competition "Dora", where he performed as an invited reserve, led him to the ESC. That something big was in the works was immediately apparent after the release of the video for the song, which had millions of views on the ESC's official channel, as well as numerous social networks. The infectious rhythm of the lyrics, which speak about the leading problems of today's youth, such as existence, life in multigenerational families, leaving the family home and mental health, have been widely recognized. In addition, the story of a young man from a small country that shows the challenges of life in rural areas, imbued with tradition (Istrian costumes, tablets), gastronomy (food and drink), images of picturesque landscapes of Istrian peninsula that united impressive video content, is one of the best-told stories about Croatia in the form of a music video. An energetic performance at the ESC, during which everyone in the hall was as one, and the second place won became a historic success for Croatia in this music competition that will be difficult to surpass. Finally, we must not forget the communication phenomenon of Baby Lasagna – a modest and self-effacing young man, a student of public relations who was not changed by the sudden media attention and who left us all with numerous life and communication lessons. Simple, spontaneous, authentic, always ready to communicate and joke, are just some of the characteristics that this young man showed in statements before and after the victory, then in numerous posts on social networks, all accompanied by sincere emotions. These are the key ingredients of successful storytelling through music, a medium that we all understand so well and that connects us, and which shows how to build or strengthen a national brand using the example of a spectacle such as the Eurovision Song Contest.

REFERENCES

A. D. (2024a). Baby Lasagna ususret Dori: Bit će toplo i vatreno, hrt.hr. https://magazin.hrt.hr/zabava/baby-lasagna-0-11372792

A. D. (2024b). Rim Tim Tagi Dim izazov osvojio mreže, zaplesali HRT-ovci, Bembo i političari, hrt.hr. https://magazin.hrt.hr/zabava/izazov-1-11400953

Anholt, S. (2003). *Brand New Justice: How branding places and products can help the developing world.* Elsevier Butterworth-Heinemann.

Anholt, S. (2007). *Competitive Identity. The New Brand Management for Nations, Cities and Regions.* Palgrave Macmillan., DOI: 10.1057/9780230627727

Arsenault, N. (2019). The Power of Stories in Tourism. In Jelinčić, D. A., & Mansfeld, Y. (Eds.), *Creating and Managing Experiences in Cultural Tourism* (pp. 173–179). World Scientific., DOI: 10.1142/10809

Baker, C., Atkinson, D., Grabher, B., & Howcroft, M. (2024). *Soft power, cultural relations and conflict through Eurovision and other mega-events: a literature review.* British Council., DOI: 10.57884/MB1H-DT68

Balci, B. (2015). Between ambition and realism. In Agadjanian, A., Jödicke, A., & van der Zweerde, E. (Eds.), *Religion, Nation and Democracy in the South Caucasus* (pp. 255–258). Routledge.

Bebek, V. (2023). Prisjetili smo se svih pobjednika Dore i pronašli stare fotke u arhivi, gloria.hr, https://www.gloria.hr/gl/scena/price/prisjetili-smo-se-svih-pobjednika-dore-i-pronasli-stare-fotke-u-arhivi-15304873

Bekcan, U., & Uz, P. (2021). Evaluation of Eurovision Song Contest as a Cultural Impact Tool. *Tarih Kültür ve Sanat Arastirmalari Dergisi, 10*(1), 84–97. DOI: 10.7596/taksad.v10i1.3009

Benković, Z. (2011). Tisuću i jedna noć konzum-(n)acije. Narodna umjetnost: hrvatski časopis za etnologiju i folkloristiku, 48(2), 63-82 https://hrcak.srce.hr/clanak/111474

Berger, A. A. (1997). *Narratives in popular culture, media and everyday life.* Sage Publications.

Borko, B. (2017). What Lies Underneath the LOVEly Image of sLOVEnia? The construction of Slovenia and its national identity through nation branding on the website “I feel Slovenia”. Master Thesis. Sweden: JÖNKÖPING UNIVERSITY School of Education and Communication. https://www.diva-portal.org/smash/record.jsf?pid=diva2%3A1114834&dswid=-4772

Bovée C. L., & Thill, J. V. (2012). Suvremena poslovna komunikacija. Zagreb: MATE d.o.o.

Bryman, A. (2016). *Social Research Methods* (4th ed.). Oxford University Press Inc., New York.

Butković, H., & Šelo Šabić, S. (2023). The Challenges of Euroscepticism in Croatia. *Ten Years After EU Accession, On-line Journal Modelling the New Europe.*, (42), 81–108. DOI: 10.24193/OJMNE.2023.42.05

Colombo, C. (2024). Who is Baby Lasagna? Meet the Croatia Eurovision 2024 entry. RadioTimes.com., https://www.radiotimes.com/tv/entertainment/baby-lasagna-eurovision-2024-croatia-profile-age-instagram-explained/

CroatiansOnline. (2024) The American ambassador supported Baby Lasagna, watch the video! croatiansonline.com, https://croatiansonline.com/en/American-ambassador-supported-baby-lasagna,-watch-the-video/ 11062025

Croatiaweek (2023). Croatia ranks in Top 5 as best country to live in Europe in 2023, https://www.croatiaweek.com/croatia-ranks-in-top-5-as-best-country-to-live-in-europe-in-2023/#:~:text=%E2%80%9CCroatia%20has%20a%20low%20cost,%2C%20Portugal%2C%20Netherlands%20and%20Slovenia

Ćuk, D. (2024). Baby Lasagna pobijedio je na Dori! Ostao u šoku: 'Hvala svima! Dao sam sve od sebe!', Večernji.hr, https://www.vecernji.hr/showbiz/uskoro-uzivo-veceras-biramo-hrvatskog-predstavnika-na-euroviziji-u-svedskoj-1749082

Dragomir, M., & Túñez López, M. (2024). How public service media are changing in the platform era: A comparative study across four European countries. European Journal of Communication, 39(6), 608-624. (Original work published 2024)DOI: 10.1177/02673231241290062

Dnevnik.hr. (2024). Komunikacijski stručnjak o uspjehu Baby Lasagne: "To je europski fenomen, Hrvatska zbog njega konačno ima priliku...". dnevnik.hr. https://dnevnik.hr/vijesti/hrvatska/bozo-skoko-komentirao-marketinski-potencijal-hrvatske-zbog-uspjeha-baby-lasagne---848248.html

Domazet, I., & Hanić, A. (2012). "Promotion of Serbian Natinal Image in the Light of EU Accession," Book Chapters. In Teixeira, P., Duarte, A. P., Redzepagic, S., & Eric, D. (Eds.), *European Integration Process in Western Balkan Countries* (1st ed., Vol. 1, pp. 58–607). Institute of Economic Sciences.

Enciklopedija.hr. (2025). Pejačević, Dora, enciklopedija.hr. https://enciklopedija.hr/clanak/pejacevic-dora

Eurosong.hr. (2025). Dora. eurosong.hr. https://eurosong.hr/povijest/povijest-dore/uvod-u-doru/#:~:text=Prva%20takva%20promjena%20dogodila%20se,Dore%20nastavila%20se%20i%202001

Eurovisionfun.com. (2024). Croatia: Baby Lasagna wins SF1 Eurovision Audience Poll! eurovisionfun.com https://eurovisionfun.com/en/2024/05/croatia-baby-lasagna-wins-sf1-eurovision-audience-poll/

Falck, C. (2024). European Media's Role in Nation Branding: A Case Study of Swedish and British Coverage of Ukraine's 2016 and 2022 Eurovision Participation. Södertörn University, School of Social Sciences, Journalism. https://www.diva-portal.org/smash/record.jsf?pid=diva2%3A1867332&dswid=1319

Fan, Y. (2006). Branding the Nation: What is Being Branded? *Journal of Vacation Marketing*, *12*(1), 5–14.

Felknerová, P. (2014). Nation Branding as a Soft Power Building Tool. The Case of Germany. Master Thesis. Praha: Univerzita Karlova v Praha. https://dspace.cuni.cz/bitstream/handle/20.500.11956/61185/DPTX_2012_1_11230_0_322674_0_128374.pdf?sequence=1

Fergusson, N. (2004). *Colossus: The Price of America's Empire*. Penguin Press.

Filipović, L. (2018). 'Predsjednica radi dobru stvar, Hrvatsku treba brendirati, samo smo mi crni u glavi', tportal.hr. https://www.tportal.hr/biznis/clanak/predsjednica-radi-dobru-stvar-hrvatsku-treba-brendirati-samo-smo-mi-crni-u-glavi-foto-20181101/print

Fisher, D., & Smith, S. (2011). Cocreation is chaotic: What it means for marketing when no one has control. *Marketing Theory*, *11*(3), 325–350.

Fricker, K., & Gluhovic, M. (2013). Introduction: Eurovision and the 'new' Europe, 10. In Fricker, K., & Gluhovic, M. (Eds.), *Performing the 'New' Europe: Identities, Feelings, and Politics in the Eurovision Song Contest*. Palgrave Macmillan.

Furjan, M. (2024). Koliko je Baby Lasagna utjecao na promociju Hrvatske? Evo što kaže HTZ, index.hr. https://www.index.hr/magazin/clanak/koliko-je-baby-lasagna-utjecao-na-promociju-hrvatske-evo-sto-kaze-htz/2565013.aspx

Georgiou, M. (2008). "In the End, Germany will Always Resort to Hot Pants": Watching Europe Singing, Constructing the Stereotype. *Popular Communication*, *6*(3), 141–154. DOI: 10.1080/15405700802198188

Giles, D. (2003). *Media Psychology, 1 st edition*. Routledge.

Gotal, M. (2015). Kulturna diplomacija Republike Hrvatske, Polemos: časopis za interdisciplinarna istraživanja rata i mira, XVIII(36), 141-162. https://hrcak.srce.hr/clanak/231005

Grgić, D. (2025). Baby Lasagna je Ponos Hrvatske, hrt.hr, https://magazin.hrt.hr/price-iz-hrvatske/baby-lasagna-je-ponos-hrvatske-12105189

Grmuša, T., & Mori, H. (2020). The Role of Stereotypes in the Creation of National Image: The Image of Croatia held by Japanese People. *Communication Management Review.*, *5*(1), 26–47. DOI: 10.22522/cmr20200154

Grmuša, T., Tomulić, A. M., & Anđelić, V. (2020). Uloga strateškog komuniciranja u brendiranju turističke destinacije na primjeru Međimurske županije. In Peručić, D., Lekić, R., & Dabo, K. (Eds.), *U potrazi za zajedničkim nazivnikom: komunikacija, turizam, nacionalna kultura i brend* (pp. 26–41). Veleučilište Edward Bernays.

Grubiša, D. (2012). Hrvatski referendum za Europsku uniju: anatomija zakašnjelog (ne)uspjeha. Politička misao: časopis za politologiju. 49(2), 45-72.

Güvendik, E. (2020). Music in Political Culture: The Eurovision Song Contest. Etnomüzikoloji Dergisi/Ethnomusicology Journal, 3(1), 96-103.

Hill, A. (2023). *Digital Storytelling and Ethics. Collaborative Creation and Facilitation.* Routledge.

Hocking, B. (2013). The ministry of foreign affairs and the national diplomatic system. In Kerr, P., & Wiseman, G. (Eds.), *Diplomacy in a Globalizing World: Theories and Practices* (pp. 123–140). Oxford University Press.

Hou, D. (2024). Origin and Development: History of Storytelling. *Dean & Francis*, *1*(9), 1–4. DOI: 10.61173/xkvvf133

HUOJ. (2025). Izaberite najboljeg Komunikatora 2024., istaknite Antikomunikaciju godine! huoj.hr. https://www.huoj.hr/magazin/vijesti/izaberite-najboljeg-komunikatora-istaknutite-antikomunikaciju-godine/

I. B. (2024). Baby Lasagna ruši rekorde: Njegov nastup na Dori sada je najgledaniji, tportal.hr. https://www.tportal.hr/showtime/clanak/baby-lasagna-rusi-rekorde-njegov-nastup-na-dori-sada-je-najgledaniji-foto-20240224

Index Magazin. (2024a). Nastup Baby Lasagne na Dori skupio 3 milijuna pregleda, na kladionicama ima 19 posto, index.hr. https://www.index.hr/magazin/clanak/nastup-baby-lasagne-na-dori-skupio-3-milijuna-pregleda-na-kladionicama-ima-19-posto/2549231.aspx

Index Magazin. (2024b). "Cijela dvorana je pjevala s njim": Ovo su komentari na nastup Baby Lasagne, index.hr, https://www.index.hr/magazin/clanak/cijela-dvorana-je-pjevala-s-njim-ovo-su-komentari-na-nastup-baby-lasagne/2563038.aspx

Index Magazin. (2024c). Baby Lasagna dobio još jedno priznanje fanova Eurosonga, evo o čemu se radi, index.hr. https://www.index.hr/magazin/clanak/baby-lasagna-osvojio-nagradu-obozavatelja-za-najbolji-kostim-na-eurosongu/2566384.aspx

Index Magazin. (2024d). Ovaj graf s Googlea najbolje pokazuje koliko je Baby Lasagna zainteresirao svijet, index.hr. https://www.index.hr/magazin/clanak/ovaj-graf-s-googlea-najbolje-pokazuje-koliko-je-baby-lasagna-zainteresirao-svijet/2542852.aspx

Ismayilov, M. (2012). State, identity, and the politics of music: Eurovision and nation-building in Azerbaijan. *Nationalities Papers*, *40*(6), 833–851. DOI: 10.1080/00905992.2012.742990

Ivanković, J., Mitrović, M., & Plantić Tadić, D. (2024). Analysis of the Perception of the Republic of Croatia as a Brand: Recommendations for Developing a Nation Branding Strategy. Suvremene teme: međunarodni časopis za društvene i humanističke znanosti, 15(1), 59-77 DOI: 10.46917/st.15.1.3

Jagodzinski, K. (2025). Global Soft Power Index 2025: The shifting balance of global Soft Power. brandfinance.com. https://brandfinance.com/insights/global-soft-power-index-2025-the-shifting-balance-of-global-soft-power

Jambrač, J. (2020). Croatian Post-Socialist Transition or Transformation: Lost in Translation. *HKJU-CCPA*, *20*(4), 649–676.

Jelinčić, D. A. (2019). Creating Experiences in Cultural Tourism: From Sightseeing to Engaged Emotional Action. In In Jelinčić, D. A., & Mansfeld, Y. (Eds.), *Creating and Managing Experiences in Cultural Tourism* (pp. 3–17). World Scientific., DOI: 10.1142/10809

Jordan, P. (2015). The Modern Fairy Tale: Nation Branding, National Identity and the Eurovision Song Contest in Estonia. European Journal of Communication, 30(1), 118. (Original work published 2015)DOI: 10.1177/0267323114567273k

Jugo, D., Skoko, B., & Petrović, M. (2021). Krizno komuniciranje u Hrvatskoj 2020.: izvori informacija, povjerenje u institucije i meka moć država. Sociologija i prostor: časopis za istraživanje prostornoga i sociokulturnog razvoja, 59 (3, 222), 349-370. , https://hrcak.srce.hr/clanak/393693DOI: 10.5673/sip.59.3.1

Kampmann, A., & Pedell, B. (2022). Using storytelling to promote organizational resilience: An experimental study of different forms of risk communication. Schmalenbach Journal of Business Research (SBUR), ISSN 2366-6153, Springer, Heidelberg, 74(4), 695-725. DOI: 10.1007/s41471-022-00143-x

Kersan-Škabić, I., & Tomić, D. (2009). Prepoznavanje euroskepticizma u Hrvatskoj – studija istraživanja stavova studentske populacije, Economic research -. *Ekonomska Istrazivanja*, *22*(4), 100–117.

Klasnić, K., & Rukavina, I. (2011). Što utječe na sliku Hrvatske u inozemstvu? Mišljenja građana Republike Hrvatske. Socijalna ekologija: journal for environmental thought and sociological research = Socijalna ekologija: Zeitschrift für Umweltgedanken und soziologische. *Forschung*, *20*(2), 131–145. https://hrcak.srce.hr/clanak/105385

Kuyucu, M. (2011). *Türkiye'nin Eurovision Serüveni*. Esen Kitap.

Labaš, D., & Grmuša, T. (2011). Istinitost i objektivnost u informaciji i društveno štetne komunikacijske forme. Kroatologija: časopis za hrvatsku kulturu Fakulteta hrvatskih studija Sveučilišta u Zagrebu, 2(2), 87-121.

Leško, L. (2019). Pregled nacionalnih modela sportske diplomacije u svijetu i perspektiva razvoja hrvatskog modela sportske diplomacije. Političke perspektive: časopis za istraživanje politike, 9(1): 87-108. , https://hrcak.srce.hr/clanak/331381DOI: 10.20901/pp.9.1.04

Lippmann, W. (2007). *Public opinion*. NuVision. (Original work published 1922)

L.M.B. (2024). Kakva čast: Baby Lasagna osvojio je nagradu za najbolju pjesmu Eurosonga! tportal.hr. https://www.tportal.hr/showtime/clanak/kakva-cast-baby-lasagna-osvojio-je-nagradu-za-najbolju-pjesmu-eurosonga-foto-20240509

Lund, F. N., Cohen, S. A., & Scarles, C. (2018). The power of social media storytelling in destination branding. *Journal of Destination Marketing & Management*, *8*, 271–280.

McKean, M. (2024). The power of storytelling in communications: Maximising impact with logic and emotion. drpgroup.com. https://www.drpgroup.com/en/blog/the-power-of-storytelling-in-communications-maximising-impact-with-logic-and-emotion

MVEP.GOV.HR. (2024). Baby Lasagna played in Dublin, mvep.gov.hr, https://mvep.gov.hr/news-100537/baby-lasagna-played-in-dublin/275166

Milenković, V. & Stamenković, S. (2013). Performans između spektakla i umjetnosti. In medias res, 2 (2), 148-161.

Milišić, R. (1997). *Čija je Amerika?* Izvori.

Miletić, M. (2003). *Menadžment medija.* FMMSP.

Morgan, N., & Pritchard, A. (2004). Meeting the destination branding challenge. In Morgan, N., Pritchard, A., & Pride, R. (Eds.), *Destination Branding, Creating the unique destination proposition.* Elsevier Butterworth-Heinemann.

Morić, D. A. (2025). Ksenija Urličić samo za tportal: ' Dora se vratila doma, ondje gdje pripada', tportal.hr. Retrieved March 2, 2025, from https://www.tportal.hr/showtime/clanak/ksenija-urlicic-samo-za-tportal-pobijedit-ce-huljic-foto-20250302

Mucundorfeanu, M. (2017). *The Creative Process Behind the Advertising Discourse.* Hochschulverlag Mittweida, Mittweida.

Mucundorfeanu, M. (2018). The Key Role of Storytelling in the Branding Process. [Babe -Bolyai University.]. *The Journal of Medical Research, 11*(1 (30)). DOI: 10.24193/jmr.30.3

Muir, E. (2024). Eurovision fans proclaim Croatia's Baby Lasagna favourite to win. Independent.co.uk., https://www.independent.co.uk/arts-entertainment/eurovision/baby-lasagna-eurovision-song-who-marko-purisic-b2543530.html

Murray, S. (2018). *Sport Diplomacy, origins, theory and practice.* Routledge: Taylor & Francis.

Newman, N., & Fletcher, R. Robertson, Craig, T., Arguedas, A. R. & Nielsen, R. K. (2024). Reuters Institute Digital News Report 2024. Oxford: Reuters Institute for the Study of Journalism. DOI: 10.60625/risj-vy6n-4v57

Novčić Korać, B., Damnjanović, V., & Popesku, M. (2012). Serbia brand identity: Perspectives of residents and diaspora. *EuroMed Journal of Business, 7*(3), 256–267. DOI: 10.1108/14502191211265316

Novčić Korać, B., Bradić Martinović, A., & Miletić, B. (2020). Constructing a nation branding model: The case of Serbia. *Geographica Pannonica, 24*(4), 311–324. DOI: 10.5937/gp24-28279

Noy, C. (2012). Narratives and counter-narratives: Contesting a tourist site in Jerusalem, In J. Tivers & T. Rakić (eds.), Narratives of Travel and Tourism (pp. 135-150). England: Ashgate publishing limited.

Noya, J. (2006). The symbolic power of nations. *Place Branding and Public Diplomacy*, *2*(1), 53–67.

Nye, J. S. (2004). *Soft Power: The Means to Success in World Politics*. PublicAffairs.

Nye, J. S. (2009). Get smart. Combining Hard and Soft Power. *Foreign Affairs*, *88*(4), 160–163.

O'Neill, J. W. (2002). The Role of Storytelling in Affecting Organizational Reality in the Strategic Management Process. *Journal of Behavioral and Applied Management*, *4*(1), 4–18.

Perić, N. (2011). Branding the State and the Nation (the case of the Republic of Serbia). *Technics Technologies Education Management*, *6*(2), 361–367.

Popović, G., Grmuša, T., & Prpić, H. (2011). Izvještavanje o Europskoj uniji u hrvatskim dnevnim novinama: Završetak hrvatskih pristupnih pregovora. *Informatologia*, *44*(4), 309–322.

Popović, G., Grmuša, T. & Popović, M. (2013). Awareness of European Union and Completion of Croatia's Accesion Negotiation Among University Students. Informatologia 46(2), 122-138.Reardon, K. K. (1986). Interpersonal Communication: Where Minds Meet. Wadsworth Pub Co.

Rocco, F. (1993). *Rječnik marketinga*. Masmedia.

Ruzzier, M. K., & Petek, N. (2012). Country Brand I Feel Slovenia:First Response from Locals. *Economic Research-Ekonomska Istraživanja*, *25*(2), 465–484. DOI: 10.1080/1331677X.2012.11517518

Pandžić Skoko, M. (2023). Uspon i pad američkog sna kao ključnog aduta meke moći Sjedinjenih Američkih Država, Communication. *Management Review*, *1*(8), 6–29. https://hrcak.srce.hr/clanak/442191. DOI: 10.22522/cmr20220183

Porin, org. (2025). Utemeljitelji Porina https://www.porin.org/?q=content/utemeljitelji-porina

Prasetyo, Y. (2017). From Storytelling to Social Change: The Power of Story in the Community Building. *SSRN*: https://ssrn.com/abstract=3094947 , DOI: 10.2139/ssrn.3094947

Pertiwi, E., & Sanusi, P. A. (2023). Storytelling in the Digital Age: Examining the Role and Effectiveness in Communication Strategies of Social Media Content Creators? *Palakka Media and Islamic Communication*, *4*(1), 25–34. DOI: 10.30863/palakka.v4i1.5082

Rosenberg, T. (2020). Rising Like the Eurovision Song Contest: On Kitsch, Camp, and Queer Culture. *Lambda Nordica, 25*(2), 93–113. DOI: 10.34041/ln.v25.676

Rožman, K. (2024). Baby Lasagna o finalu, pobjedniku Nemu, bodovima žirija... 'Ponosan sam, dali smo najbolje od sebe', jutarnji.hr. https://www.jutarnji.hr/scena/domace-zvijezde/baby-lasagna-o-finalu-pobjedniku-nemu-bodovima-zirija-ponosan-sam-dali-smo-najbolje-od-sebe-15459730

Sammer, P. (2015). Storytelling. Die Zukunft von PR und Marketing, dpunkt. verlag, Heidelberg.

Savage, M. (2024). Eurovision 2024: Your guide to all 37 songs. bbc.com, https://www.bbc.com/news/articles/crgy7l6er7vo

Simmonds, L. (2024). Baby Lasagna boosts Croatian Tourism, Total-Croatia-News.com, Retrieved June 12, 2025, from https://total-croatia-news.com/news/baby-lasagna-boosts-croatian-tourism/ 10062025

Sinčić Ćorić, D. (2019, May). Branding Croatia Project. Paper presented at Communication Management Forum. Zagreb: Edward Bernays University of Applied Sciences.

Skoko, B. (2009). Država kao brend. Upravljanje nacionalnim identitetom. Zagreb: Matica hrvatska.

Skoko, B., & Kovačić, V. (2009). Koncept meke moći država i njegova primjena na Republiku Hrvatsku. Polemos: časopis za interdisciplinarna istraživanja rata i mira, XII (23), 29-49. https://hrcak.srce.hr/clanak/73543

Skoko, B. (2012). *The Image of Bosnia and Herzegovina and its Citizens in Croatia and Serbia*. Friedrich Ebert Stiftung.

Skoko, B. (2017). Communication Strategies and Branding Attempts of Selected Countries Created upon the Disintegration of the Former Yugoslavia. Sociologija i prostor: časopis za istraživanje prostornoga i sociokulturnog razvoja, 55(1), 5-31.DOI: 10.5673/sip.55.1.1

Skoko, B., & Hlača, A. (2020). Šport kao meka moć države: važnost športske diplomacije na primjeru Hrvatske. South Eastern European Journal of Communication, 2(2), 7-20. , https://hrcak.srce.hr/clanak/359865DOI: 10.47960/2712-0457.2020.2.2.7

Skoko, B., & Primorac, M. (2021). Filmska industrija kao segment meke moći država na primjeru Južne Koreje, Kine i SAD-a. South Eastern European Journal of Communication, 3(2), 7-20., , https://hrcak.srce.hr/clanak/397993DOI: 10.47960/2712-0457.2021.2.3.7

Skoko, B., Ježovita, J., & Plenković, M. (2022). Imidž Hrvatske iz perspektive hrvatskih iseljenika i njihovih potomaka u različitim dijelovima svijeta. Kroatologija: časopis za hrvatsku kulturu Fakulteta hrvatskih studija Sveučilišta u Zagrebu, 13(1-2): 167-187. https://hrcak.srce.hr/clanak/408046

Skoko, B., & Frka Petešić, Z. (2023). *Hrvatska u 30 priča*. Naklada Ljevak.

Stasiak, A. (2019). Creating Tourism Experiences — Theoretical Foundations. In Jelinčić, D. A., & Mansfeld, Y. (Eds.), *Creating and Managing Experiences in Cultural Tourism* (pp. 17–41). World Scientific., DOI: 10.1142/10809

Suvremena.hr. (2019). Završen CommForum2019: Kontinuirano brendiranje ključ je za podizanje prepoznatljivosti Hrvatske u svijetu. suvremena.hr. https://suvremena.hr/zavrsen-commforum2019-kontinuirano-brendiranje-kljuc-je-za-podizanje-prepoznatljivosti-hrvatske-u-svijetu/

Šarčević, A. (2023). Sjećate li ih se? Ovo su svi pobjednici Dore od 1993. godine, 24sata.hr. https://www.24sata.hr/show/sjecate-li-ih-se-ovo-su-svi-pobjednici-dore-od-1993-godine-890604

Təlišman-Košuta, N. (2017). Shaping Destination Identity: Challenges of Branding Croatia. In Dwyer, L., Tomljenović, R., & Čorak, S. (Eds.), *Evolution of Destination Planning and Strategy: The Rise of Tourism in Croatia* (pp. 67–78). The Palgrave Macmillan.

Tomić, I. (2022). Sportska diplomacija. South Eastern European Journal of Communication, 4(1), 45-55., , https://hrcak.srce.hr/clanak/411792DOI: 10.47960/2712-0457.2022.1.4.45

Tuđman, M. (2013). Izvještajne službe i meka moć. National Security and the Future 14(1), 9-22, https://hrcak.srce.hr/clanak/185535

V. G. (2025). Godina obilježavanja 1100. obljetnice Hrvatskoga Kraljevstva, hrt.hr. https://magazin.hrt.hr/kultura/godina-obiljezavanja-1100-obljetnice-hrvatskoga-kraljevstva-11940320

Večernji.hr (2024). Stranci o Baby Lasagni: 'Pošaljite njega na Euroviziju, molim vas', večernji.hr, https://www.vecernji.hr/showbiz/baby-lasagna-na-youtubeu-je-najgledaniji-iz-drugog-polufinala-a-evo-sto-o-njemu-kazu-stranci-1748895

Varlaj, S., Grmuša, T., & Vuković, D. (2021). The Role of Corporate Values and Corporate Culture in the Untypical Times of the Covid-19 Pandemic // 3rd International conference on decision making for small and medium-sized enterprises: conference proceedings. Opava: Karviná: Silesian University in Opava, School of Business Administration in Karviná, 2021. p. 672-680.

Von Stackerberg, P., & Jones, R. E. (2014). Tales of Our Tomorrows: Transmedia Storytelling and Communicating About the Future. *Journal of Futures Studies, 18*(3), 57–76. https://jfsdigital.org/wp-content/uploads/2014/04/183-A05.pdf

Vuletic, D. (2018). *Postwar Europe and the Eurovision Song Contest.* Blooms-bury Academic.

Wimmer, R. D., & Dominick, J. R. (2014). Mass Media Research An Introduction. 10th Edition, Wadsworth, Cengage Learning, Boston.

Zavišić, S. (2024). Andrija Jarak o bodovima Eurosong žirija: 'Nisam teoretičar zavjere, ali jedna stvar se nikad prije nije dogodila', jutarnji.hr, https://www.jutarnji.hr/scena/domace-zvijezde/andrija-jarak-o-bodovima-eurosong-zirija-nisam-teoreticar-zavjere-ali-jedna-stvar-se-nikad-prije-nije-dogodila-15461259?cx_linkref=jl_ia_vezane

Zgurić, B. (2021). Politički i društveno-kulturni narativi u turskim serijama: između nenamjernog instrumenta meke moći i tihog oružja za vođenje kulturnog rata? Anali Hrvatskog politološkog društva: časopis za politologiju, 18(1), 233-254. DOI: 10.20901/an.18.05

Zimand-Sheiner, D., & (Hilik)Limor, Y. (2017). The exodus myth in commercial advertisements in Israeli secular and religious printed press 1948–2008. *Israel Affairs, 23*(5), 808–827. DOI: 10.1080/13537121.2017.1343861

Zimand-Sheiner, D. (2024). Four Dimensions of Brand Storytelling: Framework for Managing and Analyzing Online Brand Stories. *International Journal of Business Communication, 0*(0). DOI: 10.1177/23294884241261362

KEY TERMS AND DEFINITIONS

Baby Lasagna: real name Marko Purišić. Croatian representative at the ESC 2024, who won second place in a tense final with the song 'Rim Tim Tagi Dim', thus ensuring Croatia's historic success at this competition.

Country branding: managing a country's image and reputation to ensure competitive advantage and global recognition.

Croatia: the youngest member of the European Union, a country that in its 30 years of existence as an independent democratic state has gone through a transformational path from NATO membership to EU membership. A leader in Southeast Europe, a dominantly positive image based on a rich cultural heritage, natural beauty, individuals who have indebted the world with their inventions and sporting successes.

Dora: a music competition in Croatia that selects the national representative for the Eurovision Song Contest. It is held and organized by the public broadcasting service (HRT). It is named after the famous Croatian composer Dora Pejačević.

Eurovision Song Contest (ESC): a music competition to select the best song in Europe. Founded in 1956 as an attempt to culturally unify Europe after World War II, it has grown into a global television spectacle that brings together the masses and contributes to strengthening interculturalism, communication and togetherness.

Identity: the image we have of ourselves. We distinguish between personal, business, organizational and national identity.

Image: the image that others create of us as an individual, organization, and country.

Promotion: one of the basic marketing activities aimed at increasing the visibility of a product/service/person/country/brand and raising awareness about it.

Soft power: the concept of influencing others to induce desired behavioral outcomes. It is used in the process of branding a country and its international positioning.

Storytelling: a form of communication that relies on the use of stories and visuals that stimulate the listener's imagination and emotions. Today, it has multiple possibilities of use: communication, marketing, political.

ENDNOTE

1 Combined metholodology for leading the group disscussions (scenario planning, branding, mrketing, organisational psychology), small group discussions, plennary discussions, matrix-analaysis, mind-mappiing, story-telling technique and competitive analysis, Capstone's model and Brand Key model for nation brands, On spot analysis, instant documentation of the process, qualitative and quantitative research methodlogy and external review (Sinčić Ćorić, 2019).

APPENDIX

Below are fan comments on Baby Lasagna's performance at the Eurovision Song Contest 2024:

"Croatia, please. This is your first win, don't screw up. Let's go Baby Lasagna - said one fan." (Večernji.hr, 2024).

„ "Baby Lasagna is the favorite. The winner", "I don't know what the others were like, but Baby Lasagna was great. And the whole hall sings with him. Bravo!" and "I heard the audience all the way to Greece", are some of the comments from fans." (Index Magazin, 2024b).

"Rim Tim Tagi Dim is so special. Baby Lasagna for the win," (Muir, 2024)

"Croatia. Baby Lasagna. Silly lyrics. Silly outfits. Silly staging. Very catchy. Very Eurovision." (Muir, 2024)

Compilation of References

10Haber. (2023, July 23). CHP yönetimi ile Halk TV'nin kavgası büyüyor. https://10haber.net/siyaset/chp-ile-halk-tv-arasindaki-gerilim-buyuyor-program-iptal-edildi-223265/

A. D. (2024a). Baby Lasagna ususret Dori: Bit će toplo i vatreno, hrt.hr. https://magazin.hrt.hr/zabava/baby-lasagna-0-11372792

A. D. (2024b). Rim Tim Tagi Dim izazov osvojio mreže, zaplesali HRT-ovci, Bembo i političari, hrt.hr. https://magazin.hrt.hr/zabava/izazov-1-11400953

Aaker, D. A. (1991). *Managing Brand Equity: Capitalizing on the Value of a Brand Name*. Free Press.

Aaker, D. A. (1996). *Building strong brands*. Free Press.

Aaker, D. A. (1996). Measuring Brand Equity across Products and Markets. *California Management Review*, *38*(3).

Aaker, D. A. (2004). *Brand portfolio strategy: Creating relevance, differentiation, energy, leverage, and clarity*. Simon and Schuster.

AB 101: Historical figures in generative art — A. Michael Noll (2022, January 8). https://medium.com/the-link-art-blocks/ab-101-historical-figures-in-generative-art-a-michael-noll-5a23ea78ac41

AB 101: Historical figures in generative art — Georg Nees (2021, December 5). https://medium.com/the-link-art-blocks/ab-101-historical-figures-in-generative-art-georg-nees-6b006e62126a

AB 101: Historical figures in generative art — Herbert W. Franke (2022, January 30). https://medium.com/the-link-art-blocks/ab-101-historical-figures-in-generative-art-herbert-w-franke-48911e977096

Adams, G., Estrada-Villalta, S., Sullivan, D., & Markus, H. R. (2019). The psychology of neoliberalism and the neoliberalism of psychology. *The Journal of Social Issues*, *75*(1), 189–216. https://psycnet.apa.org/doi/10.1111/josi.12305. DOI: 10.1111/josi.12305

Ailawadi, K. L., & Keller, K. L. (2004). Understanding retail branding: Conceptual insights and research priorities. *Journal of Retailing*, *80*(4), 331–342.

Akbay, B. (2021-present). Refik Anadol'la makine hatıraları sergi turu [machine memories with Refik Anadol exhibition tour]. YouTube. https://www.youtube.com/watch?v=-_gTYr_zFT4 (In Turkish)

Akın, L. (2014). Jenerik Marka İsimlerin Oluşumu ve TDK Sözlüğüne Giriş Şekilleri, Uluslararası Sosyal Araştırmalar Dergisi, Cilt: 7, Sayı: 31.

Albalawi, Y., & Sixsmith, J. (2015). Agenda setting for health promotion: Exploring an adapted model for the social media era. *JMIR Public Health and Surveillance*, *1*(2), e21. Advance online publication. DOI: 10.2196/publichealth.5014 PMID: 27227139

Alexander, B. (2011). *The New Digital Storytelling: Creating Narratives with New Media*. Praeger. DOI: 10.5040/9798216979456

Allbirds. (2025). Mother nature made us do it. https://www.allbirds.com/pages/our-story

Almakaty, S. (2025). *A comprehensive and critical literature review on framing theory in the digital media age. Preprints.* https://www.preprints.org/manuscript/202504.1728/v1

Alqahtani, M. M., Alanazi, A. M., Algarni, S. S., Aljohani, H., Alenezi, F. K., Alotaibi, T. F., & Ismaeil, T. T. (2024). Unveiling the Influence of AI on Advancements in Respiratory Care: Narrative Review. *Interactive Journal of Medical Research*, *13*(1), e57271. DOI: 10.2196/57271 PMID: 39705080

Althusser, L. (2003). *İdeoloji ve devletin ideolojik aygıtları*. İthaki Publishing.

Althusser, L. (2019). *Devletin ideolojik aygıtları* (Tümertekin, A., Trans.). İthaki Publications.

Altun, F. (2006). *M. McLuhan ve J. Baudrillard'ın medya kuramlarının karşılaştırmalı çözümlemesi* [Comparative analysis of the media theories of M. McLuhan and J. Baudrillard] [Doctoral thesis] Istanbul University Social Sciences Enstitute, İstanbul. https://nek.istanbul.edu.tr/ekos/TEZ/41475.pdf

AMA. (2025). Branding. https://www.ama.org/topics/brand-and-branding/

Anadolu Ajansı, A. (2024). *Muhabir*. Anadolu Ajansı.

Andrade, R. F. C. (2021). *Luxury brand communication on social media. Management with Specialization in Marketing, at the Universidade Católica*. Portuguesa.

Anholt, S. (2003). *Brand New Justice: How branding places and products can help the developing world*. Elsevier Butterworth-Heinemann.

Anholt, S. (2006). *Competitive identity: The new brand management for nations, cities and regions*. Palgrave Macmillan.

Anholt, S. (2007). *Competitive Identity. The New Brand Management for Nations, Cities and Regions*. Palgrave Macmillan., DOI: 10.1057/9780230627727

Arendt, H. (1963). *Eichmann in Jerusalem: A Report on the Banality of Evil*. Viking Press.

Arendt, H. (1998). *The Human Condition*. University of Chicago Press. DOI: 10.7208/chicago/9780226924571.001.0001

Arsenault, N. (2019). The Power of Stories in Tourism. In Jelinčić, D. A., & Mansfeld, Y. (Eds.), *Creating and Managing Experiences in Cultural Tourism* (pp. 173–179). World Scientific., DOI: 10.1142/10809

Artun, A. (2021, March 29). Refik Anadol ve algoritma sanatı [Refik Anadol and the art of algorithm]. *Skopbülten*. https://www.e-skop.com/skopbulten/refik-anadol-ve-algoritma-sanati/6111

Artun, A. (2011). *Çağdaş Sanatın Örgütlenmesi: Estetik ve Modernizmin Tasfiyesi* [The Organization of Contemporary Art: Aesthetics and the Liquidation of Modernism]. İletişim Publishing.

Aschbrenner, K. A., Naslund, J. A., Tomlinson, E. F., Kinney, A., Pratt, S. I., & Brunette, M. F. (2019). Adolescents' use of digital technologies and preferences for mobile health coaching in public mental health settings. *Frontiers in Public Health*, *7*, 178. DOI: 10.3389/fpubh.2019.00178 PMID: 31312629

Asur, S. A., Huberman, B., Szabo, G., & Wang, C. (2021). Trends in social media: persistence and decay. *Proceedings of the International AAAI Conference on Web and Social Media*, 5(1), 434-437. https://doi.org/DOI: 10.1609/icwsm.v5i1.14167

Atalay, D. G. (2022). Insider Conversations: Film Making in the Age of Digital Media. In Tetik, T., Atalay, D. G., & Ulusoy, N. (Eds.), *Turkish Cinema and Television Industry in the Digital Streaming Era* (pp. 63–72). Peter Lang.

Atam, Z. (2009). Critical Thoughts on the New Turkish Cinema. In Bayrakdar, D., Kotaman, A., & Uğursoy, A. S. (Eds.), *Cinema and Politics: Turkish Cinema and The New Europe* (pp. 202–220). Cambridge Scholars Publishing.

Atik, A. (2006). *Türkiye'de özel televizyon haberciliğinde eğlendiren bilgi süreci ve örnek program Show TV Ana Haber Kuşağı* (Unpublished Doctoral Dissertation). Istanbul University Social Sciences Institute. DÜNYA. (2024, January 25). *FOX TV'den NOW TV'ye geçişin nedeni 71,3 milyar dolarlık anlaşma*. https://www.dunya.com/gundem/fox-tvden-now-tvye-gecisin-nedeni-713-milyar-dolarlik-anlasma-haberi-717941

Avello Martínez, R., Gajderowicz, T., & Gómez Rodríguez, V. G. (2024). Is ChatGPT helpful for graduate students in acquiring knowledge about digital storytelling and reducing their cognitive load? An experiment.

Aytekin, M., & Akar, D. (2018). Cinema and Social Media: Role of Media in Movie Publicities in Turkish Cinema Industry. In Dogan, B. Ö., & Ünlü, D. G. (Eds.), *Handbook of Research on Examining Cultural Policies Through Digital Communication* (pp. 1–30). IGI Global., DOI: 10.4018/978-1-5225-6998-5.ch001

Aziz, A. (2013). *Sosyal Bilimlerde Araştırma Yöntemleri ve Teknikleri*. Nobel.

Bahadır, H., Tüfekci, A., & Çakır, H. (2021). Dijital hikâye anlatımının disiplinlerarası öğretim bağlamında kullanım durumları. *Muğla Sıtkı Koçman Üniversitesi Eğitim Faculty Journal*, *8*(2), 635–654.

Baker, C., Atkinson, D., Grabher, B., & Howcroft, M. (2024). *Soft power, cultural relations and conflict through Eurovision and other mega-events: a literature review*. British Council., DOI: 10.57884/MB1H-DT68

Balci, B. (2015). Between ambition and realism. In Agadjanian, A., Jödicke, A., & van der Zweerde, E. (Eds.), *Religion, Nation and Democracy in the South Caucasus* (pp. 255–258). Routledge.

Bal, D., & Onay, A. (2018). Yeni Medya ve Dijital Hikaye Anlatıcılığının Geleceği. *International Symposium Communication in the Millennium*, 863-875.

Bali, R. (2002). *Tarzı-ı hayattan life style'a yeni seçkinler, yeni mekanlar, yeni yaşamlar*. İletişim Publications.

Bamford. (2015). Ben & Jerry's pushing green message with Save Our Swirled. https://www.thegrocer.co.uk/news/ben-and-jerrys-pushing-green-message-with-save-our-swirled/523992.article

Bansal, G., Nawal, A., Chamola, V., & Herencsar, N. (2024). Revolutionizing visuals: The role of generative AI in modern image generation. *ACM Transactions on Multimedia Computing Communications and Applications*, *20*(11), 1–22. DOI: 10.1145/3689641

Barbosa, B., Simões, D., & Leal, F. (2022). Young adults' views on digital storytelling campaigns. *Innovar (Universidad Nacional de Colombia)*, *32*(83), 63–74.

Barger, R. N. (2008). Introduction. In *Computer Ethics: A Case-based Approach* (pp. 1–15). Cambridge University Press.

Barkman, C. (2024). *Narrative complexity in videogames* [Doctoral dissertation, Swinburne University of Technology]. Swinburne Research Bank.

Baudrillard, J. (1998). *The consumer society*. SAGE Publications Ltd, https://doi .org/, S., & Rivers, I. (2015). *Mental health in the digital age*. Palgrave Macmillan. DOI: 10.4135/9781526401502Bauman

Baudrillard, J. (2004). *Tüketim toplumu. (Trans. H. Deliçaylı ve F.Keskin)*. Ayrıntı Puclications.

Bebek, V. (2023). Prisjetili smo se svih pobjednika Dore i pronašli stare fotke u arhivi, gloria.hr, https://www.gloria.hr/gl/scena/price/prisjetili-smo-se-svih-pobjednika-dore-i-pronasli-stare-fotke-u-arhivi-15304873

Begby, E. (2024). From Belief Polarization to Echo Chambers: A Rationalizing Account. *Episteme (Edinburgh)*, *21*(2), 519–539. DOI: 10.1017/epi.2022.14

Beguš, N. (2024). Experimental narratives: A comparison of human crowdsourced storytelling and ai storytelling. *Humanities & Social Sciences Communications*, *11*(1), 1–22. DOI: 10.1057/s41599-024-03868-8

Beins, B. C. (2008). Why we believe: Fostering critical thought and scientific literacy in research methods. In Dunn, D. S., Halonen, J. S., & Smith, R. A. (Eds.), *Teaching critical thinking in psychology: A handbook of best practices* (pp. 199–210). Wiley Blackwell., DOI: 10.1002/9781444305173.ch17

Bekcan, U., & Uz, P. (2021). Evaluation of Eurovision Song Contest as a Cultural Impact Tool. *Tarih Kültür ve Sanat Arastirmalari Dergisi*, *10*(1), 84–97. DOI: 10.7596/taksad.v10i1.3009

Belda-Medina, J., & Goddard, M. (2024). AI-driven digital storytelling: A strategy for creating English as a foreign language (EFL) materials.

Belova, A. (2021). Storytelling in advertising and branding. *Cognition, Communication. Discourse (Berkeley, Calif.)*, (22), 13–26.

Benjamin, L. T. (1986). Why don't they understand us? A history of psychology's public image. *The American Psychologist, 41*(9), 941–946. DOI: 10.1037/0003-066X.41.9.941 PMID: 17154720

Benković, Z. (2011). Tisuću i jedna noć konzum-(n)acije. Narodna umjetnost: hrvatski časopis za etnologiju i folkloristiku, 48(2), 63-82 https://hrcak.srce.hr/clanak/111474

Berger, A. A. (1997). *Narratives in popular culture, media and everyday life*. Sage Publications.

Berksü, Ö. Z. (2021). Gucci: Bir marka hikayesi. https://www.oggusto.com/moda/markalar-ve-tasarimcilar/gucci-bir-marka-hikayesi

Best, P., Manktelow, R., & Taylor, B. (2014). Online communication, social media and adolescent wellbeing: A systematic narrative review. *Children and Youth Services Review, 41*, 27–36. DOI: 10.1016/j.childyouth.2014.03.001

Beverland, M. (2006). The Freal thing: Branding authenticity in the luxury wine trade. *Journal of Business Research, 59*, 251–258.

Beydâvî. (2013). Beydavî Interpretatşon: Envâru't-Tenzîl ve Esrâru't-Te'vîl. Trans. Abdülvehhab Öztürk. 3. Volume. İstanbul: Kahraman Publishing.

Bilici, S., & Yilmaz, R. M. (2024). The effects of using collaborative digital storytelling on academic achievement and skill development in biology education. *Education and Information Technologies, 29*(15), 20243–20266. DOI: 10.1007/s10639-024-12638-7

Binark, M. (2007). *Yeni Medya Çalışmaları. M. Binark içinde, Yeni Medya Çalışmaları*. Dipnot.

Blackett, T. (2003). What is a Brand? In R. Clifton, & J. Simmons (Ed.), Brands and Branding (ss. 13-26). London: Profile Books.

Blumler, J. G., & Katz, E. (1974). *The uses of mass communications*. Sage Publications., DOI: 10.1086/268277

Bogost, I. (2008). The rhetoric of video games. In Salen, K. (Ed.), *The ecology of games: Connecting youth, games, and learning* (pp. 117–140). MIT Press.

Borko, B. (2017). What Lies Underneath the LOVEly Image of sLOVEnia? The construction of Slovenia and its national identity through nation branding on the website "I feel Slovenia". Master Thesis. Sweden: JÖNKÖPING UNIVERSITY School of Education and Communication. https://www.diva-portal.org/smash/record.jsf?pid=diva2%3A1114834&dswid=-4772

Bostan, B. (2022). Dijital oyunlar ve interaktif anlatı (Digital games and interactive narrative). Press and Publishing Industry and Trade Inc.

Bouchardon, S. (2014). *La Valeur Heuristique De La Littérature Numérique*. Hermann.

Bourdieu, P. (1987). Legitimation and structured interests in Weber's sociology of religion. In Lash, S., & Whimster, S. (Eds.), *Max Weber, rationality and modernity* (Turner, C., Trans.; pp. 119–136). Allen & Unwin.

Bovée C. L., & Thill, J. V. (2012). Suvremena poslovna komunikacija. Zagreb: MATE d.o.o.

Bredava, A. (2021). Why everybody loves M&Ms: A marketing success story of a brand mascot. https://awario.com/blog/mms-marketing-mascot/

Brooks, A. (2023). Popular psychology. In *A suspicious science: The uses of psychology* (pp. 90–157). Academic.

Brownell, J., & Kurtz, Z. (2022). The power of storytelling at patagonia. https://blog.uvm.edu/si-mba/2022/05/27/the-power-of-storytelling-at-patagonia/

Bryman, A. (2016). *Social Research Methods* (4th ed.). Oxford University Press Inc., New York.

Bucci, S., Schwannauer, M., & Berry, N. (2019). The digital revolution and its impact on mental health care. *Psychology and Psychotherapy: Theory, Research and Practice*, *92*(2), 277–297. DOI: 10.1111/papt.12222 PMID: 30924316

Bucher, T. (2020). The right-time web: Theorizing the virologic of algorithmic media. *New Media & Society*, *22*(9), 1699–1714. DOI: 10.1177/1461444820913560

Butković, H., & Šelo Šabić, S. (2023). The Challenges of Euroscepticism in Croatia. *Ten Years After EU Accession, On-line Journal Modelling the New Europe.*, (42), 81–108. DOI: 10.24193/OJMNE.2023.42.05

Buzkan, E. (2023). *Şah-ı Mar- The Children of the Şahmaran* (1st ed.). Destek Publishing.

Caferoğlu, A. (1988). *Türk Kavimleri*. Enderun Publishing.

Cai, S., & Xu, Y. C. (2011). Designing not just for pleasure: Effects of web site aesthetics on consumer shopping value. *International Journal of Electronic Commerce*, *15*(4), 159–188. DOI: 10.2753/JEC1086-4415150405

Calleja, G. (2011). *In-game: From immersion to incorporation*. MIT Press. DOI: 10.7551/mitpress/8429.001.0001

Cameron, D. (2007). *The myth of Mars and Venus: Do men and women really speak different languages?* Oxford University Press.

Caplan, L. (2020, January 3). The social conscience of generative art, *Art in Amerika.* https://www.artnews.com/art-in-america/features/max-bense-gustav-metzger-generative-art-1202674265/

Carr, D. M. (2020, May 4). The Formation of Genesis 1-11. Oxford University Press. http://books.google.ie/books?id=FcDgDwAAQBAJ&printsec=frontcover&dq=genesis&hl=&cd=10&source=gbs_api

Cassuto, U. (1997). *A Commentary on the Book of Exodus.* The Hebrew University Magnes Press.

Çelik Varol, M. (2022). *Lüks tüketimde ikinci el.* Orion Yayınevi.

Chen, F., Wyer, R. S., & Shen, H. (2015). The interactive effects of affect and shopping goal on information search and product evaluations. *Journal of Experimental Psychology. Applied, 21*(4), 429–442. DOI: 10.1037/xap0000059 PMID: 26460676

Chevalier, M., & Mazzalovo, G. (2008). *Luxury Brand Management: A World of Privilege.* Wiley.

Choi, B., Kim, H., & Huh-Yoo, J. (2021). Seeking mental health support among college students in video-based social media: Content and statistical analysis of YouTube videos. *JMIR Formative Research, 5*(11), e31944. Advance online publication. DOI: 10.2196/31944 PMID: 34762060

Chubb, J., Reed, D., & Cowling, P. (2024). Expert views about missing AI narratives: Is there an AI story crisis? *AI & Society, 39*(3), 1107–1126. DOI: 10.1007/s00146-022-01548-2 PMID: 36039046

Chuo, F. (2017). History at a glance: the story of patek philippe. https://deployant.com/history-at-a-glance-the-story-of-patek-philippe/

Çıblak, N. (2007). *Tarsus Kültürünün Tanıtımında Şahmaran Efsanelerinin Önemi.* Ç.Ü. Social Sciences Institute Journal.

Ciğerci, F. M., & Yıldırım, M. (2024). From Freytag pyramid story structure to digital storytelling: Adventures of pre-service teachers as story writers and digital story tellers. *Education and Information Technologies, 29*(5), 5697–5720. DOI: 10.1007/s10639-023-12042-7

Ciulu, A. (2024). Luxury brand storytelling: crafting narratives that resonate. https://www.sublimio.com/luxury-brand-storytelling/

Clark, C. (2012). *Personal Branding*. http://illinois.edu/2059/personal_branding_2012.pdf

Clover, J. C. (2015). *Men, Women and Chain Saws: Gender in the modern horror film*. Princeton University Press. DOI: 10.1515/9781400866113

Cohen, H. (2013). 5 Image storytelling tips brands need. https://heidicohen.com/images-how-to-tell-your-brand-story-examples/

Coleman, R., McCombs, M., Shaw, D., & Weaver, D. (2009). Agenda setting. In Wahl-Jorgensen, K., & Hanitzsch, T. (Eds.), *The handbook of journalism studies* (pp. 167–180). Routledge.

Colombo, C. (2024). Who is Baby Lasagna? Meet the Croatia Eurovision 2024 entry. RadioTimes.com., https://www.radiotimes.com/tv/entertainment/baby-lasagna-eurovision-2024-croatia-profile-age-instagram-explained/

Conway, K. (2012). Cultural Translation, Long-form Journalism, and Readers' Responses to the Muslim Veil. *Meta: Translators'. Journal*, (57), 997–1012.

Cook, A. J., Moore, K., & Steel, G. D. (2004). The Taking of a Position: A Reinterpretation of the Elaboration Likelihood Model. *Journal for the Theory of Social Behaviour*, *34*(4), 315–331. DOI: 10.1111/j.1468-5914.2004.00252.x

Cooper, S. P. (1988). "Zen's Two Silences." *InsightTimer Blog*. https://insighttimer.com/blog/zens-two-silences

Cooper, S. P. (2023). *Psychoanalysis and Zen Buddhism: A Realizational Perspective*. Routledge. DOI: 10.4324/9781003289821

Cordón, L. A. (2005). *Popular psychology: An encyclopedia*. Greenwood Press. DOI: 10.5040/9798400699191

Çoruhlu, Y. (1994). *Türk Sanatında Görülen Yılan Tasvirlerinin Sembolizmi*. Turkish World History Journal.

Cosgrove, L., & Karter, J. M. (2018). The poison in the cure: Neoliberalism and contemporary movements in mental health. *Theory & Psychology*, *28*(5), 669–683. DOI: 10.1177/0959354318796307

CroatiansOnline. (2024) The American ambassador supported Baby Lasagna, watch the video! croatiansonline.com, https://croatiansonline.com/en/American-ambassador-supported-baby-lasagna,-watch-the-video/ 11062025

Croatiaweek (2023). Croatia ranks in Top 5 as best country to live in Europe in 2023, https://www.croatiaweek.com/croatia-ranks-in-top-5-as-best-country-to-live-in-europe-in-2023/#:~:text=%E2%80%9CCroatia%20has%20a%20low%20cost,%2C%20Portugal%2C%20Netherlands%20and%20Slovenia

Crowther, P. (2008). Ontology and aesthetics of digital art. *The Journal of Aesthetics and Art Criticism*, *66*(2), 161–170. https://www.jstor.org/stable/40206323. DOI: 10.1111/j.1540-6245.2008.00296.x

Ćuk, D. (2024). Baby Lasagna pobijedio je na Dori! Ostao u šoku: 'Hvala svima! Dao sam sve od sebe!', Večernji.hr, https://www.vecernji.hr/showbiz/uskoro-uzivo-veceras-biramo-hrvatskog-predstavnika-na-euroviziji-u-svedskoj-1749082

Cuncic, A. (2023) What Is Pop Psychology? *Very Well Mind.* https://www.verywellmind.com/what-is-pop-psychology-5195653

Cunningham, D. (2004). How the sublime became "now": Time, modernity and aesthetics in Lyotard's rewriting of Kant. *Canadian Journal of Continental Philosophy*, *8*(3), 549–571. https://westminsterresearch.westminster.ac.uk/download/d2a7f877f0f5c20d11e1fffe409dfd3655db9d8223db312f2c562a265ff689b6/875498/Cunningham_2004_final.pdf. DOI: 10.5840/symposium20048341

Currid, J. D. (1997). *Ancient Egypt and the Old Testament*. Baker Books.

D'Ambrosio. (2023). *"Orientation to Profiles: Identity in a Digitized World." How Does the Digitization of Our World Change Our Orientation.R.G. Mueller& W.Stegmaier (edt).* Orientation Press.

Dahlan, N. F. (2024). Media and Culture: The role of media and social media in the formation and dissemination of popular, local, global and international culture. *Journal of Studies on Art, Culture and Society*, 1(1), 13–17. Retrieved from https://jacs.professorline.com/index.php/journal/article/view/3

Dai, Y., Lee, J., & Kim, J. W. (2024). AI vs. human voices: How delivery source and narrative format influence the effectiveness of persuasion messages. *International Journal of Human-Computer Interaction*, *40*(24), 8735–8749. DOI: 10.1080/10447318.2023.2288734

Dale, R., & Reiter, E. (2000). *Building Applied Natural Language Generation.* Cambridge University Press.

Dauenhauer, B. P. (1980). *Silence: The Phenomenon and Its Ontological Significance*. Indiana University Press.

De Choudhury, M., & De, S. (2014, May). Mental health discourse on Reddit: Self-disclosure, social support, and anonymity. In *Proceedings of the International AAAI Conference on Web and Social Media, 8*(1), 71–80. DOI: 10.1609/icwsm.v8i1.14526

de Lima, E. S., Casanova, M. A., & Furtado, A. L. (2024). Imagining from images with an AI storytelling tool. *arXiv preprint arXiv:2408.11517.*

De Santo, M. (2024). Digital narratives of mental health: Investigating medical communication on TikTok. *Textus, 36*(3), 97–120. DOI: 10.7370/115625

De Vos, J. (2011). Psychologization or the discontents of psychoanalysis. *Psychoanalysis, Culture & Society, 16*(4), 354–372. DOI: 10.1057/pcs.2010.29

De Vos, J. (2012). *Psychologisation in times of globalisation.* Routledge. DOI: 10.4324/9780203115459

Debener, T., & Gudin, S. (2003). Encyclopedia Of Rose Science. Three-Volume Set, Burlington, Elsevier Science, sect.2 45.

Diakopoulos, N. (2019). *Automating the News: How Algorithms Are Rewriting the Media.* Harvard University Press. DOI: 10.4159/9780674239302

Dijk, T. A. (2006). *The Network Society Social Aspect Of New Media.* Sega.

Dirlik, A. (2003). Global modernity? Modernity in an age of global capitalism. *European Journal of Social Theory, 6*(3), 275–292. DOI: 10.1177/13684310030063001

Djafarova, E., & Trofimenko, O. (2019). 'Instafamous'–credibility and self-presentation of micro-celebrities on social media. *Information Communication and Society, 22*(10), 1432–1446. DOI: 10.1080/1369118X.2018.1438491

Dnevnik.hr. (2024). Komunikacijski stručnjak o uspjehu Baby Lasagne: "To je europski fenomen, Hrvatska zbog njega konačno ima priliku...". dnevnik.hr. https://dnevnik.hr/vijesti/hrvatska/bozo-skoko-komentirao-marketinski-potencijal-hrvatske-zbog-uspjeha-baby-lasagne---848248.html

Doğan, B., Ersöz, S. Ş., & Şahin, C. (2022). Kripto sanatı ve NFT [Crypto Art and NFT]. *Tarih Kültür ve Sanat Arastirmalari Journal, 11*(1), 1–12. DOI: 10.7596/taksad.v10i4.3127

Domazet, I., & Hanić, A. (2012). "Promotion of Serbian Natinal Image in the Light of EU Accession," Book Chapters. In Teixeira, P., Duarte, A. P., Redzepagic, S., & Eric, D. (Eds.), *European Integration Process in Western Balkan Countries* (1st ed., Vol. 1, pp. 58–607). Institute of Economic Sciences.

Donzé, P. Y., & Wubs, B. (2019). Storytelling and the making of a global luxury fashion brand: Christian Dior. *International Journal of Fashion Studies*, *6*, 83–102.

Dove. (2024). Dove real beauty sketches. https://www.dove.com/us/en/campaigns/purpose/real-beauty-sketches.html

Dragomir, M., & Túñez López, M. (2024). How public service media are changing in the platform era: A comparative study across four European countries. European Journal of Communication, 39(6), 608-624. (Original work published 2024)DOI: 10.1177/02673231241290062

Dreamertalin. (2023). https://dreamertalin.medium.com/storytelling-in-open-world-games-part-2-c1409fee2606

Dube, J. (2000). *Online Storytelling Forms.* cyberjournalist.net: Retrieved from cyberjournalist.net/online-storytelling-forms

Dubois, B., & Paternault, C. (1995). Understanding the World of Luxurious Brands. *Journal of Marketing*, *59*(4), 75–91.

Duran, E., & Topbaşoğlu, N. (2017). Hikaye anlatıcılığı ve eğitimde kullanımı. *IJLA*, *14*, 109–124.

Ea.com. (n.d.). https://www.ea.com/games/the-sims?isLocalized=true

Eco, U. (2006). *Güzelliğin Tarihi* [History of Beauty]. (Akkoyunlu, A. C., Trans.). Doğan Publishing. (Original work published 2004)

Effie. (2018). IKEA & Mother London, The wonderful everyday. https://www.effie.org/insights/ikea-mother-london-the-wonderful-everyday/

Ekebring, K., & Mellqvist, C. (2019). *Luxury brands' storytelling on social media.* Department of Business Studies, Uppsala University.

Ekşioğlu Sarılar, N. B. (2020). Neo-liberal politikaların medya ve kamu hizmeti yayıncılığına etkisi. *İnsan ve İnsan*, 7(26), 41–64. https://doi.org/DOI: 10.29224/insanveinsan.791980

Ekşioğlu Sarılar, N. B. (2018). 1950'lerden bugüne haber perspektifinde dönüşen haber sunucusu profili: Spiker–anchor. *Yeni Medya Electronic Journal*, *2*(2), 63–72.

Ekşioğlu Sarılar, N. B. (2021). *Medya, iktidar, demokrasi: Sansür ve otosansür.* Kriter Publishing.

Elmquist, D. L., & McLaughlin, C. L. (2018). Social media use among adolescents coping with mental health. *Contemporary School Psychology*, *22*(4), 503–511. DOI: 10.1007/s40688-017-0167-5

Emergent Narratives. (2015). https://multiverse-narratives.com/2015/05/07/emergent-narratives-in-games/

Enciklopedija.hr. (2025). Pejačević, Dora, enciklopedija.hr. https://enciklopedija.hr/clanak/pejacevic-dora

English, A., & Stengel, B. (2010). Exploring fear: Rousseau, Dewey, and Freire on fear and learning. *Educational Theory*, *60*(5), 521–542. DOI: 10.1111/j.1741-5446.2010.00375.x

Entman, R. M. (1993). Framing: Toward clarification of a fractured paradigm. *Journal of Communication*, *43*(4), 51–58. DOI: 10.1111/j.1460-2466.1993.tb01304.x

Erdağı, D. Ö. (2024). Evil in Turkish Muslim horror film: The demonic in "Semum.". *SN Social Sciences*, *4*(27), 1–22. DOI: 10.1007/s43545-024-00832-w

Erdoğan, İ. (1999). Popüler kültür, kültür alanında egemenlik ve mücadele. Güngör, N (Eds.) Popüler Kültür ve İktidar (pp. 18-53). Ankara: Vadi Publications.

Ergen, R. C. (2015). Dior and I filminde bilmeniz gereken 8 gerçek. https://vogue.com.tr/moda-haber/dior-and-i-filminde-bilmeniz-gereken-8-gerce

Ersümer, A. (2013). *Klasik Anlatı Sineması*. Hayalperest Publishing.

Escalas, J. E. (2004). Imagine yourself in the product: Mental simulation, narrative transportation, and persuasion. *The Journal of Consumer Research*, *30*(2), 249–269.

Escalas, J. E. (2004). Narrative processing: Building consumer connections to brands. *Journal of Consumer Psychology*, *14*(1-2), 168–180.

Esports, D. O. T. (2024). https://dotesports.com/minecraft/news/minecraft-player-brings-stunning-real-world-creations-to-game-using-actual-map-data

Eurosong.hr. (2025). Dora. eurosong.hr. https://eurosong.hr/povijest/povijest-dore/uvod-u-doru/#:~:text=Prva%20takva%20promjena%20dogodila%20se,Dore%20nastavila%20se%20i%202001

Eurovisionfun.com. (2024). Croatia: Baby Lasagna wins SF1 Eurovision Audience Poll! eurovisionfun.com https://eurovisionfun.com/en/2024/05/croatia-baby-lasagna-wins-sf1-eurovision-audience-poll/

Evren, F. B. (2024). *Açık dünya oyunlarında oyuncu odaklı hikaye anlatımı: The Witcher 3: Wild Hunt örneği* [Player-focused storytelling in open-world games: The case of The Witcher 3: Wild Hunt]. Sanat & Tasarım Dergisi.

Fadak, A. S., & Khozium, M. O. (2020). Dialogue generation for digital interactive storytelling. *International Journal of Future Generation Communication and Networking, 13*(4), 4451–4460.

Falck, C. (2024). European Media's Role in Nation Branding: A Case Study of Swedish and British Coverage of Ukraine's 2016 and 2022 Eurovision Participation. Södertörn University, School of Social Sciences, Journalism. https://www.diva-portal.org/smash/record.jsf?pid=diva2%3A1867332&dswid=1319

Fan, M., Cui, X., Hao, J., Ye, R., Ma, W., Tong, X., & Li, M. (2024, May). StoryPrompt: Exploring the Design Space of an AI-Empowered Creative Storytelling System for Elementary Children. In *Extended Abstracts of the CHI Conference on Human Factors in Computing Systems* (pp. 1-8).

Fan, Y. (2006). Branding the Nation: What is Being Branded? *Journal of Vacation Marketing, 12*(1), 5–14.

Farca, G. (2010). *Narratives in video games* [Unpublished manuscript]. Augsburg Phil. Hist University, Englische Literaturwissenschaft.

Featherstone, M. (1991). *Consumer culture and postmodernism.* Sage Publications.

Febriandy, R. K., & Revolusi, P. (2024). Digital storytelling as political image construction in the 2024 presidential election campaign: Case study of the tiktok account@ gibran_rakabuming. *The International Journal of Social Sciences (Islamabad), 4*(2), 191–204.

Feinstein, B. A., Hershenberg, R., Bhatia, V., Latack, J. A., Meuwly, N., & Davila, J. (2013). Negative social comparison on Facebook and depressive symptoms: Rumination as a mechanism. *Psychology of Popular Media Culture, 2*(3), 161–170. DOI: 10.1037/a0033111

Felknerová, P. (2014). Nation Branding as a Soft Power Building Tool. The Case of Germany. Master Thesis. Praha: Univerzita Karlova v Praha. https://dspace.cuni.cz/bitstream/handle/20.500.11956/61185/DPTX_2012_1_11230_0_322674_0_128374.pdf?sequence=1

Feng, X., Wang, P., Wang, S., & Zhang, K. (2024). *A study on the construction of brand storytelling and the emotional connection of generation z.* Dean & Francis.

Ferenczi, A. (2024, Jun 9). The art and science of Alexander Mordvintsev. https://www.katevassgalerie.com/blog/the-art-and-science-of-alexander-mordvintsev

Fergie, G., Hunt, K., & Hilton, S. (2016). Social media as a space for support: Young adults' perspectives on producing and consuming user-generated content about diabetes and mental health. *Social Science & Medicine, 170*, 46–54. DOI: 10.1016/j.socscimed.2016.10.006 PMID: 27750067

Fergusson, N. (2004). *Colossus: The Price of America's Empire*. Penguin Press.

Feucht, C. (2025). *Self-diagnosis goes viral: Exploring the impact of social media on women's mental health practices* [Doctoral dissertation, The Ohio State University].

Filipović, L. (2018). 'Predsjednica radi dobru stvar, Hrvatsku treba brendirati, samo smo mi crni u glavi', tportal.hr. https://www.tportal.hr/biznis/clanak/predsjednica-radi-dobru-stvar-hrvatsku-treba-brendirati-samo-smo-mi-crni-u-glavi-foto-20181101/print

Fine, G. A., & Manning, P. (2000). Erving Goffman. In Ritzer, G. (Ed.), *Blackwell Companion to Major Social Theorists* (pp. 457–485).

Fisher, D., & Smith, S. (2011). Cocreation is chaotic: What it means for marketing when no one has control. *Marketing Theory, 11*(3), 325–350.

Fitzpatrick, K. K., Darcy, A., & Vierhile, M. (2017). Delivering cognitive behavior therapy to young adults with symptoms of depression and anxiety using a fully automated conversational agent (Woebot): A randomized controlled trial. *JMIR Mental Health, 4*(2), e19. DOI: 10.2196/mental.7785 PMID: 28588005

Fog, K., Budtz, C., & Yakaboylu, B. (2005). *Branding through storytelling. Storytelling*. Branding in Practice.

Freud, S. (2007). *(1915). Thoughts For The Times On War And Death, The Standart Edition of the Complete Psychological Works of Sigmund Freud* (Vol. XIV). The Hogarth Press.

Fricker, K., & Gluhovic, M. (2013). Introduction: Eurovision and the 'new' Europe, 10. In Fricker, K., & Gluhovic, M. (Eds.), *Performing the 'New' Europe: Identities, Feelings, and Politics in the Eurovision Song Contest*. Palgrave Macmillan.

Friedrich, C. D. (1818). *The Wanderer Above the Sea of Fog*. Oil Painting.

Furjan, M. (2024). Koliko je Baby Lasagna utjecao na promociju Hrvatske? Evo što kaže HTZ, index.hr. https://www.index.hr/magazin/clanak/koliko-je-baby-lasagna-utjecao-na-promociju-hrvatske-evo-sto-kaze-htz/2565013.aspx

Furnham, A., & Hughes, D. J. (2014). Myths and misconceptions in popular psychology: Comparing psychology students and the general public. *Teaching of Psychology, 41*(3), 256–261. DOI: 10.1177/0098628314537984

Gabbard, G. (2001). Psychotherapy in Hollywood Cinema. *Australasian Psychiatry, 9*(4), 365–369. DOI: 10.1046/j.1440-1665.2001.00365.x

García, E., & Whittinghill, D. (2011). The Aesthetic Legacy of Aldo Giorgini. *Leonardo, 44*(4), 309–316. https://www.jstor.org/stable/20869493. DOI: 10.1162/LEON_a_00207

Garreton, M., Morini, F., Moyano, D., Grün, G.-C., Parra, D., & Dörk, M. (2023). Data Stories of Water: Studying the Communicative Role of Data Visualizations within Long-form Journalism. *Eurographics Conference on Visualization (EuroVis) 2023*, 99-110. DOI: 10.1111/cgf.14815

Gazete Duvar. (2023, June 27). Fatih Portakal'ın iç sesinden öfke çıktı: Canlı yayında 'dış ses'i azarladı. https://www.gazeteduvar.com.tr/fatih-portakalin-ic-sesinden-ofke-cikti-canli-yayinda-dis-sesi-azarladi-haber-1625687

George, A., Sandars, N. K., & Pasco, R. (2003). The epic of Gilgamesh (A. George, Trans.). Penguin Classics.

Georgiou, M. (2008). "In the End, Germany will Always Resort to Hot Pants": Watching Europe Singing, Constructing the Stereotype. *Popular Communication, 6*(3), 141–154. DOI: 10.1080/15405700802198188

Gerbner, G. (1998). Cultivation analysis: An overview. *Mass Communication & Society, 1*(3–4), 175–194. DOI: 10.1080/15205436.1998.9677855

Gierl, H., & Huettl, V. (2010). Are scarce products always more attractive? The interaction of different types of scarcity signals with products' suitability for conspicuous consumption. *International Journal of Research in Marketing, 27*(3), 225–235. DOI: 10.1016/j.ijresmar.2010.02.002

Giles, D. (2003). *Media Psychology, 1 st edition*. Routledge.

Girgin, A. (2008). *Gazeteciliğin Temel İlkeleri*. İstanbul: Der.

Gjinali, V., & Tunca, E. A. (2020). A General Look on the Impact of Turkish Horror Movies: An Exploratory Study on the Opinions of Youth on Horror Movies. *SAGE Open, 10*(4), 1–11. DOI: 10.1177/2158244020979701

Goffman, E. (1959). *The presentation of self in everyday life*. Doubleday.

Goffman, E. (1974). *Frame analysis: An essay on the organization of experience*. Harper & Row.

González Romo, Z., Garcia Medina, I., & Plaza Romero, N. (2017). Storytelling and social networking as tools for digital and mobile marketing of luxury fashion brands. *International Journal of Interactive Mobile Technologies.*, *11*(6), 136–149. DOI: 10.3991/ijim.v11i6.7511

Gooding, P. (2019). Mapping the rise of digital mental health technologies: Emerging issues for law and society. *International Journal of Law and Psychiatry*, *67*, 101498. Advance online publication. DOI: 10.1016/j.ijlp.2019.101498 PMID: 31785726

Görgülü, T. (2015). *Islamic Motifs in Turkish Horror Films* [M.A Thesis]. Bahçeşehir University.

Goss, K. F. (1979). Consequences of diffusion of innovations. *Rural Sociology*, *44*(4), 754–772.

Gotal, M. (2015). Kulturna diplomacija Republike Hrvatske, Polemos: časopis za interdisciplinarna istraživanja rata i mira, XVIII(36), 141-162. https://hrcak.srce.hr/clanak/231005

Gourlet, P., Ricci, D., & Crépel, M. (2024). Reclaiming artificial intelligence accounts: A plea for a participatory turn in artificial intelligence inquiries. *Big Data & Society*, *11*(2), 20539517241248093. DOI: 10.1177/20539517241248093

Gramsci, A. (1971). *Selections from the prison notebooks* (Hoare, Q., & Nowell Smith, G., Eds. & Trans.). International Publishers.

Grgić, D. (2025). Baby Lasagna je Ponos Hrvatske, hrt.hr, https://magazin.hrt.hr/price-iz-hrvatske/baby-lasagna-je-ponos-hrvatske-12105189

Grmuša, T., & Mori, H. (2020). The Role of Stereotypes in the Creation of National Image: The Image of Croatia held by Japanese People. *Communication Management Review.*, *5*(1), 26–47. DOI: 10.22522/cmr20200154

Grmuša, T., Tomulić, A. M., & Anđelić, V. (2020). Uloga strateškog komuniciranja u brendiranju turističke destinacije na primjeru Međimurske županije. In Peručić, D., Lekić, R., & Dabo, K. (Eds.), *U potrazi za zajedničkim nazivnikom: komunikacija, turizam, nacionalna kultura i brend* (pp. 26–41). Veleučilište Edward Bernays.

Grow, P. (2018). Power of Storytelling | Warby Parker knows that storytelling is vital to their identity. https://www.pamelagrow.com/10335/power-storytelling-warby-parker-knows-storytelling-vital-identity/

Grubiša, D. (2012). Hrvatski referendum za Europsku uniju: anatomija zakašnjelog (ne)uspjeha. Politička misao: časopis za politologiju. 49(2), 45-72.

Güney, E., & Uysal, S. (2021). Jeneratif sanat: Nöroplastisite ve derin öğrenme ilişkisinde post dijital dönüşümler [Generative art: Post-digital transformations in the relationship between neuroplasticity and deep learning. *Yıldız Journal Art and Design*, 8(2), 62-74. https://yjad.yildiz.edu.tr

Güngör, N. (2011). *İletişim Kuramlar Yaklaşımlar.* Siyasal Publishing.

Güntan, S., & Ar, B. (2014). Recreating the past: Historical narratives and virtual environments of video games. Journal of Spatial Research, Istanbul Technical University.

Guntuku, S. C., Sherman, G., Stokes, D. C., Agarwal, A. K., Seltzer, E., Merchant, R. M., & Ungar, L. H. (2020). Tracking mental health and symptom mentions on Twitter during COVID-19. *Journal of General Internal Medicine, 35*(9), 2798–2800. DOI: 10.1007/s11606-020-05988-8 PMID: 32638321

Güregen, E. S. (2020). *Mobil oyunlarda hikaye anlatımının oyun deneyimine etkisi* [The impact of storytelling on the gaming experience in mobile games] [Master's thesis, Istanbul University Institute of Social Sciences]. Istanbul University Institutional Repository.

Güvendik, E. (2020). Music in Political Culture: The Eurovision Song Contest. Etnomüzikoloji Dergisi/Ethnomusicology Journal, 3(1), 96-103.

Habermas, J. (1977). Hannah Arendt's Communications Concept of Power. *Social Research, 44*(1), 3–24. https://insighttimer.com/blog/zens-two-silences/

Habib, M. Y., & ElTarabishi, M. (2024). The role of Artificial Intelligence in shaping the future of Media production and the application of Algorithm bias theory in Storytelling. *Journal of Media and Interdisciplinary Studies, 3*(8), 1–28. DOI: 10.21608/jmis.2024.299137.1033

Hall, S. (1980). Encoding/decoding. In Hall, S., Hobson, D., Lowe, A., & Willis, P. (Eds.), *Culture, media, language* (pp. 128–138). Routledge.

Hall, S. (1988). *The hard road to renewal: Thatcherism and the crisis of the left.* Verso.

Hall, S. (2010). Encoding, decoding 1. In Marris, P., & Thornham, S. (Eds.), *Media studies: A reader* (2nd ed., pp. 569–599). NYU Press.

Hall, S. (2017). *Temsil: Kültürel temsiller ve anlamlandırma uygulamaları (S. İrvan* (Güner, İ. Ed. & Trans.). Pinhan Publishing.

Hamm, M. P., Newton, A. S., Chisholm, A., Shulhan, J., Milne, A., Sundar, P., Ennis, H., Scott, S. D., & Hartling, L. (2015). Prevalence and effect of cyberbullying on children and young people: A scoping review of social media studies. *JAMA Pediatrics, 169*(8), 770–777. DOI: 10.1001/jamapediatrics.2015.0944 PMID: 26098362

Harari, Y. N. (2024). *Neksus, taş devri'nden yapay zekaya bilgi ağlarının kısa tarihi* [Nexus: a brief history of information networks from the stone age to AI]. (Şentuğ, Ç., Trans.). Kolektif Publishing. (Original work published 2024)

Haridakis, P., & Humphries, Z. (2019). Uses and gratifications. In Stacks, D. W., Salwen, M. B., & Eichhorn, K. C. (Eds.), *An integrated approach to communication theory and research* (pp. 139–154). Routledge., DOI: 10.4324/9780203710753-13

Hartmann, T. (2016). Parasocial interaction, parasocial relationships, and well-being. In Reinecke, L., & Oliver, M. B. (Eds.), *The Routledge handbook of media use and well-being* (pp. 131–144). Routledge.

Harva, U. (1933,January1). Altain suvun uskonto. http://books.google.ie/books?id =P8ssHQAACAAJ&dq=Altain+Suvun+Uskonto&hl=&cd=1&source=g s_api.

Hermansson, F. (2005). *The Service Branding Model: Small Service Firms' Approach to Building Brand Equity* (Yayınlanmamış Yüksek Lisans Tezi). Jönköping University, İsveç.

Hernandez-Martinez, P., & Keane, T. (2024). Learning mathematics and its relevance through a digital storytelling assessment task at university. *International Journal of Mathematical Education in Science and Technology*, •••, 1–17.

Herskovitz, S., & Crystal, M. (2010). The essential brand persona: Storytelling and branding. *The Journal of Business Strategy, 31*(3), 21–22.

High, S. (2010). Telling stories: A reflection on oral history and new media. *Power and Protest*, 38(1), 101-112. https://www.jstor.org/stable/40650320

Highton-Williamson, E., Priebe, S., & Giacco, D. (2015). Online social networking in people with psychosis: A systematic review. *The International Journal of Social Psychiatry, 61*(1), 92–101. DOI: 10.1177/0020764014556392 PMID: 25381145

Hill, A. (2023). *Digital Storytelling and Ethics. Collaborative Creation and Facilitation*. Routledge.

Hocking, C. (2007). Ludonarrative dissonance in BioShock: The problem of what the game is about. *Click Nothing*. https://clicknothing.typepad.com/click_nothing/ 2007/10/ludonarrative_d.html

Hocking, B. (2013). The ministry of foreign affairs and the national diplomatic system. In Kerr, P., & Wiseman, G. (Eds.), *Diplomacy in a Globalizing World: Theories and Practices* (pp. 123–140). Oxford University Press.

Holbrook, M. B., & Hirschman, E. C. (1982). The experiential aspects of consumption: Consumer fantasies, feelings, and fun. *The Journal of Consumer Research, 9*(2), 132–140. https://www.jstor.org/stable/2489122. DOI: 10.1086/208906

Holmes, D. (2013). *Communication theory: Media, technology and society* (2nd ed.). SAGE Publications.

Hooke, S. H. (2004, January 1). *Middle Eastern Mythology*. Courier Corporation. http://books.google.ie/books?id=YSUnmTKWhtkC&printsec=frontcover&dq=Hooke,+Samuel+Henry&hl=&cd=3&source=gbs_api

Hopkinson, G. C., & Hogarth-Scott, S. (2001). What happened was... broadening the agenda for storied research. *Journal of Marketing Management, 17*(1-2), 27–47.

Hopper, B. (2024). A case study on airbnb's belong anywhere campaign. https://thebrandhopper.com/2024/07/29/a-case-study-on-airbnb-belong-anywhere-campaign/

Hopper.E. (1972). "Automat." Oil painting.

Horkheimer, M., & Adorno, T. W. (2002). *Dialectic of enlightenment: Philosophical fragments (G. S. Noerr* (Jephcott, E. Ed. & Trans.). Stanford University Press.

Horton, D., & Richard Wohl, R. (1956). Mass communication and para-social interaction: Observations on intimacy at a distance. *psychiatry, 19*(3), 215-229. DOI: 10.1080/00332747.1956.11023049

Hou, D. (2024). Origin and Development: History of Storytelling. *Dean & Francis, 1*(9), 1–4. DOI: 10.61173/xkvvf133

Howell, P. (2025). Brand storytelling is not about what you make, but what you make happen. https://businessofstory.com/brand-storytelling-not-make-make-happen/

Hoyer, W. D., & Stokburger-Sauer, N. E. (2012). The role of aesthetic taste in consumer behavior. *Journal of the Academy of Marketing Science, 40*(1), 167–180. DOI: 10.1007/s11747-011-0269-y

Hudders, L., Pandelaere, M., & Vyncke, P. (2013). Consumer meaning making: The meaning of luxury brands in a democratised luxury world. *International Journal of Market Research, 55*(3), 391–412.

Hughes, M., Bendoni, W. K., & Pehlivan, E. (2016). Storygiving as a co-creation tool for luxury brands in the age ofthe internet: A love story by Tiffany and thousands of lovers. *Journal of Product and Brand Management, 25*(4), 357–364.

HUOJ. (2025). Izaberite najboljeg Komunikatora 2024., istaknite Antikomunikaciju godine! huoj.hr. https://www.huoj.hr/magazin/vijesti/izaberite-najboljeg-komunikatora-istaknutite-antikomunikaciju-godine/

I. B. (2024). Baby Lasagna ruši rekorde: Njegov nastup na Dori sada je najgledaniji, tportal.hr. https://www.tportal.hr/showtime/clanak/baby-lasagna-rusi-rekorde-njegov-nastup-na-dori-sada-je-najgledaniji-foto-20240224

Illouz, E. (2008). *Saving the modern soul: Therapy, emotions, and the culture of self-help*. Univ of California Press. DOI: 10.1525/9780520941311

Index Magazin. (2024a). Nastup Baby Lasagne na Dori skupio 3 milijuna pregleda, na kladionicama ima 19 posto, index.hr. https://www.index.hr/magazin/clanak/nastup-baby-lasagne-na-dori-skupio-3-milijuna-pregleda-na-kladionicama-ima-19-posto/2549231.aspx

Index Magazin. (2024b). "Cijela dvorana je pjevala s njim": Ovo su komentari na nastup Baby Lasagne, index.hr, https://www.index.hr/magazin/clanak/cijela-dvorana-je-pjevala-s-njim-ovo-su-komentari-na-nastup-baby-lasagne/2563038.aspx

Index Magazin. (2024c). Baby Lasagna dobio još jedno priznanje fanova Eurosonga, evo o čemu se radi, index.hr. https://www.index.hr/magazin/clanak/baby-lasagna-osvojio-nagradu-obozavatelja-za-najbolji-kostim-na-eurosongu/2566384.aspx

Index Magazin. (2024d). Ovaj graf s Googlea najbolje pokazuje koliko je Baby Lasagna zainteresirao svijet, index.hr. https://www.index.hr/magazin/clanak/ovaj-graf-s-googlea-najbolje-pokazuje-koliko-je-baby-lasagna-zainteresirao-svijet/2542852.aspx

Inkster, B., Sarda, S., & Subramanian, V. (2018). An empathy-driven, conversational artificial intelligence agent (Wysa) for digital mental well-being: Real-world data evaluation mixed-methods study. *JMIR mHealth and uHealth, 6*(11), e12106. Advance online publication. DOI: 10.2196/12106 PMID: 30470676

İnternet Araştırmaları Koordinatörlüğü. (2024, February). Türkiye Dijital 2024: Türkiye'nin nüfus, internet, sosyal medya, mobil, e-ticaret ve dijital pazarlama göstergeleri. https://www.guvenliweb.org.tr/dosya/3degJ.pdf

Işık, S.Y (2018). "Yılan, Su, Söz: Kadın Düşmanlığı ile Belirsizlik Korkusu Arasındaki İlişikiye Dair Bir Yorum Denemesi". Folklor Edebiyat Journal. Volume: 24. No: 93. ss. 177-196.)

Ismayilov, M. (2012). State, identity, and the politics of music: Eurovision and nation-building in Azerbaijan. *Nationalities Papers*, *40*(6), 833–851. DOI: 10.1080/00905992.2012.742990

Ivanković, J., Mitrović, M., & Plantić Tadić, D. (2024). Analysis of the Perception of the Republic of Croatia as a Brand: Recommendations for Developing a Nation Branding Strategy. Suvremene teme: međunarodni časopis za društvene i humanističke znanosti, 15(1), 59-77 DOI: 10.46917/st.15.1.3

Jagodzinski, K. (2025). Global Soft Power Index 2025: The shifting balance of global Soft Power. brandfinance.com. https://brandfinance.com/insights/global-soft-power-index-2025-the-shifting-balance-of-global-soft-power

Jambrač, J. (2020). Croatian Post-Socialist Transition or Transformation: Lost in Translation. *HKJU-CCPA*, *20*(4), 649–676.

Jansz, J. (2004). Psychology and society: An overview. In Brock, A. C. (Ed.), *A social history of psychology* (pp. 12–44). Wiley.

Jao, C. Y., Chen, C. H., & Yeh, H. C. (2024). Exploring the effects of cross-cultural collaborating on bilingual digital storytelling on students' intercultural learning. *Interactive Learning Environments*, *32*(10), 6815–6832. DOI: 10.1080/10494820.2023.2286386

Jenkins, H. (2007). Official Weblog of Henry Jenkins. 11. 12.2015. *TransmediaStorytelling*101:http://henryjenkins.org/2007/03/transmedia_storytelling_101.html

Jenkins, H., Lashley, M., & Creech, B. (2017). Voices for a New Vernacular: A Forum on Digital Storytelling Interview with Henry Jenkins. *International Journal of Communication*, 1061-1068.

Jenkins, M., & Gravestock, P. (2009). *Digital Storytelling Synthesis.* (Çevrim İçi): digitalstorytellingsynthesis.journo.com.tr. (2016, 04 26). journo.com.tr. journo.com.tr: Retrieved from journo.com.tr/yeni-medya-caginda-haberi-anlatabilmenin-9-yolu

Jenkins, H. (2002). Game design as narrative architecture. In Wardrip-Fruin, N., & Harrigan, P. (Eds.), *First person: New media as story, performance, and game* (pp. 118–130). MIT Press.

Jenkins, H. (2006). *Convergence culture: Where old and new media collide.* New York University Press.

Jenkins, H. (2009). *Confronting the challenges of participatory culture: Media education for the 21st century.* MIT Press. DOI: 10.7551/mitpress/8435.001.0001

Jenkins, H. (2016). *Cesur Yeni Medya: Teknolojiler ve Hayran Kültürü* (Yeğengil, N., Trans.). Communication Publishing.

Jeong, S. (2016). Digital Auteurism in Film Criticism. *Film Criticism, 40*(1), 1–2. DOI: 10.3998/fc.13761232.0040.116

Jiang, J. (2024). "Emotions are what will draw people in": A study of critical affective literacy through digital storytelling. *Journal of Adolescent & Adult Literacy, 67*(4), 253–263. DOI: 10.1002/jaal.1322

Jiang, X., Liu, L., Wu-Ouyang, B., Chen, L., & Lin, H. (2024). Which storytelling people prefer? Mapping news topic and news engagement in social media. *Computers in Human Behavior, 158*, 108248. DOI: 10.1016/j.chb.2024.108248

Jin, C. (2021). Game narrative conveyed through visual elements in digital games [Master's thesis, University of Skövde]. University of Skövde Digital Repository.

Jordan, P. (2015). The Modern Fairy Tale: Nation Branding, National Identity and the Eurovision Song Contest in Estonia. European Journal of Communication, 30(1), 118. (Original work published 2015)DOI: 10.1177/0267323114567273k

Jugo, D., Skoko, B., & Petrović, M. (2021). Krizno komuniciranje u Hrvatskoj 2020.: izvori informacija, povjerenje u institucije i meka moć država. Sociologija i prostor: časopis za istraživanje prostornoga i sociokulturnog razvoja, 59 (3, 222), 349-370. , https://hrcak.srce.hr/clanak/393693DOI: 10.5673/sip.59.3.1

Kalsın, B. (2017). *Tüm Boyutlarıyla İnternet Haberciliği*. Gece.

Kampmann, A., & Pedell, B. (2022). Using storytelling to promote organizational resilience: An experimental study of different forms of risk communication. Schmalenbach Journal of Business Research (SBUR), ISSN 2366-6153, Springer, Heidelberg, 74(4), 695-725. DOI: 10.1007/s41471-022-00143-x

Kang, J. A., Hong, S., & Hubbard, G. T. (2020). The role of storytelling in advertising: Consumer emotion, narrative engagement level, and word-of-mouth intention. *Journal of Consumer Behaviour, 19*(1), 47–56. https://doi.org/10.1002/cb.1793

Kant, I., & Bernard, J. H. (1914). *Kant's Critique of judgement* (2nd ed., rev). Macmillan.

Kapferer, J. N. (2012). *The New Strategic Brand Management: Advanced Insights and Strategic Thinking*. Kogan Page Publishers.

Kapferer, J. N., & Bastien, V. (2009). *The luxury strategy: break the rules of marketing to build luxury brands*. Kogan Page Publishers.

Kapferer, J. N., & Bastien, V. (2015). *The luxury strategy: Break the rules of marketing to build luxury brands* (2nd ed.). Kogan Page Publishers.

Kars, N. (2015). *Radyo-televizyon haberciliği*. Der Publishing.

Kasemsarn, K., Sawadsri, A., Harrison, D., & Nickpour, F. (2024). Museums for Older Adults and Mobility-Impaired People: Applying Inclusive Design Principles and Digital Storytelling Guidelines—A Review. *Heritage*, *7*(4), 1893–1916. DOI: 10.3390/heritage7040090

Katz, D. L.Academic Psychology Books. (2022). Don't judge a book by its cover: A case study and comparative analysis of popular vs. academy psychology books. *Journal of Scientific Exploration*, *36*(2), 233–250. Advance online publication. DOI: 10.31275/20222463

Kaufman, B. (2003). Stories that sell, stories that tell. *The Journal of Business Strategy*, *24*(2), 11–15. http://dx.doi.org/10.1108/02756660310508155

Kauppinen-Raisanen, H., Bjork, P., Lonnstrom, A., & Jauffret, M. N. (2018). How consumers' need for uniqueness, self-monitoring, and social ıdentity affect their choices when luxury brands visually shout versus whisper. *Journal of Business Research*, *84*, 72–81. DOI: 10.1016/j.jbusres.2017.11.012

Kaya, Z. (2019). *Yeni Medyada Haber Anadolu Ajansında Haberin Yapısal Dönüşümü*. Gece Akademi.

Kaye, H. (2012). Gothic Film. In *A New Companion to The Gothic* (First, pp. 239–251). Wiley-Blackwell. DOI: 10.1002/9781444354959.ch17

Kazaz, M., & Kartal, H. (2013). "Turkish Cinema vs. Religion" Religious Elements Used in Post-Millennium Turkish Horror Films. *Book of Proceedings: International Symposium on Language and Communication: Exploring Novelties*, 1289–1301.

Keles, B., McCrae, N., & Grealish, A. (2020). A systematic review: The influence of social media on depression, anxiety and psychological distress in adolescents. *International Journal of Adolescence and Youth*, *25*(1), 79–93. DOI: 10.1080/02673843.2019.1590851

Keller, K. L. (2013). Strategic brand management: Building, measuring and managing brand equity. *Pearson Education*.4.th Edition. ISBN: 978-0-13-266425-7.

Keller, K. L. (2013). *Strategic brand management: Building, measuring, and managing brand equity*. Pearson Education.

Kendrick, M., & Early, M. (2025). Digital storytelling and intersectional identities: Youth with refugee experiences (re) claiming life stories. *International Multilingual Research Journal, 19*(2), 99–115. DOI: 10.1080/19313152.2024.2332119

Kennedy Krieger Institute. (2024). Tips for navigating mental health content on social media. *Kennedy Krieger.* https://www.kennedykrieger.org/community/parent-education/tips-for-navigating-mental-health-content-on-social-media

Kersan-Škabić, I., & Tomić, D. (2009). Prepoznavanje euroskepticizma u Hrvatskoj – studija istraživanja stavova studentske populacije, Economic research -. *Ekonomska Istrazivanja, 22*(4), 100–117.

Kholifah, W., & Hamzah, H. (2025). Harnessing AI for Writing Excellence: Exploring ToolBaz. com and Gender Differences in Enhancing Twelfth Graders' Narrative Skills. *AL-ISHLAH: Jurnal Pendidikan, 17*(1), 524–534. DOI: 10.35445/alishlah.v17i1.6563

Kirişci, M. (2015). Korkusuz Türk Sineması [Com]. *Oteki Sinema [Fearless Turkish Cinema. Oteki Cinema].* https://www.otekisinema.com/korkusuz-turk-sinemasi/

Kısa Dalga. (2022, November 27). AKP'nin daveti üzerinden Türkiye'de gazeteciliğin güncel fotoğrafı. https://kisadalga.net/haber/detay/akpnin-daveti-uzerinden-turkiyede-gazeteciligin-guncel-fotografi_47878

Kızılca, M. (2015). Türk Korku Sineması'na Genel Bir Bakış. Oteki Sinema [An Overview of Turkish Horror Cinema. Oteki Cinema] [Com]. *otekisinema.* https://www.otekisinema.com/turk-korku-sinemasina-genel-bir-bakis/

Klasnić, K., & Rukavina, I. (2011). Što utječe na sliku Hrvatske u inozemstvu? Mišljenja građana Republike Hrvatske. Socijalna ekologija: journal for environmental thought and sociological research = Socijalna ekologija: Zeitschrift für Umweltgedanken und soziologische. *Forschung, 20*(2), 131–145. https://hrcak.srce.hr/clanak/105385

Klevjer, R. (2006). *What is the avatar? Fiction and embodiment in avatar-based singleplayer computer games* [Doctoral dissertation, University of Bergen]. University of Bergen Open Research Archive.

Koçer, Z. (2019). The Monstrous-feminine and Masculinity as Abjection in Turkish Horror Cinema: An Analysis of Haunted (Musallat, Alper Mestçi, 2007). In S. Holland, R. Shail, & S. Gerrard (Eds.), *Gender and Contemporary Horror in Film* (pp. 151–165). Emerald Publishing Limited. DOI: 10.1108/978-1-78769-897-020191011

Koch, T., Arendt, F., & Maximilian, L. (2017). Media effects: Cumulation and duration. *The international encyclopedia of media effects*, 1-11. DOI: 10.1002/9781118783764.wbieme0217

Ko, E., & Megehee, C. M. (2012). Fashion marketing of luxury brands: Recent research issues and contribution. *Journal of Business Research*, *65*(10), 1395–1398.

Ko, E., & Megehee, C. M. (2012). Fashion Marketing of Luxury Brands: Recent Research Issues and Contributions. *Journal of Business Research*, *65*, 1395–1398. DOI: 10.1016/j.jbusres.2011.10.004

Kolmes, K. (2012). Social media in the future of professional psychology. *Professional Psychology, Research and Practice*, *43*(6), 606–612. DOI: 10.1037/a0028678

Kongar, E. (2004, May 3). Üç güzeller. https://www.kongar.org/medyanotu/101_Uc_Guzeller.php

Kosakarika, S. (2023). Brand storytelling techniques arousing emotional bonds in different customer groups based on cluster analysis. *Kasetsart Journal of Social Sciences*, *44*, 281–292.

Kotler, P., & Pfoertsch, W. (2006). *B2B Brand Management*. Springer.

Küngerü, A. (2016). "Bir İfade Aracı Olarak Dijital Öykü Anlatımı", *Abant Cultural Researches Journal (AKAR)*, Volume 1, Number 2.

Kurian, N., & Saad, C. (2024). Where technology meets empathy: Using digital storytelling, gaming, and AI to teach about peace and human rights. *Communication and education: Promoting peace and democracy in times of crisis and conflict*, 148-163.

Kuyucu, M. (2011). *Türkiye'nin Eurovision Serüveni*. Esen Kitap.

L.M.B. (2024). Kakva čast: Baby Lasagna osvojio je nagradu za najbolju pjesmu Eurosonga! tportal.hr. https://www.tportal.hr/showtime/clanak/kakva-cast-baby-lasagna-osvojio-je-nagradu-za-najbolju-pjesmu-eurosonga-foto-20240509

Labaš, D., & Grmuša, T. (2011). Istinitost i objektivnost u informaciji i društveno štetne komunikacijske forme. Kroatologija: časopis za hrvatsku kulturu Fakulteta hrvatskih studija Sveučilišta u Zagrebu, 2(2), 87-121.

Lachance, M. J., Beaudoin, P., & Robitaille, J. (2003). Adolescents' brand sensitivity in apparel: Influence of three socialization agents. *International Journal of Consumer Studies*, *27*(1), 47–57.

Lack, C. W., & Rousseau, J. (2022). Mental health, pop psychology, and the misunderstanding of clinical psychology. *Academic Questions, 35*(4), 519–534. DOI: 10.1016/B978-0-12-818697-8.00052-2

Lang, C., & Armstrong, C. M. J. (2018). Collaborative consumption: The influence of fashion leadership, need for uniqueness, and materialism on female consumers' adoption of clothing renting and swapping. *Sustainable Production and Consumption, 13*, 37–47. DOI: 10.1016/j.spc.2017.11.005

Laughey, D. (2021). *Medya çalışmaları teoriler ve yaklaşımlar* [Media studies theories and approaches]. Kalkedon yayınları. (Original work published 2009)

Laughlin, V. A. (2015). A Brief Overview of al-Jinn within Islamic Cosmology and Religiosity. *Journal of Adventist Mission Studies, 11*(1), 67–78. DOI: 10.32597/jams/vol11/iss1/9/

Lavander, A. (2010). Digital culture. In S. Bay-Cheng, C. Kattenbelt, A. Lavander, R. Nelson (Eds.), *Mapping intermediality in performance* (pp. 125-134). Amsterdam University Press. http://www.jstore.org/stable/j.ctt46mwjd.23

Laverty, M. J. (2011). Can you hear me now? Jean-Jacques Rousseau on listening education. *Educational Theory, 61*(2), 155–169. DOI: 10.1111/j.1741-5446.2011.00397.x

Lee, A., Yang, J., Mizerski, R., & Lambert, C. (2015). *The Strategy of Global Branding and Brand Equity*. Routledge.

Lego Education. (2025). Rebuild the world with storytelling. https://education.lego.com/en-us/rebuild-the-world-with-storytelling-/

Leško, L. (2019). Pregled nacionalnih modela sportske diplomacije u svijetu i perspektiva razvoja hrvatskog modela sportske diplomacije. Političke perspektive: časopis za istraživanje politike, 9(1): 87-108. , https://hrcak.srce.hr/clanak/331381DOI: 10.20901/pp.9.1.04

Leung, F. F., Gu, F. F., & Palmatier, R. W. (2022). Online influencer marketing. *Journal of the Academy of Marketing Science, 50*(2), 226–251. DOI: 10.1007/s11747-021-00829-4

Lilienfeld, S. O., Lynn, S. J., Ruscio, J., & Beyerstein, B. L. (2009). *50 great myths of popular psychology: Shattering widespread misconceptions about human behavior*. John Wiley & Sons.

Lilienfeld, S. O., Lynn, S. J., Ruscio, J., & Beyerstein, B. L. (2017). *From inquiry to understanding* (4th ed.). Pearson.

Lin, P. H. (2005). A dream of digital art: Beyond the myth of contemporary computer technology in visual arts. *Visual Arts Research, 31*(1), 4–12. https://www.jstor.org/stable/20715364

Lippmann, W. (2007). *Public opinion.* NuVision. (Original work published 1922)

Lofton, K. (2011). *Oprah: The gospel of an icon.* University of California Press. DOI: 10.1525/9780520948242

Lossin, R. H. (2023, March 17). Refik Anadol'un MoMA Sergisi Üzerine: Teknoloji, Sanat, Propaganda [On Refik Anadol's MoMA exhibition: technology, art, propaganda] (E. Gen Trans.). *Skopbülten.* https://www.e-skop.com/skopbulten/refik-anadolun-moma-sergisi-uzerine-teknoloji-sanat-propaganda/6558

Loughran, T. (2023). Sex, relationships and 'everyday psychology' on British magazine problem pages, c. 1960–1990. *Medical Humanities, 49*(2), 203–213. DOI: 10.1136/medhum-2022-012497 PMID: 36549861

Luhmann, N. (2012). *Introduction to Systems Theory.* Polity Press.

Lund, F. N., Cohen, S. A., & Scarles, C. (2018). The power of social media storytelling in destination branding. *Journal of Destination Marketing & Management, 8*, 271–280.

Lundqvist, A., Liljander, V., Gummerus, J., & Van Riel, A. (2013). The Impact of storytelling on the consumer brand experience: The case of a firm-originated story. *Journal of Brand Management, 20*, 283–297. DOI: 10.1057/bm.2012.15

Maden, J. (2024). Iris Murdoch: "Unselfing" is Crucial for Living a Good Life". *Philosophy Break.* https://philosophybreak.com/articles/iris-murdoch-unselfing-is-crucial-for-living-a-good-life/. Access: 10.02.2025.

Madsen, O. J. (2015). Optimizing the self: Social representations of self-help. In Parker, I. (Ed.), *Handbook of critical psychology* (pp. 222–230). Routledge.

Mandung, F. (2024). The influence of storytelling techniques in digital marketing on brand loyalty: A consumer psychology perspective. *Golden Ratio of Marketing and Applied Psychology of Business, 5*, 66–78.

Manovich, L. (2018). *AI Aesthetics.* https://monoskop.org/images/6/66/Manovich_Lev_AI_Aesthetics_2018.pdf

Manovich, L. (2001). *The Language of New Media.* MIT Press.

Marconi, F. (2024). Yapay Zekâ ve Gazeteciliği Geleceği. (A. Açıkgöz, Çev.) Ankara: AA Kitap.

Marwick, A. E. (2015). Instafame: Luxury selfies in the attention economy. *Public Culture*, *27*(1), 137–160. DOI: 10.1215/08992363-2798379

Maxqda.com. (2025). *Maxqda.com*. Retrieved from https://www.maxqda.com/tr

McCashin, D., & Murphy, C. M. (2023). Using TikTok for public and youth mental health: A systematic review and content analysis. *Clinical Child Psychology and Psychiatry*, *28*(1), 279–306. DOI: 10.1177/13591045221106608 PMID: 35689365

McCombs, M. E., Shaw, D. L., & Weaver, D. H. (2018). New directions in agenda-setting theory and research. In Fortner, R. S., & Fackler, P. M. (Eds.), *Advances in foundational mass communication theories* (pp. 131–152). Routledge. DOI: 10.4324/9781315164441-9

McCormack, J., Bown, O., Dorin, A., McCabe, J., Monro, G., & Whitelaw, M. (2014). Ten questions concerning generative computer art. *Leonardo*, *47*(2), 135–141. https://www.jstor.org/stable/43834149. DOI: 10.1162/LEON_a_00533

McEvoy, E. (2007). Gothic Traditions. In Spooner, C., & McEvoy, E. (Eds.), *The Routledge Companion to Gothic* (pp. 7–9). Routledge.

McKean, M. (2024). The power of storytelling in communications: Maximising impact with logic and emotion. drpgroup.com. https://www.drpgroup.com/en/blog/the-power-of-storytelling-in-communications-maximising-impact-with-logic-and-emotion

McKenna, S., Riche, N., Lee, B., Boy, J., & Meyer, M. (2017). Visual Narrative Flow: Exploring Factors Shaping Data Visualization Story Reading Experiences. *Computer Graphics Forum*, *36*(3), 377–387. DOI: 10.1111/cgf.13195

McQuail, D., & Windahl, S. (2005). *Kitle iletişim çalışmalarında iletişim modelleri. Trans. Konca Kumlu*. İmge Publishing.

Medium. (2017). Apple's art of storytelling. https://medium.com/@absofx/apple-and-the-art-of-storytelling-fd782af8596f

Medium. (2019). Glossier's brand storytelling and the democratization of beauty. https://medium.com/@itmovesit/glossiers-brand-storytelling-and-the-democratization-of-beauty-fc5cab75716c

Metin, O., & Ünal, Ş. (2022). İçerik analizi tekniği: Iletişim bilimlerinde ve sosyolojide doktora tezlerinde kullanımı. *Anadolu Üniversitesi Sosyal Bilimler Dergisi*, *22*(2), 273–294.

Michel, J. P., & Ladd, M. (2015). "Snow Fall"-ing Special Collections and Archives. *Journal of Web Librarianship*, *9*(2-3), 212–131. DOI: 10.1080/19322909.2015.1044689

Mighall, R. (1999). *A Geography of Victorian Gothic Fiction*. Oxford University Press.

Milenković, V. & Stamenković, S. (2013). Performans između spektakla i umjetnosti. In medias res, 2 (2), 148-161.

Miletić, M. (2003). *Menadžment medija*. FMMSP.

Milišić, R. (1997). *Čija je Amerika?* Izvori.

Miller, T. G. (1984). Goffman, social acting, and moral behavior. *Journal for the Theory of Social Behaviour, 14*(2), 141–164. DOI: 10.1111/j.1468-5914.1984.tb00492.x

Mills, A. J., & John, J. (2021). Brand stories: Bringing narrativetheory to brand management. *Journal of Strategic Marketing, 28*, 1–9.

Milton, A., Ajmani, L., DeVito, M. A., & Chancellor, S. (2023, April). "I see me here": Mental health content, community, and algorithmic curation on TikTok. In *Proceedings of the 2023 CHI conference on human factors in computing systems* (pp. 1-17). DOI: 10.1145/3544548.3581489

Monro, G. (2009). Emergence and generative art. *Leonardo, 5*(42), 476–477. https://www.jstor.org/stable/40540082. DOI: 10.1162/leon.2009.42.5.476

Montoya, P. (2002). *The brand called you: Make your business stand out in today's competitive marketplace*. McGraw-Hill.

Moorhead, S. A., Hazlett, D. E., Harrison, L., Carroll, J. K., Irwin, A., & Hoving, C. (2013). A new dimension of health care: Systematic review of the uses, benefits, and limitations of social media for health communication. *Journal of Medical Internet Research, 15*(4), e85. Advance online publication. DOI: 10.2196/jmir.1933 PMID: 23615206

Morgan, N., & Pritchard, A. (2004). Meeting the destination branding challenge. In Morgan, N., Pritchard, A., & Pride, R. (Eds.), *Destination Branding, Creating the unique destination proposition*. Elsevier Butterworth-Heinemann.

Morić, D. A. (2025). Ksenija Urličić samo za tportal: ' Dora se vratila doma, ondje gdje pripada', tportal.hr. Retrieved March 2, 2025, from https://www.tportal.hr/showtime/clanak/ksenija-urlicic-samo-za-tportal-pobijedit-ce-huljic-foto-20250302

Morris, R. L. (1977). The Airport Project: A survey of the techniques for psychic development advocated by popular books. In J. D. Morris, W. G. Roll., & R. L. Morris (Eds.), *Research in parapsychology* (pp. 54–56). Scarecrow Press.

Morse, M. (1998). Televizyonda haberci kişiliği ve inandırıcılık / Geçiş sürecindeki haberler üzerine düşünceler. In Modleski, T. (Ed.), *Eğlence incelemeleri* (Gürbilek, N., Trans.; pp. 87–88). Metis Publishing.

Moskalewicz, M. (2024). *Hannah Arendt's Ambiguous Storytelling. Temporality, Judgment and the Philosophy of History*. Bloomsbury.

Mucundorfeanu, M. (2018). The key role of storytelling in the branding process. *Journal of Media Research*. Vol. 11, Issue 1(30). p. 42-54.

Mucundorfeanu, M. (2017). *The Creative Process Behind the Advertising Discourse*. Hochschulverlag Mittweida, Mittweida.

Mucundorfeanu, M. (2018). The Key Role of Storytelling in the Branding Process. [Babe -Bolyai University.]. *The Journal of Medical Research, 11*(1 (30)). DOI: 10.24193/jmr.30.3

Muir, E. (2024). Eurovision fans proclaim Croatia's Baby Lasagna favourite to win. Independent.co.uk., https://www.independent.co.uk/arts-entertainment/eurovision/baby-lasagna-eurovision-song-who-marko-purisic-b2543530.html

Murdoch, I. (1993). *Metaphysics as a Guide to Morals*. Allen Lane, Penguin Press.

Murphy, P. I. (2015). New Ikea campaign focuses on everyday heroes. https://www.retaildive.com/news/new-ikea-campaign-focuses-on-everyday-heroes/374081/

Murray, J. H. (2017). *Hamlet on the holodeck: The future of narrative in cyberspace* (Updated ed.). MIT Press.

Murray, C. E. (2015). Self-help and the helpless subject: Samuel Smiles and biography's objects. *Nineteenth-Century Literature, 69*(4), 481–508. DOI: 10.1525/ncl.2015.69.4.481

Murray, J. H. (1997). *Hamlet On The Holodeck: The Future Of Narrative in Cyberspace*. MIT Press.

Murray, S. (2018). *Sport Diplomacy, origins, theory and practice*. Routledge: Taylor & Francis.

Mutlu, E. (1991). *Televizyonu Anlamak*. Gündoğan.

Mutlugün, A., & Topuz, M.Y.(2020). New Position of Storytelling in the Context of Digital Narration. *International Journal of Humanities and Research*, February, Year 4, Issue:4, Volume 3.

MVEP.GOV.HR. (2024). Baby Lasagna played in Dublin, mvep.gov.hr, https://mvep.gov.hr/news-100537/baby-lasagna-played-in-dublin/275166

Nader, K., Toprac, P., Scott, S., & Baker, S. (2024). Public understanding of artificial intelligence through entertainment media. *AI & Society*, *39*(2), 713–726. DOI: 10.1007/s00146-022-01427-w PMID: 35400854

Naghdi, A. (2024). https://dreamfarmstudios.com/blog/what-is-transmedia/, E.T.

Nam, K. A. (2015). High-context and low-context communication. The SAGE encyclopedia of intercultural competence, 377-381.

Naslund, J. A., Bondre, A., Torous, J., & Aschbrenner, K. A. (2020). Social media and mental health: Benefits, risks, and opportunities for research and practice. *Journal of Technology in Behavioral Science*, *5*(3), 245–257. DOI: 10.1007/s41347-020-00134-x PMID: 33415185

Naughty Dog. (2013). *The Last of Us* [Video game]. Sony Computer Entertainment.

Nazari, M. (2015). "Zen Buddhism." *Philosophy of Religion*. https://www.academia.edu/19495154/Zen_Buddhism

Nehring, D., Alvarado, E., Hendriks, E. C., & Kerrigan, D. (2016). *Transnational popular psychology and the global self-help industry: The politics of contemporary social change*. Palgrave Macmillan. DOI: 10.1057/9780230370869

Nesser, C. (2019). Characteristics of visual storytelling advertisement-*From a Millennial & Communication Professional point of view,* Bachelor Thesis, Faculty of Behavioral. Management and Science.

Newman, N., & Fletcher, R. Robertson, Craig, T., Arguedas, A. R. & Nielsen, R. K. (2024). Reuters Institute Digital News Report 2024. Oxford: Reuters Institute for the Study of Journalism. DOI: 10.60625/risj-vy6n-4v57

Newman, J. (2013). *Videogames* (2nd ed.). Routledge.

Ngoi, S., Tan, K. H., Alias, J., & Mat, N. (2024). Digital storytelling to improve english narrative writing skills. *International Journal of Academic Research in Business & Social Sciences*, *14*(4), 546–560. DOI: 10.6007/IJARBSS/v14-i4/21249

Nouri, M. (2018). *The power of influence: Traditional celebrity vs social media influencer* (Student thesis, Santa Clara University). *Pop Culture Intersections*, 32. https://scholarcommons.scu.edu/engl_176/32

Novčić Korać, B., Bradić Martinović, A., & Miletić, B. (2020). Constructing a nation branding model: The case of Serbia. *Geographica Pannonica*, *24*(4), 311–324. DOI: 10.5937/gp24-28279

Novčić Korać, B., Damnjanović, V., & Popesku, M. (2012). Serbia brand identity: Perspectives of residents and diaspora. *EuroMed Journal of Business*, *7*(3), 256–267. DOI: 10.1108/14502191211265316

Noy, C. (2012). Narratives and counter-narratives: Contesting a tourist site in Jerusalem, In J. Tivers & T. Rakić (eds.), Narratives of Travel and Tourism (pp. 135-150). England: Ashgate publishing limited.

Noya, J. (2006). The symbolic power of nations. *Place Branding and Public Diplomacy*, *2*(1), 53–67.

NTV. (2018, March 22). Hürriyet, Kanal D, CNN Türk ve Posta'yı Demirören Grubu alıyor (Erdoğan Demirören kimdir?). https://www.ntv.com.tr/ekonomi/hurriyet-kanal-d-cnn-turk-ve-postayi-demiroren-grubu-aliyor-erdogan-demiroren-kimdir%2CXg4DGSoZoUCH5YNVwt8dCg

Nueno, J. L., & Quelch, J. A. (1998). The Mass Marketing of Luxury. *Business Horizons*, *39*(6), 61–68.

Nunn, H., & Biressi, A. (2010). 'A trust betrayed': Celebrity and the work of emotion. *Celebrity Studies*, *1*(1), 49–64. DOI: 10.1080/19392390903519065

Nye, J. S. (2004). *Soft Power: The Means to Success in World Politics*. PublicAffairs.

Nye, J. S. (2009). Get smart. Combining Hard and Soft Power. *Foreign Affairs*, *88*(4), 160–163.

O'Gieblyn, M. (2023). *Tanrı insan hayvan makine: Teknoloji, metafor ve anlam arayışı* [God, human, animal, machine: Technology, metaphor, and the search for meaning]. (Sarıalioğlu, F., Trans.). Altın Kitaplar Publishing. (Original work published 2021)

O'Keefe, D. J. (2013). The elaboration likelihood model. In Dillard, J. P., & Shen, L. (Eds.), *The SAGE handbook of persuasion: Developments in theory and practice* (2nd ed., pp. 137–149). Sage Publications, Inc.

O'Neill, J. W. (2002). The Role of Storytelling in Affecting Organizational Reality in the Strategic Management Process. *Journal of Behavioral and Applied Management*, *4*(1), 4–18.

Ökmen, Y. E. (2021). *Gelenekselden Dijitale Hikâye Anlatıcılığı: Youtube Örneği*, İstanbul University Social Science Institute, Radio, TV and Cinema Department, Unpublished Doctoral Dissertation. Sarı, Gülşah. (2017). "Transmedya Hikâye Anlatıcılığı Kötü Çocuk Örneği", *Abant Cultural Researhes Journal (AKAR)*. Volume 2, No. 4.

Öncel, Ş. (2004, Eylül 1). Jenerik Markanın Sonu mu Geliyor? *Capital* http://www.capital.com.tr/yonetim/pazarlama/jenerik-markanin-sonu-mu-geliyor-haberdetay-1614 sayfasından alınmıştır.

Orkan, S. (2022). The Use of Digital Effects on Storytelling in Turkish Cinema. *MEDIAJ*, *5*(2), 356–369. DOI: 10.33464/mediaj.1162233

Owen, D., Lynham, A. J., Smart, S. E., Pardiñas, A. F., & Camacho Collados, J. (2024). AI for Analyzing Mental Health Disorders Among Social Media Users: Quarter-Century Narrative Review of Progress and Challenges. *Journal of Medical Internet Research*, *26*, e59225. Advance online publication. DOI: 10.2196/59225 PMID: 39546783

Oyunlastirma.co. (2023). https://oyunlastirma.co/makale/gamfed-turkiye-kaptanlari-karya-kortel-ve-sule-kucuk-yaziyor-dijital-oyun-ve-oyunlastirmada-hikaye-tasarimi-narrative-design-for-gamification

Ozcelik, A. B., & Levi, E. (2020). Choosing the right influencer for your brand. In Yesiloglu, S., & Costello, J. (Eds.), *Influencer marketing* (pp. 79–97). Routledge. DOI: 10.4324/9780429322501-8

Özdemir, Z., & Çetinkaya, A. (2019). *Dijital Çağda Habercilik Kuram ve Uygulamada Yeni Yönelimler.* İstanbul: Der.

Özdemir., H. (1998). "Geleneksel Kültürümüzde Şahmaran", V. *International Folk Culture Congress Folk Literature Section Papers*, v.2.Ankara. p.252.

Özkantar, M. Ö. (2022). Woman Depiction in Turkish Horror Films: A Semiotic Analysis as Part of the Concept of "Alterity.". *Intermedia International E-Journal*, *9*(17), 154–169. DOI: 10.56133/intermedia.1099340

Pablos, T. G. (2015). Game design and emergent storytelling: The construction of new narrative models in early Japanese videogames. *KYOTO Conference.*

Pandžić Skoko, M. (2023). Uspon i pad američkog sna kao ključnog aduta meke moći Sjedinjenih Američkih Država, Communication. *Management Review*, *1*(8), 6–29. https://hrcak.srce.hr/clanak/442191. DOI: 10.22522/cmr20220183

Paquette, A. A., Yang, B., & Long, Y. (2017). *How is storytelling used to strengthen a brand? Strategic Brand Management* (3rd ed.). Student Papers.

Pavlik, J. V. (2013). Yeni Medya ve Gazetecilik. Ankara: Phoenix.

Pavlik, J. V., & Pavlik, J. (2017). Understanding Quality in Digital Storytelling: A Theoretically Based Analysis of the Interactive Documentary. *Springer International Publishing*, 381-396.

Pearce, C. (2005). Theory wars: An argument against arguments in the so-called ludology/narratology debate. In *DiGRA Conference Proceedings*. Digital Games Research Association.

Pereira, G. (2019). Brand storytelling: A three-dimensional perspective. *Henry Stewart Publications 2045-855x. Journal of Brand Strategy*, *8*(2), 146–159.

Pereira, G. (2019). Brand storytelling: A three-dimensional perspective. *Journal of Brand Strategy*, *8*(2), 146–159. DOI: 10.69554/CEWY2163

Perić, N. (2011). Branding the State and the Nation (the case of the Republic of Serbia). *Technics Technologies Education Management*, *6*(2), 361–367.

Perry, A., & Wisnom, D. (2003). *Markanın DNA'sı, Çev. Zeynep Yılmaz*. Media Cat Yayınları.

Pertiwi, E., & Sanusi, P. A. (2023). Storytelling in the Digital Age: Examining the Role and Effectiveness in Communication Strategies of Social Media Content Creators? *Palakka Media and Islamic Communication*, *4*(1), 25–34. DOI: 10.30863/palakka.v4i1.5082

Petty, R. E., & Cacioppo, J. T. (1986). The elaboration likelihood model of persuasion. In Berkowitz, L. (Ed.), Vol. 19, pp. 123–205). Advances in experimental social psychology. Academic Press.

Picard, M. (1952).*The World of Silence*. H.Regnery. Original from University of California.

Pierosara, S. (2024). Narrative autonomy and artificial storytelling. *AI & Society*, *39*(4), 1785–1794. DOI: 10.1007/s00146-022-01595-9

Pillai, P. (1992). Rereading Stuart Hall's encoding/decoding model. *Communication Theory*, *2*(3), 221–233. DOI: 10.1111/j.1468-2885.1992.tb00040.x

Popović, G., Grmuša, T. & Popović, M. (2013). Awareness of European Union and Completion of Croatia's Accesion Negotiation Among University Students. Informatologia 46(2), 122-138.Reardon, K. K. (1986). Interpersonal Communication: Where Minds Meet. Wadsworth Pub Co.

Popović, G., Grmuša, T., & Prpić, H. (2011). Izvještavanje o Europskoj uniji u hrvatskim dnevnim novinama: Završetak hrvatskih pristupnih pregovora. *Informatologia*, *44*(4), 309–322.

Porin, org. (2025). Utemeljitelji Porina https://www.porin.org/?q=content/utemeljitelji-porina

Prada. (2025). Galleria 1913. https://www.prada.com/tr/tr/pradasphere/places/galleria-1913.html

Prasetyo, Y. (2017). From Storytelling to Social Change: The Power of Story in the Community Building. *SSRN*: https://ssrn.com/abstract=3094947 , DOI: 10.2139/ssrn.3094947

Prensky, M. (2001). Digital Natives, Digital Immigrants, Part 1. *On the Horizon*, *9*(5), 1–6. DOI: 10.1108/10748120110424816

Pretorius, C., McCashin, D., & Coyle, D. (2022). Mental health professionals as influencers on TikTok and Instagram: What role do they play in mental health literacy and help-seeking? *Internet Interventions : the Application of Information Technology in Mental and Behavioural Health*, *30*, 100591. Advance online publication. DOI: 10.1016/j.invent.2022.100591 PMID: 36458161

Procter, J. (2004). *Stuart Hall*. Routledge. Schudson, M. (2001). The objectivity norm in American journalism. *Journalism*, *2*(2), 149–170. DOI: 10.1177/146488490100200201

Pulizzi, J. (2012). The rise of storytelling as the new marketing. *Journal of Publishing Research Quarterly*, *28*(2), 116–123. DOI: 10.1007/s12109-012-9264-5

Putri, S. D. G., Purnomo, E. P., & Khairunissa, T. (2024). Echo chambers and algorithmic bias: The homogenization of online culture in a smart society. In *SHS Web of Conferences* (Vol. 202, p. 05001). EDP Sciences. DOI: 10.1051/shsconf/202420205001

Rachman, R., Hamid, M. A., Wijaya, B. K., Wibowo, S. E., & Intan, D. N. (2024). Brand storytelling in the digital age: Challenges and opportunities in online marketing. *Jurnal Ekonomi*, *13*(01), 355–364.

Rafique, S., Khan, M. H., & Bilal, H. (2022). A critical analysis of pop culture and media. *Global Regional Review*, *VII*(I), 173–184. DOI: 10.31703/grr.2022(VII-I).17

Rapp, D. (1988). The reception of Freud by the British press: General interest and literary magazines, 1920–1925. *Journal of the History of the Behavioral Sciences*, *24*(2), 191–201. DOI: 10.1002/1520-6696(198804)24:2<191::AID-JHBS2300240206>3.0.CO;2-X PMID: 3286754

Rawal, A. (2018). Gucci's art of storytelling. https://medium.com/@anahatrawal/guccis-art-of-storytelling-e5451cc9d976

Red Dead Redemption II. (2018). https://www.mmorpg.com/videos/not-so-mmo-red-dead-redemption-2-official-gameplay-video-2000113375

Reddit.(2019). https://www.reddit.com/r/truegaming/comments/dsqy4z/a_masterpiece_in_interactive_storytelling_how_the/

Rey, P. J. (2012). Alienation, exploitation, and social media. *The American Behavioral Scientist, 56*(4), 399–420. DOI: 10.1177/0002764211429367

Richards, J. (1982). Spreading the gospel of self-help: G. A. Henty and Samuel Smiles. *Journal of Popular Culture, 16*(2), 52–65. DOI: 10.1111/j.0022-3840.1982.00052.x

Roberts, J. A., & David, M. E. (2023). Instagram and TikTok flow states and their association with psychological well-being. *Cyberpsychology, Behavior, and Social Networking, 26*(2), 80–89. DOI: 10.1089/cyber.2022.0117 PMID: 36716180

Robin, B. R. (2016). The Power of Digital Storytelling to Support Teaching and Learning. *Digital Education Review*, 17-29. scrolli.co. (2025). Scrolli.co: Retrieved from www.scrolli.co

Rocco, F. (1993). *Rječnik marketinga*. Masmedia.

Rodríguez-López, R. (2023, July 18). Self-help or self-governance? The role of the psy-disciplines in neoliberalism. *Mad in America*. https://www.madinamerica.com/2023/07/self-help-or-self-governance-the-role-of-the-psy-disciplines-in-neoliberalism/

Rogers, E. M. (1962). *Diffusion of Innovations*. Free Press.

Rogers, E. M., & Picot, A. (1986). *Impact Of New Communication Technologies. E. M. Rogers, & F. Belle içinde, The Media Revolution in America and Europe*. Ablex Publishing Corporation Norwood.

Rojek, C. (2015). *Presumed intimacy: Parasocial interaction in media, society and celebrity culture*. John Wiley & Sons.

Rolex. (2015). About rolex. https://www.rolex.com/tr/about-rolex/history/1905-1919

Rolex. (2025). Making history with rolex. https://www.rolex.org/perpetual/making-history-with-rolex

Romero, A. (2024). How Spotify Wrapped Turns Your Year of Music into a Viral Sensation. https://medium.com/we-are-storytellers/how-spotify-wrapped-turns-your-year-of-music-into-a-viral-sensation-8ee33da89d5d

Rosenberg, T. (2020). Rising Like the Eurovision Song Contest: On Kitsch, Camp, and Queer Culture. *Lambda Nordica, 25*(2), 93–113. DOI: 10.34041/ln.v25.676

Rosen, G. M. (1987). Self-help treatment books and the commercialization of psychotherapy. *The American Psychologist, 42*(1), 46–51. DOI: 10.1037/0003-066X.42.1.46 PMID: 3565914

Rosen, R. D. (1977). *Psychobabble: Fast talk and quick cure in the era of feeling*. Atheneum.

Rosenthal, B., & Brito, E. P. (2017). The brand meaning co-creation process on Facebook. *Marketing Intelligence & Planning, 35*(7), 923–936. https://doi.org/10.1108/MIP-09-2016-0171

Roshni Rehab Centre. (2024). The destructive impact of social media addiction on society. *Roshni Rehabilitation Centre*. https://www.roshnirehabilitationcentre.com/post/thedestructiveimpactofsocialmediaaddictiononsociety

Ross, S. (2011). The encoding/decoding model revisited. Paper presented at the *Annual Meeting of the International Communication Association*, Boston.

Rousseau, J. J. (1918). Émile or Treatise on Education. (W.H.Payne,Trans) New York and London. D.Appleton Company.

Rousseau, J. J. (1979). *Emile: Or, On Education* (Bloom, A., Trans.). Basic Books.

Rousseau, J. J. (1992). *The Reveries of the Solitary Walker* (Charles, E., Trans.). Hackett Publishing Company., https://www.scribd.com/document/555838753/Rousseau-Reveries-of-the-Solitary-Walker-Butterworth

Roy, B. (2023). Standardization of Culture: A Constructed Ideology for Dominion and Power Maintenance.

Rožman, K. (2024). Baby Lasagna o finalu, pobjedniku Nemu, bodovima žirija... 'Ponosan sam, dali smo najbolje od sebe', jutarnji.hr. https://www.jutarnji.hr/scena/domace-zvijezde/baby-lasagna-o-finalu-pobjedniku-nemu-bodovima-zirija-ponosan-sam-dali-smo-najbolje-od-sebe-15459730

Rubio-Hurtado, M. J., Fuertes-Alpiste, M., Martínez-Olmo, F., & Quintana, J. (2022). Youths' posting practices on social media for digital storytelling. Journal of new approaches in educational research, 11(1), 97-113.

Ruggiero, T. E. (2000). Uses and Gratifications Theory in the 21st Century. *Mass Communication & Society, 3*(1), 3–37. DOI: 10.1207/S15327825MCS0301_02

Ruzzier, M. K., & Petek, N. (2012). Country Brand I Feel Slovenia:First Response from Locals. *Economic Research-Ekonomska Istraživanja, 25*(2), 465–484. DOI: 10.1080/1331677X.2012.11517518

Ryan, M. L. (2003). *Narrative as virtual reality: Immersion and interactivity in literature and electronic media*. Johns Hopkins University Press.

Ryder, B. (2021). The magical realism of Tesla. *The Economist*. https://www.economist.com/business/2021/04/29/the-magical-realism-of-tesla

Saifa, S. (2023). *The use of storytelling in luxury brands on social media. Bachelor of Arts Program in Journalism (Media Studies) International Program Faculty of Journalism and Mass Communication*. Thammasat University.

Sakman, S. (2021). *Dijital oyun tasarımında görsel retorik* [Visual rhetoric in digital game design]. International Social Mentality and Researcher Thinkers Journal.

Salen, K., & Zimmerman, E. (2004). *Rules of play: Game design fundamentals*. MIT Press.

Salt, A. (2006). *Ansiklopedi Semboller*. Ruh ve Madde Publishing.

Sammer, P. (2015). Storytelling. Die Zukunft von PR und Marketing, dpunkt. verlag, Heidelberg.

Sanabria Zepeda, J. C., Olivo Montaño, P. G., Artemova, I., & Argüelles Cruz, A. J. (2024). Prospective narratives on global issues: An AI-based pedagogical model for assessing complex thinking. *JOTSE: Journal of Technology and Science Education, 14*(1), 184–199. DOI: 10.3926/jotse.2445

Šarčević, A. (2023). Sjećate li ih se? Ovo su svi pobjednici Dore od 1993. godine, 24sata.hr. https://www.24sata.hr/show/sjecate-li-ih-se-ovo-su-svi-pobjednici-dore-od-1993-godine-890604

Savage, M. (2024). Eurovision 2024: Your guide to all 37 songs. bbc.com, https://www.bbc.com/news/articles/crgy7l6er7vo

Schell, J. (2008). *The art of game design: A book of lenses*. Morgan Kaufmann. DOI: 10.1201/9780080919171

Schimmel, A. (1996). Deciphering The Signs of God: A Phenomenological Approach to Islam. Oxford University Press. Vol 7. No. 1 January. p. 70-72.

Schmitt, B. (2012). The consumer psychology of brands. *Journal of Consumer Psychology, 22*, 7–17.

Serrat, O. (2008). Storrytelling. *Knowledge Solutions*. October, 10. p. 1-4.

Serrat, O. (2017). Storytelling. In Knowledge Solutions (pp. 839-842). Springer. DOI: 10.1007/978-981-10-0983-9_91

Shahbazi, N. (2024). https://pixune.com/blog/transmedia-storytelling/, E.T.

Shakespeare, W. (1993). *Macbeth.* Dover Publications.

Shapiro, S. L. (2009). The integration of mindfulness and psychology. *Journal of Clinical Psychology*, *65*(6), 555–560. DOI: 10.1002/jclp.20602 PMID: 19340826

Shinkle, E. (2013). Video games and the technological sublime. In N. Llewellyn, C. Riding (Eds.). *The art of the sublime*, Tate Research Publication. https://www.tate.org.uk/art/research-publications/the-sublime/eugenie-shinkle-video-games-and-the-technological-sublime-r1136830

Shrum, L. J. (2017). Cultivation theory: Effects and underlying processes. In Rössler, P. (Ed.), *The international encyclopedia of media effects* (Vol. 1, pp. 1–12). Wiley. DOI: 10.1002/9781118783764.wbieme0040

Siddals, S., Coxon, A., & Torous, J. (2024). " It just happened to be the perfect thing": Real-life experiences of generative AI chatbots for mental health. *NPJ Mental Health Research*, 48. DOI: 10.21203/rs.3.rs-4612612/v1

Silva. (2024). Christian dior and coco chanel's ınfamous rift. https://www.elledecor.com/life-culture/a46583225/dior-chanel-rivalry-history/

Simaku, X. (2022). Netflix and Chill: An analysis of Turkish Generation Z viewers on The New Hedonistic Product. *İletişim Kuram Ve Araştırma Dergisi, 58*, 170–184. DOI: 10.47998/ikad.1004162

Simmonds, L. (2024). Baby Lasagna boosts Croatian Tourism, Total-Croatia-News.com, Retrieved June 12, 2025, from https://total-croatia-news.com/news/baby-lasagna-boosts-croatian-tourism/ 10062025

Şimşek, B. (2018). *Dijital Hikâye Anlatımı Kavramlar ve Türkiye Deneyimi*. Alternatif Bilişim.

Sinčić Ćorić, D. (2019, May). Branding Croatia Project. Paper presented at Communication Management Forum. Zagreb: Edward Bernays University of Applied Sciences.

Singh, A., Sethu, S. G., & Chaudhary, R. (2024). Artificial Intelligence in Storytelling: A Critical Analysis of Narrative Authenticity, Cultural Impact, and the Future of Creative Industries. *Library of Progress-Library Science, Information Technology & Computer, 44*(3).

Skoko, B. (2009). Država kao brend. Upravljanje nacionalnim identitetom. Zagreb: Matica hrvatska.

Skoko, B. (2017). Communication Strategies and Branding Attempts of Selected Countries Created upon the Disintegration of the Former Yugoslavia. Sociologija i prostor: časopis za istraživanje prostornoga i sociokulturnog razvoja, 55(1), 5-31.DOI: 10.5673/sip.55.1.1

Skoko, B., & Hlača, A. (2020). Šport kao meka moć države: važnost športske diplomacije na primjeru Hrvatske. South Eastern European Journal of Communication, 2(2), 7-20. , https://hrcak.srce.hr/clanak/359865DOI: 10.47960/2712-0457.2020.2.2.7

Skoko, B., & Kovačić, V. (2009). Koncept meke moći država i njegova primjena na Republiku Hrvatsku. Polemos: časopis za interdisciplinarna istraživanja rata i mira, XII (23), 29-49. https://hrcak.srce.hr/clanak/73543

Skoko, B., & Primorac, M. (2021). Filmska industrija kao segment meke moći država na primjeru Južne Koreje, Kine i SAD-a. South Eastern European Journal of Communication, 3(2), 7-20., , https://hrcak.srce.hr/clanak/397993DOI: 10.47960/2712-0457.2021.2.3.7

Skoko, B., Ježovita, J., & Plenković, M. (2022). Imidž Hrvatske iz perspektive hrvatskih iseljenika i njihovih potomaka u različitim dijelovima svijeta. Kroatologija: časopis za hrvatsku kulturu Fakulteta hrvatskih studija Sveučilišta u Zagrebu, 13(1-2): 167-187. https://hrcak.srce.hr/clanak/408046

Skoko, B. (2012). *The Image of Bosnia and Herzegovina and its Citizens in Croatia and Serbia*. Friedrich Ebert Stiftung.

Skoko, B., & Frka Petešić, Z. (2023). *Hrvatska u 30 priča*. Naklada Ljevak.

Smith, D. M., & Moore, A. W. (2011). *Narrative in video games: Theories and case studies*. Game Studies.

Snyder, C. R. (1992). Product scarcity by need for uniqueness interaction: A consumer Catch-22 carousel? *Basic and Applied Social Psychology*, *13*(1), 9–24. DOI: 10.1207/s15324834basp1301_3

Soodo. (2025). Nike: The masters of storytelling. https://soodo.co/the-power-of-storytelling-how-nike-inspires-action-with-every-ad/

Sortiraparis. (2023). Louis Vuitton: modaevinin tarihçesi ve Paris'teki haberler. https://www.sortiraparis.com/tr/hobiler/alisveris/articles/306728-louis-vuitton-modaevinin-tarihcesi-ve-paris-teki-haberler

Sözcü. (2023, March 1). SÖZCÜ televizyonu yayın hayatına başladı. https://www.sozcu.com.tr/sozcu-televizyonu-yayin-hayatina-basladi-wp7610389

Srisan, K. (2024). The art of storytelling with hermes. https://www.hashtaglegend.com/th-en/the-art-of-storytelling-with-hermes

Stegmaier, W. (2019). *What is Orientation:A Philosophical Investigation* (Mueller, R. G., Trans.). De Gruyter. DOI: 10.1515/9783110575149

Subitha N.., G., M. S., & C., T. (2024). Influence of social media ınfluencers on buying behavior of college students in ernakulam district. *Journal of Lifestyle and SDGs Review*, 4(4), e03539. https://doi.org/DOI: 10.47172/2965-730X.SDGsReview.v4.n04.pe03539

Suvremena.hr. (2019). Završen CommForum2019: Kontinuirano brendiranje ključ je za podizanje prepoznatljivosti Hrvatske u svijetu. suvremena.hr. https://suvremena.hr/zavrsen-commforum2019-kontinuirano-brendiranje-kljuc-je-za-podizanje-prepoznatljivosti-hrvatske-u-svijetu/

Tanilli, S. (2009). *Nasıl bir demokrasi istiyoruz.* Cumhuriyet Publishing.

Tariq, M. U. (2025). *AI-Driven Learning and Engagement in Higher Education.* IGI Global., DOI: 10.4018/979-8-3693-4074-5

Tariq, M. U. (2025). AI-Driven Personalized Learning: Revolutionizing Student Engagement and Teacher Efficiency in Education 5.0. In Mobo, F. (Ed.), *AI and Emerging Technologies for Emergency Response and Smart Cities* (pp. 75–96). IGI Global Scientific Publishing., DOI: 10.4018/979-8-3693-9770-1.ch004

Tariq, M. U. (2025). Bridging Generations: Digital Transformation and Its Multifaceted Impact Across Societal Sectors. In Anshari, M., Almunawar, M., & Ordóñez de Pablos, P. (Eds.), *Impacts of Digital Technologies Across Generations* (pp. 1–22). IGI Global Scientific Publishing., DOI: 10.4018/979-8-3693-6366-9.ch001

Tariq, M. U. (2025). Co-Living With Augmented Digital Beings-Navigating the Intersection of AI and Everyday Life. In Moutinho, L., & Martins, L. (Eds.), *Impacts of Sensetech on Society* (pp. 187–206). IGI Global Scientific Publishing., DOI: 10.4018/979-8-3693-7147-3.ch009

Tariq, M. U. (2025). Unlocking Competitive Edge: Harnessing the Power of Collaborative Innovation. In Martínez-Falcó, J., Sánchez-García, E., & Marco-Lajara, B. (Eds.), *Open Innovation Strategies for Effective Competitive Advantage* (pp. 315–344). IGI Global Scientific Publishing., DOI: 10.4018/979-8-3693-9266-9.ch011

Taylor, C. (2007). *A Secular Age*. Harvard University Press.

Telišman-Košuta, N. (2017). Shaping Destination Identity: Challenges of Branding Croatia. In Dwyer, L., Tomljenović, R., & Čorak, S. (Eds.), *Evolution of Destination Planning and Strategy: The Rise of Tourism in Croatia* (pp. 67–78). The Palgrave Macmillan.

Teraiya, V., Namboodiri, S., & Jayswal, R. (2023). The impact of storytelling advertising on consumer advertising experiences and brand equity. *Journal of Management Review and Transformation*. Volume 2, Issue 1. e-ISSN: 2583-5076.

Teraiya, V., Namboodiri, S., & Jayswal, R. (2023, May).. . *First Published*, *5*, 231160591. DOI: 10.1177/jmrt

Thakkar, A., Gupta, A., & De Sousa, A. (2024). Artificial intelligence in positive mental health: A narrative review. *Frontiers in Digital Health*, *6*, 1280235. DOI: 10.3389/fdgth.2024.1280235 PMID: 38562663

The Game Awards. (2020). Game of the year winners. https://thegameawards.com/

The University of British Columbia. (2018). Data pseudonymization. Retrieved from: https://researchdata.library.ubc.ca/share/anonymize-and-de-identify/data-pseudonymization/

The Witcher. (2015). The Witcher 3: Wild Hunt, [Video game]. https://www.thewitcher.com/en/witcher2

Thestraitstimes. (2025). https://www.straitstimes.com/life/entertainment/how-minecraft-became-the-biggest-video-game-in-the-world

Thomas, S. (2024). AI and actors: Ethical challenges, cultural narratives and industry pathways in synthetic media performance. *Emerging Media*, *2*(3), 523–546. DOI: 10.1177/27523543241289108

Thomson, M., Maclnnis, D. J., & Park, C. W. (2005). The ties that bind: Measuring the strength of consumers' emotional attachments to brands. *Journal of Consumer Psychology*, *15*(1), 77–91.

Timisi, N. (2003). *Yeni İletişim Teknolojileri ve Demokrasi*. Dost.

Tiryaki, S., & Kaya, E. (2019). Sosyal medyanın gri yüzü. In Livberber, T., & Tiryaki, S. (Eds.), *Sosyal medya çalışmaları: Kuram, söylem, pratik* (pp. 239–262). Literaturk Academia.

Tjärnhage, A., Söderström, U., Norberg, O., Andersson, M., & Mejtoft, T. (2023). The Impact of Scrollytelling on the Reading Experience of Long-Form Journalism. *European Conference in Cognitive Ergonomics*. DOI: 10.1145/3605655.3605683

Tomaselli, K. (2016). Encoding/decoding, the transmission model and a court of law. *International Journal of Cultural Studies, 19*(1), 59–70. DOI: 10.1177/1367877915599611

Tomić, I. (2022). Sportska diplomacija. South Eastern European Journal of Communication, 4(1), 45-55., , https://hrcak.srce.hr/clanak/411792DOI: 10.47960/2712-0457.2022.1.4.45

Törenli, N. (2005). *Yeni Medya, Yeni İletişim Ortamı*. Bilim ve Sanat.

Tosun, P., Uslu, A., & Erul, E. (2025). Connecting through chatbots: Residents' insights on digital storytelling, place attachment, and value co-creation. *Current Issues in Tourism, 28*(4), 561–584. DOI: 10.1080/13683500.2024.2316857

Tuđman, M. (2013). Izvještajne službe i meka moć. National Security and the Future 14(1), 9-22, https://hrcak.srce.hr/clanak/185535

Tunalı, İ. (2010). *Estetik* [Aesthetics]. Remzi Publishing. (Original work published 1989)

Türkdoğan, O., & Gökçe, O. (2015). *Sosyal Bilimlerde Araştırma Yöntemleri*. Çizgi.

Turkish Grand National Assembly (1983). *2954 sayılı Türkiye Radyo ve Televizyon Kanunu*. https://www.tcmevzuat.com/normlar/2954-sayili-turkiye-radyo-ve-televizyon-kanunu/

Turner, G. (2010). *Ordinary people and the media: The demotic turn*. SAGE Publications. DOI: 10.4135/9781446269565

Tutar, C. (2015). Türk Korku Sinemasının Yapısal Engelleri: Sosyo-Kültürel Bir Bakış. Gümüşhane University [Structural Barriers of Turkish Horror Cinema: A Socio-Cultural Perspective. Gumushane University]. *E-Journal of Faculty of Communication, 3*(2), 247–274. DOI: 10.19145/guifd.33671

Ueda, S. (1995). Silence and Words in Zen Buddhism. *Diogenes, 43*(170), 1–21. DOI: 10.1177/039219219504317001

Ukeni, S. C. (2022). Strategy behind the business success of amazon: a case study. *Texila International Journal of Management*. p.1-16. ISSN: 2520-310X.

Ültay, E., Akyurt, H., & Ültay, N. (2021). Sosyal bilimlerde betimsel içerik analizi. *IBAD Sosyal Bilimler Dergisi*, (10), 188–201. DOI: 10.21733/ibad.871703

Upthrust. (2024). https://upthrust.co/2025/01/mass-effect-trilogy-retrospective-how-it-redefined-storytelling-for-sci-fi-rpgs

Ussher, J. (2013). Media representations of psychology: Denigration and popularization, or worthy dissemination of knowledge? In Smart, B. (Ed.), *Social scientists meet the media* (pp. 123–137). Routledge.

Uygur, T. (2021, March 13). Refik Anadol NASA'nın 60 yıllık arşivlerini görselleştirip sergi açtı… uzaya sanatsal bakış [Refik Anadol visualized 60 years of NASA archives and opened an exhibition... an artistic view of space]. *Hürriyet Cumartesi.* https://www.hurriyet.com.tr/kelebek/hurriyet-cumartesi/refik-anadol-nasanin-60-yillik-arsivlerini-gorsellestirip-sergi-acti-uzaya-sanatsal-bakis-41761577

Uzun, Ö. (2016). *Canlandırma Sinemasında Transmedya Hikâye Anlatım Örneği Olarak Shrek Serisi,* Marmara University Social Sciences, Unpublished Doctoral Dissertation. https://www.chip.com.tr/makale/sahmaran-dizisi-konusu-ne-oyunculari-kimler-netflixin-yeni-yerli-dizisi-mercek-altinda_155606.html, E.T.10.04.2024

V. G. (2025). Godina obilježavanja 1100. obljetnice Hrvatskoga Kraljevstva, hrt.hr. https://magazin.hrt.hr/kultura/godina-obiljezavanja-1100-obljetnice-hrvatskoga-kraljevstva-11940320

Van Pinxteren, M. M., Pluymaekers, M., & Lemmink, J. G. (2020). Human-like communication in conversational agents: A literature review and research agenda. *Journal of Service Management, 31*(2), 203–225. DOI: 10.1108/JOSM-06-2019-0175

Vara, C. F. (2019). *Introduction to game analysis* (2nd ed.). Routledge. DOI: 10.4324/9781351140089

Varlaj, S., Grmuša, T., & Vuković, D. (2021). The Role of Corporate Values and Corporate Culture in the Untypical Times of the Covid-19 Pandemic // 3rd International conference on decision making for small and medium-sized enterprises: conference proceedings. Opava: Karviná: Silesian University in Opava, School of Business Administration in Karviná, 2021. p. 672-680.

Večernji.hr (2024). Stranci o Baby Lasagni: 'Pošaljite njega na Euroviziju, molim vas', večernji.hr, https://www.vecernji.hr/showbiz/baby-lasagna-na-youtubeu-je-najgledaniji-iz-drugog-polufinala-a-evo-sto-o-njemu-kazu-stranci-1748895

Vogue. (2018). Gucci Garden hakkında. https://vogue.com.tr/metropol/gucci-garden-hakkinda

Von Stackerberg, P., & Jones, R. E. (2014). Tales of Our Tomorrows: Transmedia Storytelling and Communicating About the Future. *Journal of Futures Studies, 18*(3), 57–76. https://jfsdigital.org/wp-content/uploads/2014/04/183-A05.pdf

Vuitton, L. (2025). The spirit of travel by jean lariviere. https://hk.louisvuitton.com/eng-hk/magazine/articles/louis-vuitton-jean-lariviere

Vuletic, D. (2018). *Postwar Europe and the Eurovision Song Contest.* Blooms-bury Academic.

Vural, İ. (2003). *"Anchor" as a professional persona in television journalism – An evaluation in terms of source characteristics and a situational analysis of its practice in Turkey* (Unpublished doctoral dissertation). Anadolu University, Institute of Social Sciences, Eskişehir.

Waddell, T. (2014). Shrink-wrapped television: Simulated therapy, disclosure, and the lure of 'plausible doubt. In Hillis, K., Petit, M., & McCallum, K. D. (Eds.), *Eavesdropping* (pp. 129–143). Routledge. DOI: 10.4324/9781315739526-9

Wala, H. H. (2015). *Meine Marke. Was Unternehmen authentisch, unverwechselbar und lagfristig erfolgreich macht, 7.th updated edition.* Redline Verlag.

Wang, C., & Zhang, P. (2012). The evolution of social commerce: The people, management, technology, and information dimensions. *Communications of the Association for Information Systems, 31*, 105–127. DOI: 10.17705/1CAIS.03105

Wang, Y., Kong, S., Li, M., & Liu, L. (2022). Need for uniqueness moderates the effectiveness of different types of scarcity appeals. *Frontiers in Psychology, 13*, 890350. DOI: 10.3389/fpsyg.2022.890350 PMID: 36507003

Wardley, K. J. (2010). "Learning to be silent: theological and philosophical reflections on silence and transcendence." *Culture and Transcendence: Shifting Religion and Spirituality in Philosophy Theology, Art and Politics.* VU Amsterdam, 28-29th October, pp.1-23.

Warrell, D. A. (2010). *Guidelines of the Management of Snake Bites.* World Health Organization.

Weil, S. (1952). *The need for roots: prelude to a declaration of duties towards mankind.* Routledge.

Weiner, R. (2002). An ode to Ann Landers and Dear Abby. *Public Relations Quarterly, 47*(3), 7.

Wejnert, B. (2002). Integrating models of diffusion of innovations: A conceptual framework. *Annual Review of Sociology, 28*(1), 297–326. DOI: 10.1146/annurev.soc.28.110601.141051

Wenders, W. (2023). *Perfect Days.* Master Mind Limited and Spoon Inc.

Werner, E. T. (1994). Edward T. Chalmers, Myths and Legends of China. Courier Corporation. p. 252.

Wiecek, A., Wentzel, D., & Landwehr, J. R. (2019). The aesthetic fidelity effect. *International Journal of Research in Marketing*, *36*(4), 580–597. DOI: 10.1016/j.ijresmar.2019.03.002

Wikipedia. (2018). https://en.wikipedia.org/wiki/Red_Dead_Redemption_2

Williams, R. (1985). Keywords: A vocabulary of culture and society (Rev. and expanded ed.). Oxford University Press.

Wimmer, R. D., & Dominick, J. R. (2014). Mass Media Research An Introduction. 10th Edition, Wadsworth, Cengage Learning, Boston.

Wiseman, E. (2021, October 17). Conspirituality: The dark side of wellness – how it all got so toxic. *The Guardian*. https://www.theguardian.com/lifeandstyle/2021/oct/17/eva-wiseman-conspirituality-the-dark-side-of-wellness-how-it-all-got-so-toxic

Wittgenstein, L. (1961). *Tractatus logico-philosophicus.* (D.F.Pears-B.F.McGuinness, Çev.). London: Routledge-Kegan Paul. "Wu". *Oxford Reference.* https://www.oxfordreference.com/display/10.1093/oi/authority.20110803125126659.Access: 15.02.2025.

Wolf, C., & Godulla, A. (2016). Potentials of digital longforms in journalism. A survey among mobile Internet users about the relevance of online devices, Internet-specific qualities, and modes of payment. *Journal of Media Business Studies*, *13*(4), 199–221. DOI: 10.1080/16522354.2016.1184922

Woodruff, A., Shelby, R., Kelley, P. G., Rousso-Schindler, S., Smith-Loud, J., & Wilcox, L. (2024, May). How knowledge workers think generative ai will (not) transform their industries. In *Proceedings of the 2024 CHI Conference on Human Factors in Computing Systems* (pp. 1-26). DOI: 10.1145/3613904.3642700

Woodside, A. G., Sood, S., & Miller, K. E. (2008). When consumers and brands talk: Storytelling theory and research in psychology and marketing. *Psychology and Marketing*, *25*(2), 97–145. https://doi.org/10.1002/mar.20203

Works, V. (2023). Dior marka hikayesi. https://www.vscoworks.com/blog/dior-marka-hikayesi

Xu, C. (2020, Nowember 10). *Algorithmic Art: Beyond the Artist. Illumine Magazine.* https://illumin.usc.edu/algorithmic-art-beyond-the-artist/

Yadav,P., Gupta P.K.,Upamannyu, N.Kr. (2022). Influence of social reference group and personality traits on automobile buying decision: a research on youth, ınspira-*Journal of Modern Management & Entrepreneurship (JMME)* 207, Impact Factor: 6.280, Volume 12, No. 01, January-March 2022, pp. 207-216

Yang, Y., Tang, Y., Zhang, Y., & Yang, R. (2021, September 6). Exploring the relationship between visual aesthetics and social commerce through visual information adoption unimodel. *Frontiers in Psychology, 12*, 700180. DOI: 10.3389/fpsyg.2021.700180 PMID: 34552529

Yılmaz, B. F. (2020). Lüks Markalamada Sanatın Kullanılmasının Sosyal Medyada Yansımaları. Istanbul University Social Sciences Institute, Unpublished Master's Thesis.

Yılmaz, İ. (2021, April 05). Yeni medya sanatı ve anten tartışması [New media art and antenna discussion]. *Hürriyet.* (https://www.hurriyet.com.tr/yazarlar/ihsan-yilmaz/yeni-medya-sanati-ve-anten-tartismasi-41780110

Yılmaz, T., & Canbaz, E. (2019). Hikâye odaklı video oyunlarda çevirinin rolü: The Last of Us üzerine bir değerlendirme [The role of translation in story-driven video games: An evaluation of The Last of Us]. Journal of Translation Studies and Applications, *27*, 35–55.

YouTube. (2012). *Report from Vietnam (1968)* [Video]. YouTube. https://web.archive.org/web/20120227183438/http://www.youtube.com/watch?v=Nn4w-ud-TyE&gl=US&hl

Zamora. (2025). Unraveling allbirds' strategic narrative. https://zamora.design/unraveling-allbirds-strategic-narrative/

Zavišić, S. (2024). Andrija Jarak o bodovima Eurosong žirija: 'Nisam teoretičar zavjere, ali jedna stvar se nikad prije nije dogodila', jutarnji.hr, https://www.jutarnji.hr/scena/domace-zvijezde/andrija-jarak-o-bodovima-eurosong-zirija-nisam-teoreticar-zavjere-ali-jedna-stvar-se-nikad-prije-nije-dogodila-15461259?cx_linkref=jl_ia_vezane

Zeithaml, V. A., Bitner, M. J., & Gremler, D. D. (2018). *Services marketing: Integrating customer focus across the firm.* McGraw-Hill Education.

Zgurić, B. (2021). Politički i društveno-kulturni narativi u turskim serijama: između nenamjernog instrumenta meke moći i tihog oružja za vođenje kulturnog rata? Anali Hrvatskog politološkog društva: časopis za politologiju, 18(1), 233-254. DOI: 10.20901/an.18.05

Zhao, X., Ma, Z., & Ma, R. (2024). Analyzing narrative contagion through digital storytelling in social media conversations: An AI-powered computational approach. *New Media & Society*, •••, 14614448241285445. DOI: 10.1177/14614448241285445

Zimand-Sheiner, D. (2024). Four Dimensions of Brand Storytelling: Framework for Managing and Analyzing Online Brand Stories. *International Journal of Business Communication*, *0*(0). DOI: 10.1177/23294884241261362

Zimand-Sheiner, D., & (Hilik)Limor, Y. (2017). The exodus myth in commercial advertisements in Israeli secular and religious printed press 1948–2008. *Israel Affairs*, *23*(5), 808–827. DOI: 10.1080/13537121.2017.1343861

Zimmer, F., Scheibe, K., Stock, M., & Stock, W. G. (2019). *Echo chambers and filter bubbles of fake news in social media: Man-made or produced by algorithms? In 8th Annual Arts*. Humanities, Social Sciences & Education Conference.

Zurn, M. (2010). "Fall of the Berlin Wall": Globalisation and the Future of Europe. New Zealand International Review, 35(3), 2–7. https://search.informit.org/doi/10.3316/informit.062924525552962

About The Contributors

Nur Emine Koç has a BA and MA degree in English Language and Literature. She completed her PhD in Communication Studies at Maltepe University in 2016. From 2002 to 2009, she worked as an English teacher at universities and as a counselor for students and parents. In 2010, she continued her career as a lecturer at İstanbul Aydın University and after receiving her degree as an assistant professor in 2016, she has not only taught various types of courses to vocational school, BA, MA and PhD students, but has also taken on many administrative tasks, such as being the deputy head of the Department of Communication Studies. Such as deputy head of the Vocational School of Foreign Languages, head of the Department of Foreign Languages and Cultures, head of the Department of Applied English and Translation, head of the Department of English Translation, deputy head of the Center for New Media and Application and Research. After numerous studies in the field of new media, Koç has been the head of the Department of New Media and Communication for BA and MA students at the Faculty of Communication at İstanbul Aydın University since 2020. She is also a volunteer supervisor for the analysis of films and TV series for the "Let's End Violence Together" platform. She received her Assoc. Prof. in Communication Sciences in March 2022.

Mine Demirtaş completed her Master's degree in Journalism and Public Relations at Marmara University Institute of Social Sciences in 1990 and her PhD in 1996. In 2015, she became an Associate Professor in Public Relations. Her research interests include film censorship, public relations films, media studies, management, corporate social responsibility, sponsorship and media research. He is currently working at Beykent University, Faculty of Communication, Department of Media and Communication.

***

Ayşe Nesrin Akören completed her undergraduate education in the Department of Fine Arts Education, Painting and Crafts Education, Graphics Department in 1986 at Marmara University AEF. She completed her MA in 1989 and her PhD in 2012 at the Istanbul Technical University, Institute of Social Sciences, Art History Program in the field of Multi-Disciplinary. Her MA thesis is 'Contemporary Graphic Art and Promotional Graphics in Turkey from the Beginning to the Present' and her PhD thesis is 'Urban Presentation of Outdoor Graphics and the Istanbul Example (1980-2010)'. In her PhD thesis, she has been developing her expertise on digital arts and new generation artistic productions since the process in which she interpreted the studies on new generation applications in a field-specific way. She worked as a full-time faculty member in the Department of Cartoon and Animation at Maltepe University, Republic of Turkey. She passed the Associate Professorship exam in 2022 and has been teaching applied and theoretical courses as the head of the Digital Game Design department at Doğuş University since that year. Assoc. Prof. Dr. Ayşe Nesrin Akören, in addition to her domestic education, received Cartoon training at Kingsway College in England and did her field internships in the United States. She also worked as a Junior Animator at Amblin Studio in London, England for a short period. She also won the Model Animation Display and Monetary Incentive Award from Channel Four TV in England at that time. Her main areas of interest in her writings and practical works are: Digital design, Photography, Film Documentary studies, Cartoons, 2D Animation and Digital Games.

Nazan Alioglu, BA, Philosophy (Istanbul University, 1991); MA, Socio-Cultural Structure of the European Community (Istanbul University, 1994). Thesis topic: "Historicism and Aesthetic Formation in Benedetto Croce"; PhD, Communication Sciences (Marmara University, 1998). Thesis topic: "The Compulsory Realism of Art: Art as a Subject of Cultural Consumption in Contemporary Mass Communication". Her research interests are aesthetics, philosophy of art, cultural theories, and cultural studies. She has a book titled "New Media Art and Aesthetics" and a joint book titled "An Essay on the Problem of Meaning in Contemporary Art". She works as a full-time faculty member and department head at the Department of Television Reporting and Programming, Faculty of Communication, Istanbul Beykent University.

Merve Celik-Varol, was born in Ankara. In 2013, she graduated from Yaşar University, Faculty of Communication, Department of Public Relations and Advertising, where she studied with scholarship and in English. In 2016, she graduated from Istanbul University, Institute of Social Sciences, New Media and Communication Management Master's Programme with Thesis with her thesis titled 'Factors Affecting Consumer Attitudes and Behaviours in Online

Shopping: A Research on the Students of the Department of Communication Arts of the Foundation University'. In the same year, she enrolled in Istanbul University, Institute of Social Sciences, Public Relations and Publicity Doctorate Programme. In 2021, she was entitled to receive the title of 'Doctor' with her doctoral thesis titled 'The Transformation of Hedonic Attitudes of Digital Consumers in Luxury Brand Usage: A Review on Second-Hand Fashion Sites'. Between 2015-2020, he worked as a Research Assistant at Istanbul Kültür University, Faculty of Art and Design, Department of Communication Arts. Since 2021, Varol has been working as 'Assoc. Prof. Dr.' at Beykent University, Faculty of Communication, Department of Public Relations and Advertising, and in 2024, he was awarded the title of 'associate professor' in the field of Public Relations. Varol is currently working on 'public relations', 'integrated marketing communication', 'consumer behaviour' and 'consumer culture'.

Tuğba Gülal is a PhD holder and currently works at Radio, Television and Cinema Department of Faculty of Communication at Istanbul Aydın University in Türkiye.Dr. Gülal was educated at Istanbul University and graduated with Bachelor degree in English-Turkish Translation and Interpreting.Following her Bachelor, Dr.Tuğba then attended Istanbul University, Translation studies department and gained her M.A. degree with honors degree with thesis about analysis of news text translations and gendered discourse. In June,2023, Dr. Gülal attained an M.A. degree from Wuhan University, Department of Philosophy and her master study has been fully funded by China Scholarship Council. Besides, in February,2024,she completed her PhD in Media studies with summa cum laude and her dissertation focuses on epistemology of news reporting studies. Before completing her PhD, Gülal stayed in Germany and UK for academic research. Nowadays, Gülal focuses on philosophy of communication, contemporary political philosophy issues and Confucian virtue ethics and prepares a book chapter about Asia and Iris Murdoch for Palgrave Macmillan.

Ahmet Serkan Okay graduated from the Department of Public Relations and Advertising at Istanbul University Faculty of Communication in 2010. In 2015, he completed his master's degree in Journalism at Atatürk University with a thesis titled "Glokal Reklam in the Context of Cultural Imperialism". He began his doctorate studies in Journalism at Istanbul University in 2017 and completed his dissertation titled "The Production and Transformation of Content from Traditional to Digital: A Research in the Context of Digital Journalism" in 2021. Ahmet Serkan Okay started his academic career in 2016 as a Research Assistant at Istanbul Medipol University Faculty of Communication. In 2021, he became a Dr. Assistant Professor at Istanbul Medipol University Faculty of Communication, Department of New

Media and Communication. His areas of expertise include digital journalism, advertising, graphic design, and cultural imperialism. He continues to teach courses on internet journalism, consumer behavior, page design, and media literacy, among other subjects. Ahmet Serkan Okay was born in 1988 in Erzurum.

Aman Deep Singh joined Nirma University in February 2022 as an assistant professor (English) in the Department of Humanities and Social Sciences. Before joining Nirma University, Dr Aman Deep Singh worked as assistant professor at Indian Institute of Information Technology (IIIT) Vadodara for two and half years and taught subjects like English communication, Technical Writing, and Science Fiction.He did his Doctorate from the Central University of Rajasthan, post-graduation in English from Pondicherry University, and a Bachelorette in English Honors from the University of Delhi. His area of specialism includes Science Fiction Studies, Creative Writing, ELT, Literary theory and Criticism.

Muhammad Usman Tariq has more than 16+ year's experience in industry and academia. He has authored more than 200+ research articles, 110+ case studies, 150+ book chapters and several books other than 4 patents. He is founder and CEO of The Case HQ, a unique repository for courses, narrative and video case studies. He has been working as a consultant and trainer for industries representing six sigma, quality, health and safety, environmental systems, project management, and information security standards. His work has encompassed sectors in aviation, manufacturing, food, hospitality, education, finance, research, software and transportation. He has diverse and significant experience working with accreditation agencies of ABET, ACBSP, AACSB, WASC, CAA, EFQM and NCEAC. Additionally, Dr. Tariq has operational experience in incubators, research labs, government research projects, private sector startups, program creation and management at various industrial and academic levels. He is Certified Higher Education Teacher from Harvard University, USA, Certified Online Educator from HMBSU, Certified Six Sigma Master Black Belt and has been awarded PFHEA, SFSEDA, SMIEEE, and CMBE.

Asena Temelli Cosgun, In 2023, she completed her doctoral studies at Marmara University, Department of Advertising, with a thesis titled "A Study on the Consumption Practices of the New Middle Class from Pierre Bourdieu's Perspective." She earned her master's degree in 2019 from the Department of Advertising and Promotion at Marmara University. Asena Temelli Coşgun began her academic career in the same year and currently works as an Assistant Professor in the Department of Public Relations and Advertising at the Faculty of Communication, Istanbul Medipol

University. Her research interests include cultural studies, advertising, consumer behavior, social media, and marketing.

Erdem Varol, He was born in 1984 in Samsun. In 2011, she graduated from Ege University, Faculty of Communication, Department of Journalism. In 2016, he received his master's degree from Marmara University, Institute of Social Sciences, Public Relations Master's Programme with a thesis titled 'The Relationship between Shopping Centres and Consumption Society in Urban Culture'. In the same year, she enrolled in Marmara University, Institute of Social Sciences, Advertising and Publicity Doctorate Programme, and in 2023, she graduated from the said doctoral programme with the thesis titled "Happiness as a Consumption Object: A Research on the Use of Happiness in Advertisements", he was entitled to receive the title of doctor. Varol, who worked as a Research Assistant at Marmara University, Faculty of Communication, Department of Public Relations and Publicity between 2013-2023, has been working as an Assistant Professor at Marmara University, Faculty of Communication, Department of Public Relations and Publicity as of July 2025. He continues his studies on subjects such as 'Consumption Culture', 'Consumer Behaviour', 'Advertising'.

Index

A

Advertising 9, 12, 18, 19, 29, 52, 231, 234, 235, 239, 240, 248, 253, 255, 257, 261, 264, 268, 271, 273, 278, 279, 280, 287, 291, 293, 295, 300, 321, 340, 375
Aesthetics 7, 9, 10, 12, 20, 197, 199, 204, 209, 210, 211, 212, 213, 214, 215, 216, 218, 219, 221, 225, 226, 228, 231, 242, 253, 278, 282, 283, 285, 286, 292, 295, 298, 306, 307, 320
Algorithmic Art 199, 206, 207, 223, 228
Anchor 28, 31, 32, 33, 34, 35, 38, 44, 46, 50, 52, 54, 55
Artificial Intelligence 1, 6, 8, 11, 16, 19, 24, 25, 26, 83, 141, 143, 145, 146, 148, 151, 155, 156, 161, 163, 164, 166, 197, 198, 199, 200, 201, 203, 204, 206, 207, 209, 210, 211, 212, 217, 218, 219, 220, 221, 222, 223, 276, 327

B

Baby Lasagna 333, 336, 360, 361, 362, 363, 364, 365, 367, 368, 369, 370, 371, 372, 373, 374, 375, 377, 379, 381
Branching 19, 62, 63, 64, 72, 74, 75, 76, 83
Branding 3, 9, 18, 32, 229, 232, 233, 235, 237, 238, 247, 248, 249, 257, 258, 259, 260, 261, 262, 263, 271, 295, 306, 307, 314, 333, 334, 336, 338, 339, 340, 341, 342, 343, 345, 346, 348, 350, 351, 353, 354, 356, 366, 367, 369, 371, 373, 374, 375, 376, 377, 378, 379, 380

C

Consumer Behaviour 261

D

Data Art 199, 202
Digital Age 5, 11, 15, 25, 27, 68, 91, 142, 143, 145, 163, 198, 199, 200, 209, 211, 213, 218, 221, 229, 240, 270, 272, 308, 318, 323, 376
Digital Auteurism 88, 89, 91, 93, 94, 110, 112
Digital Games 57, 58, 60, 68, 71, 79, 80, 82, 83, 84, 85, 148
Digital Journalism 141, 142, 143, 144, 145, 146, 148, 150, 155, 156, 158, 161, 166
Digital Platforms 21, 87, 88, 89, 90, 91, 94, 98, 105, 106, 107, 112, 115, 116, 117, 119, 124, 136, 143, 145, 147, 148, 150, 155, 246, 268, 275, 285, 288, 292, 293, 299, 300, 305, 313, 319
Digital Storytelling 1, 4, 5, 20, 23, 24, 25, 26, 90, 108, 110, 112, 118, 141, 147, 148, 149, 155, 156, 163, 166, 167, 168, 197, 198, 199, 201, 202, 205, 212, 213, 214, 215, 216, 218, 225, 267, 268, 269, 270, 271, 276, 277, 279, 280, 281, 295, 297, 339, 372
Dubai Chocolate 267, 278, 287, 288, 289, 290, 293

E

Eurovision Song Contest 333, 335, 336, 353, 354, 359, 360, 361, 362, 363, 365, 367, 368, 369, 371, 372, 373, 377, 379, 380, 381

F

Fashion Marketing 229, 230, 231, 232, 237, 245, 247, 248, 249, 254, 257, 258, 262

G

Generative Art 197, 198, 199, 200, 202, 203, 204, 205, 206, 207, 209, 210, 211, 212, 214, 216, 223, 224, 226, 227, 228
Generative Content 26
Genre Evolution 112
Gothic 87, 88, 90, 91, 92, 93, 95, 96, 97, 101, 104, 107, 108, 109, 110, 111, 112, 213

I

Interactive Narratives 26, 62, 82, 99, 148, 150

L

Linear 1, 2, 4, 5, 6, 16, 19, 57, 59, 60, 61, 64, 67, 72, 73, 74, 76, 77, 99, 145, 147, 149, 153, 154, 162, 165, 320
Listening 75, 171, 172, 173, 174, 175, 176, 177, 178, 183, 185, 186, 189, 190, 192, 193, 194, 195, 270
Long Scrolling Narrative 149, 150, 152, 156, 160, 166
Ludonarrative Dissonance 79, 80, 81, 82, 85
Luxury Brands 229, 230, 231, 232, 236, 237, 245, 246, 247, 248, 250, 257, 258, 260, 261, 262, 264, 296

M

Mental Health 26, 299, 300, 301, 302, 305, 306, 307, 308, 309, 310, 311, 312, 314, 315, 316, 317, 318, 319, 320, 321, 323, 324, 325, 326, 327, 328, 329, 331, 367

N

Narrative 1, 2, 3, 4, 5, 6, 7, 8, 10, 11, 12, 13, 14, 15, 16, 17, 19, 20, 21, 22, 23, 25, 26, 27, 28, 29, 33, 35, 37, 38, 39, 41, 42, 44, 45, 46, 47, 48, 49, 50, 52, 53, 57, 58, 59, 60, 61, 62, 63, 64, 67, 68, 71, 72, 73, 74, 75, 76, 77, 78, 79, 80, 81, 82, 83, 84, 85, 86, 87, 88, 89, 90, 91, 93, 94, 96, 98, 99, 103, 104, 105, 106, 107, 108, 109, 112, 118, 119, 124, 127, 136, 138, 141, 145, 146, 147, 148, 149, 150, 151, 152, 153, 154, 155, 156, 158, 159, 160, 161, 162, 165, 166, 168, 184, 199, 202, 219, 231, 238, 239, 241, 242, 243, 244, 245, 246, 250, 253, 255, 256, 257, 260, 261, 265, 269, 271, 272, 277, 279, 280, 304, 319, 323, 329, 337, 338, 339, 342, 354, 356
nation branding 235, 333, 340, 342, 343, 350, 351, 369, 371, 373, 375
Netflix 11, 12, 13, 18, 19, 88, 89, 90, 98, 106, 107, 108, 111, 112, 115, 116, 117, 120, 121, 124, 125, 126, 128, 131, 132, 133
New Media 5, 19, 26, 37, 54, 85, 87, 91, 97, 99, 110, 112, 116, 117, 118, 120, 143, 144, 147, 148, 167, 168, 201, 202, 203, 204, 218, 219, 227, 228, 309, 311, 324, 337, 366
News Production 141, 142, 144, 145, 146, 147, 148, 149, 151, 154, 155, 156, 161, 163, 165, 166

P

performative 171, 173, 174, 175, 179, 180, 181, 182, 183, 184, 185, 189, 192, 193, 194
Personalization 2, 6, 10, 17, 18, 26, 231
philosophy of communication 174, 175, 176, 177, 185, 191
Popular Psychology 300, 301, 302, 303, 305, 306, 307, 308, 309, 310, 311, 312, 313, 314, 318, 320, 324, 325, 327, 329, 331
Presenter 32, 33, 38, 39, 45, 50, 52
promotion 12, 90, 91, 225, 241, 247, 252, 278, 279, 280, 323, 333, 335, 336, 344, 345, 356, 358, 362, 365, 370, 380
Pseudoscience 299, 314, 317, 321, 331
Psychologization 300, 303, 325, 332
Psychotainment 299, 303, 304, 320, 332

R

Refik Anadol 197, 199, 202, 204, 205, 207, 210, 214, 216, 218, 219, 220, 221, 222, 223, 224, 225, 226, 227, 228

S

Sahmaran 115, 116, 117, 121, 123, 124, 125, 126, 127, 128, 129, 131, 132, 133, 136, 139

Self-Help 299, 300, 301, 302, 305, 312, 314, 318, 319, 320, 326, 328, 329, 330, 332
Social Media 5, 6, 8, 11, 12, 18, 20, 24, 26, 29, 35, 38, 44, 45, 49, 51, 52, 90, 99, 110, 120, 143, 144, 146, 149, 150, 161, 184, 207, 208, 216, 220, 230, 232, 235, 238, 239, 240, 249, 253, 258, 259, 260, 264, 268, 269, 270, 272, 273, 274, 275, 276, 277, 278, 279, 280, 281, 282, 283, 284, 285, 286, 287, 288, 289, 290, 291, 292, 293, 295, 297, 299, 300, 301, 305, 306, 307, 308, 309, 311, 312, 313, 314, 315, 316, 317, 318, 319, 320, 323, 324, 325, 326, 327, 328, 329, 330, 331, 339, 346, 347, 361, 364, 374, 376
soft power 333, 336, 342, 343, 344, 345, 346, 347, 351, 352, 354, 366, 369, 371, 373, 376, 380
Storytelling 1, 2, 3, 4, 5, 6, 7, 9, 10, 11, 12, 13, 14, 15, 16, 17, 18, 19, 20, 21, 23, 24, 25, 26, 27, 37, 53, 57, 58, 59, 60, 62, 64, 65, 66, 67, 72, 73, 74, 75, 76, 77, 82, 83, 84, 85, 86, 87, 88, 89, 90, 91, 93, 94, 95, 96, 97, 98, 99, 100, 106, 107, 108, 109, 110, 111, 112, 115, 116, 117, 118, 119, 120, 121, 124, 125, 136, 138, 141, 145, 146, 147, 148, 149, 150, 151, 152, 153, 154, 155, 156, 159, 163, 165, 166, 167, 168, 171, 174, 180, 181, 183, 184, 185, 187, 188, 196, 197, 198, 199, 200, 201, 202, 204, 205, 206, 212, 213, 214, 215, 216, 218, 220, 224, 225, 229, 230, 231, 232, 236, 237, 238, 239, 240, 241, 242, 243, 244, 245, 246, 247, 248, 249, 250, 253, 254, 255, 256, 257, 258, 260, 261, 262, 263, 264, 265, 267, 268, 269, 270, 271, 272, 273, 276, 277, 279, 280, 281, 291, 292, 293, 295, 297, 300, 301, 302, 306, 308, 315, 317, 318, 320, 333, 334, 335, 336, 337, 338, 339, 342, 366, 367, 368, 372, 374, 375, 376, 377, 379, 380

T

tacet sui 171, 174, 185, 188, 189, 191, 192, 193, 194
Technological Determinism 197, 199, 215, 216, 224
Technological Sublime 197, 199, 212, 213, 214, 215, 219, 224, 228
Television 2, 27, 28, 29, 31, 32, 33, 34, 36, 38, 51, 52, 55, 89, 90, 92, 98, 106, 108, 110, 118, 119, 120, 121, 136, 142, 150, 268, 302, 303, 304, 309, 312, 331, 335, 344, 353, 354, 359, 364, 365, 367, 380
Television Journalism 29, 32, 55
Transmedia Storytelling 5, 6, 11, 90, 115, 116, 117, 119, 120, 121, 124, 136, 338, 379
Turkish Horror Cinema 87, 88, 89, 91, 92, 93, 94, 95, 96, 97, 99, 101, 102, 103, 104, 105, 107, 108, 111

V

voice 4, 6, 9, 18, 34, 35, 39, 41, 51, 60, 75, 91, 132, 171, 176, 177, 178, 194

www.ingramcontent.com/pod-product-compliance
Lightning Source LLC
LaVergne TN
LVHW062327300926
849161LV00007B/1606